DEAN HAYES

MANCHESTER UNITED

THE FOOTBALL FACTS

THE ULTIMATE GUIDE TO THE GREATEST
FOOTBALL CLUB ON EARTH

JOHN BLAKE

Published by John Blake Publishing Ltd,
3 Bramber Court, 2 Bramber Road,
London W14 9PB, England

www.johnblakepublishing.co.uk

First published in paperback in 2009

ISBN: 978-1-84454-795-1

British Library Cataloguing-in-Publication Data:

A catalogue record for this book is available from the British Library.

Design by www.envydesign.co.uk

Printed in Great Britain by CPI Bookmarque, Croydon, CR0 4TD

1 3 5 7 9 10 8 6 4 2

Papers used by John Blake Publishing are natural, recyclable products
made from wood grown in sustainable forests. The manufacturing
processes conform to the environmental regulations of the country
of origin.

Every attempt has been made to contact the relevant copyright-holders,
but some were unobtainable. We would be grateful if the appropriate
people could contact us.

CONTENTS

DID YOU KNOW?

The only occasion on which two brothers have scored in the same game for United – or rather Newton Heath – occurred in the old Football Alliance, before the club was admitted to the Football League. In April 1890, Jack and Roger Doughty both scored against Small Heath, the future Birmingham City.

When Manchester United were still known as Newton Heath, they arrived at Stoke on 7 January 1893 without goalkeeper Warner, who had missed his train. Three different players – Stewart, Fitzsimmons and Clements – all had a turn in goal. United scored first but lost 7-1.

For their first two seasons in the Football League, Newton Heath played in red-and-white quartered jerseys and blue shorts.

Harry Stafford was the only player to captain both Newton Heath and Manchester United. He was the Heathens' captain from 1896 to 1902 and United's first-ever captain.

On Christmas Day 1902 Herbert Birchenough played in goal for United in a 1-1 draw with Manchester City in Division Two. On Boxing Day, Birchenough was replaced in goal by James Whitehouse for their 2-2 draw with Blackpool. The following day United used their third consecutive goalkeeper in three successive League games over three consecutive days when James Saunders was put in goal for a 2-1 win over Barnsley. All three matches were played at Clayton.

On the last day of the 1907/08 season United beat Preston North End

2-1 to win the First Division Championship for the first time in the club's history. In winning the Championship, United set a then season record for the most League points, 52.

Jimmy Turnbull, Manchester United's Scottish centre-forward, was sent off in two consecutive matches in 1909.

The quickest United hat-trick was probably by Ernie Goldthorpe at Notts County on 10 February 1923, when he scored three times between the 62nd and 66th minutes.

Albert Pape travelled to Old Trafford with his team Clapton Orient on 7 February 1925, but was actually transferred to United an hour before the kick-off. He then played in the match and scored for the Reds in a 4-2 win.

Manchester United persuaded Stockport County to allow amateur wing-half Hughie McLenahan to join them in 1927 in exchange for three freezers of ice cream! United scout Louis Rocca arranged for these to be given to the County club to raise club funds at their bazaar.

Manchester United suffered 12 consecutive defeats at the start of the 1930/31 Division One season – still a record!

Towards the end of the 1933/34 season United were in danger of being relegated to the Third Division (North). In an attempt to change their fortunes they changed their colours to cherry hoops on white. In their decisive match at Millwall they won 2-0 but when the new season began the club's old colours reappeared.

When Irish international goalkeeper Tommy Breen made his United debut against Leeds United in November 1936 he conceded a goal after just 60 seconds, before he had even touched the ball.

In 1936/37 Manchester United had five professional goalkeepers all born in different countries – John Breedon and Leonard Langford (England), John Clunie (Scotland), Tommy Breen (Ireland) and Roy John (Wales).

When the fans turned up at Maine Road for United's 'home' game against Blackpool on 22 February 1947 they discovered that there was no match programme. This was due to a printers' strike.

During the 1947/48 season, Manchester United conceded more League goals at home (27) than they conceded away (21).

When Manchester United won the FA Cup in 1948, John Anderson, playing for the Reds against Blackpool at Wembley, hit a surprise shot from 40 yards, fell as he connected with the ball and did not see it enter the net. Neither did Pathe News cameras nor photographers stationed behind the goal.

Charlie Mitten scored three penalties for United in a 7-0 First Division home win over Aston Villa on 8 March 1950. He also netted a fourth goal in the game. At the end of the season, Mitten left England to play football in Colombia.

At the beginning of the 1951/52 season, Jack Rowley scored three hat-tricks in 22 days for United. On the opening day of the season he scored all three in a 3-3 draw with West Bromwich Albion. Four days later he netted another treble in a 4-2 defeat of Middlesbrough and then on 8 September he scored three in a 4-0 win over Stoke. In between he netted a further five times for a total of 14 goals in seven League games.

John Aston senior won the League Championship with United in 1952. Fifteen years later his son, John Aston junior, won the Championship with the club. They are the only father and son combination to win the English First Division title with the same club.

When Tommy Taylor joined Manchester United in March 1953 from Barnsley the agreed fee was £30,000, but because Matt Busby did not want to burden the young centre-forward with a £30,000 price tag, he paid £29,999 for him and gave the tea lady the other £1.

The Manchester United team that won the First Division Championship in 1955/56 had an average age of only 22.

United won the League title by 11 points from runners-up Blackpool in 1956, which effectively remains the best winning margin of all-time. It translates into 16 points under the present three-points-for-a-win system and thus surpasses Everton's 13-point margin in 1985.

Old Trafford's floodlights were switched on for the first time in a League game against Bolton Wanderers on 25 March 1957.

On 4 September 1957 United travelled to Goodison Park for a First Division encounter with Everton. The game ended 3-3 but the crowd of 72,077 set an all-time high attendance for a midweek Football League game.

Nobby Stiles had the misfortune to score two own goals in games against Manchester City – at Old Trafford on 23 September 1961 and at Maine Road on 21 January 1967. In the first game he also scored for United.

Denis Law is the only Manchester United player to have scored a hat-trick in each of the three major European competitions. Overall 'The King' scored 18 hat-tricks during his time at Old Trafford including a record seven during the 1963/64 season.

In November 1966, David Herd's hat-trick against Sunderland was scored past three different goalkeepers. Jim Montgomery, who went off injured, then Charlie Hurley and finally John Parke.

United's longest undefeated home League run is 37 games, between 27 April 1966 and 20 January 1968.
United's League match at Arsenal in March 1967 was watched by 28,000 on closed-circuit TV screens at old Trafford – the first time that pictures of a game had been relayed in this way.

George Best is the youngest ever Footballer of the Year. He was only 21 when he was awarded the title in 1968.

United took part in the first ever penalty shoot-out in English football. On 5 August 1970 United drew 1-1 with Hull City in the Watney Cup. The game was decided on penalties with United progressing to the final with a 4-3 win.

On 7 February 1970, George Best returned from suspension and was in the United side that faced Northampton Town at the County Ground in the 5th round of the FA Cup. Time after time he carved his way through the Cobblers' defence, scoring two hat-tricks in the process as United ran out 8-2 winners.

In July 1971 the Football League closed Old Trafford for two weeks following a knife-throwing incident during the home match against Newcastle United the previous season.

In 1971 George Best escaped suspension when United used TV film footage as evidence at an FA hearing – the first time a player was acquitted in this way.

Halfway through the 1973/74 season, Alex Stepney, Manchester United's goalkeeper, was the side's leading goalscorer with two penalties!

In January 1974 a programme was printed for an FA Cup replay involving United at Plymouth Argyle. Yet no replay was needed, since United had won the tie at Old Trafford 1-0. Plymouth had printed the programme in advance as a precaution against power cuts during the three-day week.

At Maine Road on 13 March 1974 United's Lou Macari and Manchester City's Mike Doyle were dismissed together. Both players refused to leave the pitch and to resolve matters the referee Clive Thomas had to take both teams off for five minutes. The game eventually resumed without either player.

Denis Law scored his last goal in first-class football on 27 April 1974 at Old Trafford when he was playing for Manchester City. Scoring towards the end of the match, he sent his former club United into Division Two.

On 19 August 1975, United keeper Alex Stepney was taken to hospital during an away game with Birmingham City with a dislocated jaw, apparently sustained by shouting at a team-mate!

The youngest FA Cup Final goalscorer was Norman Whiteside. He was 18 years 19 days old when he scored against Brighton & Hove Albion in the 1983 replay. He is also the youngest goalscorer in a Wembley Cup Final – aged 17 years 324 days when he scored against Liverpool in that season's League Cup Final.

In 1990 United had one League point deducted after a brawl erupted during the home defeat by Arsenal that October. Arsenal had two points deducted. This was the first time League sides had been disciplined in this way.

Manchester United won the FA Cup in 1990 by playing all their games away from home.

In 1993 it took a Frenchman, Eric Cantona, to become the first player to win English League Championship medals in successive seasons with different clubs. In all Cantona won Championship medals in four consecutive seasons – 1991 with Marseille, 1992 with Leeds United and 1993 and 1994 with the Reds. His 1996 medal was therefore his fifth in six seasons.

In 1994 United became the first club to win the League, FA Cup and Charity Shield in the same season.

Andy Cole set a Premiership record when he scored five goals for Manchester United against Ipswich Town in United's 9-0 victory in the 1994/95 season. The victory set another Premiership record as the biggest win.

Eric Cantona suffered the longest suspension in modern times after his attack on a spectator during a Premiership match at Crystal Palace on 25 January 1995. He was banned from football by the FA for eight months.

Peter Schmeichel scored for Manchester United against Rotor Volgograd in the UEFA Cup first round second leg on 26 September 1995.

David Beckham's 57-yard strike against Wimbledon at Selhurst Park on 17 August 1996 is the longest successful attempt at goal since the Premiership was formed in 1992.

In August 1998 Manchester United launched its own television channel. MUTV broadcasts six hours a day, seven days a week from a studio at Old Trafford. The channel is available through subscription and shows live youth and reserve team games and friendlies, but not Premiership matches.

Nick Culkin made his debut in goal for Manchester United away against Arsenal on 22 August 1999. When the referee blew his whistle for full-time, he'd been on the pitch for a mere 12 seconds and he never got another game!

United's Tim Howard saved two penalties on his debut in the 2003 FA Community Shield, denying Arsenal's Giovanni van Bronckhorst and Robert Pires. United won the Shield on penalties.

CHAPTER ONE

THE MANCHESTER UNITED STORY

Manchester United – a name associated with flair and passion – started life as Newton Heath some 130 years ago. But how did it all begin?

It was a group of carriage and wagon workers from the Lancashire and Yorkshire railway who began it all in 1878 when they were granted permission and funds from the Dining Room Committee of the Lancashire and Yorkshire Railway Company to start their own football team. The men chose the title 'Newton Heath LYR' for the team (the LYR being Lancashire and Yorkshire Railway). Newton Heath LYR were given a pitch on a stretch of land in North Road, close to the railway yard. It was a bumpy, stony pitch in summer and a muddy, heavy swamp in the rainy months of the year. But the men of Newton Heath LYR didn't care!

At first the games were mostly inter-departmental or occasionally against other railway workers carried along the lines from places such as Earlstown, Middleton, Oldham and St Helens. Gradually the team began to grow in stature and reputation and eventually found that it dominated most of the local domestic competition. There were a number of other clubs in the area and a Manchester Cup competition was launched in 1885, which Newton Heath LYR entered and reached the final. The following year they again competed but this time they won the competition. In 1887, Newton Heath LYR again reached the final of the Manchester Cup, only to lose, but the club was now ready for a major step in its history as the game of football itself took off.

In 1888, the Football League was formed, its 12 members having a strong northern domination but with other clubs from the Midlands also involved. Newton Heath didn't consider themselves a strong enough outfit to compete with the elite of the game but they were certainly growing in stature and it became quite clear that the opposition being provided locally was not strong enough to test the 'Heathens'. In 1888, Newton Heath had the proud record of not losing a game at home until October, when a team of touring Canadians came to Manchester and beat them before a crowd of 3,000 spectators in what was the first 'international' game ever played at North Road.

In 1889, Newton Heath joined other clubs on the verge of the Football League to form the Football Alliance In their first season, the club finished in eighth place and also played in the first round of the FA Cup. Sadly for the Heathens they had the misfortune to be drawn away to the cup holders, Preston North End, who beat them 6-1. The only consolation for Newton Heath was that they had at least scored against the 'Invincibles' which is more than many of the Football League clubs had done the previous season.

In 1890 came another major step in the history of Newton Heath. They began to sever their links with the railway company and the letters 'LYR' were dropped from their title. Even so, there was still a strong connection with the railways, though in fact the club was no longer supported by the social committee of the Lancashire and Yorkshire Railway. Most of the club's players still worked for the railways and of course, it was this that had made the club a success in the first place. At the time it was thought that a job on the railways was a job for life and being able to offer a talented footballer work in the Manchester area allowed the football club to attract men from all parts of the British Isles.

Though professionalism in football had started some three years before the formation of the Football League, a number of Newton Heath's players earned money by playing for the club. The Heathens had attracted a number of players who were highly rated in the game, Welshmen like the Doughty brothers, Jack and Roger, who found work in the local railway depot and whose football skills eventually earned them international honours.

Jack Powell was one player who had a quite remarkable rise to fame. He was completely new to the game of football when the Welsh club Druids signed him but it was also obvious from watching him play that he had a bright future. He had made just three appearances when he was selected to play for Wales against England in 1879 – eight years later he registered as a professional with Newton Heath.

At the end of the 1889/90 season, Stoke had finished bottom of the Football League having been successful in only three games throughout the entire season. Having found life in the League a struggle both on and off the field, they asked if they could stand down and were replaced by Sunderland from the Football Alliance.

In their second season in the Football Alliance, Newton Heath sadly did no better than they had in their first. Once again winning seven games, five of them at North Road, their biggest win was 6-3 against Crewe, but they went down 8-2 on their visit to Nottingham Forest. Sunderland, meanwhile, had impressed in the Football League, finishing in seventh place, just six points adrift of the champions Everton. The Wearsiders' strength was further emphasised the following season when they won the title!

That season was also one of great significance for Newton Heath, for with Darwen now out of the Alliance and Stoke back in the higher section, two new clubs filled their places – Lincoln City and Ardwick FC from Manchester. Ardwick of course eventually became Manchester City, and the first time the two great Manchester rivals met under senior league conditions was to be 10 October 1891 when Newton Heath triumphed 3-1 at North Road, courtesy of two goals by Farman and one from Donaldson. Strangely the two sides had met the previous week in an FA Cup qualifying round when the Heathens won 5-1. The league win over Ardwick marked another milestone for Newton Heath as it was the first time since being elected to the Alliance that the team had celebrated three successive victories. Nottingham Forest won the title but Newton Heath were runners-up.

Then, in 1892, the Football League again decided that it should enlarge. It divided into two divisions, the League becoming the First Division and expanding to 16 clubs, whilst a Second Division was formed by clubs from the Alliance and other clubs such as Woolwich Arsenal, Northwich Victoria and Rotherham. Nottingham Forest and Newton Heath were invited to join the First Division. So the Heathens, who had struggled for those first two seasons in the Alliance, had reached a pinnacle at just the right time and were now one of the game's elite teams. They may have been elite by status, but they were certainly not one of the game's rich clubs, however, staggering from financial problem to financial problem.

The Heathens' first campaign in the Football League was one of direct comparison with their situation off the field. They struggled, yet they survived. Newton Heath's first game in the First Division was against Blackburn Rovers, a formidable force. Rovers had won the FA Cup three times and Newton Heath approached the fixture with some trepidation. The match, at Blackburn's ground, saw Newton Heath go down 4-3 with their goals being scored by Donaldson, Coupar and Farman. The Newton Heath side for that historic game was: Warner, Clements, Brown, Perrins, Stewart, Erentz, Farman, Coupar, Donaldson, Carson and Matthieson.

A week later, the city of Manchester witnessed its first Football League match, the Heathens drawing 1-1 with Burnley, with Scot Robert Donaldson again getting on the scoresheet. Newton Heath failed to win any of their opening six League games and suffered heavy defeats at the hands of Everton (6-0) Burnley (4-0) and West Bromwich Albion (4-0). However, when victory did come, it came in style. Newton Heath's first-ever Football League win was against Wolverhampton Wanderers whom they beat 10-1. Even so, more defeats followed and with victories few and far between, the club finished 16th – bottom of the table – some five points adrift of the next club, Accrington Stanley.

The Football League had decided that at the end of the season, the three bottom clubs in the new First Division would meet the top three clubs in the Second Division for the right to play in the top flight the following year. Small Heath, later to become Birmingham City, had finished top of the Second Division, so it was they who met the Heathens at Stoke for the deciding match. Farman's goal earned Newton Heath a 1-1 draw and in the replay at Bramall Lane, he netted a hat-trick in a 5-2 win that secured the club's place in the First Division for the 1893/94 season.

In 1893, Newton Heath left the mud of their North Road ground for Bank Street in Clayton, where they played amidst the toxic fumes of a chemical works which ran alongside the pitch. While the move to Clayton meant a good walk for many of the club's supporters, Newton Heath at least had a ground to call its own.

The Heathens' second season in the Football League was to have a significant effect on the future of the club. Newton Heath won their first League game on their new ground, beating Burnley 3-2. Their first defeat of the season came at West Bromwich Albion, but the return match at

Bank Street was to lead to a strange turn of events which would seriously affect the club's financial position.

Football had by now become extremely popular and newspapers assigned correspondents to cover games. After the Heathens had beaten West Bromwich Albion 4-1, the *Birmingham Daily Gazette* published the following report: 'It wasn't football, it was simply brutality and if these are the tactics Newton Heath are compelled to adopt to win their matches, the sooner the Football Association deal severely with them the better it will be for the game generally.' Newton Heath's officials were sent a cutting of the story and were furious. They decided to take the newspaper, and its writer William Jephcott, to court.

In March 1894, after a season of football that saw Newton Heath still fighting for survival, the Manchester Civil Court judge granted Newton Heath one farthing in damages and ordered both clubs to pay their own costs. This was a body blow for the Heathens. After that game against the Baggies, Newton Heath won only three further matches, so it came as no surprise when they were once again involved in the end-of-season Test Matches.

Liverpool had topped the Second Division Championship and faced Newton Heath at Blackburn's Ewood Park ground. The game ended 2-0 in favour of the Merseyside outfit and they were promoted from the Second Division, whilst Newton Heath became the first ever club to be relegated.

Newton Heath ended their first campaign in the Second Division in third place, again qualifying for the Test Matches, but this time they lost to Stoke, whose season had ended with them third from bottom of the First Division.

After finishing 6th in 1895/96, the following season Newton Heath found that the play-off system had been changed to a mini-league among the qualifying clubs. Newton Heath were again among the teams in the play-offs, finishing the season as runners-up in the League. They first played the First Division's bottom club Burnley, then after winning and losing to them, faced Sunderland. They drew 1-1 at Bank Street but then lost 2-0 in the north-east and stayed down.

A season later, the Test Matches were abandoned completely in favour of automatic promotion of the top two clubs, and relegation of the bottom two. Burnley and Newcastle United moved up to replace Stoke and Blackburn Rovers, leaving the two Manchester clubs, City and

Newton Heath, in third and fourth places in the Second Division. In the seasons leading up to the turn of the century, the Heathens had missed promotion to the First Division by two places in two successive seasons, and had seen their financial position worsen.

Newton Heath had ended the 1900/01 season in 10th place and with attendances falling away, the club badly needed cash. It was decided to organise a grand bazaar in St James' Hall in Oxford Street and here one man and his dog stepped into the creation of a legend.

A St Bernard dog, with a barrel fastened to its collar, was one of the major attractions at the show. One night after the place had closed, the dog apparently knocked over part of a stall in the centre of the room. A hurried search revealed that the dog had broken loose and a fireman on duty in the hall saw two eyes staring at him in the darkness. He had no idea it was the dog and rushed out of the side entrance to the building. The St Bernard went out the same way.

What happened next has, over the years, become greatly distorted, with parts added to give the story even more impact! The animal was found by a friend of Mr James Taylor and was seen by Mr JH Davies, who fancied buying it. The making of the bargain led to a meeting between of Mr Davies – a self-made man with an eye for investment – and Harry Stafford, the club's right-back and captain. The latter, knowing the trouble in which the club was in, asked Mr Davies for a contribution to club funds. This led to Newton Heath changing hands.

Early in 1902, Newton Heath's creditors could wait no longer. The club had debts of £2,670 and was on the verge of bankruptcy. A creditors' meeting was held and though there were no new tradesmen's debts outstanding since the date of the winding-up order, the club still needed £2,000 to make it solvent again. Harry Stafford got to his feet and told the meeting that he knew where he could get hold of the money. Stafford told the packed New Islington Hall that he had met four businessmen who were each willing to invest £500, but who in turn would require a direct interest in the running of the club. The club's directors were forced into agreement by the creditors and the four men – J Brown of Denton, W Deakin of Manchester together with James Taylor and John Henry Davies, all of whom eventually came forward with their proposals.

On 28 April 1902, Newton Heath FC was no more – it was replaced by Manchester United Football Club. The selection of the new title was not entirely straightforward, though. Manchester Central was suggested but it was decided that it sounded too much like a railway station. Also suggested and rejected was Manchester Celtic before Louis Rocca hit upon the name of Manchester United which was unanimously adopted.

The curtain came down on Newton Heath as the club finished 15th in the Second Division. The following season, as Manchester United, new spirit and new players took them to fifth position in the Second Division but unfortunately they were forced to look on with some envy as their rivals Manchester City won promotion.

The 1903/04 season began with a 2-2 home draw against Bristol City and defeats at the hands of both Burnley and Port Vale. This disappointing start led to a call for action from the club's supporters. In September 1903, the club's first real manager arrived on the scene, Ernest Mangnall, and he was to play an important part in the building of the Manchester United of today. At the end of his first season in charge, United were third in the Second Division table, two places ahead of his former club Burnley. It was a season in which the new manager used 28 players as he searched for the right blend.

The following season began well; in fact, it took on record-breaking proportions after a mixed start. United drew 2-2 with Port Vale on the opening day of the season and beat Bristol City 4-1 before going down at home to Bolton Wanderers on 17 September 1904. They then went on a run of games which saw them not lose any of their next 18 fixtures – 16 wins and two draws – until February 1905. Under Mangnall, United finished their second season in third place, missing promotion for the second year by one place. But the backbone of United's first successful side was being created by the manager. Goalkeeper Harry Moger was signed from Southampton, Jack Picken from Plymouth Argyle and Charlie Roberts from Grimsby Town. Roberts was to later captain the side from his position at centre-half and was a revolutionary in that he wore shorts at a time when players were encouraged to keep their knees covered!

In 1905/06, Ernest Mangnall's third full season in charge, United won promotion to the First Division, finishing runners-up to Bristol City, the two clubs changing places with Nottingham Forest and Wolves. That year United also reached the FA Cup quarter-finals, after victories over Staple Hill, Norwich City and Aston Villa. They were then beaten by Woolwich

Arsenal 3-2. It was quite obvious to the thousands of supporters following the team that real success was sure to come soon.

In 1904, United's rivals Manchester City had thrilled half the people of the city by finishing runners-up to Sheffield Wednesday in the First Division and defeating Bolton Wanderers 1-0 to win the FA Cup. Ironically, it was the backbone of the City side which was to turn Manchester United into a footballing power, after a very shrewd piece of negotiation by Ernest Mangnall.

A year after City's victory in the Cup Final, one of their star players, the legendary Billy Meredith, was suspended from the game for three years, firstly for trying to bribe an Aston Villa player to throw a game and then for illegally trying to obtain payment from City while under suspension – when his punishment included a ban on even going to the club's home ground. Even though the suspension prevented Meredith from playing until April 1908, in May 1906 Ernest Mangnall signed him for a fee of £500. It would turn out to be money well spent.

United started their first campaign in the First Division well enough, winning at Bristol City, drawing with Derby and Notts County and then beating Sheffield United at Bramall Lane. Despite this early promise, Mangnall was constantly on the look-out for new players in an effort to compete with their rivals from across the city.

Then a bombshell hit the game. A Football Association inquiry, which had been investigating the activities of many clubs, discovered that Manchester City had been making illegal payments to their players. Five Manchester City directors were forced to resign and 17 players – many from City's FA Cup-winning squad – were banned from playing for City for life. In a move unheard of before, or, for that matter, since, the club had to sell most of their playing staff or face expulsion from the Football League.

With Billy Meredith having already been signed by United, the spotlight fell on one of the game's best full-backs, Herbert Burgess. He was wanted by Bolton, Everton and Newcastle United but it was Mangnall who beat them in the race for his signature. City announced a meeting at the Queen's Hotel in Manchester's Piccadilly, where clubs interested in their players were invited to attend.

The United boss had no intention of competing against rival clubs, many of them much richer than the Reds, so he made arrangements to approach the players he wanted before the meeting even started. The other clubs did not like this at all and Everton made an official protest to the FA about their loss of Burgess to United – who also signed forward Jimmy Bannister and the prolific goalscorer Alec 'Sandy' Turnbull.

Billy Meredith's suspension was adjusted to end at the same time as his former Manchester City team-mates' and on New Year's Day 1907, a crowd of over 40,000 turned up at Bank Street to see United's new quartet of players in action against Aston Villa. They weren't disappointed as Sandy Turnbull got the only goal of the game and United went on to end the season in eighth place in the First Division.

In 1907/08, Manchester United won the League Championship for the first time, a feat their rivals Manchester City had failed to achieve. They won the title in fine style, finishing nine points ahead of both Aston Villa and Manchester City. United won 23 of their 38 games and only let their form slip once the Championship had been secured.

That summer, United played in Europe. The club decided to take its players on a summer tour to Hungary and Austria and were one of the first northern sides to play on the continent. As Champions of England, they were a great attraction. Earlier in the Championship-winning season, United's players had been pelted with both mud and stones as they left Bradford City's ground and there had been reports of similar outbreaks of hooliganism at United's game with Sheffield Wednesday. But these were nothing compared to United's not-so-amicable 'friendly' in Hungary.

The Reds had first played a combined Vienna Sport and Vienna FC team, and won comfortably 4-0 before travelling on by train to Budapest for two games against Ferencvaros. United won the first meeting 6-2, but having seen their side score twice against the English champions, the Hungarian supporters came to the second match hoping for at least a draw. United started the game in roaring style, and the Hungarian fans applauded in admiration, but the Reds continued to pile on the pressure and the scene turned sour as the referee sent off three United players and a mini-riot developed. Eventually the police got everything under control and United finished the game with eight players and a 7-0 win.

It didn't end there, however. As the United team left the field they were attacked by the crowd. Stones were hurled from the terraces, players were spat on and police finally had to charge the crowd with swords drawn to disperse the throng. The players left the ground under police escort and were on their way back to their hotel in a row of coaches when the rioters attacked again. Several United players sustained head wounds before the police again got the crowd under control. United were glad to get back to England and although the Hungarian incident made headline news for several weeks, it was quickly forgotten as rumours strengthened that the club was about to move from Bank Street to a new ground.

The following season, 1908/09, was not quite as successful in the League, but it was a completely different story in the FA Cup competition. The Cup campaign opened at Bank Street with a game against Brighton & Hove Albion – the Southern League side being beaten 1-0. In the second round, United were again drawn at home, this time to Everton – the Reds again winning by the only goal of the game scored by Halse. Drawn at home for a third successive tie, United thrashed Blackburn Rovers 6-1. For the first time in that season's FA Cup competition, United were drawn away from at home at Second Division Burnley. The Reds were losing 1-0 when the game was abandoned because of a blinding snowstorm. Four days later, United beat the Clarets 3-2. United were now in the semi-finals where their opponents were Newcastle United, a side well on its way to winning the League Championship. The game was played at Bramall Lane but another 1-0 win courtesy of another Harold Halse goal took the Reds into the FA Cup Final.

United's opponents in the final, held at Crystal Palace, were Bristol City. Before the big match, Ernest Mangnall had taken his players away from the distractions of Manchester, where supporters had caught 'Cup Fever' for the first time. With both United and Bristol City being teams who played in red jerseys and white shorts, the FA made them select neutral colours. Bristol chose blue and white while United announced they would play in all white with a thin red line at the neck and the wrists with the red rose of Lancashire on the breast. Sandy Turnbull scored the only goal and man-of-the-match Billy Meredith added another Cup-Winners' medal to the one he won with City in 1904.

United had ended that 1908/09 season in 13th place in the League, but the Cup win meant success for Ernest Mangnall's men for the second time. However, before the start of the 1909/10 season, the game of football went through a major change and the men of Manchester were largely responsible for it!

In 1908 the Reds had played a game against Newcastle United to raise funds for their union, and they had done so against the wishes of both the League and the FA. For the next year, the Players' Union sought affiliation to the Federation of Trades Unions and just before the start of the 1909/10 season was due to begin, matters reached crisis point.

Five days before the start of the new campaign, representatives of the League clubs met in Birmingham and decided that any player admitting to being a member of the union should be suspended, have his wages stopped and be banned from taking part in any game. The move by the League and the FA was to try to prevent a strike. However, it almost caused one! Instead of persuading players that being part of a union would not be of any help to then, it convinced footballers all over the UK that the only way for them to achieve their aims of better pay and conditions was to be part of such a body.

Ernest Mangnall and the United board summoned the players to a meeting where they were told about the League directive. Some discussion followed and the United players said they would like it to be thoroughly understood that they had no grievance whatever with the club but they were fighting for what they believed to be a just principle and therefore they intended to retain their membership of the Players' Union.

The United committee then held a meeting and decided to contact their opponents on the opening day, Bradford City, so as to cause them no inconvenience, to tell them that because the United players were determined to remain members of the Players' Union, the club had no players and therefore couldn't fulfil their league game against the Bantams. Two days before the new season was due to begin, most clubs were claiming to have signed enough amateurs to get fixtures underway – but not United.

On 31 August 1909, the eve of the new football season, the authorities had a change of heart and gave in. The Players' Union was recognised, the suspensions were lifted and the arrears of pay were allowed. In the eyes of many, this was one of Manchester United's most important victories. Had they not stayed together, then their cause would have been lost.

The 1909/10 season went reasonably well but on 22 January 1910, the Reds played their last game at bank Street in front of a crowd of just 7,000 or so loyal supporters. They beat Spurs 5-0 – a fine way to say goodbye to a ground which had held many memories for both the players and the club's followers.

The move to Old Trafford took place during mid-season and the club's opening game at their new ground on 19 February 1910 saw Liverpool as their visitors. The formal opening of the ground took place during the week before the first match, after equipment had been moved into the new offices from the old ground at Clayton. The move came just in time because two days before the Liverpool fixture, fierce gales struck the Manchester area and the old wooden grandstand at Bank Street was blown down, wreckage spilling across the road and damaging houses opposite. As for the game itself, the Merseysiders spoiled the celebrations by winning 4-3.

The 1909/10 campaign ended with the Reds in fifth place but a year later they were crowned League Champions once more. Under the direction of Ernest Mangnall, they had won the League Championship of 1907/08, become the first winners of the FA Charity Shield (which was introduced in 1908) and the Manchester Cup the same year, and had won the FA Cup in 1909. The Championship of 1910/11 would be their final peak under the man whose role in Manchester football is one of unquestionable importance.

The team that took the title in 1910/11 by just one point from Aston Villa was quite different from the one which earned the title three years earlier. Enoch 'Knocker' West had joined the Reds from Nottingham Forest and he netted 19 goals during the course of the League season. Other new faces included goalkeeper Hugh Edmonds, and full-backs Arthur Donnelly and Leslie Hofton. The title race reached an exciting climax on the last Saturday of the season when Aston Villa, leading the table by a point, were away to Liverpool and United were at home to Sunderland. On that last day, Liverpool, lying in the bottom half of the table, pulled off a remarkable victory at Villa Park, winning 3-1, while United thrashed Sunderland 5-1 to win the title. United's victory in the FA Charity Shield of 1911, when they beat Southern League Swindon Town 8-4, marked the end of a great era for the club.

After the 1911/12 season in which United finished 13th in the First Division and excited the FA Cup in the fourth round, they also lost manager Ernest Mangnall who had been in charge throughout their successful years – he left to join Manchester City!

Mangnall's place as secretary-manager was taken by JJ Bentley and under his guidance, United finished fourth in the League in 1912/13. It was around this time that many players who had been part of those Championship-winning sides were reaching the end of their playing days. By the end of the 1913/14 season, only Duckworth, Meredith, Stacey, Turnbull, Wall and West were left and by the end of the following season, in which the club escaped relegation by just one point, United's crowds had dropped to below an average of 15,000.

Though Ernest Mangnall had often been referred to in newspaper articles as United's 'manager' his actual title was secretary and it wasn't until 1914 that the club's first official manager was appointed. John Robson, who arrived at Old Trafford from Brighton & Hove Albion in December of that year, worked under secretary Bentley and took charge of all playing arrangements.

The First World War brought the game of football to a standstill and had an adverse effect on Manchester United, the club being faced with massive overheads for the maintenance of Old Trafford. The hostilities also robbed the club of one of its star players. Sandy Turnbull was killed in France and when football resumed in 1919, there was a very different United line-up for the first game against Derby County, a match United drew 1-1.

Attendances gradually began to rise but United's finish of 12th in 1919/20 did little to inspire. A year later John Chapman replaced Robson as manager and he also filled the secretarial role. Then at the end of the 1921/22 season came the final blow for the Reds, when they were relegated after winning just eight of their 42 games.

By the time the club played its first game in the Second Division for 16 years, none of the great players of the pre-war years remained, with Billy Meredith having left the club in the season prior to the relegation. United ended the 1922/23 campaign in fourth place, having had hopes of immediate promotion until defeats at Blackpool and at home to Leicester City saw them slip out of contention.

After a season in which United finished in mid-table, the club won promotion back to the top flight in 1924/25. Prior to the start of the campaign, a combined United and City side played an Everton and Liverpool side as a testimonial for Ernest Mangnall, who had decided to retire from football management and take up a career in journalism.

The Reds finished the season as runners-up to Leicester City, whom they beat on the opening day of the campaign. The improvement was maintained the following season as the Reds finished a creditable ninth in the First Division. That season saw United progress to the FA Cup semi-finals where they met Manchester City at Bramall Lane. Although City won 3-0, they then lost 1-0 to Bolton in the final and were relegated to the Second Division!

It was around this time that new stars began to emerge for the Reds: Joe Spence, an outside-right who went to play in a record 510 League and Cup games in his 14 years with the club; Frank Barson, a towering centre-half who had been a blacksmith before turning professional and Clarrie Hilditch a wing-half who went on to become the club's player-manager in 1926/27 as the Reds sought a new manager to succeed John Chapman.

In 1927 John Henry Davies died – the man who had saved the club from slipping out of existence in 1902 and played a very important part in the creation of Manchester United.

Former referee Herbert Bamlett was appointed as United's boss – in fact, he had been the youngest to take charge of an FA Cup Final when at the age of only 32, he officiated in the 1914 showpiece. However, under Bamlett, United slipped slowly down the First Division – they were 15th in 1926/27; 18th in 1927/28; 12th in 1928/29; 17th in 1929/30 and then in 1930/31 they were relegated after finishing bottom of the First Division.

After losing 4-3 at home to Aston Villa on the opening day of the season, United followed this with eleven more successive defeats so that by the end of October, their record read:

P	W	D	L	F	A	Pts
12	0	0	12	14	49	0

United also had massive debts and therefore couldn't afford to sign any new players, but even so they plunged recklessly into the transfer market, adding to their own downfall by doing so. By the end of the campaign they had conceded a massive 115 goals, winning just six times at Old Trafford, so it was no surprise that they went down.

Despite being in the Second Division, the club still found themselves fighting for their lives. They lost their opening couple of games to Bradford City at Valley Parade and at home to Southampton in front of very sparse crowds. In fact, only 3,507 turned up for the opening game of the campaign. Herbert Bamlett had lost his job towards the end of the relegation season and the post was filled, albeit temporarily, by club secretary Walter Crickmer. By December 1931, Manchester United were again in dire trouble. Deep in debt and unable to pay off instalments on the loan made to the club to build Old Trafford, and also with no chance of paying for players they had obtained from other clubs, the Reds faced bankruptcy. In Christmas week, the players went to pick up their wages but were told that there was no money available.

James W Gibson, whose company was a major garment producer, had a great love of sport and he was persuaded to help the club. Gibson met United's directors, laid down his terms and agreed to help the club out on the understanding that he would become chairman and be able to elect his own colleagues on to the board. The directors had little choice; they agreed to Gibson's proposals and so once again the club was saved from extinction.

A new manger, Scott Duncan, was appointed and he spent money on new players as he tried to build a strong side, but whether the former Rangers and Newcastle player spent wisely is debatable. In the season in which they almost faded into obscurity United finished 12th in the Second Division; a year later they had moved up to sixth but then in 1933/34, even Gibson's money couldn't prevent them from falling to the lowest point in the club's history, just one point away from the Third Division. In fact, United's future hung by the most slender of threads as late as the final day of the campaign – 5 May 1934.

Lincoln City were bottom and nothing could save the Imps from being relegated. United were above them, seven points better off and a point behind their opponents on that final day, Millwall. The Reds played their hearts out and with goals from Manley and Cape they won 2-0 to save themselves from the drop.

The 1934/35 season began with Scott Duncan's new players in the United line-up. Much improved performances brought the crowds flocking back to Old Trafford as the club finished fifth in Division Two. A season later and the Reds had something to celebrate as they won the Second Division title. Scott Duncan's side had achieved the title with a tremendous run-in to the end of the campaign, stringing together 19 games without a defeat and clinching promotion with a 3-2 win over local rivals Bury at Gigg Lane. The club's only defeat after the beginning of the year, apart from a 2-0 FA Cup loss at Stoke had been to lose by the only goal of the game at Bradford City. Constantly being able to field a virtually unchanged side was a great help as the club returned to the top flight for the first time since the start of the decade.

However, their stay was a short one! By the end of the 1936/37 season, United had won only ten games, eight of them at Old Trafford, and just a season after celebrating their promotion from the Second Division, they were back there.

The club continued to yo-yo between divisions – in 1937/38 they won promotion back to the First Division as runners-up to Aston Villa, although United did it by the skin of their teeth. Sheffield United had exactly the same record as the Reds but their goal average of 1.738 was slightly inferior to United's 1.952 – the Reds went up and the Blades stayed down with Coventry City only a point behind in third.

Scott Duncan had resigned in November 1937 and Walter Crickmer was given the reins for another spell as the club's temporary manager. A month before he had resigned, Duncan had brought Jack Rowley to the club from Bournemouth and with Louis Rocca having spotted young Irishman Johnny Carey and Stan Pearson breaking into the side, things were beginning to look up for the Reds. In the game against Chesterfield, Tommy Bamford scored four times in a 7-1 win. United lost just five more games over the course of the season after that defeat of the Spireites to win promotion.

United ended the 1938/39 season in 14th place in the First Division, but it was events outside football which would have a long-lasting effect on the Old Trafford club.

At the outbreak of the Second World War, football was suspended. In March 1941 the Luftwaffe put paid to all the efforts of James Gibson and those at the club. Old Trafford was bombed. Manchester City quickly offered to help their neighbours, proposing that Maine Road could be used as a temporary home for United until Old Trafford could be rebuilt.

When the game began again after years of friendlies and makeshift matches – though United did win the 1942 Football League North Cup and were runners-up in 1945 – the club would start again in the First

Division with a new manager, Matt Busby. The genial Scot wasted little time and right from the outset showed the character and judgement that eventually became legendary.

In 1946/47, football returned to a national league instead of being divided into northern and southern regional leagues. United finished the season as runners-up to Liverpool in the League Championship. Busby's talented collection of vastly experienced players actually finished runners-up in each of the first three seasons of league football following the hostilities. Even if the club did miss out on the title, that was impressive consistency.

The Reds were not to be denied a deserved honour, though, giving Busby his first trophy by winning the 1948 FA Cup Final against Blackpool. The game was regarded as one of the competition's classic finals. United dominated the competition from the start and reached the Wembley final by scoring 18 goals in the five ties. In the third round at Aston Villa, United found themselves a goal down after 13 seconds without having touched the ball! It was probably the worst thing Villa could have done for by the interval, United were leading 5-1. Villa fought back creditably to 5-4 but United had the last word when Pearson netted to make it 6-4. United then beat Liverpool 3-0, Charlton Athletic 2-0, Preston North End 4-1 and Derby County in the semi-final 3-1 to set up the Wembley meeting with Blackpool whom they beat 4-2.

After finishing as runners-up in the League three years on the trot, then fourth, followed by another second place, the 'nearly men' of Manchester United finally cracked it. The Reds won the 1951/52 League Championship, four points clear of runners-up Tottenham Hotspur. They were very prolific up front, with Jack Rowley netting 30 goals and Stan Pearson 22.

Jack Rowley opened the Championship-winning season in superb form, scoring hat-tricks in the first two games of the campaign – a 3-3 draw at West Bromwich Albion and a 4-2 home defeat of Middlesbrough. However, United weren't invincible and suffered a 1-0 defeat at Bolton. The early pace-setters were Portsmouth but the south coast club fell away to leave United. Arsenal and Spurs as the fancied teams. The Gunners in fact were chasing a League and Cup double – they did reach Wembley but lost 1-0 to Newcastle United. In the League, Arsenal hit Championship form just after Christmas until the end of April with an unbeaten run.

United matched them except for another double defeat in matches at Huddersfield Town and Portsmouth.

The three clubs were almost neck and neck on the final laps with the Reds just edging it. The destiny of the League Championship was decided on the final day of the season with Arsenal visiting Old Trafford. The London club's goal difference was inferior – they needed to win 7-0 – but in the event United proved worthy champions, beating the Gunners 6-1 with Rowley netting another treble. United finished on 57 points with both Spurs and Arsenal four points behind. After coming so close to the title for five years, it was a fitting peak for the club and established Matt Busby as a manager of style and perception.

After winning the League title in 1951/52, Busby not surprisingly kicked off the following season with his winning team but after a handful of games it was obvious that the first great post-war side had passed its peak. Busby realised that he had to start making changes and bringing in new players. Always in his mind had been the dream of a team based on youngsters that he had brought up in his way. The result was that as well as having Jimmy Murphy as his right-hand man, he had Joe Armstrong signing the best schoolboy players he could find throughout the whole of Ireland and Billy Behan in Dublin and Bob Bishop and Bob Harper in Belfast didn't miss much in the way of talent.

United began to dominate the FA Youth Cup, winning the competition for five successive seasons, beginning from its inception in the 1952/53 season. The result was that towards the end of that disappointing campaign, players such as Dennis Viollet, Bill Foulkes, Duncan Edwards, Jackie Blanchflower and Jeff Whitefoot started to get the odd first team game.

In 1953/54, the Busby Babes, as they became known, finished fourth in the First Division and the following season, fifth but after that everything began to fall into place and in 1955/56 they won the League Championship by a remarkable 11 points from runners-up Blackpool – and that with a team whose average age was barely 22!

The Reds were at the forefront of the 1955/56 Championship race right from the start, though they didn't go to the top of the table until December following a 2-1 home win over Sunderland. In the second-half of the season, United lost just two games and clinched the title with two games to spare by beating their nearest rivals Blackpool 2-1. Tommy

Taylor's tally of 25 goals was backed up by 20 from Viollet and their winning margin of 11 points equalled the record shared in the previous century by Preston North End, Sunderland and Aston Villa.

United were in peak form and they won the Championship again in 1956/57, this time finishing eight points clear of second-placed Spurs. During the course of that campaign whenever Taylor or Viollet was injured, Bobby Charlton would play. He made his debut against Charlton at The Valley, scoring twice in a 4-2 win. He finished the season with 10 goals in 14 League appearances – clearly one for the future! It was certainly a high-scoring season with United topping the hundred mark – Whelan leading the way with 26 goals, with Taylor on 22 and Viollet 16.

Towards the end of the campaign, Busby had to ring the changes because of the club's FA Cup commitments. In that competition they went to Wembley and came within a whisker of achieving the elusive League and FA Cup double. Just six minutes into the final against Aston Villa, Reds keeper Ray Wood was carried off the field suffering from a smashed cheekbone. Northern Ireland international winger Peter McParland had headed the ball into Wood's arms and it seemed like a routine matter for the keeper to kick it clear. But McParland, perhaps fired up by the occasion, kept on coming and crashed into the United goalkeeper. Jackie Blanchflower took over in goal and the rest of his defence performed heroics to keep the match goalless at half-time. Tommy Taylor scored with a fine header but McParland turned from villain to Villa's hero with two second-half goals.

As Champions in 1955/56, United were invited to enter the following season's European Cup competition. Busby was keen to take part and in their first-ever European match against Anderlecht in Brussels, the Reds won 2-0 with goals from Viollet and Taylor. The return leg was played at Maine Road – the Old Trafford floodlights not yet being ready. That night, the Reds would have beaten any club side in the world but nobody could have envisaged the 10-0 scoreline with Viollet (4) Taylor (3) Whelan (2) and Berry the goalscorers. In the next round, United faced Borussia Dortmund and after a 3-2 home win, the Reds played out a goalless draw in Germany to go through to the quarter-finals. Atletico Bilbao had not been beaten at home in any competition for three years and when they led United 3-0 at half-time, the tie looked dead and buried. Though Taylor and Viollet pulled it back to 3-2, the Spanish outfit responded with two goals to lead 5-2 with five minutes to go. Billy Whelan then scored a wonder goal in the dying moments to give the Reds hope in the second leg. Two goals from Viollet and a third by Taylor levelled the scores and with just two minutes to go Johnny Berry fired home United's fourth goal in a marvellous second-leg display. United's semi-final opponents were Real Madrid. They were the greatest team in the world and after beating United 3-1 at the Bernabeu Stadium held the Reds to a 2-2 draw to go through to the final 5-3 on aggregate.

As United readied themselves for another treble bid in season 1957/58, their hopes were to come crashing to the ground on the snow and ice of Munich in what was to be one of the saddest seasons in British football.

There is no knowing what the Reds might have achieved in 1957/58, and the seasons thereafter, but for the Munich disaster. At the time of the tragedy, United were trying to win the League Championship for a third successive season and had already reached the fifth round of the FA Cup and the quarter-finals of the European Cup, having beaten Shamrock Rovers and Dukla Prague.

The Busby Babes flew out of Manchester to face Red Star Belgrade in the second leg of the quarter-final tie, having won the first encounter at Old Trafford 2-1. Five days before the Munich tragedy, United had played Arsenal at Highbury and had beaten the Gunners 5-4 in one of the best displays of attacking football ever seen in the Football League. As the tie in Belgrade approached, the Reds had also made progress in the FA Cup with victories over Workington and Ipswich Town. The run up to the second leg was encouraging for just days before their triumph at Highbury, United had thumped Bolton Wanderers 7-2.

The game against Red Star saw United up against 11 desperate footballers and a fiercely partisan 52,000 crowd as well as facing some bizarre refereeing decisions from Austrian official Karl Kainer. United survived the Battle of Belgrade, however, drawing the game 3-3 and winning through to their second successive European Cup semi-final.

The twin-engined Elizabethan plane bringing the players back to Manchester stopped off at Munich to refuel. As the plane tried to take off it came to a halt, the problem being a very rich mixture of fuel which had caused the engines to over-accelerate. A second take-off attempt was given by air traffic control, and for a second time the plane came to a halt. The United party left the plane to wait in the lounge, during which time it began to snow quite heavily. On the third attempt, the plane left the runway, but then crashed through a fence and crossed a road before the port wing hit a house. The wing and part of the plane's tail were ripped off and the house caught fire. The plane's cockpit struck a tree and the starboard side of the fuselage hit a wooden hut containing a truck loaded with tyres and fuel.

Matt Busby was badly hurt and was taken away injured, whilst Bill Foulkes and Harry Gregg helped the injured, including Bobby Charlton and Dennis Viollet. It was not until the following day that the full horror of the air crash became evident.

The Busby babes were no more – players of the calibre of Roger Byrne, Tommy Taylor, Mark Jones, Geoff Bent, Liam Whelan, David Pegg and Eddie Colman had been killed instantly whilst club secretary Walter Crickmer, first team trainer Tom Curry and coach Bert Whalley also lost their lives. Duncan Edwards and Johnny Berry were both critically injured and fighting for their lives, whilst manager Matt Busby had suffered extensive injuries. Duncan Edwards sadly lost his fight for life, and Johnny Berry and Jackie Blanchflower were two of nine players who survived, but neither played again.

The following weekend, United were due to play League leaders Wolverhampton Wanderers at Old Trafford and though the club faced a long journey home, it was thought that they would close the four-point gap at the top of the table. But of course, following the Munich crash, the game was postponed until later in the season.

Jimmy Murphy was given the job of rebuilding the club. Life had to go on despite the tragedy, and Manchester United would play again.

In the days following Munich, Manchester mourned its famous footballing heroes as their bodies were flown home to lie overnight in the club's gymnasium under the main grandstand before being passed on to relatives for the funerals. Thousands of supporters turned out to pay their last respects. Where families had requested that funerals should be private, United fans stayed away from gravesides, but lined the routes to look on in silence as the corteges passed.

To give United a chance of surviving in football, the FA waived its rule which 'cup-ties' a player once he has played in an FA Cup round in a particular season. The rule prevents him from playing for another club in the same competition, so if he is transferred to a new club, he can't play in the competition until the following season. But United's need for 'new' players was desperate, and Murphy began the rebuilding by signing Blackpool's Ernie Taylor.

Some 13 days after Munich, United took to the field again in their postponed FA Cup fifth round tie against Sheffield Wednesday. On a night of immense emotion, the crowd of 60,000 openly wept. Harry Gregg and Bill Foulkes were the only familiar names but United's new boys gave a great account of themselves and, with Shay Brennan scoring twice on his debut, won 3-0. United had reached the quarter-finals of the FA Cup but, two days after that cup tie, Duncan Edwards lost his fight for survival and the sadness of Munich resurfaced.

Just a day after Edwards's death, they were plunged back into League football as a crowd of 66,124 packed into Old Trafford to witness a 1-1 draw with Nottingham Forest. The patched-up side won only one of their remaining 14 League games but still finished in a commendable 9th place. However, in the FA Cup it was a different story. After drawing 2-2 at West Bromwich Albion, a Bobby Charlton goal gave them a 1-0 victory in the replay. Then it was back to the Midlands and Villa Park for a 2-2 draw in the semi-final against Fulham. The replay at Highbury saw Alex Dawson net a hat-trick in a 5-3 win. United's opponents in the final were Bolton Wanderers, and though Bobby Charlton crashed a shot against the Bolton upright, two goals from Nat Lofthouse - one most controversial - gave the Wanderers the Cup.

Five days after losing to Bolton, United faced AC Milan in the European Cup semi-final first leg at Old Trafford. They were without Bobby Charlton, who had been picked to play for England in a friendly against Portugal on the same night! The patched-up Reds fought bravely to win 2-1, but it was a slim lead to take to the San Siro Stadium for the second leg and United, after being pelted with cabbages and carrots by the 80,000-strong crowd, went down 4-0.

In 1958/59, United's hopes of a another Wembley trip were soon ended when they were knocked out in the third round by Norwich City, but in the League, the Reds finished as runners-up to Wolverhampton Wanderers - it was an incredible achievement. After taking a little while to settle, the team won 11 games out of 12 between November and February to make the title chase a two-horse race. United netted over a hundred League goals with Bobby Charlton scoring 29 and Dennis Viollet 21. Charlton scored a hat-trick in a 5-2 win over Chelsea on the opening day of the season and when he and Viollet hit scoring form together, the Reds were unstoppable. The two of them shared four goals in the games against Blackburn and Portsmouth, both of which were won by a 6-1 margin.

Viollet's best season in terms of goals scored came in 1959/60 as United, hoping to build on their position of runners-up, could only finish 7th. It was hardly the fault of the United forward who broke Jack Rowley's club scoring record by notching 32 League goals. United again topped 100 goals for the season with Viollet being well supported by Charlton 18, Dawson 15 and 13 from new signing Albert Quixall. The Reds were far too erratic to win the title, scoring four one week but conceding four the next! Things came to a head when the Reds travelled to Newcastle United and lost 7-3. This forced Busby's hand and he signed Maurice Setters to stiffen the midfield and left-back Noel Cantwell who later became a most influential captain.

There was certainly no instant success with United unable to improve on 7th place in 1960/61 and making a fourth round FA Cup exit. A drop to 15th place the following season was compensated for by a run to the FA Cup semi-finals, where the Reds went down 3-1 to Spurs at Hillsborough. Just before the start of that 1961/62 season, Busby had bought David Herd and he had responded by scoring 14 goals but in the summer of 1962, he spent again, splashing out £115,000 to sign Denis Law from Italian side Torino. With Law and Herd supported by Charlton and Quixall and youngsters Johnny Giles and Nobby Stiles forcing their way into the side, United were hoping for great things. But still the balance wasn't quite right, and Busby went out and signed Pat Crerand from Celtic.

Though it was too late to pull things back – United finished in their worst-ever position under Busby of 19th – they sailed through every round of the FA Cup without needing a replay. Their opponents in the Wembley final were Leicester City and with the Foxes having finished fourth in the First Division, United were the underdogs. Denis Law gave United the lead before two goals from David Herd helped United win 3-1. The victory more than made up for the club's disappointing League form and finally buried the memory of their two Wembley defeats in 1957 and 1958. The Reds now looked forward to the 1963/64 season in a more confident mood.

Denis Law was to enjoy his best scoring season for United in a campaign which was also significant for the League debut of a certain George Best. Law scored a total of 46 goals in League and Cup competitions, including 30 in the League from the same number of appearances. This undoubtedly helped the Reds to finish as runners-up to Liverpool. Law also scored 10 in six FA Cup ties as United reached the semi-finals, only to lose to West Ham United, and eight in ten games in the European Cup-Winners' Cup. The Reds exited the European Cup-Winners' Cup in a most disappointing fashion – after beating Sporting Lisbon 4-1 in the first leg at Old Trafford, they squandered their three-goal advantage and were beaten 5-0 in the return leg.

Matt Busby still felt that United needed a top-class winger and so in the summer of 1964 he bought the experienced England international John Connelly from Burnley for a fee of £60,000. He was the final piece in the jigsaw that turned a team of runners-up into champions. In 1964/65, the Reds pipped Leeds United to the League Championship title – in the days when goal average settled the issue if two teams were level on points, United won by the narrow margin of 0.686 of a goal!

In fact, the Reds still had a game in hand when they knew they had won the title, so the last game of the season against Aston Villa at Villa Park was of little importance and United duly lost. They were League Champions for the first time since Munich. Connelly certainly played his part, scoring 15 goals from his position at outside-right whilst Law led the way with 28, well supported by Herd with 20. Best playing wide on the left also reached double figures and whilst the forwards inevitable attracted the headlines, United's defence only conceded 39 goals. The highlight of the season was undoubtedly the 7-0 thrashing of Aston Villa with Denis Law netting four of the goals. The club also did well in other competitions that season – in fact they were chasing a treble for most of the campaign – reaching the semi-finals of both the European Fairs Cup and FA Cup.

United were again determined to make an impression on three fronts in 1965/66 and although they certainly succeeded in doing so, they failed to actually land a trophy. Back in their beloved European Cup, United reached the semi-finals only to be beaten by Partizan Belgrade. That European season will be remembered for an incredible performance in the quarter-finals against Benfica in Lisbon, which was inspired by George

Best, who came home having been dubbed 'El Beatle'. The Irishman destroyed the Portuguese champions with one of the finest individual displays ever seen in European football. The Reds reached the semi-finals of the FA Cup, too, despite one or two scares along the way, but a hectic season caught up with them when they went down 1-0 to Everton at Burnden Park just three days after the European tie against Partizan Belgrade. Though United were always up among the leading teams in the race for the League title and put in a tremendous late finish, including beating Aston Villa 6-1, they had to be content with 4th place.

In the close season, Matt Busby signed a new goalkeeper, Alex Stepney, from Chelsea. He was probably the biggest single factor behind the winning of the 1966/67 League Championship, the Reds finishing four points clear of runners-up Nottingham Forest. The club clinched the title in spectacular fashion, winning 6-1 at West Ham United to take the honours with a match to spare. United went through the season unbeaten at home, although at the turn of the year it was still a three-horse race with Liverpool and Nottingham Forest also in contention. United played out a goalless draw at Anfield, after which Liverpool slipped out of the title race. At one stage, Forest were only a point behind the Reds but the decisive fixture at Old Trafford saw Denis Law score the game's only goal. A total of over a million fans watched United's home games – the highest attendance figures since the Second World War – but it wasn't just winning the title that brought supporters flocking to watch the club, it was the quality of the team's football coupled with all the personalities in the United side.

Despite losing their opening game of the 1967/68 season, United then went 11 games without defeat and just after the turn of the year, the Reds held a five-point lead at the top of the First Division. However, following a third round FA Cup exit at the hands of Spurs, the side then lost five of their next eight games to allow Manchester City into the title race. The Blues also beat United 3-1 at Old Trafford. The two Manchester clubs were level on points as they went into their final matches but United four days away from their European Cup semi-final second leg, lost 2-1 at home to Sunderland whilst City won 4-3 at Newcastle to take the Championship.

United's 1967/68 European Cup campaign opened with an easy tie against the Hibernian part-timers of Malta. D Sadler and Denis Law each scored twice in a 4-0 win whilst the return in Malta ended goalless on a rock-hard sandy pitch. United's opponents in the next round were Sarajevo and in a match in which George Best was repeatedly chopped down, United returned from Yugoslavia with another goalless draw. A 2-1 win in the return took the Reds into the quarter-finals were they faced Polish side Gornik Zabrze. After a 2-0 first-leg win at Old Trafford, United played the second-leg on a snow covered pitch with snow still falling and though they went down 1-0, they had won through to the semi-finals for the fourth time in their history. United's opponents were their old friends and rivals, Real Madrid. The Reds took a 1-0 lead to Madrid, courtesy of a George Best goal but by half-time in the return game, the Spanish outfit had built up a 3-1 lead. With time running out, Sadler reduced the arrears on the night but level on aggregate and then Bill Foulkes netted a third goal to book United's place in the final with what was to be his only European Cup goal.

Manchester United's European Cup Final opponents at Wembley were Benfica. The Reds took the lead with a goal from captain Bobby Charlton, only for the Portuguese champions to hit back. Extra-time was required and again United took the initiative. Best scored their second, followed by a third from birthday boy Brian Kidd, just 19 and in the team as a replacement for Denis Law, who was out with a broken leg. Bobby Charlton completed the 4-1 victory. It was a wonderful moment for all those with United in their hearts – dedicated to those killed or injured at Munich.

The following year, the Reds attempted to win the unofficial 'world title' by defeating Argentinian side Estudiantes in the World Club Championship. In a bad-tempered match over two spiteful legs, United were defeated 2-1 on aggregate. Nobby Stiles received his marching orders in the first leg and George Best was sent off in the second.

Despite their successful season, it was clear that some United players were no longer in their prime and that changes would have to be made. Matt Busby thought long and hard about whether he wanted to remain in charge as manager but he was still at the helm when the 1968/69 season opened. Three games were lost in the opening month of August and though Busby signed Willie Morgan to bolster the team, Law and Best's goal returns were down on previous seasons and United ended the season in 11th place. Midway through the campaign, Busby decided he would 'go upstairs' to become general manager and let a new man run the team. The club solved the problem by looking within their own staff and decided to promote Wilf McGuinness to the position of chief coach.

Denis Law hit a hat-trick in a 3-1 win at Waterford as United began their defence of the European Cup and Law then went one better by netting four in a 7-1 second leg win. Law was on fire and scored twice in a 3-0 defeat of Anderlecht, but then United nearly gave the tie away when they lost 3-1 in Belgium. The Reds were back to their best for the quarter-final tie with Rapid Vienna, though, winning 3-0 at Old Trafford before playing out a goalless draw in Austria. United's semi-final opponents were AC Milan but after losing 2-0 in the first leg in the San Siro, the Reds were up against it. Though United won 1-0 at Old Trafford it wasn't enough and they went out 2-1 on aggregate. Sadly, an unruly element in the Stretford End began to hurl all sorts of missiles and rubbish onto the pitch and the club were ordered to erect a screen behind their goals before playing in European competition again. But there was no need to start work immediately, for it would be another eight years before the Reds qualified for a European return!

After drawing the opening game of the 1969/70 season 2-2 at Crystal Palace, United suffered three successive defeats – the fans were starting to worry. McGuinness was unlucky in that for most of the season he was without Nobby Stiles, recovering from a cartilage operation and problems with his knee. Though the team then began to hold their own, there were lapses like a 4-0 beating at Manchester City and a 5-1 reversal at Newcastle, immediately avenged by a 7-0 thumping of West Bromwich Albion at Old Trafford in the next match. The team did McGuinness proud in reaching the semi-finals of both the FA and League Cups including an 8-2 win at Northampton Town in the former. This game belonged to George Best, who scored six of United's goals.

United's opponents in the FA Cup semi-final were Leeds United and it took three encounters before a goal was scored! After the sides had battled vainly to score at both Hillsborough and Villa Park, it took a Billy Bremner goal to separate the sides in the third meeting at Burnden Park. In the League Cup, United met rivals Manchester City over two legs. The Blues won the first-leg at Maine Road 2-1 and following a 2-2 draw at Old Trafford, it was they who went through to the final 4-3 on aggregate. United finished 8th in the League and though they beat Watford 2-0 in a match for third place between the losing FA Cup semi-finalists, it counted for little when measured against the Reds' ambitions.

On paper, Manchester United still had a top-class team but they made a disastrous start to the 1970/71 season. They then picked up, proving they were still capable of producing winning performances. They again reached the League Cup semi-final but couldn't master their Third Division opponents, Aston Villa, and went out of the competition. The defeat signalled the end of Wilf McGuinness's reign and following a 4-4 draw at Derby County three days later, he was relieved of his duties. Sir Matt was put back in temporary charge and despite the Reds being bundled out of the FA Cup at Middlesbrough, he helped the team claw their way back up the table to again finish 8th.

Frank O'Farrell was the next man to take charge, in June 1971. His United side got off to a brilliant start, losing just one of their opening 14 games. By early October they were top of the First Division. However, in November they went out of the League Cup at Stoke and after three successive draws the following month came seven successive defeats – including 5-1 at Leeds – and United slipped down the table at an alarming rate. O'Farrell realised he had to turn to the transfer market and so he brought Martin Buchan and Ian Storey-Moore to Old Trafford. There were also continuing off-field problems with George Best, but United ended the season with a 3-0 defeat of Stoke – who also knocked United out of the FA Cup – and a third successive 8th place finish.

United made a very disappointing start to the 1972/73 season and slumped to the bottom of the First Division. Despite winning two games following a morale-sapping defeat in the Manchester derby, United crashed 5-0 at Crystal Palace – it was O'Farrell's last game in charge.

There was a need for a dynamic personality and bold leadership and when the United board appointed O'Farrell's successor – Tommy Docherty – they found just the man. The Doc's first challenge was to keep the Reds in the top flight, while gradually replacing the fading legends of the 1960s. The rebuilding started immediately, with George Graham and Alex Forsyth joining the playing staff and Tommy Cavanagh being drafted in as coach. Celtic's Lou Macari followed after the club had been knocked out of the FA Cup. Bobby Charlton hinted that he might retire at the end of the season, whilst Denis Law and Tony Dunne looked to be on their way out of Old Trafford. There was a slight improvement in United's fortunes over the rest of the campaign and they narrowly avoided relegation by finishing in 18th place.

During the summer of 1973, there was much speculation about the future make-up of the Football League. The League Secretary, Alan Hardaker, put forward a revolutionary scheme in which he proposed a reduction in the number of clubs in the top flight to 20, with three promotion and relegation places instead of two. While the scheme as a whole was not considered it was decided to adopt the three-up-and-three-down idea for 1973/74.

United went through a spell during the 1973/74 season that was even worse than the previous campaign and by the turn of the year, they were just one position higher than they had been 12 months previously – 21st! Though Charlton and Law had left Old Trafford – the latter going to rivals Manchester City – George Best had decided to return to the fold. However, by the New Year, Best had gone again and goalkeeper Alex Stepney was the club's leading scorer after being appointed penalty-taker by the Doc. In the first Manchester derby at Maine Road – a game that ended goalless – Lou Macari and Mike Doyle began throwing punches at one another. Referee Clive Thomas ordered them both off but they refused to go! Thomas marched both teams off and it seemed that the game would be abandoned, but both teams returned minutes later without the two offenders.

The club were hanging on to their First Division status by their fingertips but after three successive victories the real drama came on 27 April 1974 when United, with two games left to play, entertained Manchester City. Norwich City were bottom of the table with 29 points. United were above them on 32, two points behind Southampton. Just above the Saints were Birmingham City on 35 points. If Birmingham lost what was their last game and United could win both of theirs, they could still survive. However, with the game against City goalless, United legend Denis Law back-heeled the ball over the line to relegate his former club!

Manchester United were in the Second Division after the glory years of the 1960s, the brilliance of the 1950s and the building of the 1940s – the unthinkable had become a reality.

To Tommy Docherty's credit, the Reds bounced back very quickly. They won their first four games to top the division and stayed at the top for the whole season. Stuart 'Pancho' Pearson scored 17 League goals and

Lou Macari netted the goal that clinched promotion in the game against Southampton at the Dell. One of the best signings Docherty made that season was Steve Coppell, whose arrival signalled the end for United winger Willie Morgan. The Scottish player left after a series of much publicised incidents, and then a televised condemnation of Docherty led to Morgan being sued by his former manager for slander. The case was eventually heard in 1978 and this led to Docherty being charged with perjury after withdrawing from the first battle. The United boss appeared at the Old Bailey three years later and was found not guilty.

United's start to the 1975/76 season was remarkable, as back in the First Division they won five of their first six games. Docherty knew though that he still needed to improve his squad and in November 1975 he bought the exciting winger Gordon Hill from Millwall. Though United's League form slipped, they had a great run in the FA Cup, reaching the final against already-relegated Southampton. The final was an anti-climax to a successful season as former United midfielder Jim McCalliog created the only goal of the game for Bobby Stokes's shot to beat Alex Stepney. The day after the final, thousands turned out to welcome back United's defeated players and, as Docherty said, 'If this is what they do when we come back without the Cup, what's it going to be like next year?'

The 1976/77 season saw United leading the First Division at one stage, but then they went eight games without a victory and slumped to 17th position. Out came Docherty's chequebook and Jimmy Greenhoff, older brother of Brian, arrived from Stoke City. The Reds, having beaten Ajax in the first round of the UEFA Cup, went out at the next stage, defeated by Juventus. Though Everton had knocked United out of the League Cup, they did well in the FA Cup, reaching the final. Their opponents were the all-conquering Liverpool who had already won the League – United finished 6th – and were aiming to complete the third leg of a League, FA Cup and European Cup treble. It was a party atmosphere at Wembley but Liverpool's party fell flat with goals from Stuart Pearson and Jimmy Greenhoff winning the cup for United for the fourth time.

The joy of that win didn't last long for Tommy Docherty, however. Just 44 days later, he was sacked when it emerged he had set up home with the wife of the club's physiotherapist Laurie Brown. He was replaced as manager by Dave Sexton.

The 1977/78 season could have had no better start for Sexton with

Lou Macari netting a hat-trick in a 4-1 home win over Birmingham City. Even so, this was the team that Tommy Docherty had built and United fans were quick to remind the new manager of the fact by chanting the Doc's name at regular intervals. But over the course of the season, Sexton's side were inconsistent and ended the campaign in 10th place, in spite of him signing Joe Jordan and Gordon McQueen.

In the European Cup-Winners' Cup, United's first round tie with St Etienne was fought on two fronts, on and off the field. In France, United drew 1-1 but the real drama was happening on the terraces where the French club had ignored all of United's appeals for fan segregation. Fighting broke out and riot police were called in. UEFA decided to throw the Reds out of the competition, but the decision was revoked after an appeal. United were ordered to play their 'home' leg in a neutral stadium at least 200 km from Old Trafford. They chose Plymouth, where they beat the French side 2-0. United came to grief in the next round, however, at the hands of FC Porto. The Reds went down 4-0 in Portugal but won the return 5-2 to make it a fighting farewell.

The following season,1978/79, saw United celebrate their centenary year with a 4-0 win over Real Madrid, but they continued their indifferent performances in the League and finished 9th. An early exit in the League Cup at the hands of Third Division Watford was more than compensated for when the Reds reached Wembley for a third FA Cup Final in four years. The match against Arsenal proved to be one of the most dramatic finals of all time. Trailing 2-0 with just four minutes to go, United scored twice through Gordon McQueen and Sammy McIlroy and it looked like extra-time was looming. However, Alan Sunderland scored a last-minute winner, to the delight of those who had made the short journey from Highbury. One of the Gunners' other goalscorers that day would later make history for United as the first man to score in an FA Cup Final for two different teams – Frank Stapleton.

The start to the new season was one of the best in several years and by the turn of the year, the lowest position that the Reds had occupied was third – there was optimism that the 13-year gap since the club last won the Championship might be bridged. Sadly, in February 1980, club chairman Louis Edwards died of a heart attack and was succeeded by his son Martin. The battle for the Championship continued between United and Liverpool, but one scoreline caused much concern when Ipswich beat the Reds 6-0 – a match in which Gary Bailey also saved two penalties. However, United recovered to win eight of their last ten League games, but they still finished as runners-up to the Merseyside club.

During the summer of 1980, Dave Sexton tried unsuccessfully to buy Republic of Ireland star Liam Brady from Arsenal. He was at the end of his contract and the Gunners had put a fee of £1.5 million on the player. There was strong speculation that he would sign for the Old Trafford club but in the end he joined Italian giants Juventus.

Not only was there no Brady, but the injury jinx which had hit the club during pre-season training continued with McQueen, Wilkins and Jordan missing much of the campaign. The injuries became a millstone round Sexton's neck and scoring goals became a major problem. Following early exits from the UEFA and League Cups, Sexton signed Garry Birtles from Nottingham Forest, but he struggled in front of goal. It was Forest who knocked the Reds out of the FA Cup, leaving them with just the Championship to play for. The return of McQueen to the heart of the defence showed United what they'd been missing and the club produced seven successive victories at the end of the campaign to finish 8th. But it was too late to save Sexton, who lost his job.

Sexton's replacement was Ron Atkinson, who had shown at West Bromwich Albion that he was capable of producing a first-class team with limited resources. His arrival at Old Trafford brought swift changes – out went coaches Harry Gregg and Jack Crompton and physio Laurie Brown, to be replaced by Mick Brown as his right-hand man, Eric Harrison as youth coach and Jim Headridge as physio. Sadly Headridge collapsed and died at the Cliff Training Ground within a year of joining the club. The new manager signed Frank Stapleton from Arsenal and, shortly after the season got underway, broke the British transfer record to recruit Bryan Robson from his former club for £1.5 million and her spent around a third of that to sign another ex-Albion man in Remi Moses. United failed in the two domestic cup competitions but ended the season in 3rd place in the First Division to qualify for the following season's UEFA Cup.

Though the 1982/83 season was not to be their year in the race for the Championship, it was a different story in the domestic cup competitions. In Europe, United fell at the first hurdle, going out of the UEFA Cup to Valencia. United progressed to the final of the League Cup where their opponents were runaway League leaders Liverpool. Though Norman

Whiteside scored a great goal after 12 minutes, Moran and McQueen picked up injuries and Liverpool equalised through Alan Kennedy. United held out to force extra-time but went down 2-1 to a Ronnie Whelan goal. United also reached Wembley in the FA Cup, facing lowly Brighton & Hove Albion. With the score 2-2, the game went into extra-time and Gary Bailey saved United's day when he threw himself at the feet of Gordon Smith when it seemed certain the Seagulls' player would score. In the replay it was all one-way traffic with Robson (2) Muhren and Whiteside scoring United's goals in a 4-0 win.

The side began the 1983/84 season playing attractive football, and eight wins and just two defeats in the opening 11 games saw them sitting on top of the First Division. The Reds exited the Milk Cup in the fourth round, beaten by Oxford United in a third meeting. Their defence of the FA Cup was no luckier as United were beaten 2-0 by Third Division Bournemouth. The United fans chanted 'Atkinson Out!' – this to a manager who had won the FA Cup and Charity Shield the previous season and whose club at the time were lying second in the table to Liverpool. After defeating Dukla Prague and Spartak Varna, United faced Barcelona. They lost 2-0 at the Nou Camp but won 3-0 at Old Trafford, beating Barcelona (and Maradona) 3-2. United went out in the semi-final to Juventus but a finish of fourth in the League gave them another shot at the UEFA Cup the following season.

After four draws at the start of the season, the Reds began to win, beating Newcastle United 5-0 and moving into the second round of the UEFA Cup, but they were inconsistent. They beat West Ham United 5-1 but two games later went down 5-0 at Everton. The club's next game in the League Cup was also against Everton – it proved a disastrous night for John Gidman who headed the only goal of the game past his own keeper, Gary Bailey. The team then began to string some results together and by the turn of the year and moved up to third place in the League behind Everton and Spurs. Injuries then began to take their toll and though the League title looked out of their grasp, they made good progress in the FA Cup. After an emphatic revenge win over Bournemouth, the Reds beat Coventry, Blackburn and West Ham to reach the semi-final where their opponents were Liverpool. Mark Hughes kept United's hopes of a League and Cup double alive by netting a hat-trick in a 4-0 defeat of Aston Villa. He went on to be voted Young Footballer of the Year.

The gap at the top of the table between United and Everton had been narrowed to four points though the Reds went out of the UEFA Cup in a penalty shoot-out to Hungarian side Videoton. In the FA Cup semi-final, United met Liverpool at Goodison Park and were denied a win by the referee overruling a linesman's flag and allowing Liverpool's late equaliser to stand. In the replay at Maine Road, United won 2-1. They fell away in the League to finish 4th but it was a different story in the 1985 Wembley final.

Everton had, just days before, won the European Cup-Winners' Cup. The FA Cup Final was to become an historic game. With the match still goalless, United's Kevin Moran brought down Peter Reid. The referee saw it as a clear offence and United's popular Irishman became the first player to be sent off in an FA Cup Final. United's 10-men forced the game into extra time. It was then that Norman Whiteside produced a moment of magic, curling an unstoppable shot past Neville Southall to win the FA Cup.

United began their 1985/86 season by setting a new club record for successive victories – not surprisingly ten games, ten wins resulted in the Reds topping the First Division. The club had qualified for Europe but there were no foreign competitions that season following the Heysel Stadium tragedy, when rioting at the Liverpool v Juventus European Cup Final had led to the deaths of 39 Italian supporters. United's run of victories ended with a draw at Luton but it was November before they lost their first League game, going down 1-0 to Sheffield Wednesday. After this defeat, United were knocked out of the League Cup by Liverpool but by the turn of the year, they were still top of the League. United made progress in the FA Cup too but were beaten in the fifth round by West Ham United following a replay. In a season wrecked by injuries, the Reds finished the campaign in 4th place in the First Division, filling that spot for the third successive year.

When the 1986/87 season began, Bryan Robson was still recovering from surgery required to repair his damaged shoulder and Mark Hughes had joined Barcelona in a £1.8 million transfer deal. A 7-2 aggregate win over Port Vale in the League gave hope for a good season but by the time the next round came round, United had won only three of their opening 12 games and were at the foot of the table. In the next round of the League Cup, United drew 0-0 at home to Southampton, but the replay at The Dell, which United lost 4-1 was the club's final game under Ron Atkinson.

Martin Edwards was quick to appoint a new man and only hours after Atkinson's sacking, the chairman flew to Scotland to talk to Aberdeen's manager Alex Ferguson. Atkinson had given the supporters a successful team but had failed to win over their hearts. Five wins and four draws including a win at Anfield lifted the club away from the relegation zone. After an FA Cup defeat by Coventry, United spent the rest of the season in mid-table, finishing the campaign in 11th place, their lowest position since the relegation season of 1973/74. But there were signs beginning to show that the following season would have more to offer.

One of manager Ferguson's new close season signings was Brian McClair from Celtic and he soon began to repay his transfer fee and by the turn of the year had scored 14 goals. An injury to Paul McGrath forced the United boss into the transfer market again in December and the target this time was Norwich City's Steve Bruce. United entered 1988 with optimism, especially after they had beaten reigning champions Everton at Old Trafford to move into 4th place. Liverpool stood in their way and as they were unbeaten, it seemed nothing could stand in their way. United exited both cup competitions – a soul-destroying defeat at Oxford United in the League Cup and a 2-1 fifth round FA Cup reversal against Arsenal, a match in which McClair missed a penalty two minutes from time. The Scot made amends in the League game against Luton, by notching his 20th League goal – the first United player to reach this total since George Best twenty years earlier. After drawing 3-3 at Anfield against the champions elect, United finished the season as runners-up after cutting down a 17-point lead to just a three-game difference. The club's total of 81 points was their biggest tally since the introduction of three points for a win.

In the close season, Ferguson splashed out a record £750,000 for Scottish international goalkeeper Jim Leighton whilst another Scottish international, Arthur Albiston, was given a free transfer after eleven years with the club. The close season also saw the return of Mark Hughes, a player the fans had never wished to see leave in the first place. Though Leighton started well, his confidence was dented in a much publicised incident when he dropped a harmless cross from Southampton's Graham Baker over his shoulder and into the net. But the goalkeeper wasn't solely responsible for United's dip in form. The club had been knocked out of the League Cup by Wimbledon and had lost at home to Nottingham Forest in the quarter-finals of the FA Cup. Ferguson realised that the team had little chance of gaining honours and gave young players an opportunity. The season, which United finished in 11th place, ended with murmurings of unrest on the terraces.

There then came a period in the club's history when its activities off the field received as much attention as those on it. On the eve of the 1989/90 season, news broke that businessman Michael Knighton was to buy the majority shareholding in the club. Knighton stole the headlines on the opening day of the season when an Old Trafford crowd of 47,000 gave him a rapturous welcome as he performed a ball juggling act. The showbiz start rubbed off on the players who beat new champions Arsenal 4-1. Ferguson had been criticised for his summer selling of Norman Whiteside and Paul McGrath but with the season only a few games old, he splashed a record £2.3 million on Middlesbrough's Gary Pallister and a few weeks alter £2 million on Paul Ince of West Ham United. Though the team could only finish in 13th position, the FA Cup became their saving grace.

Having beaten Nottingham Forest in the third round with a goal from young striker Mark Robins, the Reds progressed to the semi-finals where they faced Second Division Oldham Athletic. After two epic contests, United triumphed and took their place in the Cup Final. Their opponents were Crystal Palace, who had already caused one upset that season by beating Liverpool in the semi-final. After a gripping 3-3 draw, Ferguson caused a surprise by dropping Leighton in favour of Les Sealey for the replay four days later. Sealey was in inspired form until Neil Webb picked out the run of Lee Martin, the full-back became the unlikeliest of heroes and gave the Reds their seventh FA Cup success.

The following season, though United's League form improved, they were still well short of winning the title, finishing in 6th place. The club's hopes of repeating their FA Cup success had foundered after wins over Queen's Park Rangers and Bolton, when they lost in the fifth round at Norwich City. Things were going well in both the League and European Cup-Winners' Cups and after defeating Liverpool, Arsenal and Leeds United on the way to the Wembley League Cup Final, they started as favourites against Sheffield Wednesday. United lost 1-0, though, their downfall stemming from the fact that they had underestimated their more modest opponents.

The Cup win opened the way for United to be back playing in Europe. During the ban, the Reds had been denied European football three times, missing the Cup-Winners' Cup of 1985/86 and the UEFA Cup competition of 1986/87 and 1988/89. This was Alex Ferguson's first European campaign as United manager and having succeeded in the Cup-Winners' Cup with Aberdeen, he was determined to repeat that feat. United beat Pecsi Munkas, Wrexham, Montpellier and Legia Warsaw to reach the final against Barcelona. The game was to be staged in Rotterdam despite efforts to have it moved to a larger stadium and for Mark Hughes the final meant so much – it was against his former club. Two goals by the Welshman sealed the match 2-1 in Fergie's favour, 23 years after the club's previous triumph in Europe.

Despite success in other competitions, United were still searching for the first League Championship in over a quarter of a century. There was some further European success when United beat European Champions Red Star Belgrade in the Super Cup thanks to a Brian McClair goal. However, the club's attempt to retain their European Cup-Winners' crown fell at the second round stage following defeat by Atletico Madrid. Despite a fourth round FA Cup exit, the Reds reached the League Cup Final at Wembley where another McClair goal gave United a 1-0 win over a Nottingham Forest side containing a young Roy Keane. The signing of goalkeeper Peter Schmeichel for a fee of £500,000 had helped United's push towards the League summit, only for them to falter over the critical Easter fixtures and be overtaken by Leeds United who took the First Division title, four points clear of the Reds.

The summer of 1992 saw a transformation in the game with the launch of the new FA Premier League, following a breakaway by the top-flight clubs from the Football League. United's start to the campaign was anything but emphatic and by the beginning of November they had been dumped out of the League Cup and Europe – beaten on penalties in the first round by Torpedo Moscow – talk of a crisis was again rife at Old Trafford. The solution and saviour came in the form of French international Eric Cantona who stunned Leeds fans by accepting a £1.2 million move to United. His goals galvanised the Reds attack and the Frenchman went on to become the first player to win successive League

Championship medals with different clubs. Despite a disappointing fourth round FA Cup defeat at the hands of Sheffield United, United marched on to win the inaugural Premiership title, helped by their nearest rivals Aston Villa losing 1-0 at home to Oldham.

The 1993/94 season will long be remembered at Old Trafford for two momentous events – the death of its father figure, Sir Matt Busby, and the winning of the League and Cup double. The season started with new signing Roy Keane on show in the FA Charity Shield against Arsenal, a match United won in a penalty shoot-out. Progress in both the Champions' and League Cups was steady if not spectacular, while in the League, United went from strength to strength, leading by 11 points by the end of November. The European dream ended when following a 3-3 draw at home to Galatasaray, United could only draw 0-0 in Turkey to go out on away goals. To make matters worse, Cantona was dismissed after the final whistle for remarks made to the referee.

All thoughts of titles and Cups were forgotten on 20 January 1994 when Busby died. The football family united in mourning and at the next home game against Everton, a lone Scots piper led the teams onto the pitch in utter silence, a true reflection of the former manager's lasting influence.

United reached the League Cup Final but had to make do without Peter Schmeichel, who was suspended following his sending-off in the FA Cup quarter-final win over Charlton Athletic. Cantona was dismissed against Swindon and Arsenal in consecutive matches. His subsequent five-match ban upset the balance of the side and they went down 3-1 to Aston Villa in the League Cup Final. Cantona, who was the PFA Player of the Year, returned to score both goals in a 2-0 win over Manchester City and United retained their title with two games to spare. The icing on the cake came at Wembley with a runaway 4-0 win over Chelsea, though the match was much closer than the scoreline suggests.

United's target in 1994/95 was the European Champions League, but despite preserving their unbeaten home European record, they suffered a couple of defeats on their travels including a 4-0 crushing at Barcelona and went out of Europe. Early inconsistency in the League was remedied by a period of ten successive home wins and without a goal conceded in 1,135 minutes of football, United topped the League with Blackburn in close proximity. United's inferior goal difference to Rovers was wiped out during a 9-0 annihilation of Ipswich town with Andy Cole scoring five of the goals. Despite their consistency, United could not hold back Rovers, although a winning goal on the final day at West ham would have taken the title to Old Trafford again. As it was, United finished as runners-up. They reached the FA Cup Final again but went down 1-0 to Everton.

Whatever the Reds did or did not on the pitch, their good name was severely dented by Frenchman Eric Cantona. Dismissed four times, he was sent for 120 days' community service after landing a kick on an aggressive supporter in January 1995. Cantona was also fined £20,000 and suspended from all football for eight months.

Considering the success that Alex Ferguson had brought to the club, he had to withstand a fair amount of criticism and questioning of his wisdom after allowing star players Paul Ince, Andrei Kanchelskis and Mark Hughes to be sold for a combined fee of £13.5 million, just after the club had surrendered the Championship to Blackburn.

After a disappointing start to the 1995/96 campaign, United embarked on a fine 10-match unbeaten run which saw them close in on leaders Newcastle United. But a series of indifferent results meant that by the end of January, the Magpies were 12 points clear of United. The Reds' response was magnificent, with 31 of the next available 33 points coming their way, including a vital and enthralling 1-0 victory at St James' Park. With Cantona scoring some stunning goals, United took over pole position as Newcastle faltered. A 3-0 success at Middlesbrough on the final day of the season confirmed United's third title in four years.

Disappointing showings in the League and UEFA Cup were more than compensated for by the club's run to the FA Cup Final, where they became only the sixth club to reach the Wembley showpiece in three consecutive seasons. The final against Liverpool was a dismal affair, decided almost fittingly and in accordance with the script by Footballer of the Year Eric Cantona as United became the first side to complete the domestic League and Cup double twice.

United started the following season in spectacular fashion with a 4-0 destruction of Newcastle in the Charity Shield and followed it with a 3-0 opening day success over Wimbledon, which included David Beckham's classic long-range goal. Early results took United to the top of the League but then heavy defeats – 5-0 at Newcastle and 6-3 at Southampton, which made Peter Schmeichel look like a mere mortal –

saw United lose pole position. The club then went on a 16-match unbeaten run, however, which included five straight victories and when Liverpool were crushed 3-1 at Anfield, a fourth title in five years was virtually assured. After early exits in the two domestic Cup competitions, United were given a football lesson by Juventus, whose 1-0 win at Old Trafford saw the end of their 41-year undefeated record at Old Trafford in European competitions. However, United still qualified for the knockout stages and reached the semi-finals where they went out to Borussia Dortmund.

Up until the midway stage of the 1997/98 season, United looked on course for an unprecedented third League and Cup double, following excellent form in the Champions League group matches. Prior to Christmas the Reds had lost just one Premiership match and had won five of their six Champions League fixtures. Possibly with one eye on Europe, United's League form dipped and they went on to suffer more defeats than in any of the previous five years of the Premiership. Even so, the Reds still handed out a number of thrashings – Barnsley 7-0, Sheffield Wednesday 6-1, Wimbledon 5-2 and Blackburn Rovers 4-0. At one stage, United held a seemingly impregnable 11-point lead. Arsenal's win at Old Trafford meant that the Gunners had cut United's lead to six points and the North London club had three games in hand. United's disappointing end-of-season run-in handed the title to Arsène Wenger's side. Poor showings in the League and FA Cup were followed by United reaching the Champions League quarter-finals were they lost to Monaco on the away goals rule.

Manchester United swept all before them during the 1998/99 season as they achieved what many had believed to be the impossible by adding the Champions League trophy to the domestic double. Courtesy of a last-day-of-the-season victory over Spurs, United lifted the Premiership title for the fifth time in seven seasons and with a comfortable 2-0 victory over Newcastle in the FA Cup Final completed an unprecedented third domestic double.

High points were numerous but there were also some games during which the dream could have died, particularly in the Cup competitions. In the FA Cup, Liverpool were stunned at Old Trafford as Dwight Yorke and Ole Gunnar Solskjaer scored last-minute goals to reverse a seemingly lost cause, while Peter Schmeichel's semi-final penalty save from Dennis Bergkamp also proved decisive prior to Ryan Giggs's breathtaking solo goal. United's European venture looked destined to end in failure as Juventus, after drawing at Old Trafford, took a two-goal semi-final lead in Italy before Ferguson's side seized an historic 3-2 triumph. But the most astonishing comeback was saved for the final itself when the 90th anniversary of Sir Matt Busby's birth was celebrated in momentous fashion as United won the Champions League Cup in Barcelona with two heart-stopping late goals.

The treble became a quadruple later in the year when Sir Alex Ferguson's men travelled to Tokyo to compete for the Inter-Continental Cup. Roy Keane's goal against Palmeiras of Brazil bestowed upon United the title of World Club Champions. Officially, at the end of the millennium, the biggest football club in the world had also become the best! Alex Ferguson was awarded a Knighthood for his services to football.

In 1999/2000, United won their sixth Premiership title in eight years. While their performance didn't quite match that of the previous season, when they went on an unbeaten run of 33 matches on their way to completing the treble, another Premier League trophy was a just reward. With a forced winter break while the team was playing in the inaugural FIFA Club World Championship in Brazil, United were able to resume without too much of a problem. From then on, freed from the task of defending their FA Cup success (United chose not to compete in the 1999/2000 FA Cup competition) and out of the League Cup, which had never really interested them anyway, the Reds had just two goals in their sights – the Premier League and the Champions League. After losing to Real Madrid in the Champions League, United, with Roy Keane taking both the PFA and Football Writers' Player of the Year awards, won the title by a massive 18 points from second-placed Arsenal.

Manchester United will be poorly served by the history books in years to come as the 10-point winning margin of their seventh Premier League title fails to tell the full story of the 2000/01 campaign. There were still five matches to play when United won the title for a third time in a row – a record hat-trick of titles since the Premiership began in 1992. With the League already wrapped up, the Reds lost three of their remaining fixtures to give entirely the wrong picture of the season. Sir Alex Ferguson had manipulated the squad system to perfection, with not one player being ever-present. The United boss then announced his impending retirement, only to backtrack and decide to stay.

Trafford Council unveiled a plaque in October 2000 to mark the great debt that Manchester United Football Club owed to James Gibson and his family. Fittingly, it was placed on the railway bridge next to Old Trafford, Mr Gibson having arranged for the station to be used for United fans to travel to see their heroes play.

Having signed Juan Sebastian Veron from Lazio for a fee of £28 million, a British transfer record, Ferguson later strengthened the side with the purchase of Ruud van Nistelrooy from PSV Eindhoven. The club finished in 3rd place in the Premiership, though, never recovering from an erratic start in which they sometimes looked unbeatable and on other occasions seemed strangely inept! Having waited a year for van Nistelrooy to recover full fitness, both club and player were well rewarded when the freescoring Dutchman was voted Player of the Year by his peers.

Despite making their worst start ever to a League campaign, Manchester United went on to win their eighth Premiership title in eleven years. Of course, the Championship is a marathon and not a sprint – although they were six points adrift of leaders Arsenal after only six games, United judged their final spurt perfectly. A 6-2 win at Newcastle United took United to the top and there they stayed, finishing the campaign five points clear of the Gunners. They did lose at home to Arsenal in the FA Cup and to Real Madrid in the Champions League quarter-final, but they reached the League Cup Final where they lost 2-0 to Liverpool.

In 2003/04, United made a poor start to the Premiership campaign and as well as taking just two League points from a possible 12, they were also knocked out of the Champions League by the eventual winners Porto. Even so, a gap developed between the top three and the rest of the Premiership and the Reds, who occupied third spot at the end of the season, were 15 points ahead of 4th-placed Liverpool. Midway through the season, £30 million capture Rio Ferdinand was punished by the FA for failing to attend a mandatory drugs test at Carrington and was suspended for eight months. Without Rio in their ranks, United won the FA Cup for a record eleventh time, beating Millwall 3-0 in the final at the Millennium Stadium.

In the 2004 close season, American Michael Glazer took control of the club. At the end of the following season, a campaign in which United finished 3rd in the Premiership, the Reds were back at Cardiff's

Millennium Stadium to face Arsenal in the FA Cup Final. Despite a dominant display from United, for whom Cristiano Ronaldo and Wayne Rooney were outstanding, the game ended goalless with Arsenal winning the resultant penalty shoot-out.

The 2005/06 season, in which United finished as runners-up to Chelsea – the Stamford Bridge club winning their second successive Championship title – saw the Old Trafford club win silverware when they beat Wigan Athletic 4-0 in the League Cup Final. Ruud van Nistelrooy had scored 21 League goals, though he wasn't as potent as in previous seasons, despite notching up his 150th goal for the club. United's late season ground improvements meant that another Premiership record was broken when the first crowd of over 70,000 attended the home game against Arsenal.

Chelsea were aiming to win their third successive Premiership title in 2006/07 but United wrested the Championship away from the Blues with a six-point finishing margin between the teams. Though the Reds lost more games than Chelsea – five to the London club's three – they did have a superior goal average with Ronaldo and Rooney proving a potent force. United lost out to AC Milan in the Champions League semi-final and to Chelsea in the FA Cup Final but the main aim all along had been to snatch the title back from Stamford Bridge. While the whole squad performed admirably, the player that took most of the plaudits was Cristiano Ronaldo, who collected 13 personal honours during the season including PFA Player of the Year and Young Player of the Year.

One of the most thrilling seasons in the 16-year history of the Premiership ended with Manchester United lifting the trophy for the 10th time but during the early part of the campaign, United could not buy a win.

After draws with Reading and Portsmouth, United lost to local rivals Manchester City at Eastlands. Cristiano Ronaldo was missing following his suspension after a red card against Pompey and it was the club's worst start to a campaign since the first Premier League season in 1992/93.

United's response to the City defeat was to squeeze out four consecutive 1-0 victories prior to showing they meant business by scoring four goals in four successive games. United continued to dominate proceedings and at the turn of the year they won their fifth league game in a row to go seven points clear of Chelsea. Arsenal took over at the top of the table but their lead was short-lived as United's 6-0 demolition of Newcastle took them back on top on goal difference. Then, in February, things started to go wrong for the Gunners and though United had lost for a second time to rivals City, on the day of the Munich memorial, a 5-1 win at Newcastle shifted the momentum in United's favour.

United's march towards the title gathered pace and by April they led the chasing pack by five points with six games to play. The league table suggested the title race was as good as over but the fixture list argued otherwise. United came from a goal behind to beat Arsenal at Old Trafford but then lost 2-1 at Chelsea. Now, only United's healthy goal difference stood between the two sides. United beat West Ham 4-1 and Chelsea won 2-0 at Newcastle. The final day saw United win 2-0 at Wigan while Chelsea could only draw 1-1 at home to Bolton. For United the win was a culmination of a season's hard work – it had started poorly but ultimately had a happy ending.

In the UEFA Champions League, United strolled through their group games before beating Lyon and AS Roma to reach the semi-finals. After a goalless draw against Barcelona in the Nou Camp, it took a searing, swerving strike from Paul Scholes to book United's place in the final. It was certainly heart-in-the-mouth stuff followed by jubilation at the final whistle. The Reds' opponents in the Moscow final were Chelsea but United clinched the trophy – and a Premiership and Champions League double – following a dramatic penalty shoot-out after the game had ended all square at 1-1 after extra-time. Sir Alex Ferguson put it down to fate, the success coming 50 years after the Munich disaster had torn the Busby Babes apart.

Before the start of the 2008/9 season, United once again contested the FA Community Shield (formerly the Charity Shield), beating FA Cup winners Portsmouth on penalties after the game had ended 0-0. The season started relatively slowly for the Reds, with a 1-1 draw with Newcastle United and a slim1-0 victory against Portsmouth at Fratton Park, before United beat Liverpool 2-1 at Anfield and drew 1-1 with Chelsea at Old Trafford. By the end of September things were picking up, though, and October saw solid wins against Blackburn, West Brom and West Ham, as well as a 3-0 drubbing of Celtic in the Champions League group stage. Newly-promoted Hull City gave the Reds a shock at Old Trafford on the first day of November, but United ground out a 4-3 win in a compelling game, thanks to two goals from Cristiano Ronaldo and two more from Michael Carrick and Nemanja Vidic. On 15 November United produced a spectacular display to thrash Stoke City 5-0, and the last day of the month saw the Reds overcome bitter rivals Manchester City 1-0. December produced yet more good results, including victory in the Club World Cup in Japan, where United beat LDU Quito 1-0 to lift their first piece of competitive silverware for the season.

United won all their games except one in January 2009, and many began to speculate on whether they were capable of winning an incredible five trophies in one season – the Premier League, FA Cup, Champions League, League Cup and Club World Cup. Their only defeat of the month came as they went down 1-0 in the League Cup semi-final first leg at Derby County. Meanwhile, on 27 January, Edwin van der Sar set a new club and Premier League record for clean sheets, having gone 11 games and 1,032 minutes without conceding a goal. Four days later, he broke the overall English league record of 1,103 minutes. This incredible run continued until 4 March, when a goalkeeping error by Van der Sar allowed Peter Løvenkrands of Newcastle United to score after 9 minutes. Van der Sar had gone 1,311 minutes without conceding a goal.

On 1 March, United picked up their second piece of silverware, beating Tottenham Hotspur in another penalty shoot-out to lift the League Cup trophy. The game had finished 0-0 after 90 minutes, but United won the shoot-out convincingly. Things were going well until 14 March, when Liverpool visited Old Trafford. In the most shocking result of United's season, they were beaten 4-1 by their Merseyside rivals, and a 2-0 defeat to Fulham followed. It looked as if United's title challenge may be faltering – Liverpool were close behind them in second place and looked to be entering a rich vein of form. The title race continued to be almost too close to call, but on 16 May United sealed their 11th Premier League title, and 18th English League title, with a 0-0 draw at Arsenal. This brought them level with Liverpool, who had also won 18 League titles in their history.

United had also booked themselves a place in the Champions League final, overcoming Jose Mourinho's Inter Milan side in the quarter-finals and fierce rivals Arsenal in the semi-finals. Their opponents would be Barcelona, regarded by many as the greatest team in the world. Neutrals were thrilled by the prospect of a Manchester United/Barcelona showdown, and United fans were hopeful of seeing their team become the first to lift the Champions League trophy two years running since the European Cup's rebranding in1992. Sadly those hopes were dashed in the final on 27 May, as Barcelona easily overcame a weary-looking United side 2-0, with goals from Samuel Eto'o and the celebrated Lionel Messi. There was good news for United, though, as Ryan Giggs, who had played his 800th game for the club in United's semi-final victory over Arsenal on 29 April, was voted PFA Player of the Year for the first time in his career. Sadly the five trophy wins never materialised, but a Club World Cup, League Cup and Premier League treble still marked an extremely successful season for United.

CHAPTER TWO

THE PLAYERS

⚽ JAMES WARNER Goalkeeper

Born	Lozells, Birmingham April 1865	
Clubs	Milton FC; Aston Villa; Newton Heath; Walsall Town Swifts	
	A	G
1892/93	22	0
Total	**22**	**0**

⚽ JOHN ERNEST CLEMENTS Full-back

Clubs	Nottingham St Saviours; Notts County; Newton Heath; Rotherham Town; Newcastle United	
	A	G
1892/93	24	0
1893/94	12	0
Total	**36**	**0**

⚽ JAMES BROWN Full-back

Clubs	Dundee Our Boys; Newton Heath; Dundee	
	A	G
1892/93	7	0
Total	**7**	**0**

⚽ GEORGE PERRINS Half-back

Born	Birmingham, 24 February 1873	
Clubs	Birmingham St George; Newton Heath; Luton Town; Chatham; Stockport County	
	A	G
1892/93	28	0
1893/94	27	0

	A	G
1894/95	25	0
1895/96	12	0
Total	**92**	**0**

⚽ WILLIAM S STEWART Half-back

Born   Coupar Angus, Perthshire, 11 February 1872
Died   Dundee, June 1945
Clubs   Dundee Our Boys; Warwick County; Newton Heath; Luton Town; Millwall Athletic; Luton Town; Thames Ironworks; Dundee

	A	G
1892/93	29	4
1893/94	25	0
1894/95	22	1
Total	**76**	**5**

⚽ FRED C ERENTZ Full-back

Born   Dundee 1870
Died   Haughton Green, Denton, 6 April 1938
Clubs   Dundee Our Boys; Newton Heath

	A	G
1892/93	29	0
1893/94	22	2
1894/95	28	1
1895/96	24	0
1896/97	27	0
1897/98	28	1
1898/99	32	1
1899/1900	34	2
1900/01	31	0
1901/02	25	2
Total	**280**	**9**

⚽ ALFRED H FARMAN Forward

Born   Kings Norton, Birmingham, April 1869
Clubs   Birmingham Excelsior; Aston Villa; Bolton Wanderers; Newton Heath

	A	G
1892/93	28	10

1893/94	18	8
1894/95	5	0
Total	**51**	**18**

⚽ JAMES COUPAR Forward

Born	Dundee
Clubs	Dundee Our Boys; Newton Heath; St Johnstone; Rotherham Town; Luton Town; Swindon Town; Linfield; Swindon Town; Newton Heath

	A	G
1892/93	21	5
1901/02	11	4
Total	**32**	**9**

⚽ ROBERT DONALDSON Forward

Clubs	Airdrieonians; Blackburn Rovers; Newton Heath; Luton Town; Glossop North End; Ashford

	A	G
1892/93	26	16
1893/94	24	7
1894/95	27	15
1895/96	17	7
1896/97	29	9
1897/98	8	2
Total	**131**	**56**

⚽ ADAM CARSON Forward

Clubs	Glasgow Thistle; Newton Heath; Ardwick; Liverpool

	A	G
1892/93	13	3
Total	**13**	**3**

⚽ WILLIAM MATHIESON Forward

Clubs	Clydesdale FC; Newton Heath; Rotherham Town

	A	G
1892/93	8	0
1893/94	2	2
Total	**10**	**2**

⚽ **ANDREW MITCHELL** Full-back

Clubs	Airdrieonians; Newton Heath; Burton Swifts		
		A	G
	1892/93	29	0
	1893/94	25	0
	Total	**54**	**0**

⚽ **WILLIAM HOOD** Forward

Clubs	Newton Heath		
		A	G
	1892/93	21	5
	1893/94	12	1
	Total	**33**	**6**

⚽ **JAMES HENDRY** Forward

Clubs	Alloa Athletic; Newton Heath		
		A	G
	1892/93	2	1
	Total	**2**	**1**

⚽ **JOSEPH KINLOCH** Forward

Clubs	Newton Heath		
		A	G
	1892/93	1	0
	Total	**1**	**0**

⚽ **JAMES COLVILLE** Forward

Clubs	Annbank; Newton Heath; Fairfield; Notts County; Annbank		
		A	G
	1892/93	9	1
	Total	**9**	**1**

⚽ **THOMAS FITZSIMMONS** Forward

Born	Annbank, 21 October 1870
Clubs	Annbank; Newton Heath; Annbank; St Mirren; Annbank; Fairfield; Glossop North End; Fairfield; Oldham County; Chorley; Wigan County; Annbank

	A	G
1892/93	18	5
1893/94	9	1
Total	**27**	**6**

⚽ ARTHUR HENRYS Half-back

Clubs   Newton Heath; Notts Jardines; Newton Heath; Leicester Fosse; Notts County

	A	G
1892/93	3	0
Total	**3**	**0**

⚽ JOHN DAVIES Goalkeeper

Clubs   Newton Heath

	A	G
1892/93	7	0
Total	**7**	**0**

⚽ JOSEPH CASSIDY Forward

Born   Dalziel, Lanarkshire, 30 July 1872
Clubs   Motherwell Athletic; Blythe FC; Newton Heath; Glasgow Celtic;
Newton Heath; Manchester City; Middlesbrough; Workington

	A	G
1892/93	4	0
1894/95	8	8
1895/96	19	16
1896/97	28	17
1897/98	30	14
1898/99	34	19
1899/1900	29	16
Total	**152**	**90**

⚽ JOSEPH WILLIAM FALL Goalkeeper

Born   Miles Platting, Manchester, 16 January 1872
Clubs   Middlesbrough Ironopolis; Newton Heath; Small Heath; Altrincham

	A	G
1893/94	23	0
Total	**23**	**0**

⚽ WILLIAM R DAVIDSON Half-back

Clubs	Annbank; Newton Heath		
		A	G
	1893/94	28	1
	1894/95	12	1
	Total	**40**	**2**

⚽ JAMES RANKIN McNAUGHT Half-back

Born   Dumbarton, 8 June 1870
Died   West Ham, London, March 1919
Clubs   Dumbarton; Linfield; Newton Heath; Tottenham Hotspur; Maidstone

		A	G
	1893/94	26	1
	1894/95	26	2
	1895/96	28	3
	1896/97	30	4
	1897/98	30	2
	Total	**140**	**12**

⚽ JOHN PEDEN Forward

Born   Belfast, 11 March 1865
Clubs   Linfield; Newton Heath; Sheffield United; Belfast Distillery; Linfield

		A	G
	1893/94	28	7
	Total	**28**	**7**

⚽ WILLIAM THOMPSON Forward

Clubs	Dumbarton; Aston Villa; Newton Heath		
		A	G
	1893/94	3	0
	Total	**3**	**0**

⚽ DAVID PRINCE Forward

Clubs	Newton Heath		
		A	G
	1893/94	2	0
	Total	**2**	**0**

⚽ JOHN GRAHAM Forward

Clubs	Blyth FC; Newton Heath		
		A	G
	1893/94	4	0
	Total	**4**	**0**

⚽ WILLIAM CECIL CAMPBELL Forward

Clubs	Royal Arsenal; Preston North End; Middlesbrough; Darwen; Blackburn Rovers; Newton Heath; Notts County; Newark		
		A	G
	1893/94	5	1
	Total	**5**	**1**

⚽ CHARLES ROTHWELL Forward

Clubs	Newton Heath		
		A	G
	1893/94	1	0
	1894/95	1	1
	Total	**2**	**1**

⚽ JOHN CLARKIN Forward

Born	Neilston, Renfrew		
Clubs	Neilston FC; Glasgow Thistle; Newton Heath; Blackpool		
		A	G
	1893/94	12	5
	1894/95	29	11
	1895/96	26	7
	Total	**67**	**23**

⚽ SAMUEL PARKER Forward

Born	Hurlford, near Kilmarnock		
Clubs	Hurlford FC; Newton Heath; Burnley; Southport Central; Hurlford FC; Kilmarnock Athletic		
		A	G
	1893/94	11	0
	Total	**11**	**0**

⚽ WILLIAM DOUGLAS Goalkeeper

Born   Dundee
Clubs   Dundee Our Boys; Ardwick; Newton Heath; Derby County; Blackpool;
             Warmly FC; Dundee

	A	G
1893/94	7	0
1894/95	30	0
1895-96	18	0
Total	**55**	**0**

⚽ JOHN M DOW Full-back

Born   Dundee, 1873
Clubs   Dundee Our Boys; Dundee; Newton Heath; Fairfield; Glossop North End;
             Luton Town; Middlesbrough; West Ham United; Luton Town

	A	G
1893/94	2	0
1894/95	27	5
1895/96	19	1
Total	**48**	**6**

⚽ HERBERT HENRY STONE Half-back

Born   St Albans, April 1873
Clubs   Newton Heath; Ashton North End

	A	G
1893/94	2	0
1894/95	4	0
Total	**6**	**0**

⚽ JOHN McCARTNEY Full-back

Born   Glasgow
Died   18 January 1933
Clubs   Cartvale FC; Thistle FC; Glasgow Rangers; Cowlairs FC; Newton Heath;
             Luton Town; Barnsley

	A	G
1894/95	18	1
Total	**18**	**1**

⚽ RICHARD SMITH Forward

Born   Bolton
Clubs   Halliwell Rovers; Heywood central; Newton Heath; Halliwell Rovers;
        Wigan County; Newton Heath; Bolton Wanderers; Wigan United

	A	G
1894/95	29	19
1895/96	28	9
1896/97	14	3
1897/98	5	1
1899/1900	12	2
1900/01	5	1
Total	**93**	**35**

⚽ JAMES PETERS Forward

Clubs   Heywood Central; Newton Heath; New Brompton; Sheppey United

	A	G
1894/95	30	7
1895/96	16	6
Total	**46**	**13**

⚽ GEORGE MILLAR Forward

Clubs   Glasgow Perthshire; Newton Heath; Chatham

	A	G
1894-95	6	5
Total	**6**	**5**

⚽ DAVID McFETTERIDGE Forward

Clubs   Bolton Wanderers; Cowlairs FC; Newton Heath; Stockport County

	A	G
1894/95	1	0
Total	**1**	**0**

⚽ JAMES CAIRNS (1) Full-back

Clubs   Ardwick; Newton Heath

	A	G
1894/95	1	0
Total	**1**	**0**

⚽ **WILLIAM LONGAIR** Half-back

Born	Dundee, 19 July 1870	
Died	28 November 1926	
Clubs	Rockwell FC; Dundee East End; Dundee; Newton Heath; Dundee;	
	Sunderland; Burnley; Dundee; Brighton United; Dundee	

	A	G
1894/95	1	0
Total	**1**	**0**

⚽ **DAVID FITZSIMMONS** Half-back

Born	Annbank, Ayrshire	
Clubs	Annbank FC; Newton Heath; Fairfield; Chorley; Wigan County;	
	Newton Heath	

	A	G
1895/96	26	0
1899/1900	2	0
Total	**28**	**0**

⚽ **WALTER CARTWRIGHT** Half-back

Born	Nantwich, January 1871	
Clubs	Nantwich FC; Heywood Central; Crewe Alexandra; Newton Heath	

	A	G
1895/96	27	2
1896/97	25	0
1897/98	27	1
1898/99	33	2
1899/1900	25	0
1900/01	31	0
1901/02	29	3
1902/03	22	0
1903/04	9	0
Total	**228**	**8**

⚽ **WILLIAM JOHN KENNEDY** Forward

Clubs	Ayr Parkhouse; Newton Heath; Stockport County; Greenock Morton	

	A	G
1895/96	29	11

1896/97	1	0
Total	**30**	**11**

⚽ JOHN AITKEN Forward

Born   Scotland
Clubs   5th King's Rifle Volunteers (Dumfries); Newton Heath

	A	G
1895/96	2	1
Total	**2**	**1**

⚽ JAMES COLLINSON Full-back

Born   Newton Heath
Clubs   Newton Heath

	A	G
1895/96	13	1
1896/97	-	-
1897/98	10	4
1898/99	21	9
1899/1900	7	2
1900/01	11	0
Total	**62**	**16**

⚽ JOSEPH ARTHUR RIDGWAY Goalkeeper

Born   Chorlton-cum-Hardy, Manchester, 25 April 1873
Clubs   West Manchester; Newton Heath; Rochdale Town

	A	G
1895/96	6	0
1896/97	5	0
1897/98	3	0
Total	**14**	**0**

⚽ R STEPHENSON Forward

Clubs   Talbot FC; Newton Heath; Northern Nomads

	A	G
1895/96	1	1
Total	**1**	**1**

⚽ JAMES VANCE Forward

Clubs: Annbank FC; Newton Heath; Fairfield FC; Annbank FC

	A	G
1895/96	10	1
1896/97	1	0
Total	**11**	**1**

⚽ JOHN WHITNEY Half-back

Clubs: Newton Heath

	A	G
1895/96	2	0
1896/97	-	-
1897/98	-	-
1898/99	-	-
1899/1900	-	-
1900/01	1	0
Total	**3**	**0**

⚽ WALTER WHITTAKER Goalkeeper

Born: Manchester, 20 September 1878
Died: Swansea, 2 June 1917
Clubs: Molyneaux FC; Buxton; Molyneaux FC; Newton Heath; Fairfield;
Grimsby Town; Reading; Blackburn Rovers; Grimsby Town;
Derby County; Brentford; Reading; Clapton Orient; Exeter City;
Swansea Town

	A	G
1895/96	3	0
Total	**3**	**0**

⚽ HARRY STAFFORD Full-back

Born: Crewe, 1869
Clubs: Southport Central; Crewe Alexandra; Newton Heath

	A	G
1895/96	4	0
1896/97	24	0
1897/98	25	0
1898/99	33	0

1899/1900	31	0
1900/01	30	0
1901/02	26	0
1902/03	10	0
Total	**183**	**0**

⚽ LEVI WILLIAM DRAYCOTT Half-back

Born   Newhall, Derby, 15 February 1869
Clubs   Stoke; Burton Wanderers; Newton Heath; Bedminster; Bristol Rovers; Wellingborough; Luton Town

	A	G
1896/97	29	5
1897/98	21	0
1898/99	31	1
Total	**81**	**6**

⚽ CAESAR AUGUSTUS LLEWELYN JENKYNS Half-back

Born   Builth Wells, 24 August 1866
Died   Birmingham, 23 July 1941
Clubs   Small Heath St Andrews; Walsall Swifts; Unity Gas FC; Small Heath; Woolwich Arsenal; Newton Heath; Walsall; Coventry City; Unity Gas FC; Saltney Wednesday

	A	G
1896/97	27	5
1897/98	8	0
Total	**35**	**5**

⚽ WILLIAM BRYANT Forward

Born   Rotherham, 1874
Clubs   Rotherham town; Newton Heath; Blackburn Rovers

	A	G
1896/97	29	3
1897/98	29	10
1898/99	32	10
1899/1900	19	4
Total	**109**	**27**

⚽ **WILLIAM 'RIMMER' BROWN** Forward

Clubs	Stalybridge Rovers; Chester; Newton Heath; Stockport County; Hurst Ramblers		
		A	G
	1896/97	7	2
	Total	**7**	**2**

⚽ **JOSEPH WETHERELL** Goalkeeper

Clubs	Newton Heath		
		A	G
	1896/97	2	0
	Total	**2**	**0**

⚽ **FRANCIS 'FRANK' BARRETT** Goalkeeper

Born	Dundee, 2 August 1872		
Died	August 1907		
Clubs	Dundee Harp; Dundee; Newton Heath; New Brighton Tower; Arbroath; Manchester City; Dundee; Aberdeen		
		A	G
	1896/97	23	0
	1897/98	27	0
	1898/99	34	0
	1899/1900	34	0
	Total	**118**	**0**

⚽ **MATTHEW GILLESPIE** Forward

Born	Strathclyde, Glasgow, 24 December 1869		
Clubs	Strathclyde FC; Leith Athletic; Lincoln City; Newton Heath		
		A	G
	1896/97	17	2
	1897/98	19	3
	1898/99	28	7
	1899/1900	10	5
	Total	**74**	**17**

⚽ **HENRY BOYD** Forward

Born	Pollokshaws, Scotland 1868

Clubs   Sunderland Albion; Burnley; West Bromwich Albion; Royal Arsenal;
          Newton Heath; Falkirk

	A	G
1896/97	10	5
1897/98	30	22
1898/99	12	5
Total	**52**	**32**

☺ WILLIAM MORGAN Half-back

Clubs   Horwich FC; Newton Heath; Bolton Wanderers; Watford;
          Leicester Fosse; New Brompton; Newton Heath Athletic

	A	G
1896/97	2	0
1897/98	9	1
1898/99	24	2
1899/1900	30	0
1900/01	33	3
1901/02	33	0
1902/03	12	0
Total	**143**	**6**

☺ WILLIAM DUNN Forward

Born   Middlesbrough
Clubs   South Bank; Newton Heath

	A	G
1897/98	10	0
Total	**10**	**0**

☺ FRANCIS EDGAR WEDGE Forward

Born   Dudley, 28 July 1876
Clubs   Manchester Talbot; Newton Heath; Chorlton-cum-Hardy FC

	A	G
1897/98	2	2
Total	**2**	**2**

☺ JAMES CARMAN Forward

Clubs   Oldham County FC; Newton Heath;

	A	G
1897/98	3	1
Total	**3**	**1**

⚽ HENRY BERNT ERENTZ Full-back

Born   Dundee, 17 September 1874
Died   Dundee, 19 July 1947
Clubs   Dundee; Oldham County FC; Newton Heath; Tottenham Hotspur;
          Swindon Town

	A	G
1897/98	6	0
Total	**6**	**0**

⚽ OWEN JOHN JONES Forward

Born   Bangor, North Wales, 1871
Died   Crewe, 23 September 1955
Clubs   Bangor; Crewe Alexandra; Chorley; Newton Heath; Bangor; Earlstown;
          Stalybridge Rovers

	A	G
1897/98	2	0
Total	**2**	**0**

⚽ ROBERT TURNER Defender

Clubs   Newton Heath; Brighton United; Fulham; Glentoran

	A	G
1898/99	2	0
Total	**2**	**0**

⚽ JAMES CAIRNS Forward

Clubs   Stevenston Thistle; Glossop North End; Lincoln City; Newton Heath;
          Berry's Association

	A	G
1898/99	1	0
Total	**1**	**0**

⚽ W OWEN Forward

Clubs   Holywell FC; Newton Heath

	A	F
1898/99	1	0
Total	**1**	**0**

⚽ JOHN TURNER Half-back

Clubs	Gravesend United; Newton Heath

	A	G
1898/99	3	0
Total	**3**	**0**

⚽ WILLIAM HENRY BROOKS Forward

Born   Stalybridge, 30 July 1873
Clubs   Stalybridge Rovers; Newton Heath; Stalybridge Rovers; Newton Heath;
         Stalybridge Rovers

	A	G
1898/99	3	3
Total	**3**	**3**

⚽ JAMES CONNACHAN Forward

Born   Duntocher, Scotland, 1876
Clubs   Glasgow Perthshire; Duntocher Hibernian; Glasgow Celtic;
         Airdrieonians; Newton Heath; Glossop North End; Leicester Fosse;
         Nottingham Forest; Morton; Renton; Brittania FC (Canada);
         Dumbarton Harp

	A	G
1898/99	4	0
Total	**4**	**0**

⚽ JOHN CUNNINGHAM Forward

Born   Glasgow
Clubs   Benburb FC; Burnley; Glasgow Hibernian; Glasgow Celtic;
         Partick Thistle; Heart of Midlothian; Glasgow Rangers; Glasgow Thistle;
         Preston North End; Sheffield United; Aston Villa; Newton Heath;
         Wigan County; Barrow

	A	G
1898/99	15	2
Total	**15**	**2**

⚽ FRANCIS PEPPER Half-back

Born   Sheffield, 2 July 1875
Clubs   Greasborough FC; Sheffield United; Newton Heath; Barnsley;
        Doncaster Rovers; South Kirkby

	A	G
1898/99	7	0
Total	**7**	**0**

⚽ ROBERT WALKER Defender

Clubs   Newton Heath

	A	G
1898/99	2	0
Total	**2**	**0**

⚽ WA 'BOGIE' ROBERTS Forward

Clubs   Newton Heath

	A	G
1898/99	3	1
1899/1900	6	1
Total	**9**	**2**

⚽ JOHN GOURLAY Half-back

Born   Scotland 1879
Clubs   Annbank; Newton Heath

	A	G
1898/99	1	0
Total	**1**	**0**

⚽ JAMES HOPKINS Forward

Born   Manchester
Clubs   Berry's Association; Newton Heath

	A	G
1898/99	1	0
Total	**1**	**0**

⚽ EDWIN LEE Forward

Clubs   Hurst Ramblers; Newton Heath

	A	G
1898/99	7	4
1899/1900	4	1
Total	**11**	**5**

⚽ WILLIAM GRIFFITHS Half-back

Born	Manchester
Clubs	Berry's Association; Newton Heath; Atherton Church House

	A	G
1898/99	7	0
1899/1900	33	3
1900/01	31	4
1901/02	29	5
1902/03	25	4
1903/04	30	11
1904/05	2	0
Total	**157**	**27**

⚽ GEORGE RADCLIFFE Forward

Clubs	Newton Heath

	A	G
1898/99	1	0
Total	**1**	**0**

⚽ WILLIAM JAMES JACKSON Forward

Born	Flint, 27 January 1876
Died	Flint, 25 March 1954
Clubs	Flint; Rhyl; Flint; St Helen's Recreation; Newton Heath; Barrow; Burnley; Flint

	A	G
1899/1900	32	7
1900/01	29	5
Total	**61**	**12**

⚽ ALFRED AMBLER Half-back

Born	Manchester
Clubs	Hawktown Juniors; Newton Heath; Colne; Stockport County; Exeter City; Colne

	A	G
1899/1900	9	1
1900/01	1	0
Total	**10**	**1**

⚽ JAMES BAIN Forward

Clubs   Dundee; Newton Heath

	A	G
1899/1900	2	1
Total	**2**	**1**

⚽ JOSEPH CLARK Forward

Clubs   Dundee; Newton Heath

	A	G
1899/1900	9	0
Total	**9**	**0**

⚽ F SAWYER Forward

Clubs   Newton Heath; Chorley

	A	G
1899/1900	2	0
Total	**2**	**0**

⚽ PETER BLACKMORE Forward

Clubs   Newton Heath

	A	G
1899/1900	1	0
Total	**1**	**0**

⚽ ROBERT PARKINSON Forward

Born   Preston, Lancashire, 25 April 1873
Clubs   Nottingham Forest; Newton Heath

	A	G
1899/1900	15	7
Total	**15**	**7**

⚽ JOSEPH HEATHCOTE Forward

Clubs	Berry's Association; Newton Heath		
		A	G
	1899/1900	1	0
	1900/01	3	0
	1901/02	3	0
	Total	**7**	**0**

⚽ GILBERT GODSMARK Forward

Born	Derby, 16 January 1877		
Died	South Africa, February 1901		
Clubs	Ashford FC; Newton Heath		
		A	G
	1899/1900	9	4
	Total	**9**	**4**

⚽ G FOLEY Forward

Clubs	Ashford FC; Newton Heath		
		A	G
	1899/1900	7	1
	Total	**7**	**1**

⚽ TOM LEIGH Forward

Clubs	Derby County; Burton Swifts; New Brighton Tower; Newton Heath		
		A	G
	1899/1900	9	1
	1900/01	34	14
	Total	**43**	**15**

⚽ EDWARD HOLT Forward

Clubs	Newton Heath Athletic; Newton Heath		
		A	G
	1899/1900	1	1
	Total	**1**	**1**

⚽ JOHN GRUNDY Forward

Born	Egerton, Bolton	
Clubs	Wigan County; Newton Heath; Halliwell Rovers; Newton Heath	

	A	G
1899/1900	1	1
1900/01	10	2
Total	**11**	**3**

⚽ JAMES PATRICK GARVEY Goalkeeper

Born	Hulme, Manchester, 23 January 1878
Clubs	Wigan County; Newton Heath; Middleton FC; Stalybridge Rovers; Southport Central; Bradford City

	A	G
1900/01	6	0
Total	**6**	**0**

⚽ ALFRED JOHN SCHOFIELD Forward

Born	Liverpool
Clubs	Everton; Newton Heath

	A	G
1900/01	29	7
1901/02	29	4
1902/03	16	3
1903/04	26	6
1904/05	24	4
1905/06	23	4
1906/07	10	2
Total	**157**	**30**

⚽ REGINALD OPENSHAW LAWSON Forward

Born	Bolton, 15 November 1880
Clubs	Halliwell St Pauls; Cheshire College; Newton Heath; Bolton Wanderers; Southport Central

	A	G
1900/01	3	0
Total	**3**	**0**

⚽ JAMES WHITEHOUSE Goalkeeper

Born	Birmingham, 27 April 1873
Died	7 February 1934

Clubs	Albion Swifts; Birmingham St George; Grimsby Town; Aston Villa; Bedminster; Grimsby Town; Newton Heath; Manchester City; Third Lanark; Hull City; Southend United		
		A	G
	1900/01	29	0
	1901/02	23	0
	1902/03	7	0
	Total	**59**	**0**

☺ JAMES FISHER Forward

Born	Scotland		
Clubs	East Stirlingshire; St Bernard FC; Aston Villa; Kings Park FC; Newton Heath		
		A	G
	1900/01	25	1
	1901/02	17	1
	Total	**42**	**2**

⚽ WILSON GREENWOOD Forward

Born	Padiham, Lancashire, 1868		
Died	Padiham, 1943		
Clubs	Blue Star; Brierfield; Accrington; Sheffield United; Rossendale; Rochdale Athletic; Warmley; Grimsby Town; Newton Heath		
		A	G
	1900/01	3	0
	Total	**3**	**0**

⚽ HUGH MORGAN Forward

Born	Lanarkshire		
Clubs	Harthill Thistle; Airdrieonains; Sunderland; Bolton Wanderers; Newton Heath; Manchester City; Accrington Stanley; Blackpool		
		A	G
	1900/01	20	4
	Total	**20**	**4**

⚽ WILLIAM BOOTH Forward

Born	Manchester

Clubs	Edge Lane FC; Newton Heath		
		A	G
	1900/01	2	0
	Total	**2**	**0**

⚽ JAMES VINCENT HAYES Full-back

Born	Miles Platting, Manchester, 25 April 1879		
Clubs	Newton Heath Athletic; Newton Heath; Brentford; Manchester United; Bradford; Rochdale		
		A	G
	1900/01	1	0
	1901/02	16	1
	1902/03	2	0
	1903/04	21	0
	1904/05	22	1
	1908/09	22	0
	1909/10	30	0
	1910/11	1	0
	Total	**115**	**2**

⚽ SAMUEL JOHNSON Forward

Clubs	Tonge FC; Newton Heath; Heywood FC		
		A	G
	1900/01	1	0
	Total	**1**	**0**

⚽ HUBERT HENRY LAPPIN Forward

Born	Manchester, 16 January 1879		
Died	Liverpool May 1925		
Clubs	Springfield FC; Oldham Athletic; Newton Heath; Grimsby Town; Rossendale United; Clapton Orient; Chester; Birmingham; Chirk; Hurst FC; Macclesfield FC		
		A	G
	1900/01	1	0
	1901/02	21	3
	1902/03	5	1
	Total	**27**	**4**

⚽ JOHN BANKS Half-back

Born	West Bromwich, May 1871	
Died	Barrow-in-Furness, January 1947	
Clubs	Oldbury Town; West Bromwich Albion; Newton Heath;	
	Plymouth Argyle; Leyton; Exeter City	

	A	G
1901/02	27	0
1902/03	13	0
Total	**40**	**0**

⚽ WILLIAM WILLIAMS Forward

Clubs	Everton; Blackburn Rovers; Bristol Rovers; Newton Heath	

	A	G
1901/02	4	0
Total	**4**	**0**

⚽ STEPHEN PRESTON Forward

Born	Manchester	
Clubs	Newton Heath; Stockport County; Manchester United	

	A	G
1901/02	29	11
1902/03	4	3
Total	**33**	**14**

⚽ WILLIAM SMITH Forward

Clubs	Stockport County; Manchester City; Stockport County; Newton Heath	

	A	G
1901/02	16	0
Total	**16**	**0**

⚽ WILLIAM HIGGINS Half-back

Born	Smethwick, Staffordshire, 1870	
Clubs	Woodfield FC; Albion Swifts; Birmingham St George; Grimsby Town;	
	Bristol City; Newcastle United; Middlesbrough; Newton Heath	

	A	G
1901/02	10	0
Total	**10**	**0**

⚽ WILLIAM RICHARDS Forward

Born	West Bromwich, 15 November 1874
Died	February 1926
Clubs	Wordesley FC; Singers FC (Coventry); West Bromwich Standard; West Bromwich Albion; Newton Heath; Stourbridge FC; Halesowen Town

	A	G
1901/02	9	1
Total	**9**	**1**

⚽ JAMES SAUNDERS Goalkeeper

Born	Birmingham
Clubs	Glossop; Middlesbrough; Newton Heath; Nelson; Lincoln City; Chelsea; Watford; Lincoln Liberal Club FC

	A	G
1901/02	11	0
1902/03	1	0
Total	**12**	**0**

⚽ JAMES HIGSON Forward

Clubs	Manchester Wednesday; Newton Heath

	A	G
1901/02	5	1
Total	**5**	**1**

⚽ GEORGE O'BRIEN Forward

Clubs	Newton Heath

	A	G
1901/02	1	0
Total	**1**	**0**

⚽ THOMAS HERBERT READ Full-back

Born	Manchester
Clubs	Stretford FC; Manchester City; Manchester United

	A	G
1902/03	27	0
1903/04	8	0
Total	**35**	**0**

⚽ CHARLES HENRY RICHARDS Forward

Born   Burton-on-Trent, 9 August 1875
Clubs   Gresley Rovers; Notts County; Nottingham Forest; Grimsby Town;
        Leicester Fosse; Manchester United; Doncaster Rovers

	A	G
1902/03	8	1
Total	**8**	**1**

⚽ ERNEST 'DICK' PEGG Forward

Born   Leicester, 28 July 1878
Died   Leicester, 11 June 1916
Clubs   Leicester Fosse; Loughborough Town; Kettering FC; Reading;
        Preston North End; Manchester United; Fulham; Barnsley

	A	G
1902/03	28	7
1903/04	13	6
Total	**41**	**13**

⚽ JOHN HOPE PEDDIE Forward

Born   Southside, Glasgow, 21 March 1877
Died   Detroit, United States, 1928
Clubs   Benburb FC; Third Lanark; Newcastle United; Manchester United;
        Plymouth Argyle; Manchester United; Heart of Midlothian

	A	G
1902/03	30	11
1904/05	32	17
1905/06	34	18
1906/07	16	6
Total	**112**	**52**

⚽ FREDERICK WILLIAMS Forward

Born   Manchester
Clubs   Hanley Swifts; South Shore; Blackpool; Manchester City;
        Manchester United

	A	G
1902/03	8	0
Total	**8**	**0**

⚽ DANIEL JAMES HURST Forward

Born	Cockermouth, 2 October 1876		
Clubs	Black Diamonds FC; Workington; Blackburn Rovers; Workington;		
	Manchester City; Manchester United		

	A	G
1902/03	16	4
Total	**16**	**4**

⚽ WILLIAM BUNCE Full-back

Born	Rochdale
Clubs	Rochdale Athletic; Stockport County; Manchester United

	A	G
1902/03	2	0
Total	**2**	**0**

⚽ HERBERT BIRCHENOUGH Goalkeeper

Born	Crewe, 30 July 1874
Clubs	Crewe Alexandra; Burslem Port Vale; Glossop; Manchester United;
	Crewe Alexandra

	A	G
1902/03	25	0
Total	**25**	**0**

⚽ HERBERT ROTHWELL Full-back

Born	Manchester
Clubs	Newton Heath Athletic; Glossop North End; Manchester United;
	Manchester City; Newton Heath Athletic; Failsworth FC

	A	G
1902/03	22	0
Total	**22**	**0**

⚽ ARTHUR BEADSWORTH Forward

Born	Leicester, 12 October 1876
Clubs	Hinckley Town; Leicester Fosse; Preston North End; Manchester United;
	Swindon Town; New Brompton; Burton United

	A	G
1902/03	9	1
Total	**9**	**1**

⚽ WILLIAM HENRY BALL Half-back

Born   West Derby, Liverpool 11 April 1876
Clubs Liverpool South End; Rock Ferry FC; Blackburn Rovers; Everton;
       Notts County; Blackburn Rovers; Manchester United

	A	G
1902/03	4	0
Total	**4**	**0**

⚽ ALEXANDER LEEK BROWN DOWNIE Half-back

Born   Dunoon, 1876
Died   Withington, Manchester, 9 December 1953
Clubs Glasgow Perthshire; Third Lanark; Bristol City; Swindon Town;
       Manchester United; Oldham Athletic; Crewe Alexandra;
       Old Chorltonians

	A	G
1902/03	22	5
1903/04	29	4
1904/05	32	1
1905/06	34	0
1906/07	19	2
1907/08	10	0
1908/09	23	0
1909/10	3	0
Total	**172**	**12**

⚽ LAWRENCE SMITH Forward

Born   Manchester 1881
Died   Garston, Liverpool 23 September 1912
Clubs Manchester United; New Brompton; Earlstown FC

	A	G
1902/03	8	1
Total	**8**	**1**

⚽ **THOMAS MORRISON** Forward

Born	Belfast 1874		
Clubs	Stormont FC; Glentoran; Burnley; Glasgow Celtic; Burnley;		
	Manchester United; Colne FC		

		A	G
	1902/03	20	7
	1903/04	9	0
	Total	**29**	**7**

⚽ **ALEXANDER BELL** Half-back

Born	Cape Town, South Africa, 1882		
Died	Chorlton-cum-Hardy, 30 November 1934		
Clubs	Ayr Spring Vale; Ayr Westerlea; Ayr Parkhouse; Manchester United;		
	Blackburn Rovers; Clackmannan FC		

		A	G
	1902/03	5	1
	1903/04	6	1
	1904/05	29	1
	1905/06	36	2
	1906/07	35	2
	1907/08	35	1
	1908/09	20	2
	1909/10	27	0
	1910/11	27	0
	1911/12	32	0
	1912/13	26	0
	Total	**278**	**10**

⚽ **THOMAS ARTHUR ARKESDEN** Forward

Born	Warwick, 28 July 1878		
Died	Hulme, Manchester, 25 June 1921		
Clubs	Burton Wanderers; Derby County; Burton United; Manchester United;		
	Gainsborough Trinity		

		A	G
	1902/03	9	2
	1903/04	26	11
	1904/05	28	15

	A	G
1905/06	7	0
Total	**70**	**28**

⚽ JOHN CHRISTIE Full-back

Born   Manchester
Clubs   Sale Holmefield; Manchester United; Manchester City; Bradford;
          Croydon Common; Brentford

	A	G
1902/03	1	0
Total	**1**	**0**

⚽ ERNEST STREET Forward

Born   Manchester
Clubs   Sale Holmefield; Manchester United; Sale Holmefield

	A	G
1902/03	1	0
Total	**1**	**0**

⚽ ARTHUR GEORGE MARSHALL Full-back

Born   Liverpool, 2 October 1881
Clubs   Crewe Alexandra; Leicester Fosse; Stockport County;
          Manchester United; Portsmouth

	A	G
1902/03	6	0
Total	**6**	**0**

⚽ JOHN FITCHETT Full-back

Born   Chorlton, 28 October 1874
Clubs   Talbot FC; Bolton Wanderers; Southampton; Manchester United;
          Plymouth Argyle; Manchester United; Fulham; Sale Holmfield;
          Barrow; Exeter City

	A	G
1902/03	5	1
1904/05	11	0
Total	**16**	**1**

⚽ HARRY CLEAVER Forward

Clubs	Desborough FC; Manchester United		
		A	G
	1902/03	1	0
	Total	**1**	**0**

⚽ JOHN WILLIAM SUTCLIFFE Goalkeeper

Born	Shibden near Halifax, 14 April 1868		
Died	Bradford 7 July 1947		
Clubs	Bolton Wanderers; Millwall Athletic; Manchester United;		
	Plymouth Argyle		
		A	g
	1903/04	21	0
	Total	**21**	**0**

⚽ ROBERT BONTHRON Full-back

Born	Dundee 1884		
Clubs	Raith Athletic; Raith Rovers; Dundee; Manchester United; Sunderland;		
	Northampton Town; Birmingham; Leith Athletic		
		A	G
	1903/04	33	1
	1904/05	32	0
	1905/06	26	2
	1906/07	28	0
	Total	**119**	**3**

⚽ ALEXANDER ROBERTSON Half-back

Clubs	Hibernian; Manchester United		
		A	G
	1903/04	24	0
	1904/05	8	1
	Total	**32**	**1**

⚽ WILLIAM McCARTNEY Forward

Born	Newmilns, Ayrshire	
Clubs	Rutherglen Glencairn; Ayr; Hibernian; Manchester United;	
	West Ham United; Broxburn; Lochgelly United; Clyde; Broxburn; Clyde	

	A	G
1903/04	13	1
Total	**13**	**1**

⚽ RALPH GAUDIE Forward

Born   Guisborough, 16 January 1876
Clubs   South Bank; Sheffield United; Aston Villa; Woolwich Arsenal;
       Manchester United

	A	G
1903/04	7	0
Total	**7**	**0**

⚽ THOMAS ROBERTSON Forward

Clubs   East Benhar; Heatherbell; Motherwell; Fauldhouse;
       Heart of Midlothian; Liverpool; Heart of Midlothian; Dundee;
       Manchester United; Bathgate

	A	G
1903/04	3	0
Total	**3**	**0**

⚽ ALEXANDER 'SANDY' ROBERTSON Forward

Born   Dundee 1878
Clubs   Dundee Violet; Dundee FC; Middlesbrough; Manchester United; Bradford

	A	G
1903/04	27	10
1904/05	1	0
Total	**28**	**10**

⚽ THOMAS BLACKSTOCK Full-back

Born   Kirkcaldy 1882
Died   Clayton, Manchester 8 April 1907
Clubs   Dunniker Rangers; Blue Bell FC; Raith Athletic; Cowdenbeath;
       Manchester United

	A	G
1903/04	1	0
Total	**1**	**0**

⚽ WILLIAM GRASSAM Forward

Born	Larbert, Stenhousemuir, 20 November 1878	
Clubs	Redcliffe Thistle; Glasgow Maryhill; Burslem Port Vale; West Ham United;	
	Glasgow Celtic; Manchester United; Leyton FC; West Ham United; Brentford	

	A	G
1903/04	23	11
1904/05	6	2
Total	**29**	**13**

⚽ HENRY HERBERT MOGER Goalkeeper

Born	Southampton, September 1879
Died	Manchester 20 June 1927
Clubs	Forest Swifts; Freemantle; Southampton; Manchester United

	A	G
1903/04	13	0
1904/05	32	0
1905/06	27	0
1906/07	38	0
1907/08	29	0
1908/09	36	0
1909/10	36	0
1910/11	25	0
1911/12	6	0
Total	**242**	**0**

⚽ RICHARD DUCKWORTH Half-back

Born	Collyhurst, Manchester
Clubs	Rossall Mission; Stretford FC; Newton Heath Alliance; Manchester United

	A	G
1903/04	1	1
1904/05	8	6
1905/06	10	0
1906/07	28	2
1907/08	35	0
1908/09	33	0
1909/10	29	0
1910/11	22	2

1911/12	26	0
1912/13	24	0
1913/14	9	0
Total	**225**	**11**

⚽ HENRY WILKINSON Forward

Born | Bury 1883
Clubs | Newton Heath Alliance; Manchester United; Hull City; West Ham United; Manchester United; Haslingden FC; St Helens Recreation FC; Bury; Oswaldtwistle Rovers; Rochdale

	A	G
1903/04	8	0
Total	**8**	**0**

⚽ HUGH KERR Forward

Born | 1882
Clubs | Ayr; Manchester United

	A	G
1903/04	2	0
Total	**2**	**0**

⚽ PROCTOR HALL Forward

Born | Blackburn, 23 January 1884
Clubs | Oswaldtwistle Rovers; Manchester United; Brighton & Hove Albion; Aston Villa; Bradford City; Luton Town; Chesterfield Town; Hyde FC; Newport County; Mardy FC

	A	G
1903/04	8	2
Total	**8**	**2**

⚽ JOSEPH SCHOFIELD Forward

Born | Wigan
Clubs | Bryn Central; Ashton Town; Manchester United; Stockport County; Luton Town

	A	G
1903/04	2	0
Total	**2**	**0**

⚽ CHARLES ROBERTS Half-back

Born	Darlington, 6 April 1883	
Died	Manchester, 7 August 1939	
Clubs	Rise Carr Rangers; Darlington St Augustine's; Sheffield United;	
	Bishop Auckland; Grimsby Town; Manchester United; Oldham Athletic	

	A	G
1903/04	2	0
1904/05	28	5
1905/06	34	4
1906/07	31	2
1907/08	32	2
1908/09	27	1
1909/10	28	4
1910/11	33	1
1911/12	32	2
1912/13	24	1
Total	**271**	**22**

⚽ GEORGE LYONS Forward

Clubs	Black Lane Temperance; Manchester United; Oldham Athletic;	
	Rossendale United; Salford United	

	A	G
1903/04	2	0
1905/06	1	0
Total	**3**	**0**

⚽ WILLIAM HARTWELL Forward

Born	Kettering 1885	
Clubs	Kettering Town; Manchester United; Northampton Town	

	A	G
1903/04	1	0
1904/05	2	0
Total	**3**	**0**

⚽ JOHN THOMAS ALLAN Forward

Born	South Shields, 16 January 1883	
Clubs	Bishop Auckland; Manchester United; Bishop Auckland	

	A	G
1904/05	27	16
1905/06	5	5
1906/07	3	0
Total	**35**	**21**

⚽ CHARLES MACKIE Forward

Clubs   Aberdeen; Manchester United; West Ham United; Aberdeen; Lochgelly United

	A	G
1904/05	5	3
Total	**5**	**3**

⚽ HENRY WILLIAMS Forward

Born   Farnworth, Bolton 1883

Clubs   Walkden St Marys; Turton FC; Bury; Bolton Wanderers; Burnley; Manchester United; Leeds City

	A	G
1904/05	22	6
1905/06	10	1
Total	**32**	**7**

⚽ JOHN HARRY 'CLEM' BEDDOW Forward

Born   Burton-on-Trent, 31 October 1885

Clubs   Trent Rovers; Burton United; Manchester United; Burnley

	A	G
1904/05	9	1
1905/06	21	11
1906/07	3	0
Total	**33**	**12**

⚽ RICHARD WOMBWELL Forward

Born   Nottingham, 28 July 1877

Clubs   Bulwell FC; Ilkeston Town; Derby County; Bristol City; Manchester United; Heart of Midlothian; Brighton & Hove Albion; Blackburn Rovers; Ilkeston United

	A	G
1904/05	8	1
1905/06	25	2
1906/07	14	0
Total	**47**	**3**

ROBERT VALENTINE Goalkeeper

Clubs Manchester United

	A	G
1904/05	2	0
1905/06	8	0
Total	**10**	**0**

RICHARD HOLDEN Full-back

Born Middleton, 12 June 1885
Clubs Parkfield Central; Tonge FC; Manchester United

	A	G
1904/05	1	0
1905/06	27	0
1906/07	27	0
1907/08	26	0
1908/09	2	0
1909/10	7	0
1910/11	8	0
1911/12	6	0
1912/13	2	0
Total	**106**	**0**

JOHN BARCLAY PICKEN Forward

Born Hurlford, Ayrshire 1880
Died Devonport, Plymouth 31 July 1952
Clubs Hurlford Thistle; Kilmarnock Shawbank; Bolton Wanderers;
Plymouth Argyle; Manchester United; Burnley; Bristol City

	A	G
1905/06	33	20
1906/07	26	4
1907/08	8	1

1908/09	13	3
1909/10	19	7
1910/11	14	4
Total	**113**	**39**

☻ CHARLES SAGAR Forward

Born   Daisy Hill, Bolton, 28 March 1878
Died   Bolton 4 December 1919
Clubs   Edgworth Rovers; Turton Rovers; Bury; Manchester United;
        Atherton FC; Haslingden

	A	G
1905/06	20	16
1906/07	10	4
Total	**30**	**20**

☻ ARCHIBALD MONTGOMERY Goalkeeper

Born   Chryston, Lanark 1871
Died   January 1922
Clubs   Chryston Athletic; Glasgow Rangers; Bury; Manchester United; Bury

	A	G
1905/06	3	0
Total	**3**	**0**

☻ JAMES ARTHUR DYER Forward

Born   Blacker Hill, Barnsley, 24 August 1883
Clubs   Wombwell FC; Barnsley; Doncaster Rovers; Ashton Town;
        Manchester United; West Ham United; Bradford; Wombwell FC

	A	G
1905/06	1	0
Total	**1**	**0**

☻ ERNARD DONAGHY Forward

Born   Londonderry
Clubs   Derry Celtic; Manchester United; Derry Celtic; Burnley

	A	G
1905/06	3	0
Total	**3**	**0**

⚽ GEORGE WALL Forward

Born	Bolden Colliery near Sunderland, 20 February 1885	
Died	Manchester 1962	
Clubs	Bolden Royal Rovers; Whitburn; Jarrow; Barnsley; Manchester United;	
	Oldham Athletic; Hamilton Academicals; Rochdale; Ashton National;	
	Manchester Ship Canal FC	

	A	G
1905/06	6	3
1906/07	38	11
1907/08	36	19
1908/09	34	11
1909/10	32	14
1910/11	26	5
1911/12	33	3
1912/13	36	10
1913/14	29	11
1914/15	17	2
Total	**287**	**89**

⚽ HORACE ELFORD BLEW Full-back

Born	Wrexham, 16 January 1878	
Died	Wrexham, 1 February 1957	
Clubs	Rhostyllen; Wrexham; Druids; Bury; Manchester United;	
	Manchester City; Brymbo	

	A	G
1905/06	1	0
Total	**1**	**0**

⚽ WILLIAM YATES Forward

Born	Birmingham 1883	
Clubs	Aston Villa; Brighton & Hove Albion; Manchester United;	
	Heart of Midlothian; Portsmouth; Coventry City	

	A	G
1906/07	3	0
Total	**3**	**0**

⚽ FRANKLIN CHARLES BUCKLEY Half-back

Born	Urmston, Manchester, 9 November 1882
Died	Walsall, 22 December 1964
Clubs	Aston Villa; Brighton & Hove Albion; Manchester United; Aston Villa; Manchester City; Birmingham; Derby County; Bradford City

		A	G
	1906/07	3	0
	Total	**3**	**0**

⚽ ARTHUR YOUNG Forward

Born	Scotland
Clubs	Hurlford Thistle; Manchester United

		A	G
	1906/07	2	0
	Total	**2**	**0**

⚽ WILLIAM ALEXANDER BERRY Forward

Born	Sunderland 1882
Clubs	Oakhill; Sunderland Royal Rovers; Sunderland; Tottenham Hotspur; Manchester United; Stockport County; Sunderland Royal Rovers

		A	G
	1906/07	9	0
	1907/08	3	1
	1908/09	1	0
	Total	**13**	**1**

⚽ ALEXANDER WILLIAM MENZIES Centre-forward

Born	Blantyre, Lanark, 25 November 1882
Clubs	Blantyre Victoria; Heart of Midlothian; Arthurlie; Heart of Midlothian; Manchester United; Luton Town; Dundee

		A	G
	1906/07	17	4
	1907/08	6	0
	Total	**23**	**4**

⚽ HERBERT BURGESS Full-back

Born	Openshaw, Manchester, October 1883

Died	Manchester, July 1954		
Clubs	Gorton St Francis; Openshaw United; Edge Lane FC; Moss Side FC;		
	Glossop; Manchester City; Manchester United		
		A	G
	1906/07	17	0
	1907/08	27	0
	1908/09	4	0
	1909/10	1	0
	Total	**49**	**0**

⚽ WILLIAM HENRY MEREDITH Forward

Born	Black Park near Chirk, 30 July 1874		
Died	Withington, Manchester, 19 April 1958		
Clubs	Black Park, Chirk; Northwich Victoria; Manchester City;		
	Manchester United; Stalybridge Celtic		
		A	G
	1906/07	16	5
	1907/08	37	10
	1908/09	34	0
	1909/10	31	5
	1910/11	35	5
	1911/12	35	3
	1912/13	22	2
	1913/14	34	2
	1914/15	26	0
	1919/20	19	2
	1920/21	14	1
	Total	**303**	**35**

⚽ ALEXANDER 'SANDY' TURNBULL Forward

Born	Hurlford near Kilmarnock, 1884		
Died	Arras, France, 3 May 1917		
Clubs	Hurlford Thistle; Manchester City; Manchester United		
		A	G
	1906/07	15	6
	1907/08	30	25
	1908/09	19	5

1909/10	26	13
1910/11	35	18
1911/12	30	7
1912/13	35	10
1913/14	17	4
1914/15	13	2
Total	**220**	**90**

⚽ JAMES BANNISTER Forward

Born   Leyland, 20 September 1880

Clubs   Leyland Temperance; Leyland FC; Chorley; Manchester City;
Manchester United; Preston North End; Burslem Port Vale; Heywood FC

	A	G
1906/07	4	1
1907/08	36	5
1908/09	16	1
1909/10	1	0
Total	**57**	**7**

⚽ JOSEPH WILLIAMS Forward

Born   Crewe

Clubs   Macclesfield; Manchester United

	A	G
1906/07	3	1
Total	**3**	**1**

⚽ ERNEST THOMSON Half-back

Born   Blackburn 1884

Clubs   Darwen FC; Manchester United; Nelson; Cardiff City; Nelson

	A	G
1907/08	3	0
1908/09	1	0
Total	**4**	**0**

⚽ JAMES McLACHLAN TURNBULL Forward

Born   East Plain, Bannockburn, 23 May 1884

Clubs   East Stirlingshire; Dundee; Falkirk; Rangers; Preston North End; Leyton FC;

Manchester United; Bradford; Chelsea; Manchester United; Hurst FC

	A	G
1907/08	26	10
1908/09	22	17
1909/10	19	9
Total	**67**	**36**

⚽ GEORGE WILLIAM STACEY Full-back

Born   Thorpe Hesley, Rotherham, 25 April 1887
Clubs   Thorpe Hesley FC; Sheffield Wednesday; Thornhill United; Barnsley;
         Manchester United

	A	G
1907/08	18	1
1908/09	32	0
1909/10	32	0
1910/11	36	0
1911/12	29	2
1912/13	36	1
1913/14	34	1
1914/15	24	4
Total	**241**	**9**

⚽ KERR WHITESIDE Half-back

Born   Scotland 1887
Clubs   Irvine Victoria; Manchester United; Hurst FC

	A	G
1907/08	1	0
Total	**1**	**0**

⚽ JOHN McGILLIVRAY Half-back

Born   Broughton
Clubs   Berry's Association; Manchester United; Southport Central; Stoke; Dartford

	A	G
1907/08	1	0
1908/09	2	0
Total	**3**	**0**

⚽ THOMAS CARTER WILSON Forward

Born	Preston, 20 October 1877
Died	Blackpool, 30 August 1940
Clubs	Fishwick Ramblers; Ashton-in-Makerfield FC; West Manchester FC; Ashton Town; Ashton North End; Oldham County; Swindon Town; Blackburn Rovers; Swindon Town; Millwall Athletic; Aston Villa; Queen's Park Rangers; Bolton Wanderers; Leeds City; Manchester United

	A	G
1907/08	1	0
Total	**1**	**0**

⚽ HERBERT BROOMFIELD Goalkeeper

Born	Audlem near Nantwich, 11 December 1878
Clubs	Northwich Wednesday; Northwich Victoria; Bolton Wanderers; Manchester United; Manchester City; Manchester United

	A	G
1907/08	9	0
Total	**9**	**0**

⚽ EDWARD DALTON Full-back

Clubs	Pendlebury FC; Manchester United; Pendlebury FC; St Helens Recs

	A	G
1907/08	1	0
Total	**1**	**0**

⚽ HAROLD JAMES HALSE Forward

Born	Stratford, East London, 1 January 1886
Died	Colchester, 25 March 1949
Clubs	Newportians FC; Wanstead FC; Barking Town; Clapton Orient; Southend United; Manchester United; Aston Villa; Chelsea; Charlton Athletic

	A	G
1907/08	6	4
1908/09	29	14
1909/10	27	6
1910/11	23	9
1911/12	24	8
Total	**109**	**41**

⚽ AARON HULME Full-back

Born	Manchester 30 April 1883
Died	Failsworth, Manchester, November 1933
Clubs	Newton Heath Alliance; Colne FC; Oldham Athletic; Manchester United; Nelson; Hyde FC; St Helens Recs; Newton Heath Alliance

	A	G
1907/08	1	0
1908/09	3	0
Total	**4**	**0**

⚽ DAVID CHRISTIE Forward

Born	Scotland 1885
Clubs	Hurlford FC; Manchester United

	A	G
1908/09	2	0
Total	**2**	**0**

⚽ HAROLD PAYNE HARDMAN Forward

Born	Kirkmanshulme, Manchester, 4 April 1882
Died	Sale, Cheshire 9 June 1965
Clubs	Blackpool; Everton; Manchester United; Bradford City; Stoke; Manchester United

	A	G]
1908/09	4	0
Total	**4**	**0**

⚽ THOMAS WALTER WILCOX Goalkeeper

Born	Stepney, 1881
Died	Blackpool, September 1962
Clubs	Millwall Athletic; Cray Wanderers; Woolwich Arsenal; Norwich City; Blackpool; Manchester United; Carlisle United; Goole Town; Abergavenny

	A	G
1908/09	2	0
Total	**2**	**0**

⚽ OSCAR HORACE LINKSON Full-back

Born	New Barnet 25 April 1888

		A	G
Died	France, December 1916		
Clubs	Barnet & Alston; The Pirates FC; Manchester United; Shelbourne		
	1908/09	10	0
	1910/11	7	0
	1911/12	21	0
	1912/13	17	0
	Total	**55**	**0**

⚽ JOSEPH CURRY Half-back

		A	G
Born	Newcastle-on-Tyne 23 January 1887		
Clubs	Scotswood FC; Manchester United; Southampton; West Stanley		
	1908/09	8	0
	1910/11	5	0
	Total	**13**	**0**

⚽ GEORGE TURNER LIVINGSTONE Forward

		A	G
Born	Dumbarton, 5 May 1876		
Died	Helensburgh, 15 January 1950		
Clubs	Sinclair Swifts; Artizan Thistle; Heart of Midlothian; Sunderland; Glasgow Celtic; Liverpool; Manchester City; Glasgow Rangers; Manchester United		
	1908/09	11	3
	1909/10	16	0
	1910/11	10	0
	1911/12	1	0
	1912/13	2	1
	1913/14	3	0
	Total	**43**	**4**

⚽ ERNEST PAYNE Forward

		A	G
Clubs	Worcester City; Manchester United		
	1908/09	2	1
	Total	**2**	**1**

⚽ ANTHONY DONNELLY Full-back

Born	Middleton, 30 April 1886
Died	Oldham 25 April 1947
Clubs	Parkfield Lads; Rhodes Church; Heywood United; Manchester United; Heywood United; Glentoran; Heywood United; Chester; Southampton; Middleton Borough

	A	G
1908/09	1	0
1909/10	4	0
1910/11	15	0
1911/12	13	0
1912/13	1	0
Total	**34**	**0**

⚽ JOSEPH BERTRAM FORD Forward

Born	Northwich 7 May 1886
Clubs	Witton Albion; Crewe Alexandra; Manchester United; Nottingham Forest; Goole Town

	A	G
1908/09	4	0
1909/10	1	0
Total	**5**	**0**

⚽ JOHN JOSEPH QUIN Forward

Born	Barrhead, Renfrewshire 1890
Clubs	Xaverian College; Higher Broughton FC; Cheetham Hill FC; Manchester City; Manchester United; Nelson; Chorley; Eccles Borough; Grimsby Town; Clyde; Ayr United

	A	G
1908/09	1	0
1909/10	1	0
Total	**2**	**0**

⚽ SAMUEL PRINCE BLOTT Forward

Born	London 1 January 1886
Died	Southend 16 January 1969
Clubs	Southend United; Bradford; Southend United; Manchester United;

Plymouth Argyle; Newport County

	A	G
1909/10	10	1
1910/11	1	0
1911/12	6	0
1912/13	2	1
Total	**19**	**2**

⚽ ELIJAH ROUND Goalkeeper

Born   Stoke-on-Trent, January 1882
Clubs   Mexborough; Barnsley; Oldham Athletic; Manchester United;
           Worksop Town; Mexborough

	A	G
1909/10	2	0
Total	**2**	**0**

⚽ THOMAS PERCY HOMER Forward

Born   Winson Green, Birmingham 1 April 1886
Clubs   Soho Caledonians; Erdington FC; Aston Villa; Kidderminster Harriers;
           Manchester United

	A	G
1909/10	17	8
1910/11	7	6
1911/12	1	0
Total	**25**	**14**

⚽ ARTHUR WHALLEY Half-back

Born   Rainford, 17 February 1886
Died   Wythenshawe, Manchester 23 November 1952
Clubs   Bryn Central; Blackpool; Manchester United; Southend United;
           Charlton Athletic; Millwall

	A	G
1909/10	9	0
1910/11	15	0
1911/12	5	0
1912/13	26	4
1913/14	18	2

1914/15	1	0
1919/20	23	0
Total	**97**	**6**

⚽ EDWARD CONNOR Forward

Born   Liverpool 1884
Died   January 1955
Clubs   Eccles Borough; Walkden Central; Manchester United; Sheffield United; Bury; Exeter City; Rochdale; Chesterfield; Saltney Athletic

	A	G
1909/10	8	1
1910/11	7	1
Total	**15**	**2**

⚽ ARTHUR HENRY HOOPER Forward

Born   Brierley Hill, 18 January 1889
Clubs   Kidderminster Harriers; Manchester United; Crystal Palace

	A	G
1909/10	2	1
1910/11	2	0
1913/14	3	0
Total	**7**	**1**

⚽ ENOCH JAMES WEST Forward

Born   Hucknall Torkard, Nottinghamshire 31 March 1886
Clubs   Sheffield United; Hucknall Constitutional; Nottingham Forest; Manchester United

	A	G
1910/11	35	19
1911/12	32	17
1912/13	36	21
1913/14	30	6
1914/15	33	9
Total	**166**	**72**

⚽ JOHN SHELDON Forward

Born   Clay Cross, Derbyshire April 1887

Died	Manchester 19 March 1943	
Clubs	Nuneaton FC; Manchester United; Liverpool	
	A	G
1910/11	5	0
1911/12	5	0
1912/13	16	1
Total	**26**	**1**

⚽ HUGH EDMONDS Goalkeeper

Born	Chryston, Ayrshire 1884	
Clubs	Hamilton Academical; Belfast Distillery; Linfield; Bolton Wanderers; Manchester United; Glenavon; Belfast Distillery	
	A	G
1910/11	13	0
1911/12	30	0
Total	**43**	**0**

⚽ LESLIE BROWN HOFTON Full-back

Born	Sheffield, April 1888	
Clubs	Kiveton Park FC; Worksop Town; Denaby United; Glossop; Manchester United; Denaby Main	
	A	G
1910/11	9	0
1911/12	7	0
1920/21	1	0
Total	**17**	**0**

⚽ JAMES HODGE Defender

Born	Stenhousemuir, 5 July 1891	
Died	Chorlton-cum-Hardy 2 September 1970	
Clubs	Stenhousemuir; Manchester United; Millwall Athletic; Norwich City; Southend United	
	A	G
1910/11	2	0
1911/12	10	0
1912/13	19	0
1913/14	28	0

1914/15	4	0
1919/20	16	2
Total	**79**	**2**

⚽ GEORGE WALTER ANDERSON Forward

Born   Cheetham, Manchester January 1893
Clubs   Broughton St James'; Broughton Wellington; Salford United; Bury;
            Manchester United

	A	G
1911/12	1	0
1912/13	24	12
1913/14	32	15
1914/15	23	10
Total	**80**	**37**

⚽ MICHAEL HAMILL Forward

Born   Belfast 19 January 1885
Died   July 1943
Clubs   St Paul's Swifts; Belfast Rangers; Belfast Celtic; Manchester United;
            Manchester City; Fall River (Boston USA); Coats FC (Rhode Island
            USA); Belfast Celtic

	A	G
1911/12	16	1
1912/13	15	1
1913/14	26	0
Total	**57**	**2**

⚽ PATRICK McCARTHY Forward

Born   Chester 1888
Clubs   Chester; Skelmersdale United; Manchester United;
            Skelmersdale United; Tranmere Rovers; Chester

	A	G
1911/12	1	0
Total	**1**	**0**

⚽ EZRA JOHN ROYALS Goalkeeper

Born   Fenton, Staffordshire January 1882

Clubs	Chesterton White Star; Manchester United; Northwich Victoria	
	A	G
1911/12	2	0
1913/14	5	0
Total	**7**	**0**

⚽ THOMAS ALBERT NUTTALL Forward

Born   Bolton, 16 January 1889
Clubs   Heywood United; Manchester United; Everton; St Mirren; Northwich Victoria;
        Southend United; Leyland FC; Northwich Victoria

	A	G
1911/12	6	2
1912/13	10	2
Total	**16**	**4**

⚽ ALFRED CAPPER Forward

Born   Northwich, January 1891
Clubs   Northwich Victoria; Manchester United; Witton Albion; Sheffield Wednesday;
        Brentford

	A	G
1911/12	1	0
Total	**1**	**0**

⚽ FRANK KNOWLES Half-back

Born   Hyde, April 1891
Clubs   Hyde FC; Stalybridge Celtic; Manchester United; Hartlepool United;
        Manchester City; Stalybridge Celtic; Ashington; Stockport County;
        Newport County; Queen's Park Rangers; Ashton National; Macclesfield

	A	G
1911/12	7	0
1912/13	2	0
1913/14	18	1
1914/15	19	0
Total	**46**	**1**

⚽ ROBERT HUGHES BEALE Goalkeeper

Born   Maidstone, 8 January 1884

		A	G
Died	Dymchurch near Folkestone 5 October 1950		
Clubs	Maidstone United; Brighton & Hove Albion; Norwich City;		
	Manchester United; Gillingham; Manchester United		
	1912/13	37	0
	1913/14	31	0
	1914/15	37	0
	Total	**105**	**0**

⚽ THOMAS SAVILL GIPPS Half-back

		A	G
Born	Walthamstow, January 1888		
Clubs	Walthamstow FC; Tottenham Hotspur; Barrow; Manchester United		
	1912/13	2	0
	1913/14	11	0
	1914/15	10	0
	Total	**23**	**0**

⚽ JOHN WILLIAM MEW Goalkeeper

		A	G
Born	Sunderland, 30 March 1889		
Died	Barton Irwell, October 1963		
Clubs	Marley Hill St Cuthbert's; Blaydon United; Marley Hill United;		
	Manchester United; Barrow		
	1912/13	1	0
	1913/14	2	0
	1914/15	1	0
	1919/20	42	0
	1920/21	40	0
	1921/22	41	0
	1922/23	41	0
	1923/24	12	0
	1925/26	6	0
	Total	**186**	**0**

⚽ WILLIAM HUNTER Forward

Born   Sunderland

Clubs   Sunderland West End; Liverpool; Sunderland; Lincoln City; South Shields;
         Barnsley; Manchester United; Clapton Orient; Exeter City

	A	G
1912/13	3	2
Total	**3**	**2**

ARTHUR CASHMORE Forward

Born   Birmingham 30 October 1893
Clubs   Sparkhill Avondale; Bromsgrove Rovers; Stourbridge FC;
         Manchester United; Oldham Athletic; Darlaston FC; Cardiff City;
         Notts County; Darlaston FC; Nuneaton FC; Shrewsbury Town

	A	G
1913/14	3	0
Total	**3**	**0**

THOMAS CHORLTON Full-back

Born   Heaton Mersey 1882
Clubs   All Saints FC; Northern FC; Stockport County; Accrington Stanley;
         Liverpool; Manchester United; Stalybridge Celtic

	A	G
1913/14	4	0
Total	**4**	**0**

WILFRED WOODCOCK Forward

Born   Ashton-under-Lyne, January 1892
Clubs   Abbey Hey FC; Stalybridge Celtic; Manchester United; Manchester City;
         Stockport County; Wigan Borough

	A	G
1913/14	11	2
1914/15	19	7
1919/20	28	11
Total	**58**	**20**

JOSEPH HAYWOOD Half-back

Born   Wednesbury 1893
Clubs   Hindley Central; Manchester United

	A	G
1913/14	14	0
1914/15	12	0
Total	**26**	**0**

⚽ JAMES THOMSON Forward

Born   Dumbarton
Clubs   Clydebank; Renton FC; Manchester United; Dumbarton Harp; St Mirren

	A	G
1913/14	6	1
Total	**6**	**1**

⚽ ARTHUR POTTS Forward

Born   Cannock, Staffordshire 26 May 1888
Died   South Staffordshire, January 1981
Clubs   Willenhall Swifts; Manchester United; Wolverhampton Wanderers;
          Walsall; Bloxwich Strollers; Dudley town; Red White & Blue

	A	G
1913/14	6	1
1914/15	17	4
1919/20	4	0
Total	**27**	**5**

⚽ ROBERT ROBERTS Full-back

Born   Earlstown, Lancashire 1892
Clubs   Altrincham; Manchester United

	A	G
1913/14	2	0
Total	**2**	**0**

⚽ JOHN HODGE Defender

Born   Stenhousemuir
Clubs   Stenhousemuir; Manchester United

	A	G
1913/14	4	0
1914/15	26	0
Total	**30**	**0**

⚽ EDWARD KEARNEY HUDSON Full-back

Born   Bolton 16 January 1887
Clubs   Walkden Central; Manchester United; Stockport County; Aberdare

	A	G
1913/14	9	0
1914/15	2	0
Total	**11**	**0**

⚽ JOSEPH PATRICK NORTON Forward

Born   Leicester July 1890
Clubs   Leicester Imperial; Nuneaton Town; Stockport County; Nuneaton Town;
       Manchester United; Leicester City; Bristol Rovers; Swindon Town;
       Kettering Town; Atherstone Town' Hinckley United; Ashby Town

	A	G
1913/14	8	0
1914/15	29	3
Total	**37**	**3**

⚽ JAMES EDWARD 'GEORGE' TRAVERS Forward

Born   Newtown, Birmingham 15 November 1888
Died   Smethwick 31 August 1946
Clubs   Bilston United; Rowley United; Wolverhampton Wanderers; Birmingham;
       Aston Villa; Queen's Park Rangers; Leicester Fosse; Barnsley;
       Manchester United; Swindon Town; Millwall Athletic; Norwich City;
       Gillingham; Nuneaton Town; Cradley St Luke's; Bilston United

	A	G
1913/14	13	4
1914/15	8	0
Total	**21**	**4**

⚽ JOCELYN 'JOSH' ROWE Full-back

Born   Kingston-upon-Thames
Clubs   Dublin Bohemians; Manchester United; Dublin Bohemians;
       Kingstonians FC

	A	G
1913/14	1	0
Total	**1**	**0**

⚽ GEORGE HUNTER Half-back

Born	Peshawar, India 1885
Died	February 1934
Clubs	Maidstone; Croydon Common; Aston Villa; Oldham Athletic; Chelsea; Manchester United; Portsmouth

		A	G
	1913/14	7	0
	1914/15	15	2
	Total	**22**	**2**

⚽ PATRICK O'CONNELL Half-back

Born	Dublin 1887
Clubs	Belfast Celtic; Sheffield Wednesday; Hull City; Manchester United; Dumbarton; Ashington

		A	G
	1914/15	34	2
	Total	**34**	**2**

⚽ SAMUEL PERCY COOKSON Half-back

Born	Bargoed, January 1891
Clubs	Bargoed Town; Manchester United

		A	G
	1914/15	12	0
	Total	**12**	**0**

⚽ WALTER SPRATT Full-back

Born	Huddersfield 2 October 1892
Clubs	Rotherham Town; Brentford; Manchester United; Brentford; Sittingbourne; Elsecar Main

		A	G
	1914/15	12	0
	1919/20	1	0
	Total	**13**	**0**

⚽ ARTHUR ALLMAN Full-back

Born	Milton, Staffordshire 24 December 1890
Died	Milton, Staffordshire 22 December 1956

Clubs   Smallthorne; Shrewsbury Town; Wolverhampton Wanderers;
Swansea Town; Manchester United; Millwall Athletic; Port Vale;
Aberaman; Crewe Alexandra; Aberaman

	A	G
1914/15	12	0
Total	**12**	**0**

⚽ ALBERT PRINCE Forward

Clubs   Stafford Rangers; Manchester United

	A	G
1914/15	1	0
Total	**1**	**0**

⚽ JAMES MONTGOMERY Half-back

Born   Craghead
Clubs   Glossop; Manchester United

	A	G
1914/15	11	0
1919/20	14	1
1920/21	2	0
Total	**27**	**1**

⚽ CHARLES WILLIAM MOORE Full-back

Born   Cheslyn Hay, Staffordshire 3 June 1898
Clubs   Hednesford Town; Manchester United

	A	G
1919/20	36	0
1920/21	26	0
1922/23	12	0
1923/24	42	0
1924/25	40	0
1925/26	33	0
1926/27	30	0
1927/28	25	0
1928/29	37	0
1929/30	28	0
Total	**309**	**0**

☺ JOHN SILCOCK Full-back

Born	New Springs, Wigan 15 January 1898		
Died	Ashton-under-Lyne 28 June 1966		
Clubs	Atherton FC; Manchester United; Oldham Athletic; Droylsden United		
		A	G
	1919/20	40	0
	1920/21	37	1
	1921/22	36	0
	1922/23	37	0
	1923/24	8	0
	1924/25	29	0
	1925/26	33	0
	1926/27	26	0
	1927/28	26	0
	1928/29	27	1
	1929/30	21	0
	1930/31	25	0
	1931/32	35	0
	1932/33	27	0
	1933/34	16	0
	Total	**423**	**2**

☺ CLARENCE GEORGE 'LAL' HILDITCH Half-back

Born	Hartford, Cheshire 2 June 1894		
Clubs	Hartford FC; Witton Albion; Altrincham; Manchester United		
		A	G
	1919/20	32	2
	1920/21	34	1
	1921/22	29	0
	1922/23	32	1
	1923/24	41	0
	1924/25	4	0
	1925/26	28	1
	1926/27	16	0
	1927/28	5	0
	1928/29	11	1
	1929/30	27	1

1930/31	25	0
1931/32	17	0
Total	**301**	**7**

⚽ JOSEPH WATERS SPENCE Forward

Born   Throckley, Northumberland 15 December 1898
Died   31 December 1966
Clubs   Throckley Celtic; Manchester United; Bradford City; Chesterfield

	A	G
1919/20	32	14
1920/21	15	7
1921/22	35	15
1922/23	35	11
1923/24	36	10
1924/25	42	5
1925/26	39	7
1926/27	40	18
1927/28	38	22
1928/29	36	5
1929/30	42	12
1930/31	35	6
1931/32	37	19
1932/33	19	7
Total	**481**	**158**

⚽ FRED HOPKIN Forward

Born   Dewsbury, Yorkshire 23 September 1895
Died   Darlington March 1970
Clubs   Darlington; Manchester United; Liverpool; Darlington; Redcar Borough

	A	G
1919/20	39	5
1920/21	31	3
Total	**70**	**8**

⚽ THOMAS MEEHAN Half-back

Born   Harpurhey, Manchester 28 July 1896
Died   London 18 August 1924

Clubs	Newton FC; Walkden Central; Rochdale; Manchester United; Chelsea

	A	G
1919/20	36	2
1920/21	15	4
Total	**51**	**6**

⚽ WILLIAM EDWARD TOMS Forward

Born	Manchester 19 May 1896
Clubs	Altrincham; Eccles Borough; Manchester United; Plymouth Argyle; Oldham Athletic; Coventry City; Stockport County; Wrexham; Crewe Alexandra; Great Harwood; Winsford United; CWS Margarine Works

	A	G
1919/20	12	3
1920/21	1	0
Total	**13**	**3**

⚽ JOHN BARTON GRIMWOOD Half-back

Born	Marsden near South Shields 25 October 1898
Died	Childswickham, Worcestershire 26 December 1977
Clubs	Marsden Rescue FC; South Shields; Manchester United; Aldershot Town; Blackpool; Altrincham; Taylor Bros

	A	G
1919/20	22	1
1920/21	25	4
1921/22	28	0
1922/23	36	0
1923/24	22	2
1924/25	39	1
1925/26	7	0
1926/27	17	0
Total	**196**	**8**

⚽ FRANK CHARLES HODGES Forward

Born	Nechells Green, Birmingham 26 January 1891
Died	Southport 5 June 1985
Clubs	Alum Roch All Souls; Birmingham City Gas; Birmingham;

Manchester United; Wigan Borough; Crewe Alexandra;
Winsford United

	A	G
1919/20	18	4
1920/21	2	0
Total	**20**	**4**

⚽ THOMAS FORSTER Half-back

Born   Northwich April 1894
Clubs   Northwich Victoria; Manchester United; Northwich Victoria

	A	G
1919/20	5	0
1920/21	26	0
1921/22	4	0
Total	**35**	**0**

⚽ GEORGE BISSETT Forward

Born   Cowdenbeath 25 January 1897
Clubs   Glencraig Thistle; Third Lanark; Manchester United;
        Wolverhampton Wanderers; Pontypridd; Southend United

	A	G
1919/20	22	6
1920/21	18	4
Total	**40**	**10**

⚽ JAMES WILSON ROBINSON Outside-left

Born   Belfast 8 January 1898
Clubs   Manchester United; Tranmere Rovers

	A	G
1919/20	2	0
1920/21	7	2
1921/22	12	1
Total	**21**	**3**

⚽ CYRIL BARLOW Full-back

Born   Newton Heath 22 January 1889
Clubs   Newton Heath Parish Church; Northern Nomads; Manchester United;
        New Cross FC

	A	G
1919/20	7	0
1920/21	19	0
1921/22	3	0
Total	**29**	**0**

⚽ FRANCIS EDGAR 'FRANK' HARRIS Half-Back

Born   Urmston, Manchester 1 December 1899
Clubs Urmston Congregational; Urmston Old Boys; Manchester United

	A	G
1919/20	7	1
1920/21	26	1
1921/22	13	0
Total	**46**	**2**

⚽ JOHN WILLIAMSON Half-back

Born   Manchester
Clubs Manchester United; Bury; Crewe Alexandra; British Dyestuffs

	A	G
1919/20	2	0
Total	**2**	**0**

⚽ JOHN PRENTICE Forward

Born   Glasgow 1900
Clubs Manchester United; Swansea Town; Tranmere Rovers; Hurst FC

	A	G
1919/20	1	0
Total	**1**	**0**

⚽ GEORGE DOUGLAS SAPSFORD Forward

Born   Broughton, Manchester 10 March 1896
Died   Abingdon, Oxfordshire 17 October 1970
Clubs Clarendon FC; Manchester United; Preston North End; Southport

	A	G
1919/20	2	0
1920/21	21	7

	A	G
1921/22	29	9
Total	**52**	**16**

⚽ WILLIAM GOODWIN Forward

Born	Staveley 1892
Clubs	Old Staveley Primitives; Chesterfield FC; Blackburn Rovers; Exeter City; Manchester United; Southend United; Dartford

	A	G
1920/21	5	1
1921/22	2	0
Total	**7**	**1**

⚽ GEORGE WILLIE SCHOFIELD Forward

Born	Southport 6 August 1896
Clubs	Manchester United; Crewe Alexandra; Altofts WR Colliery

	A	G
1920/21	1	0
Total	**1**	**0**

⚽ JOSEPH MYERSCOUGH Forward

Born	Galgate, Lancashire 8 August 1893
Died	Scotforth near Lancaster 29 July 1975
Clubs	Lancaster Town; Manchester United; Bradford; Lancaster Town; Rossendale United; Morecambe

	A	G
1920/21	13	5
1921/22	7	0
1922/23	13	3
Total	**33**	**8**

⚽ HARRY DOXFORD LEONARD Forward

Born	Sunderland July 1886
Died	Derby 3 November 1951
Clubs	Sunderland North End, Southwick FC; Newcastle United; Grimsby Town; Middlesbrough; Derby County; Manchester United; Heanor Town

	A	G
1920/21	10	5
Total	**10**	**5**

⚽ THOMAS MILLER Forward

Born	Motherwell 29 June 1890
Died	Glasgow 3 September 1958
Clubs	Larkhall Hearts; Glenview; Larkhall United; Hamilton Academical; Liverpool; Manchester United; Heart of Midlothian; Torquay United; Hamilton Academical; Raith Rovers

	A	G
1920/21	25	7
Total	**25**	**7**

⚽ EDWARD PARTRIDGE Forward

Born	Lye, Worcestershire 13 February 1891
Died	Manchester 1973
Clubs	Stembermill St Marks; Ebbw Vale FC; Manchester United; Halifax Town; Manchester Central; Altrincham; Crewe Alexandra

	A	G
1920/21	28	7
1921/22	37	4
1922/23	30	0
1923/24	5	0
1924/25	1	0
1925/26	3	0
1926/27	16	0
1927/28	23	5
1928/29	5	0
Total	**148**	**16**

⚽ ALFRED STEWARD Goalkeeper

Born	Manchester 18 September 1898
Clubs	Stalybridge Celtic; Manchester United; Heaton Park FC; Manchester United; Manchester North End; Altrincham

	A	G
1920/21	2	0

1921/22	1	0
1922/23	1	0
1923/24	30	0
1924/25	42	0
1925/26	35	0
1926/27	42	0
1927/28	10	0
1928/29	37	0
1929/30	39	0
1930/31	38	0
1931/32	32	0
Total	**309**	**0**

⚽ **WILLIAM EWART HARRISON** Forward

Born   Wybunbury, Staffordshire 27 December 1886
Clubs   Hough United; Crewe South End; Willaston White Star; Crewe Alexandra;
        Wolverhampton Wanderers; Manchester United; Port Vale; Wrexham

	A	G
1920/21	23	3
1921/22	21	2
Total	**44**	**5**

⚽ **CHARLIE RADFORD** Full-back

Born   Walsall 19 March 1900
Died   Wolverhampton July 1924
Clubs   Walsall; Manchester United

	A	G
1920/21	1	0
1921/22	26	0
1922/23	34	1
1923/24	30	0
Total	**91**	**1**

⚽ **FRANK BERNARD BRETT** Full-back

Born   King's Norton; 10 March 1899
Died   Chichester, 21 July 1988
Clubs   Redditch; Aston Villa; Manchester United; Aston Villa; Northampton Town;

Brighton & Hove Albion; Tunbridge Wells Rangers; Hove FC

	A	G
1921/22	10	0
Total	**10**	**0**

⚽ SAMUEL RAYMOND BENNION Half-back

Born	Summer Hill, Wrexham 1 September 1896
Died	Burnley 12 March 1968
Clubs	Ragtimes FC; Chrichton's Athletic; Manchester United; Burnley

	A	G
1921/22	15	0
1922/23	14	0
1923/24	34	0
1924/25	17	0
1925/26	7	0
1926/27	37	0
1927/28	36	1
1928/29	34	0
1929/30	28	0
1930/31	36	1
1931/32	28	0
Total	**286**	**2**

⚽ JOHN SCOTT Half-back

Born	Motherwell
Clubs	Hamilton Academical; Bradford; Manchester United; St Mirren

	A	G
1921/22	23	0
Total	**23**	**0**

⚽ RICHARD SAMUEL GIBSON Forward

Born	Holborn, London January 1889
Clubs	Sultan FC; Birmingham; Manchester United

	A	G
1921/22	11	0
Total	**11**	**0**

⚽ ARTHUR WILLIAM LOCHHEAD Forward

Born   Busby, Lanarkshire 8 December 1897
Clubs   Heart of Midlothian; Manchester United; Leicester City

	A	G
1921/22	31	8
1922/23	34	13
1923/24	40	14
1924/25	37	13
1925/26	5	2
Total	**147**	**50**

⚽ PERCY SCHOFIELD Forward

Born   Bolton
Clubs   Eccles Borough; Manchester United; Eccles United; Hurst FC

	A	G
1921/22	1	0
Total	**1**	**0**

⚽ NEIL McBAIN Half-back

Born   Campbeltown, Argyllshire 15 November 1895
Died   13 May 1974
Clubs   Campbeltown Academical; Hamilton Academical; Ayr United; Manchester United; Everton; St Johnstone; Liverpool; Watford

	A	G
1921/22	21	0
1922/23	21	2
Total	**42**	**2**

⚽ WILLIAM HENDERSON Forward

Born   Edinburgh 1898
Died   Rosyth 1964
Clubs   St Bernards; Airdrieonians; Manchester United; Preston North End; Clapton Orient; Heart of Midlothian; Morton; Torquay United; Exeter City

	A	G
1921/22	10	2
1922/23	2	1

	1924/25	22	14
	Total	**34**	**17**

⚽ JOHN THOMAS HOWARTH Full-back

Born	Darwen, Lancashire 1899		
Clubs	Darwen; Manchester United		
		A	G
	1921/22	4	0
	Total	**4**	**0**

⚽ WALTER TAYLOR Forward

Born 1901

Clubs	New Mills FC; Manchester United		
		A	G
	1921/22	1	0
	Total	**1**	**0**

⚽ GEORGE HASLAM Half-Back

Born	Turton, Bolton 25 April 1898		
Clubs	Darwen; Manchester United; Portsmouth; Ashton National; Whitchurch;		
	Lancaster Town; Chorley; Burscough Rangers; Northwich Victoria		
		A	G
	1921/22	1	0
	1923/24	7	0
	1924/25	1	0
	1925/26	9	0
	1926/27	4	0
	1927/28	3	0
	Total	**25**	**0**

⚽ HENRY THOMAS Forward

Born	Swansea 28 February 1901		
Clubs	Swansea Town; Porth FC; Manchester United; Merthyr Town; Abercarn FC		
		A	G
	1921/22	3	0
	1922/23	18	0
	1923/24	6	0

1924/25	3	0
1925/26	29	5
1926/27	16	0
1927/28	13	2
1928/29	19	4
1929/30	21	1
Total	**128**	**12**

⚽ JAMES PUGH Full-back

Born   Hereford 1898
Clubs   Brighton & Hove Albion; Abertillery; Manchester United; Wrexham

	A	G
1921/22	1	0
1922/23	1	0
Total	**2**	**0**

⚽ JOHN WOOD Forward

Born   Leven, Fife 1900
Clubs   Hibernian; Dunfermline Athletic; Lochgelly United; Dumbarton;
          Manchester United; Lochgelly United; St Mirren; East Stirlingshire

	A	G
1922/23	15	1
Total	**15**	**1**

⚽ HARRY WILLIAMS Forward

Born   Hucknall Torkard, Nottinghamshire 1899
Clubs   Hucknall Olympic; Sunderland; Chesterfield; Manchester United;
          Brentford

	A	G
1922/23	5	2
Total	**5**	**2**

⚽ FRANK BARSON Half-Back

Born   Grimethorpe, Sheffield 10 April 1891
Died   Winson Green, Birmingham 13 September 1968
Clubs   Albion FC; Cammell Laird FC; Barnsley; Aston Villa; Manchester United;
          Watford; Hartlepool United; Wigan Borough; Rhyl Athletic

	A	G
1922/23	31	0
1923/24	17	0
1924/25	32	0
1925/26	28	2
1926/27	21	2
1927/28	11	0
Total	**140**	**4**

⚽ DAVID LYNER Forward

Born	Belfast
Clubs	Owen O'Cork FC; Glentoran; Belfast Distillery; Glentoran; Manchester United; Kilmarnock; Queen's Island; Clydebank; Mid Rhondda; New Brighton

	A	G
1922/23	3	0
Total	**3**	**0**

⚽ WILLIAM ISAAC SARVIS Forward

Born	Merthyr Tydfil 30 July 1898
Died	Llanelli 22 March 1968
Clubs	Merthyr Town; Manchester United; Bradford City; Walsall

	A	G
1922/23	1	0
Total	**1**	**0**

⚽ DAVID BAIN Forward

Born	Rutherglen 5 August 1900
Clubs	Rutherglen Glencairn; Manchester United; Everton; Bristol City; Halifax Town; Rochdale

	A	G
1922/23	4	1
1923/24	18	8
Total	**22**	**9**

⚽ ERNEST HOLROYD GOLDTHORPE Forward

Born	Middleton, Leeds 8 June 1898

Clubs	Bradford City; Leeds United; Bradford City; Manchester United; Rotherham United	
	A	G
1922/23	22	13
1923/24	4	1
1924/25	1	1
Total	**27**	**15**

☺ HERBERT REDVERS CARTMAN Forward

Born	Bolton 28 February 1900	
Clubs	Waterloo Temperance; Bolton Wanderers; Manchester United; Tranmere Rovers; Brighton & Hove Albion; Stockport County; Chorley; Burscough Rangers; Westhoughton Collieries	
	A	G
1922/23	3	0
Total	**3**	**0**

☺ JOHN BARBER Forward

Born	Salford 8 January 1901	
Died	Manchester 30 March 1961	
Clubs	Clayton FC; Manchester United; Southport; Halifax Town; Rochdale; Stockport County; Hull City; Stockport County; Bacup Borough	
	A	G
1922/23	2	0
1923/24	1	1
Total	**3**	**1**

☺ WILFRED LIEVESLEY Forward

Born	Netlerthorpe, Staveley 6 October 1902	
Clubs	Staveley Old Boys; Derby County; Manchester United; Exeter City; Wigan Borough; Cardiff City	
	A	G
1922/23	2	0
Total	**2**	**0**

☺ KENNETH MacDONALD Forward

Born	Llanrwst, Denbighshire 24 April 1898

Clubs	Inverness Citadel; Inverness Clachnacuddin; Aberdeen; Caerau; Cardiff City; Manchester United; Bradford; Hull City; Halifax Town; Coleraine; Walker Celtic; Spennymoor United; Walker Celtic; Blyth Spartans	
	A	G
1922/23	2	1
1923/24	7	1
Total	**9**	**2**

⚽ FRANK DRURY MANN Half-Back

Born	Newark, Nottinghamshire 4 March 1891	
Clubs	Newark Castle United; Newark Castle Rovers; Newark Town; Leeds City; Lincoln City; Aston Villa; Huddersfield Town; Manchester United; Mossley FC; Meltham Mills FC	
	A	G
1922/23	10	0
1923/24	25	3
1924/25	32	0
1925/26	34	0
1926/27	14	0
1927/28	26	0
1928/29	25	1
1929/30	14	1
Total	**180**	**5**

⚽ ALBERT HENRY BROOME Forward

Born	Unsworth, Lancashire January 1900	
Clubs	Northern Nomads; Oldham Athletic; Manchester United; Oldham Athletic; Welshpool FC; Stockport County; Mossley	
	A	G
1922/23	1	0
Total	**1**	**0**

⚽ DAVID ELLIS Forward

Born	Kirkcaldy 1900
Clubs	Glasgow Ashfield; Airdrieonians; Maidstone United; Manchester United; St Johnstone; Bradford City; Arthurlie FC

	A	G
1923/24	11	0
Total	**11**	**0**

⚽ FRANCIS COMBER McPHERSON Forward

Born   Barrow-in-Furness 14 May 1901
Died   Davyhulme, Manchester 5 March 1953
Clubs   Barrow Shipbuilders FC; Partick Thistle; Chesterfield Municipal; Barrow;
Manchester United; Manchester Central; Watford; Reading; Watford; Barrow

	A	G
1923/24	34	1
1924/25	38	7
1925/26	29	16
1926/27	32	15
1927/28	26	6
Total	**159**	**45**

⚽ FRED KENNEDY Forward

Born   Bury 2 October 1902
Died   Failsworth, Lancashire 15 November 1963
Clubs   Rossendale United; Manchester United; Everton; Middlesbrough; Reading;
Oldham Athletic; Rossendale United; Northwich Victoria; Racing Club de Paris;
Blackburn Rovers; Racing Club de Paris; Stockport County

	A	G
1923/24	6	1
1924/25	11	3
Total	**17**	**4**

⚽ WILLIAM DENNIS Full-back

Born   Mossley 21 September 1896
Clubs   Stalybridge Celtic; Blackburn Rovers; Stalybridge Celtic; Manchester
United; Chesterfield; Wigan Borough; Macclesfield; Hurst FC

	A	G
1923/24	3	0
Total	**3**	**0**

⚽ **SIDNEY TYLER** Full-back

Born	Wolverhampton 7 December 1904	
Died	Walsall 25 January 1971	
Clubs	Stourbridge FC; Manchester United; Wolverhampton Wanderers; Gillingham; Millwall; Colwyn Bay United; Chamberlain & Hookham	

	A	G
1923/24	1	0
Total	**1**	**0**

⚽ **THOMAS GABLE SMITH** Forward

Born	Whitburn, Co Durham 18 October 1900	
Died	Whitburn, Co Durham 21 February 1934	
Clubs	Marsden Villa; Whitburn FC; South Shields; Leicester City; Manchester United; Northampton Town; Norwich City; Whitburn FC	

	A	G
1923/24	12	4
1924/25	31	5
1925/26	30	3
1926/27	10	0
Total	**83**	**12**

⚽ **JAMES MILLER** Forward

Born	Greenock 1900	
Clubs	Port Glasgow Athletic; St Mirren; Greenock Morton; Grimsby Town; Manchester United; York City; Boston Town; Shirebrook FC	

	A	G
1923/24	4	1
Total	**4**	**1**

⚽ **SIDNEY EVANS** Forward

Born	Darlaston	
Clubs	Darlaston FC; Cardiff City; Manchester United; Pontypridd	

	A	G
1923/24	6	2
Total	**6**	**2**

☺ THOMAS JONES Full-back

Born	Penycae, near Wrexham 6 December 1899	
Died	Cefn, Wrexham 20 February 1978	
Clubs	Acrefair; Druids; Everton; Oswestry Town; Manchester United;	
	Scunthorpe & Lindsay United	

	A	G
1924/25	15	0
1925/26	10	0
1926/27	21	0
1927/28	33	0
1928/29	0	0
1929/30	16	0
1930/31	5	0
1931/32	12	0
1932/33	10	0
1933/34	39	0
1934/35	27	0
1935/36	0	0
1936/37	1	0
Total	**189**	**0**

☺ JAMES HANSON Forward

Born	Manchester 6 November 1904	
Clubs	Manchester YMCA; Bradford Parish FC; Stalybridge Celtic;	
	Manchester North End; Manchester United	

	A	G
1924/25	3	3
1925/26	24	5
1926/27	21	5
1927/28	30	10
1928/29	42	19
1929/30	18	5
Total	**138**	**47**

☺ CHRISTOPHER TAYLOR Forward/Half-Back

Born	Small Heath, Birmingham July 1904
Clubs	Evesham Town; Redditch FC; Manchester United; Hyde United

	A	G
1924/25	1	0
1925/26	6	6
1926/27	0	0
1927/28	2	0
1928/29	3	0
1929/30	16	0
Total	**28**	**6**

⚽ JAMES BAIN Half-Back

Born	Rutherglen 6 February 1902
Died	Polegate, Sussex 22 December 1969
Clubs	Rutherglen Glencairn; Glasgow Strathclyde; Manchester United; Manchester Central; Brentford

	A	G
1924/25	1	0
1925/26	2	0
1926/27	0	0
1927/28	1	0
Total	**4**	**0**

⚽ ALBERT ARTHUR PAPE Forward

Born	Elescar, near Wath-on-Dearne 13 June 1897
Died	Doncaster 18 November 1955
Clubs	Wath Athletic; Bolton upon Dearne FC; Rotherham County; Notts County; Clapton Orient; Manchester United; Fulham; Rhyl Athletic; Hurst FC; Darwen; Manchester Central; Hartlepool United; Halifax Town; Burscough Rangers; Horwich RMI; Nelson

	A	G
1924/25	16	5
1925/26	2	0
Total	**18**	**5**

⚽ CLATWORTHY RENNOX Forward

Born	Shotts, Lanarkshire 25 February 1900
Clubs	Dykehead; Wishaw; Clapton Orient; Manchester United; Grimsby Town

	A	G
1924/25	4	0
1925/26	34	17
1926/27	22	7
Total	**60**	**24**

✪ RICHARD IDDON Forward

Born   Tarleton, Lancashire 22 June 1901
Clubs   Tarleton FC; Leyland; Preston North End; Chorley; Manchester United;
        Chorley; Morecambe; New Brighton; Lancaster Town; Horwich RMI;
        Altrincham

	A	G
1925/26	1	0
1926/27	1	0
Total	**2**	**0**

✪ CHARLES HANNAFORD Forward

Born   Finsbury Park, London 8 January 1896
Died   Aylesbury, Buckinghamshire 28 July 1970
Clubs   Tufnell Park; Maidstone United; Millwall; Charlton Athletic;
        Clapton Orient; Manchester United; Clapton Orient

	A	G
1925/26	4	0
1926/27	7	0
Total	**11**	**0**

✪ JAMES McCRAE Half-Back

Born   Bridge of Weir, Renfrewshire 8 March 1897
Clubs   Clyde; West Ham United; Bury; Wigan Borough; New Brighton;
        Manchester United; Watford; Third Lanark

	A	G
1925/26	9	0
Total	**9**	**0**

✪ JOHN HALL Forward

Born   Bolton 1905
Clubs   Lincoln City; Accrington Stanley; Manchester United

	A	G
1925/26	3	0
Total	**3**	**0**

⚽ ERIC SWEENEY Forward

Born	Rock Ferry, Birkenhead 3 October 1905
Clubs	Flint Town; Manchester United; Charlton Athletic; Crewe Alexandra; Carlisle United

	A	G
1925/26	3	1
1926/27	13	3
1927/28	4	1
1928/29	6	1
1929/30	1	0
Total	**27**	**6**

⚽ JOSEPH EMMANUEL ASTLEY Full-back

Born	Dudley, 30 April 1899
Died	Manchester October 1967
Clubs	Cradley Heath; Manchester United; Notts County; Northwich Victoria; Hyde United

	A	G
1925/26	1	0
1926/27	1	0
Total	**2**	**0**

⚽ WILLIAM WHITE INGLIS Full-back

Born	Kirkcaldy 2 March 1894
Died	Sale, Cheshire 20 January 1968
Clubs	Kirkcaldy United; Raith Rovers; Sheffield Wednesday; Manchester United; Northampton Town

	A	G
1925/26	7	1
1926/27	6	0
1927/28	0	0
1928/29	1	0
Total	**14**	**1**

⚽ LANCELOT HOLLIDAY RICHARDSON Goalkeeper

Born	Tow Law, Co Durham April 1899	
Died	Cordoba, Argentina 22 February 1958	
Clubs	Shildon Athletic; South Shields; Manchester United; Reading; Rowlands Gill FC	

	A	G
1925/26	1	0
1926/27	0	0
1927/28	32	0
1928/29	5	0
Total	**38**	**0**

⚽ RONALD HAWORTH Forward

Born	Lower Darwen, Lancashire 10 March 1901	
Died	Blackburn October 1973	
Clubs	Blackburn Rovers; Hull City; Manchester United; Darwen	

	A	G
1926/27	2	0
Total	**2**	**0**

⚽ JOHN THOMAS WILSON Half-Back

Born	Leadgate, 8 March 1897	
Clubs	Leadgate St Ives; Leadgate United; Newcastle United; Leadgate Park; Durham City; Stockport County; Manchester United; Bristol City	

	A	G
1926/27	21	0
1927/28	33	0
1928/29	19	1
1929/30	28	1
1930/31	20	1
1931/32	9	0
Total	**130**	**3**

⚽ WILLIAM CHAPMAN Forward

Born	Murton Co Durham 21 September 1902	
Died	Murton Co Durham 2 December 1967	
Clubs	Murton Celtic; Murton PM; Hetton PM; Sunderland; Murton Democrats; Sheffield Wednesday; Manchester United; Watford; Murton Colliery	

	A	G
1926/27	17	0
1927/28	9	0
Total	**26**	**0**

⚽ THOMAS HARRIS Forward

Born	Ince-in-Makerfield 18 September 1905
Clubs	Skelmersdale United; Manchester United; Wigan Borough; Rotherham United; Crewe Alexandra; Chorley; Burton Town; Prescot Cables

	A	G
1926/27	4	1
Total	**4**	**1**

⚽ ALBERT CHARLES SMITH Forward

Born	Glasgow 1900
Clubs	Petershill FC; Manchester United; Preston North End; Dolphin FC; Carlisle United

	A	G
1926/27	5	1
Total	**5**	**1**

⚽ CHARLES WILLIAM RAMSDEN Forward

Born	South Normanton 16 January 1903
Clubs	South Normanton Colliery; Rotherham United; Manchester United; Stockport County; Manchester North End; Witton Albion; Gresham & Craven

	A	G
1927/28	2	0
1928/29	5	3
1929/30	0	0
1930/31	7	0
Total	**14**	**3**

⚽ DAVID REES WILLIAMS Forward

Born	Abercanaid near Merthyr Tydfil 1900
Died	Abercanaid near Merthyr Tydfil 30 December 1963

Clubs	Pentrebach FC; Merthyr Town; Sheffield Wednesday;
	Manchester United; Thames Association; Aldershot; Merthyr Town; Glenavon

	A	G
1927/28	13	2
1928/29	18	0
Total	**31**	**2**

⚽ WILLIAM GIFFORD JOHNSTON Forward

Born	Edinburgh 16 January 1901
Clubs	Dalkeith Thistle; Selby Town; Huddersfield Town; Stockport County;
	Manchester United; Macclesfield; Manchester United; Oldham Athletic;
	Frickley Colliery

	A	G
1927/28	31	8
1928/29	12	5
1931/32	28	11
Total	**71**	**24**

⚽ HUGH McLENAHAN Half-Back

Born	West Gorton, Manchester 23 March 1909
Died	Macclesfield May 1988
Clubs	Ambrose FC; Longsight; Ashton Brothers; Stalybridge Celtic; Blackpool;
	Stockport County; Manchester United; Notts County

	A	G
1927/28	10	1
1928/29	1	0
1929/30	10	6
1930/31	21	1
1931/32	11	0
1932/33	24	2
1933/34	22	0
1934/35	10	1
1935/36	0	0
1936/37	3	0
Total	**112**	**11**

⚽ GEORGE NICOL Forward

Born   Saltcoats 1905
Clubs   Ardrossan Winton Rovers; Kilwinning FC; Saltcoats Victoria;
        Manchester United; Brighton & Hove Albion; Glenavon; Gillingham

	A	G
1927/28	4	2
1928/29	2	0
Total	**6**	**2**

⚽ WILLIAM EDWARD RAWLINGS Forward

Born   Andover, Hampshire 3 January 1896
Died   Chandlers Ford 25 September 1972
Clubs   Andover FC; Southampton; Manchester United; Port Vale; New Milton;
        Newport (Isle of Wight)

	A	G
1927/28	12	10
1928/29	19	6
1929/30	4	3
Total	**35**	**19**

⚽ ARCHIBALD DANIEL FERGUSON Forward

Born   Flint, 25 January 1904
Clubs   Rhyl Athletic; Manchester United; Reading; Accrington Stanley;
        Chester; Halifax Town; Stockport County; Macclesfield

	A	G
1927/28	4	0
Total	**4**	**0**

⚽ WILLIAM DALE Full-back

Born   Manchester 17 February 1905
Died   Manchester 20 June 1987
Clubs   Sandbach Ramblers; Manchester United; Manchester City;
        Ipswich Town; Norwich City

	A	G
1928/29	19	0
1929/30	19	0
1930/31	22	0

	A	G
1931/32	4	0
Total	**64**	**0**

☺ CHARLES WILLIAM SPENCER Half-back

Born Washington, Co Durham 4 December 1899
Died York 9 February 1953
Clubs Glebe Rovers; Washington Chemical Works; Newcastle United;
Manchester United; Tunbridge Wells Rangers; Wigan Athletic

	A	G
1928/29	36	0
1929/30	10	0
Total	**46**	**0**

☺ HENRY BOWATER ROWLEY Forward

Born Bilston, Staffordshire 23 January 1904
Clubs Southend United; Shrewsbury Town; Manchester United;
Manchester City; Oldham Athletic; Manchester United; Burton Town;
Gillingham

	A	G
1928/29	25	5
1929/30	40	12
1930/31	29	7
1931/32	1	0
1934/35	24	8
1935/36	37	19
1936/37	17	4
Total	**173**	**55**

☺ THOMAS JOSEPH REID Forward

Born Motherwell 15 August 1905
Died Prescot, Liverpool 1972
Clubs Blantyre Victoria; Clydebank; Liverpool; Manchester United;
Oldham Athletic; Barrow; Rhyl Athletic

	A	G
1928/29	17	14
1929/30	13	5
1930/31	30	17

	A	G
1931/32	25	17
1932/33	11	10
Total	**96**	**63**

⚽ THOMAS BOYLE Forward

Born	Sheffield January 1897	
Clubs	Bullcroft Colliery; Sheffield United; Manchester United; Macclesfield; Northampton Town	

	A	G
1928/29	1	0
1929/30	15	6
Total	**16**	**6**

⚽ JOHN THOMAS BALL Forward

Born	Banks, Southport 13 September 1907	
Died	Luton 6 February 1976	
Clubs	Croston FC; Southport; Darwen; Chorley; Manchester United; Sheffield Wednesday; Manchester United; Huddersfield Town; Luton Town; Excelsior Roubaix (France); Luton Town; Vauxhall Motors; St Albans City; Biggleswade	

	A	G
1929/30	23	11
1933/34	18	5
1934/35	6	1
Total	**47**	**17**

⚽ GEORGE HERBERT McLACHLAN Forward

Born	Glasgow 21 September 1902	
Clubs	Clyde; Cardiff City; Manchester United; Chester	

	A	G
1929/30	23	2
1930/31	42	2
1931/32	28	0
1932/33	17	0
Total	**110**	**4**

⚽ ARTHUR CHESTERS Goalkeeper

Born	Salford 14 February 1910
Clubs	Irlam o'the Heights; Bangor City; Sedgley Park; Manchester United; Exeter City; Crystal Palace; Rochdale

	A	G
1929/30	3	0
1930/31	4	0
1931/32	2	0
Total	**9**	**0**

⚽ ARTHUR WARBURTON Forward

Born	Whitefield, near Bury 30 October 1903
Died	Bury 21 April 1978
Clubs	Sedgley Park; Manchester United; Burnley; Nelson; Fulham; Queen's Park Rangers

	A	G
1929/30	2	1
1930/31	18	5
1931/32	7	3
1932/33	6	1
1933/34	2	0
Total	**35**	**10**

⚽ ARTHUR THOMSON Forward

Born	West Stanley July 1903
Clubs	West Stanley FC; Derby County; Morecambe FC; Huddersfield Town; Manchester United; Southend United; Coventry City; Tranmere Rovers

	A	G
1929/30	1	0
1930/31	2	1
Total	**3**	**1**

⚽ FRANK WILLIAMS Half-Back

Born	Kearsley, Lancashire 1908
Clubs	Stalybridge Celtic; Manchester United; Stalybridge Celtic; Manchester United; Altrincham

	A	G
1930/31	3	0
Total	**3**	**0**

⚽ JOHN MELLOR Full-back

Born	Oldham 1905
Clubs	Failsworth Trinity; Witton Albion; Manchester United; Cardiff City

	A	G
1930/31	35	0
1931/32	33	0
1932/33	40	0
1933/34	5	0
1934/35	1	0
1935/36	0	0
1936/37	2	0
Total	**116**	**0**

⚽ JAMES BULLOCK Forward

Born	Gorton, Manchester 25 March 1902
Died	Stockport 9 March 1977
Clubs	Gorton FC; Crewe Alexandra; Manchester City; Crewe Alexandra; Southampton; Chesterfield; Manchester United; Dundalk; Llanelly; Hyde United

	A	G
1930/31	10	3
Total	**10**	**3**

⚽ THOMAS ALBERT PARKER Half-Back

Born	Eccles, Lancashire 22 November 1906
Died	Manchester 11 November 1964
Clubs	Manchester United; Bristol City; Carlisle United; Stalybridge Celtic

	A	G
1930/31	9	0
1931/32	8	0
Total	**17**	**0**

⚽ STANLEY HUGH GALLIMORE Forward

Born	Bucklow Hill, Cheshire 14 April 1910
Clubs	Witton Albion; Manchester United; Altrincham; Northwich Victoria

	A	G
1930/31	28	5
1931/32	25	6
1932/33	12	5
1933/34	7	3
Total	**72**	**19**

⚽ GEORGE LYDON Half-Back

Born	Newton Heath, Manchester 24 June 1902
Died	Failsworth, Lancashire 12 August 1953
Clubs	Nelson United; Mossley; Manchester United; Southport; Burton Tower; Hurst; Great Harwood

	A	G
1930/31	1	0
1931/32	2	0
Total	**3**	**0**

⚽ SAMUEL HOPKINSON Forward

Born	Killamarsh near Sheffield 9 February 1902
Clubs	Rotherham County; Shirebrook; Chesterfield; Shirebrook; Ashton National; Manchester United; Tranmere Rovers

	A	G
1930/31	17	4
1931/32	19	5
1932/33	6	1
1933/34	9	0
Total	**51**	**10**

⚽ JOHN JAMES FERGUSON Forward

Born	Rowlands Gill, Newcastle-on-Tyne 1904
Clubs	Grimsby Town; Workington; Spen Black & White; Wolverhampton Wanderers; Watford; Burton Town; Manchester United; Derry City; Gateshead United

	A	G
1931/32	8	1
Total	**8**	**1**

⚽ HERBERT HARRY MANN Forward

Born   Nuneaton, Warwickshire 30 December 1907
Clubs   Griff Colliery; Derby County; Grantham Town; Manchester United;
            Ripley Town

	A	G
1931/32	13	2
Total	**13**	**2**

⚽ HAROLD DEAN Forward

Born   Hulme, Manchester 1908
Clubs   Old Trafford FC; Manchester United; Mossley

	A	G
1931/32	2	0
Total	**2**	**0**

⚽ MATTHEW ROBINSON Forward

Born   Felling, Co Durham 1909
Clubs   Pelaw FC; Cardiff City; Manchester United; Chester; Barrow

	A	G
1931/32	10	0
Total	**10**	**0**

⚽ THOMAS MANLEY Half-Back

Born   Northwich, Cheshire 7 October 1912
Clubs   Brunner Mods FC; Norley United; Northwich Victoria;
            Manchester United; Brentford

	A	G
1931/32	3	0
1932/33	19	0
1933/34	30	2
1934/35	30	9
1935/36	31	14
1936/37	31	5

1937/38	21	7
1938/39	23	3
Total	**188**	**40**

⚽ WILLIAM RIDDING Forward

Born	Heswall, Cheshire 4 April 1911
Died	Bolton 20 September 1981
Clubs	Heswall PSA; Tranmere Rovers; Manchester City; Manchester United; Northampton Town; Tranmere Rovers; Oldham Athletic

	A	G
1931/32	14	3
1932/33	23	11
1933/34	5	0
Total	**42**	**14**

⚽ JOHN WHITTLE Forward

Born	Leigh, Lancashire 1910
Clubs	Hindsford FC; Manchester United; Rossendale United; Fleetwood; Hindsford FC

	A	G
1931/32	1	0
Total	**1**	**0**

⚽ ERNEST VINCENT Half-back

Born	Seaham Harbour, Co Durham 28 October 1907
Died	Bircotes, near Worksop 2 June 1978
Clubs	Dawdon Colliery; Hyhope Colliery; Seaham Harbour; Washington Colliery; Southport; Manchester United; Queen's Park Rangers; Doncaster Rovers

	A	G
1931/32	16	0
1932/33	40	1
1933/34	8	0
Total	**64**	**1**

⚽ LESLIE LIEVESLEY Half-Back

Born	Staveley July 1911
Died	Superga, Italy 4 May 1949

Clubs	Rossington Main Colliery; Doncaster Rovers; Manchester United;		
	Chesterfield; Torquay United; Crystal Palace		
		A	G
	1931/32	2	0
	Total	·2	0

⚽ LOUIS ANTONIO PAGE Forward

Born	Kirkdale, Liverpool 27 March 1899		
Died	Birkenhead 12 October 1959		
Clubs	South Liverpool; Stoke; Northampton Town; Burnley; Manchester United;		
	Port Vale; Yeovil & Petters United		
		A	G
	1931/32	9	0
	1932/33	3	0
	Total	12	0

⚽ JOHN MOODY Goalkeeper

Born	Heeley, Sheffield 1 November 1903		
Clubs	Hathersage FC; Sheffield United; Arsenal; Bradford; Doncaster Rovers;		
	Manchester United; Chesterfield		
		A	G
	1931/32	8	0
	1932/33	42	0
	Total	50	0

⚽ GEORGE ARTHUR FITTON Forward

Born	Melton Mowbray 30 May 1902		
Died	Kinver September 1984		
Clubs	Kinver Swifts; Kinver FC; Cookley St peters; Kidderminster Harriers;		
	West Bromwich Albion; Manchester United; Preston North End;		
	Coventry City; Kidderminster Harriers		
		A	G
	1931/32	8	2
	1932/33	4	0
	Total	12	2

⚽ WILLIAM McDONALD Forward

Born   Coatbridge, Lanarkshire 1904
Clubs   Coatbridge FC; Dundee; Broxburn United; Laws Scotia FC; Airdrieonians;
        Manchester United; Tranmere Rovers; Coventry City; Plymouth Argyle

	A	G
1931/32	2	0
1932/33	21	4
1933/34	4	0
Total	**27**	**4**

⚽ ARTHUR RICHARD BLACK Forward

Born   Glasgow 1905
Clubs   Greenock Morton; Manchester United; St Mirren

	A	G
1931/32	3	2
1932/33	1	0
1933/34	4	1
Total	**8**	**3**

⚽ JAMES BROWN Forward

Born   Kilmarnock 31 December 1908
Clubs   Plainfield FC; Bayonne Rovers (New Jersey); Newark Skeeters; New York Giants;
        Brooklyn Wanderers; Manchester United; Brentford; Tottenham Hotspur;
        Guildford City; Clydebank

	A	G
1932/33	25	10
1933/34	15	7
Total	**40**	**17**

⚽ THOMAS FRAME Half-Back

Born   Burnbank 5 September 1902
Died   Paisley 17 January 1987
Clubs   Burnbank Athletic; Cowdenbeath; Manchester United; Southport;
        Rhyl Athletic; Bridgnorth Town

	A	G
1932/33	33	2

	A	G
1933/34	18	2
Total	**51**	**4**

⚽ WILLIAM STEWART CHALMERS Forward

Born Mount Florida, Glasgow 5 March 1907
Clubs Queen's Park; Heart of Midlothian; Manchester United;
   Dunfermline Athletic

	A	G
1932/33	22	1
1933/34	12	0
Total	**34**	**1**

⚽ WILLIAM TODD STEWART Forward

Born Glasgow 1908
Clubs Shettlestone Juniors; Cowdenbeath; Manchester United; Motherwell

	A	G
1932/33	21	3
1933/34	25	4
Total	**46**	**7**

⚽ ERNEST WILLIAM HINE Forward

Born Smithy Cross near Barnsley 9 April 1901
Died Huddersfield April 1974
Clubs New Mills FC; Staincross Station; Barnsley; Leicester City;
   Huddersfield Town; Manchester United; Barnsley

	A	G
1932/33	14	5
1933/34	33	6
1934/35	4	1
Total	**51**	**12**

⚽ NEIL HAMILTON DEWAR Forward

Born Lochgilphead, Argyllshire 11 November 1908
Clubs Lochgilphead United; Third Lanark; Manchester United;
   Sheffield Wednesday; Third Lanark

	A	G
1932/33	15	6

1933/34	21	8
Total	**36**	**14**

⚽ ANDREW MITCHELL Forward

Born	Coxhoe, Co Durham 20 April 1907
Died	Blackburn 3 December 1971
Clubs	Crook Town; Sunderland; Notts County; Darlington; Manchester United; Hull City; Northampton Town; Rossendale United

	A	G
1932/33	1	0
Total	**1**	**0**

⚽ HENRY TOPPING Full-back

Born	Manchester, 16 October 1908
Clubs	Manchester United; Barnsley; Macclesfield

	A	G
1932/33	5	0
1933/34	6	1
1934/35	1	0
Total	**12**	**1**

⚽ HERBERT HEYWOOD Forward

Born	Little Hulton, Lancashire 1909
Clubs	Turton FC; Oldham Athletic; Northwich Victoria; Manchester United; Tranmere Rovers; Altrincham; Wigan Athletic; Astley & Tyldesley Colliery

	A	G
1932/33	1	0
1933/34	3	2
Total	**4**	**2**

⚽ CHARLES EMMANUEL HILLAM Goalkeeper

Born	Burnley 6 October 1908
Clubs	Clitheroe; Nelson; Clitheroe; Burnley; Manchester United; Clapton Orient; Southend United; Chingford Town

	A	G
1933/34	8	0
Total	**8**	**0**

⚽ GEORGE VOSE Half-back

Born	St Helens 4 October 1911		
Died	Wigan 20 June 1981		
Clubs	Peasley Cross Athletic; Manchester United; Runcorn		

		A	G
	1933/34	17	1
	1934/35	39	0
	1935/36	41	0
	1936/37	26	0
	1937/38	33	0
	1938/39	39	0
	1939/40	2	0
	Total	**197**	**1**

⚽ CHARLES McGILLIVRAY Forward

Born	East Whitburn, West Lothian 5 July 1912
Died	7 November 1986
Clubs	Ayr United; Glasgow Celtic; Manchester United; Motherwell; Dundee; Heart of Midlothian; Albion Rovers; Morton; Dunfermline Athletic; Dundee United; Hibernian; Dundee United

	A	G
1933/34 8	0	
Total **8**	**0**	

⚽ ROBERT EDWARD GREEN Forward

Born	Tewkesbury, Gloucestershire 1909
Died	Cheltenham, Gloucestershire
Clubs	Bournemouth; Derby County; Manchester United; Stockport County; Cheltenham Town

	A	G
1933/34 9	4	
Total **9**	**4**	

⚽ WALTER McMILLEN Half-back

Born	Belfast 24 November 1913
Clubs	Carrickfergus; Cliftonville; Arsenal; Manchester United; Chesterfield; Millwall; Tonbridge FC

	A	G
1933/34	23	1
1934/35	4	1
Total	**27**	**2**

⚽ JOHN HALL Goalkeeper

Born   Failsworth, Lancashire 23 October 1912
Clubs   Failsworth FC; Newton Heath Loco; Manchester United; Tottenham Hotspur;
        Stalybridge Celtic; Runcorn; Stalybridge Celtic

	A	G
1933/34	23	0
1934/35	8	0
1935/36	36	0
Total	**67**	**0**

⚽ DAVID BYRNE Forward

Born   Ringsend, Dublin 28 April 1905
Clubs   St Brendan's; Shamrock Rovers; Bradford City; Shelbourne; Shamrock Rovers;
        Sheffield United; Shamrock Rovers; Manchester United; Coleraine; Larne;
        Shamrock Rovers; Hammond Lane FC; Brideville FC; Shelbourne

	A	G
1933/34	4	3
Total	**4**	**3**

⚽ GEORGE WILLIAM NEVIN Full-back

Born   Lintz Co Durham 16 December 1907
Died   Sheffield January 1973
Clubs   Dipton United; Lintz Colliery; Whitehead-Le-Rangers; Newcastle United;
        Sheffield Wednesday; Manchester United; Sheffield Wednesday; Burnley;
        Lincoln City; Rochdale

	A	G
1933/34	4	0
Total	**4**	**0**

⚽ THOMAS MANNS Wing-half

Born   Rotherham 1910
Clubs   Eastwood United WMC; Rotherham United; Burnley; Manchester United;

Clapton Orient; Carlisle United; Yeovil & Petters United

	A	G
1933/34	2	0
Total	**2**	**0**

⚽ PERCY NEWTON Half-back

Born   Whitchurch 1911
Clubs   Whitchurch FC; Chester; Sandbach Ramblers; Manchester United; Tranmere Rovers

	A	G
1933/34	2	0
Total	**2**	**0**

⚽ WILLIAM BEHAN Goalkeeper

Born   Dublin 3 August 1911
Died   Dublin   November 1991
Clubs   Shelbourne; Manchester United; Shelbourne; Shamrock Rovers

	A	G
1933/34	1	0
Total	**1**	**0**

⚽ ALPHONSO AINSWORTH Inside-forward

Born   Manchester 31 July 1913
Died   Rochdale 25 April 1975
Clubs   Ashton United; Manchester United; New Brighton; Congleton Town

	A	G
1933/34	2	0
Total	**2**	**0**

⚽ JOHN HACKING Goalkeeper

Born   Blackburn 22 December 1897
Died   Accrington 1 June 1955
Clubs   Grimshaw Park Co-operative; Blackpool; Fleetwood; Oldham Athletic; Manchester United; Accrington Stanley

	A	G
1933/34	10	0
1934/35	22	0
Total	**32**	**0**

✪ JOHN GRIFFITHS Full-back

Born   Fenton, Staffordshire 15 September 1911
Clubs   Shirebrook FC; Wolverhampton Wanderers; Bolton Wanderers; Manchester United

	A	G
1933/34	10	0
1934/35	40	0
1935/36	41	1
1936/37	18	0
1937/38	18	0
1938/39	35	0
1939/40	3	0
Total	**168**	**1**

✪ WILLIAM ROBERTSON Half-Back

Born   Falkirk 20 April 1911
Clubs   Third Lanark; Ayr United; Stoke; Manchester United; Reading

	A	G
1933/34	10	0
1934/35	36	1
1935/36	1	0
Total	**47**	**1**

✪ WILLIAM McKAY Half-Back

Born   West Benhar, Lanarkshire 1907
Died   24 August (Year unknown)
Clubs   Shotts Battlefield FC; East Stirlingshire; Hamilton Academical;
              Bolton Wanderers; Manchester United; Stalybridge Celtic

	A	G
1933/34	10	0
1934/35	38	3
1935/36	35	0
1936/37	29	4
1937/38	37	7
1938/39	20	1
1939/40	2	0
Total	**171**	**15**

⚽ **GEORGE MUTCH** Forward

Born   Aberdeen 21 September 1912

Clubs   Avondale FC; Banks o'Dee; Arbroath; Manchester United;
Preston North End; Bury; Southport

	A	G
1934/35	40	18
1935/36	42	21
1936/37	28	7
1937/38	2	0
Total	**112**	**46**

⚽ **THOMAS JOHN JONES** Forward

Born   Tonypandy, Glamorgan 6 December 1909

Clubs   Mid Rhondda; Tranmere Rovers; Sheffield Wednesday;
Manchester United; Watford; Guildford City

	A	G
1934/35	20	4
Total	**20**	**4**

⚽ **LEONARD LANGFORD** Goalkeeper

Born   Sheffield 30 May 1899

Died   Stockport 26 December 1973

Clubs   Attercliffe Victory; Rossington Colliery; Nottingham Forest;
Manchester City; Manchester United

	A	G
1934/35	12	0
1935/36	3	0
Total	**15**	**0**

⚽ **WILLIAM OWEN** Forward

Born   Northwich 17 September 1906

Died   Newport 26 March 1981

Clubs   Northwich Victoria; Macclesfield; Manchester United; Reading;
Exeter City; Newport County

	A	G
1934/35	15	1

1935/36	2	0
Total	**17**	**1**

🔵 THOMAS BAMFORD Forward

Born	Port Talbot 2 September 1905
Died	Wrexham 12 December 1967
Clubs	Cardiff Docks XI; Cardiff Wednesday; Bridgend Town; Wrexham; Manchester United; Swansea Town

	A	G
1934/35	19	9
1935/36	27	16
1936/37	29	14
1937/38	23	14
Total	**98**	**53**

⚽ WILLIAM BRYANT Forward

Born	Shildon 26 November 1913
Died	Durham West District October 1975
Clubs	Cockfield FC; Wolverhampton Wanderers; Wrexham; Manchester United; Bradford City; Altrincham; Stalybridge Celtic;

	A	G
1934/35	24	6
1935/36	21	8
1936/37	37	10
1937/38	39	12
1938/39	27	6
1939/40	3	2
Total	**151**	**44**

🔵 WILLIAM PORTER Full-back

Born	Fleetwood, Lancashire July 1905
Died	Ashton-under-Lyne 28 April 1946
Clubs	Windsor Villa FC; Fleetwood; Oldham Athletic; Manchester United; Hyde United

	A	G
1934/35	15	0
1935/36	42	0

	1936/37	2	0
	1937/38	2	0
	Total	**61**	**0**

⚽ WILLIAM GILLESPIE BOYD Forward

Born   Cambuslang, 27 November 1905
Died   Bristol 14 December 1967
Clubs   Regent Star; Larkhill Thistle; Clyde; Sheffield United; Manchester United; Workington; Luton Town; Southampton; Weymouth

		A	G
	1934/35	6	4
	Total	**6**	**4**

⚽ JOHN NORMAN BREEDON Goalkeeper

Born   South Hiendley near Barnsley, 29 December 1907
Clubs   South Hiendley; Barnsley; Sheffield Wednesday; Manchester United; Burnley

		A	G
	1935/36	3	0
	1936/37	1	0
	1937/38	9	0
	1938/39	22	0
	1939/40	3	0
	Total	**38**	**0**

⚽ JAMES BROWN Half-Back

Born   Leith 1907
Clubs   Wishaw YMCA; East Fife; Burnley; Manchester United; Bradford Park Avenue

		A	G
	1935/36	40	0
	1936/37	31	0
	1937/38	28	1
	1938/39	3	0
	Total	**102**	**1**

⚽ REGINALD ARTHUR CHESTER Forward

Born   Long Eaton, Nottinghamshire 21 November 1904
Died   Long Eaton, Nottinghamshire 24 April 1977

Clubs	Long Eaton Rangers; Notts County; Mansfield Town; Peterborough & Flertton United; Stamford Town; Long Eaton Rangers; Aston Villa; Manchester United; Huddersfield Town; Darlington; Arnold Town; Woodborough United

	A	G
1935/36	13	1
Total	**13**	**1**

⚽ RONALD JOHNSON FERRIER Forward

Born	Cleethorpes 26 April 1914
Died	Cleethorpes 11 October 1991
Clubs	Grimsby Wanderers; Grimsby Town; Manchester United; Oldham Athletic; Lincoln City; Grimsby Town; Lysaghts Sports

	A	G
1935/36	7	0
1936/37	6	1
1937/38	5	3
Total	**18**	**4**

⚽ HUBERT REDWOOD Full-back

Born	St Helens, Lancashire July 1913
Died	St Helens, Lancashire October 1943
Clubs	Sherdley Albion; Manchester United

	A	G
1935/36	1	0
1936/37	21	0
1937/38	29	2
1938/39	35	1
1939/40	3	0
Total	**89**	**3**

⚽ DAVID MIDDLETON ROBBIE Forward

Born	Motherwell 6 October 1899
Died	Bury 4 December 1978
Clubs	Bathgate FC; Bury; Plymouth Argyle; Manchester United; Margate; Luton Town

	A	G
1935/36	1	0
Total	**1**	**0**

⚽ JOHN VICTOR WASSALL Forward

Born	Shrewsbury 11 February 1917	
Clubs	Wellington Town; Manchester United; Stockport County	

	A	G
1935/36	2	0
1936/37	7	1
1937/38	9	1
1938/39	27	4
1939/40	1	0
Total	**46**	**6**

⚽ BENJAMIN MORTON Forward

Born	Sheffield October 1910	
Clubs	Stourbridge FC; Wolverhampton Wanderers; Stourbridge FC; Manchester United; Torquay United; Swindon Town; Stourbridge FC	

	A	G
1935/36	1	0
Total	**1**	**0**

⚽ HERBERT WHALLEY Half-Back

Born	Ashton-under-Lyne 6 August 1912	
Died	Munich 6 February 1958	
Clubs	Ferguson & Pailins FC; Stalybridge Celtic; Manchester United	

	A	G
1935/36	2	0
1936/37	19	0
1937/38	6	0
1938/39	2	0
1939/40	1	0
1946/47	3	0
Total	**33**	**0**

⚽ CHARLES RICHARD GARDNER Forward

Born	Birmingham, January 1913	
Clubs	Evesham Town; Birmingham; Notts County; Stourbridge; Manchester United; Sheffield United	

	A	G
1935/36	12	1
1936/37	4	0
Total	**16**	**1**

✪ THOMAS LANG Forward

Born	Larkhall near Motherwell 3 April 1906
Clubs	Larkhall Thistle; Newcastle United; Huddersfield Town; Manchester United; Swansea Town; Queen of the South; Ipswich Town

	A	G
1935/36	4	1
1936/37	8	0
Total	**12**	**1**

✪ WILLIAM RONALD 'Roy' JOHN Goalkeeper

Born	Briton Ferry near Neath 29 January 1911
Died	Port Talbot 12 July 1973
Clubs	Briton Ferry Athletic; Swansea Town; Walsall; Stoke; Preston North End; Sheffield United; Manchester United; Newport County; Swansea Town

	A	G
1936/37	15	0
Total	**15**	**0**

✪ JAMES McCLELLAND Forward

Born	Dysart near Kirkcaldy 11 May 1902
Clubs	Rosslyn; Raith Rovers; Southend United; Middlesbrough; Bolton Wanderers; Preston North End; Blackpool; Bradford; Manchester United

	A	G
1936/37	5	1
Total	**5**	**1**

✪ WILLIAM GEORGE ROUGHTON Full-back

Born	Manchester 11 December 1909
Died	Southampton 7 June 1989
Clubs	Droylsden FC; Huddersfield Town; Manchester United; Exeter City

	A	G
1936/37	33	0

	1937/38	39	0
	1938/39	14	0
	Total	**86**	**0**

⚽ JOHN ERNEST THOMPSON Forward

Born   Newbiggin, Northumberland 30 July 1909
Clubs   Stakeford United; Ashington; Bradford; Carlisle United; Bristol City;
        Bath City; Blackburn Rovers; Manchester United; Gateshead; York City

		A	G
	1936/37	2	1
	1937/38	1	0
	Total	**3**	**1**

⚽ THOMAS BREEN Goalkeeper

Born   Belfast 27 April 1917
Clubs   Drogheda United; Belfast Celtic; Manchester United; Belfast Celtic;
        Linfield; Shamrock Rovers; Newry Town; Glentoran

		A	G
	1936/37	26	0
	1937/38	33	0
	1938/39	6	0
	Total	**65**	**0**

⚽ WALTER WINTERBOTTOM Half-Back

Born   Oldham 1914
Clubs   Royton Amateurs FC; Manchester City; Mossley FC; Manchester United;
        Mossley FC

		A	G
	1936/37	21	0
	1937/38	4	0
	Total	**25**	**0**

⚽ REGINALD LLOYD HALTON Forward

Born   Buxton, Derbyshire 11 July 1916
Died   Buxton, Derbyshire March 1988
Clubs   Cheddington Mental Hospital; Manchester United; Notts County; Bury;
        Chesterfield; Leicester City; Scarborough Town; Goole Town

	A	G
1936/37	4	1
Total	**4**	**1**

⚽ HENRY BAIRD Forward

Born   Belfast 17 August 1913
Died   22 May 1973
Clubs   Bangor FC; Dunmurry FC; Linfield; Manchester United; Huddersfield Town;
       Ipswich Town

	A	G
1936/37	14	3
1937/38	35	12
Total	**49**	**15**

⚽ WILLIAM HERBERT WRIGGLESWORTH Forward

Born   South Elmshall 12 November 1912
Clubs   Frickley Colliery; Chesterfield; Wolverhampton Wanderers;
       Manchester United; Bolton Wanderers; Southampton; Reading;
       Burton Albion; Scarborough

	A	G
1936/37	7	1
1937/38	4	1
1938/39	12	3
1939/40	3	1
1946/47	4	2
Total	**30**	**8**

⚽ GEORGE WILLIE GLADWIN Half-Back

Born   Chesterfield 28 March 1907
Clubs   Worksop Town; Doncaster Rovers; Manchester United

	A	G
1936/37	8	1
1937/38	7	0
1938/39	12	0
Total	**27**	**1**

⚽ ROBERT MURRAY Forward

Born	Edinburgh 1914	
Clubs	Newtongrange Star; Heart of Midlothian; Manchester United; Bath City; Colchester United	
	A	G
1937/38	4	0
Total	**4**	**0**

⚽ JOHN JOSEPH CAREY Full-back

Born	Dublin 23 February 1919	
Died	August 1995	
Clubs	Home Farm FC; St James' Gate; Manchester United	
	A	G
1937/38	16	3
1938/39	32	6
1939/40	2	1
1946/47	31	0
1947/48	37	1
1948/49	41	1
1949/50	38	1
1950/51	39	0
1951/52	38	3
1952/53	32	1
Total	**306**	**17**

⚽ JOHN FREDERICK ROWLEY Forward

Born	Wolverhampton 7 October 1920	
Clubs	Wolverhampton Wanderers; Cradley Heath FC; Bournemouth; Manchester United; Plymouth Argyle	
	A	G
1937/38	25	9
1938/39	38	10
1946/47	37	26
1947/48	39	23
1948/49	39	20
1949/50	39	20
1950/51	39	14

	A	G
1951/52	40	30
1952/53	26	11
1953/54	36	12
1954/55	22	7
Total	**380**	**182**

⚽ STANLEY CLARE PEARSON Forward

Born   Salford 11 January 1919
Clubs   Manchester United; Bury; Chester

	A	G
1937/38	11	2
1938/39	9	1
1939/40	3	1
1946/47	42	19
1947/48	40	18
1948/49	39	14
1949/50	41	15
1950/51	39	18
1951/52	41	22
1952/53	39	16
1953/54	11	2
Total	**315**	**128**

⚽ DAVID GWILYM JONES Half-Back

Born   Ynysddu Monmouth 23 November 1914
Died   Swindon 30 May 1988
Clubs   Ynysddu; Tottenham Hotspur; Cardiff City; Fulham; Newport County;
        Wigan Athletic; Manchester United; Swindon Town; Cheltenham Town

	A	G
1937/38	1	0
Total	**1**	**0**

⚽ ROBERT EDWARD SAVAGE Half-Back

Born   Louth, Lincolnshire January 1912
Died   Wallasey, Cheshire 30 January 1964
Clubs   Lincoln City; Liverpool; Manchester United; Wrexham

	A	G
1937/38	4	0
Total	**4**	**0**

⚽ JOHN SMITH Forward

Born	Batley, Yorkshire 17 February 1915
Clubs	Whitehall Printers; Dewsbury Moor Welfare; Huddersfield Town; Newcastle United; Manchester United; Blackburn Rovers; Port Vale; Macclesfield

	A	G
1937/38	17	8
1938/39	19	6
1939/40	1	0
Total	**37**	**14**

⚽ CHARLES CRAVEN Forward

Born	Boston, Lincolnshire 2 December 1909
Died	Solihull 30 March 1972
Clubs	Boston Trinity; Boston Town; Boston United; Grimsby Town; Manchester United; Birmingham; Tamworth; Sutton Town

	A	G
1938/39	11	2
Total	**11**	**2**

⚽ JOHN WARNER Half-Back

Born	Trelaw, Tonypandy 21 September 1911
Died	Tonypandy 4 October 1980
Clubs	Aberaman; Swansea Town; Manchester United; Oldham Athletic; Rochdale

	A	G
1938/39	29	0
1939/40	3	0
1946/47	34	1
1947/48	15	0
1948/49	3	0
1949/50	21	0
Total	**105**	**1**

⚽ JOHN JAMES HANLON Forward

Born   Manchester 12 October 1917
Clubs   Manchester United; Bury; Northwich Victoria; Rhyl

	A	G
1938/39	27	12
1939/40	1	0
1946/47	27	7
1947/48	8	1
1948/49	1	0
Total	**64**	**20**

⚽ NORMAN TAPKEN Goalkeeper

Born   Wallsend, Northumberland 21 February 1914
Clubs   Wallsend Thermal Welfare; Newcastle United; Manchester United;
        Darlington; Shelbourne

	A	G
1938/39	14	0
Total	**14**	**0**

⚽ LEONARD BRADBURY Forward

Born   Northwich July 1914
Clubs   Northwich Victoria; Manchester United; Northwich Victoria; Corinthians;
        Moor Green FC; Corinthians

	A	G
1938/39	2	1
Total	**2**	**1**

⚽ THOMAS DOUGAN Forward

Born   Holytown, Lanarkshire 1913
Clubs   Tunbridge Wells Rangers; Plymouth Argyle; Manchester United;
        Heart of Midlothian; Kilmarnock; Dunfermline Athletic

	A	G
1938/39	4	0
Total	**4**	**0**

⚽ BEAUMONT ASQUITH Forward

Born   Painthorpe 16 September 1910

Died	Barnsley 12 April 1977	
Clubs	Painthorpe Albion; Barnsley; Manchester United; Bradford City;	
	Scarborough	

	A	G
1939/40	1	0
Total	**1**	**0**

🌑 ALLENBY CHILTON Half-back

Born	South Hylton, Co Durham 16 September 1918	
Died	Hull 16 June 1996	
Clubs	Hylton Colliery; Seaham Colliery; Liverpool; Manchester United;	
	Grimsby Town	

	A	G
1939/40	1	0
1946/47	41	1
1947/48	41	0
1948/49	42	0
1949/50	35	1
1950/51	38	0
1951/52	42	0
1952/53	42	0
1953/54	42	1
1954/55	29	0
Total	**353**	**3**

🌑 JOHN CROMPTON Goalkeeper

Born	Newton Heath, Manchester 18 December 1921	
Clubs	Manchester YMCA; Newton Heath Loco; Goslings FC; Oldham Athletic;	
	Manchester City; Manchester United	

	A	G
1946/47	29	0
1947/48	37	0
1948/49	41	0
1949/50	27	0
1950/51	2	0
1951/52	9	0
1952/53	25	0

1953/54	15	0
1954/55	5	0
1955/56	1	0
Total	**191**	**0**

⚽ WILLIAM McGLEN Half-Back

Born   Bedlington 27 April 1921
Clubs   Blyth Spartans; Manchester United; Lincoln City; Oldham Athletic

	A	G
1946/47	33	1
1947/48	13	0
1948/49	23	1
1949/50	13	0
1950/51	26	0
1951/52	2	0
Total	**110**	**2**

⚽ HENRY COCKBURN Half-Back

Born   Ashton-under-Lyne 14 September 1923
Clubs   Goslings FC; Manchester United; Bury; Peterborough United;
         Corby Town; Sankey's Wellington; Oldham Athletic

	A	G
1946/47	32	0
1947/48	26	1
1948/49	36	0
1949/50	35	1
1950/51	35	0
1951/52	38	2
1952/53	22	0
1953/54	18	0
1954/55	1	0
Total	**243**	**4**

⚽ JAMES DELANEY Forward

Born   Cleland, Lanarkshire 3 September 1914
Died   Cleland, Lanarkshire 26 September 1989
Clubs   Cleland St Mary's; Wishaw Juniors; Stoneyburn Juniors; Glasgow Celtic;

Manchester United; Aberdeen; Falkirk; Derry City; Cork Athletic; Elgin City

	A	G
1946/47	37	8
1947/48	36	8
1948/49	36	4
1949/50	42	4
1950/51	13	1
Total	**164**	**25**

⚽ CHARLES MITTEN Forward

Born	Rangoon, Burma 17 January 1921
Clubs	Dunblane Rovers; Strathallan Hawthorn; Manchester United;
	Sante Fe (Bogota); Fulham; Mansfield Town

	A	G
1946/47	20	8
1947/48	38	8
1948/49	42	18
1949/50	42	16
Total	**142**	**50**

⚽ JOHN ASTON Senior Full-back

Born	Prestwich, Manchester 3 September 1921
Clubs	Mujacs FC; Manchester United

	A	G
1946/47	21	0
1947/48	42	0
1948/49	39	0
1949/50	40	0
1950/51	41	15
1951/52	18	4
1952/53	40	8
1953/54	12	2
Total	**253**	**29**

⚽ JOSEPH WALTON Full-back

Born	Manchester 5 June 1925
Clubs	Manchester United; Preston North End; Accrington Stanley

	A	G
1946/47	15	0
1947/48	6	0
Total	**21**	**0**

⚽ JOHN MORRIS Forward

Born   Radcliffe, Lancashire 27 September 1923
Clubs   Mujacs FC; Manchester United; Derby County; Leicester City;
        Corby Town; Kettering Town

	A	G
1946/47	24	8
1947/48	38	18
1948/49	21	6
Total	**83**	**32**

⚽ RONALD STEWART BURKE Forward

Born   Dormanstown, Yorkshire 13 August 1921
Clubs   St Albans City; Luton Town; Manchester United; Huddersfield Town;
        Rotherham United; Exeter City; Tunbridge Wells Rangers; Biggleswade Town

	A	G
1946/47	13	9
1947/48	6	1
1948/49	9	6
Total	**28**	**16**

⚽ CLIFFORD COLLINSON Goalkeeper

Born   Middlesbrough 3 March 1920
Died   September 1990
Clubs   Urmston Boys Club; Manchester United

	A	G
1946/47	7	0
Total	**7**	**0**

⚽ HAROLD WORRALL Full-back

Born   Northwich 19 November 1918
Clubs   Winsford United; Manchester United; Swindon Town

	A	G
1946/47	1	0
1947/48	5	0
Total	**6**	**0**

⚽ EDWARD BUCKLE Forward

Born   Southwark, London 28 October 1924
Clubs   Manchester United; Everton; Exeter City; Prestatyn; Dolgellau

	A	G
1946/47	5	3
1947/48	3	1
1948/49	5	2
1949/50	7	0
Total	**20**	**6**

⚽ WILLIAM FIELDING Goalkeeper

Born   Broadhurst near Hyde 17 June 1915
Clubs   Broadbottom YMCA; Hurst FC; Cardiff City; Bolton Wanderers;
         Manchester United

	A	G
1946/47	6	0
Total	**6**	**0**

⚽ THOMAS LOWRIE Half-Back

Born   Glasgow 14 January 1928
Clubs   Glasgow YMCA; Troon Athletic; Manchester United; Aberdeen; Oldham Athletic

	A	G
1947/48	2	0
1948/49	8	0
1949/50	3	0
Total	**13**	**0**

⚽ JOHN BALL Full-back

Born   Ince near Wigan 13 March 1925
Clubs   Wigan Athletic; Manchester United; Bolton Wanderers

	A	G
1947/48	1	0

1948/49	8	0
1949/50	13	0
Total	**22**	**0**

⚽ JOSEPH DALE Forward

Born Northwich 3 July 1921
Clubs Witton Albion; Manchester United; Port Vale; Witton Albion

	A	G
1947/48	2	0
Total	**2**	**0**

⚽ JAMES KENNETH PEGG Goalkeeper

Born Salford 4 January 1926
Clubs Manchester United; Torquay United; York City

	A	G
1947/48	2	0
Total	**2**	**0**

⚽ JOHN ANDERSON Half-Back

Born Salford 11 October 1921
Clubs Manchester United; Nottingham Forest; Peterborough United

	A	G
1947/48	18	1
1948/49	15	0
Total	**33**	**1**

⚽ SAMUEL LYNN Half-Back

Born St Helens, Lancashire 25 December 1920
Clubs Peasley Cross St Josephs; Manchester United; Bradford

	A	G
1947-48	3	0
1948-49	0	0
1949-50	10	0
Total	**13**	**0**

⚽ **ROBERT BERESFORD 'BERRY' BROWN** Goalkeeper

| Born | West Hartlepool 6 September 1927 |
| Clubs | Manchester United; Doncaster Rovers; Hartlepool United |

	A	G
1947/48	4	0
Total	**4**	**0**

⚽ **LAWRENCE CASSIDY** Forward

| Born | Manchester 10 March 1923 |
| Clubs | Manchester United; Oldham Athletic |

	A	G
1947/48	1	0
1948/49	1	0
1949/50	0	0
1950/51	1	0
1951/52	1	0
Total	**4**	**0**

⚽ **JOHN DENNIS DOWNIE** Forward

| Born | Lanark 19 July 1925 |
| Clubs | Lanark ATC; Bradford; Manchester United; Luton Town; Hull City; King's Lynn; Wisbech Town; Mansfield Town; Darlington; Hyde United; Mossley; Stalybridge Celtic |

	A	G
1948/49	12	5
1949/50	18	6
1950/51	29	10
1951/52	31	11
1952/53	20	3
Total	**110**	**35**

⚽ **BRIAN BIRCH** Forward

| Born | Salford 18 November 1931 |
| Clubs | Manchester United; Wolverhampton Wanderers; Lincoln City; Boston United; Barrow; Exeter City; Oldham Athletic; Rochdale; Boston United; Mossley |

	A	G
1949/50	1	0

1950/51	8	4
1951/52	2	0
Total	**11**	**4**

⚽ THOMAS BOGAN Forward

Born	Glasgow 18 May 1920
Died	23 September 1993
Clubs	Strathclyde; Blantyre Celtic; Renfrew; Hibernian; Glasgow Celtic; Preston North End; Manchester United; Aberdeen; Southampton; Blackburn Rovers; Macclesfield Town

	A	G
1949/50	18	4
1950/51	11	3
Total	**29**	**7**

⚽ JOHN IGNATIUS 'SONNY' FEEHAN Goalkeeper

Born	Dublin 17 September 1926
Clubs	Bohemians; Waterford; Manchester United; Northampton Town; Brentford

	A	G
1949/50	12	0
Total	**12**	**0**

⚽ RAYMOND ERNEST WOOD Goalkeeper

Born	Hebburn-on-Tyne, Co Durham 11 June 1931
Died	Bexhill 7 July 2002
Clubs	Newcastle United; Darlington; Manchester United; Huddersfield Town; Bradford City; Barnsley

	A	G
1949/50	1	0
1950/51	0	0
1951/52	0	0
1952/53	12	0
1953/54	27	0
1954/55	37	0
1955/56	41	0
1956/57	39	0
1957/58	20	0

| | 1958/59 | 1 | 0 |
| | **Total** | **178** | **0** |

⚽ JOSEPH GERARD LANCASTER Goalkeeper

Born   Stockport 28 April 1926
Clubs   Heaton Norris Old Boys; Manchester United; Accrington Stanley;
        Northwich Victoria

		A	G
	1949/50	2	0
	Total	**2**	**0**

⚽ FRANK CLEMPSON Forward

Born   Salford 27 May 1930
Clubs   Manchester United; Stockport County; Chester; Hyde United

		A	G
	1949/50	1	0
	1950/51	2	0
	1951/52	8	2
	1952/53	4	0
	Total	**15**	**2**

⚽ THOMAS McNULTY Full-back

Born   Salford 30 December 1929
Clubs   Manchester United; Liverpool; Hyde United

		A	G
	1949/50	2	0
	1950/51	4	0
	1951/52	24	0
	1952/53	23	0
	1953/54	4	0
	Total	**57**	**0**

⚽ JEFFREY WHITEFOOT Half-Back

Born   Cheadle, Cheshire 31 December 1933
Clubs   Manchester United; Grimsby Town; Nottingham Forest

| | | A | G |
| | 1949/50 | 1 | 0 |

1950/51	2	0
1951/52	3	0
1952/53	10	0
1953/54	38	0
1954/55	24	0
1955/56	15	0
Total	**93**	**0**

⚽ REGINALD ARTHUR ALLEN Goalkeeper

Born   Marylebone, London 3 May 1919
Clubs   Corona FC; Bromley; Queen's Park Rangers; Manchester United; Altrincham

	A	G
1950/51	40	0
1951/52	33	0
1952/53	2	0
Total	**75**	**0**

⚽ EDWARD McILVENNY Half-Back

Born   Greenock, Renfrewshire 21 October 1924
Clubs   Morton; Wrexham; Fairhill Club (USA); Philadelphia Nationals (USA);
          Manchester United; Waterford

	A	G
1950/51	2	0
Total	**2**	**0**

⚽ THOMAS RICHARD DONALD 'DON' GIBSON Half-Back

Born   Manchester 12 May 1929
Clubs   Manchester United; Sheffield Wednesday; Leyton Orient; Buxton

	A	G
1950/51	32	0
1951/52	17	0
1952/53	20	0
1953/54	7	0
1954/55	32	0
Total	**108**	**0**

⚽ HENRY 'HARRY' McSHANE Forward

Born   Holytown, Lanarkshire 8 April 1920

Clubs   Bellshill Athletic; Blackburn Rovers; Huddersfield Town; Bolton Wanderers; Manchester United; Oldham Athletic; Chorley; Wellington Town; Droylsden

	A	G
1950/51	30	7
1951/52	12	1
1952/53	5	0
1953/54	9	0
Total	**56**	**8**

⚽ WILLIAM REDMAN Full-back

Born   Manchester 29 January 1928

Clubs   Manchester United; Bury; Buxton FC

	A	G
1950/51	16	0
1951/52	18	0
1952/53	1	0
1953/54	1	0
Total	**36**	**0**

⚽ MARK JONES Half-Back

Born   Barnsley 15 June 1933

Died   Munich 6 February 1958

Clubs   Manchester United

	A	G
1950/51	4	0
1951/52	3	0
1952/53	2	0
1953/54	0	0
1954/55	13	0
1955/56	42	1
1956/57	29	0
1957/58	10	0
Total	**103**	**1**

⚽ CLIFFORD BIRKETT Forward

Born   Haydock 17 September 1933
Clubs   Manchester United; Southport; Crompton Recs; Wigan Rovers; Macclesfield Town

	A	G
1950/51	9	2
Total	**9**	**2**

⚽ JAMES ERNEST BOND Forward

Born   Preston 4 May 1929
Clubs   Preston North End; Leyland Motors; Manchester United;
           Carlisle United; Cowdenbeath

	A	G
1951/52	19	4
1952/53	1	0
Total	**20**	**4**

⚽ JOHN JAMES BERRY Forward

Born   Aldershot 1 June 1926
Died   15 September 1994
Clubs   Aldershot YMCA; Birmingham City; Manchester United

	A	G
1951/52	36	6
1952/53	40	7
1953/54	37	5
1954/55	40	3
1955/56	34	4
1956/57	40	8
1957/58	20	4
Total	**247**	**37**

⚽ JOHN WALTON Forward

Born   Horwich near Bolton 21 March 1928
Clubs   Plymouth Argyle; Saltash United; Bury; Manchester United; Bury;
           Burnley; Coventry City; Kettering Town; Chester

	A	G
1951/52	2	0
Total	**2**	**0**

⚽ ROGER WILLIAM BYRNE Full-back

Born   Gorton, Manchester 8 February 1929
Died   Munich 6 February 1958
Clubs   Manchester United

	A	G
1951/52	24	7
1952/53	40	2
1953/54	41	3
1954/55	39	2
1955/56	39	3
1956/57	36	0
1957/58	26	0
Total	**245**	**17**

⚽ JOHN BLANCHFLOWER Half-Back

Born   Belfast 7 March 1933
Clubs   Boyland FC; Manchester United

	A	G
1951/52	1	0
1952/53	1	0
1953/54	27	13
1954/55	29	10
1955/56	18	3
1956/57	11	0
1957/58	18	0
Total	**105**	**26**

⚽ JOHN SCOTT Forward

Born   Belfast 22 December 1933
Died   Manchester June 1978
Clubs   Boyland FC; Ormond Star FC; Manchester United; Grimsby Town; York City; Margate

	A	G
1952/53	2	0
1953/54	0	0
1954/55	0	0
1955/56	1	0
Total	**3**	**0**

⚽ EDWARD LEWIS Forward

| Born | Manchester 3 January 1935 |
| Clubs | Goslings FC; Manchester United; Preston North End; West Ham United; Leyton Orient; Folkestone Town |

	A	G
1952/53	10	7
1953/54	6	1
1954/55	0	0
1955/56	4	1
Total	**20**	**9**

⚽ JOHN PETER DOHERTY Forward

| Born | Manchester 12 March 1935 |
| Clubs | Manchester United; Leicester City; Rugby Town; Altrincham |

	A	G
1952/53	5	2
1953/54	0	0
1954/55	0	0
1955/56	16	4
1956/57	3	0
1957/58	1	1
Total	**25**	**7**

⚽ DAVID PEGG Forward

Born	Doncaster 20 September 1935
Died	Munich 6 February 1958
Clubs	Manchester United

	A	G
1952/53	19	4
1953/54	9	0
1954/55	6	1
1955/56	35	9
1956/57	37	6
1957/58	21	4
Total	**127**	**24**

⚽ **WILLIAM ANTHONY FOULKES** Defender

Born	St Helens, Lancashire 5 January 1932		
Clubs	Manchester United		
		A	G
	1952/53	2	0
	1953/54	32	1
	1954/55	41	0
	1955/56	26	0
	1956/57	39	0
	1957/58	42	0
	1958/59	32	0
	1959/60	42	0
	1960/61	40	0
	1961/62	40	0
	1962/63	41	0
	1963/64	41	1
	1964/65	42	0
	1965/66	33	0
	1966/67	33	4
	1967/68	24	1
	1968/69	10	0
	1969/70	3	0
	Total	**563**	**7**

⚽ **THOMAS TAYLOR** Forward

Born	Barnsley 29 January 1932		
Died	Munich 6 February 1958		
Clubs	Smithies United; Barnsley; Manchester United		
		A	G
	1952/53	11	7
	1953/54	35	22
	1954/55	30	20
	1955/56	33	25
	1956/57	32	22
	1957/58	25	16
	Total	**166**	**112**

⚽ DUNCAN EDWARDS Half-Back

Born	Dudley, Worcestershire 1 October 1936
Died	Munich 21 February 1958
Clubs	Manchester United

	A	G
1952/53	1	0
1953/54	24	0
1954/55	33	6
1955/56	33	3
1956/57	34	5
1957/58	26	6
Total	**151**	**20**

⚽ ROBERT LESLIE OLIVE Goalkeeper

Born	Salford 27 April 1928
Clubs	Manchester United

	A	G
1952/53	2	0
Total	**2**	**0**

⚽ DENNIS SYDNEY VIOLLET Forward

Born	Manchester 20 September 1933
Died	United States 6 March 1999
Clubs	Manchester United; Stoke City; Baltimore Bays (USA); Witton Albion; Linfield

	A	G
1952/53	3	1
1953/54	29	11
1954/55	34	20
1955/56	34	20
1956/57	27	16
1957/58	22	16
1958/59	37	21
1959/60	36	32
1960/61	24	15
1961/62	13	7
Total	**259**	**159**

⚽ COLIN WEBSTER Forward

Born	Cardiff 17 July 1932	
Clubs	Avenue Villa; Cardiff Nomads; Cardiff City; Manchester United; Swansea Town;	
	Newport County; Worcester City; Merthyr Tydfil; Porthmadog	

	A	G
1953/54	1	0
1954/55	17	8
1955/56	15	4
1956/57	5	3
1957/58	20	6
1958/59	7	5
Total	**65**	**26**

⚽ NOEL WILLIAM McFARLANE Forward

Born	Bray, Co Wicklow 20 December 1934
Clubs	Manchester United; Waterford

	A	G
1953/54	1	0
Total	**1**	**0**

⚽ IAN DENZIL GREAVES Full-back

Born	Shaw, near Oldham 26 May 1932	
Clubs	Oldham Athletic; Buxton United; Manchester United; Lincoln City;	
	Oldham Athletic; Altrincham	

	A	G
1954/55	1	0
1955/56	15	0
1956/57	3	0
1957/58	12	0
1958/59	34	0
1959/60	2	0
Total	**67**	**0**

⚽ PATRICK ANTHONY KENNEDY Full-back

Born	Dublin 9 October 1934
Clubs	Johnville; Manchester United; Blackburn Rovers; Southampton;
	Oldham Athletic

	A	G
1954/55	1	0
Total	**1**	**0**

🕸 FRED GOODWIN Half-Back

Born   Heywood, Lancashire 28 June 1933
Clubs   Manchester United; Leeds United; Scunthorpe United

	A	G
1954/55	5	0
1955/56	8	0
1956/57	6	0
1957/58	16	0
1958/59	42	6
1959/60	18	1
Total	**95**	**7**

🕸 ALBERT JOSEPH SCANLON Forward

Born   Manchester 10 October 1935
Clubs   All Saints FC; Manchester United; Newcastle United; Lincoln City;
              Mansfield Town; Belper Town

	A	G
1954/55	14	4
1955/56	6	1
1956/57	5	2
1957/58	9	3
1958/59	42	16
1959/60	31	7
1960/61	8	1
Total	**115**	**34**

🕸 GEOFFREY BENT Full-back

Born   Salford 27 September 1932
Died   Munich 6 February 1958
Clubs   Manchester United

	A	G
1954/55	2	0
1955/56	4	0

	1956/57	6	0
	Total	**12**	**0**

⚽ WILLIAM 'LIAM' WHELAN Forward

Born	Dublin 1 April 1935		
Died	Munich 6 February 1958		
Clubs	Home Farm FC; Manchester United		
		A	G
	1954/55	7	1
	1955/56	13	4
	1956/57	39	26
	1957/58	20	12
	Total	**79**	**43**

⚽ WALTER WHITEHURST Half-Back

Born	Manchester 7 June 1934		
Clubs	Manchester United; Chesterfield; Crewe Alexandra; Macclesfield Town; Mossley		
		A	G
	1955/56	1	0
	Total	**1**	**0**

⚽ WILFRED McGUINNESS Half-Back

Born	Manchester 25 October 1937		
Clubs	Manchester United		
		A	G
	1955/56	3	1
	1956/57	13	0
	1957/58	7	0
	1958/59	39	1
	1959/60	19	0
	Total	**81**	**2**

⚽ EDWARD COLMAN Half-Back

Born	Salford 1 November 1936
Died	Munich 6 February 1958
Clubs	Manchester United

	A	G
1955/56	25	0
1956/57	36	1
1957/58	24	0
Total	**85**	**1**

⚽ RONALD COPE Half-Back

Born   Crewe 5 October 1934
Clubs   Manchester United; Luton Town; Northwich Victoria; Winsford United

	A	G
1956/57	2	0
1957/58	13	0
1958/59	32	2
1959/60	40	0
1960/61	6	0
Total	**93**	**2**

⚽ ROBERT CHARLTON Forward

Born   Ashington, Northumberland 11 October 1937
Clubs   Manchester United; Preston North End; Waterford

	A	G
1956/57	14	10
1957/58	21	8
1958/59	38	29
1959/60	37	18
1960/61	39	21
1961/62	37	8
1962/63	28	7
1963/64	40	9
1964/65	41	10
1965/66	38	16
1966/67	42	12
1967/68	41	15
1968/69	32	5
1969/70	40	12

	A	G
1970/71	42	5
1971/72	40	8
1972/63	36	6
Total	**606**	**199**

⚽ ANTHONY HAWKSWORTH Goalkeeper

Born   Sheffield 15 January 1938
Clubs   Manchester United

	A	G
1956/57	1	0
Total	**1**	**0**

⚽ GORDON CLAYTON Goalkeeper

Born   Chadsmoor, Staffordshire 3 November 1936
Died   Stretford, Manchester 29 September 1991
Clubs   Manchester United; Tranmere Rovers; Sankey's; Radcliffe Borough

	A	G
1956/57	2	0
Total	**2**	**0**

⚽ ALEXANDER DOWNIE DAWSON Forward

Born   Aberdeen 21 February 1940
Clubs   Manchester United; Preston North End; Bury; Brighton & Hove Albion;
        Brentford; Corby Town

	A	G
1956/57	3	3
1957/58	12	5
1958/59	11	4
1959/60	22	15
1960/61	28	16
1961/62	4	2
Total	**80**	**45**

⚽ ERNEST PETER JONES Full-back

Born   Salford 30 November 1937
Clubs   Manchester United; Wolverhampton Wanderers; Manchester United;
        Wrexham; Stockport County; Altrincham

	A	G
1957/58	1	0
Total	**1**	**0**

⚽ JOHN DAVID GASKELL Goalkeeper

Born   Orrell, Lancashire 5 October 1940
Clubs   Manchester United; Wigan Athletic; Wrexham

	A	G
1957/58	3	0
1958/59	0	0
1959/60	9	0
1960/61	10	0
1961/62	21	0
1962/63	18	0
1963/64	17	0
1964/65	5	0
1965/66	8	0
1966/67	5	0
Total	**96**	**0**

⚽ HENRY 'HARRY' GREGG Goalkeeper

Born   Magherafelt, Co Derry 25 October 1932
Clubs   Linfield Rangers; Linfield Swifts; Coleraine; Doncaster Rovers;
        Manchester United; Stoke City

	A	G
1957/58	19	0
1958/59	41	0
1959/60	33	0
1960/61	27	0
1961/62	13	0
1962/63	24	0
1963/64	25	0
1964/65	26	0
1965/66	2	0
Total	**210**	**0**

⚽ KENNETH MORGANS Forward

		A	G
Born	Swansea 16 March 1939		
Clubs	Manchester United; Swansea Town; Newport County; Cwmbran Town		
	1957/58	13	0
	1958/59	2	0
	1959/60	0	0
	1960/61	2	0
	Total	**17**	**0**

⚽ STANLEY CROWTHER Half-Back

		A	G
Born	Bilston, Staffordshire 3 September 1935		
Clubs	West Bromwich Albion; Bilston Town; Aston Villa; Manchester United; Chelsea; Brighton & Hove Albion; Rugby Town; Hednesford Town		
	1957/58	11	0
	1958/59	2	0
	Total	**13**	**0**

⚽ ERNEST TAYLOR Forward

		A	G
Born	Sunderland 2 September 1925		
Died	Birkenhead 9 April 1985		
Clubs	Hylton Colliery; Newcastle United; Blackpool; Manchester United; Sunderland; Altrincham; Derry City		
	1957/58	11	2
	1958/59	11	0
	Total	**22**	**2**

⚽ MARK PEARSON Forward

		A	G
Born	Ridgeway, Derbyshire 28 October 1939		
Clubs	Manchester United; Sheffield Wednesday; Fulham; Halifax Town		
	1957/58	8	0
	1958/59	4	1
	1959/60	10	3
	1960/61	27	7

1961/62	17	1
1962/63	2	0
Total	**68**	**12**

⚽ SEAMUS ANTHONY 'SHAY' BRENNAN Full-back

Born   Manchester 6 May 1937
Died   9 June 2000
Clubs   Manchester United; Waterford

	A	G
1957/58	5	0
1958/59	1	0
1959/60	29	0
1960/61	41	0
1961/62	41	2
1962/63	37	0
1963/64	17	0
1964/65	42	0
1965/66	28	0
1966/67	16	0
1967/68	13	1
1968/69	13	0
1969/70	9	0
Total	**292**	**3**

⚽ ROBERT HARROP Half-Back

Born   Manchester 25 August 1936
Clubs   Manchester United; Tranmere Rovers; Ramsgate FC

	A	G
1957/58	5	0
1958/59	5	0
Total	**10**	**0**

⚽ THOMAS RUSSELL FERRIE HERON Forward

Born   Irvine, Ayrshire 31 March 1936
Clubs   Queen's Park; Kilmarnock; Portadown; Manchester United; York City; Altrincham; Droylsden

	A	G
1957/58	1	0
1958/59	0	0
1959/60	1	0
1960/61	1	0
Total	**3**	**0**

⚽ ALBERT QUIXALL Forward

Born	Sheffield 9 August 1933
Clubs	Sheffield Wednesday; Manchester United; Oldham Athletic; Stockport County; Altrincham; Radcliffe Borough

	A	G
1958/59	33	4
1959/60	33	13
1960/61	38	13
1961/62	21	10
1962/63	31	7
1963/64	9	3
Total	**165**	**50**

⚽ WARREN BRADLEY Forward

Born	Hyde, Cheshire 20 June 1933
Died	6 June 2007
Clubs	Durham City; Bolton Wanderers; Bishop Auckland; Manchester United; Bury; Northwich Victoria; Macclesfield; Bangor City; Macclesfield

	A	G
1958/59	24	12
1959/60	29	8
1960/61	4	0
1961/62	6	0
Total	**63**	**20**

⚽ JOSEPH CAROLAN Full-back

Born	Dublin 8 September 1937
Clubs	Home Farm FC; Manchester United; Brighton & Hove Albion; Tonbridge; Canterbury City

	A	G
1958/59	23	0
1959/60	41	0
1960/61	2	0
Total	**66**	**0**

⚽ REGINALD JOHN HUNTER Forward

Born Colwyn Bay 25 October 1938
Clubs Colwyn Bay; Manchester United; Wrexham; Bangor City

	A	G
1958/59	1	0
Total	**1**	**0**

⚽ MICHAEL JOHN GILES Inside-forward

Born Cabra, Dublin 6 November 1940
Clubs Colombus FC; Dublin City; Stella Maris; Leprechauns FC; Home Farm FC; Manchester United; Leeds United; West Bromwich Albion; Shamrock Rovers; Philadelphia Fury (USA)

	A	G
1959/60	10	2
1960/61	23	2
1961/62	30	2
1962/63	36	4
Total	**99**	**10**

⚽ MAURICE EDGAR SETTERS Half-Back

Born Honiton, Devon 16 December 1936
Clubs Exeter City; West Bromwich Albion; Manchester United; Stoke City; Coventry City; Charlton Athletic

	A	G
1959/60	17	0
1960/61	40	4
1961/62	38	3
1962/63	27	1
1963/64	32	4
1964/65	5	0
Total	**159**	**12**

⚽ NORBERT LAWTON Half-Back

Born   Newton Heath, Manchester 25 March 1940
Clubs   Manchester United; Preston North End; Brighton & Hove Albion; Lincoln City

	A	G
1959/60	3	0
1960/61	1	0
1961/62	20	6
1962/63	12	0
Total	**36**	**6**

⚽ FRANK HAYDOCK Half-back

Born   Eccles 29 November 1940
Clubs   Blackpool; Manchester United; Charlton Athletic; Portsmouth; Southend United

	A	G
1960/61	4	0
1961/62	1	0
1962/63	1	0
Total	**6**	**0**

⚽ JAMES JOSEPH NICHOLSON Half-Back

Born   Belfast 27 February 1943
Clubs   Boyland FC; Manchester United; Huddersfield Town; Bury; Mossley;
        Stalybridge Celtic

	A	G
1960/61	31	5
1961/62	17	0
1962/63	10	0
Total	**58**	**5**

⚽ NORBERT PETER 'NOBBY' STILES Half-Back

Born   Collyhurst, Manchester 18 May 1942
Clubs   Manchester United; Middlesbrough; Preston North End

	A	G
1960/61	26	2
1961/62	34	7
1962/63	31	2
1963/64	17	0

1964/65	41	0
1965/66	39	2
1966/67	37	3
1967/68	20	0
1968/69	41	1
1969/70	8	0
1970/71	17	0
Total	**311**	**17**

⚽ IAN MOIR Forward

Born   Aberdeen 30 June 1943
Clubs   Manchester United; Blackpool; Chester; Wrexham; Shrewsbury Town;
         Wrexham

	A	G
1960/61	8	1
1961/62	9	0
1962/63	9	1
1963/64	18	3
1964/65	1	0
Total	**45**	**5**

⚽ ANTHONY PETER DUNNE Full-back

Born   Dublin 24 July 1941
Clubs   Shelbourne; Manchester United; Detroit Express (USA); Bolton Wanderers

	A	G
1960/61	3	0
1961/62	28	0
1962/63	25	0
1963/64	40	0
1964/65	42	0
1965/66	40	1
1966/67	40	0
1967/68	37	1
1968/69	33	0
1969/70	33	0
1970/71	35	0
1971/72	34	0

1972/73	24	0
Total	**414**	**2**

⚽ NOEL CANTWELL Full-back

Born	Cork 28 February 1932
Died	8 September 2005
Clubs	Western Rovers; Cork Athletic; West Ham United; Manchester United

	A	G
1960/61	24	0
1961/62	17	2
1962/63	25	1
1963/64	28	0
1964/65	2	1
1965/66	23	2
1966/67	4	0
Total	**123**	**6**

⚽ WILLIAM RONALD BRIGGS Goalkeeper

Born	Belfast 29 March 1943
Clubs	Manchester United; Swansea Town; Bristol Rovers

	A	G
1960/61	1	0
1961/62	8	0
Total	**9**	**0**

⚽ MICHAEL JOHN PINNER Goalkeeper

Born	Boston, Lincolnshire 16 February 1934
Clubs	Wyberton Rangers; Notts County; Pegasus; Aston Villa; Sheffield Wednesday; Queen's Park Rangers; Manchester United; Hendon FC; Chelsea Casuals; Chelsea; Arsenal; Swansea City; Leyton Orient; Belfast Distillery

	A	G
1960/61	4	0
Total	**4**	**0**

⚽ DAVID GEORGE HERD Forward

Born	Hamilton, Lanarkshire 15 April 1934
Clubs	Stockport County; Arsenal; Manchester United; Stoke City; Waterford

	A	G
1961/62	27	14
1962/63	37	19
1963/64	30	20
1964/65	37	20
1965/66	37	24
1966/67	28	16
1967/68	6	1
Total	**202**	**114**

⚽ SAMUEL THOMAS McMILLAN Forward

Born   Belfast 29 September 1941
Clubs   Manchester United; Wrexham; Southend United; Chester;
        Stockport County; Oswestry Town

	A	G
1961/62	11	6
1962/63	4	0
Total	**15**	**6**

⚽ JOHN PHILIP CHISNALL Forward

Born   Stretford, Manchester 27 October 1942
Clubs   Manchester United; Liverpool; Southend United; Stockport County

	A	G
1961/62	9	1
1962/63	6	1
1963/64	20	6
Total	**35**	**8**

⚽ DENIS LAW Forward

Born   Aberdeen 24 February 1940
Clubs   Huddersfield Town; Manchester City; Torino (Italy); Manchester United;
        Manchester City

	A	G
1962/63	38	23
1963/64	30	30
1964/65	36	28
1965/66	33	15

	A	G
1966/67	36	23
1967/68	23	7
1968/69	30	14
1969/70	11	2
1970/71	28	15
1971/72	33	13
1972/73	9/2	1
Total	**309**	**171**

☺ PATRICK TIMOTHY CRERAND Half-Back

Born	Glasgow 19 February 1939
Clubs	Duntocher Hibernian; Glasgow Celtic; Manchester United

	A	G
1962/63	19	0
1963/64	41	1
1964/65	39	3
1965/66	41	0
1966/67	39	3
1967/68	41	1
1968/69	35	1
1969/70	25	1
1970/71	24	0
Total	**304**	**10**

☺ DENNIS ALAN WALKER Forward

Born	Northwich, Cheshire 26 October 1944
Clubs	Manchester United; York City; Cambridge United; Poole Town

	A	G
1962/63	1	0
Total	**1**	**0**

☺ DAVID SADLER Midfield/Forward

Born	Yalding, Kent 5 February 1946
Clubs	Maidstone United; Manchester United; Miami Toros (USA); Preston North End

	A	G
1963/64	19	5
1964/65	6	1

1965/66	10	4
1966/67	36	5
1967/68	41	3
1968/69	29	0
1969/70	40	2
1970/71	32	1
1971/72	37	1
1972/73	19	0
1973/74	3	0
Total	**272**	**22**

⚽ GEORGE BEST Forward

Born	Belfast 22 May 1946
Died	25 November 2005
Clubs	Manchester United; Dunstable Town; Stockport County; Cork Celtic; Los Angeles Aztecs (USA); Fulham; Los Angeles Aztecs (USA); Fort Lauderdale Strikers (USA); Hibernian; San Jose Earthquakes (USA); Bournemouth; Brisbane Lions (Australia)

	A	G
1963/64	17	4
1964/65	41	10
1965/66	31	9
1966/67	42	10
1967/68	41	28
1968/69	41	19
1969/70	37	15
1970/71	40	18
1971/72	40	18
1972/73	19	4
1973/74	12	2
Total	**361**	**137**

⚽ GRAHAM MOORE Forward

Born	Cascade near Hengoed, Glamorgan 7 March 1941
Clubs	Bargoed YMCA; Cardiff City; Chelsea; Manchester United; Northampton Town; Charlton Athletic; Doncaster Rovers

	A	G
1963/64	18	4
Total	**18**	**4**

⚽ WILLIAM JOHN ANDERSON Forward

Born   Liverpool 24 January 1947
Clubs   Manchester United; Aston Villa; Cardiff City; Portland Timbers (USA)

	A	G
1963/64	2	0
1964/65	0	0
1965/66	6	0
1966/67	1	0
Total	**9**	**0**

⚽ WILFRED TRANTER Half-Back

Born   Pendlebury, Manchester 5 March 1945
Clubs   Manchester United; Brighton & Hove Albion; Baltimore Bays (USA);
Fulham; St Louis Stars (USA)

	A	G
1963/64	1	0
Total	**1**	**0**

⚽ JOHN MICHAEL CONNELLY Forward

Born   St Helens, Lancashire 18 July 1938
Clubs   St Helens Town; Burnley; Manchester United; Blackburn Rovers; Bury

	A	G
1964/65	42	15
1965/66	32	5
1966/67	6	2
Total	**80**	**22**

⚽ PATRICK ANTHONY JOSEPH DUNNE Goalkeeper

Born   Dublin 9 February 1943
Clubs   Everton; Shamrock Rovers; Manchester United; Plymouth Argyle;
Shamrock Rovers

	A	G
1964/65	37	0

	A	G
1965/66	8	0
Total	**45**	**0**

⚽ JOHN HERBERT NORTON FITZPATRICK Defender

Born   Aberdeen 18 August 1946
Clubs   Manchester United

	A	G
1964/65	2	0
1965/66	4	0
1966/67	3	0
1967/68	17	0
1968/69	30	3
1969/70	20	3
1970/71	35	2
1971/72	1	0
1972/73	5	0
Total	**117**	**8**

⚽ JOHN ASTON Junior Forward

Born   Manchester 28 June 1947
Clubs   Manchester United; Luton Town; Mansfield Town; Blackburn Rovers

	A	G
1964/65	1	0
1965/66	23	4
1966/67	30	5
1967/68	37	10
1968/69	13	2
1969/70	22	1
1970/71	20	3
1971/72	9	0
Total	**155**	**25**

⚽ ROBERT NOBLE Full-back

Born   Manchester 18 December 1945
Clubs   Manchester United

	A	G
1965/66	2	0

	1966/67	29	0
	Total	**31**	**0**

⚽ JAMES RYAN Forward

Born   Stirling 12 May 1945
Clubs   Corrie Hearts; Manchester United; Luton Town; Dallas Tornados (USA)

		A	G
	1965/66	4	1
	1966/67	5	0
	1967/68	8	2
	1968/69	6	1
	1969/70	1	0
	Total	**24**	**4**

⚽ ALEXANDER CYRIL STEPNEY Goalkeeper

Born   Mitcham, Surrey 18 September 1942
Clubs   Achilles FC; Fulham; Tooting & Mitcham; Chelsea; Manchester United;
        Dallas Tornados (USA); Altrincham

		A	G
	1966/67	35	0
	1967/68	41	0
	1968/69	38	0
	1969/70	37	0
	1970/71	22	0
	1971/72	39	0
	1972/73	38	0
	1973/74	42	2
	1974/75	40	0
	1975/76	38	0
	1976/77	40	0
	1977/78	23	0
	Total	**433**	**2**

⚽ BRIAN KIDD Forward

Born   Collyhurst, Manchester 29 May 1949
Clubs   Manchester United; Arsenal; Manchester City; Everton; Bolton Wanderers;
        Atlanta Chiefs (USA); Fort Lauderdale Strikers (USA); Minnesota Strikers (USA)

	A	G
1967/68	38	15
1968/69	29	1
1969/70	33	12
1970/71	25	8
1971/72	34	10
1972/73	18	4
1973/74	21	2
Total	**203**	**52**

⚽ FRANCIS BURNS Defender

Born   Glenboig, Lanarkshire 17 October 1948
Clubs   Manchester United; Southampton; Preston North End; Shamrock Rovers

	A	G
1967/68	36	2
1968/69	16	0
1969/70	32	3
1970/71	20	0
1971/72	17	1
Total	**121**	**6**

⚽ FRANK KOPEL Full-back

Born   Falkirk 28 March 1949
Clubs   Manchester United; Blackburn Rovers; Dundee United

	A	G
1967/68	2	0
1968/69	8	0
Total	**10**	**0**

⚽ ALAN EDWIN GOWLING Forward

Born   Stockport 16 March 1949
Clubs   Manchester United; Huddersfield Town; Newcastle United;
        Bolton Wanderers; Preston North End

	A	G
1967/68	5	1
1968/69	2	0
1969/70	7	3

1970/71	20	8
1971/72	37	6
Total	**71**	**18**

⚽ JOHN JAMES RIMMER Goalkeeper

Born   Southport 10 February 1948
Clubs   Manchester United; Swansea City; Arsenal; Aston Villa; Swansea City;
          Hamrun Spartans (Malta)

	A	G
1967/68	1	0
1968/69	4	0
1969/70	5	0
1970/71	20	0
1971/72	0	0
1972/73	4	0
Total	**34**	**0**

⚽ WILLIAM MORGAN Forward

Born   Sauchie near Alloa 2 October 1944
Clubs   Burnley; Manchester United; Burnley; Bolton Wanderers;
          Chicago Sting (USA); Minnesota Kicks (USA); Blackpool

	A	G
1968/69	29	6
1969/70	35	7
1970/71	25	3
1971/72	35	1
1972/73	39	3
1973/74	41	2
1974/75	34	3
Total	**238**	**25**

⚽ CARLO DOMENICO SARTORI Midfield

Born   Calderzone, Italy 10 February 1948
Clubs   Manchester United; Bologna (Italy); Lecce (Italy); Rimini (Italy); Trento (Italy)

	A	G
1968/69	13	0
1969/70	17	2

1970/71	7	2
1971/72	2	0
Total	**39**	**4**

⚽ STEVEN ROBERT JAMES Defender

Born   Coseley near Wolverhampton 29 November 1949
Clubs   Manchester United; York City; Kidderminster Harriers; Tipton Town

	A	G
1968/69	21	1
1969/70	2	0
1970/71	13	0
1971/72	37	1
1972/73	22	0
1973/74	21	2
1974/75	13	0
Total	**129**	**4**

⚽ DANIEL JOSEPH 'DON' GIVENS Forward

Born   Dublin 9 August 1949
Clubs   Dublin Rangers; Manchester United; Luton Town; Queen's Park Rangers;
            Birmingham City; Bournemouth; Sheffield United; Xamax Neuchatel (Switzerland)

	A	G
1969/70	8	1
Total	**8**	**1**

⚽ PAUL FRANCIS EDWARDS Defender

Born   Shaw near Oldham 7 October 1947
Clubs   Manchester United; Oldham Athletic; Stockport County; Ashton United

	A	G
1969/70	19	0
1970/71	30	0
1971/72	4	0
1972/73	1	0
Total	**54**	**0**

⚽ JOHN FRANCOMBE 'IAN' URE Defender

Born   Ayr 7 December 1939

Clubs	Ayr Albion; Dalry Thistle; Dundee; Arsenal; Manchester United; St Mirren		
		A	G
	1969/70	34	1
	1970/71	13	0
	Total	**47**	**1**

☻ TERENCE ANTHONY YOUNG Midfield/Defender

Born	Urmston, Manchester 24 December 1952		
Clubs	Manchester United; Charlton Athletic; York City; Bangor City		
		A	G
	1970/71	1	0
	1971/72	7	0
	1972/73	30	0
	1973/74	29	1
	1974/75	15	0
	1975/76	1	0
	Total	**83**	**1**

☻ WILLIAM WATSON Full-back

Born	Motherwell 4 December 1949		
Clubs	Manchester United; Huddersfield Town; Miami Toros (USA); Burnley; Motherwell		
		A	G
	1970/71	8	0
	1971/72	0	0
	1972/73	3	0
	Total	**11**	**0**

☻ SAMUEL BAXTER McILROY Midfield

Born	Belfast 2 August 1954		
Clubs	Manchester United; Stoke City; Manchester City; Orgyte (Sweden); Bury; Preston North End		
		A	G
	1971/72	16	4
	1972/73	10	0
	1973/74	29	6
	1974/75	42	7
	1975/76	41	10

	A	G
1976/77	40	2
1977/78	39	9
1978/79	40	5
1979/80	41	6
1980/81	32	5
1981/82	12	3
Total	**342**	**57**

⚽ MARTIN McLEAN BUCHAN Defender

Born   Aberdeen 6 March 1949
Clubs   Banks o'Dee; Aberdeen; Manchester United; Oldham Athletic

	A	G
1971/72	13	1
1972/73	42	0
1973/74	42	0
1974/75	41	0
1975/76	42	0
1976/77	33	0
1977/78	28	1
1978/79	37	2
1979/80	42	0
1980/81	26	0
1981/82	27	0
1982/83	3	0
Total	**376**	**4**

⚽ IAN STOREY-MOORE Forward

Born   Ipswich 17 January 1945
Clubs   Nottingham Forest; Manchester United; Burton Albion; Chicago Sting (USA)

	A	G
1971/72	11	5
1972/73	26	5
1973/74	2	1
Total	**39**	**11**

⚽ JOHN PATRICK CONNAUGHTON Goalkeeper

Born   Wigan 23 September 1949

Clubs	Manchester United; Halifax Town; Torquay United; Sheffield United; Port Vale; Altrincham	
	A	G
1971/72	3	0
Total	**3**	**0**

⚽ IAN RICHARD DONALD Full-back

Born	Aberdeen 28 November 1951	
Clubs	Banks o'Dee; Manchester United; Partick Thistle; Arbroath	
	A	G
1972/73	4	0
Total	**4**	**0**

⚽ RONALD WYN DAVIES Forward

Born	Caernarfon 20 March 1942	
Clubs	Llanberis FC; Caernarfon Town; Wrexham; Bolton Wanderers; Newcastle United; Manchester City; Manchester United; Blackpool; Crystal Palace; Stockport County; Arcadia Shepherds (South Africa); Crewe Alexandra; Bangor City	
	A	G
1972/73	16	4
Total	**16**	**4**

⚽ EDWARD JOHN MacDOUGALL Forward

Born	Inverness 8 January 1947	
Clubs	Liverpool; York City; Bournemouth; Manchester United; West Ham United; Norwich City; Southampton; Bournemouth; Detroit Express (USA); Blackpool; Salisbury; Poole Town; Totton; Gosport Borough; Athena (Australia)	
	A	G
1972/73	18	5
Total	**18**	**5**

⚽ GEORGE GRAHAM Midfield

Born	Bargeddie, Lanarkshire 30 November 1944	
Clubs	Aston Villa; Chelsea; Arsenal; Manchester United; Portsmouth; Crystal Palace; California Surf (USA)	
	A	G
1972/73	18	1

1973/74	24	1
1974/75	1	0
Total	**43**	**2**

⚽ ALEXANDER FORSYTH Full-back

Born   Swinton, Lanarkshire 5 February 1952
Clubs   Partick Thistle; Manchester United; Glasgow Rangers; Motherwell;
        Hamilton Academical

	A	G
1972/73	8	0
1973/74	19	1
1974/75	39	1
1975/76	28	2
1976/77	4	0
1977/78	3	0
Total	**101**	**4**

⚽ JAMES ALLAN HOLTON Central Defender

Born   Lesmahagow, Lanarkshire 11 April 1951
Died   Baginton near Coventry 5 October 1993
Clubs   West Bromwich Albion; Shrewsbury Town; Manchester United; Sunderland;
        Coventry City; Detroit Express (USA); Sheffield Wednesday

	A	G
1972/73	15	3
1973/74	34	2
1974/75	14	0
Total	**63**	**5**

⚽ LUIGI 'LOU' MACARI Forward

Born   Edinburgh 4 June 1949
Clubs   Kilwinning Amateurs; Glasgow Celtic; Manchester United;
        Swindon Town

	A	G
1972/73	16	5
1973/74	35	5
1974/75	38	11
1975/76	36	12

1976/77	38	9
1977/78	32	8
1978/79	32	6
1979/80	39	9
1980/81	38	9
1981/82	11	2
1982/83	9	2
1983/84	5	0
Total	**329**	**78**

✪ MICHAEL PAUL MARTIN Midfield

Born   Dublin 9 July 1951
Clubs   Home Farm FC; Bohemians; Manchester United; West Bromwich Albion;
            Newcastle United; Vancouver Whitecaps (Canada); Willingdon FC; Cardiff City;
            Peterborough United; Rotherham United; Preston North End

	A	G
1972/73	16	2
1973/74	16	0
1974/75	8	0
Total	**40**	**2**

✪ TREVOR ANDERSON Forward

Born   Belfast 3 March 1951
Clubs   Portadown; Manchester United; Swindon Town; Peterborough United; Linfield

	A	G
1972/73	7	1
1973/74	12	1
Total	**19**	**2**

✪ PETER FLETCHER Forward

Born   Manchester 2 December 1953
Clubs   Manchester United; Hull City; Stockport County; Huddersfield Town

	A	G
1972/73	2	0
1973/74	5	0
Total	**7**	**0**

⚽ ARNOLD SIDEBOTTOM Half-Back Born
Barnsley 1 April 1954

Clubs   Manchester United; Huddersfield Town; Halifax Town

	A	G
1972/73	2	0
1973/74	2	0
1974/75	12	0
Total	**16**	**0**

⚽ GERARD ANTHONY DALY Midfield
Born   Cabra, Dublin 30 April 1954

Clubs   Bohemians; Manchester United; Derby County; New England Tea Men (USA); Coventry City; Leicester City; Birmingham City; Shrewsbury Town; Stoke City; Doncaster Rovers; Telford United

	A	G
1973/74	16	1
1974/75	37	11
1975/76	41	7
1976/77	17	4
Total	**111**	**23**

⚽ BRIAN GREENHOFF Defender
Born   Barnsley 28 April 1953

Clubs   Manchester United; Leeds United; Hong Kong; Rochdale

	A	G
1973/74	36	3
1974/75	41	4
1975/76	40	0
1976/77	40	3
1977/78	31	1
1978/79	33	2
Total	**221**	**13**

⚽ GEORGE BUCHAN Forward
Born   Aberdeen 2 May 1950

Clubs   Aberdeen; Manchester United; Bury; Motherwell

	A	G
1973/74	3	0
Total	**3**	**0**

⚽ CLIVE LESLIE GRIFFITHS Defender

Born   Pontypridd 22 January 1955
Clubs   Manchester United; Plymouth Argyle; Tranmere Rovers; Chicago Sting (USA);
        Tulsa Roughnecks (USA)

	A	G
1973/74	7	0
Total	**7**	**0**

⚽ STEWART MACKIE HOUSTON Full-back

Born   Dunoon, Argyllshire 20 August 1949
Clubs   Port Glasgow Rangers; Chelsea; Brentford; Manchester United;
        Sheffield United; Colchester United

	A	G
1973/74	20	2
1974/75	40	6
1975/76	42	2
1976/77	36	3
1977/78	31	0
1978/79	22	0
1979/80	14	0
Total	**205**	**13**

⚽ PAUL ANTHONY BIELBY Forward

Born   Darlington 24 November 1956
Clubs   Manchester United; Hartlepool United; Huddersfield Town

	A	G
1973/74	4	0
Total	**4**	**0**

⚽ JAMES McCALLIOG Midfield

Born   Glasgow 22 September 1946
Clubs   Chelsea; Sheffield Wednesday; Wolverhampton Wanderers;
        Manchester United; Southampton; Chicago Sting (USA); Lincoln City; Runcorn

	A	G
1973/74	11	4
1974/75	20	3
Total	**31**	**7**

⚽ STUART JAMES PEARSON Forward

Born   Hull 21 June 1949
Clubs   Hull City; Manchester United; West Ham United

	A	G
1974/75	32	17
1975/76	39	13
1976/77	39	15
1977/78	30	10
Total	**139**	**55**

⚽ ARTHUR RICHARD ALBISTON Full-back

Born   Edinburgh 14 July 1957
Clubs   Manchester United; West Bromwich Albion; Dundee; Chesterfield;
        Chester City; Molde FC (Norway)

	A	G
1974/75	2	0
1975/76	3	0
1976/77	17	0
1977/78	28	0
1978/79	33	0
1979/80	25	0
1980/81	42	1
1981/82	42	1
1982/83	38	1
1983/84	40	2
1984/85	39	0
1985/86	37	1
1986/87	22	0
1987/88	11	0
Total	**379**	**6**

⚽ DAVID McCREERY Midfield

Born   Belfast 16 September 1957

Clubs   Manchester United; Queen's Park Rangers; Tulsa Roughnecks (USA); Newcastle United; Heart of Midlothian; Hartlepool United; Coleraine; Carlisle United

	A	G
1974/75	2	0
1975/76	28	4
1976/77	25	2
1977/78	17	1
1978/79	15	0
Total	**87**	**7**

⚽ RONALD TUDOR DAVIES Forward

Born   Holywell 25 May 1942

Clubs   Chester; Luton Town; Norwich City; Southampton; Portsmouth; Manchester United; Arcadia Shepherds (South Africa); Millwall; Los Angeles Aztecs (USA); Dorchester Town; Los Angeles Aztecs (USA); Tulsa Roughnecks (USA); Seattle Sounders (USA); White Horse FC; Totton FC

	A	G
1974/75	8	0
Total	**8**	**0**

⚽ THOMAS BALDWIN Forward

Born   Gateshead 10 June 1945

Clubs   Arsenal; Chelsea; Millwall; Manchester United; Seattle Sounders (USA); Gravesend & Northfleet; Brentford

	A	G
1974/75	2	0
Total	**2**	**0**

⚽ PATRICK JOSEPH CHRISTOPHER ROCHE Goalkeeper

Born   Dublin 4 January 1951

Clubs   Shelbourne; Manchester United; Brentford; Halifax Town; Chester City; Northwich Victoria

	A	G
1974/75	2	0
1975/76	4	0
1976/77	2	0
1977/78	19	0
1978/79	14	0
1979/80	0	0
1980/81	2	0
1981/82	3	0
Total	**46**	**0**

⚽ STEPHEN JAMES COPPELL Midfield/Forward

Born   Croxteth, Liverpool 9 July 1955
Clubs   Tranmere Rovers; Manchester United

	A	G
1974/75	10	1
1975/76	39	4
1976/77	40	6
1977/78	42	5
1978/79	42	11
1979/80	42	8
1980/81	42	6
1981/82	36	9
1982/83	29	4
Total	**322**	**54**

⚽ JAMES MICHAEL NICHOLL Defender

Born   Hamilton, Ontario, Canada 28 February 1956
Clubs   Manchester United; Toronto Blizzard (USA); Sunderland; Toronto Blizzard (USA);
        Glasgow Rangers; Toronto Blizzard (USA); West Bromwich Albion;
        Glasgow Rangers

	A	G
1974/75	1	0
1975/76	20	0
1976/77	39	0
1977/78	37	2
1978/79	21	0

1979/80	42	0
1980/81	36	1
1981/82	1	0
Total	**197**	**3**

⚽ THOMAS JACKSON Midfield

Born   Belfast 3 November 1946
Clubs   Glentoran; Everton; Nottingham Forest; Manchester United; Waterford

	A	G
1975/76	17	0
1976/77	2	0
Total	**19**	**0**

⚽ ANTHONY GRIMSHAW Defender

Born   Manchester 8 December 1957
Clubs   Manchester United; Ballymena United

	A	G
1975/76	1	0
Total	**1**	**0**

⚽ GORDON ALEX HILL Forward

Born   Sunbury-on-Thames 1 April 1954
Clubs   Staines Town; Slough Town; Southall; Millwall; Chicago Sting (USA);
           Manchester United; Derby County; Queen's Park Rangers;
           Montreal Manic (Canada); Chicago Sting (USA); New York Arrows (USA);
           Kansas Comets (USA); Tacoma Stars (USA); HJK Helsinki (Finland);
           Twente Enschede (Holland); Bournemouth; Northwich Victoria;
           Stafford Rangers; Northwich Victoria; Radcliffe Borough

	A	G
1975/76	26	7
1976/77	39	15
1977/78	36	17
Total	**101**	**39**

⚽ JAMES WILLIAM KELLY Midfield

Born   Carlisle 2 May 1957
Clubs   Manchester United; Chicago Sting (USA); Los Angeles Aztecs (USA);

Tulsa Roughnecks (USA); Toronto Blizzard (USA)

	A	G
1975/76	1	0
Total	**1**	**0**

☻ PETER DAVID COYNE Forward

Born   Hartlepool 13 November 1958

Clubs   Manchester United; Ashton United; Crewe Alexandra; Hyde United; Swindon Town; Aldershot; Colne Dynamo; Glossop; Radcliffe Borough

	A	G
1975/76	2	1
Total	**2**	**1**

☻ ALAN FOGGON Forward

Born   West Pelton Co Durham 23 February 1950

Clubs   Newcastle United; Cardiff City; Middlesbrough; Rochester Lancers (USA); Hartford Bi-Centennials (USA); Manchester United; Sunderland; Southend United; Hartlepool United; Consett; Whitley Bay

	A	G
1976/77	3	0
Total	**3**	**0**

☻ COLIN WALDRON Defender

Born   Bristol 22 June 1948

Clubs   Bury; Chelsea; Burnley; Manchester United; Sunderland; Tulsa Roughnecks (USA); Philadelphia Fury (USA); Atlanta Chiefs (USA); Rochdale

	A	G
1976/77	3	0
Total	**3**	**0**

☻ ROLAND CHRISTOPHER McGRATH Midfield

Born   Belfast 29 November 1954

Clubs   Tottenham Hotspur; Millwall; Manchester United; Tulsa Roughnecks (USA); South China (Hong Kong)

	A	G
1976/77	6	0
1977/78	18	1

	A	G
1978/79	2	0
1979/80	1	0
1980/81	1	0
Total	**28**	**1**

⚽ STEVEN WILLIAM PATERSON Defender

Born   Mostodloch, Elgin 8 April1 958
Clubs   Nairn County; Manchester United; Forres Mechanics; Elgin City

	A	G
1976/77	2	0
1977/78	0	0
1978/79	2	0
1979/80	1	0
Total	**6**	**0**

⚽ JONATHAN CLARK Midfield

Born   Swansea 12 November 1958
Clubs   Manchester United; Derby County; Preston North End; Bury; Carlisle United;
        Morecambe; Rhyl

	A	G
1976/77	1	0
Total	**1**	**0**

⚽ JAMES GREENHOFF Forward

Born   Barnsley 19 June 1946
Clubs   Leeds United; Birmingham City; Stoke City; Manchester United;
        Crewe Alexandra; Toronto Blizzards (USA); Port Vale; Rochdale

	A	G
1976/77	27	8
1977/78	23	6
1978/79	33	11
1979/80	5	1
1980/81	9	0
Total	**97**	**26**

⚽ AUGUSTINE ASHLEY GRIMES Defender/Midfield

Born   Dublin 2 August 1957

Clubs	Stella Maris; Bohemians; Manchester United; Coventry City; Luton Town; Osasuna (Spain)		
		A	G
	1977/78	13	2
	1978/79	16	0
	1979/80	26	3
	1980/81	8	2
	1981/82	11	1
	1982/83	16	2
	Total	**90**	**10**

⚽ MARTYN ROGERS Defender

Born	Nottingham 26 January 1960		
Died	Ringwood, Hampshire March 1992		
Clubs	Manchester United; Queen's Park Rangers		
		A	G
	1977/78	1	0
	Total	**1**	**0**

⚽ ANDREW TIMOTHY RITCHIE Forward

Born	Manchester 28 November 1960		
Clubs	Manchester United; Brighton & Hove Albion; Leeds United; Oldham Athletic		
		A	G
	1977/78	4	0
	1978/79	17	10
	1979/80	8	3
	1980/81	4	0
	Total	**33**	**13**

⚽ JOSEPH JORDAN Forward

Born	Carluke, Lanarkshire 15 December 1951		
Clubs	Blantyre Victoria; Morton; Leeds United; Manchester United; AC Milan (Italy); Verona (Italy); Southampton; Bristol City		
		A	G
	1977/78	14	3
	1978/79	30	6
	1979/80	32	13

	A	G
1980/81	33	15
Total	**109**	**37**

GORDON McQUEEN Defender

Born   Kilbirnie, Ayrshire 26 June 1952
Clubs   Largs Thistle; St Mirren; Leeds United; Manchester United; Seiko (Hong Kong)

	A	G
1977/78	14	1
1978/79	36	6
1979/80	33	9
1980/81	11	2
1981/82	21	0
1982/83	37	0
1983/84	20	1
1984/85	12	1
Total	**184**	**20**

GARY RICHARD BAILEY Goalkeeper

Born   Ipswich 9 August 1958
Clubs   Witts University (South Africa) Manchester United; Kaiser Chiefs (South Africa)

	A	G
1978/79	28	0
1979/80	42	0
1980/81	40	0
1981/82	39	0
1982/83	37	0
1983/84	40	0
1984/85	38	0
1985/86	25	0
1986/87	5	0
Total	**294**	**0**

THOMAS SLOAN Midfield

Born   Ballymena 10 July 1959
Clubs   Ballymena United; Manchester United; Chester

	A	G
1978/79	4	0

	A	G
1979/80	5	0
1980/81	2	0
Total	**11**	**0**

⚽ MICHAEL REGINALD THOMAS Midfield

Born   Mochdre near Colwyn Bay 7 July 1954

Clubs   Wrexham; Manchester United; Everton; Brighton & Hove Albion; Stoke City; Chelsea; West Bromwich Albion; Derby County; Wichita Wings (USA); Shrewsbury Town; Leeds United; Stoke City; Wrexham; Conway United

	A	G
1978/79	25	1
1979/80	35	8
1980/81	30	2
Total	**90**	**11**

⚽ THOMAS EUGENE CONNELL Full-back

Born   Newry 25 November 1957

Clubs   Newry Town; Coleraine; Manchester United; Glentoran

	A	G
1978/79	2	0
Total	**2**	**0**

⚽ KEVIN BERNARD MORAN Defender

Born   Dublin 29 April 1956

Clubs   Bohemians; Pegasus; Manchester United; Sporting Gijon (Spain); Blackburn Rovers

	A	G
1978/79	1	0
1979/80	9	1
1980/81	32	0
1981/82	30	7
1982/83	29	2
1983/84	38	7
1984/85	19	4
1985/86	19	0
1986/87	33	0
1987/88	21	0
Total	**231**	**21**

⚽ **RAYMOND COLIN WILKINS** Midfield

Born   Hillingdon, Middlesex 14 September 1956
Clubs   Chelsea; Manchester United; AC Milan (Italy); Paris St Germain (France);
Glasgow Rangers; Queen's Park Rangers; Crystal Palace; Wycombe Wanderers;
Hibernian; Millwall; Leyton Orient

	A	G
1979/80	37	2
1980/81	13	0
1981/82	42	1
1982/83	26	1
1983/84	42	3
Total	**160**	**7**

⚽ **NIKOLA JOVANOVIC** Defender

Born   Cetinje, Yugoslavia 18 September 1952
Clubs   Red Star Belgrade; Manchester United; FC Buducnoet

	A	G
1979/80	1	0
1980/81	19	4
Total	**20**	**4**

⚽ **MICHAEL DUXBURY** Defender/Midfield

Born   Accrington 1 September 1959
Clubs   Manchester United; Blackburn Rovers; Bradford City

	A	G
1980/81	33	2
1981/82	24	0
1982/83	42	1
1983/84	39	0
1984/85	30	1
1985/86	23	1
1986/87	32	1
1987/88	39	0
1988/89	18	0
1989/90	19	0
Total	**299**	**6**

⚽ **SCOTT THOMAS McGARVEY** Forward

Born   Glasgow 22 April 1963
Clubs   Manchester United; Wolverhampton Wanderers; Portsmouth; Carlisle United;
        Grimsby Town; Bristol City; Oldham Athletic; Wigan Athletic; Mazda (Japan);
        Aris (Cyprus); Derry City; Witton Albion; Barrow

	A	G
1980/81	2	0
1981/82	16	2
1982/83	7	1
Total	**25**	**3**

⚽ **GARRY BIRTLES** Forward

Born   Nottingham 27 July 1956
Clubs   Long Eaton Rovers; Long Eaton United; Nottingham Forest; Manchester United;
        Nottingham Forest; Notts County; Grimsby Town

	A	G
1980/81	25	0
1981/82	33	11
Total	**58**	**11**

⚽ **ANTHONY GERARD WHELAN** Defender

Born   Dublin 23 November 1959
Clubs   Bohemians; Manchester United; Shamrock Rovers; Cork; Shamrock Rovers;
        Bray Wanderers; Shelbourne

	A	G
1980/81	1	0
Total	**1**	**0**

⚽ **JOHN GIDMAN** Full-back

Born   Liverpool 10 January 1954
Clubs   Liverpool; Aston Villa; Everton; Manchester United; Manchester City;
        Stoke City; Darlington

	A	G
1981/82	37	1
1982/83	3	0
1983/84	4	0
1984/85	27	3

	1985/86	24	0
	Total	**95**	**4**

⚽ FRANCIS ANTHONY STAPLETON Forward

Born	Dublin 10 July 1956		
Clubs	St Martins; Bolton Athletic; Arsenal; Manchester United; Ajax (Amsterdam); Derby County; Le Havre (France); Blackburn Rovers; Aldershot; Huddersfield Town; Bradford City		
		A	G
	1981/82	41	13
	1982/83	41	14
	1983/84	42	13
	1984/85	24	6
	1985/86	41	7
	1986/87	34	7
	Total	**223**	**60**

⚽ REMI MARK MOSES Midfield

Born	Miles Platting, Manchester 14 November 1960		
Clubs	West Bromwich Albion; Manchester United		
		A	G
	1981/82	21	2
	1982/83	29	0
	1983/84	35	2
	1984/85	26	3
	1985/86	4	0
	1986/87	18	0
	1987/88	17	0
	Total	**150**	**7**

⚽ BRYAN ROBSON Midfield

Born	Chester-le-Street 11 January 1957		
Clubs	West Bromwich Albion; Manchester United; Middlesbrough		
		A	G
	1981/82	32	5
	1982/83	33	10
	1983/84	33	12

1984/85	33	9
1985/86	21	7
1986/87	30	7
1987/88	36	11
1988/89	34	4
1989/90	20	2
1990/91	17	1
1991/92	27	4
1992/93	14	1
1993/94	15	1
Total	**345**	**74**

☻ NORMAN WHITESIDE Midfield/Forward

Born	Belfast 7 May 1965	
Clubs	Manchester United; Everton	
	A	G
1981/82	2	1
1982/83	39	8
1983/84	37	10
1984/85	27	9
1985/86	37	4
1986/87	31	8
1987/88	27	7
1988/89	6	0
Total	**206**	**47**

☻ ALAN DAVIES Forward

Born	Manchester 5 December 1961	
Died	Gower near Swansea 4 February 1992	
Clubs	Manchester United; Newcastle United; Charlton Athletic; Carlisle United; Swansea City; Bradford City; Swansea City	
	A	D
1981/82	1	0
1982/83	3	0
1983/84	3	0
Total	**7**	**0**

⚽ ARNOLDUS JOHANNUS HYACINTHUS 'ARNOLD' MUHREN Midfield

Born   Vollendam, Holland 2 June 1951
Clubs   Ajax (Amsterdam); FC Twente Enschede (Holland); Ipswich Town;
       Manchester United; Ajax (Amsterdam)

	A	G
1982/83	32	5
1983/84	26	8
1984/85	12	0
Total	**70**	**13**

⚽ PAUL McGRATH Defender

Born   Ealing, London 4 December 1959
Clubs   St Patrick's Athletic; Manchester United; Aston Villa

	A	G
1982/83	14	3
1983/84	9	1
1984/85	23	0
1985/86	40	3
1986/87	35	2
1987/88	21	2
1988/89	20	1
Total	**163**	**12**

⚽ JEFFREY ANDREW WEALANDS Goalkeeper

Born   Darlington 26 August 1951
Clubs   Darlington Cleveland Bridge; Wolverhampton Wanderers;
       Northampton Town; Darlington; Hull City; Birmingham City;
       Manchester United; Oldham Athletic; Preston North End; Altrincham;
       Barrow; Altrincham

	A	G
1982/83	5	0
1983/84	2	0
Total	**7**	**0**

⚽ LAURENCE PAUL CUNNINGHAM Forward

Born   St Mary's Archway, London 8 March 1956
Died   Madrid, Spain 15 July 1989

Clubs   Orient; West Bromwich Albion; Real Madrid (Spain); Manchester United;
           Sporting Gijon (Spain); Olympique Marseille (France); Leicester City;
           Rayo Vallecano (Spain); FC Betis (Spain); RSC Charleroi (Belgium);
           Wimbledon; Rayo Vallecano (Spain)

	A	G
1982/83	5	1
Total	**5**	**1**

⚽ ARTHUR GRAHAM Forward

Born   Castlemilk, Glasgow 26 October 1952
Clubs   Cambuslang Rangers; Aberdeen; Leeds United; Manchester United;
           Bradford City

	A	G
1983/84	37	5
Total	**37**	**5**

⚽ GARTH ANTHONY CROOKS Forward

Born   Stoke-on-Trent 10 March 1958
Clubs   Stoke City; Tottenham Hotspur; Manchester United; West Bromwich Albion;
           Charlton Athletic

	A	G
1983/84	7	2
Total	**7**	**2**

⚽ GRAEME JAMES HOGG Defender

Born   Aberdeen 17 June 1964
Clubs   Manchester United; West Bromwich Albion; Portsmouth; Heart of Midlothian

	A	G
1983/84	16	1
1984/85	29	0
1985/86	17	0
1986/87	11	0
1987/88	10	0
Total	**83**	**1**

⚽ LESLIE MARK HUGHES Forward

Born   Wrexham 1 November 1963

Clubs	Manchester United; Barcelona (Spain); Bayern Munich (Germany); Manchester United; Chelsea; Southampton; Everton; Blackburn Rovers		
		A	G
	1983/84	11	4
	1984/85	38	16
	1985/86	40	17
	1988/89	38	14
	1989/90	37	13
	1990/91	31	10
	1991/92	39	11
	1992/93	41	15
	1993/94	36	12
	1994/95	34	8
	Total	**345**	**120**

⚽ CLAYTON GRAHAM BLACKMORE Defender/Midfield

Born	Neath 23 September 1964		
Clubs	Manchester United; Middlesbrough; Bristol City; Barnsley; Notts County; Leigh RMI		
		A	G
	1983/84	1	0
	1984/85	1	0
	1985/86	12	3
	1986/87	12	1
	1987/88	22	3
	1988/89	28	3
	1989/90	28	2
	1990/91	35	4
	1991/92	33	3
	1992/93	14	0
	Total	**186**	**19**

⚽ GORDON DAVID STRACHAN Midfield

Born	Edinburgh 9 February 1957		
Clubs	Dundee; Aberdeen; Manchester United; Leeds United; Coventry City		
		A	G
	1984/85	41	15

	A	G
1985/86	28	5
1986/87	34	4
1987/88	36	8
1988/89	21	1
Total	**160**	**33**

✪ ALAN BERNARD BRAZIL Forward

Born   Glasgow 15 June 1959
Clubs   Ipswich Town; Detroit Express (USA); Tottenham Hotspur; Manchester United;
        Coventry City; Queen's Park Rangers; Witham Town; Chelmsford City;
        FC Baden (Switzerland); Chelmsford City; Southend Manor; Bury Town;
        Stambridge; Chelmsford City; Wivenhoe Town

	A	G
1984/85	20	5
1985/86	11	3
Total	**31**	**8**

✪ JESPER OLSEN Forward

Born   Fakse, Denmark 20 March 1961
Clubs   FC Naestved (Denmark); Ajax (Amsterdam); Manchester United;
        Bordeaux (France); SM Caen (France)

	A	G
1984/85	36	5
1985/86	28	11
1986/87	28	3
1987/88	37	2
1988/89	10	0
Total	**139**	**21**

✪ WILLIAM FRANCIS GARTON Defender

Born   Salford 15 March 1965
Clubs   Manchester United; Birmingham City; Salford City; Witton Albion

	A	G
1984/85	2	0
1985/86	10	0
1986/87	9	0
1987/88	6	0

1988/89	14	0
Total	**41**	**0**

⚽ STEPHEN PEARS Goalkeeper

Born	Brandon, Durham 22 January 1962
Clubs	Manchester United; Middlesbrough; Liverpool; Hartlepool United

	A	G
1984/85	4	0
Total	**4**	**0**

⚽ PETER SIMON BARNES Forward

Born	Manchester 10 June 1957
Clubs	Gatley Rangers; Manchester City; West Bromwich Albion; Leeds United; Real Betis (Spain); Coventry City; Manchester United; Manchester City; Bolton Wanderers; Port Vale; Hull City; Drogheda United; Sporting Farense (Portugal); Bolton Wanderers; Sunderland; Tampa Bay Rowdies (USA); Northwich Victoria; Wrexham; Radcliffe Borough; Mossley; Cliftonville

	A	G
1985/86	13	2
1986/87	7	0
Total	**20**	**2**

⚽ COLIN JOHN GIBSON Defender

Born	Bridport, Dorset 6 June 1960
Clubs	Portsmouth; Aston Villa; Manchester United; Port Vale; Leicester City; Blackpool; Walsall

	A	G
1985/86	18	5
1986/87	24	1
1987/88	29	2
1988/89	2	0
1989/90	6	1
Total	**79**	**9**

⚽ MARK JAMES DEMPSEY Midfield

Born	Manchester 14 January 1964

Clubs	Manchester United; Swindon Town; Sheffield United; Chesterfield; Rotherham United; Macclesfield Town		
		A	G
	1985/86	1	0
	Total	**1**	**0**

☻ CHRISTOPHER ROBERT TURNER Goalkeeper

Born	Sheffield 15 September 1958		
Clubs	Sheffield Wednesday; Lincoln City; Sunderland; Manchester United; Sheffield Wednesday; Leeds United; Leyton Orient		
		A	G
	1985/86	17	0
	1986/87	23	0
	1987/88	24	0
	Total	**64**	**0**

☻ NICHOLAS ANTHONY WOOD Forward

Born	Oldham 11 January 1966		
Clubs	Manchester United		
		A	G
	1985/86	1	0
	1986/87	2	0
	Total	**3**	**0**

☻ TERENCE BRADLEY GIBSON Forward

Born	Walthamstow 23 December 1962		
Clubs	Tottenham Hotspur; Gals (Sweden); Coventry City; Manchester United; Wimbledon; Swindon Town; Charlton Athletic; Peterborough United; Barnet		
		A	G
	1985/86	7	0
	1986/87	16	1
	Total	**23**	**1**

☻ JOHN SIVEBACK Full-back

Born	Vejle, Denmark 26 October 1961	
Clubs	Vejle Boldklub (Denmark); Manchester United; St Etienne (France); Monaco FC (France); Atlanta (Italy); Pescara (Italy)	

	A	G
1985/86	3	0
1986/87	28	1
Total	**31**	**1**

⚽ PETER DAVENPORT Forward

Born   Birkenhead 24 March 1961
Clubs   Cammel Laird FC; Everton; Nottingham Forest; Manchester United;
          Middlesbrough; Sunderland; Airdrieonians

	A	G
1985/86	11	1
1986/87	39	14
1987/88	34	5
1988/89	8	2
Total	**92**	**22**

⚽ MARK NICHOLAS HIGGINS Defender

Born   Buxton 29 September 1958
Clubs   Everton; Manchester United; Bury; Stoker City; Burnley

	A	G
1985/86	6	0
Total	**6**	**0**

⚽ GARY WALSH Goalkeeper

Born   Wigan 21 March 1968
Clubs   Manchester United; Airdrieonians; Oldham Athletic; Middlesbrough;
          Bradford City; Middlesbrough; Wigan Athletic

	A	G
1986/87	14	0
1987/88	16	0
1988/89	0	0
1989/90	0	0
1990/91	5	0
1991/92	2	0
1992/93	0	0
1993/94	3	0

	A	G
1994/95	10	0
Total	**50**	**0**

⚽ WILLIAM FRANCIS 'LIAM' O'BRIEN Midfield

Born   Dublin 5 September 1964
Clubs   Stella Maris; Bohemians; Shamrock Rovers; Manchester United;
           Newcastle United; Tranmere Rovers

	A	G
1986/87	10	0
1987/88	17	2
1988/89	3	0
Total	**31**	**2**

⚽ ANTHONY DEAN GILL Defender

Born   Bradford 6 March 1968
Clubs   Manchester United

	A	G
1986/87	1	0
1987/88	0	0
1988/89	9	1
Total	**10**	**1**

⚽ VIVIAN ALEXANDER ANDERSON Full-back

Born   Nottingham 29 August 1956
Clubs   Nottingham Forest; Arsenal; Manchester United; Sheffield Wednesday; Barnsley

	A	G
1987/88	31	2
1988/89	6	0
1989/90	16	0
1990/91	1	0
Total	**54**	**2**

⚽ BRIAN JOHN McCLAIR Midfield/Forward

Born   Airdrie 8 December 1963
Clubs   Motherwell; Glasgow Celtic; Manchester United

	A	G
1987/88	40	24

	A	G
1988/89	38	10
1989/90	37	5
1990/91	36	13
1991/92	42	18
1992/93	42	9
1993/94	26	1
1994/95	40	5
1995/96	22	3
1996/97	19	0
1997/98	13	0
Total	**355**	**88**

⚽ DEINOL WILLIAM THOMAS GRAHAM Forward

Born   Cannock, Staffordshire 4 October 1969
Clubs   Manchester United; Barnsley; Preston North End; Carlisle United;
        Stockport County; Scunthorpe United

	A	G
1987/88	1	0
1988/89	0	0
1989/90	1	0
Total	**2**	**0**

⚽ STEPHEN ROGER BRUCE Defender

Born   Corbridge, Northumberland 31 December 1960
Clubs   Gillingham; Norwich City; Manchester United; Birmingham City

	A	G
1987/88	21	2
1988/89	38	2
1989/90	34	3
1990/91	31	13
1991/92	37	5
1992/93	42	5
1993/94	41	3
1994/95	35	2
1995/96	30	1
Total	**309**	**36**

☺ LEE ANDREW MARTIN Defender

Born   Hyde, Cheshire 5 February 1968

Clubs   Manchester United; Glasgow Celtic; Bristol Rovers; Huddersfield Town

	A	G
1987/88	1	0
1988/89	24	1
1989/90	32	0
1990/91	14	0
1991/92	1	0
1992/93	0	0
1993/94	1	0
Total	**73**	**1**

☺ JAMES LEIGHTON Goalkeeper

Born   Johnstone, Renfrewshire 24 July 1958

Clubs   Dalry Thistle; Aberdeen; Manchester United; Arsenal; Reading; Dundee; Sheffield United; Hibernian; Aberdeen

	A	G
1988/89	38	0
1989/90	35	0
Total	**73**	**0**

☺ LEE STUART SHARPE Forward

Born   Halesowen 25 May 1971

Clubs   Torquay United; Manchester United; Leeds United; Bradford City; Portsmouth; Exeter City

	A	G
1988/89	22	0
1989/90	18	1
1990/91	23	2
1991/92	14	1
1992/93	27	1
1993/94	30	9
1994/95	28	3
1995/96	31	4
Total	**193**	**21**

⚽ RUSSELL PETER BEARDSMORE Midfield

Born	Wigan 28 September 1968
Clubs	Manchester United; Blackburn Rovers; Bournemouth

		A	G
	1988/89	23	2
	1989/90	21	2
	1990/91	12	0
	Total	**56**	**4**

⚽ MARK GORDON ROBINS Forward

Born	Ashton-under-Lyne, Lancashire 22 December 1969
Clubs	Manchester United; Norwich City; Leicester City; Reading;
	Deportivo Orense (Spain); Panionios (Greece); Manchester City;
	Walsall; Rotherham United; Bristol City; Sheffield Wednesday;
	Burton Albion

		A	G
	1988/89	10	0
	1989/90	17	7
	1990/91	19	4
	1991/92	2	0
	Total	**48**	**11**

⚽ MALACHY MARTIN DONAGHY Defender

Born	Belfast 13 September 1957
Clubs	Cromac Albion; Larne Town; Luton Town; Manchester United;
	Luton Town; Chelsea

		A	G
	1988/89	30	0
	1989/90	14	0
	1990/91	25	0
	1991/92	20	0
	Total	**89**	**0**

⚽ RALPH MILNE Forward

Born	Dundee 13 May 1961
Clubs	Dundee United; Charlton Athletic; Bristol City; Manchester United;
	West Ham United; Sing Tao FC (Hong Kong)

	A	G
1988/89	22	3
1989/90	1	0
Total	**23**	**3**

⚽ DAVID GRAHAM WILSON Midfield

Born   Burnley 20 March 1969
Clubs   Manchester United; Lincoln City; Charlton Athletic; Bristol Rovers

	A	G
1988/89	4	0
Total	**4**	**0**

⚽ GUILLANO MAIORANA Forward

Born   Cambridge 18 April 1969
Clubs   Histon FC; Manchester United

	A	G
1988/89	6	0
1989/90	1	0
Total	**7**	**0**

⚽ DEREK MICHAEL BRAZIL Defender

Born   Dublin 14 December 1968
Clubs   Belvedere FC; Rivermount Boys Club; Manchester United;
        Oldham Athletic; Swansea City; Cardiff City; Newport County

	A	G
1988/89	1	0
1989/90	1	0
Total	**2**	**0**

⚽ MICHAEL CHRISTOPHER PHELAN Defender/Midfield

Born   Nelson, Lancashire 24 September 1962
Clubs   Burnley; Norwich City; Manchester United; West Bromwich Albion

	A	G
1989/90	38	1
1990/91	33	1
1991/92	18	0
1992/93	11	0

1993/94	2	0
Total	**102**	**2**

☺ NEIL JOHN WEBB Midfield

Born   Reading 30 July 1963
Clubs   Reading; Portsmouth; Nottingham Forest; Manchester United;
           Nottingham Forest; Swindon Town; Grimsby Town

	A	G
1989/90	11	2
1990/91	32	3
1991/92	31	3
1992/93	1	0
Total	**75**	**8**

☺ GARY ANDREW PALLISTER Defender

Born   Ramsgate 30 June 1963
Clubs   Billingham Town; Middlesbrough; Darlington; Manchester United;
           Middlesbrough

	A	G
1989/90	35	3
1990/91	36	0
1991/92	40	1
1992/93	42	1
1993/94	41	1
1994/95	42	2
1995/96	21	1
1996/97	27	3
1997/98	33	0
Total	**317**	**12**

☺ PAUL EMERSON CARLYLE INCE Midfield

Born   Ilford, Essex 21 October 1967
Clubs   West Ham United; Manchester United; Inter Milan (Italy); Liverpool;
           Middlesbrough; Wolverhampton Wanderers

	A	G
1989/90	26	0
1990/91	31	3

1991/92	33	3
1992/93	41	6
1993/94	39	8
1994/95	36	5
Total	**206**	**25**

⚽ DAVID LLOYD 'DANNY' WALLACE Forward

Born   Greenwich, London 21 January 1964
Clubs   Southampton; Manchester United; Millwall; Birmingham City;
        Wycombe Wanderers

	A	G
1989/90	26	3
1990/91	19	3
1991/92	0	0
1992/93	2	0
Total	**47**	**6**

⚽ LESLIE JESSE SEALEY Goalkeeper

Born   Bethanl Green, London 29 September 1957
Died   19 August 2001
Clubs   Coventry City; Luton Town; Plymouth Argyle; Manchester United; Aston Villa;
        Coventry City; Birmingham City; Manchester United; Blackpool;
        West Ham United; Leyton Orient; West Ham United

	A	G
1989/90	2	0
1990/91	31	0
Total	**33**	**0**

⚽ MARK BOSNICH Goalkeeper

Born   Sydney, Australia 13 January 1972
Clubs   Croatia Sydney SFC; Manchester United; Croatia Sydney SFC; Aston Villa;
        Manchester United; Chelsea

	A	G
1989/90	1	0
1990/91	2	0
1999/2000	23	0
Total	**26**	**0**

⚽ DENIS JOSEPH IRWIN Full-back

| Born | Cork 31 October 1965 |
| Clubs | Leeds United; Oldham Athletic; Manchester United; Wolverhampton Wanderers |

	A	G
1990/91	34	0
1991/92	38	4
1992/93	40	5
1993/94	42	2
1994/95	40	2
1995/96	31	1
1996/97	31	1
1997/98	25	2
1998/99	29	2
1999/2000	25	3
2000/01	21	0
2001/02	12	0
Total	**368**	**22**

⚽ DARREN FERGUSON Midfield

| Born | Glasgow 9 February 1972 |
| Clubs | Manchester United; Wolverhampton Wanderers; Wrexham; Peterborough United |

	A	G
1990/91	5	0
1991/92	4	0
1992/93	15	0
1993/94	3	0
Total	**27**	**0**

⚽ RYAN JOSEPH GIGGS Forward

| Born | Cardiff 29 November 1973 |
| Clubs | Manchester United |

	A	G
1990/91	2	1
1991/92	38	4
1992/93	41	9

1993/94	38	13
1994/95	29	1
1995/96	33	11
1996/97	26	3
1997/98	29	8
1998/99	24	3
1999/2000	30	6
2000/01	31	5
2001/02	25	7
2002/03	36	8
2003/04	33	7
2004/05	32	5
2005/06	27	3
2006/07	30	4
2007/08	31	3
2008/09	28	2
Total	**563**	**103**

☺ NEIL ANTHONY WHITWORTH Defender

Born   Wigan 12 April 1972
Clubs   Wigan Athletic; Manchester United; Preston North End; Barnsley;
        Rotherham United; Blackpool; Kilmarnock; Wigan Athletic; Exeter City

	A	G
1990/91	1	0
Total	1	0

☺ PAUL WRATTEN Midfield

Born   Middlesbrough 29 November 1970
Clubs   Manchester United; Hartlepool United

	A	G
1990/91	2	0
Total	2	0

☺ ANDREI KANCHELSKIS Forward

Born   Kirovograd, Ukraine 23 January 1969
Clubs   Dynamo Kiev; Shakhytor Donetsk (Russia); Manchester United; Everton;
        Fiorentian (Italy); Glasgow Rangers; Manchester City; Southampton;

Al Halil (Saudi Arabia); Dynamo Moscow (Russia);
Saturn Ramenskoye (Russia)

	A	G
1990/91	1	0
1991/92	34	5
1992/93	27	3
1993/94	31	6
1994/95	30	14
Total	**123**	**28**

⚽ PETER BOLESLAW SCHMEICHEL Goalkeeper

Born   Gladsaxe, Denmark 18 November 1963
Clubs   Hvidovre (Denmark); Brondby (Denmark); Manchester United;
        Sporting Lisbon (Portugal); Aston Villa; Manchester City

	A	G
1991/92	40	0
1992/93	42	0
1993/94	40	0
1994/95	32	0
1995/96	36	0
1996/97	36	0
1997/98	32	0
1998/99	34	0
Total	**292**	**0**

⚽ PAUL ANDREW PARKER Defender

Born   West Ham 4 April 1964
Clubs   Fulham; Queen's Park Rangers; Manchester United; Derby County;
        Sheffield United; Chelsea

	A	G
1991/92	26	0
1992/93	31	1
1993/94	40	0
1994/95	2	0
1995/96	6	0
Total	**105**	**1**

⚽ DION DUBLIN Forward

Born	Leicester 22 April 1969
Clubs	Oakham United; Norwich City; Cambridge United; Manchester United; Coventry City; Aston Villa; Millwall; Leicester City; Glasgow Celtic; Norwich City

	A	G
1992/93	7	1
1993/94	8	1
Total	**11**	**2**

⚽ NICHOLAS BUTT Midfield

Born	Manchester 21 January 1975
Clubs	Manchester United; Newcastle United; Birmingham City

	A	G
1992/93	1	0
1993/94	1	0
1994/95	22	1
1995/96	32	2
1996/97	26	5
1997/98	33	3
1998/99	31	2
1999/2000	32	3
2000/01	28	3
2001/02	25	1
2002/03	18	0
2003/04	21	1
Total	**270**	**21**

⚽ ERIC CANTONA Forward

Born	Paris, France 24 May 1966
Clubs	Auxerre; Bordeaux; Marseille; Montpellier; Nimes; (France); Sheffield Wednesday; Leeds United; Manchester United

	A	G
1992/93	22	9
1993/94	34	18
1994/95	21	12
1995/96	30	14

1996/97	36	11
Total	**143**	**64**

⚽ ROY MAURICE KEANE Midfield

Born	Cork 10 August 1971
Clubs	Cobh Ramblers; Nottingham Forest; Manchester United; Glasgow Celtic

	A	G
1993/94	37	5
1994/95	25	2
1995/96	29	6
1996/97	21	2
1997/98	9	2
1998/99	35	2
1999/2000	29	5
2000/01	28	2
2001/02	28	3
2002/03	21	0
2003/04	28	3
2004/05	31	1
2005/06	5	0
Total	**326**	**33**

⚽ BENJAMIN LINDSAY THORNLEY Forward

Born	Bury, Lancashire 21 April 1975
Clubs	Manchester United; Stockport County; Huddersfield Town; Aberdeen; Blackpool; Bury

	A	G
1993/94	1	0
1994/95	0	0
1995/96	1	0
1996/97	1	0
1997/98	5	0
Total	**9**	**0**

⚽ GARY ALEXANDER NEVILLE Defender

Born	Bury, Lancashire 18 February 1975
Clubs	Manchester United

	A	G
1993/94	1	0
1994/95	18	0
1995/96	31	0
1996/97	31	1
1997/98	34	0
1998/99	34	1
1999/2000	22	0
2000/01	32	1
2001/02	34	0
2002/03	26	0
2003/04	30	2
2004/05	22	0
2005/06	25	0
2006/07	24	0
2007/08	0	0
2008/09	16	0
Total	**380**	**5**

☺ COLIN McKEE Forward

Born	Glasgow 22 August 1974
Clubs	Manchester United; Bury; Kilmarnock; Falkirk

	A	G
1993/94	1	0
Total	**1**	**0**

☺ DAVID MAY Defender

Born	Oldham, Lancashire 24 June 1970
Clubs	Blackburn Rovers; Manchester United; Huddersfield Town; Burnley

	A	G
1994/95	19	2
1995/96	16	1
1996/97	29	3
1997/98	9	0
1998/99	6	0
1999/2000	1	0
2000/01	2	0

2001/02	2	0
2002/03	1	0
Total	**85**	**6**

⚽ PAUL SCHOLES Midfield/Forward

Born	Salford 16 November 1974
Clubs	Manchester United

	A	G
1994/95	17	5
1995/96	26	10
1996/97	24	3
1997/98	31	8
1998/99	31	6
1999/2000	31	9
2000/01	32	6
2001/02	35	8
2002/03	33	14
2003/04	28	9
2004/05	31	9
2005/06	20	2
2006/07	30	6
2007/08	24	1
2008/09	21	2
Total	**416**	**98**

⚽ KEITH ROBERT GILLESPIE Forward

Born	Larne, 18 February 1975
Clubs	Manchester United; Wigan Athletic; Newcastle United; Blackburn Rovers; Wigan Athletic; Leicester City; Sheffield United; Charlton Athletic; Bradford City

	A	G
1994/95	9	1
Total	**9**	**1**

⚽ SIMON ITHEL DAVIES Midfield

Born	Winsford 23 April 1974
Clubs	Manchester United; Exeter City; Huddersfield Town; Luton Town; Macclesfield; Rochdale; Bangor City

	A	G
1994/95	5	0
1995/96	6	0
Total	**11**	**0**

⚽ KEVIN WILLIAM PILKINGTON Goalkeeper

Born   Hitchin, Hertfordshire 8 March 1974
Clubs   Manchester United; Rochdale; Rotherham United; Port Vale; Mansfield Town;
          Notts County

	A	G
1994/95	1	0
1995/96	3	0
1996/97	0	0
1997/98	2	0
Total	**6**	**0**

⚽ ANDREW ALEXANDER COLE Forward

Born   Nottingham 15 October 1971
Clubs   Arsenal; Fulham; Bristol City; Newcastle United; Manchester United;
          Blackburn Rovers; Fulham; Manchester City; Portsmouth; Birmingham City;
          Sunderland; Burnley; Nottingham Forest

	A	G
1994/95	18	12
1995/96	34	11
1996/97	20	6
1997/98	33	15
1998/99	32	17
1999/2000	28	19
2000/01	19	9
2001/02	11	4
Total	195	93

⚽ PHILIP JOHN NEVILLE Defender/Midfield

Born   Bury, Lancashire 21 January 1977
Clubs   Manchester United; Everton

	A	G
1994/95	2	0

1995/96	24	0
1996/97	18	0
1997/98	30	1
1998/99	28	0
1999/2000	29	1
2000/01	29	1
2001/02	28	2
2002/03	25	0
2003/04	31	0
2004/05	19	0
Total	**263**	**5**

⚽ DAVID ROBERT JOSEPH BECKHAM Midfield

Born   Leytonstone, Essex 2 May 1975
Clubs   Manchester United; Preston North End; Real Madrid (Spain); LA Galaxy (USA); AC Milan (Italy)

	A	G
1994/95	4	0
1995/96	33	7
1996/97	36	8
1997/98	37	9
1998/99	34	6
1999/2000	31	6
2000/01	31	9
2001/02	28	11
2002/03	31	6
Total	**265**	**62**

⚽ JOHN ANDREW O'KANE Full-back

Born   Nottingham 15 November 1974
Clubs   Manchester United; Bury; Bradford City; Everton; Burnley; Bolton Wanderers; Blackpool

	A	G
1995/96	1	0
1996/97	1	0
Total	**2**	**0**

☻ TERENCE JOHN COOKE Forward

Born   Birmingham 5 August 1976
Clubs   Manchester United; Sunderland; Birmingham City; Wrexham; Manchester City;
            Wigan Athletic; Sheffield Wednesday; Grimsby Town; Sheffield Wednesday;

	A	G
1995/96	4	0
Total	**4**	**0**

☻ WILLIAM PRUNIER Defender

Born   Montreuil, France 14 August 1967
Clubs   Auxerre; Marseille; Bordeaux; (France); Manchester United;
            FC Copenhagen (Denmark); Montpellier (France); Napoli (Italy);
            Courtrai (Belgium); Toulouse (France)

	A	G
1995/96	2	0
Total	**2**	**0**

☻ CHRISTOPHER MARTIN CASPER Defender

Born   Burnley 28 April 1975
Clubs   Manchester United; Bournemouth; Swindon Town; Reading

	A	G
1996/97	2	0
Total	**2**	**0**

☻ JORDI CRUYFF Forward

Born   Amsterdam, Holland 9 February 1974
Clubs   Barcelona (Spain); Manchester United; Celta Vigo (Spain);
            Alaves (Spain); Espanol (Spain)

	A	G
1996/97	16	3
1997/98	5	0
1998/99	5	2
1999/2000	8	3
Total	**34**	**8**

☻ JEAN RONNY JOHNSEN Defender/Midfield

Born   Sandefjord, Norway 10 June 1969

Clubs	Tonsberg; Lyn Oslo; LIllestrom (Norway); Besiktas (Turkey); Manchester United; Aston Villa; Newcastle United		
		A	G
	1996/97	31	0
	1997/98	22	2
	1998/99	22	3
	1999/2000	3	0
	2000/01	11	1
	2001/02	10	1
	Total	**99**	**7**

⚽ KAREL POBORSKY Midfield/Forward

Born	Jindinchuv-Hradec, Czechoslovakia 30 March 1972		
Clubs	Ceske Budejovice; Viktoria Zizkov; Slavia Prague (Czech Republic); Manchester United; Benfica (Portugal); Lazio (Italy); Sparta Prague (Czech Republic)		
		A	G
	1996/97	22	3
	1997/98	10	2
	Total	**32**	**5**

⚽ OLE GUNNAR SOLSKJAER Forward

Born	Kristiansund, Norway 26 February 1973		
Clubs	FK Clausenengen; Molde (Norway); Manchester United		
		A	G
	1996/97	33	18
	1997/98	22	6
	1998/99	19	12
	1999/2000	28	12
	2000/01	31	10
	2001/02	30	17
	2002/03	37	9
	2003/04	13	0
	2004/05	0	0
	2005/06	3	0
	2006/07	19	0
	Total	**235**	**91**

⚽ RAIMOND VAN DER GOUW Goalkeeper

Born   Oldenzaal, Holland 24 March 1963
Clubs   Go Ahead Eagles; Vitesse Arnhem (Holland); Manchester United; West Ham United

	A	G
1996/97	2	0
1997/98	5	0
1998/99	5	0
1999/2000	14	0
2000/01	10	0
2001/02	1	0
Total	**37**	**0**

⚽ MICHAEL CLEGG Full-back

Born   Ashton-under-Lyne 7 July 1977
Clubs   Manchester United; Ipswich Town; Wigan Athletic; Oldham Athletic

	A	G
1996/97	4	0
1997/98	3	0
1998/99	0	0
1999/2000	2	0
Total	**9**	**0**

⚽ EDWARD PAUL 'TEDDY' SHERINGHAM Forward

Born   Highams Park, London 2 April 1966
Clubs   Millwall; Aldershot; Nottingham Forest; Tottenham Hotspur; Manchester United;
        Tottenham Hotspur; Portsmouth; West Ham United; Colchester United

	A	G
1997/98	31	9
1998/99	17	2
1999/2000	27	5
2000/01	29	15
Total	**104**	**31**

⚽ HENNING BERG Defender

Born   Eidswell, Norway 1 September 1969
Clubs   KFUM Oslo; Valerengen; Lillestrom (Norway); Blackburn Rovers;
        Manchester United; Glasgow Rangers

	A	G
1997/98	27	1
1998/99	16	0
1999/2000	22	1
2000/01	1	0
Total	**66**	**2**

⚽ JOHN CHARLES KEYWORTH CURTIS Defender

Born   Nuneaton 3 September 1978
Clubs   Manchester United; Barnsley; Blackburn Rovers; Sheffield United;
Leicester City; Portsmouth; Preston North End; Nottingham Forest

	A	G
1997/98	8	0
1998/99	4	0
1999/2000	1	0
Total	**13**	**0**

⚽ RONALD WALLWORK Midfield

Born   Manchester 10 September 1977
Clubs   Manchester United; Carlisle United; Stockport County; West Bromwich Albion;
Bradford City; Barnsley

	A	G
1997/98	1	0
1998/99	0	0
1999/2000	5	0
2000/01	12	0
2001/02	1	0
Total	**19**	**0**

⚽ ERIK NEVLAND Forward

Born   Stavanger, Norway 10 November 1977
Clubs   Viking Stavanger (Norway); Manchester United; IFK Gothenburg (Sweden);
Viking Stavanger (Norway)

	A	G
1997/98	1	0
Total	**1**	**0**

⚽ WESLEY MICHAEL BROWN Defender

Born   Manchester 13 October 1979
Clubs   Manchester United

	A	G
1997/98	2	0
1998/99	14	0
1999/2000	0	0
2000/01	28	0
2001/02	17	0
2002/03	22	0
2003/04	17	0
2004/05	21	1
2005/06	19	0
2006/07	22	0
2007/08	36	1
2008/09	8	1
Total	**206**	**3**

⚽ PHILIP PATRICK MULRYNE Midfield

Born   Belfast 1 January 1978
Clubs   Manchester United; Norwich City; Cardiff City; Leyton Orient; King's Lynn

	A	G
1997/98	1	0
Total	**1**	**0**

⚽ DANIEL JOHN HIGGINBOTHAM Defender

Born   Manchester 29 December 1978
Clubs   Manchester United; Derby County; Southampton; Stoke City; Sunderland; Stoke City

	A	G
1997/98	1	0
1998/99	0	0
1999/2000	3	0
Total	**4**	**0**

⚽ JAAP STAM Defender

Born   Kampen, Holland 17 July 1972
Clubs   FC Zwolle; Cambour Leeuwarden; Willem II; PSV Eindhoven (Holland);

Manchester United; Lazio (Italy); AC Milan (Italy)

	A	G
1998/99	30	1
1999/2000	33	0
2000/01	15	0
2001/02	1	0
Total	**79**	**1**

⚽ DWIGHT EVERSLEY YORKE Forward

Born   Canaan, Tobago 3 November 1971
Clubs   Signal Hill (Tobago); Aston Villa; Manchester United; Blackburn Rovers;
           Birmingham City; Sydney FC (Australia); Sunderland

	A	G
1998/99	32	18
1999/2000	32	20
2000/01	22	9
2001/02	10	1
Total	**96**	**48**

⚽ JESPER BLOMQVIST Midfield

Born   Tavelsjo, Sweden 5 February 1974
Clubs   Tavelsjo IK; UMEA; IFK Gothenburg (Sweden); AC Milan; Parma (Italy);
           Manchester United; Everton; Charlton Athletic; Djurgarden (Sweden)

	A	G
1998/99	25	1
Total	**25**	**1**

⚽ JONATHAN GREENING Midfield

Born   Scarborough 2 January 1979
Clubs   York City; Manchester United; Middlesbrough; West Bromwich Albion

	A	G
1998/99	3	0
1999/2000	4	0
2000/01	7	0
Total	**14**	**0**

⚽ NICHOLAS CULKIN Goalkeeper

Born   York 6 July 1978
Clubs   York City; Manchester United; Hull City; Bristol Rovers; Livingston;
        Queen's Park Rangers

	A	G
1999/2000	1	0
Total	**1**	**0**

⚽ QUINTON FORTUNE Defender/Midfield

Born   Cape Town, South Africa 21 May 1977
Clubs   Mallorca (Spain); Atletico Madrid (Spain); Manchester United; Bolton Wanderers;
        Sunderland; Sheffield United; Brescia Calcio (Italy);AFC Tubize (Belgium)

	A	G
1999/2000	6	2
2000/01	7	0
2001/02	14	1
2002/03	9	0
2003/04	23	1
2004/05	17	0
Total	**76**	**5**

⚽ MASSIMO TAIBI Goalkeeper

Born   Palermo, Italy 18 February 1970
Clubs   Licata; AC Milan; Como; Calcio; Piancenza; Venezia; Reggina; (Italy);
        Manchester United

	A	G
1999/2000	4	0
Total	**4**	**0**

⚽ MIKAEL SAMY SILVESTRE Defender

Born   Chambray-les-Tours, France 9 August 1977
Clubs   Rennes (France); Inter Milan (Italy); Manchester United; Arsenal

	A	G
1999/2000	31	0
2000/01	30	1
2001/02	35	0
2002/03	34	1

	A	G
2003/04	34	0
2004/05	35	2
2005/06	33	1
2006/07	14	1
2007/08	3	0
Total	**249**	**6**

⚽ MARK ANTHONY WILSON Midfield

Born   Scunthorpe 9 February 1979
Clubs Manchester United; Wrexham; Middlesbrough; Stoke City; Swansea City;
       Sheffield Wednesday; Doncaster Rovers; Livingston; Doncaster Rovers

	A	G
1999/2000	3	0
Total	**3**	**0**

⚽ FABIEN BARTHEZ Goalkeeper

Born   Lavelanet, France 28 June 1971
Clubs Toulouse; Marseille; Monaco; (France); Manchester United; Marseille;
       Nantes (France)

	A	G
2000/01	30	0
2001/02	32	0
2002/03	30	0
Total	**92**	**0**

⚽ LUKE HARRY CHADWICK Midfield

Born   Cambridge 18 November 1980
Clubs Manchester United; Reading; Burnley; West Ham United; Stoke City;
       Norwich City; Milton Keynes Dons

	A	G
2000/01	16	2
2001/02	8	0
2002/03	1	0
Total	**25**	**2**

⚽ DAVID JONATHAN HEALY Forward

Born   Downpatrick 5 August 1979

Clubs	Manchester United; Port vale; Preston North End; Norwich City; Leeds United; Fulham; Sunderland	
	A	G
2000/01	1	0
Total	**1**	**0**

⚽ PAUL STEPHEN RACHUBKA Goalkeeper

Born   San Luis Obispo, California, USA 21 May 1981
Clubs   Manchester United; Oldham Athletic; Charlton Athletic; Huddersfield Town; MK Dons; Northampton Town; Huddersfield Town; Peterborough United; Blackpool

	A	G
2000/01	1	0
Total	**1**	**0**

⚽ ANDREW LEWIS GORAM Goalkeeper

Born   Bury, Lancashire 13 April 1964
Clubs   Oldham Athletic; Hibernian; Glasgow Rangers; Notts County; Sheffield United; Motherwell; Manchester United; Coventry City; Oldham Athletic; Queen of the South

	A	G
2000/01	2	0
Total	**2**	**0**

⚽ MICHAEL JAMES STEWART Midfield

Born   Edinburgh 26 February 1981
Clubs   Manchester United; Royal Antwerp (Belgium); Nottingham Forest; Heart of Midlothian; Hibernian

	A	G
2000/01	3	0
2001/02	3	0
2002/03	1	0
Total	**7**	**0**

⚽ BOJAN DJORDJIC Midfield

Born   Belgrade, Serbia 6 February 1982
Clubs   Bromma Pojkarna (Sweden); Manchester United; Sheffield Wednesday;

Glasgow Rangers; Plymouth Argyle; AIK (Sweden)

	A	G
2000/01	1	0
Total	**1**	**0**

⚽ RUTGERUS JOHANNES MARTINUS 'RUUD' VAN NISTELROOY Forward

Born   Oss, Holland 1 July 1976

Clubs   Den Bosch; Heerenveen; PSV Eindhoven (Holland); Manchester United;
Real Madrid (Spain)

	A	G
2001/02	31	23
2002/03	34	25
2003/04	32	20
2004/05	17	6
2005/06	35	21
Total	**160**	**95**

⚽ JUAN SEBASTIAN VERON Midfield

Born   Buenos Aires, Argentina 9 March 1975

Clubs   Estudiantes; Boca Juniors (Argentina); Sampdoria; Parma;
Lazio (Italy); Manchester United; Chelsea; Inter Milan (Italy);
Estudiantes (Argentina)

	A	G
2001/02	26	5
2002/03	25	2
Total	**51**	**7**

⚽ ROY ERIC CARROLL Goalkeeper

Born   Enniskillen 30 September 1977

Clubs   Hull City; Wigan Athletic; Manchester United; West Ham United;
Derby County

	A	G
2001/02	7	0
2002/03	10	0
2003/04	6	0
2004/05	26	0
Total	**49**	**0**

⚽ LAURENT BLANC Defender

Born   Ales, France 19 November 1965
Clubs   Montpellier (France); Napoli (Italy); Nimes; St Etienne; Auxerre (France);
          Barcelona (Spain); Marseille (France); Inter Milan (Italy); Manchester United

	A	G
2001/02	29	1
2002/03	18	0
Total	**48**	**1**

⚽ JOHN FRANCIS O'SHEA Defender

Born   Waterford 30 April 1981
Clubs   Waterford United; Bournemouth; Manchester United

	A	G
2001/02	9	0
2002/03	32	0
2003/04	33	2
2004/05	23	2
2005/06	34	1
2006/07	32	4
2007/08	28	0
2008/09	30	0
Total	**221**	**9**

⚽ DIEGO FORLAN Forward

Born   Montevideo, Uruguay 19 May 1979
Clubs   Penarol (Uruguay); Independiente (Argentina); Manchester United;
          Villareal; Atletico Madrid (Spain)

	A	G
2001/02	13	0
2002/03	25	6
2003/04	24	4
Total	**62**	**10**

⚽ RIO GAVIN FERDINAND Defender

Born   Peckham, London 7 November 1978
Clubs   West Ham United; Bournemouth; Leeds United; Manchester United

	A	G
2002/03	28	0
2003/04	20	0
2004/05	31	0
2005/06	37	3
2006/07	33	1
2007/08	35	2
2008/09	24	0
Total	**208**	**6**

⚽ DANIEL ADAM PUGH Midfield

Born   Manchester 19 October 1982
Clubs   Manchester United; Leeds United; Preston North End

	A	G
2002/03	1	0
Total	**1**	**0**

⚽ LEE PAUL ROCHE Defender

Born   Bolton 28 October 1980
Clubs   Manchester United; Wrexham; Burnley; Wrexham

	A	G
2002/03	1	0
Total	**1**	**0**

⚽ KIERAN EDWARD RICHARDSON Midfield

Born   Greenwich, London 21 October 1984
Clubs   Manchester United; West Bromwich Albion; Sunderland

	A	G
2002/03	2	0
2003/04	0	0
2004/05	2	0
2005/06	22	1
2006/07	15	1
Total	**41**	**2**

⚽ RICARDO LOPEZ Goalkeeper

Born   Madrid, Spain 31 December 1971

Clubs   Atletico Madrid; Real Valladolid (Spain); Manchester United; Racing Santander (Spain)

	A	G
2002/03	1	0
Total	**1**	**0**

⚽ TIMOTHY MATTHEW HOWARD Goalkeeper

Born   North Brunswick, New Jersey, USA 6 March 1979
Clubs   New York; New Jersey Metrostars (USA); Manchester United; Everton

	A	G
2003/04	32	0
2004/05	12	0
2005/06	1	0
Total	**45**	**0**

⚽ ERIC DANIEL DJEMBA DJEMBA Midfield

Born   Douala, Cameroon 4 May 1981
Clubs   Nantes (France); Manchester United; Aston Villa; Burnley

	A	G
2003/04	15	0
2004/05	5	0
Total	**20**	**0**

⚽ DON SANTOS AVEIRO 'CRISTIANO' RONALDO Forward

Born   Madeira, Portugal 5 February 1985
Clubs   Sporting Lisbon (Portugal); Manchester United

	A	G
2003/04	29	4
2004/05	33	5
2005/06	33	9
2006/07	34	17
2007/08	34	31
2008/09	33	18
Total	**196**	**84**

⚽ JOSE PEREIRA KLEBERSON Midfield

Born   Urai, Brazil 19 June 1979
Clubs   Nichika; PSTC; Atletico Paranaense (Brazil); Manchester United;

Besiktas (Turkey); Flamengo (Brazil)

	A	G
2003/04	12	2
2004/05	8	0
Total	**20**	**2**

⚽ DAVID BELLION Forward

Born   Sevres, France 27 November 1982
Clubs   Cannes (France); Sunderland; Manchester United; West Ham United; Nice; Bordeaux (France)

	A	G
2003/04	14	2
2004/05	10	2
Total	**24**	**4**

⚽ DARREN BARR FLETCHER Midfield

Born   Dalkeith 1 February 1984
Clubs   Manchester United

	A	G
2003/04	22	0
2004/05	18	3
2005/06	27	1
2006/07	24	3
2007/08	16	0
2008/09	23	3
Total	**130**	**10**

⚽ LOUIS SAHA Forward

Born   Paris, France 8 August 1978
Clubs   Metz (France); Newcastle United; Fulham; Manchester United; Everton

	A	G
2003/04	12	7
2004/05	14	1
2005/06	19	7
2006/07	24	8
2007/08	17	5
Total	**86**	**28**

⚽ LIAM WILLIAM PETER MILLER Midfield

Born   Cork 13 February 1981
Clubs   Ballincollig AFC; Glasgow Celtic; Manchester United; Leeds United; Sunderland

	A	G
2004/05	8	0
2005/06	1	0
Total	**9**	**0**

⚽ ALAN SMITH Forward

Born   Rothwell, Yorkshire 28 October 1980
Clubs   Leeds United; Manchester United; Newcastle United

	A	G
2004/05	31	6
2005/06	21	1
2006/07	9	0
Total	**61**	**7**

⚽ JONATHAN MICHAEL PAUL SPECTOR Full-back

Born   Chicago, Illinois (USA) 1 March 1986
Clubs   Chicago Sockers (USA); Manchester United; Charlton Athletic; West Ham United

	A	G
2004/05	3	0
Total	**3**	**0**

⚽ GABRIEL IVAN HEINZE Defender

Born   Crespo, Argentina 19 April 1978
Clubs   Newell's Old Boys (Argentina); Real Valladolid (Spain); Sporting Lisbon
         (Portugal); Paris St Germain (France); Manchester United; Real Madrid (Spain)

	A	G
2004/05	26	1
2005/06	4	0
2006/07	22	0
Total	**52**	**1**

⚽ WAYNE MARK ROONEY Forward

Born   Liverpool 24 October 1985
Clubs   Everton; Manchester United

	A	G
2004/05	29	11
2005/06	36	16
2006/07	35	14
2007/08	27	12
2008/09	30	12
Total	**157**	**65**

☺ EDWIN VAN DER SAR Goalkeeper

Born   Leiden, Holland 29 October 1970
Clubs   Noordwijk; Ajax; (Holland); Juventus (Italy); Fulham; Manchester United

	A	G
2005/06	38	0
2006/07	32	0
2007/08	29	0
2008/09	33	0
Total	**132**	**0**

☺ JI-SUNG PARK Midfield

Born   Seoul, South Korea 25 February 1981
Clubs   Kyoto Purple Sanga (Japan); PSV Eindhoven (Holland); Manchester United

	A	G
2005/06	34	1
2006/07	14	5
2007/08	12	1
2008/09	25	2
Total	**85**	**9**

☺ PHILIP ANTHONY BARDSLEY Full-back

Born   Salford 28 June 1985
Clubs   Manchester United; Burnley; Glasgow Rangers; Aston Villa;
          Sheffield United; Sunderland

	A	G
2005/06	8	0
Total	**8**	**0**

⚽ GERARD PIQUE Defender

Born   Barcelona, Spain 2 February 1987
Clubs   Manchester United; Barcelona

	A	G
2005/06	3	0
2006/07	0	0
2007/08	9	0
Total	**12**	**0**

⚽ GIUSEPPE ROSSI Forward

Born   Clifton, New Jersey, USA 1 February 1987
Clubs   Manchester United; Newcastle United; Villareal (Spain)

	A	G
2005/06	5	1
Total	**5**	**1**

⚽ PATRICE EVRA Defender

Born   Dakar, Senegal 15 May 1981
Clubs   AS Monaco (France); Manchester United

	A	G
2005/06	11	0
2006/07	24	1
2007/08	33	0
2008/09	28	0
Total	**96**	**1**

⚽ NEMANJA VIDIC Defender

Born   Subotica, Serbia 21 October 1981
Clubs   Red Star Belgrade; Spartak Subotica (Serbia); Spartak Moscow (Russia); Manchester United

	A	G
2005/06	11	0
2006/07	25	3
2007/08	32	1
2008/09	34	4
Total	**102**	**8**

⚽ DARRON GIBSON Midfielder

Born   Derry, Northern Ireland 25 October 1987
Clubs   Manchester United; Royal Antwerp (loan); Manchester United;
           Wolverhampton Wanderers (loan); Manchester United

	A	G
2005/06	0	0
2006/07	0	0
2007/08	0	0
2008/09	15	3
Total	**15**	**3**

⚽ MICHAEL CARRICK Midfield

Born   Wallsend 28 July 1981
Clubs   West Ham United; Swindon Town; Birmingham City; Tottenham Hotspur;
           Manchester United

	A	G
2006/07	33	3
2007/08	31	2
2008/09	27	4
Total	**92**	**9**

⚽ TOMASZ KUSZCZAK Goalkeeper

Born   Krosno Odrzanskie, Poland 20 March 1982
Clubs   Hertha Berlin (Germany); West Bromwich Albion; Manchester United

	A	G
2006/07	6	0
2007/08	9	0
2008/09	4	0
Total	**19**	**0**

⚽ HENRIK EDWARD LARSSON Forward

Born   Helsingborg, Sweden 20 September 1971
Clubs   Hogaborgs BK; Helsingborg IF (Sweden); Feyenoord (Holland); Glasgow Celtic;
           Barcelona (Spain); Helsingborg IF (Sweden); Manchester United

	A	G
2006/07	7	1
Total	**7**	**1**

⚽ CHRISTOPHER MARK EAGLES Midfield

Born   Hemel Hempstead 19 November 1985
Clubs   Manchester United; Watford; Sheffield Wednesday; NEC Nijimegen (Holland)

	A	G
2006/07	2	1
2007/08	4	0
Total	**6**	**0**

⚽ KIERAN CHRISTOPHER LEE Full-back

Born   Stalybridge 22 June 1988
Clubs   Manchester United

	A	G
2006/07	1	0
2007/08	0	0
Total	**1**	**0**

⚽ DONG FANGZHUO Forward

Born   Dalian, China 23 January 1985
Clubs   Dalian Saidelong; Dalian Shide (China); Manchester United;
        Royal Antwerp (Belgium)

	A	G
2006/07	1	0
2007/08	0	0
Total	**1**	**0**

⚽ JONNY EVANS Defender

Born   Belfast, Northern Ireland 2 January 1988
Clubs   Manchester United; Royal Antwerp; Sunderland (loan); Manchester United;
        Sunderland (loan); Manchester United

	A	G
2006/07	0	0
2007/08	0	0
2008/09	17	0
Total	**17**	**0**

⚽ DAVID PETER GRAY Defender

Born   Edinburgh, Scotland 4 May 1988

Clubs	Manchester United; Royal Antwerp (loan); Manchester United; Crewe Alexandra (loan); Manchester United; Plymouth Argyle (loan)	
	A	G
2006/07	0	0
2007/08	0	0
2008/09	1	0
Total	**1**	**0**

⚽ LUIS CARLOS ALMEIDA DA CUNHA 'NANI' Midfield

Born	Praia, Cape Verde 17 November 1987	
Clubs	Sporting Club Portugal; Manchester United;	
	A	G
2007/08	26	3
2008/09	12	1
Total	**38**	**4**

⚽ CARLOS ALBERTO TEVEZ Forward

Born	Buenos Aires, Argentina 5 February 1984	
Clubs	Boca Juniors; Corinthians (Brazil); West Ham United; Manchester United	
	A	G
2007/08	34	14
2008/09	29	5
Total	**63**	**19**

⚽ OWEN HARGREAVES Defender/Midfield

Born	Calgary, Alberta, Canada 20 January 1981	
Clubs	Bayern Munich; Manchester United	
	A	G
2007/08	23	2
2008/09	2	0
Total	**25**	**2**

⚽ FRAIZER CAMPBELL Forward

Born	Huddersfield, Yorkshire 13 September 1987	
Clubs	Manchester United; Hull City; Tottenham Hotspur	
	A	G
2007/08	1	0

| | 2008/09 | 1 | 0 |
| | **Total** | **2** | **0** |

⚽ ANDERSON LUIS DE ABREU OLIVEIRA Midfield

Born   Port Alegre, Brazil 13 April 1988
Clubs   Gremio (Brazil); FC Porto (Portugal); Manchester United

		A	G
	2007/08	24	0
	2008/09	17	0
	Total	**41**	**0**

⚽ DANIEL SIMPSON Defender

Born   Salford 4 January 1987
Clubs   Manchester United; Royal Antwerp (Belgium); Sunderland; Ipswich Town

		A	G
	2007/08	3	0
	2008/09	8	0
	Total	**11**	**0**

⚽ BENJAMIN ANTHONY FOSTER Goalkeeper

Born   Leamington Spa 3 April 1983
Clubs   Racing Club Warwick; Stoke City; Kidderminster Harriers; Wrexham;
           Manchester United; Watford; Manchester United

		A	G
	2007/08	1	0
	2008/09	9	0
	Total	**10**	**0**

⚽ DIMITAR BERBATOV Striker

Born   Blagoevgrad 30 January 1981
Clubs   CSKA Sofia; Bayer Leverkusen; Tottenham Hotspur; Manchester United

		A	G
	2008/09	42	14
	Total	**42**	**14**

⚽ ZORAN TO?I?Winger

Born   Zrenjanin 28 April 1987

Clubs	Budu?nost BD; Banat Zrenjanin; Partizan; Manchester United		
		A	G
	2008/09	2	0
	Total	**2**	**0**

⚽ DANNY WELBECK Forward

Born	Longsight, Manchester 26 November 1990		
Clubs	Manchester United		
		A	G
	2008/09	2	1
	Total	**2**	**1**

⚽ FÁBIO PEREIRA DA SILVA Left-Back

Born	Petrópolis, Rio de Janeiro 9 July 1990		
Clubs	Manchester United		
		A	G
	2008/09	0	0
	Total	**0**	**0**

⚽ RAFAEL PEREIRA DA SILVA Right-Back

Born	Petrópolis, Rio de Janeiro 9 July 1990		
Clubs	Manchester United		
		A	G
	2008/09	16	1
	Total	**16**	**1**

⚽ MATEUS ALBERTO CONTREIRAS GONÇLAVES Striker

Born	Luanda 7 March 1983		
Clubs	Manchester United; Hull City (loan)		
		A	G
	2008/09	3	0
	Total	**3**	**0**

⚽ RODRIGO POSSEBON Midfielder

Born	Sapucaia do Sul, Rio Grand do Sul 13 February 1989		
Clubs	Manchester United		
		A	G

	2008/09	2	0
	Total	**2**	**0**

⚽ THOMAS CLEVERLEY Midfielder

Born	Basingstoke, Hampshire 12 August 1989		
Clubs	Manchester United; Leicester City (loan)		
		A	G
	2008/09	0	0
	Total	**0**	**0**

⚽ JAMES GRANT CHESTER Defender

Born	Warrington, Cheshire 23 January 1989		
Clubs	Manchester United; Peterborough United (loan)		
		A	G
	2008/09	1	0
	Total	**1**	**0**

⚽ BEN AMOS Goalkeeper

Born	Macclesfield, England 10 April 1990		
Clubs	Manchester United		
		A	G
	2008/09	1	0
	Total	**1**	**0**

⚽ FREDERICO MACHEDA Striker

Born	Rome 22 August 1991		
Clubs	Manchester United		
		A	G
	2008/09	5	2
	Total	**5**	**2**

⚽ RICHARD ECKERSLEY Defender

Born	Salford, Manchester 12 March 1989		
Clubs	Manchester United		
		A	G
	2008/09	4	0
	Total	**4**	**0**

TOP TEN PLAYERS' PROFILES

ARTHUR ALBISTON

Arthur Albiston has the unique distinction of having made his FA Cup debut in a Wembley final when, as a 19-year-old, he was called up against Liverpool for the 1977 showpiece. Ninety minutes later, after just one Cup game, he was the proud owner of an FA Cup Winners' medal. It was Stuart Houston who had missed out through injury and though Albiston sportingly offered his winners' medal to him, it was graciously refused.

The big occasion never overawed Albiston, who had made his senior debut for United in front of a 55,000 crowd as the Reds faced Manchester City in a 1974 League Cup game.

A strong, thoughtful defender, Albiston took a couple of seasons to establish himself but after his surprise Cup Final appearance, he became a first team regular. Subsequent FA Cup Final appearances followed in 1979 – Arsenal (lost 2-3) 1983 – Brighton & Hove Albion (won 4-0 after a 2-2 draw) and 1985 – Everton (won 1-0) and he was also in United's 1983 Milk Cup Final team. Following United's defeat of Everton, Albiston became the first United player ever to win three FA Cup Winners' medals.

Capped by Scotland as a schoolboy, he went on to make his full Scottish debut in 1982 against Northern Ireland. By the mid-1980s, he had established himself in the heart of the Scottish defence and went on to collect a total of 14 caps, including a trip to Mexico for the 1986 World Cup Finals.

The Edinburgh-born defender had appeared in 482 League and Cup games for Manchester United when, in 1988, he left Old Trafford to join West Bromwich Albion. His well deserved testimonial against Manchester City was a fitting finale to his United career. After just one season at the Hawthorns, he moved on to Dundee on a free transfer. He later played for Chesterfield, Chester City and Norwegian club Molde before hanging up his boots.

He has since maintained his links with United, working with the boys at the club's school of excellence.

DAVID BECKHAM

One of a number of the famed Manchester United Class of '92 to make the breakthrough to the big time, David Beckham made his first team bow in a League Cup tie at Brighton in September 1992 but then had to wait another two years before his next taste of action. Following a loan spell at Preston North End, he replaced the departed Kanchelskis on the right-hand side of United's midfield, though manager Alex Ferguson reckoned the player's best position was in a more central role.

Possessing excellent vision, he was able to turn defence into attack with a superb range of passes. His first full season in the United side brought him both Championship and FA Cup-Winners' medals – a tremendous achievement for a 21-year-old. The following season he scored the goal of the campaign in the match against Wimbledon, when he chipped the keeper from the halfway line. Promoted to the full England side, he went from strength to strength, especially as a regular scorer of outstanding goals and ended the season as the PFA's Young Player of the Year.

Though every aspect of his life began to dominate the headlines – notably his engagement to 'Posh Spice', Victoria Adams – his form continued to earn rave notices. Thought by many to be a player who would grace the World Cup stage in France '98, he was sent-off against Argentina, effectively limiting England's chances of victory. He returned to England a marked man, and it was feared that he might have to move abroad to escape the fierce hostility shown towards him. However, demonstrating that he had the necessary character to rise above adversity, he was ever-present as United lifted the Premiership title, FA Cup and European Champions League trophy.

However, after his marriage to Victoria Adams, the back pages of the newspapers continued to portray him as either hero or villain. Taking the runners-up spot behind Rivaldo in the 2000 European Footballer of the Year, Beckham continued to juggle his showbiz lifestyle with his career as a professional footballer with great dexterity.

Made captain of England by new coach Sven Göran Eriksson who saw in him qualities that the media had missed, Beckham was instrumental in the nation reaching the World Cup Finals in 2002. He scored some stunning goals, though it was feared that a broken metatarsal would prevent him from playing in the Finals themselves.

Awarded an OBE in the 2003 Queen's Birthday Honours List, he became another superstar to join the exodus to Spain when in the summer of 2004 he signed for Real Madrid. Beckham immediately became a favourite with Real Madrid supporters. It was while with the Spanish giants that he was sent off whilst playing for England against Austria, making him the first England captain to be sent off and the first player to be sent off twice while playing for England!

Football, or soccer as it's known in the USA, delivered a major coup with the signing of David Beckham to the LA Galaxy in January 2007 and though the standard is far from that of the Premiership or La Liga, Beckham won his 100th international cap in England's friendly against France in March 2008.

In January 2009 Beckham, keen to stay match fit and in touch with European football during the MLS close season, joined AC Milan on a loan deal, initially lasting until the start of the MLS season in March. This deal was then extended, with Milan and Galaxy agreeing a unique 'timeshare' arrangement meaning that Beckham would return to Galaxy to play from mid-July until the end of the 2009 MLS soccer season.

JOHNNY BERRY

Affectionately known as 'Digger', Johnny Berry played his early football for Birmingham City and it was his displays for the St Andrew's club against United that prompted Matt Busby to sign him for a fee of £25,000 in 1951.

What an inspired signing he turned out to be. Berry came into the United team as the first wave of the Busby Babes were making their Football League debuts and his experience and willingness to help the youngsters certainly played an important part in their development. Though his United debut against Bolton Wanderers was marked by defeat, he made the right-wing position his own for the next seven seasons or so.

He was a member of the United side that won the League Championship in 1951/52 and was a key member of the side that 1955/56 and 1956/57 titles.

After being capped by England at 'B' level, Berry won four full caps, the first against Argentina in May 1953 – a match that was abandoned with the game goalless after 23 minutes. Johnny Berry was a tremendous performer who would most certainly have added to his tally of international caps had he not played in the same era as Stanley Matthews and Tom Finney.

Many players of Johnny Berry's era found that the hostilities cut short their career but Berry might well have missed out on the game of professional football had it not been for service with the Royal Artillery.

He had impressed a fellow-soldier Fred Harris who was also captain of Birmingham City and so it was at the age of 20 that he took his place in the Blues' line-up, going on to make 103 league appearances.

One of the game's bravest wingmen, he had ironically lost his place in the United side to Kenny Morgans just prior to the Munich disaster. In fact, he didn't play in the Busby Babes' last league game at Arsenal or the second leg of the ill-fated European Cup quarter-final in Belgrade but was in the squad and the aircraft. He suffered grievously with head injuries and spent the rest of that 1957/58 season in hospital. He returned to Old Trafford the following season but with little chance of playing. He returned to his home-town of Aldershot where he went into business in a sports shop with his brother Peter who had appeared for both Crystal Palace and Peterborough United.

Sadly, the crash not only ended his playing career but with a legacy that in all probability shortened his life.

GEORGE BEST

Millions of words have been written about George Best, the unknown from Belfast who became a soccer superstar. He didn't make the Irish schoolboy team because he wasn't strong or big enough but Manchester United's Northern Ireland scout Rob Bishop rated him highly and signed him up for Old Trafford. However, the 15-year-old Best was homesick and he and Eric McMordie caught the night ferry back to Belfast. Upon his return, he settled down under the paternal influence of Matt Busby and even worked afternoons for the Manchester Ship Canal Company just in case football didn't work out!

He made his League debut in September 1963, replacing Ian Moir for the game against West Bromwich Albion. After only 15 League games, Northern Ireland gave him his first cap in the match against Wales at Swansea's Vetch Field.

Best initially played wide on the left but soon began to play in a free attacking role, scoring some of the most stunning goals ever seen at Old Trafford. He won a League Championship medal in 1964/65 and again in 1966/67 but as things began to go wrong, his frustration began to show as he retaliated against harsh treatment to earn himself a reputation for indiscipline, while his taste for wine and women began to undermine his consistency on the field.

No player in the history of British football had until David Beckham been such a centre of attraction as Best, and had to cope with so much attention and publicity. With his long black hair, his beard, the fashionable clothes he wore, models and endorsements, his expensive sports cars, the house he had built for himself outside Manchester, the reputed £30,000 a year in earnings from many sources, he was essentially the product and emblem of the years which followed the abolition of soccer's maximum wage in 1961.

The peak of George Best's career came in 1968 when his team won the European Cup at Wembley, beating Benfica 4-1 after extra-time. One of those goals was a superb effort by Best, who rounded goalkeeper Henrique before coolly rolling the ball into an empty net. It was a euphoric night for Manchester United and for Best, the pinnacles of achievement in a season that saw him gain the titles of English and European Footballer of the Year.

George Best had great natural ability – one of the most gifted footballers you could wish to see. He had great speed and awareness, coupled with fantastic dribbling ability. Strong and brave, he was the complete all-round forward, netting a hat-trick for Northern Ireland in a 5-0 defeat of Cyprus.

He was however, becoming increasingly difficult to manage – missing training and failing to turn up for a match. Just before 1972, United sacked their manager Frank O'Farrell and issued a statement that George Best would remain on the transfer list and would not be selected for Manchester United again. A letter from George Best announcing his retirement crossed with this. He walked out on United several times and played his last game for them on New Year's Day 1974. Four days later he failed to turn up for training yet again and his days at Old Trafford were over.

After a spell with Stockport County, he played in the States for Los Angeles Aztecs before returning to Football League action with Fulham. He later played for Cork before returning to America with San Diego Sockers, Fort Lauderdale Strikers and san Jose Earthquakes. In 1980/81 he played Scottish League football with Hibernian and Motherwell as well as turning out for Glentoran, Bournemouth and several non-League clubs.

After a succession of glamorous girlfriends, a drink problem and several skirmishes with the law, Best served a prison sentence in 1985. Best, who later underwent a liver transplant, was a footballing genius and has gone down in history as one of world football's all-time greats.

He sadly died in November 2005, after a long battle with alcohol-related liver disease.

SHAY BRENNAN

One of the most popular players ever to wear the red shirts of Manchester United, Shay Brennan was born in Manchester of Irish parents. A member of United's FA Youth Cup winning side in 1955, he initially developed as an inside-forward before making a memorable debut at outside-left in the FA Cup tie against Sheffield Wednesday – the first game after the Munich disaster. In that fifth round game, Brennan scored twice in a 3-0 win and stayed in the side for his League debut against Nottingham Forest a few days later.

Brennan also scored in the FA Cup semi-final replay against Fulham but he missed out on a final appearance as the more senior players recovered from the injuries sustained in the crash and so became available for selection. He was also unlucky five years later when United reached the final against Leicester City for after appearing in the first four rounds of the competition he was deposed by the fast-emerging Tony Dunne.

Shay Brennan was a cool-headed full-back, with excellent positional sense and an immense amount of skill on the ball.

He remained a key part of the Manchester United side throughout the sixties and his earlier disappointments were compensated for when he appeared in the 1968 European Cup Final defeat of Benfica. He was also ever-present when the Reds won the League Championship in 1964/65 and won another First Division Championship medal two seasons later.

He made 19 full international appearances for the Republic of Ireland – being the first player born outside of Ireland to represent the boys in green under the parentage rule and in 1961 he represented the FA on two occasions in matches against the RAF and the Army.

After making over 360 first team appearances for United, Brennan became player-manager of Waterford, settling in nearby Tremore where he ran a parcel courier business. In 1986 he suffered a heart attack and successfully came through a heart by-pass operation, whilst the same year, 10,000 attended a benefit match between Shamrock Rovers and United in Dublin.

Sadly, Shay Brennan died suddenly on Wexford Golf Course at the age of 63 in June 2000.

STEVE BRUCE

A strong-tackling, determined defender, Steve Bruce played his early football for Wallsend Youth Club in Newcastle, along with Peter Beardsley but while a number of his team-mates were taken on as juniors locally, Bruce's only offer was from Gillingham. He made his debut for the Kent club against Blackpool, playing in midfield but after half-a-dozen matches, he was switched to a defensive role and soon becoming one of the Third Division's most outstanding players.

Norwich City signed him for £125,000 in the summer of 1984 and though the club were relegated at the end of his first season at Carrow Road, he won a League Cup Winners' medal as Sunderland were beaten 1-0. The following season he helped the Canaries back to the top flight as they won the Second Division Championship. He went on to play in 180 first team games for Norwich until, after a seemingly interminable wrangle with the City board, he joined Manchester United for £800,000 in December 1987.

He marked his United debut with a win against Portsmouth but also broke his nose and conceded a penalty! He soon settled into the heart of the United defence alongside Gary Pallister and in 1990 won an FA Cup-Winners' medal as United beat Crystal Palace. The following year he picked up a European Cup-Winners' Cup medal as the Reds defeated Barcelona. That 1990/91 season, he was United's leading scorer with 20 goals – and though half came from the penalty-spot, he was also extremely dangerous from set-pieces.

He won a League Cup Winners' medal in 1992 before being appointed team captain for the start of the newly formed Premiership. He then proceeded to lead United to three Premiership titles in the space of four years and also had the distinction of helping the Reds to two League and FA Cup doubles in three years.

One of England's best uncapped players, he had scored 51 goals in 414 first team games for United when his first team place began to look under threat. Bruce rejected the prospect of a lucrative testimonial at Old Trafford to join Birmingham City in June 1996, on a free transfer. Appointed club captain by manager Trevor Francis, Bruce fractured an eye socket in March 1997 forcing him to miss nine matches – even so, he was still runner-up in the Blues' Player of the Year competition. Having won the Player of the Year in 1998/99, Bruce left St Andrew's to become player-manager of Sheffield United.

Unsuccessful with the Blades, he managed Huddersfield and Wigan briefly before taking charge at Crystal Palace. After some controversy, he returned to Birmingham in 2001, this time as manager and in his first season in charge, took the club into the Premiership. He has since managed Wigan Athletic and in June 2009 took charge of Sunderland. There are some who would love him to manage Manchester United one day.

MARTIN BUCHAN

Martin Buchan stood alone as Manchester United's most influential player for more than a decade following his arrival at Old Trafford from Aberdeen in March 1972.

Buchan's independence showed at a very early age when he went to a rugby-playing school in his native Aberdeen. He refused to play the sport and instead joined a Boys Brigade soccer team. When he had turned 17, Aberdeen invited him to join them full-time and follow in the footsteps of his father who had played for the Dons just after the Second World War.

During his time at Pittodrie, Buchan played under 23 and full international football for Scotland, won a Scottish Cup medal and had been voted Scottish Footballer of the Year.

United boss Frank O'Farrell paid £125,000 for Buchan's services, and rarely have the Old Trafford club struck a better bargain. Buchan settled in extremely quickly and began turning in the classy displays that became his trademark. However, United were a struggling side and a couple of seasons later, they were relegated to the Second Division. By now, Buchan was United's captain and he led them back to the top flight at the first time of asking.

It was during the next five seasons or so that Martin Buchan reached his peak, forming two very effective central defensive partnerships, first with Brian Greenhoff and then fellow Scot Gordon McQueen. A firm tackler, Buchan also read the game well but his greatest asset was undoubtedly his terrific speed.

He was a man of principles with an uncompromising attitude which occasionally bordered on the eccentric – turning up in a collar and tie and blazer for a journey when the rest of the team and the manager turned up in shorts and summer wear. Even so, he expected those around him to meet his own high standards and once famously cuffed winger Gordon Hill round the ear because he had, in his view as skipper, failed to fulfil his defensive duties!

He took United to Wembley three times and led the team to their notable FA Cup final victory over Liverpool in 1977. In that game despite not being fully fit, Buchan completely snuffed out the threat of Kevin Keegan as United ran out 2-1 winners.

During the early 1980s, Martin Buchan began to face increasing fitness problems and in 1983 he moved on to play for Oldham Athletic. He had been at Boundary Park for just one season when injury forced his retirement. He later had a spell as manager of Burnley but it was a short-lived attempt and after working for a sports manufacturer, he became an adviser with the PFA.

ROGER BYRNE

One of the most accomplished defenders in football history, Roger Byrne started out as a wing-half and was converted to a left-winger – the position he played for United's reserves – before making his Football League debut at left-back in the match against Liverpool at Anfield in the 1951/52 season. It was the first time he had ever worn the No.3 shirt!

That season, United won the Championship and Byrne was so impressive that he kept his place in the side until six matches from the end of the campaign. Then after a couple of defeats, Matt Busby opted for experiment and Byrne found himself back in his former position of left-wing. He responded with seven goals in six games as the Reds romped to the League Championship without losing another game.

The following season, he asked for a transfer because he didn't like playing on the wing but was soon returned to the left-back spot. It was obvious that he had found his true position, though his ability to support his forwards remained one of his special qualities. He went on to play the same role for England in 33 consecutive internationals from his debut in 1954 until his death at Munich.

Byrne replaced Johnny Carey as United captain in 1954. He was a natural leader, a father figure – very much respected by the Busby Babes. He led United to consecutive League Championships in 1955/56 and 1956/57 and to the FA Cup Final in this latter season but their hopes of the 'double' were dashed by Aston Villa.

After that defeat, Byrne felt able to comment cheerfully 'Never mind, we'll be back next year'. With hindsight it was a poignant remark as of course the Reds bravely returned to Wembley in 1958 but Byrne, killed at Munich, did not.

Roger Byrne was a player who would have stood out in any company, in any era. Some eight months after losing his life in the carnage at Munich, Byrne's wife, Joy, gave birth to their son – christened Roger in loving memory.

ERIC CANTONA

Eric Cantona holds a special place in the hearts of all Manchester United supporters. The fans hailed him as *Le Dieu*, the God who led their team to the promised land of the League Championship after 26 frustrating years without winning the title.

Having played for Auxerre, Martigues, Marseille, Montpellier and Nimes in his native France, Eric Cantona's career was going nowhere significant except to achieve notoriety as the enfant terrible of French football! He had virtually to flee his own country in order to find another club willing to take him on and even when he arrived in England, it proved difficult.

It hadn't worked out for the Frenchman at Sheffield Wednesday, where he had a brief trial, and despite helping Leeds United to the League Championship, the Yorkshire club's manager Howard Wilkinson clearly didn't rate his work-rate or contribution to their success very highly, or he wouldn't have sold him to United for a mere £1.2 million.

At Old Trafford, it was a completely different story as everything fell into place. As soon as he pulled on the United shirt midway through the 1992/93 season, the team was transformed and they lost only two games after the turn of the year on their way to the inaugural Premiership title.

One of the world's most gifted footballers, Cantona strutted proudly on to the United stage, helping the Reds follow up their title success with the hallowed League and FA Cup double the following season. There might well have been a third successive title but for the Frenchman's eight-month ban after attacking a lout who had goaded him in the match against Crystal Palace at Selhurst Park in January 1995. Even Alex Ferguson thought it would be impossible for him to resume his Premiership career after this episode but the player expressed an interest in staying and the manager supported him.

The upshot was yet another Premiership title with Cantona's goals winning match after match as Newcastle's vast lead was steadily overhauled. During the course of that 1995/96 season, Cantona was made United captain and it was he who scored the only goal of that season's FA Cup Final as Everton were beaten 1-0. The following season his form for the first time since his arrival, began to falter. A week after leading United to the 1996/97 Premiership title, Cantona announced his retirement.

The popular Frenchman was just 31 when he left Old Trafford, eventually settling in Barcelona after retiring from all but beach football and trying his hand as an actor. He achieved success on the big screen in 2009, playing himself in Ken Loach's acclaimed film *Looking for Eric.*

JOHNNY CAREY

The undisputed architect of Manchester United's 'second coming' in the years after World War Two was Matt Busby, but his right-hand man and representative on the pitch was Johnny Carey.

The genial Irishman had an illustrious playing career at club and international level which was followed by a successful but largely under-rated series of managerial appointments. Above all else though, Carey had an unrivalled reputation for sportsmanship, which won the respect of team-mates and opponents and made him a natural choice as captain.

Carey joined United from Dublin club St James's Gate in November 1936 for just £250. He was spotted by United's chief scout at the time, Louis Rocca, who had gone to watch another player. It was allegedly only Carey's third game of football but Rocca was so keen that the 17-year-old was signed before he even had time to take off his boots! In 1937/38 he helped United win promotion to the First Division and appeared in 53 games before the war intervened. After army service, he returned to a bomb-devastated Old Trafford and began a seven-year run with the first of Busby's great sides.

He captained United's 1948 FA Cup winning team and the one which finally lifted the League Championship in 1951/52 after several near misses. By the time he retired in 1953, Carey had made 344 appearances and scored 18 goals for United.

He was also capped 29 times by the Republic of Ireland – including leading his country to a famous 2-0 win over England at Goodison Park in 1949 – and played seven times for Northern Ireland. Carey also captained the Rest of Europe against Great Britain in 1947 and was voted Footballer of the Year in 1949 and Sportsman of the Year in 1950.

Carey was a man so versatile that he figured in nine different positions for the Reds, ten if you include the occasion he pulled on the goalkeeper's jersey when Jack Crompton was taken ill at an away match. He was also versatile on the international stage, appearing in seven different positions for the Republic of Ireland.

After hanging up his boots, he could have stayed at Old Trafford in a coaching capacity but he chose to move into management with Blackburn Rovers. At Ewood Park, Carey took Rovers into the First Division and this success led to his appointment as Everton manager in 1958. This was the one club where he failed to make an impact. From Merseyside he went to Brisbane Road and guided Leyton Orient into the top flight for the first and only time. He then had five seasons in charge of Nottingham Forest, leading them to runners-up spot in the First Division in 1966/67.

He left football for a textile machine company and ended his working days in the Treasurer's Office of Trafford Borough Council. His retirement was spent in Bramall, Cheshire, where he could indulge in his passion for golf and make regular visits to his beloved Old Trafford.

BOBBY CHARLTON

Manchester United gave Bobby Charlton his debut against Charlton Athletic at Old Trafford on 6 October 1956 and he scored twice in a 4-2 win. Even so, Matt Busby felt that the young striker needed time to mature. Yet only 14 months later he was caught up in the Munich air crash, being thrown some 50 yards and escaping with just a deep cut to his head.

After his return to Old Trafford, it didn't take him long to reach the footballing heights, for within a little over two months he made his international debut against Scotland, marking the occasion with a spectacular goal. By 1966 and the World Cup Finals in England, Charlton's skills had reached their full maturity. He opened England's scoring with a typical long-distance blast and went on to score some thrilling goals in the tournament including both goals in England's 2-1 semi-final win over Portugal. At the end of that season, he won both the Footballer of the Year and the European players' awards.

The nephew of the legendary Newcastle United centre-forward Jackie Milburn, Bobby Charlton joined United straight from school and was a member of the sides that won the FA Youth Cup in 1953/54, 1954/55 and 1955/56. In his first full season of 1958/59 he scored 28 goals in 38 League games and helped the Reds beat Leicester City in the 1963 FA Cup Final. Charlton was also a key figure in the club's League Championship successes of 1964/65 and 1966/67. In May 1968 he scored two goals in the emotionally charged European Cup Final against Benfica at Wembley as United won 4-1.

After 106 caps and 49 goals, his international career ended in Mexico in dramatic fashion. He was substituted in order to keep him fresh for the semi-finals as England led West Germany 2-0, but it wasn't to be, the Germans running out winners 3-2.

He pulled on a Manchester United shirt for the last time at Stamford Bridge in 1973, setting appearance records for both club and country – his tally for United being 247 goals in 754 League and Cup games.

Charlton joined Preston North End as player-manager but didn't have the same success off the pitch as he'd enjoyed on it and he duly retired. He was an active director of Wigan Athletic, whom he managed for a brief spell at the end of the 1982/83 season, before establishing the famous Bobby Charlton soccer schools for children.

Knighted in 1994 for his services to football, he has helped make Manchester United the most famous club in the world and was without doubt one of the most talented and popular footballers of all time.

STEVE COPPELL

Steve Coppell was studying economics at Liverpool University when Tranmere Rovers rated him highly enough to place him as an amateur in their Third Division side. He caught the eye of former Liverpool boss Bill Shankly who recommended him to Manchester United. The Old Trafford club's scouts Johnny Carey and Jimmy Murphy both had a look at the 18-year-old winger and Tommy Docherty did the rest, signing him for £40,000 with another £20,000 to come after 20 League appearances.

Coppell arrived at Old Trafford in March 1975, just in time to help the Reds clinch promotion back to the First Division. Back in the top flight, Coppell quickly established himself as one of United's key players and progressed to international level almost immediately, appearing once for the England under-23 side before making his full debut against Italy in November 1977.

Able to wriggle past defenders, race to the line and send over a perfect cross, he could also chase back and provide cover for his defenders. His efforts at United were rewarded with an FA Cup Winners' medal in 1977 as the Reds beat Liverpool 2-1.

His exhilarating football for United in seasons 1975/76 and 1976/77 when he formed an exciting wing tandem with Gordon Hill became more subdued in later seasons when some defenders worked out how to combat his direct running. He switched to a more central midfield role where he was an ever-present for four seasons – his work rate, determination and overall contribution to the team effort were immense.

Steve Coppell was noted for his all-action never-say-die attitude but his career was brought to an early end by a tackle from the Hungarian defender Joseph Toth at Wembley in 1981. He struggled on for another 14 months, producing some of his best-ever football and undergoing three operations, but there was no way back. He was able to play in the first four games of the 1982 World Cup Finals but the problems flared up again in the match against West Germany and though he played in a further two games for England, he subsequently retired on medical advice.

He was soon snapped up to become the Football League's youngest manager when he was appointed at Crystal Palace. A former chairman of the PFA, has also served as chief executive of the League Managers Association. Coppell has manager Brentford, Manchester City and Brighton and Hove Albion as well as four different periods in charge at Selhurst Park but is now manager of Reading, whom he led into the Premiership in 2005/06.

PAT CRERAND

It was often said that when Pat Crerand played well, Manchester United played well. A midfield playmaker, it was the Scot's ability to create openings that prompted United boss Sir Matt Busby to bring him down from Parkhead for a fee of £56,000 in February 1963.

Having joined Celtic from Duntocher Hibs in 1957, he soon won a place in the Parkhead club's side and during his time with the Hoops won 11 of his 16 full international caps for Scotland. He also represented the Scottish League and appeared in the 1961 Scottish Cup Final which Celtic lost 2-0 to Dunfermline Athletic after a replay.

An utter gentleman off the park, Pat Crerand often had a formidable temper in the heat of the battle. Whilst with Celtic, he was ordered off playing for Scotland against Czechoslovakia in Bratislava in May 1961 for an alleged head-butt and was involved in the fracas against Uruguay at Hampden a year later, when an unidentified Scotland player punched the referee in a melee!

Within months of his arrival at Old Trafford, Crerand had won an FA Cup-Winners' medal after the Reds beat Leicester City 3-1 – a perfect pass from the Scotsman enabled Law to score the first goal with Herd scoring the other two.

Crerand was a thoughtful player with a firm belief in attacking, constructive football; he initiated numerous attacks with long, shrewd passes. His strong compact build gave him scope to tackle swiftly and firmly – and began to give United a more balanced look. Any lack of pace was more than compensated for by his superb distribution skills. 'Paddy' Crerand was an architect, sweeping out accurate crossfield passes of 40 and 50 yards to his forwards.

Along with Bobby Charlton and Nobby Stiles, he formed the midfield that drove Manchester United to victory in the European Cup. He also went on to collect two League Championship medals in 1964/65 and 1966/67, his creative skills being a big factor behind United's success throughout the 1960s. After United's 4-3 win at Maine Road in the final game of the 1970/71 season, he decided to retire. He had played in 392 first team games for the Reds and though he only scored 15 goals, he made many more.

He then joined United's coaching staff before, in January 1973 becoming the club's assistant-manager. He left Old Trafford in July 1976 to become manager at Northampton Town, where he stayed for six months before leaving the game to run a public house in Altrincham.

TONY DUNNE

Tony Dunne was a centre-forward in his junior days in Dublin with St Finbar's and Tara United. He then joined Shelbourne but a few weeks after winning an FAI Cup Winners' medal in April 1960, he was on his way to Manchester United for a knock-down price of £5,000.

He worked his way up through the ranks at Old Trafford before claiming a regular first team spot in place of Noel Cantwell midway through the 1961/62 season. That breakthrough signalled the beginning of his career as one of the greatest full-backs the game has ever seen.

With the Republic of Ireland using Noel Cantwell's physical presence at centre-forward, Dunne won the first of his 33 international caps against Austria in Dublin in April 1962. In his early days with the Republic, he played right-back but his best performances at national level came when he was paired with his United team-mate Shay Brennan. He was an important player in the Irish team which narrowly missed out on qualification for the 1966 World Cup Finals. The pinnacle of Dunne's international career came three years later when he was appointed captain of the Republic of Ireland for the first time. The honour came shortly after he had been named Ireland's Player of the Year.

Tony Dunne had 13 seasons at Old Trafford, during which he turned out for he Reds in 530 League and Cup games. He picked up League Championship medals in 1964/65 and 1966/67, an FA Cup Winners' medal after United's 3-1 victory over Leicester City in 1963 and a European Cup Winners' medal in 1968. This match, where the Reds defeated Portuguese champions Benfica 4-1 after extra-time is regarded by football pundits as one of the greatest displays of Dunne's career.

In April 1973, Tony Dunne was one of six players – including Denis Law – to be freed by United boss Tommy Docherty and the following August he was transferred to Bolton Wanderers. In five seasons at Burnden Park, Dunne played in 192 League and Cup games. In his final season in the Football League, 1977/78, he won a Second Division Championship medal with the Wanderers.

He then jetted off to the United States to play for Detroit Express in the NASL. Tony Dunne, who still follows the fortunes of both United and the Wanderers, manages the golf driving range he built in Altrincham shortly after hanging up his boots.

DUNCAN EDWARDS

Snatched from under the noses of several Midlands clubs, Duncan Edwards began his career with Manchester United. Once at Old Trafford he soon impressed, making an immediate impact in the newly launched FA Youth Cup in 1952/53. He played a big part in helping United establish themselves as the masters of the Youth Cup, as they won the competition for five successive seasons following its inception – Edwards playing in the first three.

United gave him his League debut against Cardiff City at Old Trafford on 4 April 1953 at the tender age of 16 years and 185 days. United lost 4-1 and he didn't play again that season, but the following year he strode majestically into action as Matt Busby unveiled his Busby Babes.

He played superbly as the youthful Reds won the League Championship in the successive seasons of 1955/56 and 1956/57 and scored in United's remarkable 5-4 First Division win at Arsenal just before the team flew out to Belgrade for their European Cup quarter-final against Red Star and the fateful refuelling stop at Munich.

Duncan Edwards was the youngest-ever England player when he was given his first cap against Scotland in April 1955 at the age of 18 years 183 days – a match England won 7-2. After England beat West Germany 3-1 in the Olympic Stadium in Berlin in 1956, he became known as 'Boom Boom' on account of the power he packed into his shots. Receiving the ball on the left of his own penalty area from keeper Reg Matthews, he beat one man and advanced to the halfway line. He beat another, then three more inside the German half and then, from fully 30 yards out, he hit a left-footer into the roof of the net like a rocket!

'Big Dunc' was the golden youth who could well have become the greatest soccer immortal of them all had his career not been cut short scarcely after it had begun. The Munich Air Crash in February 1958 not only crushed the might of a fine Manchester United side but denied supporters the world over the opportunity of watching this Black Country boy so dedicated to the game he loved. After 15 days fighting as valiantly for his life as he had fought on a football field, he died aged only 21.

RIO FERDINAND

A consummate central defender who possesses strength in the air and neat skills on the ground, he began his career with West Ham United, making his Hammers debut against Sheffield Wednesday in the final game of the 1995/96 season.

Following a loan spell at Bournemouth he consistently impressed over the next couple of seasons and was selected in England's squad for the World Cup qualifier against Moldova in September 1997, only for Glenn Hoddle to send him home following a drink-driving charge. However, he soon became a regular in the England squad, quite unfairly being compared to Bobby Moore at both club and international level.

He remained a steady figure in the West Ham back four until he was eventually sold to Leeds United in November 2000 for a new club-record fee of £18 million. It made him the world's most costly defender.

Ferdinand soon settled into the Elland Road club's side, his partnership with Lucas Radebe at the heart of the defence coinciding with an upturn in fortunes for the Yorkshire club. His leadership qualities impressed David O'Leary so much that he appointed him captain. However, despite a good World Cup, Leeds' new boss Terry Venables sold him to Manchester United for a fee of £30 million.

After missing a number of games through injury he began to show the kind of form that had persuaded Sir Alex Ferguson to part with that huge cheque. However, in December 2003, he was banned by the FA for eight months for failing to attend a drugs test – his absence in the United defence being clearly felts in the remaining months of the season. Stepping back onto the Premiership stage, his subsequent performances suggested he'd never been away and he was rewarded with a place in the PFA Premiership team of the season.

He won a Carling Cup Winners' medal in 2006 as United beat Wigan Athletic 4-0 at the Millennium Stadium and League Championship winners' medals 2006/07, 2007/08 and 2008/9, and his central defensive partnership with Nemanja Vidic has been outstanding. He also picked up a Champions League winners' medal as he helped United to their third European Cup victory in May 2008.

BILL FOULKES

Bill Foulkes was the rock upon which Sir Matt Busby built the recovery of Manchester United following the Munich air crash.

His father was a miner at St Helens as well as playing for the town team at Rugby League. Bill too worked down the mine and was recruited playing for Whiston Boys/ Club at the age of 17, though only as a part-timer. Two years' National Service didn't help his cause but eventually he made his United debut at right-back in the game against Liverpool in 1952. In those days he was a rather raw and ungainly defender and it was in the No.2 shirt that he won his one and only full international cap for England against Northern Ireland two years later. In 1955 he played in two England under-23 matches and for the Football League but that was the extent of his representative football.

Foulkes was a strong and reliable defender, giving United sterling service during his 18 years in the first team. He survived Munich to become the backbone of the Reds' defence after being converted into a centre-half. Captain of the new look United side in the 1958 FA Cup Final, when they lost 2-0 to Bolton Wanderers, he gained compensation for two losers' medals (having been in the United side that lost to Aston Villa) when in 1963, United beat Leicester City 3-1.

Though not a great goalscorer – only nine goals in his United career – he was on the scoresheet in United's 3-3 draw with Real Madrid that put the club into the 1968 European Cup Final where they beat Benfica. Foulkes played the last of his 682 first team games against Southampton at the start of the 1969/70 season. He had won four League Championship medals, played in three FA Cup Finals and been a member of United's European Cup-winning team.

On retirement he was appointed the club's youth team coach and a year later promoted to reserve-team coach. He then went to America to manage Chicago Stings and later Tulsa Roughnecks before taking charge of Norwegian side Lillestrom and finally Japanese side Mazda.

Still living in Sale, Bill Foulkes became the first chairman of the Association of Former Manchester United players and continues to represent Japanese football interests in this country and working for the Football for Life programme helping youngsters who fail to make the grade at professional football clubs.

RYAN GIGGS

There is probably no more thrilling sight than to see Ryan Giggs flying down the left-wing with the ball seemingly tied to his bootlaces.

Although he was born in Cardiff, Ryan Giggs was brought up in Manchester, where his father played rugby league after a successful career in rugby union. Before United snapped him up as a trainee in the summer of 1990, he was actually at Manchester City's School of Excellence and captained England schoolboys against Scotland at Old Trafford! Enquiries were made to establish whether he might be eligible to play for the England team proper, but no English relatives were uncovered so Giggs went on to represent Wales at the senior level.

Although Ryan's talent was obvious, United were careful to develop him slowly. They were reluctant to throw him into the first team week after week and it wasn't until 1991 that he became a permanent member of the United side. He made his League debut for United as a substitute against Everton at Old Trafford in March 1991. He played just once more that season in the local derby against Manchester City when he scored the only goal of the game.

In October 1991, Giggs's appearance as a substitute for Wales against West Germany in a European Championship qualifier made him the youngest ever player to be capped by Wales, until Ryan Green. He was just 17 years and 332 days old. His first start at international level came in 1993 against Belgium in a World Cup qualifier when he opened the scoring with a superb free-kick from outside the area. He set another record when he became the first player to win the PFA's Young Player of the Year award in successive seasons, a feat he achieved in 1991/92 and 1992/93.

Giggs is still blessed with the pace to outstrip most full-backs and with the two-footed ability to go inside or outside his marker whenever he chooses. He also has the confidence and the power to go on and finish his own good work when the opportunity arises and has scored a number of spectacular goals.

In 1996, at the age of 22, he became the youngest player to appear in two double-winning sides (he won the first with United in 1994, aged 20). One of his greatest games for United came in the 1996/97 season against Porto at Old Trafford, a performance that was compared to George Best's legendary night against Benfica some 31 years earlier. In 1998/99 he scored the all-important equaliser against Juventus in the European Cup semi-final before netting after a wondrous 60-yard run against Arsenal in the FA Cup semi-final replay. It prompted United boss Sir Alex Ferguson to say 'It was the goal of a genius', while Ryan described it as probably the best he has scored for the club.

At the peak of his form and having scored his 100th goal for the club, he was an inspirational figure during United's treble-winning season in 1999 and has since helped the Reds to further success in winning League and Cup honours. In 2009 he played his 800th game for the club and won his 11th Premier League winners' medal, as well as being voted PFA Player of the Year, an accolade that, surprisingly, he had never won before.

HARRY GREGG

Harry Gregg began his career with Dundalk and was a part-timer with Linfield and Coleraine before he was snapped up by Doncaster Rovers in the summer of 1951. He had made 93 appearances for the Belle Vue club when in December 1957 Manchester United manager Matt Busby signed him for what was then a record fee for a goalkeeper of £23,000.

The New Year began well for Gregg and United. A 3-2 home win over Red Star Belgrade in the European Cup was followed by a 3-3 draw in Belgrade. The Irishman was in superb form, saving shot after shot that by rights should have seen the Reds out of the competition. However, his form was such that United won a place in the European Cup semi-finals. The day after the 3-3 draw, tragedy struck when United's plane crashed on the runway at Munich Airport, killing many of the players. Harry Gregg crawled from the wreckage and as the plane's crew shouted for people to get away from the aircraft for fear of fire, he returned to the plane and helped some of the passengers to safety including a 22-month old baby girl.

Remarkably three weeks later, Gregg played in the 3-0 win over Sheffield Wednesday in the FA Cup and three months later in the Final against Bolton Wanderers. He had a great contest with Bolton and England centre-forward Nat Lofthouse but there was to be no fairy tale ending as the Wanderers won 2-0. Gregg was the victim of the controversial challenge made by Lofthouse, who bundled both Gregg and the ball over the line!

Despite his disappointments at Wembley, Gregg had a superb World Cup as Northern Ireland qualified for the 1958 Finals in Sweden. The team flew to Sweden but with Munich still fresh in his mind, Gregg went by ferry. He was outstanding despite picking up a number of injuries to help his side reach the quarter-finals where they lost to France.

Gregg continued his superb displays for United and Northern Ireland until December 1966 when he joined Stoke City on a permanent basis after a loan period at the Victoria Ground.

In 1967 he became manager of Shrewsbury Town, later taking over the reins of both Swansea and Crewe Alexandra. In 1984 he was appointed assistant to former Red Lou Macari at Swindon Town but departed less than a year later after the two former United stars allegedly ended up not speaking to each other! He is now back in Northern Ireland, where he runs a hotel in Portstewart.

DAVID HERD

David Herd was the son of Alex Herd, the Scottish international who won an FA Cup-Winners' medal with Manchester City in 1934. David Herd signed for Stockport County just after his 17th birthday and played in the same forward line as his father. Arsenal soon showed an interest in him after he was demobbed following two years National Service and in August 1954 he joined the Gunners for a fee of £10,000.

After a couple of seasons in the Arsenal reserves, he won a regular first team place in 1956/57, and over the next five seasons, he led the Gunners' goalscoring charts. His best season in terms of goals scored was 1960/61 when he netted 29 League goals including four hat-tricks – the largest return by an Arsenal player since Ronnie Rooke's 33 in 1947/48. Eventually though he became disillusioned by Arsenal's poor form and in July 1961 he was transferred to Manchester United for £35,000.

Bought by Busby to replace Dennis Viollet as the process of rebuilding continued after Munich, Herd ended the first of his seven seasons at Old Trafford as top-scorer with 14 League goals. However, once he had settled in and Denis Law had joined the club a year later, the former Arsenal man reeled off seasonal totals of 19, 20, 20 and 24 before breaking his leg in March of the following season with his tally at 16 and looking like he would it his best year.

One of the most underrated players ever to play for United – overshadowed by Law, Charlton and Best – he is one of a select band of forwards who has averaged better than a goal every two games. In all competitions for the Reds he scored 144 goals in 263 appearances. Two of his goals came in the 1963 FA Cup Final win over Leicester City as United ran out 3-1 winners. Herd was also an instrumental player in the club's Championship successes of 1964/65 and 1966/67.

His broken leg in March 1967 saw him fade from the scene at Old Trafford just before the Reds won the European Cup in 1968.

After United he had two years playing for Stoke City though he stayed in the Manchester area to establish a successful garage business in Davyhulme. After a spell managing Lincoln City, Herd also continued his highly successful cricket career with local clubs sides like Cheadle Hulme, Timperley and Brooklands. Nowadays he is still a keen committee man with the Association of former United players.

MARK HUGHES

Although he had to wait for his chance at Old Trafford, Hughes made an encouraging start, scoring four goals in his first seven appearances towards the end of the 1983/84 season. He also played in Manchester United's European Cup-Winners' Cup tie against Barcelona at the Nou Camp Stadium. He crowned a remarkable first season bys coring on his Wales debut against England at the Racecourse Ground.

The following season he was United's No.1 striker, scoring 25 goals in all competitions, the best individual scoring performance at Old Trafford for 13 years. It wasn't just the number of goals that he scored but the style of them. The glorious leaping volley which flew past Spain's Arconada will linger long in the memory, while his winner in the FA Cup semi-final against Liverpool was a perfectly placed low shot. He ended the campaign with an FA Cup Winners' medal and not unexpectedly was voted the PFA Young Player of the Year.

At the start of the 1985/86 season, United went 15 games before suffering their first defeat – Hughes scored 10 goals in that run as the Reds raced to the top of the League. It is little wonder that soon every scout in Europe was visiting Old Trafford to see his talents. When United's results fell away, Sparky was sold to Barcelona for £2.3 million. But he did keep one foot in the Old Trafford camp, stating that when he did come back to England, Manchester United were the only club he would join.

In fact, Hughes found Spanish football difficult and in his second season he was loaned out to Bayern Munich where he was much happier. On 11 November 1987, Hughes played in two important matches on the same day! He played for Wales against Czechoslovakia in Prague in a European Championship match before being flown to Bayern's Olympic Stadium – though the match was already underway, he came on in the second half to help Bayern to victory.

Alex Ferguson had wanted to re-sign Hughes before he was loaned out to Bayern and in the summer of 1988, he clinched the deal for a player who never really should have been allowed to leave Old Trafford in the first place.

Hughes soon readjusted to the Football League and was duly honoured by his peers when he was voted PFA Player of the Year. He added a second FA Cup winners' medal to his collection in 1990 as United beat Crystal Palace. In 1991 he was part of the United team that won the European Cup-Winners' Cup, scoring the crucial goal in the 2-1 defeat of Barcelona.

Also that year he became the only British player to have been twice voted PFA Player of the Year.

As he was a great favourite with the United fans, his £1.5 million transfer to Chelsea in the summer of 1995 came as a great shock particularly as he was thought to have signed a new two-year contract with United. Whilst at Stamford Bridge, Hughes was awarded the MBE in the 1998 New Years Honours List and helped the London club win both the FA Cup and European Cup-Winners' Cup before joining Southampton. He later had brief spells with Everton and Blackburn Rovers, whom he helped win the 2002 League Cup before hanging up his boots.

After throwing himself into the Welsh national team manager's job in 2000, he left to take over the reins of Blackburn Rovers, keeping the Ewood Park club in the upper echelons of the Premiership. He is currently manager of Manchester City.

DENIS IRWIN

It is hard to believe that Denis Irwin, probably the best transfer bargain of Alex Ferguson's time as Manchester United, was once released on a free transfer by Leeds United.

He was quickly snapped up by Oldham Athletic and in his first season at Boundary Park, helped the Latics reach the play-offs. Irwin stayed with Oldham for four years, highlights coming in 1989/90, his last season at Boundary Park. Oldham reached the League Cup Final, going down to Nottingham Forest. They were involved in two thrilling FA Cup semi-finals against Manchester United before losing out to a Mark Robins goal in extra-time.

The United boss was so impressed that during the 1990 close season, Irwin moved to Old Trafford for a fee of £625,000. His first season with the Reds was certainly one to remember, for not only did he win the first of 56 international caps for the Republic of Ireland but helped United win the European Cup-Winners' Cup by beating Barcelona in the final. In 1991/92 he switched to left-back and helped United win the League Cup, whilst the following season he missed just two games as the Reds won the Premiership title – the trophy returning to Old Trafford after a 26-year gap.

Although his 'quiet-man' image made him one of United's least-high profile players, his overall contribution to the side was beyond reproach. In 1995/96 he helped United win the Premiership and the FA Cup, once again proving to be 'Mr Dependable'. A specialist goalscorer from set pieces, Irwin won another Premiership medal the following season and scored a well-taken goal for the Republic in their World Cup play-off match against Belgium.

In 1998/99, a red card in the game against Liverpool ruled him out of that season's FA Cup Final but in one of the club's best-ever campaigns, he was delighted to add a European Cup and a fifth Premiership League winners' medal to his collection of honours. During the course of the following season, Irwin celebrated a few milestones – first becoming United's top man in Europe when he surpassed Peter Schmeichel's 17-match record in the Champions League.

Winning his sixth Premiership title medal, he went on to celebrate his 500th senior game at Old Trafford on St Patrick's Day and establish a new club record with his 70th appearance in European competition. Allowed to leave Old Trafford in the summer of 2002, he joined Wolves.

His first season at Molineux ended with his selection for the PFA's First Division team of the season. He thought long and hard about retiring but gave it one more season. On 15 May 2004, he was given a tremendous ovation as he retired after a long and successful career spanning some 900-odd club appearances.

ROY KEANE

A footballer who provoked extreme reactions, Roy Keane was signed by Nottingham Forest manager Brian Clough from Cobh Ramblers in 1990. He ended his first season at the City Ground by playing in the FA Cup Final which Forest lost 2-1 to Spurs. The disappointment was tempered somewhat when he was recognised at full international level, playing for the Republic of Ireland against Chile. He confirmed his progress in 1991/92 as Forest reached the finals of the League Cup and Zenith Data Cup.

Once it became clear that Forest's days in the top flight were numbered, Keane made it clear that he intended to stay in the Premiership. It looked as if he would join Blackburn Rovers but once Manchester United joined the chase, there was only one club in it. United originally offered £3.5 million and refused to increase their bid but Forest wanted £4 million before Keane's contract expired. The period of intransigence was broken when Alex Ferguson increased his offer by a further £250,000 – it was a British record transfer fee. In his first season at Old Trafford, Keane helped United to the League and Cup 'double'.

Following an outstanding 1994 World Cup, Keane's appearances for the national side became all too rare as a series of niggling injuries caused his absence.

In 1995/96, Keane was again producing brilliant competitive performances in midfield. His greatest display was reserved for the FA Cup Final against Liverpool when he won the prestigious man-of-the-match award – he also won a Premiership medal as United won their second-ever double. The following season he missed a number of games through injury but still ended the campaign as the proud possessor of a third Premiership medal as United surged to their fourth title win in five years.

Keane was sent-off playing for the Republic of Ireland in what was manager Mick McCarthy's first match in charge.

He was appointed Manchester United captain prior to the start of the 1997/98 season but suffered cruciate knee ligament damage following a challenge with Leeds United's Alf-Inge Haaland. He returned to full fitness in 1998/99, leading the Reds to success in the FA Cup and Premiership. A yellow-card offence against Juventus in the semi-final of the European Cup ruled him out of the final. After signing a new contract he led the Reds to another Premiership title. Fittingly he won both the PFA and the Football Writers' Player of the Year awards. Keane won his sixth Premiership Championship medal in 2000-01 and remained a cornerstone of the Republic of Ireland team.

Controversy followed as the well-publicised spat with Mick McCarthy ruled him out of the World Cup Finals and an announcement signalled his retirement from the international scene! He quickly put the furore over his autobiography behind him and led United to another Premiership title. He then ended his enforced absence from the national team but after criticising a number of his United team-mates, he parted company with the club. After a brief spell with Glasgow Celtic, he became manager of Sunderland and guided the Black Cats into the Premier League. After a poor start to their second top-flight season, however, Keane left Sunderland and became manager of Ipswich Town.

BRIAN KIDD

An exhilarating forward when playing to the peak of his form, Brian Kidd hit the heights of his career when it had barely started. On his 19th birthday, in 1968, he lined up alongside such greats as Bobby Charlton and George Best to score a goal in Manchester United's famous European Cup Final victory over Benfica at Wembley.

Kidd was speedy, had great attacking flair and was capable of scoring with either foot or with his head. He won two England caps before leaving Old Trafford to join Arsenal for a fee of £110,000.

After two years at Highbury in which he was top scorer in both campaigns, Kidd was anxious to return north and in June 1976 he jumped at the chance of joining Manchester City for £100,000. He finished his first season at Maine Road as the club's top scorer with 21 goals and topped the charts again twelve months later with 16. In March 1979 he was on the move again, this time to Everton for £150,000. With the Goodison club he had the unwelcome distinction of becoming only the second player since the Second World War to be dismissed in an FA Cup semi-final when he was sent-off against West Ham United. Shortly afterwards he signed for Bolton Wanderers but his stay at Burnden Park was brief and he went to play in the NASL with Fort Lauderdale, Atlanta Chiefs and Minnesota Strikers.

Kidd returned to these shores to play non-League football as player-manager of Barrow before becoming assistant-manager of Preston North End. He took over the reins when Tommy Booth left before returning to Old Trafford to work in community football. That led him into youth development with the club itself and a key role when Sir Alex Ferguson decided to revamp the scouting and coaching set-up. Following the departure of Archie Knox to become coach at Glasgow Rangers, Ferguson officially appointed Kidd as his assistant-manager and first team coach. He played a key role in the development of players such as David Beckham, Ryan Giggs and Paul Scholes and helped the club win the League Cup, Premiership and FA Cup.

In the year 2000, after flirting with the possibility of becoming manager of Manchester City, he left to take charge at Blackburn Rovers, only to quit after the Ewood Park club were relegated. He returned to football as youth coach at Leeds, later promoted by David O'Leary to coach the first team, but left following the appointment of Peter Reid.

He was named as assistant to England boss Sven Göran Eriksson but had to leave this role prior to Euro 2004 after being diagnosed with prostate cancer. Thankfully he made a full recovery and joined Neil Warnock at Sheffield United as his assistant. When Warnock was fired, Kidd stayed on with new boss Bryan Robson but when Robbo parted company with the Blades in February 2008, Kidd left as well. He is currently assistant manager at Portsmouth.

DENIS LAW

Denis Law was one of the greatest strikers and characters in the modern game yet when he arrived at Huddersfield Town from Aberdeen in 1956 he was a thin, bespectacled 16-year-old who looked nothing like a footballer. A year after joining Huddersfield Town, Law became the youngest player at 18 years and 236 days to represent Scotland in modern times when he made his debut against Wales. He stayed with the Yorkshire club until March 1960 when Manchester City paid Huddersfield £55,000 for his services. It was a League record surpassing the previous record by £10,000.

On 28 January 1961, Law produced a display of a lifetime to score six goals in a fourth round FA Cup tie, only for the referee to abandon the game with 21 minutes to play! His six goals against Luton Town at Kenilworth Road came within the space of 48 minutes but the conditions were worsening so the referee abandoned the game.

In July 1961, Italian giants Torino paid City £100,000 for Law's skills. It was the first time that a British club had been involved in a six-figure transfer. A year later he joined Manchester United when they became the first British club to pay over £100,000 for a player. He could score goals from impossible situations and his blond hair and one arm raised to salute a goal helped establish the Lawman legend.

On 3 November 1962 he scored four goals for United against Ipswich Town and rounded off a superb first season by scoring at Wembley in United's 3-1 FA Cup Final victory over Leicester City. He was tops corer in the Championship season of 1964–65 with 28 goals and he top-scored again with 23 when the Reds won the League again two years later.

Denis Law holds the record for the most hat-tricks scored in European Cup competitions by anyone playing for a Football League club. After his goals had helped United to the two League titles, he was unfortunate in having to watch the 4-1 European Cup Final triumph against Benfica from his hospital bed after a knee operation. Though his disciplinary record prevented him from being voted Footballer of the Year, the English writers' counterparts on the continent voted him European Footballer of the Year in 1964.

Law shares the Scotland scoring record with Kenny Dalglish, 30 goals but in 55 appearances against Dalglish's 102. He is also the only Scottish player to have scored four goal for his country on two occasions – against Northern Ireland ion 1962 and Norway in 1963.

He later enjoyed an Indian summer with Manchester City after returning to Maine Road in the summer of 1973. Ironically his last goal was a cheeky back-heel which consigned United to the Second Division – never had he taken less pleasure from a goal.

BRIAN McCLAIR

Brian McClair was a good professional: reliable, uncomplaining, versatile, rarely injured and a great influence in the dressing-room.

He went south to sign as an apprentice with Aston Villa in the summer of 1980 but was not offered a professional contract and returned to Scotland to join his local club, Motherwell. After his goals helped the Steelmen win promotion, Billy McNeill signed him for Celtic in the summer of 1983. His first season at Parkhead saw him find the net 23 times in 35 League games and in a total of 175 games for the club, he scored 121 goals. He also won a Scottish Cup medal in 1985 and Premiership Division Championship medal in 1985/86.

Desperate to re-establish themselves at the forefront of English football and to replace Mark Hughes, Manchester United signed him during the close season for a fee of £850,000. In his first season at Old Trafford he became the first player since George Best in 1967-68 to notch up more than 20 Football League goals in a season with 24 strikes including a hat-trick against Derby County. Following the return of Hughes, the two of them formed a formidable partnership, culminating in United beating Crystal Palace in the 1990 FA Cup Final.

The following year the Reds beat Barcelona 2-1 to win the European Cup-Winners' Cup and in 1992, McClair – nicknamed 'Choccy' as his name rhymed with éclair - scored the winner in the League Cup Final against Nottingham Forest. In 1992/93 he played for most of United's inaugural Premiership winning season in midfield and over the next couple of seasons he continued in that position where his canny skills and remarkable vision gave the side that extra dimension.

A great clubman, he went on to earn a deserved testimonial in 1996/97, a season which ended with him winning his fourth League Championship medal. The following season, McClair, who was by then United's senior professional, spent most of the campaign on the bench and in the close season of 1998, after scoring 128 goals in 474 games, signed for Motherwell, the club he started out with.

He never quite re-established his old reputation and when Blackburn Rovers asked him to be their assistant-manager, he returned to the north-west. He later left Ewood Park and is now back at his beloved Old Trafford as the club's Youth Academy Director.

PAUL McGRATH

One of the most controversial and surprising characters ever to pull on a red shirt, Paul McGrath was born in London and was only was only two months old when his Irish-born mother took him back to the place of her birth. After playing his early football for Pearse Rovers and Dalkey United, McGrath stepped up to play in the League of Ireland with St Patrick's Athletic. He was a revelation and in 1981/82 he was voted the PFAI 'Player of the Year'.

Manchester United's Irish scout Billy Behan liked what he saw and in April 1982, McGrath was on his way to Old Trafford for a bargain £30,000 plus extra payments for first team and international appearances.

It was midway through the 1984/85 season before McGrath established himself as a first team regular with United – a season in which international recognition for the Republic of Ireland also came his way. At the end of that season, he claimed an FA Cup winners' medal after a commanding display at the heart of United's defence in the 10-man victory over Everton.

When Jack Charlton was appointed Republic of Ireland team manager, McGrath played in the majority of his matches, playing in a new pivotal role – a midfield sweeper playing just in front of the back four. The switch proved a huge success with the Boys in Green qualifying for the 1988 European Championships with McGrath scoring in the last to qualifiers against Luxembourg and Bulgaria.

During his time at Old Trafford, McGrath was plagued by injury, perhaps an indication of the way he played and in only one season managed to play more than half the matches. Though twice voted Player of the Year by United fans, life very rarely ran smoothly for the big Irishman. By the time Alex Ferguson had replaced Ron Atkinson, McGrath was becoming just as well-known for drinking bouts and a car crash!

He asked United for a transfer because he said he was bored and not long afterwards, much to most supporters' surprise, he got his wish. He was sold to Aston Villa for £450,000 and then surprised everyone by continuing to play at the highest level despite the threat of his knees seizing up completely. His new surroundings at Villa Park seemed to agree with him and after maintaining his fitness through a programme of exercises devised by the Villa physio, enjoyed a seven season run in the first team. In 1992-93 he helped Villa finish runners-up to Manchester United in the newly formed Premiership and was voted PFA Player of the Year.

At international level, he won 83 caps for the Republic of Ireland, helping them to the final stages of both the 1990 and 1994 World Cups. Having reverted to his preferred position of centre-half, he gave his best performance in a green shirt in the 1-0 defeat of Italy in USA '94.

After parting company with Villa, he had brief spells with Derby County and Sheffield United before hanging up his boots in 1998.

SAMMY McILROY

As with so many Belfast schoolboys, Manchester United was the only team Sammy McIlroy set his sights on and he followed in the footsteps of George Best, crossing the Irish Sea to Manchester as a 15-year-old.

Signing with the distinction of being the last Busby Babe, McIlroy announced his arrival in the Reds' first team in bold print in 1971 with a sizzling debut in which he scored one goal and got two 'assists' in United's derby fixture at Maine Road which finished in a 3-3 draw. Yet the fairytale soon turned sour and a motorcycle accident kept him sidelined for over half the 1972/73 season.

Once restored to full fitness, McIlroy claimed a regular place in the United side under Tommy Docherty that was destined for relegation. McIlroy, who'd won his first international cap against Spain in February 1972, soon became an important part of the Northern Ireland side as he was United's.

He won 88 caps and was an integral part of the most glorious chapter in Northern Ireland's soccer history – which in part explains why he was awarded the MBE – as they went on to World Cup glory in Spain in 1982 and Mexico in 1986.

A midfielder full of energy and attacking purpose whose inspiration was important as United clinched the Second Division Championship, played in the 1976 FA Cup Final and won a winners' medal the following year. In 1979 he scored United's second goal in the FA Cup Final defeat to Arsenal as he made a jinking run through the Gunners' defence before unleashing a bending shot past his Northern Ireland colleague Pat Jennings. At the end of one of the most dramatic of finals, McIlroy captured the mood of the United players; 'It was like picking eight draws and then finding the pools coupon in your pocket.'

Though McIlroy was a permanent fixture in the Northern Ireland side, United's new manager Ron Atkinson didn't see him as part of Manchester United's future plans and in February 1982 after scoring 69 goals in 408 games, he joined Stoke City for £350,000.

A free transfer later saw him quit Stoke for the other half of Manchester but he played just a dozen games in blue. He next tried his luck in Sweden with Orgryte before joining Bury and then another spell abroad in Austria with VFB Molding was followed by a period with Preston North End.

After hanging up his boots, McIlroy became manager of Macclesfield whom he led to two Conference titles and victory in the 1996 FA Trophy. After winning promotion to the Football League, McIlroy took the Silkmen into Division Two in his first season in the competition. On parting company with Macclesfield in 2000, he took over the reins of the national side before later managing Stockport County. McIlroy is now in charge of Morecambe.

LOU MACARI

Born in Edinburgh of Italian parents, Lou Macari began his career with Celtic, winning League Championship medals in 1970 and 1972. He was a Scottish Cup winner in 1971 and 1972 and a League Cup finalist in 1971, 1972 and 1973. Having scored 57 goals in 102 games and shortly after signing a five-year contract, he asked for a transfer and in January 1973 he became one of the many Scottish players recruited for Manchester United by Tommy Docherty. The £200,000 paid by United was a record fee for a Scottish player at the time.

A player of great flair, Lou Macari was part of United's attractive side of the mid-1970s. However, at the end of his first full season at Old Trafford, United were relegated from the top flight for the first time in 37 years. Macari scored the only goal of the victory over Southampton which secured the club's promotion back to the First Division at the first time of asking.

Then, after playing in the 1976 FA Cup Final defeat by Southampton, he had a hand in the victory over Liverpool the following year, when his shot was deflected over the line by Jimmy Greenhoff for the winning goal. Then in 1979, he was back at Wembley when United lost 3-2 to Arsenal but by the mid-1980s, he had made way for younger men.

Lou Macari won 24 Scottish caps and scored five goals for his country but he had a poor 1978 World Cup in Argentina and the SFA responded to an outburst in the press that he never wanted to play for Scotland again, by imposing a life ban.

In June 1984, Macari left Old Trafford to join Swindon Town as player-manager. Towards the end of his first season at the County Ground, he was sacked after a row with his assistant Harry Gregg. Six days later he was reinstated and went on to steer the club from the Fourth to the Second Division in two seasons. In the summer of 1989, Macari took over the reins at West Ham United but lasted only seven months as the FA charged him, along with Swindon chairman Brian Hillier, with unauthorised betting on a Robins match.

Macari later returned to management, taking Birmingham City to a Leyland Daf Final and then Stoke City to the Autoglass Trophy Final and the Second Division Championship. In November 1993 he left the Victoria Ground to manage Celtic but within four months he was back at Stoke. Remaining with the Potters until 1997 he later managed Huddersfield Town but is now involved in working as a match analyser for both television and radio.

BILLY MEREDITH

The most famous of all Welsh footballers, Billy Meredith's figures are staggering. He played first-class football for no less than 30 years from 1894 when at 19 he joined Manchester City from Chirk, his home-town just across the Shropshire–Wales border, to 1924 when he played in every tie in City's run to the FA Cup semi-final. He played in 367 League games for Manchester City and another 303 – almost a career in itself – for Manchester United between 1906 and 1921 and scored 181 League and 56 Cup goals.

On leaving school, Meredith, the youngest of 10 children, went to work in the pits as a pony driver and continued to work there even after joining Manchester City. Having played his early football with Wrexham, he entered the Football League with Northwich Victoria before joining City. In 1904 he scored the only goal of the FA Cup Final as City beat Bolton Wanderers before in 1906 moving across the city to Manchester United.

It was money that led to his move to Manchester United. Eighteen City players, Meredith among them, were suspended for receiving 'illegal payments'. Immediately after the suspension, he moved to United and within a few years had won another FA Cup medal as United beat Bristol City 1-0 in 1909 and League Championship medals in 1907/08 and 1910/11.

He was a prominent member of the Players' Union and a leading light in their struggle with the FA in 1909.

After appearing in 332 League and Cup games, United gave him a free transfer at the age of 47 and he rejoined Manchester City an incredible 27 years after he'd first worn their colours. Two years later, as his 50th birthday approached, there was further proof of the veteran Welshman's remarkable stamina as he helped City reach the FA Cup semi-finals. His final appearance came at the end of April 1925.

At an age when many coaches are contemplating retirement, Meredith joined their ranks. In 1931 he returned to Old Trafford in a coaching capacity, at a time when the club was going through a period of turmoil. He retained more affection for United than the Maine Road club and throughout his later years, often visited the ground to watch the team in action. As late as 1950, funds were made available from Old Trafford to help him overcome a small financial problem.

Meredith, who was the first man to win Welsh and FA Cup winners' medals still holds the record as the oldest player to appear in an international match.

'Old Skinny', as he was popularly known, was said never to play without a toothpick in his mouth. His stamina remained in life as it had on the field and he was 81 when he died in 1958, just two months after the Munich air disaster.

KEVIN MORAN

The name 'Kevin Moran' will be in football's record books forever, but the central defender would gladly opt out of his place in the game's history: the first man to be sent-off in an FA Cup Final. Durham referee Peter Willis was the man who ensured the Irishman's infamy when he controversially dismissed him in the 1985 FA Cup Final against Everton.

Moran was a noted Gaelic footballer but it was his ability as a soccer player which induced Manchester United boss Dave Sexton to pay a nominal fee to Dublin's Pegasus FC for his transfer in February 1978. The tough-tackling defender made his debut against Southampton in April 1979, becoming a first team regular in 1980/81.

He had by then made his full international debut, being called into the Republic of Ireland team against Switzerland in April 1980. The appointment of Eoin Hand as national coach did nothing to hinder the United defender's progress as he went on to win 71 caps.

Moran's bravery became legendary at Old Trafford as he literally gave blood in the Reds' cause – collecting over 100 stitches in what were mostly facial injuries. As a United player he won two FA Cup winners' medals in 1983 and 1985, though he was denied his medal in the latter final until a few weeks later.

Under Jack Charlton, Moran was appointed the Republic's captain, playing a major role in the nation's qualification for the 1988 European Championships and was included in the squad for the tournament in West Germany, appearing in all three of Ireland's games. By then he had joined Spanish club Sporting Gijon on a free transfer, later returning to Football League action with Blackburn Rovers. Whilst at Ewood Park, he helped Rovers win their place in the Premiership by beating Leicester City in the Division two play-off final in May 1992.

Moran remained a key figure throughout the reign of Jack Charlton and was ever-present at Italia '90. He was in the Irish squad for the 1994 World Cup Finals but injury prevented him from adding to his total number of caps and at the end of the tournament he decided to retire.

Kevin Moran is still linked to Old Trafford as a committee member of the Association of Former Manchester United players and was chairman in the year 2000. He also works with Pro-Active Sports Management representing players and in their hospitality division.

GARY NEVILLE

Manchester United full-back Gary Neville's rise to fame and international honours was nothing short of meteoric. Furthermore, his adaptability in filling two positions has ensured his place in the national side. When his younger brother Phil, now with Everton, joined him in the England side, they were the first brothers from the same club to represent England since Nottingham Forest's Frank and Fred Foreman in 1899!

Gary Neville first came to prominence as captain of Manchester United's successful Class of '92 which captured the FA Youth Cup. He made his Football League debut for the Reds in the final home game of the 1993/94 season against Coventry City but had already made a brief appearance from the bench in European competition.

An injury to Paul Parker allowed him to establish himself in the United side and by the end of the 1994/95 campaign, Terry Venables had included him the England international squad. A most versatile defender, able to play on either flank or at the heart of the defence, he has won a host of honours with United including seven Premiership titles and the European Cup.

He continued to be a consistent and vital cog in the United side, while at international level he has, despite the emergence of Micah Richards and a number of injuries, taken his tally of caps to 85. Sadly, he missed out on a place in England's 2002 World Cup Finals after breaking a metatarsal bone in his left foot.

On his return to action, Neville's goal as stand-in United skipper against Basle in the Champions League came on his 77th outing in European football – more than any other player in the competition's history.

It is as a right-back that Gary Neville has made his name, bringing single-minded commitment and an unswerving determination to the role. Form nay years he played directly behind his good friend David Beckham and when Becks left to play for Real Madrid, Neville senior didn't always look as comfortable until the arrival of Ronaldo.

Though he was injured for much of the 2007/08 season, Gary Neville has Manchester United in his bones and few more players have displayed more passion in the club's cause. He returned to the side in 2008/9, making 29 appearances as United won their 18th League title. Sir Alex Ferguson has retained faith with him for many years now and that shows not the slightest sign of wavering – Gary Neville will be around for a good few years to come!

STAN PEARSON

Stan Pearson had every attribute of a classic inside-forward: creative, skilful, and a superb passer of the ball, yet he was an outstanding goalscorer.

He joined Manchester United straight from school in Salford and made his League debut for the Reds in November 1937 aged 18, in a 7-1 win at Chesterfield. United won promotion at the end of that season but it wasn't until after the Second World War that he made a big impression on the football scene.

A clever footballer, he linked superbly with Jack Rowley to form the most dangerous of strike forces. He hit the first of his five hat-tricks for United in September1946 as they beat Liverpool 5-0 at Old Trafford. His second came in the last match of the following season as United beat Blackburn 4-1. He was a consistent scorer, with 1951/52 being his best season as he scored 22 goals in 41 games. He could spray out some marvellous sweeping passes and was equally good enough to get on the end of the resultant crosses.

When United won the FA Cup in 1948, Stan Pearson played a leading role. There were one or two scares along the way for the Reds, the first being in the third round tie at Aston Villa. Villa scored straight from the kick-off but United gave the Midlands club a footballing lesson, going in at half-time 5-1 up! Villa pulled it back to 5-4 before Pearson chipped in with a late goal which knocked the stuffing out of the home side. A magical hat-trick from Pearson in the semi-final encounter with Derby County took United to Wembley where he added another goal in a 4-2 win for the Reds.

Pearson who won eight full caps for England and represented the Football League, scored149 goals in 350 appearances for United but with Matt Busby's youth policy beginning to bring great success, he ended his 17-0year career with the club and in February 1954, he signed for Bury.

At Gigg Lane he scored 56 goals in 122 games before joining Chester City where he eventually succeeded John Harris as the Cestrians manager. After a couple of years at the helm, he resigned and took over a newsagent's in Prestbury, coaching and managing the East Cheshire League side at the same time.

CHARLIE ROBERTS

Charlie Roberts was one of the great names in the club's early history. The Darlington-born defender first starred with Bishop Auckland before he joined Grimsby Town but after just one season with the Mariners he was snapped up by the United manager Ernest Mangnall in April 1904 for £600. For a player with less than a year's experience in first-class football it was a great deal of money but he proved to be a wonderful investment.

Roberts was for many years captain of Manchester United, inspiring them to two League Championships and the FA Cup during their first-ever run of glory.

Roberts was to spend 10 seasons with United, making 299 League and Cup appearances and scoring 23 goals. He was the backbone of a fine United side, a centre-half who was not only brave and combative but above all a footballer. He was also extremely fast and was said to be able to run the 100 yards in 11 seconds when the world record stood at 9.6 seconds. The great Italian manager Votorio Pozzo, who was a regular visitor to United when he lived in England, even fashioned his World Cup winning side of 1934 around the style of Charlie Roberts.

The United manager Ernest Mangnall gave Charlie Roberts the freedom to play as he wished and he responded with both confidence and responsibility. Yet Charlie Roberts was not always the easiest of characters – he was without doubt his own man.

He was a founding member and a leading light of the Players' trade union and one of the most determined when the United players came out on strike in 1909. He was also one of the first players to wear his shorts above his thighs when everyone else had them dangling around their knees – something which regularly brought him into trouble with the game's authorities. This probably explains why such an outstanding player was only capped three times by England.

Shortly after his mentor, Ernest Mangnall left Old Trafford, Roberts too departed, joining Oldham Athletic in the summer of 1913. It was certainly United's loss as they dropped into the First Division relegation zone while the Latics almost clinched the title.

The outbreak of the First World war brought an end to Charlie Roberts' playing career although he was later tempted out of retirement to manage Oldham. He found the job extremely stressful and after just 18 months, he quit and returned to the peace and quiet of his newsagent's shop.

BRYAN ROBSON

Not for nothing was Bryan Robson known as Captain Marvel – he was so outstanding that United at times were tagged a one-man team!

Robson began his career with West Bromwich Albion, where his skills were best expressed in midfield as he provided the ideal service for Regis and Cunningham. He suffered a major setback during the course of the 1976/77 season when he broke his leg no fewer than three times! Doggedly he fought back and when Albion boss Ron Atkinson took charge of Manchester United he returned to the Hawthorns and broke the existing transfer record by paying £1.5 million to take Robson to Old Trafford.

It was hardly surprising that they made the signing into a public ceremony out on the Old Trafford pitch. His United League debut came the following game against Manchester City at Maine Road. The following season he reached two Cup Finals at Wembley with the Reds – his move had been justified.

Initially a back four player, he developed to such an extent that his powerful surges from midfield into the penalty area became his trademark. His midfield brilliance earned him a place in England's 1982 World Cup squad. He scored England's first goal in their opening game against France in a record 27 seconds. Robson, who won 90 caps for England, took into the international game, all the physical aggression needed to withstand the pressures of the English Football League, yet he also had a natural class, working as hard as two men in midfield and possessing great stamina that allowed him to get into goalscoring positions.

It is perhaps as captain that Robson made his greatest impression, both for Manchester United and England. He led the Reds to FA Cup Final victories and was the two-goal hero of the 1983 4-0 replay win over Brighton. In 1986, United refused Robson permission to undergo surgery after he dislocated his shoulder when he ran into the electricity box controlling Old Trafford's undersoil hearing as he typically went full pelt after a cross. It continued to let him down as United kept playing him in a vain attempt to claim the title.

He later led United to victory over Barcelona in Rotterdam as the Reds deservedly lifted the European Cup-Winners' Cup and went on to score 100 goals in 465 games for United before being appointed player-manager of Middlesbrough in 1994. It was a remarkable achievement when one considers that in an injury-hit career, he broke his leg four times, suffered three dislocated shoulders, torn ankle ligaments, broken nose and concussion!

Robson steered Boro into the Premiership as First Division champions in his first season on Teesside and though they were relegated the next season, they managed to reached both the FA Cup and League Cup finals. In 1997/98 Robson inspired Middlesbrough to win promotion to the top flight but in 2001 he parted company with the club. After that he managed Bradford City, West Bromwich Albion and more recently Sheffield United, but Robson is now back at Old Trafford as an ambassador, working alongside Bobby Charlton to promote the club's commercial and charitable aims.

CRISTIANO RONALDO

Following his arrival at old Trafford from Sporting Lisbon, Cristiano Ronaldo started the 2003/04 season with a massive task in hand. Not only was he hailed as Britain's most expensive teenager, he also became heir apparent to the No.7 shirt, last worn by a certain David Beckham.

The Portuguese winger was expected to take time to settle in England but made an immediate impact with a stunning debut against Bolton Wanderers at Old Trafford. While he did not always replicate that level of performance in his first season, his tricks were always entertaining at the very least. With the club's Premiership title challenge fading, his importance to the team was becoming more evident with each game. He ended the season on a high with a goal in the FA Cup Final and helping Portugal to the Euro 2004 Final where they lost to Greece.

He continued to live up to Sir Alex Ferguson's praises the following season and was a regular in the United side throughout another action-packed campaign. In fact, Ronaldo's superb season was one of the highlights in an otherwise poor season at Old Trafford.

The 2005/06 season was a mixed one for him, with off-field troubles and heartbreak affecting his form on it. However, he improved after the turn of the year and helped Manchester United to become the first team to score 1,000 goals in the Premiership since its inception in 1992 –

heading home an injury-time winner against Middlesbrough at the Riverside. Ronaldo also featured strongly for Portugal during the 2006 World Cup Finals, making a major contribution as the team reached the semi-final stage for the first time since 1966.

He returned from the World Cup as something of a sacrificial lamb following Wayne Rooney's dismissal in England's match against Portugal. Never one to be fazed by crowd reaction, he really came to the fore as a potent strike force as United went in search of their ninth Premiership title. During the course of the campaign, United confirmed that Ronaldo had signed a new five-year deal with United, making him the highest paid player in the club's history – £120,000 a week! He was awarded the titles of PFA Player and PFA Young Player and he was also named in the PFA Premiership Team of the Year. Also chosen as the 2007 Portuguese Footballer of the Year and the Football Writers' Footballer of the Year he scored his 50th goal for the Reds against Manchester City – a decisive strike as United reclaimed their Premiership crown for the first time in four years.

Ronaldo continued to improve and in 2007/08 was by far the best player in the Premiership, winning the PFA Player of the Year award for a second successive season. He scored his first Manchester United hat-trick in the 6-0 hammering of Newcastle United, going on to score a magnificent 38 goals over the course of a season in which United retained the Premiership title and lifted the Champions League trophy.

Speculation followed about his future with United as Real Madrid reportedly launched a bid to sign him, but he committed himself to the Reds and helped them to another Premier League title in 2008/9, as well as victory in the Carling Cup. In June 2009, Real Madrid finally got their man, breaking all previous transfer records to secure Ronaldo's services for an unprecedented £80 million.

WAYNE ROONEY

The player Sir Alex Ferguson describes as 'the best young player I have seen in my time' burst onto the national stage in October 2002 following a ten-minute cameo appearance for Everton against unbeaten Premiership champions Arsenal. The then 16-year-old came off the bench in the 81st minute with game deadlocked at 1-1. Within minutes he had beaten David Seaman with a wicked, dipping, swerving drive from 25 yards.

He became England's youngest-ever player, aged 17 years and 111 days when he made his international debut against Australia on 12 February 2003. The following year he became England's youngest goalscorer, when aged 17 years 317 days, he broke Michael Owen's record, netting in the 2-1 defeat of Macedonia.

Rooney joined Manchester United in August 2004 for a fee of £20 million. A sensational hat-trick for the Reds in the Champions League heralded his arrival on the Old Trafford stage, whilst a highly notable contribution came against Arsenal at Old Trafford which ended the Gunners' 49-game unbeaten Premiership run. Also on his 19th birthday he netted the winner in the game against Liverpool at Anfield. As his first season with the club drew to a close, he missed out on his first major honour in the FA Cup Final against Arsenal. However, he topped off a magnificent display by being rewarded with the man-of-the-match award to go with his PFA Young Player of the Year award.

Perhaps Wayne Rooney's best performance in 2005/06 came in the 4-0 Carling Cup Final defeat of Wigan Athletic at the Millennium Stadium when he netted twice. Having been honoured with the PFA Young Player of the Year award for the second year running, he also won a place in the PFA Premiership Team of the Year and won the Sir Matt Busby Player of the Year award from the United supporters. However, his world soon came crashing down when he suffered a fractured metatarsal on the verge of the World Cup Finals but to the relief of all he was able to resume his place in the side during the group matches. He never really got going, though, and his red card in the quarter-final against Portugal ended both his own and effectively England's involvement in the tournament.

Following the shock sale of Ruud van Nistelrooy, Rooney cemented an impressive partnership with Louis Saha and though there was speculation about his fitness and confidence on the pitch, this was put to rest when he netted a superb hat-trick against Bolton Wanderers at the Reebok. From then on he remained in the peak of form and doubts about his ability to find the net in Europe were well banished as he netted four goals in the Champions League latter stages – home and away against AS Roma and a brace at Old Trafford against AC Milan.

Rooney helped the Reds to Premiership titles in 2007/8 and 2008/9 and the Champions League in 2008, as he continues at a rate which causes either exhilaration or consternation, depending on who you support!

JACK ROWLEY

Manchester United's Jack Rowley was renowned for his ferocity and accuracy in striking a ball, both on the ground and in the air, which netted him 208 goals in 422 League and FA Cup appearances despite a long break from the game as a soldier.

Born into a footballing family – his father was a goalkeeper for Walsall – Jack Rowley started out as a left-winger, becoming part of Major Frank Buckley's famous nursery at Wolves. However, Wolves didn't rate him too highly and he was allowed to join Bournemouth. He had scored 10 goals in 11 games for the Cherries when Manchester United paid £3,000 for his services.

After playing his first game against Sheffield Wednesday, Rowley decided he needed time to settle into his new surroundings and asked to play for the reserves. A few weeks later, he returned to first team action and scored four goals as United beat Swansea 5-1.

During the war years, he guested for Spurs, Wolves and Irish club, Distillery. He played for Spurs one week and scored seven goals and then a few days later got eight out of eight for Wolves! Dubbed 'The Gunner' because his shot was reckoned to be the hardest of his day, his style was both strong and aggressive.

He dominated United's scoring in the early post-war years, especially on the big occasions – he hit two in the 1948 FA Cup Final victory over Blackpool. He started the 1951/52 season in fine style, scoring a hat-trick in each of the first two games. Indeed after only seven games, he had rattled in an incredible 14 goals. He ended the season with 30 in 40 League Championship-winning fixtures – a United record until it was broken by Dennis Viollet in 1959/60.

After 18 years with United, he was granted a free transfer and joined Plymouth Argyle as player-manager. He took the Pilgrims into the Second Division in 1958/59 before his next job at Boundary Park where he took Oldham up to the Third Division. After an unbelievable cloak and dagger campaign, he was sacked and went to Holland, succeeding Vic Buckingham as manager of Ajax Amsterdam. After the Dutch side finished as runners-up, his contract wasn't renewed and he returned to these shores for managerial spells with Wrexham, Bradford and Oldham again.

On ending his involvement with the game he took a sub-post office at Shaw near Oldham. Jack was the brother of that brilliant goalscorer,

Arthur. Amazingly, they both scored their 200th League goal on the same day – 22 October 1955 – it was Jack who reached the milestone first by 12 minutes!

PETER SCHMEICHEL

One of the greatest goalkeepers in the game's history, Peter Schmeichel is the son of a Polish musician who emigrated to Denmark. His father wanted him to be a pianist but football called. As a young boy, he was a Manchester United fan who trained wearing a Gary Bailey replica kit!

Schmeichel first came to United's attention when they were in Spain on a winter break. Danish side Brondby were staying in the same hotel and the two teams shared a training pitch. United boss Sir Alex Ferguson had been told about this giant of a goalkeeper breaking through in Danish football and one day he stopped behind to watch him. Schmeichel's great enthusiasm as well as his obvious competence impressed the United manager and though Brondby turned down United's first approach, the Reds went back as his contract began to run out and signed him for a fee of £505,000.

He made his debut against Notts County in August 1991 and after surviving a rather nervy start, ended his first season by winning a League Cup medal but missing out on a League Championship medal in the closing weeks of the campaign. Apart from the occasional lapses in concentration he proved to be the answer to a problem position for United since the departure of Jim Leighton.

He played for Denmark in the 1992 European Championship Finals in Sweden, as last minute participants following the expulsion of Yugoslavia. Despite being unprepared for the tournament, the Danes confounded everyone by defeating France and Holland before beating Germany in the final. Schmeichel became a national hero when saving a Marco van Basten penalty in the semi-final shoot-out.

He returned to Old Trafford where he became a dominating character who proved himself outstanding in one-on-one situations, spreading himself to pull off seemingly impossible saves. He helped United power their way to the inaugural Premiership title, keeping 23 cleans sheets and at one time going 626 minutes without conceding a goal! In 1993/94 he added a second FA Premiership and an FA Cup winners' medal to his collection. He missed out on the League Cup final due to suspension, after being sent off in the FA Cup sixth round tie against Charlton Athletic. Prior to his last season with United of 1998/99, Schmeichel picked up further Premiership medals in 1995/96 and 1996/97, and another FA Cup winners' medal in 1996.

Having shocked United fans by announcing that 1998/99 would be his last season with the club, he produced a series of inspiring performances throughout the campaign including an outstanding display against
Inter Milan in the Champions League quarter-final. He also saved an FA Cup semi-final penalty against Arsenal which took the Reds through to Wembley and with Roy Keane being suspended from the Champions League Final against Bayern Munich, he captained United to their historic treble

On leaving Old Trafford he had two seasons in Portugal with Sporting Lisbon, helping them win the Portuguese Premier League in his first season with the club. He then returned to English football with Aston Villa where he became the first goalkeeper to score in the Premiership. He later ended his career at Manchester City where he maintained his record of never ever being on the losing side in a Manchester derby! His son, Kasper, is now on Manchester City's books as a goalkeeper.

PAUL SCHOLES

A central midfielder whose imaginative distribution makes him the fulcrum of the Manchester United side, Paul Scholes meteoric rise delighted Sir Alex Ferguson so much tat he likened the young United player to a young Kenny Dalglish.

During the club's 1995/96 League and FA Cup double-winning campaign, he scored 11 goals in his first 23 outings – an amazing feat when one considers that he only completed five of those games. He went on to score 14 goals from 18 starts to finish ahead of Andy Cole as runner-up to Eric Cantona in the goalscoring charts. He came on for Cole in the FA Cup Final win over Liverpool to collect another medal having already received one following the Championship success.

Despite the arrival of several big-money stars, Scholes continued to hold down a regular place in the United side and won the first of 66 caps for England when he played against South Africa in 1997. Having come of age on the international front, he was England's Man-of-the-Match in the opening game of France '98, scoring in the 2-0 win over Tunisia and appearing in all four games. He then netted a hat-trick playing for England against Poland in a European Championship qualifier at Wembley the year after.

His yellow card offence in the European Cup semi-final against Juventus ruled him out of the 1999 Final. Despite his immense disappointment, he remained one of United's key players and played an inspiring role in the FA Cup Final at Wembley, scoring the club's deciding goal, which completed the second leg of the treble. The following season he sacrificed the sunnier climes of Brazil for the inaugural World Club Championship, to undergo a hernia operation. He came back fully refreshed to help United win another Premiership title, scoring a hat-trick against West Ham United in the process.

England's Player of the Year in 1999/2000 he continued to impress for both club and country, winning yet another Premiership winners' medal in 2000/01. United's next Premiership title came their way in 2002/03, a campaign in which Scholes scored a majestic hat-trick against Newcastle United to take the Reds to the top of the table. The match against Blackburn saw him net twice including his 100th goal for the club. Scholes picked up another FA Cup winners' medal in 2004 following a 3-0 win over Millwall and was instrumental in helping them return the following season where they lost to Arsenal in a penalty shoot-out.

He has since continued to demonstrate his ability as one of United's best-ever midfield players, helping the Reds win three Premiership titles in a row in 2006/07, 2007/08 and 2008/9 as well as scoring the spectacular goal that took the club into the 2008 Champions League Final. Playing in the 2008 final was particularly memorable for Scholes, as he had missed the chance to play in the historic 1999 final. Having helped United to another Premier League title and Champions League final, he came on as a substitute in United's disappointing 2-0 defeat to Barcelona in 2009.

OLE GUNNAR SOLSKJAER

Ole Gunnar Solskjaer was the least known of Alex Ferguson's 1996 summer signings when he joined the Old Trafford club from Molde. Over the following seasons, the Norwegian striker proved himself to be not only a top-class striker but a loyal, uncomplaining player – perfect for a club like Manchester United.

In a memorable week following his arrival, he netted a brace of goals for the reserves, then scored on his Premiership debut against Blackburn, going on to end the campaign as the club's leading scorer and pick up a Premier League winners' medal. He had a torrid time with injuries in 1997/98, finding himself confined mainly to the bench after his lengthy spell out of the side, though the club recognised his talent by offering him a new seven-year contract which he duly signed. Yet weeks later, the club accepted a £5.5 million offer from Spurs only for the deal to fall through – Alex Ferguson was delighted to see him stay!

Though the Norwegian coach warned him he was risking his international future by refusing to leave Old Trafford, Solskjaer responded in the only way he knew how – by scoring goals. He continued to hit the headlines with 17 strikes in 17 games including four in ten minutes against Nottingham Forest – the record for a substitute. Having helped United win the League and FA Cup, he certainly showed his true worth in the Champions League Final at the Nou Camp. With only seconds remaining and United heading for an extra-time showdown against Bayern Munich, Ole forced home a dramatic winner to write himself into Old Trafford folklore.

His appetite for goals didn't diminish after that and in 1999/2000 he scored four in a 5-1 win against Everton. Though almost half of his appearances were from the bench, he more than played his part in helping United retain their Premiership title. He was content to play his usual waiting game as the Reds won a third consecutive Premiership title and penned a new contract for United. He started most of the games in 2001/02 and scored 25 goals in all competitions including a hat-trick against Bolton as he and Ruud van Nistelrooy's partnership developed along truly prolific lines. The following season saw him score his 100th goal for the club as United and Arsenal fought all the way for the Premiership title – United eventually finishing five points ahead of the Gunners.

He was then missing from the side for 16 months after suffering knee ligament damage but shortly after his return to first team action, he fractured a cheekbone during a reserve-team game.

Happily, despite another operation on his knee, he returned to help United win the Premiership in 2006/07 but at the end of the season he announced his retirement from the game. Ole is still at Old Trafford as manager of the reserve team, and was honoured with a testimonial match against Espanyol in August 2008, which United won 2-1 with Ole coming on as a second-half substitute.

JOE SPENCE

In 14 years at Old Trafford, Joe Spence created a club record of 481 League appearances which was to remain unbeaten until Bill Foulkes passed the total some 40 years later.

In his first season of schools football, the young Joe Spence scored 42 of his team's 49 goals. He was a coal miner from the age of just 13 and four years later joined the Army. Whilst serving with the Machine Gun Corps, he helped his battalion to win the Army Cup. On his demob, he returned to his Northumberland home and played for Newburn and Scotswood before signing for Manchester United in March 1919. He scored four goals in his first game as United beat Bury 5-1 in a Lancashire Section match.

When League soccer resumed following the hostilities in August of that year, Spence who played at either outside-right or centre-forward, made his Football League debut for United in the season's opening match against Derby County. Though he failed to score on that occasion, he ended his first season as United's top scorer. During his time at Old Trafford, Spence was either top or joint-top scorer on seven occasions.

He netted his first hat-trick for the club in the first Manchester derby of 1921/22 as United beat City 3-1 and two seasons later went one better in scoring four of United's goals in a 5-1 home win over Crystal Palace. His best season in terms of goals scored was 1927/28 when his total of 22 League goals including hat-tricks in the 5-0 defeat of Derby County and the final day 6-1 thrashing of Liverpool. The prolific United forward also netted another four-goal haul in 1929/30 as West Ham United were beaten 4-2.

He played once for the Football League and was capped twice by England during his stay at Old Trafford.

In June 1933 he moved to Bradford City, signing for Chesterfield two years later. It was whilst he was with the Spireites that he won his first major honour, helping the Saltergate club lift the Third Division (North) Championship. His final total of 613 appearances constituted a Football

League record at the time, as did his appearances in 19 of 20 inter-war seasons. On his retirement, he remained in the Chesterfield area, working and scouting for his former club.

ALEX STEPNEY

Goalkeeper Alex Stepney began his career with non-League Tooting & Mitcham before turning professional with Millwall in 1963. The Lions were relegated to the Fourth Division at the end of Stepney's first season but the ever-dependable keeper helped them bounce back at the first attempt and then into the Second Division. He had made 150 appearances for Millwall and played three times for the England under-23 side, when in May 1966, Tommy Docherty signed him for Chelsea, for a then goalkeeping record fee of £50,000.

However, four months later, having made just one League appearance for the Stamford Bridge club, Stepney, who'd been signed as cover for an unsettled Peter Bonetti, he was transferred to Manchester United for £55,000 – a further record for a keeper. At least Chelsea made a profit out of the deal, but given the magnificent service that Stepney gave to United, the Blues must have regretted letting him go.

Stepney made his United debut in the Manchester derby, a Denis Law goal giving the Reds a 1-0 win. In his first season at Old Trafford, United lifted the League Championship and then in 1968, the European Cup. It was the heroics of Alex Stepney, with two instinctive saves from Eusebio in the closing minutes of normal time, which kept United alive in the final against Benfica. The extra-time goals will always be the highlight of this famous victory but Stepney's part should never be forgotten.

Alex Stepney was a permanent reassuring feature in Manchester United's side – a solid if unspectacular keeper. Though he was never ranked alongside such contemporaries as Peter Shilton or Pat Jennings, there have been few more reliable and loyal servants to the club.

During the latter stages of the club's relegation season of 1973/74, Stepney was employed by manager Tommy Docherty as the club's penalty-taker. He successful converted two spot-kicks which at the halfway mark of the season made him joint-top scorer!

Stepney's additional honours with Manchester United included a Second Division Championship medal in 1974/75 and successive FA Cup

Final appearances in 1976 – when Southampton beat United 1-0 – and 1977 when United beat Liverpool 2-1.

After his long service with the Reds, Stepney, who appeared in 535 first team games, joined Dallas Tornadoes in February 1979 and also had a spell with non-League Altrincham before retiring.

Subsequently he worked as a licensee, managed a far and van rental company and did commercial work for Stockport County and Rochdale prior to him crossing the great divide to work for Peter Reid's Manchester City as goalkeeping coach. He lost his job when he was sacked with manager Joe Royle.

NOBBY STILES

Though Nobby Stiles wasn't the most elegant of performers, it was the only way he knew how to play and coupled with his outstanding ability to read the game, he was a key member of Manchester United's defence throughout the successful Sixties.

Hailing from Collyhurst – Manchester's most productive football area – the England schoolboy international made his League debut for United at the age of 18 in a 1-1 draw against Bolton Wanderers at Burnden Park in October 1960. He shared in the club's successful 1963 FA Cup run, though he didn't win a place in the final side. He was though a virtual ever-present in each of the club's two League Championship-winning seasons of 1964/65 and 1966/67.

He wore the No.4 shirt throughout England's triumphant World Cup in 1966. He made his mark as a world-class player with his brilliant covering, especially against Portugal's Eusebio in the semi-final. No-one will forget Nobby's antics after England had won the World Cup. He put the trophy on his head and danced with delight.

It has been said that many of Nobby's awkward-looking tackles in the early days were probably because he wasn't wearing his spectacles and that his tackling only improved after he was fitted with contact lenses! After United won the European Cup in 1968, Nobby's standing in the game was at a peak, but his earlier bad boy image was reflected by his pen picture in the match programme, when the Reds played Estudiantes in the World Club Championship; he was described as 'brutal, badly intentioned and a bad sportsman.'

The fans abroad certainly didn't like Nobby, for in his time, he was called an assassin in South America, spat at in Italy and hit on the head by a bottle in Madrid! Playing without his false teeth made him look like Dracula and according to the French, who met him in the 1966 World Cup tournament, he was twice as dangerous! Possessing a reputation for fierce tackling, his tigerish play as a wing-half earned him the respect of team-mates and opponents alike. Known to his team-mates as 'Happy', he worked hard for the team, his enthusiasm rubbing off on to other people.

At the age of 27 he suffered two cartilage operations and in May 1971, United accepted a £20,000 offer from Middlesbrough. After two seasons at Ayresome Park, he moved to Deepdale to play for Bobby Charlton's Preston North End side. He only played for one season but spent another seven years there, three as coach and the last four as manager. On leaving North End he teamed up with his brother-in-law Johnny Giles at Vancouver Whitecaps before following him to West Bromwich Albion in a similar capacity.

In 1988 United boss Alex Ferguson brought him back to Old Trafford as junior youth coach. However, his popularity and success – one of just a handful of players to have won both World Cup and European Cup winners' medals – forced to him give up his United role and drew him into a full-time career as an after-dinner speaker.

TOMMY TAYLOR

Tommy Taylor was the natural successor to Jack Rowley with his penetrating stride, fierce shooting and powerful heading.

When he wasn't starring for the Army, Taylor was plying his trade with Barnsley, who were struggling in the lower reaches of the Second Division. He was just the type of player that Manchester United needed, but he was also wanted by several other clubs – Manchester City, Cardiff City, Chelsea and West Bromwich Albion had all made offers. The chase finally ended when Barnsley chairman Joe Richards said 'The fee for Tommy Taylor is £30,000'. Matt Busby felt that big fees sometimes affect players and offered £29,999, which was accepted!

Taylor made his debut for United against Preston North End in March 1953, scoring two goals in the Reds' 5-2 win. He ended the season with seven goals in 11 games and in the close season, he toured South America with an FA XI, playing against Argentina, Chile and Uruguay.

During the course of the following season, he scored 23 goals including hat-tricks in the wins over Blackpool and Sheffield Wednesday, the latter by 5-2 on Christmas Day.

Tommy Taylor was the ideal centre-forward, strong and sure both in the air and on the ground. He seemed to climb and then hover in space – it was no wonder he won the ball almost every time. He held the forward line together superbly. When he headed the ball, it went where he wanted it to go and he could shoot as well – inside the box he was devastating.

A week after making his England debut in the abandoned game against Argentina, he scored his first goal for his country. Although he played twice in the 1954 World Cup Finals, he didn't really establish himself as an England regular until he replaced Nat Lofthouse in 1956.

When United won the League title in 1955/56, Tommy Taylor scored 25 League goals from 33 appearances including four in the 5-2 beating of Cardiff City. In all matches the following season, he scored 34 goals from 44 games including a hat-trick in United's 10-0 win over Anderlecht in a second-leg European Cup tie – the League title going to Old Trafford again. He picked up an FA Cup runners-up medal and scored United's late goal in a 2-1 defeat by Aston Villa.

He had helped England qualify for the 1958 World Cup Finals in Sweden but by the time they came round, he had tragically lost his life in the Munich disaster. In 189 first team games for United, he had scored 128 goals. His had been a magnificent career, which saw him score a goal every 125 minutes of his playing days. Taylor also scored 16 goals in 19 internationals including two hat-tricks. His early death dealt an irreparable blow to football in this country.

SANDY TURNBULL

Alex 'Sandy' Turnbull was one of several Manchester City players, banned by the FA in 1906 over an illegal payments scandal, who played for United once their suspensions were lifted.

A native of Hurlford, a mining village on the outskirts of Kilmarnock, Turnbull's career could have been all so different. In the summer of 1902, he had agreed terms with Bolton Wanderers but in the period between the arrival of the necessary papers, he received a better off from Manchester City and went back on his promise to the Wanderers.

One of the most accurate headers of a ball, Turnbull scored many goals for City from the countless Billy Meredith crosses – it was to be a prolific partnership that was to continue throughout his career. During his time with Manchester City, Turnbull, who was known as 'Turnbull the Terrible' won a Second Division Championship medal in 1902/03 and an FA Cup winners' medal in 1904 when City beat Bolton Wanderers 1-0.

Following the lifting of the ban, Sandy Turnbull joined Manchester United along with three other former City players in Meredith, Bannister and Burgess. They all made their debut on New Year's Day 1907 in a 1-0 defeat of Aston Villa, Turnbull scoring the game's only goal. The following season he was United's leading scorer with 25 goals in 30 League outings as the club surged to their very first League Championship. His total included all four in a 4-2 defeat of Arsenal and hat-tricks in the wins over Liverpool and Blackburn Rovers. He also became the first player ever sent off in a United v City derby match.

Sandy Turnbull also scored the only goal of the 1909 FA Cup Final as United beat Bristol City, ramming the ball over the line after a shot by Harold Halse had rebounded from the crossbar. It was the first time that the Reds had lifted the trophy.

When United won the League Championship for a second time in 1910/11, Turnbull netted 18 goals. He continued to score on a regular basis until 1914/15, the last of his nine seasons with the club. He had been awarded a benefit match along with George Stacey in April 1914 – the derby against Manchester City at Old Trafford, a match the visitors won 1-0. Sadly, Turnbull's fine career ended under a cloud with a life ban for betting irregularities. In 1915 he joined the Footballers' Battalion and during active service in France was killed in the Arras sector in 1917.

RUUD van NISTELROOY

Prolific Dutch international striker Ruud van Nistelrooy began his career with Den Bosch were he was converted from a central defender to centre-forward. Moving on to Heerenveen, he spent just one season there before moving to PSV Eindhoven for £6.3 million, then the record transfer sum between two Dutch teams. In each of his first two seasons with PSV, van Nistelrooy topped the Eredivisie scoring charts, winning the Dutch Player of the Year award in 1998/99.

Just days after his £18.5 million transfer to Manchester United in the summer of 2000 was shelved after United's medical staff had found problems with his medial ligaments, van Nistelrooy suffered a knee injury during a training session. When the transaction was finalised in April 2001, the Reds were forced to pay PSV an additional £500,000 for the player's services. After he successfully passed a medical, van Nistelrooy joined United for a total of £19 million and signed a five-year contract with the reigning Premiership champions.

During his first season at Old Trafford, van Nistelrooy scored 36 goals in all competitions, including both a Premiership and club record eight-game consecutive scoring streak. Included in that total were 10 Champions League goals as he ended his debut season as the PFA Player of the Year.

An archetypal centre-forward, blessed with all-round technique – powerful in the air and packing a fearsome shot in either foot, van Nistelrooy seemed determined to smash every Manchester United record going. In Europe alone, he notched a remarkable 14 goals in 11 games, thus with the previous season's tally, eclipsing the all-time club record previously held by Andy Cole. He also scored 25 goals in the Premiership including hat-tricks against Newcastle United, Fulham and Charlton Athletic.

His goalscoring prowess continued at a phenomenal rate when he set two new records at the start of the 2003/04 season. A nicely executed goal against Bolton on the opening day of the season was his ninth in nine games – a Premiership record and 11 out of 11 – a new United record. He later equalled Denis Law's 28-goal European record with a strike against Stuttgart. Having scored his 100th goal for the club against Everton, he then netted a hat-trick for Holland in their Euro 2004 play-off match against Scotland.

He missed a large part of the following season due to a hernia operation and though he wasn't fully match fit, he still managed to beat Denis Law's European scoring record by notching his 29th goal against Olympique Lyon. He then entered centre stage by scoring all four of United's goals against Sparta Prague in the Champions League – it was his first-ever hat-trick in Europe. He then continued to notch important goals despite being sidelined by constant injury problems but despite netting twice in the FA Cup semi-final defeat of Newcastle he was unable to help United beat Arsenal in the final.

Described by Alex Ferguson as the best striker he's ever worked with, van Nistelrooy ended the 2005/06 season as United's top scorer with 25 goals. Strangely left on the bench for a number of League games and the Carling Cup Final against Wigan, van Nistelrooy, who had scored 150 goals in his five seasons at Old Trafford, moved to Real Madrid for a fee of £12.3 million. Whilst in Spain, he announced his retirement from international football having scored 30 goals in 59 games but continued to find the net on a regular basis for the Spanish giants, helping them to two successive La Liga titles.

DENNIS VIOLLET

There could have been a snag to Dennis Viollet becoming a Manchester United player – he lived near Maine Road and his parents were supporters of Manchester City! Yet after Matt Busby, Jimmy Murphy and Bert Whalley had chatted with the family, both parents seemed happy for Dennis to wear the red of United.

Viollet made his League debut as a replacement for Stan Pearson in a 2-1 win at Newcastle United in April 1953.

Frail in appearance, his skills and stamina belied his frame. Viollet was a player who snapped up the half-chances at a terrific rate. In his 13 years with United, he scored seven hat-tricks; the first coming in October 1954 as the Reds won a remarkable match at Stamford Bridge, beating Chelsea 6-5. He then proceeded to score a hat-trick in each of the next six seasons, though he was on the losing side at Turf Moor in October 1960 when United lost 5-3 to Burnley.

He won League Championship medals with United in 1955/56 and 1956/57 and an FA Cup runners-up medal – when as a survivor of the Munich air crash, he recovered just in time to line-up against Bolton Wanderers in the 1958 final. In 1959/60 he scored 32 League goals – it is still a United record. In all matches for United he scored 178 goals, 159 of them coming in 259 League games. Viollet was a compelling performer at inside or centre-forward, possessing superb ball control, a delicate body-swerve and a powerful shot. He played in 12 European ties for the Reds, scoring 13 goals but in January 1962 he left Old Trafford in a surprise £25,000 transfer to Stoke City.

Viollet represented the Football League in the late fifties and was capped twice by the full England team in 1960 and 1961.

In five-and-a-half years at the Victoria Ground, he added 59 League goals in 182 appearances, helping the Potters to the Second Division Championship in 1962/63. He then spent 18 months in the United States, playing in the NASL with Baltimore Bays. He returned to these shores to play for non-League Witton Albion but six months later he joined Linfield as their player-manager and won an Irish FA Cup winners' medal. He later coached at Preston and then Crewe, managing the Gresty Road outfit for six months in 1971.

On returning to the States he set up the Dennis Viollet Dolphin Soccer Camps in addition to fulfilling his duties as head coach of Jacksonville University.

BILLY WHELAN

Known as Billy or Liam, he was spotted by Manchester United's legendary Irish scout Billy Behan whilst playing for Dublin club Home Farm and rushed into the final of the 1953 FA Youth Cup as a replacement for the injured John Doherty. He scored in each leg of the two-legged final as United beat Wolves 7-1 at Old Trafford and drew 2-2 at Molineux.

His ball control was a delight to witness and his overall command of the game's skills was a model for any young footballer to study. He made his United League debut in a 2-0 win at Preston North End in March 1955 and scored his first goal the following week on his home debut as Sheffield United were beaten 5-0.

Having helped United win the League Championship title in 1955/56, he made his full international debut for the Republic of Ireland in a 4-1 defeat of Holland in Rotterdam in May 1956, at a time when away victories for the national side were at a premium.

In 1956/57, the Reds retained the League Championship and were runners-up to Aston Villa in that season's FA Cup Final. He had a major say in keeping the title at Old Trafford that season with a remarkable 26 goals in 39 appearances including a well-taken hat-trick in a 3-1 win at Burnley. In that season's European Cup, United had reached the quarter-final where they faced Athletico Bilbao. The Spanish side were leading 5-2 in the first leg when Whelan scored a most important third goal to put the Reds back in the tie. United won the return 3-0 and thanks to Whelan's goal took the tie 6-5 on aggregate. Whelan netted another treble on the opening day of the 1957/58 campaign as United won 3-0 at Leicester City.

The artist of the pre-Munich United side, he was vying for the No.8 shirt with Bobby Charlton at the time of the Munich air crash. Charlton had played in the last seven League games before the tragedy. Although Whelan did not play in the game against Red Star Belgrade, he was a member of the squad that made that trip and was one of those who lost their lives.

In his relatively short playing career, Billy Whelan, who averaged a goal in every other match, achieved more than most players achieve in a lifetime in the game.

NORMAN WHITESIDE

Norman Whiteside was always ahead of his time both in terms of skill and physical development. He scored a century of goals per season when playing schoolboy football. He was discovered by United's Belfast scout Rob Bishop and signed by the Reds when he was 15. Ever since he was a boy, he had been tall and strongly built and his confidence to take on all-comers in passing, running, shooting or tackling earned him comparisons with George Best!

A few weeks after having made his League debut for United as a 16-year-old substitute in a 1-0 win over Brighton, Whiteside stepped out to make his World Cup debut for Northern Ireland in 1982 with the confidence of a player who had been around and seen it all. Yet he was just 17 years and 41 days old and the youngest player ever to appear in a World Cup Finals tournament.

Whiteside soon demonstrated his keen scoring ability at the highest level in 1983 when he scored for United in the League Cup Final against Liverpool and in their 4-0 win over Brighton in the FA Cup Final replay.

In 1983, AC Milan offered Manchester United £1.5 million for Whiteside. Manager Ron Atkinson and chairman Martin Edwards agreed to the deal but Whiteside wanted to continue his career at Old Trafford. After that he became even more of a key man in the United set-up. Originally a centre-forward, modelling himself on Joe Jordan, he now used his power and strength in midfield. He often outshone Bryan Robson and took over the captaincy when Robson was injured. It was from a position deep on the right that he found the space to set himself up to score the only goal in the 1985 FA Cup Final against Everton.

His performances for Northern Ireland were equalling telling. He scored the goal in Ireland's astonishing defeat of West Germany in Hamburg in 1983 and laid the groundwork for Jimmy Quinn's goal in Bucharest which gave Northern Ireland qualification at Romania's expense for the 1986 World Cup Finals in Mexico, where he became the youngest player to appear in two finals.

On the domestic scene, White side began to lose his form and became increasingly upset by injuries. When Alex Ferguson took over as team manager and decided the team needed an overhaul, Whiteside's days at Old Trafford were numbered. In the summer of 1989 with 67 goals in 292 League and Cup games to his name, Norman Whiteside left United and moved to Everton in the hope of putting sparkle back into his game.

His appearances at Goodison were however, limited by injury and in 1992 he decided to call it a day and retire – still only in his mid-twenties. He was then a full-time student at Salford University where he qualified as a chiropodist. He also plays in occasional charity matches and undertakes after-dinner speaking.

CHAPTER FOUR

THE MANAGERS

ERNEST MANGNALL 1903 to 1912

Ernest Mangnall had an unquenchable thirst for success. He also had the ability to motivate players and the powers to both spot and nurture any emerging talent.

He joined United from Burnley as successor to James West as secretary in 1903. It was Mangnall along with the club's first great benefactor, JH Davies who transformed Manchester United into one of the giants of the First Division, a team to be both feared and respected.

He brought a number of players to Clayton, including Charlie Roberts, Dick Duckworth and Harry Moger and within three years, he had produced a promotion-winning team. In 1907 when a number of Manchester City players were suspended because of an illegal payments scandal, Mangnall swooped to sign four great players in Sandy Turnbull, Herbert Burgess, Jimmy Bannister and the mercurial Billy Meredith. With these players in their ranks, United won the League Championship for the first time in 1907-08, the FA Cup in 1909 and another League title in 1910/11.
When United's great team began to wane, Mangnall moved to manage the club's greatest rivals Manchester City in 1912.

United's playing record under Ernest Mangnall:

P	W	D	L	F	A	Success Rate
334	181	66	87	614	424	64%

JOHN ROBSON 1914 to 1921

John Robson was the first official to assume the mantle of manager. Although Ernest Mangnall was the first man to actually fill the post, his title was that of secretary as was his successor John Bentley.

On Bentley's resignation in 1916, Robson took on both the role of secretary and manager as the Reds soldiered on through the regional leagues of wartime football. Robson had joined United from Brighton & Hove Albion towards the end of 1914, this after spells at Middlesbrough and Crystal Palace. He remained in charge of the Old Trafford club until he was forced to retire through ill-health in 1921. His seven-year reign makes him the club's third longest serving manager after Alex Ferguson and Matt Busby.

Throughout John Robson's managerial career at Old Trafford, United remained a First Division club – albeit with a four season break because of the First World War – but they were definitely on the decline when Robson was forced to quit his post. Immediately upon is registration, John Robson was appointed assistant to his successor, John Chapman.

United's playing record under John Robson:

P	W	D	L	F	A	Success Rate
134	40	41	53	179	201	45%

JOHN CHAPMAN 1921 to 1926

When United manager John Robson resigned in October 1921, John Chapman was appointed as the club's new boss with Robson staying on at Old Trafford as his assistant. Chapman had been in charge of Airdrieonians but on his arrival he found United to be a team struggling in the First Division.

His presence made no immediate impact. Indeed. In his first 15 games in charge, the Reds won just one match! The season finished with them bottom of the First Division and it took Chapman a further three seasons before he returned them to the top flight.

United's first season back in Division One saw them finish ninth and Chapman's side gave the Old Trafford faithful some hope of success when he led them to their first FA Cup semi-final since they won the trophy in 1909. Unfortunately Manchester City ended their dreams of a first Wembley final.

Though he had made a number of good signings for the club including Frank Barson, Frank Mann, Jim Hanson and Frank McPherson, United never really challenged for the title that their fans were hoping for.

In October 1926, five years after the club had appointed Chapman, they received a letter from the FA telling them that John Chapman was to be suspended forthwith from all involvement with football because of alleged improper conduct whilst acting as the club's secretary-manager.

The full details of the charges brought against Chapman were never made public but United had little option but to dispense with their manager's services.

United's playing record under John Chapman:

P	W	D	L	F	A	Success Rate
207	80	55	72	268	248	52%

CLARENCE HILDITCH 1926 to 1927

Clarrie Hilditch spent 16 seasons with Manchester United without ever winning a major honour. Beginning his career as a centre-forward with Witton Albion, he joined United from Altrincham in 1916. During the First World War he served as a London-based clerk in a cavalry regiment. When League football resumed in 1919/20, Hilditch went straight into the United side as for the next five seasons was a virtual ever-present at the heart of the Reds' defence. He played for England against Wales in a 1919 Victory International and against South Africa in the 1920 Commonwealth international.

When John Chapman was suspended and subsequently sacked by the United board, Hilditch stepped into the breach as the club's player-manager – the only such appointment in the club's history.

During his short spell in charge, Hilditch was reluctant to select himself and without his wholehearted displays in the centre of defence, United began to slip.

Herbert Bamlett was appointed United's next manager in 1927 when Hilditch immediately made himself available for first team selection. He continued to serve the Old Trafford club until his retirement in 1932.

United's playing record under Clarence Hilditch:

P	W	D	L	F	A	Success Rate
30	10	8	12	34	42	47%

HERBERT BAMLETT 1927 to 1931

United were struggling in the lower reached of the First Division when Herbert Bamlett replaced player-manager Clarrie Hilditch in April 1927.

Prior to entering the world of football management, Bamlett had been one of the country's top referees. One of several top-class officials to come from the north-east, he was just 32 years old when he took charge of the 1914 FA Cup Final between Burnley and Liverpool at Crystal Palace. He was also the referee for the United v Burnley FA Cup quarter-final of 1908/09 which he abandoned with 18 minutes to play with the Reds trailing 1-0. United went on to win the re-arranged game and of course the FA Cup.

Bamlett started his managerial career with Oldham Athletic and was in charge at both Wigan Athletic and Middlesbrough before arriving at Old Trafford.

Though he was in charge of United for four seasons, things on the field of play hardly improved and though he brought in prolific marksmen in the shape of Tommy Reid and Henry Rowley, United finished bottom of the First Division in 1930/31 – this after losing their first 12 games and conceding a total of 115 games. Therefore it came as no surprise when at the end of that very depressing campaign, Bamlett and United parted company.

United's playing record under Herbert Bamlett:

P	W	D	L	F	A	Success Rate
171	52	39	80	260	361	42%

WALTER CRICKMER 1931 to 1932 and 1937 to 1945

Although he never actually assumed the title of manager, Walter Crickmer twice combined his duties as the club's secretary with that of team selection.

Without doubt, Crickmer was one of the finest administrators in Manchester United's history, first taking charge of team affairs along with scout Louis Rocca prior to the start of the 1931-32 season, between the reigns of Herbert Bamlett and Scott Duncan. United finished the campaign in mid-table in the Second Division.

After Scott Duncan resigned in 1937, United were again without a manager until the appointment of the great Matt Busby and again the board turned to Crickmer. Not only did he help out with the playing affairs but his job also saw him take charge of United through the troubled years of 1939–1945.

It was Walter Crickmer who, in 1938, was largely responsible for the formation of the famous Manchester United youth policy that has served the club well in the subsequent years. Sadly, Walter Crickmer, who had first joined United as secretary in 1926, lost his life in the Munich Air disaster after 38 years at Old Trafford.

United's playing record under Walter Crickmer:

P	W	D	L	F	A	Success Rate
112	45	30	37	195	175	54%

SCOTT DUNCAN 1932 to 1937

Scott Duncan, who played his football for Dumbarton, Glasgow Rangers and Newcastle United, was offered the post of Manchester United manager in August 1932 for a salary reported to be in the region of £800 per annum.

Duncan had once played for the Reds during the First World War regional league games and had managed both Hamilton and Cowdenbeath before arriving at Old Trafford.

In his first couple of seasons at the club, he spent a great deal of money on new signings – players that included Scottish internationals Neil Dewar from Third Lanark and Stewart Chalmers from Cowdenbeath together with Irish international David Byrne from Shamrock Rovers and Welsh international Tommy Bamford from Wrexham.

After United narrowly avoided relegation in 1933/34, Duncan came under fire from both newspapers and supporters for the club – despite these new faces – failing to produce the goods. However, two years later, Duncan steered the Reds to the Second Division title but they weren't really equipped for life in the top flight and after just one season, they were relegated.

After the first 14 games of the 1938/39 season, Duncan resigned and took over the reins at Ipswich Town who were then a Southern League club. He took them into the Football League and in 1953/54 they won the Third Division (South) title but were relegated the following year and he left the club soon afterwards.

United's playing record under Scott Duncan:

P	W	D	L	F	A	Success Rate
224	89	50	85	361	341	51%

SIR MATT BUSBY 1945 to 1969 and 1970 to 1971

The one-minute silent tribute to Sir Matt Busby before United's Premiership match against Everton at Old Trafford on 22 January 1994 marked a moving and emotional farewell to a football legend.

Appointed in 1945, the great manager had been associated with United for 49 years and had steered the Reds to its finest hour and also lived through the saddest period in the club's history.

The son of a Scottish miner, Busby was a stylish wing-half with both Manchester City and Liverpool before the Second World War and although he won only one full cap for Scotland, he skippered his country in a number of wartime internationals.

When appointed, he inherited a club with no home for Old Trafford had been badly damaged in the hostilities. His team played their home matches at Maine Road as he began to rebuild from the ashes. The first of the tracksuit managers, he led his side to runners-up spot in the League in the first two seasons after the war but in 1947/48 they went on to win the FA Cup beating Blackpool 4-2. United finished as League runners-up twice more in 1948/49 and 1950/51 but in 1951/52 they won their first Championship for 41 years.

In their first six seasons under Busby's leadership, United never finished lower than fourth in Division One. With Jimmy Murphy by his side, the two of them discovered some outstanding raw talent in Roger Byrne, Duncan Edwards, Tommy Taylor and Bobby Charlton.

In 1955/56, Busby's brilliant young team won the title by 11 points from Blackpool. They repeated the feat in 1956/57 this time beating Spurs and Preston to the title. That season they almost did the League and Cup 'double' but lost 2-1 to Aston Villa in a final dominated by controversy. In that season's European Cup, they gave a good account of themselves by reaching the semi-finals where they lost to Real Madrid.

The following season, Busby's European Cup dream was shattered by the Munich disaster where the United boss suffered injuries so severe that he was administered the Last Rites. He also had to suffer the cruel knowledge that he had lost many of his young players.

After being absent from his desk for half a year, he and Murphy began to assemble a new Manchester United – Law, Herd, Crerand and Cantwell were drafted in as the Reds won the FA Cup again in 1963 and the League Championship in 1964/65. Another League title two years later set the stage for another attempt at the European Cup and this time the United manager's dream was realised with a magnificent victory over Benfica.

He made way for Wilf McGuinness but retained the post of General manager. When McGuinness was relieved of his job in December 1970, Busby took charge once more. Knighted after the Benfica success, he left the manager's chair in 1971 after which he maintained close links with the club and the city of Manchester. He was made a Freeman of Manchester in 1967, appointed a United director and then the club's president.

United's playing record under Sir Matt Busby:

P	W	D	L	F	A	Success Rate
972	480	231	261	1942	1361	61%

JIMMY MURPHY 1958

Welsh international wing-half Jimmy Murphy played the majority of his League football for West Bromwich Albion. During the Second World War, he served in Italy, where he met Matt Busby and when the Scot was offered the United manager's job in 1945, Murphy joined him. Initially he was employed as the club's coach but he was always Busby's right-hand man and in 1955 he was officially appointed the club's assistant-manager.

Shortly afterwards he became the Wales national team manager and his coaching talents were recognised when he was offered a lucrative post with Italian giants Juventus.

When the United party flew to Belgrade for the tie with Red Star, Murphy missed the trip because he was on international duty with the Welsh team for a World Cup qualifier at Ninian Park. In the wake of the Munich disaster, Murphy took charge of United and led them to the 1958 FA Cup Final where they lost 2-0 to Bolton Wanderers. In August of that year, he made way for the return of Matt Busby. The Welshman had been a tower of strength in the months following the tragedy.

Murphy resigned as assistant-manager, although he continued to scout for the club he had served for over a quarter-of-a-century.

United's playing record under Jimmy Murphy:

P	W	D	L	F	A	Success Rate
14	1	5	8	12	28	25%

WILF McGUINNESS 1969 to 1970

One of the players to emerge from United's highly successful youth team of the 1950s, he appeared in three FA Youth Cup Finals and captained the England youth team. His playing career ended at the age of 22 after he broke a leg in a Central League game and he joined United's training staff.

He was involved in the preparation of several England teams including the 1966 World Cup squad and in April 1969 it was announced that he was being appointed United's chief coach in readiness for Matt Busby's retirement at the end of the season.

In June 1969 he was given the manager's job but the concept of promoting from within did not work and he had probably found it difficult to manage players who were established internationals and who had achieved a lot more than him as a player.

In December 1970 he reverted to trainer-coach of the club's reserve team before later managing the Greek club, Aris Salonika and then York City. Also a part of the Bury coaching staff and he has been much sought after since for his wit as an after-dinner speaker.

United's playing record under Wilf McGuinness:

P	W	D	L	F	A	Success Rate
64	19	25	20	90	95	49%

FRANK O'FARRELL 1971 to 1972

Republic of Ireland international wing-half Frank O'Farrell began his career with West Ham United before moving to the north-west with Preston North End. He was an important member of the North End side that finished as runners-up in the First Division in 1957-58, later leaving to play Southern League football for Weymouth.

His League management career began at Torquay United before he took charge at Leicester City. He took the then Filbert Street club to the 1969 FA Cup Final and led them to the Second Division Championship in 1970-71.

O'Farrell took over as Manchester United manager in the summer of 1971 and in his first season in charge, United finished eighth in the First Division. It was a disappointing end to a campaign which had seen them five points clear at the top of the League at Christmas.

During his time at old Trafford, O'Farrell spent quite a lot of money on players with Ted MacDougall and Ian Storey-Moore both costing £200,000 and Martin Buchan £150,000. But with the chequebook failing to halt United's slide the following season, he paid the price and was replaced by the irrepressible Tommy Docherty.

On parting company with the Reds, O'Farrell coached the Iranian national team, later managing Cardiff City before returning to Plainmoor for another spell in charge of Torquay. He then had a spell as the Devon club's general manager.

United's playing record under Frank O'Farrell:

P	W	D	L	F	A	Success Rate
64	24	16	24	89	95	50%

TOMMY DOCHERTY 1972 to 1977

The irrepressible Tommy Docherty, one of the best known characters in soccer, was dedicated, dynamic, reckless, ruthless, seldom predictable and always controversial!

Having started his playing career with Glasgow Celtic, he soon moved to Preston North End where he acquired then nickname 'The Doc' – having the cure for most inside-forwards rash enough to press for personal attention. He soon won full international honours for Scotland, going on to win 25 caps. He spent eight seasons at Deepdale before he was allowed to join Arsenal for £28,000 in August 1958. Tragically ironic for Docherty was his misfortune in breaking a leg when playing for the Gunners against North End!

Stamford Bridge was his next port of call, Docherty being signed as player-coach. When manager Ted Drake left, Docherty became caretaker-boss before taking the job permanently in January 1962. He could not prevent Chelsea's relegation but they bounced straight back the following term. The League Cup was won in 1965 and the Doc also took Chelsea to their first Wembley FA Cup Final. Docherty resigned in 1967 to become manager of Rotherham United but within a year he had been lured back to London with Queen's Park Rangers He sensationally quit after just 29 days in charge, taking over the reins at Aston Villa. Though he was hugely popular at Villa Park, he was sacked in January 1970 with the Midlands club lying bottom of the Second Division. The following month he was off to Portugal to manage Porto before in 1971 he was appointed Scotland's national team manager. But then in December 1972, he accepted the offer to manage Manchester United.

Certainly the United job seemed to suit him and he assembled some exciting sides during his time at Old Trafford. Although he steered them clear of relegation, they dropped into the Second Division in 1974, winning the title at the first attempt the following season. In 1975/76 the Reds finished third in the First Division and reached the FA Cup Final only to lose to Second Division Southampton. They won the trophy the following year, beating Liverpool 2-1 in the final but it was Docherty's final achievement at old Trafford. He lost his job as the result of an affair with the wife of United's physiotherapist Laurie Brown. He was then in and out of court, suffering a major setback with the collapse of his libel action against Willie Morgan and Granada TV.

He later managed Derby County and Queen's Park Rangers for a second time before he moved to Australia to manage Sydney Olympic. In June 1981 he returned to manage his former club Preston North End, later ending his first-class managerial days with Wolves. Except for a brief spell in charge at Altrincham, Tommy Docherty has since earned his money as an after-dinner speaker with engagements all over the world.

United's playing record under Tommy Docherty:

P	W	D	L	F	A	Success Rate
188	84	49	55	267	208	58%

DAVE SEXTON 1977 to 1981

United appointed their fourth manager in the space of eight years in Dave Sexton. He had enjoyed a good record as manager of Chelsea, guiding the Stamford Bridge club to an FA Cup Final replay victory over Leeds United in 1970 as well as to the European Cup-Winners' Cup Final the following year.

As manager of Queen's Park Rangers, he took the Loftus Road club to within a whisker of the League Championship in 1975/76. The Manchester United board of directors saw Sexton as the ideal person to replace Docherty, especially in the wake of the scandal which had surrounded the Scotsman's departure.

United had nothing to show at the end of Sexton's first year at the helm and despite investing almost £1 million in the likes of Scottish internationals Joe Jordan and Gordon McQueen, the club finished in mid-table. The club's league fortunes changed a little in 1978/79 and Sexton led them to Wembley for the third time in four seasons. It was a memorable final but for all the wrong reasons for United fans. Trailing 2-0, the club clawed their way back into the game with two late goals only for Arsenal to grab a dramatic winner.

In 1979/80, Dave Sexton broke United's transfer record by paying £825,000 for Chelsea's ray Wilkins. It proved a wise signing as Wilkins helped United finish as runners-up to Liverpool. However, in 1980-81 after splashing out £1 million for Garry Birtles, United found themselves back in a mid-table position and with no success in either the FA or League Cup, Sexton lost his job – this despite United having won their last seven games!

Though he was obviously a good coach, there were some that said he wasn't close to his players and found it difficult to communicate at club level. After a spell managing Coventry City, he became a member of Bobby Robson's England coaching staff.

United's playing record under Dave Sexton:

P	W	D	L	F	A	Success Rate
168	70	53	45	243	197	57%

RON ATKINSON 1981 to 1986

Liverpool-born Ron Atkinson was brought up in the West Midlands. On leaving school, he worked as an apprentice engineer at the BSA tool factory. Rejected by Wolves, he signed for Aston Villa in 1956, having been spotted playing as an inside-forward for BSA Tools. Unable to make the first team at Villa Park, he was given a free transfer and joined Headington United in 1959. They changed their name to Oxford United the following year and Atkinson, converted to wing-half, captained the side to great success. They won the Southern League Championship in both the 1960/61 and 1961/62 seasons and replaced the defunct Accrington Stanley in the Football League. Atkinson served the Us for 15 years, playing in 560 matches, 383 of them in the Football League.

He began his managerial career at Kettering Town and in his first season took them to the Southern League (North Division) Championship and promotion to the Premier League.

He then joined Cambridge United and led them to the Fourth Division Championship. They were already on course for a second successive promotion when he joined West Bromwich Albion.

Atkinson led the Baggies to third place in Division One in 1979/80 and also to the UEFA Cup quarter-finals but in 1981 he replaced Dave Sexton as Manchester United manager.

He immediately went back to his former club to sign Bryan Robson for £1.5 million. In all of his seasons at Old Trafford, United did well. In 1981/82, the Reds finished third in the First Division, whilst the following season United made two Wembley appearances including defeating Brighton and Hove Albion to win the FA Cup and another third place finish in the League. In 1983-84, Atkinson's United side reached the semi-finals of the European Cup-Winners' Cup and finished fourth in the First Division. In 1985, United again won the FA Cup and though ten successive victories in 1985/86 put United well ahead of the pack, their form tailed off badly and they had to be satisfied with fourth place. The 1986/87 season opened disastrously and in November with the club fourth off the bottom, he was sacked.

After a short second spell at the Hawthorns, he was enticed to join Athletico Madrid but after just 96 days, he was sacked. In February 1989 he became manager of Sheffield Wednesday and despite suffering relegation in 1989/90 returned the club to the top flight the following season and won the League Cup.

In the summer of 1991, Atkinson turned his back on the Owls to take charge at Aston Villa. HE took the Midlands club to runners-up in the Premiership in 1992/93 and to victory in the League Cup in 1994. In 1995/96, Villa's season began to fall apart and he was sacked. After becoming manager at Coventry City, he handed the reins over to Gordon Strachan, later ending his managerial career with Nottingham Forest.

After leaving management he worked as a TV pundit but this came to an end after he was forced to resign following a racist remark. He then had spells as Director of Football with Kettering and Halesowen before leaving to pursue his business interests.

United's playing record under Ron Atkinson:

P	W	D	L	F	A	Success Rate
223	108	63	52	349	207	63%

SIR ALEX FERGUSON 1986 to present

Following a playing career spent as a bustling centre-forward with Queen's Park, St Johnstone, Dunfermline, Rangers and Ayr United, Alex Ferguson was appointed to his first managerial position at East Stirlingshire in July 1974. He moved to St Mirren in October of that year and in 1976/77, guided the Paisley club to the First Division Championship. This not surprisingly led to a number of offers from the bigger clubs north of the border and in 1978 he accepted the manager's job at Aberdeen.

It was at Pittodrie that he really began to make a name for himself as the Dons eclipsed their Old Firm rivals by taking three League titles, four Scottish Cups and a League Cup in eight seasons. Ferguson's greatest achievement with the Dons came in 1983, when he led the club to victory over Real Madrid in the European Cup-Winners' Cup.

The sad death of Jock Stein in 1986 led to Ferguson taking over the national team temporarily for the World Cup Finals in Mexico. Ferguson later turned down the opportunity to manage the national side and some other lucrative offers to move to England's top clubs, when in November 1986 he could not resist the temptation to join Manchester United.

His first three years at old Trafford did not bring him the success he had enjoyed in Scotland and it seemed at one stage that his tenure in Manchester may be short-lived. Victory in the 1990 FA Cup Final replay over Crystal Palace began an incredible run that saw the Reds win countless trophies as they dominated the English game. A European Cup-Winners' Cup followed in 1991 and League Cup in 1992 as United were edged into second place in the League by Leeds United. The following year saw the inauguration of the Premiership and with the newly-signed Eric Cantona in their side, United ended their 26-year wait with the capture of that elusive League title. Ferguson had become the first man to manage teams to Premier League titles north and south of the border.

In 1993/94, United and Ferguson repeated their success of the previous season, this time going one better, winning the League and Cup double. They almost made it an unprecedented treble but lost out to

Ron Atkinson's Aston Villa in the League Cup Final. After near misses in both the League and Cups in 1994/95, United won another 'double' in 1995/96. Another League title followed in 1996/97 before Arsenal stole the limelight from United the following season by winning the 'double' themselves.

The 1998/99 season brought an incredible triumph as Ferguson led the club to victory in the League, the FA Cup and the European Champions League – all in an incredible two-week period.

Though United didn't defend the FA Cup the following year and were knocked out of the Champions League at the quarter-final, they did retain the Premiership title by beating Arsenal by an incredible 18 points.

The following season brought United's seventh League Championship in nine years as they clinched the title with five games still yet to play – making Fergie the most successful manager in the history of English football.

Alex Ferguson became Sir Alex in 1999 (having received the OBE in 1983 and the CBE in 1995) as his achievements in football were recognised. The Scotsman made so many good signings, players such as Eric Cantona, Roy Keane, Peter Schmeichel, Andy Cole, Teddy Sheringham, Jaap Stam and Ole Gunnar Solskjaer. These, coupled with up and coming youngsters such as Ryan Giggs, David Beckham, Paul Scholes and the Neville brothers, helped United dominate the domestic game.

Having planned to retire as United's boss after the 2001/02 season, Ferguson had a change of heart and signed a new three-year deal to stay on at Old Trafford. He appointed a new assistant in Carlos Queiroz and smashed the British transfer record by paying Leeds United £30 million for Rio Ferdinand. Several injuries to key players at the beginning of the 2002-03 season saw United start the campaign off badly but they fought back to reverse Arsenal's lead at the top and snatch the Championship. At the LMA's annual dinner, Ferguson picked up the Barclaycard Manager of the Year award and not surprisingly the Premiership manager of the Decade awards.

In January 2004 Ferguson signed an extension to his contract, celebrating later in the year with an FA Cup Final victory over Millwall.

Action on the pitch the following season was overtaken by events off it as American businessman Malcolm Glazer seized control of the United board. Though the club missed the departed Roy Keane, they did win the

Carling Cup and finished runners-up in the League. In 2006/07, Ferguson and United won their ninth Premiership title but they were denied the chance of another treble or double by defeat in the FA Cup Final and Champions League semi-final.

In 2007/08, Ferguson led United to a Premiership and UEFA Champions League 'double' pipping Chelsea for the domestic title and then beating the same opposition on penalties to lift the European crown. In 2008/9, United won their 18th League title and took part in another Champions League final, unfortunately losing 2-0 to Barcelona.

He has certainly cemented his reputation as one of the game's truly great managers.

United's record under Sir Alex Ferguson

P	W	D	L	F	A	Success Rate
1276	746	302	228	2301	1142	58%

CHAPTER FIVE

FAMOUS MATCHES

MANCHESTER UNITED'S TOP 20 FAMOUS MATCHES

1	1892	Blackburn Rovers 4 Newton Heath 3
2	1894	Manchester City 2 Newton Heath 5
3	1909	Manchester United 1 Bristol City 0
4	1934	Millwall 0 Manchester United 2
5	1948	Manchester United 4 Blackpool 2
6	1956	Manchester United 10 RSC Anderlecht 0
7	1958	Arsenal 4 Manchester United 5
8	1958	Manchester United 3 Sheffield Wednesday 0
9	1966	Benfica 1 Manchester United 5
10	1968	Manchester United 4 Benfica 1
11	1974	Manchester United 0 Manchester City 1
12	1977	Manchester United 2 Liverpool 1
13	1979	Arsenal 3 Manchester United 2
14	1985	Manchester United 1 Everton 0
15	1991	Manchester United 2 Barcelona 1
16	1999	Manchester United 2 Bayern Munich 1
17	2001	Tottenham Hotspur 3 Manchester United 5
18	2003	Manchester United 4 Real Madrid 3
19	2007	Manchester United 7 AS Roma 1
20	2008	Manchester United 1 Chelsea 1

MATCH 1   **BLACKBURN ROVERS 4 NEWTON HEATH 3**
3 September 1892

Blackburn Rovers
Pennington; Murray; Forbes; Almond; Dewar; Forrest;
Chippendale; Walton; Southworth; Hall; Bowdler
Newton Heath
Warner; Clements; Brown; Perrins; Stewart; FC Erentz;
Farman; Coupar; Donaldson; Carson; Mathieson
Attendance 8,000
Referee T Helme (Farnworth)

After spending three years in the Football Alliance, Newton Heath were admitted to the Football League. The club's first taste of action in the competition they had been trying to join for a good number of years came at Ewood Park, the home of one of the leading sides of the day, Blackburn Rovers.

Rovers had four years of League experience behind them and not only that, they won the FA Cup five times. Not surprisingly, they were the clear favourites to win this opening day encounter. But when the game kicked off at 4 o'clock, the home aside were surprised by the attacking football played by the Heathens, who despite playing into the wind, were the dominant side early on.

Even so, it was Blackburn Rovers who took the lead after five minutes thanks to a fine individual goal by the prolific Jack Southworth. Two minutes later, Hall extended the home sides lead, although the Heathens defenders appealed for offside. Rovers then began to dominate the proceedings and came close to adding to their lead on a number of occasions. The game was only 15 minutes old when Hall latched on to a fine ball by Chippendale to put Blackburn 3-0 up.

Newton Heath pulled a goal back through Donaldson – their first in the Football League before a minute or so prior to half-time, Coupar broke free and rounded Pennington before rolling the ball into the empty net for the Heathens' second goal.

Sadly there was to be no great fight-back and midway through the second-half, winger Chippendale cut in from the right and beat Warner's despairing dive to restore Blackburn's two-goal lead. Newton Heath were then pinned in their own half for much of the remaining minutes of the game but shortly before full-time, Farman broke away and scored a third goal for the Heathens from an acute angle. The strike left Newton Heath's first Football League scoreline looking slightly more respectable!

MATCH 2   MANCHESTER CITY 2 NEWTON HEATH 5
3 November 1894

Manchester City
Hutchinson; H Smith; Walker; Mann; Nash; Dyer;
Meredith; Finnerhan; Rowan; Sharples; Milarvie
Newton Heath
Douglas; McCartney; F Erentz; Perrins; McNaught;
Davidson; Clarkin; Donaldson; Dow; R Smith; Peters
Attendance 14,000
Referee J Lewis (Blackburn)

The very first Football League meeting between Manchester's two major clubs took place at City's Hyde Road ground over 100 years ago. City had recently changed their name from Ardwick but United were to be known as Newton Heath for a further eight years.

The Heathens had just been relegated and all Manchester football fans eagerly awaited the first clash between the two clubs since they joined the Football League two years previously. A crowd of 14,000 braved what was a dull, miserable November day and they saw City's winger Billy Meredith who was making his home debut, put in a fine solo run before shooting narrowly wide.

It was Newton Heath who opened the scoring after five minutes when inside-left Smith's shot took a nasty deflection, sending Hutchinson the wrong way. The Heathens extended their lead after 13 minutes when the same player gave the City keeper no chance whatsoever with a powerfully struck low shot from fully 25 yards.

The rest of the first-half saw City mount attack after attack and the fact that they failed to get on the scoresheet was down to a number of fine saves in the Newton Heath goal by Douglas.

The home side found themselves reduced to 10-men shortly after the restart after full-back Smith limped off following a heavy challenge from

Peters. The Heathens went further ahead soon after wards when Clarkin netted from close range. Within the space of five minutes, Newton Heath's Smith had scored two further goals to take his personal tally to four and put Newton Heath 5-0 up.

It was another big disappointment to the home side who had lost their previous home game 4-2 to lowly Darwen and then a nine-goal thriller 5-4 at Newcastle. However, they did salvage a little pride with two late goals courtesy of Meredith and Sharples.

MATCH 3   MANCHESTER UNITED 1 BRISTOL CITY 0
24 April 1909

Manchester United
Moger; Stacey; Hayes; Duckworth; Roberts; Bell;
Meredith; Halse; J Turnbull; A Turnbull; Wall
Bristol City
Clay; Annan; Cottle; Hanlin; Wedlock; Spear; Staniforth;
Hardy; Gilligan; Burton; Hilton
Attendance 71,401
Referee J Mason (Burslem)

Despite the 1909 FA Cup Final played at Crystal Palace being a disappointing affair, the game stands out in Manchester United's history as being the first time the club won the trophy.

Even though United were below their opponents in the First Division table, they were clear favourites. They had been the previous season's League Champions and most pundits thought that their greater experience would give them the edge on the big day.

Early in the game, United's forwards mounted a number of attacks but missed several golden opportunities to open the scoring, notably one particular glaring miss from George Wall. As the game wore on though, Billy Meredith proved the difference between the teams. He was United's great motivator and he was determined to add to the winners' medal he had won with Manchester City five years earlier.

United forward Sandy Turnbull had only decided to play at the last minute when skipper Charlie Roberts persuaded him that even with a badly injured knee, he could be capable of winning the game on his own. He certainly didn't disappoint his captain and in the 22nd minute, he scored what proved to be the game's only goal.

Harold Halse's shot rebounded off the crossbar and with Bristol City keeper Clay still on the ground, Turnbull turned the ball over the line. Moments later at the other end, Moger made a fine save from City's inside-right Hardy whilst United's best effort following the goal came from wall who forced Clay into making an equally good save.

United full-back Vince Hayes also played for most of the game with a broken rib as both sides occasionally indulged in rough play. This escalated towards the end of the game and tempers began to fray as City pressed for an equaliser whilst United were cautioned for blatant time-wasting.

However, nothing could spoil the moment when Charlie Roberts became the first Manchester United captain to proudly hold aloft the FA Cup.

MATCH 4   MILLWALL 0 MANCHESTER UNITED 2
5 May 1934

Millwall
Yuill; Walsh; Pipe; Newcomb; Turnbull; Forsyth;
McCartney; Alexander; Yardley; Roberts; Fishlock
Manchester United
Hacking; Griffiths; Jones; Robertson; Vose; McKay;
Cape;McLenahan; Ball; Hine; Manley
Attendance 24,003
Referee JH Whittle (Worcester)

Manchester United travelled to Millwall on the last day of the 1933/34 season for the most crucial match in the club's history. Defeat or even a draw would see United relegated to the Third Division for the first time – and one London newspaper had had the audacity to even review the club's prospects in the lowest division.

To make things even more difficult for the Reds, Millwall were also fighting to stave off relegation to Division Three, yet for a club bear the foot of Division two, their home form was quite impressive. Lincoln City were already down and the other relegation place lay between United (32 points) MIllwall (33 points) and Swansea (33 points) – all clubs having just one game to play. United were quietly confident having not lost in their four previous games and won at both Brentford and Fulham on their previous travels to London.

The opening few minutes saw the home side launch a series of frenzied attacks on the United goal but with just eight minutes played, it was the Reds who took the lead. It was the wing pairing of Manley and Cape that did the damage. Manley played the ball out wide for Cape, who beat his marker and crossed to the far post where Manley had made good ground to head past Yuill.

United's Hine was injured in a over-the-ball challenge by Newcomb and he was a virtual passenger for the remaining three-quarters of the game. United hung on desperately to their slender lead but then two minutes after the interval, Cape put the Reds 2-0 with a powerful drive from distance.

With George Vose giving a sterling display at the heart of United's defence, they held on and it was Millwall who were relegated.

MATCH 5   MANCHESTER UNITED 4 BLACKPOOL 2
24 April 1948

Manchester United
Crompton; Carey; Aston; Anderson; Chilton;
Cockburn; Delaney; Morris; Rowley; Pearson; Mitten
Blackpool
Robinson; Shimwell; Crosland; Johnston; Hayward;
Kelly; Matthews; Munro; Mortensen; Dick; Rickett
Attendance 99,000
Referee CJ Barrick (Northampton)

It was 39 years to the day since Manchester United had last appeared in an FA Cup Final. On that occasion, the Reds beat Bristol City 1-0 in a fairly dull affair but this 1948 final was completely different, being hailed as one of the finest ever seen.

Both sides showed their intent early on and both keepers were forced into making outstanding saves. It was the Seasiders who took the lead after 12 minutes when they were awarded a penalty following Chilton's foul on Mortensen. Though the challenge was definitely an unfair one, United's players felt it had been committed outside the area. Up strode full-back Shimwell and his low drive went under the body of the diving Crompton.

A mix-up in front of goal between the Blackpool keeper and Hayward allowed Jack Rowley to nip in and level the scores just before the half-hour mark. But Blackpool regained the lead on 35 minutes when Kelly headed on a Stanley Matthews free-kick and Mortensen scored.

Matthews had been running the United defence ragged in the first-half but the Reds managed to shut him out in the second period and in a 14-minute spell, they scored three times!

In the 69th minute, Jack Rowley got between two Blackpool defenders to head home a Johnny Morris free-kick but a minute later Crompton brought off a tremendous save from Mortensen. It was the United keeper's quick clearance that brought his side their third goal. It was his long throw to Anderson that allowed the United wing-half time and space to set up Pearson who shot past the onrushing Robinson.

Seven minutes from time, United went further ahead when Anderson's centre found the back of the Blackpool net via a hefty deflection from Kelly. After what was truly a great match, United skipper Johnny Carey accepted the FA Cup from King George VI.

MATCH 6   MANCHESTER UNITED 10 RSC ANDERLECHT 0
26 September 1956

Manchester United
Wood; Foulkes; Byrne; Colman; Jones; Edwards;
Berry; Whelan; Taylor; Viollet; Pegg
RSC Anderlecht
Week; Gettemans; Culot; Hanon; De Koster; Vanderwilt;
De Dryver; Vandenbosche; Mermans; Dewael; Jurion
Attendance 40,000
Referee BM Griffiths (Newport)

Having opened their European campaign a couple of weeks earlier with a 2-0 win in the first leg in Brussels, United were confident of making further progress in the competition, even though the game was being played at City's Maine Road ground due to the Reds not having floodlights at the time.

On a very wet night, it was Anderlecht who mounted the first attack of the game but it was United who mastered the difficult muddy conditions to take the lead with a classic goal and after only nine minutes. Roger Byrne's punt upfield found David Pegg who beat several Belgian defenders before finding Tommy Taylor with an inch-perfect cross. The centre-forward headed home and then moments later toe-poked his and United's second goal.

The prolific Dennis Viollet scored United's third and fourth goals, both coming as a result of defensive errors and then completed his hat-trick with a fiercely struck shot from the edge of the penalty area.

Early in the second-half, Tommy Taylor also completed his hat-trick as the Reds went 6-0 up after he forced the ball home from close range following a goalmouth scramble. Billy Whelan added a seventh for the Reds and Viollet then scored his fourth of the game from Roger Byrne's astute pass. Johnny Berry who by his standards was having a quiet game, made it 9-0 before Billy Whelan took the score into double-figures!

Only David Pegg of United's forwards failed to get on the scoresheet but he played as well as anyone in this magnificent display. Welsh referee Mervyn Griffiths summed up the night's performance when he said 'They couldn't pick an England side to beat this United team.'

MATCH 7   ARSENAL 4 MANCHESTER UNITED 5
1 February 1958

Arsenal
Kelsey; S Charlton; Evans; Ward; Fotheringham;
Bowen; Groves; Tapscott; Herd; Bloomfield; Nutt
Manchester United
Gregg; Foulkes; Byrne; Colman; Jones; Edwards;
Morgans; R Charlton; Taylor; Viollet; Scanlon
Attendance 63,578
Referee GW Pullin (Bristol)

Manchester United and Arsenal have produced some fabulous football matches over the years and the game played at Highbury in the winter of 1958 gave a near-capacity crowd of 63,578 nine goals to savour and although they didn't know it at the time, the last opportunity to see this great United team play on English soil.

United were chasing the First Division title and by half-time in a one-sided first-half, they led the Gunners 3-0. The hugely-talented wing-half Duncan Edwards had opened the scoring firing the ball hard and low past Jack Kelsey's despairing dive. Tommy Taylor and Bobby Charlton were United's other scorers in a half that saw Arsenal's Welsh international keeper perform heroics.

The home side's fans were resigned to a heavy home defeat as the Reds looked unstoppable. But instead they saw the Gunners contribute to a most memorable second-half.

There was just half-an-hour remaining when Arsenal scored three goals in the space of just three minutes! Harry Gregg was powerless to stop David Herd's shot and then Jimmy Bloomfield netted two in quick succession – Gunners fans could hardly believe it, the scores were level.

United's answer was to fight back and Dennis Viollet headed the Reds back into the lead before Tommy Taylor made it 5-3 with a shot from a near-impossible angle. Even then Arsenal were not to be outdone and Derek Tapscott, another Welsh international in the Arsenal side made it 5-4.

As the fans poured out of Highbury, they reflected on the great game they had just seen. They could also say they had seen Roger Byrne, Duncan Edwards, Eddie Colman, Tommy Taylor and Mark Jones, for just five days later, these great players lay dead or dying following the Munich air disaster.

MATCH 8 MANCHESTER UNITED 3 SHEFFIELD WEDNESDAY 0
19 February 1958

Manchester United
Gregg; Foulkes; Greaves; Goodwin; Cope; Crowther;
Webster; E Taylor; Dawson; Pearson; Brennan
Sheffield Wednesday
Ryalls; Martin; Baker; Kay; Swan; O'Donnell; Wilkinson;
Quixall; Johnson; Froggatt; Cargill
Attendance 59,848
Referee A Bond (Middlesex)

On a night of a thousand emotions, Manchester United played their first match since the Munich air disaster, and FA Cup fifth round tie against Sheffield Wednesday.

Drafted into the United side were youngsters Alex Dawson, Ian Greaves, Freddie Goodwin, Ron Cope, Colin Webster, Mark Pearson and Shay Brennan

– their sum total of Football League experience being just 75 games. They were aided by the experience of Harry Gregg and Bill Foulkes, while the club had been given special permission by the FA to play Ernie Taylor and Stan Crowther, although technically they were ineligible.

The reception given to the teams was deafening but there was soon a hush around the Old Trafford ground as everyone stood in one minute's silence for the fallen United heroes.

United opened the scoring after 27 minutes when Wednesday keeper Ryalls made two errors. First he punched a Bill Foulkes free-kick out for a corner when the ball appeared to be sailing harmlessly wide and then he helped Shay Brennan's corner into the net! For Brennan, a young full-back who had been called up to play at outside-left, it was a moment he would never ever forget.

There was more for the popular Brennan to treasure when he put United 2-0 ahead after Pearson's shot had rebounded off the Wednesday keeper's knees. Pearson was also involved in United's third goal five minutes from the end of this pulsating game when he took the ball to the by-line before pulling it back for Alex Dawson to score.

United's 3-0 win earned them a quarter-final tie on the next step of what was an amazing journey that ended in defeat to Bolton Wanderers in the Wembley final.

MATCH 9   **BENFICA 1 MANCHESTER UNITED 5**
9 March 1966

Benfica
Costa Pereira; Carem; Germano; Cruz; Pinto; Coluna;
Augusto Silva; Eusebio; Torres; Jose Augusto; Simoes
Manchester United
Rennan; A Dunne; Crerand; Foulkes; Stiles; Best;
Law; Charlton; Herd; Connelly
Attendance 75,000
Referee C Lo Bello (Italy)

United travelled to Lisbon for their second leg tie against Portuguese giants Benfica with the narrowest of leads after winning the first leg 3-2 at Old Trafford.

Reds fans need not have worried because the mercurial George Best helped United give one of the greatest displays of attacking football ever mounted by an away side in European competition. They left Benfica, the previous season's finalists battered and bruised!

United scored three goals in the opening quarter-of-an-hour to settle the issue. The first came after six minutes when Best rose against a packed Benfica defence to head past Costa Pereira. Five minutes later, the Irish international collected a ball from David Herd and raced through the defence to hit a low shot under the keeper. Best was also involved in United's third goal when his pin-point pass was hammered home by John Connelly.

Eusebio, who had been presented with the European Footballer of the Year award before the kick-off then hit a post with a curling free-kick but on the night he looked an ordinary player compared to George Best.

Even when the home side did score, it was courtesy of an own-gaol by United full-back Shay Brennan but the Reds was so composed and in the 80th minute, Pat Crerand hit a defence-splitting pass from Denis Law to make it 4-1. In the dying moments of the game, Bobby Charlton virtually walked through a tired Benfica defence to pause before slotting home United's fifth goal.

Having seen their team humiliated, Benfica fans hurled cushions on the pitch. The 'Eagles of Lisbon' had been completely outplayed as the Reds reached what was their third semi-final. However, European glory was still a little way off.

MATCH 10   MANCHESTER UNITED 4 BENFICA 1 (after extra-time)
29 May 1968

Manchester United
Stepney; Brennan; Dunne; Crerand; Foulkes; Stiles;
Best; Kidd; Charlton; Sadler; Aston
Benfica
Henrique; Adolfo; Humberto; Jacinto; Cruz; Graca;
Coluna; Augusto; Eusebio; Torres;Simoes
Attendance 100,000
Referee C Lo Bello (Italy)

In 1968, Matt Busby realised a dream, for after three unsuccessful European Cup semi-final appearances and a tragedy that wiped out one of the finest club sides ever seen, United walked out at Wembley led by Bobby Charlton.

The first-half was a fairly uninspiring affair with neither keeper really being tested and though the second period wasn't a classic, it certainly lived up to the occasion in terms of excitement.

The Reds took the lead when David Sadler and Republic of Ireland international full-back Tony Dunne combined on the left. Sadler crossed into the box and Bobby Charlton sent a glancing header past Henrique. The goal gave United confidence and they might have gone further ahead after good work by John Aston but Sadler wasted the opportunity. Ten minutes from full-time, Benfica drew level through Graca and then with just four minutes to play, United's dream was almost shattered.

Eusebio broke free of his marker Nobby Stiles and sent in a stinging shot which United keeper Alex Stepney blocked. It was the Black Pearl's desire to score a dramatic winner, rather than the simple goal which presented itself that kept United's hopes alive.

Two minutes into the first period of extra-time and George Best scored a goal of rare brilliance, leaving the entire Benfica defence in his wake before rounding Henrique. A minute later, Brian Kidd – who was celebrating his 19th birthday – settled the issue with a header and then a third goal in the space of eight minutes from skipper Charlton gave United a 4-1 victory.

Most British football fans up and down the country savoured one of the game's most emotional nights whilst United and in particular Munich survivors Busby, Charlton and Foulkes thought back to the men who lost their lives and with it their chance of glory.

MATCH 11   MANCHESTER UNITED 0 MANCHESTER CITY 1
27 April 1974

Manchester United
Stepney; Forsyth; Houston; B Greenhoff; Holton; M Buchan; Morgan; Macari; McIlroy; McCalliog; Daly
Manchester City
Corrigan; Barrett; Donachie; Doyle; Booth; Oakes; Summerbee; Bell; Lee; Law (Hanson); Tueart

Attendance 56,996
Referee DW Smith (Stonehouse, Gloucestershire)

Manchester United went into their final home match of the 1973-74 season facing the situation that left rivals Manchester City holding the key to the Old Trafford club's immediate future. A defeat would most certainly put the Reds into the Second Division for the first time in 36 years and whilst a draw may well have secured their safety, there were many imponderables on what was the last Saturday of the League season.

A packed Old Trafford crowd gave former favourite Denis Law a warm reception on what was his last Football League appearance. The Lawman was made City captain for the day but little did United fans know that before the day was out, he would be the player who would ultimately send the Reds into the Second Division!

Apart from the final few minutes, the game itself had little to offer in terms of entertainment. Chances were few and far between with Daly and Macari going closest for United and Doyle for the visitors.

United did most of the attacking in the second-half and were unlucky to see first Doyle and then Barrett clear shots off the City line.

Then with just eight minutes remaining, Lee and Bell combined to find Law. The City man simply back-heeled the ball straight past keeper Alex Stepney and into the United net. It was to be Denis Law's last touch in League football. United fans invaded the pitch and when the game was restarted a full three minutes later, Law had been replaced by Hanson.

A second pitch invasion and a fire on the Stretford End caused referee David Smith, who was in charge of his last match, to abandon the game. The Football League ordered the result to stand and United were relegated!

MATCH 12   MANCHESTER UNITED 2 LIVERPOOL 1
21 May 1977

Manchester United
Stepney; Nicholl; Albiston; McIlroy; B Greenhoff; Buchan; Coppell; J Greenhoff; Pearson; Macari; Hill (McCreery)
Liverpool
Clemence; Neal; Jones; Smith; Kennedy; Hughes; Keegan; Case; Heighway; Johnson (Callaghan); McDermott

Attendance 100,000
Referee R Matthewson (Bolton)

After surprisingly losing the previous season's FA Cup Final to Second Division Southampton, the Reds had an even tougher-looking match when they met League Champions Liverpool in the 1977 Final. But United went on to prevent the Merseyside club from completing a League and Cup double just as they themselves had been denied 20 years earlier.

Liverpool were the better side in the first-half but despite all their pressure they couldn't find a way past United's back four and the impressive Stepney in the Reds' goal. In fact they were the better side throughout, save for a five minute spell at the start of the second-half. In the space of that five minutes, United scored two goals to Liverpool's one.

In the 50th minute, Stuart Pearson took a pass from Jimmy Greenhoff and shot low under Ray Clemence's body – a strike that showed why he was regarded as one of the game's great opportunist goalscorers.

Two minutes later, Liverpool got the goal their play deserved when Jimmy Case levelled the scores. His goal was the best of the game. Turning on the edge of the United penalty area, he hit a Joey Jones cross into the top left-hand corner of Stepney's net.

Then in the 55th minute, United were back in front with a most fortunate goal. Jimmy Greenhoff seized upon a mistake by the usually reliable Tommy Smith and his shot rebounded to Lou Macari. The Scottish international's shot could have gone almost anywhere but struck Jimmy Greenhoff and flew past Clemence!

Ray Kennedy, who had gone close for Liverpool in the first-half when his header struck a post, hit a thunderous shot against a stanchion as Liverpool pressed in the closing stages for another equaliser, but United held on and the Cup was on its way to Old Trafford.

MATCH 13   ARSENAL 3 MANCHESTER UNITED 2
12 May 1979

Arsenal
Jennings; Rice; Nelson; Talbot; O'Leary; Young; Brady; Sunderland; Stapleton; Price (Walford); Rix

Manchester United
Bailey; Nicholl; Albiston; McIlroy; McQueen; Buchan;
Coppell; J Greenhoff; Jordan; Macari; Thomas
Attendance 100,000
Referee R Challis (Tonbridge)

In an FA Cup Final that only really came to life in the last five minutes, Arsenal beat Manchester United 3-2 in one of Wembley's most memorable finishes.

Arsenal fans were ecstatic as they led 2-0 and though the United fans were still roaring their team on, deep down they knew it was an uphill battle. Then came a sensational fightback by the Reds – and ultimate agony as the Gunners came back again in one of the most rousing finales ever seen at the famous old ground.

Arsenal made the best start and took the lead after 12 minutes following some neat interplay between Brady and Stapleton. David Price broke clear and drove a low cross into the United box where Talbot and Sunderland arrived together. It was the former Ipswich man Talbot who was credited with getting the final touch. Just before half-time, Brady, who had been the architect of his side's first goal set up Arsenal's second goal for Frank Stapleton – a player later to play for United.

As the second-half wore on, the Gunners maintained their control of the match and with just four minutes left, the score remained 2-0 in Arsenal's favour.

Then the game was completely transformed. Arsenal failed to clear a free-kick and Gordon McQueen swung a boot at a loose ball and United were back in the match. Two minutes later, Sammy McIlroy cut in from the right, evaded a couple of challenges and then rolled the ball past Pat Jennings for the equaliser.

United had clawed back from the jaws of defeat, or so they thought, and extra-time looked imminent. But Liam Brady had no intention of letting the game slip now and he started the move which saw Rix take the ball down the left-wing before crossing to where Alan Sunderland was racing in to snatch a dramatic winner!

MATCH 14 MANCHESTER UNITED 1 EVERTON 0
18 May 1985

Manchester United
Bailey; Gidman; Albiston (Duxbury); Whiteside; McGrath;
Moran; Robson; Strachan; Hughes; Stapleton; Olsen
Everton
Southall; Stevens; Van den Hauwe; Ratcliffe; Mountfield;
Reid; Steven; Sharp; Gray; Bracewell; Sheedy
Attendance 100,000
Referee R Willis (Meadowfield)

In 1977, Manchester United had ended Liverpool's hopes of a League, FA Cup and European treble by winning at Wembley and in 1985 they did exactly the same to the other Merseyside outfit Everton!

The Blues had already won the Canon League trophy and the European Cup-Winners' Cup and were fully expecting to achieve what no other club had ever done – win the League and Cup double and a European trophy in the same season.

The game certainly wasn't a classic for the first 78 minutes, with both sides resorting to chancing their luck from distance but then when referee Peter Willis, a retired police inspector sent off United's Kevin Moran, the game burst into life. Willis felt that Moran's challenge on Peter Reid deserved a red card but most spectators whether at the game or watching on television, felt it was the kind of tackle seen on every ground up and down the country at the weekend. No matter, Kevin Moran became the first man to be sent-off in an FA Cup Final.

The loss of the Irishman spurred United on and even when the game went into extra-time after ninety minutes of goalless football, United's 10-men were far from finished. Wide players Olsen and Strachan in particular ran the opposition ragged with long runs deep into Everton's defence.

Ten minutes from the end of the 120 minutes of play, the Reds achieved a breakthrough. Northern Ireland international Norman Whiteside produced a curling shot which totally deceived Neville Southall in the Everton goal.

Moran had to wait a number of weeks before collecting his winners' medal as United produced one of the final's most courageous victories.

MATCH 15   MANCHESTER UNITED 2 BARCELONA 1
15 May 1991

Manchester United
Sealey; Irwin; Bruce; Pallister; Blackmore; Phelan;
Ince; Robson; McClair; Hughes; Sharpe
Barcelona
Busquets; Nando Munoz; Alexanco (Pinilla); Koeman;
Ferrer;   Bakero; Goicoechea; Salinas; Eusebio Sacristan;
M Laudrup; Beguiristain
Attendance 44,000
Referee Karlsson (Sweden)

When Manchester United arrived at the Feyenoord Stadium to face
Barcelona in the European Cup-Winners' Cup Final, they were hoping that
this would be the match to end a 23-year spell with European success.

It was the first season after the English five-year exile in Europe after
the Heysel disaster and it was most appropriate that they should be in the
final as they had been the nations first team to enter European
competition back in 1956. United had been impressive on their run top
the final but Barcelona were clear favourites, sitting top of the La Liga.
However, Mark Hughes, the player the Spanish giants rejected almost four
years previously was to prove their downfall.

United played well in the first-half but failed to score – a combination of
some good goalkeeping by Busquets and some lacklustre finishing. However,
United did take the lead after 67 minutes. Hughes was fouled on the edge of
the box. Bryan Robson took the free-kick, finding Bruce whose header downwards
looked to be going in but Hughes tore in to put the ball over the line.

Seven minutes later, the Welsh international forward broke free
from the Barca defence after an astute pass by Robson. He rounded
the Barcelona keeper but rolled his shot agonisingly wide of the far
post. But then a minute later, he made amends when scoring his and
United's second goal with an angled shot from the edge of the area –
it was the team's 100th goal of the season.

In the 79th minute, Barcelona pulled a goal back with a free kick taken
by Ronald Koeman and the next few minutes provided an anxious time
for the Reds' defence but they held firm.

In the last few seconds, Hughes looked like completing his hat-trick when he was pulled down just outside the box. The offender Nando Munoz was shown a straight red. A stray back-pass from Steve Bruce forced Clayton Blackmore into making a dramatic goal-line clearance from Michael Laudrup who had intercepted the ball and seemed certain to equalise.

United hung on to lift the trophy and Alex Ferguson was hailed as the most successful manager since Sir Matt Busby.

MATCH 16   MANCHESTER UNITED 2 BAYERN MUNICH 1
26 May 1999

Manchester United
Schmeichel; G Neville; Irwin; Johnsen; Butt; Stam; Beckham; Blomqvist (Sheringham); Cole (Solskjaer); Yorke; Giggs
Bayern Munich
Kahn; Babbel; Tarnat; Linke; Matthaus (Fink); Kuffour; Basler (Salihamidzic); Effenberg; Jancker; Zickler (Scholl); Jeremies
Attendance 90,000
Referee P Collina (Italy)

Two injury time goals from substitutes Teddy Sheringham and Ole Gunnar Solskjaer secured the European Cup for Manchester United in dramatic fashion after Bayern Munich had taken an early lead. The win saw United obtain what no English club had achieved – the treble of Premiership, FA Cup and European Cup.

For the fourth time in Europe that season, United had fallen behind after Mario Basler fired home from 25 yards – catching captain Peter Schmeichel off-guard. The set piece had been conceded after Jaap Stam collided with Carsten Jancker on the edge of the box.

Dwight Yorke then had his first chance of the game but the ball drifted inches wide of Kahn's left-hand post. It started a good period of play from United, with Bayern defending furiously. A well-floated Beckham free-kick saw Matthaus clear ff the line. The game was undoubtedly favouring the Reds but Alexander Zickler looked threatening for Bayern up front. Andy Cole scuffed another good chance on 35 minutes but at the interval United still trailed.

United's best chance of the game so far came a minute after the restart when an inch-perfect ball from Giggs found Blomqvist but the finish didn't match the build-up and the Swede fired over the bar. Moments later a long-range shot from Basler almost gave the German side a 2-0 lead but the ball shaved the top of the crossbar. Ferguson brought on Sheringham for Blomqvist with Beckham moving out to the right-wing but it was Bayern who again nearly extended their lead when Scholl chipped the ball over Schmeichel only for it to bounce off the post and directly back to the Danish keeper! With five minutes left, Bayern found the wood work again with Schmeichel beaten by an overhead kick by Jancker.

With three minutes of injury-time awarded, United looked dead and buried. But when Giggs turned a Beckham corner back into the box, Sheringham steered it home to secure an unlikely equaliser. From the kick-off United again stole possession, forcing another corner, with Solskjaer striking Sheringham's header into the roof the net.

It gave United the most thrilling of victories, with Alex Ferguson writing his name into the history books.

MATCH 17 TOTTENHAM HOTSPUR 3 MANCHESTER UNITED 5
29 September 2001

Tottenham Hotspur
Sullivan; Richards; King; Perry; Tarrico; Ziege; Freund; Anderton; Poyet; Ferdinand; Sheringham
Manchester United
Barthez; G Neville; Irwin (Silvestre); Johnsen; Blanc; Veron; Beckham; Butt (Solskjaer); Cole; Scholes; Van Nistelrooy
Attendance 36,049

Champions Manchester United staged a magnificent comeback to overwhelm Spurs at White Hart Lane. Spurs had been 3-0 up at half-time after completely outplaying the Reds in the first period. Tottenham fully deserved their interval lead. The White Hart Lane faithful cannot have seen a finer 45 minutes from their side in many years.

Spurs' five-man midfield dominated United's quartet and Ferdinand and old boy Sheringham were a constant threat in attack. New signing Dean Richards marked his debut with the opening goal after 14 minutes heading in from close range. Spurs were soon 2-0 up, with Poyet chipping the ball over a static United defence and Ferdinand spinning past Blanc as the Frenchman vainly tried to play offside. Spurs third goal came when Freund delivered a sublime right-wing cross that Ziege dived to head home from six yards.

Yet United, doubtless motivated by a forthright half-time reprimand from manager Sir Alex Ferguson were sensational in the second half.

Mikael Silvestre came on to inject pace down the left-hand side in place of Denis Irwin and Ole Gunnar Solskjaer replaced Butt as United played with three up front.

United pulled a goal back within a minute of the restart with a Cole header from Beckham's cross. United were showing far more urgency and purpose and added another when Blanc outjumped Ledley King to head a Beckham corner home. Van Nistelrooy scored the equaliser with yet another headed goal before Scholes and Solskjaer combined to play in Veron, who shot left-footed past Sullivan.

The culmination of a magnificent United comeback came three minutes from time when England captain David Beckham struck an imperious right-footed shot past Neil Sullivan from just inside the area.

MATCH 18   MANCHESTER UNITED 4 REAL MADRID 3
23 April 2003

Manchester United
Barthez; O'Shea; Silvestre (P Neville); Brown; Ferdinand; Veron (Beckham); Butt; Solskjaer; Van Nistelrooy; Keane (Fortune); Giggs

Real Madrid
Casillas; Salgado; Hierro; Helguera; Carlos; Zidane; McManaman (Portillo); Figo (Pavon); Makelele; Ronaldo (Solari) Guti

Attendance 66,708

Referee P Collina (Italy)

Ronaldo single-handedly wrecked Manchester United's Champions League dreams with a virtuoso display at Old Trafford. Real Madrid's Brazilian superstar scored a stunning hat-trick to destroy United's ambition of reaching the final on home soil the following May. Sir Alex Ferguson's men won a match liberally sprinkled with sparkling attacking football, 4-3, but Real went through 6-5 on aggregate.

Van Nistelrooy gave United early hope with a stinging drive that was well saved by Casillas. But the moment Old Trafford dreaded above all arrived after only 12 minutes when Ronaldo scored Real's crucial away goal. Guti carved open the Reds' rearguard and the Brazilian fired inside Barthez's near post. United were stunned and spent most of the first-half attempting to regain their composure and fashion a lifeline. They succeeded three minutes before the interval when Van Nistelrooy scrambled home after good work by Ole Gunnar Solskjaer.

Luis Figo posted warning signals early in the second-half when he struck the bar but it was a brief reprieve as Ronaldo was on target again after 50 minutes. United were quickly back on level terms when Helguera turned Veron's shot into his own net.

But Ronaldo was not to be denied and any lingering United ambitions ended after 58 minutes when the Brazilian marksman flashed a stunning 25-yard drive past Barthez. He was then taken off to a standing ovation from everyone inside Old Trafford.

Beckham was introduced in place of the tiring Veron and he made his point to the manager with a trademark free-kick with 20 minutes left. He then scrambled home the winner on the night but it was not enough to stop Real Madrid's march on another Champions League trophy.

MATCH 19   MANCHESTER UNITED 7 AS ROMA 1
10 April 2007

Manchester United
Van der Sar; Brown; Ferdinand; Heinze; O'Shea (Evra); Ronaldo; Fletcher; Carrick (Richardson); Giggs (Solskjaer); Rooney; Smith
AS Roma
Doni; Panucci; Mexes; Chivu; Cassetti; Wilhelmsson (Rosi); De Rossi (Faty); Vucinic; Pizarro; Mancini (Okaka Chuka); Totti
Attendance 74,476
Referee L Michel (Slovakia)

A scintillating display by Manchester United saw them tear Roma apart to reach the Champions League semi-finals. There have been many memorable performances at Old Trafford down the years but few can compare to the display Sir Alex Ferguson's men put on here.

The scuffles between fans outside the ground before kick-off were quickly forgotten once the game got underway, with the Reds looking to overturn a 2-1 deficit from the first leg.

Both sides showed attacking intentions in the opening minutes with Roma's Francesco Totti going closest with a fierce shot that fizzed past Van der Sar's right-hand post. But it was United who grabbed control of the tie with three goals in eight first-half minutes.

Carrick opened the scoring on 11 minutes when he picked up the ball from Ronaldo and bent the ball past a stationary Doni. Six minutes later it was 2-0 when Gabriel Heinze and Giggs combined before the Welshman flighted a perfect pass into the path of Smith who finished with aplomb. Rooney got in on the act soon after, timing his run superbly to slot home Giggs' low cross after the Italian side had been completely torn apart down the right flank.

A shell-shocked Roma tried to respond but their attempts to find a way back into the game only succeeded in leaving themselves more vulnerable to United's pacey attack. Ronaldo did make it 4-0 before half-time with a precise finish into the bottom corner after the Roma defence had made the mistake of inviting him to shoot.

United were quite simply superb and they did not let up after the break either. Ronaldo was in sublime form and he slid home a Giggs cross for number five before Carrick's pile driver made it 6-0 on the hour mark. Roma did get a goal back through De Rossi's neat finish but United had the final word when Evra's low shot beat Doni. Like United's first six goals, it was a fine finish and completed a magnificent victory.

MATCH 20 MANCHESTER UNITED 1 CHELSEA 1
(after extra time) Man Utd won 6-5 on penalties
21 May 2008

Manchester United
Van der Sar; Brown (Anderson); Ferdinand; Vidic; Evra; Hargreaves; Scholes (Giggs); Carrick; Ronaldo; Tevez; Rooney (Nani)
Chelsea
Cech; Essien; Carvalho; Terry; A Cole; Ballack; Makelele (Belletti); Lampard; J Cole (Anelka); Drogba; Malouda (Kalou)

Attendance 69,552

Referee Lubos Michel (Slovakia)

Manchester United won the UEFA Champions League for the third time on a night of high drama and emotion in Moscow.

The Reds' unlikely hero was Dutch goalkeeper Edwin van der Sar, with a penalty save to deny Nicolas Anelka after Chelsea skipper John Terry had missed the chance to win the trophy for the Blues by striking his own spot-kick against the post. The dramatic penalty shoot-out looked to be heading Chelsea's way after Petr Cech had saved Cristiano Ronaldo's penalty but the Chelsea captain's miss opened the door for Sir Alex Ferguson's Manchester United side.

After a disappointing start, the game turned on its head after United took a 26th minute lead through Ronaldo. Paul Scholes, who had missed United's last triumph through suspension in 1999, played a delightful interchange of passes with Wes Brown and the full-back's pin-point cross found Ronaldo at the back post. The Portuguese international sent a firm header past a static Cech to give the Reds a 1-0 lead.

Chelsea almost drew level on 33 minutes when under pressure from Michael Ballack, Ferdinand was forced to head towards his own goal where van der Sar made a superb save. But then United could have scored twice in the space of a matter of seconds. Rooney delivered a 40 yard pass into the path of Ronaldo and his cross found the head of the diving Tevez only for Cech to save. Chelsea failed to clear the loose ball and Carrick following up forced another magnificent save from the Chelsea keeper.

Then on the stroke of half-time, Michael Essien's twice-deflected shot found its way through to Frank Lampard and he made no mistake from six yards to level the scores.

In the second half, it was all Chelsea, and Drogba hit the woodwork before Ryan Giggs was introduced to make a record 759the appearance for United. The game went into extra-time and within a matter of minutes, the woodwork again came to United's rescue as Lampard crashed a left-footed shot against the crossbar. The Blues were almost made to pay dearly when Terry was forced into making a superb clearance from a goalbound Ryan Giggs shot. Drogba was then sensationally sent off for slapping Vidic as tempers began to flare.

But then the lottery of penalties ensured that the Reds clinched the trophy.

CHAPTER SIX

SEASON BY SEASON STATISTICS

1892/93

	Opposition	H/A	Score	Scorers	Attn.
1	Blackburn Rovers	A	3-4	Coupar Donaldson Farman	8,000
2	Burnley	H	1-1	Donaldson	10,000
3	Burnley	A	1-4	Donaldson	7,000
4	Everton	A	0-6		10,000
5	West Bromwich Albion	A	0-0		4,000
6	West Bromwich Albion	H	2-4	Donaldson Hood	9,000
7	Wolverhampton Wanderers	H	10-1	Donaldson 3 Stewart 3 Carson Farman Hendry Hood	4,000
8	Everton	H	3-4	Donaldson Farman Hood	4,000
9	Sheffield Wednesday	A	0-1		6,000
10	Nottingham Forest	A	1-1	Farman	6,000
11	Blackburn Rovers	H	4-4	Farman 2 Carson Hood	12,000
12	Notts County	H	1-3	Carson	8,000
13	Aston Villa	H	2-0	Coupar Fitzsimmons	7,000
14	Accrington	A	2-2	Colville Fitzsimmons	3,000
15	Bolton Wanderers	A	1-4	Coupar	3,000
16	Bolton Wanderers	H	1-0	Donaldson	4,000
17	Wolverhampton Wanderers	A	0-2		5,000
18	Sheffield Wednesday	H	1-5	Hood	4,000
19	Preston North End	A	1-2	Coupar	4,000
20	Derby County	H	7-1	Donaldson 3 Farman 3 Fitzsimmons	3,000
21	Stoke	A	1-7	Coupar	1,000
22	Nottingham Forest	H	1-3	Donaldson	8,000
23	Notts County	A	0-4		1,000

24	Derby County	A	1-5	Fitzsimmons	5,000
25	Sunderland	H	0-5		15,000
26	Aston Villa	A	0-2		4,000
27	Stoke	H	1-0	Farman	10,000
28	Preston North End	H	2-1	Donaldson 2	9,000
29	Sunderland	A	0-6		3,500
30	Accrington	H	3-3	Donaldson Fitzsimmons Stewart	3,000

● Final League Position: 16th in Division One

Test Matches

| 1 | Small Heath | N | 1-1 | Farman | 4,000 |
| 2 | Small Heath | N | 5-2 | Farman 3 Cassidy Coupar | 6,000 |

FA Cup

| 1 | Blackburn Rovers | A | 0-4 | | 7,000 |

1893/94

	Opposition	H/A	Score	Scorers	Attn.
1	Burnley	H	3-2	Farman 3	10,000
2	West Bromwich Albion	A	1-3	Donaldson	4,500
3	Sheffield Wednesday	A	1-0	Farman	7,000
4	Nottingham Forest	H	1-1	Donaldson	10,000
5	Darwen	A	0-1		4,000
6	Derby County	A	0-2		7,000
7	West Bromwich Albion	H	4-1	Peden 2 Donaldson Erentz	8,000
8	Burnley	A	1-4	Hood	7,000
9	Wolverhampton Wanderers	A	0-2		4,000
10	Darwen	H	0-1		8,000
11	Wolverhampton Wanderers	H	1-0	Davidson	5,000
12	Sheffield United	A	1-3	Fitzsimmons	2,000
13	Everton	H	0-3		6,000
14	Sunderland	A	1-4	Campbell	5,000
15	Bolton Wanderers	A	0-2		5,000
16	Aston Villa	H	1-3	Peden	8,000
17	Preston North End	A	0-2		5,000
18	Everton	A	0-2		8,000

19	Sheffield Wednesday	H	1-2	Peden	9,000
20	Aston Villa	A	1-5	Mathieson	5,000
21	Sunderland	H	2-4	McNaught Peden	10,000
22	Sheffield United	H	0-2		5,000
23	Blackburn Rovers	H	5-1	Donaldson 3 Clarkin Farmen	5,000
24	Derby County	H	2-6	Clarkin 2	7,000
25	Stoke	H	6-2	Farman 2 Peden 2 Clarkin Erentz	8,000
26	Bolton Wanderers	H	2-2	Donaldson Farman	10,000
27	Blackburn Rovers	A	0-4		5,000
28	Stoke	A	1-3	Clarkin	4,000
29	Nottingham Forest	A	0-2		4,000
30	Preston North End	H	1-3	Mathieson	4,000

• Final League Position: 16th in Division One

Test Match

1	Liverpool	N	0-2		3,000

FA Cup

1	Middlesbrough	H	4-0	Donaldson 2 Farman Peden	5,000
2	Blackburn Rovers	H	0-0 aet		18,000
2R	Blackburn Rovers	A	1-5	Donaldson	5,000

1894/95

	Opposition	H/A	Score	Scorers	Attn.
1	Burton Wanderers	A	0-1		3,000
2	Crewe Alexandra	H	6-1	Dow 2 Smith 2 Clarkin McCartney	6,000
3	Leicester Fosse	A	3-2	Dow 2 Smith	6,000
4	Darwen	A	1-1	Donaldson	6,000
5	Woolwich Arsenal	H	3-3	Donaldson 2 Clarkin	4,000
6	Burton Swifts	A	2-1	Donaldson 2	5,000
7	Leicester Fosse	H	2-2	McNaught Smith	3,000
8	Manchester City	A	5-2	Smith 4 Clarkin	14,000
9	Rotherham Town	H	3-2	Davidson Donaldson Peters	4,000
10	Grimsby Town	A	1-2	Clarkin	3,000
11	Darwen	H	1-1	Donaldson	5,000

12	Crewe Alexandra	A	2-0	Clarkin Smith	600
13	Burton Swifts	H	5-1	Peters 2 Smith 2 Dow	4,000
14	Notts County	A	1-1	Donaldson	3,000
15	Lincoln City	H	3-0	Donaldson Miller Smith	2,000
16	Burslem Port Vale	A	5-2	Clarkin Donaldson McNaught Miller Smith	1,000
17	Walsall Town Swifts	A	2-1	Miller Stewart	1,000
18	Lincoln City	A	0-3		3,000
19	Burslem Port Vale	H	3-0	Miller 2 Rothwell	5,000
20	Manchester City	H	4-1	Clarkin 2 Donaldson Smith	12,000
21	Rotherham Town	A	1-2	Erentz	2,000
22	Burton Wanderers	H	1-1	Peters	6,000
23	Grimsby Town	H	2-0	Cassidy 2	9,000
24	Woolwich Arsenal	A	2-3	Clarkin Donaldson	6,000
25	Walsall Town Swifts	H	9-0	Cassidy 2 Donaldson 2 Peters 2 Smith 2 Clarkin	6,000
26	Newcastle United	H	5-1	Cassidy 2 Smith 2 McDermidd og	5,000
27	Bury	H	2-2	Cassidy Donaldson	15,000
28	Newcastle United	A	0-3		4,000
29	Bury	A	1-2	Peters	10,000
30	Notts County	H	3-3	Cassidy Clarkin Smith	12,000

• Final League Position: 3rd in Division Two

Test Match

| 1 | Stoke | A | 0-3 | | 10,000 |

FA Cup

| 1 | Stoke | H | 2-3 | Smith Peters | 7,000 |

1895/96

	Opposition	H/A	Score	Scorers	Attn.
1	Crewe Alexandra	H	5-0	Cassidy 2 Aitken Kennedy Smith	6,000
2	Loughborough Town	A	3-3	Cassidy 2 McNaught	3,000
3	Burton Swifts	H	5-0	Donaldson 2 Cassidy 2 Kennedy	9,000
4	Crewe Alexandra	A	2-0	Smith 2	2,000
5	Manchester City	H	1-1	Clarkin	12,000

6	Liverpool	A	1-7	Cassidy	7,000
7	Newcastle United	H	2-1	Cassidy Peters	8,000
8	Newcastle United	A	1-2	Kennedy	8,000
9	Liverpool	H	5-2	Peters 3 Clarkin Smith	10,000
10	Woolwich Arsenal	A	1-2	Cassidy	9,000
11	Lincoln City	H	5-5	Clarkin 2 Cassidy Collinson Peters	8,000
12	Notts County	A	2-0	Cassidy Kennedy	3,000
13	Woolwich Arsenal	H	5-1	Cartwright 2 Clarkin Kennedy Peters	6,000
14	Manchester City	A	1-2	Cassidy	18,000
15	Notts County	H	3-0	Cassidy Clarkin Donaldson	3,000
16	Darwen	A	0-3		3,000
17	Grimsby Town	H	3-2	Cassidy 3	8,000
18	Leicester Fosse	A	0-3		7,000
19	Rotherham Town	H	3-0	Donaldson 2 Stephenson	3,000
20	Leicester Fosse	H	2-0	Kennedy Smith	1,000
21	Burton Swifts	A	1-4	Vance	2,000
22	Burton Wanderers	H	1-2	McNaught	1,000
23	Rotherham Town	A	3-2	Donaldson Kennedy Smith	1,500
24	Grimsby Town	A	2-4	Kennedy Smith	2,000
25	Burton Wanderers	A	1-5	Dow	2,000
26	Burslem Port Vale	A	0-3		3,000
27	Darwen	H	4-0	Kennedy 3 McNaught	1,000
28	Loughborough Town	H	2-0	Donaldson Smith	4,000
29	Burslem Port Vale	H	2-1	Clarkin Smith	5,000
30	Lincoln City	A	0-2		2,000

• Final League Position: 6th in Division Two

FA Cup

1	Kettering Town	H	2-1	Donaldson Smith	6,000
2	Derby County	H	1-1	Kennedy	20,000
2R	Derby County	A	1-5	Donaldson	6,000

1896/97

	Opposition	H/A	Score	Scorers	Attn.
1	Gainsborough Trinity	H	2-0	McNaught 2	4,000
2	Burton Swifts	A	5-3	Brown Bryant Cassidy	3,000

				Draycott McNaught	
3	Walsall	H	2-0	Cassidy Donaldson	7,000
4	Lincoln City	H	3-1	Cassidy 2 Donaldson	7,000
5	Grimsby Town	A	0-2		3,000
6	Walsall	A	3-2	Brown Draycott McNaught	7,000
7	Newcastle United	H	4-0	Cassidy 3 Donaldson	7,000
8	Manchester City	A	0-0		20,000
9	Small Heath	H	1-1	Draycott	7,000
10	Blackpool	A	2-4	Bryant Draycott	5,000
11	Gainsborough Trinity	A	0-2		4,000
12	Burton Wanderers	H	3-0	Cassidy 3	4,000
13	Grimsby Town	H	4-2	Cassidy 2 Donaldson Jenkyns	5,000
14	Small Heath	A	0-1		4,000
15	Notts County	A	0-3		5,000
16	Manchester City	H	2-1	Donaldson Smith	18,000
17	Blackpool	H	2-0	Cassidy 2	9,000
18	Leicester Fosse	A	0-1		8,000
19	Newcastle United	A	0-2		17,000
20	Burton Swifts	H	1-1	Donaldson	3,000
21	Loughborough Town	H	6-0	Smith 2 Boyd Donaldson Draycott Jenkyns	5,000
22	Leicester Fosse	H	2-1	Boyd Donaldson	8,000
23	Darwen	H	3-1	Cassidy 2 Boyd	3,000
24	Darwen	A	2-0	Cassidy Gillespie	2,000
25	Burton Wanderers	A	2-1	Gillespie og	3,000
26	Woolwich Arsenal	H	1-1	Boyd	3,000
27	Notts County	H	1-1	Bryant	10,000
28	Lincoln City	A	3-1	Jenkyns 3	1,000
29	Woolwich Arsenal	A	2-0	Boyd Donaldson	6,000
30	Loughborough Town	A	0-2		3,000

● Final League Position: 2nd in Division Two

Test Matches

1	Burnley	A	0-2		10,000
2	Burnley	H	2-0	Boyd Jenkyns	7,000
3	Sunderland	H	1-1	Boyd	18,000
4	Sunderland	A	0-2		6,000

FA Cup

Q1	West Manchester	H	7-0	Cassidy 2 Gillespie 2 Rothwell 2 Bryant	6,000
Q2	Nelson	H	3-0	Cassidy Donaldson Gillespie	5,000
Q3	Blackpool	H	2-2	Gillespie Donaldson	1,500
Q3R	Blackpool	A	2-1	Boyd Cassidy	1,500
1	Kettering Town	H	5-1	Cassidy 3 Donaldson 2	5,000
2	Southampton	A	1-1	Donaldson	8,000
2R	Southampton	H	3-1	Bryant 2 Cassidy	7,000
3	Derby County	A	0-2		12,000

1897/98

	Opposition	H/A	Score	Scorers	Attn.
1	Lincoln City	H	5-0	Boyd 3 Cassidy Bryant	5,000
2	Burton Swifts	A	4-0	Boyd 3 Cassidy	2,000
3	Luton Town	H	1-2	Cassidy	8,000
4	Blackpool	A	1-0	Smith	2,000
5	Leicester Fosse	H	2-0	Boyd 2	6,000
6	Newcastle United	A	0-2		12,000
7	Manchester City	H	1-1	Gillespie	20,000
8	Small Heath	A	1-2	Bryant	6,000
9	Walsall	H	6-0	Cassidy 2 Donaldson 2 Bryant Gillespie	6,000
10	Lincoln City	A	0-1		2,000
11	Newcastle United	H	0-1		7,000
12	Leicester Fosse	A	1-1	Wedge	6,000
13	Grimsby Town	H	2-1	Bryant Wedge	5,000
14	Walsall	A	1-1	Boyd	2,000
15	Manchester City	A	1-0	Cassidy	16,000
16	Gainsborough Trinity	A	1-2	Boyd	3,000
17	Burton Swifts	H	4-0	Boyd Bryant Carman McNaught	6,000
18	Woolwich Arsenal	A	1-5	FC Erentz	8,000
19	Burnley	H	0-0		7,000
20	Blackpool	H	4-0	Boyd 2 Cartwright Cassidy	4,000
21	Woolwich Arsenal	H	5-1	Bryant 2 Boyd Cassidy Collinson	6,000
22	Burnley	A	3-6	Bryant 2 Collinson	3,000
23	Darwen	A	3-2	Boyd 2 McNaught	2,000

24	Luton Town	A	2-2	Boyd Cassidy	2,000
25	Loughborough Town	H	5-1	Boyd 3 Cassidy 2	2,000
26	Grimsby Town	A	3-1	Cassidy 2 Boyd	2,000
27	Gainsborough Trinity	H	1-0	Cassidy	5,000
28	Small Heath	H	3-1	Boyd Gillespie Morgan	4,000
29	Loughborough Town	A	0-0		1,200
30	Darwen	H	3-2	Collinson 2 Bryant	4,000

• Final League Position: 4th in Division Two

FA Cup

1	Walsall	H	1-0	og	6,000
2	Liverpool	H	0-0		12,000
2R	Liverpool	A	1-2	Collinson	6,000

1898/99

	Opposition	H/A	Score	Scorers	Attn.
1	Gainsborough Trinity	A	2-0	Bryant Cassidy	2,000
2	Manchester City	H	3-0	Boyd Cassidy Collinson	20,000
3	Glossop North End	A	2-1	Bryant Cassidy	6,000
4	Walsall	H	1-0	Gillespie	8,000
5	Burton Swifts	A	1-5	Boyd	2,000
6	Burslem Port Vale	H	2-1	Bryant Cassidy	10,000
7	Small Heath	A	1-4	Cassidy	5,000
8	Loughborough Town	H	6-1	Brooks 2 Cassidy 2 Collinson 2	2,000
9	Grimsby Town	H	3-2	Brooks Cassidy Gillespie	5,000
10	Barnsley	H	0-0		5,000
11	New Brighton Tower	A	3-0	Collinson 2 Cassidy	5,000
12	Lincoln City	H	1-0	Bryant	4,000
13	Woolwich Arsenal	A	1-5	Collinson	7,000
14	Blackpool	H	3-1	Cassidy Collinson Cunningham	5,000
15	Leicester Fosse	A	0-1		8,000
16	Darwen	H	9-0	Bryant 3 Cassidy 3 Gillespie 2 og	2,000
17	Manchester City	A	0-4		25,000
18	Gainsborough Trinity	H	6-1	Collinson 2 Bryant Boyd Cartwright Draycott	2,000
19	Burton Swifts	H	2-2	Boyd Cassidy	6,000
20	Glossop North End	H	3-0	Cunningham Erentz Gillespie	12,000

21	Walsall	A	0-2		3,000
22	Burslem Port Vale	A	0-1		6,000
23	Loughborough Town	H	1-0	Bryant	1,500
24	Small Heath	H	2-0	Boyd Roberts	12,000
25	Grimsby Town	A	0-3		4,000
26	New Brighton Tower	H	1-2	Cassidy	20,000
27	Lincoln City	A	0-2		3,000
28	Woolwich Arsenal	H	2-2	Bryant Cassidy	5,000
29	Blackpool	A	1-0	Cassidy	3,000
30	Barnsley	A	2-0	Lee 2	4,000
31	Luton Town	A	1-0	Lee	1,500
32	Luton Town	H	5-0	Cartwright Cassidy Gillespie Lee Morgan	3,000
33	Leicester Fosse	H	2-2	Cassidy Gillespie	6,000
34	Darwen	A	1-1	Morgan	1,000

● Final League Position: 4th in Division Two

FA Cup

1	Tottenham Hotspur	H	1-1	Cassidy	15,000
1R	Tottenham Hotspur	A	3-5	Bryant 3	6,000

1899/1900

	Opposition	H/A	Score	Scorers	Attn.
1	Gainsborough Trinity	H	2-2	Cassidy Lee	8,000
2	Bolton Wanderers	A	1-2	Ambler	5,000
3	Loughborough Town	H	4-0	Bain Cassidy Griffiths og	6,000
4	Burton Swifts	A	0-0		2,000
5	Sheffield Wednesday	A	1-2	Bryant	8,000
6	Lincoln City	H	1-0	Cassidy	5,000
7	Small Heath	A	0-1		10,000
8	New Brighton Tower	H	2-1	Cassidy 2	5,000
9	Woolwich Arsenal	H	2-0	Jackson Roberts	5,000
10	Barnsley	A	0-0		3,000
11	Luton Town	A	1-0	Jackson	3,000
12	Burslem Port Vale	H	3-0	Cassidy 2 Jackson	5,000
13	Middlesbrough	H	2-1	Erentz Parkinson	4,000
14	Chesterfield	A	1-2	Griffiths	2,000

15	Grimsby Town	A	7-0	Bryant 2 Cassidy 2 Jackson Parkinson, og	2,000
16	Gainsborough Trinity	A	1-0	Parkinson	2,000
17	Bolton Wanderers	H	1-2	Parkinson	5,000
18	Loughborough Town	A	2-0	Jackson Parkinson	1,000
19	Burton Swifts	H	4-0	Gillespie 3 Parkinson	4,000
20	Sheffield Wednesday	H	1-0	Bryant	10,000
21	Lincoln City	A	0-1		2,000
22	Small Heath	H	3-2	Cassidy Godsmark Parkinson	10,000
23	New Brighton Tower	A	4-1	Collinson 2 Godsmark Smith	8,000
24	Grimsby Town	H	1-0	Smith	4,000
25	Woolwich Arsenal	A	1-2	Cassidy	3,000
26	Barnsley	H	3-0	Cassidy 2 Leigh	6,000
27	Leicester Fosse	A	0-2		8,000
28	Luton Town	H	5-0	Cassidy 3 Godsmark 2	6,000
29	Burslem Port Vale	A	0-1		3,000
30	Leicester Fosse	H	3-2	Gillespie Griffiths unknown	10,000
31	Walsall	H	5-0	Jackson 2 Erentz Foley Gillespie	4,000
32	Walsall	A	0-0		3,000
33	Middlesbrough	A	0-2		8,000
34	Chesterfield	H	2-1	Holt Grundy	6,000

• Final League Position: 4th in Division Two

FA Cup

Q1	South Shore	A	1-3	Jackson	3,000

1900/01

	Opposition	H/A	Score	Scorers	Attn.
1	Glossop	A	0-1		8,000
2	Middlesbrough	H	4-0	Griffiths Grundy Jackson Leigh	5,500
3	Burnley	A	0-1		4,000
4	Burslem Port Vale	H	4-0	Grundy Leigh Schofield Smith	6,000
5	Leicester Fosse	A	0-1		6,000
6	New Brighton Tower	H	1-0	Jackson	5,000
7	Gainsborough Trinity	A	1-0	Leigh	2,000
8	Walsall	H	1-1	Schofield	8,000
9	Burton Swifts	A	1-3	Leigh	2,000

10	Woolwich Arsenal	A	1-2	Jackson	8,000
11	Stockport County	A	0-1		5,000
12	Small Heath	H	0-1		5,000
13	Grimsby Town	A	0-2		4,000
14	Lincoln City	H	4-1	Leigh 2 H Morgan Schofield	4,000
15	Chesterfield	A	1-2	Hancock og	4,000
16	Blackpool	H	4-0	Griffiths Leigh W Morgan Schofield	10,000
17	Glossop	H	3-0	Leigh 2 H Morgan	8,000
18	Middlesbrough	A	2-1	Schofield 2	12,000
19	Burnley	H	0-1		10,000
20	Burslem Port Vale	A	0-2		1,000
21	Gainsborough Trinity	H	0-0		7,000
22	New Brighton Tower	A	0-2		2,000
23	Walsall	A	1-1	W Morgan	2,000
24	Burton Swifts	H	1-1	Leigh	5,000
25	Barnsley	H	1-0	Leigh	6,000
26	Woolwich Arsenal	H	1-0	Leigh	5,000
27	Leicester Fosse	H	2-3	Fisher Jackson	2,000
28	Blackpool	A	2-1	Griffiths 2	2,000
29	Stockport County	H	3-1	Leigh H Morgan Schofield	4,000
30	Lincoln City	A	0-2		5,000
31	Small Heath	A	0-1		6,000
32	Barnsley	A	2-6	Jackson W Morgan	3,000
33	Grimsby Town	H	1-0	H Morgan	3,000
34	Chesterfield	H	1-0	Leigh	1,000

• Final League Position: 10th in Division Two

FA Cup

S1	Portsmouth	H	3-0	Griffiths Jackson Stafford	5,000
1	Burnley	H	0-0		8,000
1R	Burnley	A	1-7	Schofield	4,000

1901/02

	Opposition	H/A	Score	Scorers	Attn.
1	Gainsborough Trinity	H	3-0	Preston 2 Lappin	3,000
2	Middlesbrough	A	0-5		12,000

3	Bristol City	H	1-0	Griffiths	5,000
4	Blackpool	A	4-2	Preston 2 Schofield og	3,000
5	Stockport County	H	3-3	Schofield 2 Preston	5,000
6	Burton United	A	0-0		3,000
7	Glossop	A	0-0		7,000
8	Doncaster Rovers	H	6-0	Coupar 3 Griffiths Preston og	7,000
9	West Bromwich Albion	H	1-2	Fisher	13,000
10	Woolwich Arsenal	A	0-2		3,000
11	Barnsley	H	1-0	Griffiths	4,000
12	Leicester Fosse	A	2-3	Cartwright Preston	4,000
13	Preston North End	A	1-5	Preston	2,000
14	Burslem Port Vale	H	1-0	Richards	3,000
15	Lincoln City	A	0-2		4,000
16	Preston North End	H	0-2		10,000
17	Gainsborough Trinity	A	1-1	Lappin	2,000
18	Bristol City	A	0-4		6,000
19	Blackpool	H	0-1		2,500
20	Stockport County	A	0-1		2,000
21	Burnley	H	2-0	Lappin Preston	1,000
22	Glossop	H	1-0	Erentz	5,000
23	Doncaster Rovers	A	0-4		3,000
24	Lincoln City	H	0-0		6,000
25	West Bromwich Albion	A	0-4		10,000
26	Woolwich Arsenal	H	0-1		4,000
27	Chesterfield	A	0-3		2,000
28	Barnsley	A	2-3	Cartwright Higson	2,500
29	Burnley	A	0-1		3,000
30	Leicester Fosse	H	2-0	Griffiths Hayes	2,000
31	Middlesbrough	H	1-2	Erentz	2,000
32	Burslem Port Vale	A	1-1	Schofield	2,000
33	Burton United	H	3-1	Cartwright Griffiths Preston	500
34	Chesterfield	H	2-0	Coupar Preston	2,000

• Final League Position: 15th in Division Two

FA Cup

1	Lincoln City	H	1-2	Fisher	4,000

1902/03

	Opposition	H/A	Score	Scorers	Attn.
1	Gainsborough Trinity	A	1-0	Richards	4,000
2	Burton United	H	1-0	Hurst	15,000
3	Bristol City	A	1-3	Hurst	6,000
4	Glossop	H	1-1	Hurst	12,000
5	Chesterfield	H	2-1	Preston 2	12,000
6	Stockport County	A	1-2	Pegg	6,000
7	Woolwich Arsenal	A	1-0	Beadsworth	12,000
8	Lincoln City	A	3-1	Peddie 2 Hurst	3,000
9	Small Heath	H	0-1		25,000
10	Leicester Fosse	A	1-1	Downie	5,000
11	Burnley	A	2-0	Pegg og	4,000
12	Port Vale	A	1-1	Peddie	1,000
13	Manchester City	H	1-1	Pegg	40,000
14	Blackpool	H	2-2	Downie Morrison	10,000
15	Burnley	H	2-1	Peddie Lappin	9,000
16	Gainsborough Trinity	H	3-1	Downie Peddie Pegg	8,000
17	Burton United	A	1-3	Peddie	3,000
18	Bristol City	H	1-2	Preston	12,000
19	Glossop	A	3-1	Downie Griffiths Morrison	5,000
20	Chesterfield	A	0-2		6,000
21	Blackpool	A	0-2		3,000
22	Doncaster Rovers	A	2-2	Morrison 2	4,000
23	Lincoln City	H	1-2	Downie	4,000
24	Woolwich Arsenal	H	3-0	Arkesden Peddie Pegg	5,000
25	Leicester Fosse	H	5-1	Finchett Griffiths Morrison Pegg, Smith	8,000
26	Stockport County	H	0-0		2,000
27	Preston North End	H	0-1		3,000
28	Burnley	A	4-0	Peddie 2 Griffiths Morrison	5,000
29	Manchester City	A	2-0	Peddie Schofield	30,000
30	Preston North End	A	1-3	Pegg	7,000
31	Doncaster Rovers	H	4-0	Arkesden Bell Griffiths Morrison Morrison	6,000
32	Burslem Port Vale	H	2-1	Schofield 2	8,000
33	Small Heath	A	1-2	Peddie	6,000

34	Barnsley	A	0-0		2,000

• Final League Position: 5th in Division Two

FA Cup

Q1	Accrington Stanley	H	7-0	Williams 3 Peddie Richards Pegg, Morgan	6,000
Q2	Oswaldtwistle Rovers	H	3-2	Pegg Beadsworth Williams	5,000
Q3	Southport Central	H	4-1	Pegg 3 Banks	6,000
Int	Burton United	H	1-1	Griffiths	6,000
IntR	Burton United	A	3-1	Schofield Pegg Peddie	7,000
1	Liverpool	H	2-1	Peddie 2	15,000
2	Everton	A	1-3	Griffiths	15,000

1903/04

	Opposition	H/A	Score	Scorers	Attn.
1	Bristol City	H	2-2	Griffiths 2	40,000
2	Burnley	A	0-2		5,000
3	Burslem Port Vale	A	0-1		3,000
4	Glossop	A	5-0	Griffiths 2 A Robertson Downie Arkesden	3,000
5	Bradford City	H	3-1	Pegg 3	30,000
6	Woolwich Arsenal	A	0-4		20,000
7	Barnsley	H	4-0	Pegg 2 Griffiths A Robertson	20,000
8	Lincoln City	A	0-0		5,000
9	Stockport County	H	3-1	Arkesden Grassam AJ Schofield	15,000
10	Bolton Wanderers	H	0-0		30,000
11	Preston North End	H	0-2		15,000
12	Gainsborough Trinity	H	4-2	Arkesden Duckworth Grassam A Robertson	6,000
13	Chesterfield	H	3-1	Arkesden 2 A Robertson	15,000
14	Burton United	A	2-2	Arkesden 2	4,000
15	Bristol City	A	1-1	Griffiths	8,000
16	Burslem Port Vale	H	2-0	Arkesden Grassam	10,000
17	Glossop	H	3-1	Arkesden 2 Downie	10,000
18	Bradford City	A	3-3	Griffiths 2 Downie	12,000
19	Woolwich Arsenal	H	1-0	A Robertson	40,000
20	Lincoln City	H	2-0	Downie Griffiths	8,000

21	Blackpool	A	1-2	Grassam	3,000
22	Burnley	H	3-1	Grassam 2 Griffiths	14,000
23	Preston North End	A	1-1	Arkesden	7,000
24	Grimsby Town	H	2-0	A Robertson 2	12,000
25	Stockport County	A	3-0	Hall Pegg AJ Schofield	2,500
26	Chesterfield	A	2-0	Bell, Hall	5,000
27	Leicester Fosse	A	1-0	McCartney	4,000
28	Barnsley	A	2-0	Grassam AJ Schofield	5,000
29	Blackpool	H	3-1	Grassam 2 AJ Schofield	10,000
30	Grimsby Town	A	1-3	Grassam	8,000
31	Gainsborough Trinity	A	1-0	A Robertson	4,000
32	Burton United	H	2-0	Grassam A Robertson	8,000
33	Bolton Wanderers	A	0-0		10,000
34	Leicester Fosse	H	5-2	AJ Schofield 2 Bonthron Griffiths A Robertson	7,000

• Final League Position: 3rd in Division Two

FA Cup

Int	Small Heath	H	1-1	AJ Schofield	10,000
IntR	Small Heath	A	1-1aet	Arkesden	5,000
Int2R	Small Heath	N	1-1aet	AJ Schofield	3,000
Int3R	Small Heath	N	3-1	Arkesden 2 Grassam	9,372
1	Notts County	A	3-3	Downie AJ Schofield Arkesden	12,000
1R	Notts County	H	2-1	Morrison Pegg	18,000
2	Sheffield Wednesday	A	0-6		22,051

1904/05

	Opposition	H/A	Score	Scorers	Attn.
1	Burslem Port Vale	A	2-2	Allan 2	4,000
2	Bristol City	H	4-1	Peddie Robertson Schofield Williams	20,000
3	Bolton Wanderers	H	1-2	Mackie	25,000
4	Glossop	A	2-1	Allan Roberts	6,000
5	Bradford City	A	1-1	Arkesden	12,000
6	Lincoln City	H	2-0	Arkesden Schofield	15,000
7	Leicester Fosse	A	3-0	Arkesden Peddie Schofield	7,000
8	Barnsley	H	4-0	Allan Downie Peddie Schofield	15,000

9	West Bromwich Albion	A	2-0	Arkesden Williams	5,000
10	Burnley	H	1-0	Arkesden	15,000
11	Grimsby Town	A	1-0	Bell	4,000
12	Doncaster Rovers	A	1-0	Peddie	10,000
13	Gainsborough Trinity	H	3-1	Arkesden 2 Allam	12,000
14	Burton United	A	3-2	Peddie 3	3,000
15	Liverpool	H	3-1	Arkesden Roberts Williams	40,000
16	Chesterfield	H	3-0	Allan 2 Williams	20,000
17	Burslem Port Vale	H	6-1	Allan 3 Arkesden Hayes Roberts	8,000
18	Bradford City	H	7-0	Arkesden 2 Roberts 2 Allan Peddie og	10,000
19	Bolton Wanderers	A	4-2	Allan 2 Peddie Williams	35,000
20	Bristol City	A	1-1	Arkesden	12,000
21	Glossop	H	4-1	Mackie 2 Arkesden Grassam	20,000
22	Lincoln City	A	0-3		2,000
23	Leicester Fosse	H	4-1	Peddie 3 Allan	7,000
24	Barnsley	A	0-0		5,000
25	West Bromwich Albion	H	2-0	Peddie Williams	8,000
26	Burnley	A	0-2		7,000
27	Grimsby Town	H	2-1	Allan Duckworth	12,000
28	Blackpool	A	1-0	Grassam	6,000
29	Doncaster Rovers	H	6-0	Duckworth 3 Beddow Peddie Wombwell	6,000
30	Gainsborough Trinity	A	0-0		6,000
31	Burton United	H	5-0	Duckworth 2 Peddie 2 Arkesden	16,000
32	Chesterfield	A	0-2		10,000
33	Liverpool	A	0-4		28,000
34	Blackpool	H	3-1	Allan Arkesden Peddie	4,000

• Final League Position: 3rd in Division Two

FA Cup

1	Fulham	H	2-2	Mackie Arkesden	17,000
1R	Fulham	A	0-0		15,000
2R	Fulham	N	0-1		6,000

1905/06

	Opposition	H/A	Score	Scorers	Attn.
1	Bristol City	H	5-1	Sagar 3 Beddow Picken	25,000
2	Blackpool	H	2-1	Peddie 2	7,000
3	Grimsby Town	A	1-0	Sagar	6,000
4	Glossop	A	2-1	Bell Beddow	7,000
5	Stockport County	H	3-1	Peddie 2 Sagar	15,000
6	Blackpool	A	1-0	Roberts	7,000
7	Bradford City	H	0-0		17,000
8	West Bromwich Albion	A	0-1		15,000
9	Leicester Fosse	H	3-2	Peddie 2 Sagar	12,000
10	Gainsborough Trinity	A	2-2	Bonthron 2	4,000
11	Hull City	A	1-0	Picken	14,000
12	Lincoln City	H	2-1	Picken Roberts	15,000
13	Chesterfield	A	0-1		3,000
14	Burslem Port Vale	H	3-0	Beddow Peddie og	8,000
15	Barnsley	A	3-0	Beddow Picken og	3,000
16	Clapton Orient	H	4-0	Peddie 2 Picken 2	12,000
17	Burnley	A	3-1	Beddow Peddie Picken	8,000
18	Burton United	A	2-0	Schofield 2	5,000
19	Chelsea	H	0-0		35,000
20	Bristol City	A	1-1	Roberts	18,000
21	Grimsby Town	H	5-0	Beddow 3 Picken 2	10,000
22	Leeds City	H	0-3		6,000
23	Glossop	H	5-2	Picken 2 Beddow Peddie Williams	7,000
24	Stockport County	A	1-0	Peddie	15,000
25	Bradford City	A	5-1	Beddow 2 Roberts Schofield Wombwell	8,000
26	West Bromwich Albion	H	0-0		30,000
27	Hull City	H	5-0	Picken 2 Peddie Sagar Schofield	16,000
28	Chesterfield	H	4-1	Picken 3 Sagar	16,000
29	Burslem Port Vale	A	0-1		3,000
30	Leicester Fosse	A	5-2	Peddie 3 Picken Sagar	5,000
31	Barnsley	H	5-1	Sagar 3 Bell Picken	15,000
32	Clapton Orient	A	1-0	Wall	8,000
33	Chelsea	A	1-1	Sagar	60,000
34	Burnley	H	1-0	Sagar	12,000

35	Gainsborough Trinity	H	2-0	Allen 2	20,000
36	Leeds City	A	3-1	Allen Peddie Wombwell	15,000
37	Lincoln City	A	3-2	Allen 2 Wall	1,500
38	Burton United	H	6-0	Sagar 2 Picken 2 Peddie Wall	16,000

● Final League Position: 2nd in Division Two

FA Cup

1	Staple Hill	H	7-2	Beddow 3 Picken 2 Allen Williams	7,560
2	Norwich City	H	3-0	Downie Peddie Sagar	10,000
3	Aston Villa	H	5-1	Picken 3 Sagar 2	35,500
4	Woolwich Arsenal	H	2-3	Peddie Sagar	26,500

1906/07

	Opposition	H/A	Score	Scorers	Attn.
1	Bristol City	A	2-1	Picken Roberts	5,000
2	Derby County	A	2-2	Schofield 2	5,000
3	Notts County	H	0-0		30,000
4	Sheffield United	A	2-0	Bell Downie	12,000
5	Bolton Wanderers	H	1-2	Peddie	45,000
6	Derby County	H	1-1	Bell	25,000
7	Stoke	A	2-1	Duckworth 2	7,000
8	Blackburn Rovers	H	1-1	Wall	20,000
9	Sunderland	A	1-4	Peddie	18,000
10	Birmingham	H	2-1	Peddie 2	14,000
11	Everton	A	0-3		20,000
12	Woolwich Arsenal	H	1-0	Downie	20,000
13	Sheffield Wednesday	A	2-5	Menzies Peddie	7,000
14	Bury	H	2-4	Peddie Wall	30,000
15	Manchester City	A	0-3		40,000
16	Middlesbrough	H	3-1	Wall 2 Sagar	12,000
17	Preston North End	A	0-2		9,000
18	Newcastle United	H	1-3	Menzies	18,000
19	Liverpool	H	0-0		20,000
20	Aston Villa	A	0-2		20,000
21	Bristol City	H	0-0		10,000
22	Aston Villa	H	1-0	Turnbull	40,000
23	Notts County	A	0-3		10,000

24	Sheffield United	H	2-0	Turnbull Wall	15,000
25	Bolton Wanderers	A	1-0	Turnbull	25,000
26	Newcastle United	A	0-5		30,000
27	Stoke	H	4-1	Picken 2 Meredith og	15,000
28	Blackburn Rovers	A	4-2	Meredith 2 Sagar Wall	5,000
29	Preston North End	H	3-0	Wall 2 Sagar	16,000
30	Birmingham	A	1-1	Menzies	20,000
31	Woolwich Arsenal	A	0-4		6,000
32	Sunderland	H	2-0	Turnbull Williams	12,000
33	Bury	A	2-1	Menzies Meredith	25,000
34	Liverpool	A	1-0	Turnbull	20,000
35	Manchester City	H	1-1	Roberts	40,000
36	Sheffield Wednesday	H	5-0	Wall 3 Picken Sagar	10,000
37	Middlesbrough	A	0-2		15,000
38	Everton	H	3-0	Bannister Meredith Turnbull	10,000

• Final League Position: 8th in Division One

FA Cup

1	Portsmouth	A	2-2	Picken Wall	24,329
1R	Portsmouth	H	1-2	Wall	8,000

1907/08

	Opposition	H/A	Score	Scorers	Attn.
1	Aston Villa	A	4-1	Meredith 2 Bannister Wall	20,000
2	Liverpool	H	4-0	A Turnbull 3 Wall	24,000
3	Middlesbrough	H	2-1	A Turnbull 2	20,000
4	Middlesbrough	A	1-2	Bannister	18,000
5	Sheffield United	H	2-1	A Turnbull 2	25,000
6	Chelsea	A	4-1	Meredith 2 Bannister A Turnbull	40,000
7	Nottingham Forest	H	4-0	Bannister J Turnbull Wall og	20,000
8	Newcastle United	A	6-1	Wall 2 Meredith Roberts A Turnbull J Turnbull	25,000
9	Blackburn Rovers	A	5-1	A Turnbull 3 J Turnbull 2	30,000
10	Bolton Wanderers	H	2-1	A Turnbull J Turnbull	35,000
11	Birmingham	A	4-3	Meredith 2 J Turnbull Wall	20,000
12	Everton	H	4-3	Wall 2 Meredith Roberts	30,000
13	Sunderland	A	2-1	A Turnbull 2	30,000

14	Woolwich Arsenal	H	4-2	A Turnbull 4	10,000
15	Sheffield Wednesday	A	0-2		40,000
16	Bristol City	H	2-1	Wall 2	20,000
17	Notts County	A	1-1	Meredith	11,000
18	Manchester City	H	3-1	A Turnbull 2 Wall	35,000
19	Bury	H	2-1	Meredith J Turnbull	45,000
20	Preston North End	A	0-0		12,000
21	Bury	A	1-0	Wall	29,500
22	Sheffield United	A	0-2		17,000
23	Chelsea	H	1-0	J Turnbull	20,000
24	Newcastle United	H	1-1	J Turnbull	50,000
25	Blackburn Rovers	H	1-2	A Turnbull	15,000
26	Birmingham	H	1-0	A Turnbull	12,000
27	Sunderland	H	3-0	Bell Berry Wall	15,000
28	Woolwich Arsenal	A	0-1		20,000
29	Liverpool	A	4-7	Wall 2 Bannister J Turnbull	10,000
30	Sheffield Wednesday	H	4-1	Wall 2 Halse A Turnbull	30,000
31	Bristol City	A	1-1	Wall	12,000
32	Everton	A	3-1	Halse A Turnbull Wall	17,000
33	Notts County	H	0-1		20,000
34	Nottingham Forest	A	0-2		22,000
35	Manchester City	A	0-0		40,000
36	Aston Villa	H	1-2	Picken	10,000
37	Bolton Wanderers	A	2-2	Halse Stacey	18,000
38	Preston North End	H	2-1	Halse og	8,000

• Final League Position: 1st in Division One

FA Cup

1	Blackpool	H	3-1	Wall 2 Bannister	11,747
2	Chelsea	H	1-0	A Turnbull	25,184
3	Aston Villa	A	2-0	A Turnbull Wall	12,777
4	Fulham	A	1-2	J Turnbull	41,000

1908/09

	Opposition	H/A	Score	Scorers	Attn.
1	Preston North End	A	3-0	J Turnbull 2 Halse	18,000
2	Bury	H	2-1	J Turnbull 2	16,000

3	Middlesbrough	H	6-3	J Turnbull 4 Halse Wall	25,000
4	Manchester City	A	2-1	Halse J Turnbull	40,000
5	Liverpool	H	3-2	Halse 2 J Turnbull	25,000
6	Bury	A	2-2	Halse Wall	25,000
7	Sheffield United	H	2-1	Bell 2	14,000
8	Aston Villa	A	1-2	Halse	40,000
9	Nottingham Forest	H	2-2	A Turnbull 2	20,000
10	Sunderland	A	1-6	A Turnbull	30,000
11	Chelsea	H	0-1		15,000
12	Blackburn Rovers	A	3-1	Halse J Turnbull Wall	25,000
13	Bradford City	H	2-0	Picken Wall	15,000
14	Sheffield Wednesday	H	3-1	Halse Picken J Turnbull	20,000
15	Everton	A	2-3	Bannister Halse	35,000
16	Leicester Fosse	H	4-2	Wall 3 Picken	10,000
17	Woolwich Arsenal	A	1-0	Halse	10,000
18	Newcastle United	A	1-2	Wall	35,000
19	Newcastle United	H	1-0	Halse	40,000
20	Notts County	H	4-3	Halse 2 Roberts A Turnbull	15,000
21	Preston North End	H	0-2		18,000
22	Middlesbrough	A	0-5		15,000
23	Manchester City	H	3-1	Livingstone 2 Wall	40,000
24	Liverpool	A	1-3	A Turnbull	30,000
25	Sheffield United	A	0-0		12,000
26	Nottingham Forest	A	0-2		7,000
27	Chelsea	A	1-1	Wall	30,000
28	Sunderland	H	2-2	Payne J Turnbull	10,000
29	Blackburn Rovers	H	0-3		11,000
30	Aston Villa	H	0-2		10,000
31	Sheffield Wednesday	A	0-2		15,000
32	Bristol City	H	0-1		18,000
33	Everton	H	2-2	J Turnbull 2	8,000
34	Bristol City	A	0-0		18,000
35	Notts County	A	1-0	Livingstone	7,000
36	Leicester Fosse	A	2-3	J Turnbull Wall	8,000
37	Woolwich Arsenal	H	1-4	J Turnbull	10,000
38	Bradford City	A	0-1		30,000

• Final League Position: 13th in Division One

FA Cup

		H/A	Score	Scorers	Attn.
1	Brighton & Hove Albion	H	1-0	Halse	8,300
2	Everton	H	1-0	Halse	35,217
3	Blackburn Rovers	H	6-1	A Turnbull 3 J Turnbull 3	38,500
4	Burnley	A	3-2	J Turnbull 2 Halse	16,850
SF	Newcastle United	N*	1-0	Halse	40,118
F	Bristol City	N**	1-0	A Turnbull	71,401

* Played at Bramall Lane
** Played at the Crystal Palace

1909/10

	Opposition	H/A	Score	Scorers	Attn.
1	Bradford City	H	1-0	Wall	12,000
2	Bury	H	2-0	J Turnbull 2	12,000
3	Notts County	H	2-1	J Turnbull Wall	6,000
4	Tottenham Hotspur	A	2-2	J Turnbull Wall	40,000
5	Preston North End	H	1-1	Roberts	13,000
6	Notts County	A	2-3	A Turnbull 2	11,000
7	Newcastle United	H	1-1	Wall	30,000
8	Liverpool	A	2-3	A Turnbull 2	30,000
9	Aston Villa	H	2-0	Halse A Turnbull	20,000
10	Sheffield United	A	1-0	Wall	30,000
11	Woolwich Arsenal	H	1-0	Wall	20,000
12	Bolton Wanderers	A	3-2	Homer 2 Halse	20,000
13	Chelsea	H	2-0	A Turnbull Wall	10,000
14	Blackburn Rovers	A	2-3	Homer 2	40,000
15	Nottingham Forest	H	2-6	Halse Wall	12,000
16	Sunderland	A	0-3		12,000
17	Middlesbrough	A	2-1	Homer A Turnbull	10,000
18	Sheffield Wednesday	H	0-3		25,000
19	Sheffield Wednesday	A	1-4	Wall	37,000
20	Bradford City	A	2-0	A Turnbull Wall	25,000
21	Bury	A	1-1	Homer	10,000
22	Tottenham Hotspur	H	5-0	Roberts 2 Connor Hooper Meredith	7,000
23	Preston North End	A	0-1		4,000
24	Newcastle United	A	4-3	A Turnbull Blott Roberts	20,000
25	Liverpool	H	3-4	Homer A Turnbull Wall	45,000

26	Aston Villa	A	1-7	Meredith	20,000
27	Sheffield United	H	1-0	Picken	40,000
28	Woolwich Arsenal	A	0-0		4,000
29	Bolton Wanderers	H	5-0	Halse Meredith Picken, J Turnbull Wall	20,000
30	Bristol City	H	2-1	Picken J Turnbull	50,000
31	Chelsea	A	1-1	J Turnbull	25,000
32	Bristol City	A	1-2	Meredith	18,000
33	Blackburn Rovers	H	2-0	Halse 2	20,000
34	Everton	H	3-2	J Turnbull 2 Meredith	5,500
35	Nottingham Forest	A	0-2		7,000
36	Sunderland	H	2-0	A Turnbull Wall	12,000
37	Everton	A	3-3	Homer A Turnbull Wall	10,000
38	Middlesbrough	H	4-1	Picken 4	10,000

• Final League Position: 5th in Division One

FA Cup

| 1 | Burnley | A | 0-2 | | 16,628 |

1910/11

	Opposition	H/A	Score	Scorers	Attn.
1	Woolwich Arsenal	A	2-1	Halse West	15,000
2	Blackburn Rovers	H	3-2	Meredith A Turnbull West	40,000
3	Nottingham Forest	A	1-2	A Turnbull	20,000
4	Manchester City	H	2-1	A Turnbull West	60,000
5	Everton	A	1-0	A Turnbull	25,000
6	Sheffield Wednesday	H	3-2	Wall 2 West	20,000
7	Bristol City	A	1-0	Halse	20,000
8	Newcastle United	H	2-0	Halse A Turnbull	50,000
9	Tottenham Hotspur	A	2-2	West 2	30,000
10	Middlesbrough	H	1-2	A Turnbull	35,000
11	Preston North End	A	2-0	A Turnbull West	13,000
12	Notts County	H	0-0		13,000
13	Oldham Athletic	A	3-1	A Turnbull 2 Wall	25,000
14	Liverpool	A	2-3	Roberts A Turnbull	8,000
15	Bury	H	3-2	Homer 2 A Turnbull	7,000
16	Sheffield United	A	0-2		8,000

17	Aston Villa	H	2-0	A Turnbull, West	20,000
18	Sunderland	A	2-1	Meredith A Turnbull	30,000
19	Woolwich Arsenal	H	5-0	Picken 2 West 2 Meredith	40,000
20	Bradford City	A	0-1		35,000
21	Blackburn Rovers	A	0-1		20,000
22	Bradford City	H	1-0	Meredith	40,000
23	Nottingham Forest	H	4-2	Homer Picken Wall og	10,000
24	Manchester City	A	1-1	A Turnbull	40,000
25	Everton	H	2-2	Duckworth Wall	45,000
26	Bristol City	H	3-1	Homer Picken West	14,000
27	Newcastle United	A	1-0	Halse	45,000
28	Middlesbrough	A	2-2	A Turnbull West	8,000
29	Preston North End	H	5-0	West 2 Connor Duckworth A Turnbull	25,000
30	Tottenham Hotspur	H	3-2	Meredith A Turnbull West	10,000
31	Notts County	A	0-1		12,000
32	Oldham Athletic	H	0-0		35,000
33	Liverpool	H	2-0	West 2	20,000
34	Bury	A	3-0	Homer 2 Halse	20,000
35	Sheffield United	H	1-1	West	22,000
36	Sheffield Wednesday	A	0-0		25,000
37	Aston Villa	A	2-4	Halse 2	50,000
38	Sunderland	H	5-1	Halse 2 A Turnbull West og	10,000

• Final League Position: 1st in Division One

FA Cup

1	Blackpool	A	2-1	Picken West	12,000
2	Aston Villa	H	2-1	Halse Wall	65,101
3	West Ham United	A	1-2	A Turnbull	26,000

1911/12

	Opposition	H/A	Score	Scorers	Attn.
1	Manchester City	A	0-0		35,000
2	Everton	H	2-1	Halse A Turnbull	20,000
3	West Bromwich Albion	A	0-1		35,000
4	Sunderland	H	2-2	Stacey 2	20,000
5	Blackburn Rovers	A	2-2	West 2	30,000

6	Sheffield Wednesday	H	3-1	Halse 2 West	30,000
7	Bury	A	1-0	A Turnbull	18,000
8	Middlesbrough	H	3-4	Halse A Turnbull West	20,000
9	Notts County	A	1-0	A Turnbull	15,000
10	Tottenham Hotspur	H	1-2	Halse	20,000
11	Preston North End	H	0-0		10,000
12	Liverpool	A	2-3	Roberts West	15,000
13	Aston Villa	H	3-1	West 2 Roberts	20,000
14	Newcastle United	A	3-2	West 2 Halse	40,000
15	Sheffield United	H	1-0	Halse	12,000
16	Oldham Athletic	A	2-2	A Turnbull West	20,000
17	Bolton Wanderers	H	2-0	Halse A Turnbull	20,000
18	Bradford City	H	0-1		50,000
19	Bradford City	A	1-0	West	40,000
20	Manchester City	H	0-0		50,000
21	Woolwich Arsenal	H	2-0	Meredith West	20,000
22	Everton	A	0-4		12,000
23	West Bromwich Albion	H	1-2	Wall	8,000
24	Sunderland	A	0-5		12,000
25	Sheffield Wednesday	A	0-3		25,000
26	Bury	H	0-0		6,000
27	Notts County	H	2-0	West 2	10,000
28	Preston North End	A	0-0		7,000
29	Liverpool	H	1-1	Nuttall	10,000
30	Aston Villa	A	0-6		15,000
31	Woolwich Arsenal	A	1-2	A Turnbull	14,000
32	Newcastle United	H	0-2		14,000
33	Tottenham Hotspur	A	1-1	Wall	20,000
34	Sheffield United	A	1-6	Nuttall	7,000
35	Middlesbrough	A	0-3		5,000
36	Oldham Athletic	H	3-1	West 2 Wall	15,000
37	Bolton Wanderers	A	1-1	Meredith	20,000
38	Blackburn Rovers	H	3-1	Hamill Meredith West	20,000

• Final League Position: 13th in Division One

FA Cup

1	Huddersfield Town	H	3-1	West 2 Halse	19,579

2	Coventry City	A	5-1	Halse 2 West A Turnbull Wall	17,130
3	Reading	A	1-1	West	24,069
3R	Reading	H	3-0	A Turnbull 2 Halse	29,511
4	Blackburn Rovers	H	1-1	og	59,300
4R	Blackburn Rovers aet	A	2-4	West 2	39,296

1912/13

	Opposition	H/A	Score	Scorers	Attn.
1	Woolwich Arsenal	A	0-0		11,000
2	Manchester City	H	0-1		40,000
3	West Bromwich Albion	A	2-1	Livingstone A Turnbull	25,000
4	Everton	H	2-0	West 2	40,000
5	Sheffield Wednesday	A	3-3	West 2 A Turnbull	30,000
6	Blackburn Rovers	H	1-1	Wall	45,000
7	Derby County	A	1-2	A Turnbull	15,000
8	Tottenham Hotspur	H	2-0	A Turnbull West	12,000
9	Middlesbrough	A	2-3	Nuttall 2	10,000
10	Notts County	H	2-1	Anderson Meredith	12,000
11	Sunderland	A	1-3	West	20,000
12	Aston Villa	A	2-4	Wall West	20,000
13	Liverpool	H	3-1	Anderson 2 Wall	8,000
14	Bolton Wanderers	A	1-2	Wall	25,000
15	Sheffield United	H	4-0	Anderson A Turnbull Wall West	12,000
16	Newcastle United	A	3-1	West 3	20,000
17	Oldham Athletic	H	0-0		30,000
18	Chelsea	A	4-1	West 2 Anderson Whalley	33,000
19	Chelsea	H	4-2	A Turnbull 2 Anderson Wall	20,000
20	Manchester City	A	2-0	West 2	38,000
21	Bradford City	H	2-0	Anderson 2	30,000
22	West Bromwich Albion	H	1-1	Roberts	25,000
23	Everton	A	1-4	Hamill	20,000
24	Sheffield Wednesday	H	2-0	West Whalley	45,000
25	Blackburn Rovers	A	0-0		38,000
26	Derby County	H	4-0	West 2 Anderson A Turnbull	30,000
27	Middlesbrough	H	2-3	Meredith Whalley	15,000
28	Notts County	A	2-1	Anderson A Turnbull	10,000
29	Sunderland	H	1-3	Sheldon	15,000

30	Woolwich Arsenal	H	2-0	Anderson Whalley	20,000
31	Aston Villa	H	4-0	A Turnbull Stacey Wall West	30,000
32	Bradford City	A	0-1		25,000
33	Liverpool	A	2-0	Wall West	12,000
34	Tottenham Hotspur	A	1-1	Blott	12,000
35	Bolton Wanderers	H	2-1	Anderson Wall	30,000
36	Sheffield United	A	1-2	Wall	12,000
37	Newcastle United	H	3-0	Hunter 2 West	10,000
38	Oldham Athletic	A	0-0		3,000

• Final League Position: 4th in Division One

FA Cup

1	Coventry City	H	1-1	Wall	11,500
1R	Coventry City	A	2-1	Anderson Roberts	20,042
2	Plymouth Argyle	A	2-0	Anderson Wall	21,700
3	Oldham Athletic	A	0-0		26,932
3R	Oldham Athletic	H	1-2	West	31,180

1913/14

	Opposition	H/A	Score	Scorers	Attn.
1	Sheffield Wednesday	A	3-1	A Turnbull West og	32,000
2	Sunderland	H	3-1	Anderson A Turnbull Whalley	25,000
3	Bolton Wanderers	H	0-1		45,000
4	Chelsea	A	2-0	Anderson Wall	40,000
5	Oldham Athletic	H	4-1	West 2 Anderson Wall	55,000
6	Tottenham Hotspur	H	3-1	Stacey Wall Whalley	25,000
7	Burnley	A	2-1	Anderson 2	30,000
8	Preston North End	H	3-0	Anderson 3	30,000
9	Newcastle United	A	1-0	West	35,000
10	Liverpool	H	3-0	Wall 2 West	30,000
11	Aston Villa	A	1-3	Woodcock	20,000
12	Middlesbrough	H	0-1		15,000
13	Sheffield United	A	0-2		30,000
14	Derby County	H	3-3	A Turnbull 2 Meredith	20,000
15	Manchester City	A	2-0	Anderson 2	40,000
16	Bradford City	H	1-1	Knowles	18,000
17	Blackburn Rovers	A	1-0	og	35,000

18	Everton	H	0-1		25,000
19	Everton	A	0-5		40,000
20	Sheffield Wednesday	H	2-1	Meredith Wall	10,000
21	West Bromwich Albion	H	1-0	Wall	35,000
22	Bolton Wanderers	A	1-6	West	35,000
23	Chelsea	H	0-1		20,000
24	Oldham Athletic	A	2-2	Wall Woodcock	10,000
25	Tottenham Hotspur	A	1-2	Wall	22,000
26	Burnley	H	0-1		35,000
27	Middlesbrough	A	1-3	Anderson	12,000
28	Newcastle United	H	2-2	Anderson Potts	30,000
29	Preston North End	A	2-4	Travers Wall	12,000
30	Aston Villa	H	0-6		30,000
31	Derby County	A	2-4	Anderson Travers	7,000
32	Sunderland	A	0-2		20,000
33	Manchester City	H	0-1		36,000
34	West Bromwich Albion	A	1-2	Travers	20,000
35	Liverpool	A	2-1	Travers Wall	28,000
36	Bradford City	A	1-1	Travers	10,000
37	Sheffield United	H	2-1	Anderson 2	4,500
38	Blackburn Rovers	H	0-0		20,000

• Final League Position: 14th in Division One

FA Cup

1	Swindon Town	A	0-1		18,187

1914/15

	Opposition	H/A	Score	Scorers	Attn.
1	Oldham Athletic	H	1-3	O'Connell	13,000
2	Manchester City	H	0-0		20,000
3	Bolton Wanderers	A	0-3		10,000
4	Blackburn Rovers	H	2-0	West 2	15,000
5	Notts County	A	2-4	A Turnbull Wall	12,000
6	Sunderland	H	3-0	Anderson Stacey West	16,000
7	Sheffield Wednesday	A	0-1		19,000
8	West Bromwich Albion	H	0-0		18,000
9	Everton	A	2-4	Anderson Wall	15,000

10	Chelsea	H	2-2	Anderson Hunter	15,000
11	Bradford City	A	2-4	Hunter West	12,000
12	Burnley	H	0-2		12,000
13	Tottenham Hotspur	A	0-2		12,000
14	Newcastle United	H	1-0	West	5,000
15	Middlesbrough	A	1-1	Anderson	7,000
16	Sheffield United	H	1-2	Anderson	8,000
17	Aston Villa	A	3-3	Norton 2 Anderson	10,000
18	Liverpool	A	1-1	Stacey	25,000
19	Bradford Park Avenue	H	1-2	Anderson	8,000
20	Manchester City	A	1-1	West	30,000
21	Bolton Wanderers	H	4-1	Potts 2 Stacey Woodcock	8,000
22	Blackburn Rovers	A	3-3	Woodcock 2 og	7,000
23	Notts County	H	2-2	Potts Stacey	7,000
24	Sunderland	A	0-1		5,000
25	Sheffield Wednesday	H	2-0	West Woodcock	7,000
26	West Bromwich Albion	A	0-0		10,000
27	Everton	H	1-2	Woodcock	10,000
28	Bradford City	H	1-0	Potts	14,000
29	Burnley	A	0-3		12,000
30	Tottenham Hotspur	H	1-1	Woodcock	15,000
31	Liverpool	H	2-0	Anderson 2	18,000
32	Newcastle United	A	0-2		12,000
33	Bradford Park Avenue	A	0-5		15,000
34	Oldham Athletic	A	0-1		2,000
35	Middlesbrough	H	2-2	O'Connell A Turnbull	15,000
36	Sheffield United	A	1-3	West	14,000
37	Chelsea	A	3-1	Norton West Woodcock	13,000
38	Aston Villa	H	1-0	Anderson	8,000

• Final League Position: 18th in Division One

FA Cup

| 1 | Sheffield Wednesday | A | 0-1 | | 23,248 |

1919/20

	Opposition	H/A	Score	Scorers	Attn.
1	Derby County	A	1-1	Woodcock	12,000

2	Sheffield Wednesday	H	0-0		13,000
3	Derby County	H	0-2		15,000
4	Sheffield Wednesday	A	3-1	Meehan Spence Woodcock	10,000
5	Preston North End	A	3-2	Spence 2 Meehan	15,000
6	Preston North End	H	5-1	Spence 2 Woodcock 2 Montgomery	18,000
7	Middlesbrough	A	1-1	Woodcock	20,000
8	Middlesbrough	H	1-1	Woodcock	28,000
9	Manchester City	A	3-3	Hodge Hopkin Spence	30,000
10	Manchester City	H	1-0	Spence	40,000
11	Sheffield United	A	2-2	Hopkin Woodcock	18,000
12	Sheffield United	H	3-0	Hodge Spence Woodcock	24,500
13	Burnley	A	1-2	Hodge	15,000
14	Burnley	H	0-1		25,000
15	Oldham Athletic	A	3-0	Hodge Hopkin Spence	15,000
16	Aston Villa	A	0-2		40,000
17	Aston Villa	H	1-2	Hilditch	30,000
18	Newcastle United	H	2-1	Hodge Spence	20,000
19	Liverpool	H	0-0		45,000
20	Newcastle United	A	1-2	Hilditch	45,000
21	Liverpool	A	0-0		30,000
22	Chelsea	H	0-2		25,000
23	Chelsea	A	0-1		40,000
24	West Bromwich Albion	A	1-2	Woodcock	20,000
25	Sunderland	A	0-3		25,000
26	Oldham Athletic	H	1-1	Bissett	15,000
27	Sunderland	H	2-0	Harris Hodge	35,000
28	Arsenal	A	3-0	Spence 2 Hopkin	25,000
29	West Bromwich Albion	H	1-2	Spence	20,000
30	Arsenal	H	0-1		20,000
31	Everton	H	1-0	Bissett	25,000
32	Everton	A	0-0		30,000
33	Bradford City	H	0-0		25,000
34	Bradford City	A	1-2	Bissett	18,000
35	Bradford Park Avenue	H	0-1		30,000
36	Bolton Wanderers	H	1-1	Toms	39,000
37	Bradford Park Avenue	A	4-1	Bissett Grimwood Toms	14,000

				Woodcock	
38	Bolton Wanderers	A	5-3	Bissett 2 Meredith Toms	25,000
				Woodcock	
39	Blackburn Rovers	H	1-1	Hopkin	40,000
40	Blackburn Rovers	A	0-5		30,000
41	Notts County	H	0-0		30,000
42	Notts County	A	2-0	Meredith Spence	20,000

● Final League Position: 12th in Division One

FA Cup

1	Port Vale	A	1-0	Toms	14,549
2	Aston Villa	H	1-2	Woodcock	48,600

1920/21

	Opposition	H/A	Score	Scorers	Attn.
1	Bolton Wanderers	H	2-3	Hopkin Meehan	50,000
2	Arsenal	A	0-2		40,000
3	Bolton Wanderers	A	1-1	Sapsford	35,000
4	Arsenal	H	1-1	Spence	45,000
5	Chelsea	H	3-1	Meehan 2 Leonard	40,000
6	Chelsea	A	2-1	Leonard 2	35,000
7	Tottenham Hotspur	H	0-1		50,000
8	Tottenham Hotspur	A	1-4	Spence	45,000
9	Oldham Athletic	H	4-1	Sapsford 2 Meehan Miler	50,000
10	Oldham Athletic	A	2-2	Spence, og	20,000
11	Preston North End	H	1-0	Miller	42,000
12	Preston North End	A	0-0		25,000
13	Sheffield United	H	2-1	Leonard 2	30,000
14	Sheffield United	A	0-0		18,000
15	Manchester City	H	1-1	Miller	63,000
16	Manchester City	A	0-3		35,000
17	Bradford Park Avenue	H	5-1	Miller 2 Myrescough 2 Partridge	25,000
18	Bradford Park Avenue	A	4-2	Myrescough 2 Miller Partridge	10,000
19	Newcastle United	H	2-0	Hodges, Miller	40,000
20	Aston Villa	A	4-3	Grimwood 2 Harrison Partridge	38,000
21	Aston Villa	H	1-3	Harrison	45,000
22	Newcastle United	A	3-6	Hopkin Partridge Silcock	40,000

23	West Bromwich Albion	H	1-4	Partridge	30,000
24	West Bromwich Albion	A	2-0	Myrescough Partridge	30,000
25	Liverpool	H	1-1	Grimwood	30,000
26	Liverpool	A	0-2		35,000
27	Everton	H	1-2	Meredith	30,000
28	Sunderland	H	3-0	Harrison Hilditch Robinson	40,000
29	Sunderland	A	3-2	Sapsford 2 Goodwin	25,000
30	Everton	A	0-2		38,000
31	Bradford City	H	1-1	Robinson	30,000
32	Bradford City	A	1-1	Sapsford	25,000
33	Burnley	A	0-1		20,000
34	Huddersfield Town	A	2-5	Harris Partridge	17,000
35	Burnley	H	0-3		28,000
36	Huddersfield Town	H	2-0	Bissett 2	30,000
37	Middlesbrough	A	4-2	Spence 2 Bissett Grimwood	15,000
38	Middlesbrough	H	0-1		25,000
39	Blackburn Rovers	A	0-2		18,000
40	Blackburn Rovers	H	0-1		20,000
41	Derby County	A	1-1	Bissett	8,000
42	Derby County	H	3-0	Spence 2 Sapsford	10,000

• Final League Position: 13th in Division One

FA Cup

1	Liverpool	A	1-1	Miller	40,000
1R	Liverpool	H	1-2	Partridge	30,000

1921/22

	Opposition	H/A	Score	Scorers	Attn.
1	Everton	A	0-5		30,000
2	West Bromwich Albion	H	2-3	Partridge Robinson	20,000
3	Everton	H	2-1	Harrison Spence	25,000
4	West Bromwich Albion	A	0-0		15,000
5	Chelsea	A	0-0		35,000
6	Chelsea	H	0-0		28,000
7	Preston North End	A	2-3	Lochhead Partridge	25,000
8	Preston North End	H	1-1	Spence	30,000
9	Tottenham Hotspur	A	2-2	Sapsford Spence	35,000

10	Tottenham Hotspur	H	2-1	Sapsford Spence	30,000
11	Manchester City	A	1-4	Spence	24,000
12	Manchester City	H	3-1	Spence 3	56,000
13	Middlesbrough	H	3-5	Lochhead Sapsford Spence	30,000
14	Middlesbrough	A	0-2		18,000
15	Aston Villa	A	1-3	Spence	30,000
16	Aston Villa	H	1-0	Henderson	33,000
17	Bradford City	A	1-2	Spence	15,000
18	Bradford City	A	1-1	Henderson	9,000
19	Liverpool	A	1-2	Sapsford	40,000
20	Liverpool	H	0-0		30,000
21	Burnley	H	0-1		15,000
22	Burnley	A	2-4	Lochhead Sapsford	10,000
23	Newcastle United	A	0-3		20,000
24	Sheffield United	A	0-3		18,000
25	Newcastle United	H	0-1		20,000
26	Sunderland	A	1-2	Sapsford	10,000
27	Sunderland	H	3-1	Lochhead Sapsford Spence	18,000
28	Huddersfield Town	H	1-1	Spence	30,000
29	Birmingham	A	1-0	Spence	20,000
30	Birmingham	H	1-1	Sapsford	35,000
31	Huddersfield Town	A	1-1	Sapsford	30,000
32	Arsenal	H	1-0	Spence	30,000
33	Blackburn Rovers	H	0-1		30,000
34	Blackburn Rovers	A	0-3		15,000
35	Bolton Wanderers	H	0-1		28,000
36	Arsenal	A	1-3	Lochhead	25,000
37	Bolton Wanderers	A	0-1		28,000
38	Oldham Athletic	H	0-3		30,000
39	Sheffield United	H	3-2	Harrison Lochhead Partridge	28,000
40	Oldham Athletic	A	1-1	Lochhead	30,000
41	Cardiff City	H	1-1	Partridge	18,000
42	Cardiff City	A	1-3	Lochhead	16,000

• Final League Position: 22nd in Division One

FA Cup

| 1 | Cardiff City | H | 1-4 | Sapsford | 25,726 |

1922/23

	Opposition	H/A	Score	Scorers	Attn.
1	Crystal Palace	H	2-1	Spence Wood	30,000
2	Sheffield Wednesday	A	0-1		12,500
3	Crystal Palace	A	3-2	Spence 2 Williams	8,500
4	Sheffield Wednesday	H	1-0	Spence	22,000
5	Wolverhampton Wanderers	A	1-0	Williams	18,000
6	Wolverhampton Wanderers	H	1-0	Spence	28,000
7	Coventry City	A	0-2		19,000
8	Coventry City	H	2-1	Henderson Spence	25,000
9	Port Vale	H	1-2	Spence	25,000
10	Port Vale	A	0-1		16,000
11	Fulham	H	1-1	Myrescough	18,000
12	Fulham	A	0-0		20,000
13	Clapton Orient	H	0-0		16,500
14	Clapton Orient	A	1-1	Goldthorpe	11,000
15	Bury	A	2-2	Goldthorpe 2	21,000
16	Bury	H	0-1		28,000
17	Rotherham County	H	3-0	Lochhead McBain Spence	13,500
18	Rotherham County	A	1-1	Goldthorpe	7,500
19	Stockport County	H	1-0	McBain	24,000
20	Stockport County	A	0-1		15,500
21	West Ham United	H	1-2	Lochhead	17,500
22	West Ham United	A	2-0	Lochhead 2	25,000
23	Hull City	A	1-2	Lochhead	6,750
24	Barnsley	H	1-0	Lochhead	29,000
25	Hull City	H	3-2	Goldthorpe Lochhead, og	15,000
26	Leeds United	H	0-0		25,000
27	Leeds United	A	1-0	Lochhead	24,500
28	Notts County	A	6-1	Goldthorpe 4 Myrescough 2	10,000
29	Derby County	H	0-0		27,500
30	Notts County	H	1-1	Lochhead	12,100
31	Southampton	H	1-2	Lochhead	30,000
32	Derby County	A	1-1	MacDonald	12,000
33	Bradford City	A	1-1	Goldthorpe	10,000
34	Bradford City	H	1-1	Spence	15,000
35	South Shields	H	3-0	Goldthorpe 2 Lochhead	26,000

36	Blackpool	A	0-1		21,000
37	South Shields	A	3-0	Goldthorpe 2 Lochhead	6,500
38	Blackpool	H	2-1	Lochhead Radford	20,000
39	Southampton	A	0-0		5,500
40	Leicester City	A	1-0	Bain	25,000
41	Leicester City	H	0-2		30,000
42	Barnsley	A	2-2	Lochhead Spence	8,000

• Final League Position: 4th in Division Two

FA Cup

1	Bradford City	A	1-1	Partridge	27,000
1R	Bradford City	H	2-0	Barber Goldthorpe	27,791
2	Tottenham Hotspur	A	0-4		38,333

1923/24

	Opposition	H/A	Score	Scorers	Attn.
1	Bristol City	A	2-1	Lochhead MacDonald	20,500
2	Southampton	H	1-0	Goldthorpe	21,750
3	Bristol City	H	2-1	Lochhead Spence	21,000
4	Southampton	A	0-0		11,500
5	Bury	A	0-2		19,000
6	Bury	H	0-1		43,000
7	South Shields	A	0-1		9,750
8	South Shields	H	1-1	Lochhead	22,250
9	Oldham Athletic	A	2-3	Wynne 2 ogs	12,250
10	Oldham Athletic	H	2-0	Bain 2	26,000
11	Stockport County	H	3-0	Mann 2 Bain	31,500
12	Stockport County	A	2-3	Barber Lochhead	16,500
13	Leicester City	A	2-2	Lochhead 2	17,000
14	Leicester City	H	3-0	Lochhead Mann Spence	20,000
15	Coventry City	A	1-1	Randle og	13,580
16	Leeds United	A	0-0		20,000
17	Leeds United	H	3-0	Lochhead 2 Spence	22,250
18	Port Vale	A	1-0	Grimwood	7,500
19	Port Vale	H	5-0	Bain 3 Lochhead Spence	11,750
20	Barnsley	H	1-2	Grimwood	34,000
21	Barnsley	A	0-1		12,000

22	Bradford City	A	0-0		11,500
23	Coventry City	H	1-2	Bain	7,000
24	Bradford City	H	3-0	Bain Lochhead McPherson	18,000
25	Fulham	A	1-3	Lochhead	15,000
26	Fulham	H	0-0		25,000
27	Blackpool	A	0-1		6,000
28	Blackpool	H	0-0		13,000
29	Derby County	A	0-3		12,000
30	Derby County	H	0-0		25,000
31	Nelson	A	2-0	Kennedy Spence	2,750
32	Nelson	H	0-1		8,500
33	Hull City	H	1-1	Lochhead	13,000
34	Hull City	A	1-1	Miller	6,250
35	Stoke	H	2-2	Smith 2	13,000
36	Stoke	A	0-3		11,000
37	Crystal Palace	H	5-1	Spence 4 Smith	8,000
38	Clapton Orient	A	0-1		18,000
39	Crystal Palace	A	1-1	Spence	7,000
40	Clapton Orient	H	2-2	Evans 2	11,000
41	Sheffield Wednesday	H	2-0	Lochhead Smith	7,500
42	Sheffield Wednesday	A	0-2		7,250

• Final League Position: 14th in Division Two

FA Cup

1	Plymouth Argyle	H	1-0	McPherson	35,700
2	Huddersfield Town	H	0-3		66,673

1924/25

	Opposition	H/A	Score	Scorers	Attn.
1	Leicester City	H	1-0	Goldthorpe	21,250
2	Stockport County	A	1-2	Lochhead	12,500
3	Stoke	A	0-0		15,250
4	Barnsley	H	1-0	Henderson	9,500
5	Coventry City	H	5-1	Henderson 2 Lochhead Spence McPherson	12,000
6	Oldham Athletic	A	3-0	Henderson 3	14,500
7	Sheffield Wednesday	H	2-0	McPherson Smith	29,500

8	Clapton Orient	A	1-0	Lochhead	15,000
9	Crystal Palace	H	1-0	Lochhead	27,750
10	Southampton	A	2-0	Lochhead 2	10,000
11	Wolverhampton Wanderers	A	0-0		17,500
12	Fulham	H	2-0	Henderson Lochhead	24,000
13	Portsmouth	A	1-1	Smith	19,500
14	Hull City	H	2-0	Hanson McPherson	29,750
15	Blackpool	A	1-1	Hanson	9,500
16	Derby County	H	1-1	Hanson	59,500
17	South Shields	A	2-1	Henderson McPherson	6,500
18	Bradford City	H	3-0	Henderson 2 McPherson	18,250
19	Port Vale	A	1-2	Lochhead	11,000
20	Middlesbrough	A	1-1	Henderson	18,500
21	Middlesbrough	H	2-0	Henderson Smith	44,000
22	Leicester City	A	0-3		18,250
23	Chelsea	H	1-0	Grimwood	30,500
24	Stoke	H	2-0	Henderson 2	24,500
25	Coventry City	A	0-1		9,000
26	Oldham Athletic	H	0-1		20,000
27	Clapton Orient	H	4-2	Kennedy 2 McPherson Pape	18,250
28	Crystal Palace	A	1-2	Lochhead	11,250
29	Sheffield Wednesday	A	1-1	Pape	3,000
30	Wolverhampton Wanderers	H	3-0	Spence 2 Kennedy	21,250
31	Fulham	A	0-1		16,000
32	Portsmouth	H	2-0	Lochhead Spence	22,000
33	Hull City	A	1-0	Lochhead	6,250
34	Blackpool	H	0-0		26,250
35	Derby County	A	0-1		24,000
36	Stockport County	H	2-0	Pape 2	43,500
37	South Shields	H	1-0	Lochhead	24,000
38	Chelsea	A	0-0		16,500
39	Bradford City	A	1-0	Smith	13,250
40	Southampton	H	1-1	Pape	26,500
41	Port Vale	H	4-0	Lochhead McPherson Smith Spence	33,500
42	Barnsley	A	0-0		11,250

• Final League Position: 2nd in Division Two

FA Cup

1	Sheffield Wednesday	A	0-2		35,079

1925/26

	Opposition	H/A	Score	Scorers	Attn.
1	West Ham United	A	0-1		25,630
2	Aston Villa	H	3-0	Barson Lochhead Spence	41,717
3	Arsenal	H	0-1		32,288
4	Aston Villa	A	2-2	Hanson Rennox	27,701
5	Manchester City	A	1-1	Rennox	62,994
6	Leicester City	H	3-2	Rennox 2 Lochhead	21,275
7	Liverpool	A	0-5		18,824
8	Burnley	H	6-1	Rennox 3 Hanson Hilditch Smith	17,259
9	Leeds United	A	0-2		26,265
10	Newcastle United	H	2-1	Rennox Thomas	39,651
11	Tottenham Hotspur	H	0-0		26,496
12	Cardiff City	A	2-0	McPherson 2	15,846
13	Huddersfield Town	H	1-1	Thomas	37,213
14	Everton	A	3-1	McPherson Rennox Spence	12,387
15	Birmingham	H	3-1	Barson Spence Thomas	23,539
16	Bury	A	3-1	McPherson 2 Spence	16,591
17	Blackburn Rovers	H	2-0	McPherson Thomas	33,660
18	Sunderland	A	1-2	Rennox	25,507
19	Sheffield United	H	1-2	McPherson	31,132
20	West Bromwich Albion	A	1-5	McPherson	17,651
21	Bolton Wanderers	H	2-1	Hanson Spence	38,503
22	Leicester City	A	3-1	McPherson 3	28,367
23	West Ham United	H	2-1	Rennox 2	29,612
24	Arsenal	A	2-3	McPherson Spence	25,252
25	Manchester City	H	1-6	Rennox	48,657
26	Burnley	A	1-0	McPherson	17,141
27	Leeds United	H	2-1	McPherson Sweeney	29,584
28	Tottenham Hotspur	A	1-0	Smith	25,466
29	Liverpool	H	3-3	Hanson Rennox Spence	9,214
30	Huddersfield Town	A	0-5		27,842
31	Bolton Wanderers	A	1-3	McPherson	10,794
32	Everton	H	0-0		30,058

33	Notts County	A	3-0	Rennox 2 McPherson	18,453
34	Bury	H	0-1		41,085
35	Notts County	H	0-1		19,606
36	Blackburn Rovers	A	0-7		15,870
37	Newcastle United	A	1-4	Hanson	9,829
38	Birmingham	A	1-2	Rennox	8,948
39	Sunderland	H	5-1	Taylor 3 Smith Thomas	10,918
40	Sheffield United	A	0-2		15,571
41	Cardiff City	H	1-0	Inglis	9,116
42	West Bromwich Albion	H	3-2	Taylor 3	9,974

● Final League Position: 9th in Division One

FA Cup

3	Port Vale	A	3-2	Spence 2 McPherson	14,841
4	Tottenham Hotspur	A	2-2	Spence Thomas	40,000
4R	Tottenham Hotspur	H	2-0	Spence Rennox	45,000
5	Sunderland	A	3-3	Smith 2 McPherson	50,500
5R	Sunderland	H	2-1	Smith McPherson	58,661
6	Fulham	A	2-1	Smith McPherson	28,699
SF	Manchester City	N*	0-3		46,450

*Played at Bramall Lane, Sheffield

1926/27

	Opposition	H/A	Score	Scorers	Attn.
1	Liverpool	A	2-4	McPherson 2	34,795
2	Sheffield United	A	2-2	McPherson 2	14,844
3	Leeds United	H	2-2	McPherson 2	26,378
4	Newcastle United	A	2-4	McPherson Spence	28,050
5	Arsenal	H	2-2	Hanson Spence	15,259
6	Burnley	H	2-1	Spence 2	32,593
7	Cardiff City	A	2-0	Rennox Spence	17,267
8	Aston Villa	H	2-1	Barson Rennox	31,234
9	Bolton Wanderers	A	0-4		17,869
10	Bury	A	3-0	Spence 2 McPherson	22,728
11	Birmingham	H	0-1		32,010
12	West Ham United	A	0-4		19,733
13	Sheffield Wednesday	H	0-0		16,166

14	Leicester City	A	3-2	McPherson 2 Rennox	18,521
15	Everton	H	2-1	Rennox 2	24,361
16	Blackburn Rovers	A	1-2	Spence	17,280
17	Huddersfield Town	H	0-0		33,135
18	Sunderland	A	0-6		15,385
19	West Bromwich Albion	H	2-0	Sweeney 2	18,585
20	Tottenham Hotspur	A	1-1	Spence	37,287
21	Tottenham Hotspur	H	2-1	McPherson 2	50,665
22	Arsenal	A	0-1		30,111
23	Sheffield United	H	5-0	McPherson 2 Barson Rennox Sweeney	33,593
24	Liverpool	H	0-1		30,304
25	Leeds United	A	3-2	McPherson Rennox Spence	16,816
26	Burnley	A	0-1		22,010
27	Newcastle United	H	3-1	Hanson Harris Spence	25,402
28	Cardiff City	H	1-1	Hanson	26,213
29	Aston Villa	A	0-2		32,467
30	Bolton Wanderers	H	0-0		29,618
31	Bury	H	1-2	A Smith	14,709
32	Birmingham	A	0-4		14,392
33	West Ham United	H	0-3		18,347
34	Sheffield Wednesday	A	0-2		11,997
35	Leicester City	H	1-0	Spence	17,119
36	Everton	A	0-0		22,564
37	Derby County	H	2-2	Spence 2	31,110
38	Blackburn Rovers	H	2-0	Hanson Spence	24,845
39	Derby County	A	2-2	Spence 2	17,306
40	Huddersfield Town	A	0-0		13,870
41	Sunderland	H	0-0		17,300
42	West Bromwich Albion	A	2-2	Hanson Spence	6,688

• Final League Position: 15th in Division One

FA Cup

3	Reading	A	1-1	Bennion	28,918
3R	Reading	H	2-2	Spence Sweeney	29,122
3RR	Reading	N*	1-2	McPherson	16,500

*Played at Villa Park, Birmingham

1927/28

	Opposition	H/A	Score	Scorers	Attn.
1	Middlesbrough	H	3-0	Spence 2 Hanson	44,957
2	Sheffield Wednesday	A	2-0	Hanson Partridge	17,944
3	Birmingham	A	0-0		25,863
4	Sheffield Wednesday	H	1-1	McPherson	18,759
5	Newcastle United	H	1-7	Spence	50,217
6	Huddersfield Town	A	2-4	Spence 2	17,307
7	Blackburn Rovers	A	0-3		18,243
8	Tottenham Hotspur	H	3-0	Hanson 2 Spence	13,952
9	Leicester City	A	0-1		22,385
10	Everton	A	2-5	Bennion Spence	40,080
11	Cardiff City	H	2-2	Spence Sweeney	31,090
12	Derby County	H	5-0	Spence 3 Johnston McPherson	18,304
13	West Ham United	A	2-1	McPherson Barrett og	21,972
14	Portsmouth	H	2-0	McPherson Clifford og	13,119
15	Sunderland	A	1-4	Spence	13,319
16	Aston Villa	H	5-1	Partridge 2 Johnston Spence, McPherson	25,991
17	Burnley	A	0-4		18,509
18	Bury	H	0-1		23,581
19	Sheffield United	A	1-2	Spence	11,984
20	Arsenal	H	4-1	Hanson McPherson Partridge Spence	18,120
21	Liverpool	A	0-2		14,971
22	Blackburn Rovers	H	1-1	Spence	31,131
23	Middlesbrough	A	2-1	Hanson Johnston	19,652
24	Birmingham	H	1-1	Hanson	16,853
25	Newcastle United	A	1-4	Partridge	25,912
26	Tottenham Hotspur	A	1-4	Johnston	23,545
27	Leicester City	H	5-2	Nicol 2 Spence 2 Hanson	16,640
28	Cardiff City	A	0-2		15,579
29	Huddersfield Town	H	0-0		35,413
30	West Ham United	H	1-1	Johnston	21,577
31	Everton	H	1-0	Rawlings	25,667
32	Portsmouth	A	0-1		25,400
33	Derby County	A	0-5		8,323

34	Aston Villa	A	1-3	Rawlings	24,691
35	Bolton Wanderers	A	2-3	Spence Thomas	23,795
36	Burnley	H	4-3	Rawlings 3 Williams	28,311
37	Bolton Wanderers	H	2-1	Johnston Rawlings	28,590
38	Bury	A	3-4	Johnston McLenahan Williams	17,440
39	Sheffield United	H	2-3	Rawlings Thomas	27,137
40	Sunderland	H	2-1	Hanson Johnston	9,545
41	Arsenal	A	1-0	Rawlings	22,452
42	Liverpool	H	6-1	Spence 3 Rawlings 2 Hanson	30,625

• Final League Position: 18th in Division One

FA Cup

3	Brentford	H	7-1	Hanson 4 Spence McPherson Johnston	18,538
4	Bury	A	1-1	Johnston	25,000
4R	Bury	H	1-0	Spence	48,001
5	Birmingham	H	1-0	Johnston	52,568
6	Blackburn Rovers	A	0-2		42,312

1928/29

	Opposition	H/A	Score	Scorers	Attn.
1	Leicester City	H	1-1	Rawlings	20,129
2	Aston Villa	A	0-0		30,356
3	Manchester City	A	2-2	Johnston Wilson	61,007
4	Leeds United	A	2-3	Johnston Spence	28,723
5	Liverpool	H	2-2	Hanson Silcock	24,077
6	West Ham United	A	1-3	Rawlings	20,788
7	Newcastle United	H	5-0	Rawlings 2 Hanson Johnston Spence	25,243
8	Burnley	A	4-3	Hanson 2 Spence 2	17,493
9	Cardiff City	H	1-1	Johnston	26,010
10	Birmingham	H	1-0	Johnston	17,522
11	Huddersfield Town	A	2-1	Hanson Spence	13,648
12	Bolton Wanderers	H	1-1	Hanson	31,185
13	Sheffield Wednesday	A	1-2	Hanson	18,113
14	Derby County	H	0-1		26,122
15	Sunderland	A	1-5	Rowley	15,932

16	Blackburn Rovers	H	1-4	Ramsden	19,589
17	Arsenal	A	1-3	Hanson	18,923
18	Everton	H	1-1	Hanson	17,080
19	Portsmouth	A	0-3		12,836
20	Sheffield United	H	1-1	Ramsden	22,202
21	Sheffield United	A	1-6	Rawlings	34,696
22	Leicester City	A	1-2	Hanson	21,535
23	Aston Villa	H	2-2	Hilditch Rowley	25,935
24	Manchester City	H	1-2	Rawlings	42,555
25	Leeds United	H	1-2	Sweeney	21,995
26	West Ham United	H	2-3	Reid Rowley	12,020
27	Newcastle United	A	0-5		34,134
28	Liverpool	A	3-2	Reid 2 Thomas	8,852
29	Burnley	H	1-0	Rowley	12,516
30	Cardiff City	A	2-2	Hanson Reid	13,070
31	Birmingham	A	1-1	Hanson	16,738
32	Huddersfield Town	H	1-0	Hanson	28,183
33	Bolton Wanderers	A	1-1	Hanson	17,354
34	Sheffield Wednesday	H	2-1	Reid, Rowley	27,095
35	Bury	A	3-1	Reid 2 Thomas	27,167
36	Derby County	A	1-6	Hanson	14,319
37	Bury	H	1-0	Thomas	29,742
38	Sunderland	H	3-0	Hanson Mann Reid	27,772
39	Blackburn Rovers	A	3-0	Reid 2 Ramsden	8,193
40	Arsenal	H	4-1	Reid 2 Hanson Thomas	22,858
41	Everton	A	4-2	Hanson 2 Reid 2	19,442
42	Portsmouth	H	0-0		17,728

• Final League Position: 12th in Division One

FA Cup

3	Port Vale	A	3-0	Spence Hanson Taylor	17,519
4	Bury	H	0-1		40,558

1929/30

	Opposition	H/A	Score	Scorers	Attn.
1	Newcastle United	A	1-4	Spence	43,489
2	Leicester City	A	1-4	Rowley	20,490

3	Blackburn Rovers	H	1-0	Mann	22,362
4	Leicester City	H	2-1	Ball Spence	16,445
5	Middlesbrough	A	3-2	Rawlings 3	26,428
6	Liverpool	H	1-2	Spence	20,788
7	West Ham United	A	1-2	Hanson	20,695
8	Manchester City	H	1-3	Thomas	57,201
9	Sheffield United	A	1-3	Boyle	7,987
10	Grimsby Town	H	2-5	Ball Rowley	21,498
11	Portsmouth	A	0-3		18,070
12	Arsenal	H	1-0	Ball	12,662
13	Aston Villa	A	0-1		24,292
14	Derby County	H	3-2	Ball Hanson Rowley	15,174
15	Sheffield Wednesday	A	2-7	Ball Hanson	14,264
16	Burnley	H	1-0	Rowley	9,060
17	Sunderland	A	4-2	Spence 2 Ball Hanson	11,508
18	Bolton Wanderers	H	1-1	Ball	5,656
19	Everton	A	0-0		18,182
20	Leeds United	H	3-1	Ball 2 Hanson	15,054
21	Birmingham	H	0-0		18,626
22	Birmingham	A	1-0	Rowley	35,682
23	Newcastle United	H	5-0	Boyle 2 McLachlan Rowley Spence	14,862
24	Blackburn Rovers	A	4-5	Boyle 2 Ball Rowley	23,923
25	Middlesbrough	H	0-3		21,028
26	Liverpool	A	0-1		28,592
27	West Ham United	H	4-2	Spence 4	15,424
28	Manchester City	A	1-0	Reid	64,472
29	Grimsby Town	A	2-2	Reid Rowley	9,337
30	Portsmouth	H	3-0	Reid 2 Boyle	17,317
31	Bolton Wanderers	A	1-4	Reid	17,714
32	Aston Villa	H	2-3	McLachlan Warburton	5,407
33	Arsenal	A	2-4	Ball Wilson	18,082
34	Derby County	A	1-1	Rowley	9,102
35	Burnley	A	0-4		11,659
36	Sunderland	H	2-1	McLenahan 2	13,230
37	Sheffield Wednesday	H	2-2	McLenahan Rowley	12,806
38	Huddersfield Town	H	1-0	McLenahan	26,496

39	Everton	H	3-3	McLenahan Rowley Spence	13,320
40	Huddersfield Town	A	2-2	Hilditch McLenahan	20,716
41	Leeds United	A	1-3	Spence	10,596
42	Sheffield United	H	1-5	Rowley	15,268

● Final League Position: 17th in Division One

FA Cup

| 3 | Swindon Town | H | 0-2 | | 33,226 |

1930/31

	Opposition	H/A	Score	Scorers	Attn
1	Aston Villa	H	3-4	Reid Rowley Warburton	18,004
2	Middlesbrough	A	1-3	Rowley	15,712
3	Chelsea	A	2-6	Reid Spence	48,648
4	Huddersfield Town	H	0-6		11,836
5	Newcastle United	H	4-7	Reid 3 Rowley	10,907
6	Huddersfield Town	A	0-3		14,028
7	Sheffield Wednesday	A	0-3		18,705
8	Grimsby Town	H	0-2		14,695
9	Manchester City	A	1-4	Spence	41,757
10	West Ham United	A	1-5	Reid	20,003
11	Arsenal	H	1-2	McLachlan	23,406
12	Portsmouth	A	1-4	Rowley	19,262
13	Birmingham	H	2-0	Gallimore Rowley	11,479
14	Leicester City	A	4-5	Bullock 3 McLachlan	17,466
15	Blackpool	H	0-0		14,765
16	Sheffield United	A	1-3	Gallimore	12,698
17	Sunderland	H	1-1	Gallimore	10,971
18	Blackburn Rovers	A	1-4	Rowley	10,802
19	Derby County	H	2-1	Reid Spence	9,701
20	Leeds United	A	0-5		11,282
21	Bolton Wanderers	A	1-3	Reid	22,662
22	Bolton Wanderers	H	1-1	Reid	12,741
23	Aston Villa	A	0-7		32,505
24	Leeds United	H	0-0		9,875
25	Chelsea	H	1-0	Warburton	8,966
26	Newcastle United	A	3-4	Warburton , Reid	24,835

27	Sheffield Wednesday	H	4-1	Hopkinson Reid Spence Warburton	6,077
28	Grimsby Town	A	1-2	Reid	9,305
29	Manchester City	H	1-3	Spence	39,876
30	West Ham United	H	1-0	Gallimore	9,745
31	Arsenal	A	1-4	Thomson	41,510
32	Birmingham	A	0-0		17,678
33	Portsmouth	H	0-1		4,808
34	Blackpool	A	1-5	Hopkinson	13,612
35	Leicester City	H	0-0		3,679
36	Sheffield United	H	1-2	Hopkinson	5,420
37	Liverpool	A	1-1	Wilson	27,782
38	Sunderland	A	2-1	Hopkinson Reid	13,590
39	Liverpool	H	4-1	Reid 2 McLenahan Rowley	8,058
40	Blackburn Rovers	H	0-1		6,414
41	Derby County	A	1-6	Spence	6,610
42	Middlesbrough	H	4-4	Reid 2 Bennion Gallimore	3,969

● Final League Position: 22nd in Division One

FA Cup

3	Stoke City	A	3-3	Reid 3	23,415
3R	Stoke City	H	0-0		22,013
3RR	Stoke City	N*	4-2	Hopkinson 2 Spence Gallimore	11,788
4	Grimsby Town	A	0-1		15,000

* Played at Anfield, Liverpool

1931/32

	Opposition	H/A	Score	Scorers	Attn.
1	Bradford Park Avenue	A	1-3	Reid	16,239
2	Southampton	H	2-3	Ferguson Johnston	3,507
3	Swansea Town	H	2-1	Hopkinson Reid	6,763
4	Stoke City	A	0-3		10,518
5	Tottenham Hotspur	H	1-1	Johnston	9,557
6	Stoke City	H	1-1	Spence	5,025
7	Nottingham Forest	A	1-2	Gallimore	10,166
8	Chesterfield	H	3-1	Warburton 2 Johnston	10,874
9	Burnley	A	0-2		9,719

10	Preston North End	H	3-2	Gallimore Johnston Spence	8,496
11	Barnsley	A	0-0		4,052
12	Notts County	H	3-3	Gallimore Mann Spence	6,694
13	Plymouth Argyle	A	1-3	Johnston	22,555
14	Leeds United	H	2-5	Spence 2	9,512
15	Oldham Athletic	A	5-1	Johnston 2 Spence 2 Mann	10,922
16	Bury	H	1-2	Spence	11,745
17	Port Vale	A	2-1	Spence 2	6,955
18	Millwall	H	2-0	Gallimore Spence	6,396
19	Bradford City	A	3-4	Spence 2 Johnston	13,215
20	Bristol City	H	0-1		4,697
21	Wolverhampton Wanderers	H	3-2	Hopkinson Reid Spence	33,123
22	Wolverhampton Wanderers	A	0-7		37,207
23	Bradford Park Avenue	H	0-2		6,056
24	Swansea Town	A	1-3	Warburton	5,888
25	Tottenham Hotspur	A	1-4	Reid	19,139
26	Nottingham Forest	H	3-2	Reid 3	11,152
27	Chesterfield	A	3-1	Reid 2 Spence	9,457
28	Burnley	H	5-1	Johnston 2 Ridding 2 Gallimore	11,036
29	Preston North End	A	0-0		13,353
30	Barnsley	H	3-0	Hopkinson 2 Gallimore	18,223
31	Notts County	A	2-1	Hopkinson, Reid	10,817
32	Plymouth Argyle	H	2-1	Spence 2	24,827
33	Leeds United	A	4-1	Reid 2 Johnston Ridding	13,644
34	Charlton Athletic	H	0-2		37,012
35	Oldham Athletic	H	5-1	Reid 3 Fitton Spence	17,886
36	Charlton Athletic	A	0-1		16,256
37	Bury	A	0-0		12,592
38	Port Vale	H	2-0	Reid Spence	10,916
39	Millwall	A	1-1	Reid	9,087
40	Bradford City	H	1-0	Fitton	17,765
41	Bristol City	A	1-2	Black	5,874
42	Southampton	A	1-1	Black	6,128

• Final League Position: 12th in Division Two

FA Cup

| 3 | Plymouth Argyle | A | 1-4 | Reid | 28,000 |

1932/33

	Opposition	H/A	Score	Scorers	Attn.
1	Stoke City	H	0-2		24,996
2	Charlton Athletic	A	1-0	Spence	12,946
3	Southampton	A	2-4	Reid, Campbell og	7,978
4	Charlton Athletic	H	1-1	McLenahan	9,480
5	Tottenham Hotspur	A	1-6	Ridding	23,333
6	Grimsby Town	H	1-1	Brown	17,662
7	Oldham Athletic	A	1-1	Spence	14,403
8	Preston North End	H	0-0		20,800
9	Burnley	A	3-2	Brown Gallimore Spence	5,314
10	Bradford Park Avenue	H	2-1	Reid 2	18,918
11	Millwall	H	7-1	Reid 3 Brown 2 Gallimore Spence	15,860
12	Port Vale	A	3-3	Ridding 2 Brown	7,138
13	Notts County	H	2-0	Gallimore Ridding	24,178
14	Bury	A	2-2	Brown Ridding	21,663
15	Fulham	H	4-3	Gallimore 2 Brown Ridding	28,803
16	Chesterfield	A	1-1	Ridding	10,277
17	Bradford City	H	0-1		28,513
18	West Ham United	A	1-3	Ridding	13,435
19	Lincoln City	H	4-1	Reid 3 Worthy og	18,021
20	Swansea Town	A	1-2	Brown	10,727
21	Plymouth Argyle	A	3-2	Spence 2 Reid	33,776
22	Stoke City	A	0-0		14,115
23	Plymouth Argyle	H	4-0	Ridding 2 Chalmers Spence	30,257
24	Southampton	H	1-2	McDonald	21,364
25	Tottenham Hotspur	H	2-1	Frame McDonald	20,661
26	Grimsby Town	A	1-1	Stewart	4,020
27	Oldham Athletic	H	2-0	Ridding Stewart	15,275
28	Preston North End	A	3-3	Dewar Hopkinson Stewart	15,662
29	Burnley	H	2-1	McDonald Warburton	18,533
30	Millwall	A	0-2		22,578
31	Port Vale	H	1-1	Vine	24,690
32	Notts County	A	0-1		13,018
33	Bury	H	1-3	McLenahan	27,687
34	Fulham	A	1-3	Dewar	21,477

35	Bradford Park Avenue	A	1-1	Vincent	6,314
36	Chesterfield	H	2-1	Dewar Frame	16,031
37	Nottingham Forest	A	2-3	Brown Dewar	12,963
38	Bradford City	A	2-1	Brown Hine	11,195
39	Nottingham Forest	H	2-1	Hine McDonald	16,849
40	West Ham United	H	1-2	Dewar	14,958
41	Lincoln City	A	2-3	Dewar Hine	8,507
42	Swansea City	H	1-1	Hine	9,588

• Final League Position: 6th in Division Two

FA Cup

| 3 | Middlesbrough | H | 1-4 | Spence | 36,991 |

1933/34

	Opposition	H/A	Score	Scorers	Attn.
1	Plymouth Argyle	A	0-4		25,700
2	Nottingham Forest	H	0-1		16,934
3	Lincoln City	H	1-1	Green	16,987
4	Nottingham Forest	A	1-1	Stewart	10,650
5	Bolton Wanderers	H	1-5	Stewart	21,779
6	Brentford	A	4-3	Brown 2 Frame Hine	17,180
7	Burnley	H	5-2	Dewar 4 Brown	18,411
8	Oldham Athletic	A	0-2		22,736
9	Preston North End	H	1-0	Hine	22,303
10	Bradford Park Avenue	A	1-6	Hine	11,033
11	Bury	A	1-2	Byrne	15,008
12	Hull City	H	4-1	Heywood 2 Green Hine	16,269
13	Fulham	A	2-0	Stewart Keeping og	17,049
14	Southampton	H	1-0	Manley	18,149
15	Blackpool	A	1-3	Brown	14,384
16	Bradford City	H	2-1	Dewar Barker og	20,902
17	Port Vale	A	3-2	Black Brown Dewar	10,316
18	Notts County	H	1-2	Dewar	15,564
19	Swansea Town	A	1-2	Hine	6,591
20	Millwall	H	1-1	Dewar	12,043
21	Grimsby Town	H	1-3	Vose	29,443
22	Grimsby Town	A	3-7	Byrne 2 Frame	15,801

23	Plymouth Argyle	H	0-3		12,206
24	Lincoln City	A	1-5	Brown	6,075
25	Bolton Wanderers	A	1-3	Ball	11,887
26	Brentford	H	1-3	Ball	16,891
27	Burnley	A	4-1	Cape 2 Green Stewart	9,906
28	Oldham Athletic	H	2-3	Cape Green	24,480
29	Preston North End	A	2-3	Gallimore 2	9,173
30	Bradford Park Avenue	H	0-4		13,389
31	Bury	H	2-1	Ball Gallimore	11,176
32	Hull City	A	1-4	Ball	5,771
33	Fulham	H	1-0	Ball	17,565
34	Southampton	A	0-1		4,840
35	West Ham United	H	0-1		29,114
36	Blackpool	H	2-0	Cape Hine	20,038
37	West Ham United	A	1-2	Cape	20,085
38	Bradford City	A	1-1	Cape	9,258
39	Port Vale	H	2-0	Brown McMillen	14,777
40	Notts County	A	0-0		9,645
41	Swansea Town	H	1-1	Topping	16,678
42	Millwall	A	2-0	Cape Manley	24,003

● Final League Position: 20th in Division Two

FA Cup

3	Portsmouth	H	1-1	McLenahan	23,283
3R	Portsmouth	A	1-4	Ball	18,748

1934/35

	Opposition	H/A	Score	Scorers	Attn.
1	Bradford City	H	2-0	Manley 2	27,573
2	Sheffield United	A	2-3	Ball Manley	18,468
3	Bolton Wanderers	A	1-3	Finney og	16,238
4	Barnsley	H	4-1	Mutch 3 Manley	22,315
5	Bolton Wanderers	H	0-3		24,760
6	Port Vale	A	2-3	TJ Jones Mutch	9,307
7	Norwich City	H	5-0	Cape TJN Jones McLenahan Mutch Owen	13,052
8	Swansea Town	H	3-1	Cape 2 Mutch	14,865

9	Burnley	A	2-1	Cape Manley	16,757
10	Oldham Athletic	H	4-0	Manley 2 McKay Mutch	29,143
11	Newcastle United	A	1-0	Bamford	24,752
12	West Ham United	H	3-1	Mutch 2 McKay	31,950
13	Blackpool	A	2-1	Bryant McKay	15,663
14	Bury	H	1-0	Mutch	41,415
15	Hull City	A	2-3	Bamford 2	6,494
16	Nottingham Forest	H	3-2	Mutch 2 Hine	27,192
17	Brentford	A	1-3	Bamford	21,744
18	Fulham	H	1-0	Mutch	25,706
19	Bradford Park Avenue	A	2-1	Manley Mutch	8,405
20	Plymouth Argyle	H	3-1	Bamford Bryant Rowley	24,896
21	Notts County	H	2-1	Mutch Rowley	32,965
22	Notts County	A	0-1		24,599
23	Bradford City	A	0-2		11,908
24	Southampton	H	3-0	Cape 2 Rowley	15,174
25	Sheffield United	H	3-3	Bryant Mutch Rowley	28,300
26	Barnsley	A	2-0	Bryant TJ Jones	10,177
27	Norwich City	A	2-3	Manley Rowley	14,260
28	Port Vale	H	2-1	TJ Jones Rowley	7,372
29	Swansea Town	A	0-1		8,876
30	Oldham Athletic	A	1-3	Mutch	14,432
31	Newcastle United	H	0-1		20,728
32	West Ham United	A	0-0		19,718
33	Blackpool	H	3-2	Bamford Mutch Rowley	25,704
34	Bury	A	1-0	Cape	7,229
35	Burnley	H	3-4	Boyd Cape McMillen	10,247
36	Hull City	H	3-0	Boyd 3	15,538
37	Nottingham Forest	A	2-2	Bryant 2	8,618
38	Brentford	H	0-0		32,969
39	Fulham	A	1-3	Bamford	11,059
40	Southampton	A	0-1		12,458
41	Bradford Park Avenue	H	2-0	Bamford Robertson	8,606
42	Plymouth Argyle	A	2-0	Bamford Rowley	10,767

• Final League Position: 5th in Division Two

FA Cup

3	Bristol Rovers	A	3-1	Bamford 2 Mutch	20,400
4	Nottingham Forest	A	0-0		32,862
4R	Nottingham Forest	H	0-3		33,851

1935/36

	Opposition	H/A	Score	Scorers	Attn.
1	Plymouth Argyle	A	1-3	Bamford	22,366
2	Charlton Athletic	H	3-0	Bamford Cape Chester	21,211
3	Bradford City	H	3-1	Bamford 2 Mutch	30,754
4	Charlton Athletic	A	0-0		13,178
5	Newcastle United	A	2-0	Bamford Rowley	28,520
6	Hull City	H	2-0	Bamford 2	15,739
7	Tottenham Hotspur	H	0-0		34,718
8	Southampton	A	1-2	Rowley	17,678
9	Port Vale	A	3-0	Mutch 2 Bamford	9,703
10	Fulham	H	1-0	Rowley	22,723
11	Sheffield United	H	3-1	Cape Mutch Rowley	18,636
12	Bradford Park Avenue	A	0-1		12,216
13	Leicester City	H	0-1		39,074
14	Swansea Town	A	1-2	Bamford	9,731
15	West Ham United	H	2-3	Rowley 2	24,440
16	Norwich City	A	5-3	Rowley 3 Manley 2	17,366
17	Doncaster Rovers	H	0-0		23,569
18	Blackpool	A	1-4	Mutch	13,218
19	Nottingham Forest	H	5-0	Bamford 2 Manley Mutch Rowley	15,284
20	Barnsley	H	1-1	Mutch	20,993
21	Plymouth Argyle	H	3-2	Mutch 2 Manley	20,894
22	Barnsley	A	3-0	Gardner Manley Mutch	20,957
23	Bradford City	A	0-1		11,286
24	Newcastle United	H	3-1	Mutch 2 Rowley	22,968
25	Southampton	H	4-0	Mutch 2 Bryant Curry og	23,305
26	Tottenham Hotspur	A	0-0		20,085
27	Port Vale	H	7-2	Manley 4 Rowley 2 Mutch	22,265
28	Sheffield United	A	1-1	Manley	25,852
29	Blackpool	H	3-2	Bryant Manley Mutch	18,423

30	West Ham United	A	2-1	Bryant Mutch	29,684
31	Swansea Town	H	3-0	Manley Mutch Rowley	27,580
32	Leicester City	A	1-1	Bryant	18,200
33	Norwich City	H	2-1	Rowley 2	31,596
34	Fulham	A	2-2	Bryant Griffiths	11,137
35	Doncaster Rovers	A	0-0		13,474
36	Burnley	A	2-2	Bamford 2	27,245
37	Bradford Park Avenue	H	4-0	Mutch 2 Bamford Bryant	33,517
38	Burnley	H	4-0	Bryant 2 Rowley 2	39,855
39	Nottingham Forest	A	1-1	Bamford	12,156
40	Bury	H	2-1	Lang Rowley	35,027
41	Bury	A	3-2	Manley 2 Mutch	31,562
42	Hull City	A	1-1	Bamford	4,540

• Final League Position: 1st in Division Two

FA Cup

3	Reading	A	3-1	Mutch 2 Manley	25,844
4	Stoke City	A	0-0		32,286
4R	Stoke City	H	0-2		34,440

1936/37

	Opposition	H/A	Score	Scorers	Attn.
1	Wolverhampton Wanderers	H	1-1	Bamford	42,731
2	Huddersfield Town	A	1-3	Manley	12,616
3	Derby County	A	4-5	Bamford 3 Wassall	21,194
4	Huddersfield Town	H	3-1	Bamford Bryant Mutch	26,839
5	Manchester City	H	3-2	Bamford Bryant Manley	68,796
6	Sheffield Wednesday	H	1-1	Bamford	40,933
7	Preston North End	A	1-3	Bamford	24,149
8	Arsenal	H	2-0	Bryant Rowley	55,884
9	Brentford	A	0-4		28,019
10	Portsmouth	A	1-2	Manley	19,845
11	Chelsea	H	0-0		29,859
12	Stoke City	A	0-3		22,464
13	Charlton Athletic	H	0-0		26,084
14	Grimsby Town	A	2-6	Bryant Mutch	9,844
15	Liverpool	H	2-5	Manley Thompson	26,419

16	Leeds United	A	1-2`	Bryant	17,610
17	Birmingham	H	1-2	Mutch	16,544
18	Middlesbrough	A	2-3	Halton Manley	11,790
19	West Bromwich Albion	H	2-2	McKay Mutch	21,051
20	Bolton Wanderers	H	1-0	Bamford	47,658
21	Wolverhampton Wanderers	A	1-3	McKay	41,525
22	Bolton Wanderers	A	4-0	Bryant 2 McKay 2	11,801
23	Sunderland	H	2-1	Bryant Mutch	46,257
24	Derby County	H	2-2	Rowley 2	31,883
25	Manchester City	A	0-1		64,862
26	Sheffield Wednesday	A	0-1		8,658
27	Preston North End	H	1-1	Wrigglesworth	13,225
28	Arsenal	A	1-1	Rowley	37,236
29	Brentford	H	1-3	Baird	31,942
30	Portsmouth	H	0-1		19,416
31	Chelsea	A	2-4	Bamford Gladwin	16,382
32	Stoke City	H	2-1	Baird McClelland	24,660
33	Charlton Athletic	A	0-3		25,943
34	Grimsby Town	H	1-1	Cape	26,636
35	Everton	H	2-1	Baird Mutch	30,071
36	Liverpool	A	0-2		25,319
37	Everton	A	3-2	Bryant Ferrier Mutch	28,395
38	Leeds United	H	0-0		34,429
39	Birmingham	A	2-2	Bamford 2	19,130
40	Middlesbrough	H	2-1	Bamford Bryant	17,656
41	Sunderland	A	1-1	Bamford	12,876
42	West Bromwich Albion	A	0-1		16,234

● Final League Position: 21st in Division One

FA Cup

3	Reading	H	1-0	Bamford	36,668
4	Arsenal	A	0-5		45,637

1937/38

	Opposition	H/A	Score	Scorers	Attn.
1	Newcastle United	H	3-0	Manley 2 Bryant	29,446
2	Coventry City	A	0-1		30,575

3	Luton Town	A	0-1		20,610
4	Coventry City	H	2-2	Bamford Bryant	17,455
5	Barnsley	H	4-1	Bamford 3 Manley	22,394
6	Bury	A	2-1	Ferrier 2	9,954
7	Stockport County	A	0-1		24,386
8	Southampton	H	1-2	Manley	22,729
9	Sheffield United	H	0-1		20,105
10	Tottenham Hotspur	A	1-0	Manley	31,189
11	Blackburn Rovers	A	1-1	Bamford	19,580
12	Sheffield Wednesday	H	1-0	Ferrier	16,379
13	Fulham	A	0-1		17,350
14	Plymouth Argyle	H	0-0		18,359
15	Chesterfield	A	7-1	Bamford 4 Baird Bryant Manley	17,407
16	Aston Villa	H	3-1	Bamford Manley Pearson	33,193
17	Norwich City	A	3-2	Baird Bryant Pearson	17,397
18	Swansea Town	H	5-1	Rowley 4 Bryant	17,782
19	Bradford Park Avenue	A	0-4		12,004
20	Nottingham Forest	H	4-3	Baird 2 McKay Wrigglesworth	30,778
21	Nottingham Forest	A	3-2	Bamford Bryant Carey	19,283
22	Newcastle United	A	2-2	Bamford Rowley	40,088
23	Luton Town	H	4-2	Bamford Bryant Carey McKay	16,845
24	Stockport County	H	3-1	Bamford Bryant McKay	31,852
25	Barnsley	A	2-2	Rowley Smith	7,859
26	Southampton	A	3-3	Redwood 2 Baird	20,354
27	Sheffield United	A	2-1	Bryant Smith	17,754
28	Tottenham Hotspur	H	0-1		34,631
29	West Ham United	H	4-0	Baird 2 Smith Wassell	14,572
30	Blackburn Rovers	H	2-1	Baird Bryant	30,892
31	Sheffield Wednesday	A	3-1	Baird Brown Rowley	37,156
32	Fulham	H	1-0	Baird	30,363
33	Plymouth Argyle	A	1-1	Rowley	20,311
34	Chesterfield	H	4-1	Smith 2 Bryant Carey	27,311
35	Aston Villa	A	0-3		54,654
36	Norwich City	H	0-0		25,879
37	Burnley	A	0-1		28,459
38	Swansea Town	A	2-2	Rowley Smith	13,811
39	Burnley	H	4-0	McKay 2 Baird Bryant	35,808

40	Bradford Park Avenue	H	3-1	Baird McKay Smith	28,919
41	West Ham United	A	0-1		14,816
42	Bury	H	2-0	McKay Smith	53,604

• Final League Position: 2nd in Division Two

FA Cup

3	Yeovil Town	H	3-0	Baird Bamford Pearson	49,004
4	Barnsley	A	2-2	Baird Carey	35,549
4R	Barnsley	H	1-0	Baird	33,601
5	Brentford	A	0-2		24,147

1938/39

	Opposition	H/A	Score	Scorers	Attn.
1	Middlesbrough	A	1-3	Smith	25,539
2	Bolton Wanderers	H	2-2	Craven Hubbick og	37,950
3	Birmingham	H	4-1	Smith 2 Bryant Craven	22,228
4	Liverpool	A	0-1		25,070
5	Grimsby Town	A	0-1		14,077
6	Stoke City	A	1-1	Smith	21,526
7	Chelsea	H	5-1	Carey Manley Redwood Rowley Smith	34,557
8	Preston North End	A	1-1	Bryant	25,964
9	Charlton Athletic	H	0-2		35,730
10	Blackpool	H	0-0		39,723
11	Derby County	A	1-5	Smith	26,612
12	Sunderland	H	0-1		33,565
13	Aston Villa	A	2-0	Rowley Wrigglesworth	38,357
14	Wolverhampton Wanderers	H	1-3	Rowley	32,821
15	Everton	A	0-3		31,809
16	Huddersfield Town	H	1-1	Hanlon	23,164
17	Portsmouth	A	0-0		18,692
18	Arsenal	H	1-0	Bryant	42,008
19	Brentford	A	5-2	Hanlon 2 Bryant Manley Rowley	14,919
20	Middlesbrough	H	1-1	Wassall	33,235
21	Leicester City	H	3-0	Wrigglesworth 2 Carey	26,332
22	Leicester City	A	1-1	Hanlon	21,434
23	Birmingham	A	3-3	Hanlon McKay Pearson	20,787

24	Grimsby Town	H	3-1	Rowley 2 Wassall	25,654
25	Stoke City	H	0-1		37,384
26	Chelsea	A	1-0	Bradbury	31,265
27	Preston North End	H	1-1	Rowley	41,061
28	Charlton Athletic	A	1-7	Hanlon	23,721
29	Blackpool	A	5-3	Hanlon 3 Bryant Carey	15,253
30	Derby County	H	1-1	Carey	37,166
31	Sunderland	A	2-5	Manley Rowley	11,078
32	Aston Villa	H	1-1	Wassall	28,292
33	Wolverhampton Wanderers	A	0-3		31,498
34	Everton	H	0-2		18,348
35	Huddersfield Town	A	1-1	Rowley	14,007
36	Leeds United	H	0-0		35,564
37	Portsmouth	H	1-1	Rowley	25,457
38	Leeds United	A	1-3	Carey	13,771
39	Arsenal	A	1-2	Hanlon	25,741
40	Brentford	H	3-0	Bryant Carey Wassall	15,353
41	Bolton Wanderers	A	0-0		10,314
42	Liverpool	H	2-0	Hanlon 2	12,073

● Final League Position: 14th in Division One

FA Cup

| 3 | West Bromwich Albion | A | 0-0 | | 23,900 |
| 3R | West Bromwich Albion | H | 1-5 | Redwood | 17,641 |

1946/47

	Opposition	H/A	Score	Scorers	Attn.
1	Grimsby Town	H	2-1	Mitten Rowley	41,025
2	Chelsea	A	3-0	Mitten Pearson Rowley	27,750
3	Charlton Athletic	A	3-1	Hanlon Rowley Johnson og	44,088
4	Liverpool	H	5-0	Pearson 3 Mitten Rowley	41,657
5	Middlesbrough	H	1-0	Rowley	65,112
6	Chelsea	H	1-1	Chilton	30,275
7	Stoke City	A	2-3	Delaney Hanlon	41,699
8	Arsenal	H	5-2	Hanlon 2 Rowley 2 Wrigglesworth	62,718
9	Preston North End	H	1-1	Wrigglesworth	55,395

10	Sheffield United	A	2-2	Rowley 2	35,543
11	Blackpool	A	1-3	Delaney	26,307
12	Sunderland	H	0-3		48,385
13	Aston Villa	A	0-0		53,668
14	Derby County	H	4-1	Pearson 2 Mitten Rowley	57,340
15	Everton	A	2-2	Pearson Rowley	45,832
16	Huddersfield Town	H	5-2	Mitten 2 Morris 2 Rowley	39,216
17	Wolverhampton Wanderers	A	2-3	Hanlon Delaney	46,704
18	Brentford	H	4-1	Rowley 3 Mitten	31,962
19	Blackburn Rovers	A	1-2	Morris	21,455
20	Bolton Wanderers	A	2-2	Rowley 2	28,505
21	Bolton Wanderers	H	1-0	Pearson	57,186
22	Grimsby Town	A	0-0		17,183
23	Charlton Athletic	H	4-1	Burke 2 Buckle Pearson	43,406
24	Middlesbrough	A	4-2	Pearson 2 Buckle Morris	37,435
25	Arsenal	A	2-6	Morris Pearson	29,415
26	Stoke City	H	1-1	Buckle	8,456
27	Blackpool	H	3-0	Rowley 2 Hanlon	29,993
28	Sunderland	A	1-1	Delaney	25,038
29	Aston Villa	H	2-1	Burke Pearson	36,965
30	Derby County	A	3-4	Burke 2 Pearson	19,579
31	Everton	H	3-0	Burke Delaney Warner	43,441
32	Huddersfield Town	A	2-2	Delaney Pearson	18,509
33	Wolverhampton Wanderers	H	3-1	Rowley 2 Hanlon	66,967
34	Leeds United	H	3-1	Burke 2 Delaney	41,772
35	Leeds United	A	2-0	Burke McGlen	15,528
36	Brentford	A	0-0		21,714
37	Blackburn Rovers	H	4-0	Pearson 2 Rowley Higgins og	46,196
38	Portsmouth	A	1-0	Delaney	30,623
39	Liverpool	A	0-1		48,800
40	Preston North End	A	1-1	Pearson	23,278
41	Portsmouth	H	3-0	Mitten Morris Rowley	37,614
42	Sheffield United	H	6-2	Rowley 3 Morris 2 Pearson	34,059

• Final League Position: 2nd in Division One

FA Cup

3	Bradford Park Avenue	A	3-0	Rowley 2 Buckle	26,990
4	Nottingham Forest	H	0-2		58,641

1947/48

	Opposition	H/A	Score	Scorers	Attn.
1	Middlesbrough	A	2-2	Rowley 2	39,554
2	Liverpool	H	2-0	Morris Pearson	52,385
3	Charlton Athletic	H	6-2	Rowley 4 Morris Pearson	52,659
4	Liverpool	A	2-2	Mitten Pearson	48,081
5	Arsenal	A	1-2	Morris	64,905
6	Burnley	A	0-0		37,517
7	Sheffield United	H	0-1		49,808
8	Manchester City	A	0-0		71,364
9	Preston North End	A	1-2	Morris	34,372
10	Stoke City	H	1-1	Hanlon	45,745
11	Grimsby Town	H	3-4	Mitten Morris Rowley	40,035
12	Sunderland	A	0-1		37,148
13	Aston Villa	H	2-0	Delaney Rowley	47,078
14	Wolverhampton Wanderers	A	6-2	Morris 2 Pearson 2 Delaney Mitten	44,309
15	Huddersfield Town	H	4-4	Rowley 4	59,772
16	Derby County	A	1-1	Carey	32,990
17	Everton	H	2-2	Cockburn Morris	35,509
18	Chelsea	A	4-0	Morris 3 Rowley	43,617
19	Blackpool	H	1-1	Pearson	63,683
20	Blackburn Rovers	A	1-1	Morris	22,784
21	Middlesbrough	H	2-1	Pearson 2	46,666
22	Portsmouth	H	3-2	Morris 2 Rowley	42,776
23	Portsmouth	A	3-1	Morris 2 Delaney	27,674
24	Burnley	H	5-0	Rowley 3 Mitten 2	59,838
25	Charlton Athletic	A	2-1	Morris Pearson	40,484
26	Arsenal	H	1-1	Rowley	81,962
27	Sheffield United	A	1-2	Rowley	45,189
28	Preston North End	H	1-1	Delaney	61,765
29	Stoke City	A	2-0	Buckle Pearson	36,794
30	Sunderland	H	3-1	Delaney Mitten Rowley	55,160

31	Grimsby Town	A	1-1	Rowley	12,284
32	Wolverhampton Wanderers	H	3-2	Delaney Mitten Morris	50,667
33	Aston Villa	A	1-0	Pearson	52,666
34	Bolton Wanderers	H	0-2		71,623
35	Huddersfield Town	A	2-0	Burke Pearson	38,266
36	Bolton Wanderers	A	1-0	Anderson	44,225
37	Derby County	H	1-0	Pearson	49,609
38	Manchester City	H	1-1	Rowley	71,690
39	Everton	A	0-2		44,198
40	Chelsea	H	5-0	Pearson 2 Delaney Mitten Rowley	43,225
41	Blackpool	A	0-1		32,236
42	Blackburn Rovers	H	4-1	Pearson 3 Delaney	44,439

• Final League Position: 2nd In Division One

FA Cup

3	Aston Villa	A	6-4	Pearson 2 Morris 2 Delaney Rowley	58,683
4	Liverpool*	H	3-0	Morris Rowley Mitten	74,000
5	Charlton Athletic**	H	2-0	Warner Mitten	33,312
6	Preston North End***	H	4-1	Pearson 2 Rowley Mitten	74,213
SF	Derby County****	N	3-1	Pearson 3	60,000
F	Blackpool*****	N	4-2	Rowley 2 Pearson Anderson	99,000

* Played at Goodison Park
** Played at Leeds Road Huddersfield
*** Played at Maine Road Manchester
**** Played at Hillsborough Sheffield
***** Played at Wembley Stadium

1948/49

	Opposition	H/A	Score	Scorers	Attn.
1	Derby County	H	1-2	Pearson	52,620
2	Blackpool	A	3-0	Rowley 2 Mitten	36,880
3	Arsenal	A	1-0	Mitten	64,150
4	Blackpool	H	3-4	Delaney Mitten Morris	51,187
5	Huddersfield Town	H	4-1	Pearson 2 Delaney Mitten	57,714
6	Wolverhampton Wanderers	A	2-3	Morris Rowley	42,617

7	Manchester City	A	0-0		64,502
8	Wolverhampton Wanderers	H	2-0	Buckle Pearson	33,871
9	Sheffield United	A	2-2	Buckle Pearson	36,880
10	Aston Villa	H	3-1	Mitten 2 Pearson	53,820
11	Sunderland	A	1-2	Rowley	54,419
12	Charlton Athletic	H	1-1	Burke	46,964
13	Stoke City	A	1-2	Morris	45,830
14	Burnley	H	1-1	Mitten	47,093
15	Preston North End	A	6-1	Mitten 2 Pearson 2 Morris Rowley	37,372
16	Everton	H	2-0	Delaney Morris	42,789
17	Chelsea	A	1-1	Rowley	62,542
18	Birmingham City	H	3-0	Morris Pearson Rowley	45,482
19	Middlesbrough	A	4-1	Rowley 3 Delaney	31,331
20	Newcastle United	H	1-1	Mitten	70,787
21	Portsmouth	A	2-2	McGlen Mitten	29,966
22	Derby County	A	3-1	Burke 2 Pearson	31,498
23	Liverpool	H	0-0		47,788
24	Liverpool	A	2-0	Burke Pearson	53,325
25	Arsenal	H	2-0	Burke Mitten	58,688
26	Manchester City	H	0-0		66,485
27	Aston Villa	A	1-2	Rowley	68,354
28	Charlton Athletic	A	3-2	Pearson 2 Downie	55,291
29	Stoke City	H	3-0	Downie Mitten Rowley	55,949
30	Birmingham City	A	0-1		46,819
31	Huddersfield Town	A	1-2	Rowley	17,256
32	Chelsea	H	1-1	Mitten	27,304
33	Bolton Wanderers	A	1-0	Carey	44,999
34	Burnley	A	2-0	Rowley 2	37,722
35	Bolton Wanderers	H	3-0	Rowley 2 Mitten	47,653
36	Sunderland	H	1-2	Mitten	30,640
37	Preston North End	H	2-2	Downie 2	43,214
38	Everton	A	0-2		39,106
39	Newcastle United	A	1-0	Burke	38,266
40	Middlesbrough	H	1-0	Rowley	20,158
41	Sheffield United	H	3-2	Downie Mitten Pearson	20,880
42	Portsmouth	H	3-2	Rowley 2 Mitten	49,808

• Final League Position: 2nd in Division One

FA Cup

3	Bournemouth	H	6-0	Burke 2 Rowley 2 Pearson Mitten	55,012
4	Bradford Park Avenue	H	1-1	Mitten	82,771
4R	Bradford Park Avenue	A	1-1	Mitten	30,000
4RR	Bradford Park Avenue	H	5-0	Burke 2 Rowley 2 Pearson	70,434
5	Yeovil Town	H	8-0	Rowley 5 Burke 2 Mitten	81,565
6	Hull City	A	1-0	Pearson	55,000
SF	Wolverhampton Wanderers*	N	1-1	Mitten	62,250
SF R	Wolverhampton Wanderers**	N	0-1		73,000

*Played at Hillsborough, Sheffield

** Played at Goodison Park, Liverpool

1949/50

	Opposition	H/A	Score	Scorers	Attn.
1	Derby County	A	1-0	Rowley	35,687
2	Bolton Wanderers	H	3-0	Mitten Rowley Gilles og	41,748
3	West Bromwich Albion	H	1-1	Pearson	44,655
4	Bolton Wanderers	A	2-1	Mitten Pearson	36,277
5	Manchester City	H	2-1	Pearson 2	47,760
6	Liverpool	A	1-1	Mitten	51,587
7	Chelsea	A	1-1	Rowley	61,357
8	Stoke City	H	2-2	Rowley 2	43,522
9	Burnley	A	0-1		41,072
10	Sunderland	H	1-3	Pearson	49,260
11	Charlton Athletic	H	3-2	Mitten 2 Rowley	43,809
12	Aston Villa	A	4-0	Mitten 2 Bogan Rowley	47,483
13	Wolverhampton Wanderers	H	3-0	Pearson 2 Bogan	51,427
14	Portsmouth	A	0-0		41,098
15	Huddersfield Town	H	6-0	Pearson 2 Rowley 2 Delaney Mitten	40,295
16	Everton	A	0-0		46,672
17	Middlesbrough	H	2-0	Pearson Rowley	42,626
18	Blackpool	A	3-3	Pearson 2 Bogan	27,742
19	Newcastle United	H	1-1	Mitten	30,343

20	Fulham	A	0-1		35,362
21	Derby County	H	0-1		33,753
22	West Bromwich Albion	A	2-1	Bogan Rowley	46,973
23	Arsenal	H	2-0	Pearson 2	53,928
24	Arsenal	A	0-0		65,133
25	Manchester City	A	2-1	Delaney Pearson	63,704
26	Chelsea	H	1-0	Mitten	46,954
27	Stoke City	A	1-3	Mitten	38,877
28	Burnley	H	3-2	Rowley 2 Mitten	46,702
29	Sunderland	A	2-2	Chilton Rowley	63,251
30	Charlton Athletic	A	2-1	Carey Rowley	44,920
31	Aston Villa	H	7-0	Mitten 4 Downie 2 Rowley	22,149
32	Middlesbrough	A	3-2	Downie 2 Rowley	46,702
33	Liverpool	H	0-0		43,456
34	Blackpool	H	1-2	Delaney	53,688
35	Huddersfield Town	A	1-3	Downie	34,348
36	Everton	H	1-1	Delaney	35,381
37	Birmingham City	H	0-2		47,170
38	Wolverhampton Wanderers	A	1-1	Rowley	54,296
39	Birmingham City	A	0-0		35,863
40	Portsmouth	H	0-2		44,908
41	Newcastle United	A	1-2	Downie	52,203
42	Fulham	H	3-0	Rowley 2 Cockburn	11,968

● Final League Position: 4th in Division One

FA Cup

3	Weymouth	H	4-0	Rowley 2 Pearson Delaney	38,284
4	Watford	A	1-0	Rowley	32,800
5	Portsmouth	H	3-3	Mitten 2 Pearson	53,688
5R	Portsmouth	A	3-1	Delaney Downie Mitten	49,962
6	Chelsea	A	0-2		70,362

1950/51

	Opposition	H/A	Score	Scorers	Attn.
1	Fulham	H	1-0	Pearson	44,042
2	Liverpool	A	1-2	Rowley	30,211
3	Bolton Wanderers	A	0-1		40,431

4	Liverpool	H	1-0	Downie	34,835
5	Blackpool	H	1-0	Bogan	53,260
6	Aston Villa	A	3-1	Rowley 2 Pearson	42,724
7	Tottenham Hotspur	A	0-1		60,621
8	Aston Villa	H	0-0		33,021
9	Charlton Athletic	H	3-0	Delaney Pearson Rowley	36,619
10	Middlesbrough	A	2-1	Pearson 2	48,051
11	Wolverhampton Wanderers	A	0-0		45,898
12	Sheffield Wednesday	H	3-1	Downie McShane Rowley	40,651
13	Arsenal	A	0-3		66,150
14	Portsmouth	H	0-0		41,842
15	Everton	A	4-1	Rowley 2 Aston Pearson	51,142
16	Burnley	H	1-1	McShane	39,454
17	Chelsea	A	0-1		51,882
18	Stoke City	H	0-0		30,031
19	West Bromwich Albion	A	1-0	Birch	28,146
20	Newcastle United	H	1-2	Birch	34,502
21	Huddersfield Town	A	3-2	Aston 2 Birkett	26,713
22	Fulham	A	2-2	Pearson 2	19,649
23	Bolton Wanderers	H	2-3	Aston Pearson	35,382
24	Sunderland	A	1-2	Aston	41,215
25	Sunderland	H	3-5	Bogan 2 Aston	35,176
26	Tottenham Hotspur	H	2-1	Birch Rowley	43,283
27	Charlton Athletic	A	2-1	Aston Birkett	31,978
28	Middlesbrough	H	1-0	Pearson	44,633
29	Wolverhampton Wanderers	H	2-1	Birch Rowley	42,022
30	Sheffield Wednesday	A	4-0	McShane Downie Pearson Rowley	25,693
31	Arsenal	H	3-1	Aston 2 Downie	46,202
32	Portsmouth	A	0-0		33,148
33	Everton	H	3-0	Aston Downie Pearson	29,317
34	Derby County	H	2-0	Aston Downie	42,009
35	Burnley	A	2-1	Aston McShane	36,656
36	Derby County	A	4-2	Aston Downie Pearson Rowley	25,860
37	Chelsea	H	4-1	Pearson 3 McShane	25,779
38	Stoke City	A	0-2		25,690
39	West Bromwich Albion	H	3-0	Downie Pearson Rowley	24,764

40	Newcastle United	A	2-0	Rowley Pearson	45,209
41	Huddersfield Town	H	6-0	Aston 2 McShane 2 Downie Rowley	25,560
42	Blackpool	A	1-1	Downie	22,864

• Final League Position: 2nd In Division One

FA Cup

3	Oldham Athletic	H	4-1	Pearson Aston Birch Whyte og	37,161
4	Leeds United	H	4-0	Pearson 3 Rowley	55,434
5	Arsenal	H	1-0	Pearson	55,058
6	Birmingham City	A	0-1		50,000

1951/52

	Opposition	H/A	Score	Scorers	Attn.
1	West Bromwich Albion	A	3-3	Rowley 3	27,486
2	Middlesbrough	H	4-2	Rowley 3 Pearson	37,339
3	Newcastle United	H	2-1	Downie Rowley	51,850
4	Middlesbrough	A	4-1	Pearson 2 Rowley 2	44,212
5	Bolton Wanderers	A	0-1		52,239
6	Charlton Athletic	H	3-2	Rowley 2 Downie	26,773
7	Stoke City	H	4-0	Rowley 3 Pearson	43,660
8	Charlton Athletic	A	2-2	Downie 2	28,806
9	Manchester City	A	2-1	Berry McShane	52,571
10	Tottenham Hotspur	A	0-2		70,882
11	Preston North End	H	1-2	Aston	53,454
12	Derby County	H	2-1	Berry Pearson	39,767
13	Aston Villa	A	5-2	Pearson 2 Rowley 2 Bond	47,795
14	Sunderland	H	0-1		40,915
15	Wolverhampton Wanderers	A	2-0	Pearson Rowley	46,167
16	Huddersfield Town	H	1-1	Pearson	25,616
17	Chelsea	A	2-4	Pearson Rowley	48,960
18	Portsmouth	H	1-3	Downie	35,914
19	Liverpool	A	0-0		42,378
20	Blackpool	H	3-1	Downie 2 Rowley	34,154
21	Arsenal	A	3-1	Pearson Rowley Daniels og	55,451
22	West Bromwich Albion	H	5-1	Downie 2 Pearson 2 Berry	27,584
23	Newcastle United	A	2-2	Bond Cockburn	45,414

24	Fulham	H	3-2	Berry Bond Rowley	33,802
25	Fulham	A	3-3	Bond Pearson Rowley	32,671
26	Bolton Wanderers	H	1-0	Pearson	53,205
27	Stoke City	A	0-0		36,389
28	Manchester City	H	1-1	Carey	54,245
29	Tottenham Hotspur	H	2-0	Pearson Ramsey og	40,845
30	Preston North End	A	2-1	Aston Berry	38,792
31	Derby County	A	3-0	Aston Pearson Rowley	27,693
32	Aston Villa	H	1-1	Berry	39,910
33	Sunderland	A	2-1	Cockburn Rowley	48,078
34	Wolverhampton Wanderers	H	2-0	Aston Clempson	45,109
35	Huddersfield Town	A	2-3	Clempson Pearson	30,316
36	Portsmouth	A	0-1		25,522
37	Burnley	A	1-1	Byrne	38,907
38	Liverpool	H	4-0	Byrne 2 Downie Rowley	42,970
39	Burnley	H	6-1	Byrne 2 Carey Downie Pearson Rowley	44,508
40	Blackpool	A	2-2	Byrne Rowley	29,118
41	Chelsea	H	3-0	Carey Pearson McKnight og	37,436
42	Arsenal	H	6-1	Rowley 3 Pearson 2 Byrne	53,651

• Final League Position: 1st in Division One

FA Cup

3	Hull City	H	0-2		43,517

1952/53

	Opposition	H/A	Score	Scorers	Attn.
1	Chelsea	H	2-0	Berry Downie	43,629
2	Arsenal	A	1-2	Rowley	58,831
3	Manchester City	A	1-2	Downie	56,140
4	Arsenal	H	0-0		39,193
5	Portsmouth	A	0-2		37,278
6	Derby County	A	3-2	Pearson 3	20,226
7	Bolton Wanderers	H	1-0	Berry	40,531
8	Aston Villa	A	3-3	Rowley 2 Downie	43,490
9	Sunderland	H	0-1		28,967
10	Wolverhampton Wanderers	A	2-6	Rowley 2	40,132

11	Stoke City	H	0-2		28,968
12	Preston North End	A	5-0	Aston 2 Pearson 2 Rowley	33,502
13	Burnley	H	1-3	Aston	36,913
14	Tottenham Hotspur	A	2-1	Berry 2	44,300
15	Sheffield Wednesday	H	1-1	Pearson	48,571
16	Cardiff City	A	2-1	Aston Pearson	40,096
17	Newcastle United	H	2-2	Aston Pearson	33,528
18	West Bromwich Albion	A	1-3	Lewis	23,499
19	Middlesbrough	H	3-2	Pearson 2 Aston	27,617
20	Liverpool	A	2-1	Aston Pearson	34,450
21	Chelsea	A	3-2	Doherty 2 Aston	23,261
22	Blackpool	A	0-0		27,778
23	Blackpool	H	2-1	Carey Lewis	48,077
24	Derby County	H	1-0	Lewis	34,813
25	Manchester City	H	1-1	Pearson	47,883
26	Portsmouth	H	1-0	Lewis	32,341
27	Bolton Wanderers	A	1-2	Lewis	43,638
28	Aston Villa	H	3-1	Rowley 2 Lewis	34,339
29	Sunderland	A	2-2	Lewis Pegg	24,263
30	Wolverhampton Wanderers	H	0-3		38,269
31	Stoke City	A	1-3	Berry	30,219
32	Preston North End	H	5-2	Pegg 2 Taylor 2 Rowley	52,590
33	Burnley	A	1-2	Byrne	45,682
34	Tottenham Hotspur	H	3-2	Pearson 2 Pegg	18,384
35	Sheffield Wednesday	A	0-0		36,509
36	Charlton Athletic	A	2-2	Berry Taylor	41,814
37	Cardiff City	H	1-4	Byrne	37,163
38	Charlton Athletic	H	3-2	Taylor 2 Rowley	30,105
39	Newcastle United	A	2-1	Taylor 2	38,970
40	West Bromwich Albion	H	2-2	Pearson Viollet	31,380
41	Liverpool	H	3-1	Berry Pearson Rowley	20,869
42	Middlesbrough	A	0-5		34,344

• Final League Position: 8th in Division One

FA Cup

3	Millwall	A	1-0	Pearson	35,652
4	Walthamstow Avenue	H	1-1	Lewis	34,748

| 4R | Walthamstow Avenue | A* | 5-2 | Rowley 2 Byrne Lewis Pearson | 49,119 |
| 5 | Everton | A | 1-2 | Rowley | 77,920 |

* Played at Highbury, London

1953/54

	Opposition	H/A	Score	Scorers	Attn.
1	Chelsea	H	1-1	Pearson	28,936
2	Liverpool	A	4-4	Byrne Lewis Rowley Taylor	48,422
3	West Bromwich Albion	H	1-3	Taylor	31,806
4	Newcastle United	H	1-1	Chilton	27,837
5	West Bromwich Albion	A	0-2		28,892
6	Manchester City	A	0-2		53,097
7	Middlesbrough	H	2-2	Rowley 2	18,161
8	Bolton Wanderers	A	0-0		43,544
9	Middlesbrough	A	4-1	Taylor 2 Byrne Rowley	23,607
10	Preston North End	H	1-0	Byrne	41,171
11	Tottenham Hotspur	A	1-1	Rowley	52,837
12	Burnley	H	1-2	Pearson	37,696
13	Sunderland	H	1-0	Rowley	34,617
14	Wolverhampton Wanderers	A	1-3	Taylor	40,084
15	Aston Villa	H	1-0	Berry	30,266
16	Huddersfield Town	A	0-0		34,175
17	Arsenal	H	2-2	Blanchflower Rowley	28,141
18	Cardiff City	A	6-1	Viollet 2 Berry Blanchflower Rowley Taylor	26,844
19	Blackpool	H	4-1	Taylor 3 Viollet	49,853
20	Portsmouth	A	1-1	Taylor	29,233
21	Sheffield United	H	2-2	Blanchflower 2	31,693
22	Chelsea	A	1-3	Berry	37,153
23	Liverpool	H	5-1	Blanchflower 2 Taylor 2 Viollet	26,074
24	Sheffield Wednesday	H	5-2	Taylor 3 Blanchflower Viollet	27,123
25	Sheffield Wednesday	A	1-0	Viollet	44,196
26	Newcastle United	A	2-1	Blanchflower Foulkes	55,780
27	Manchester City	H	1-1	Berry	46,379
28	Bolton Wanderers	H	1-5	Taylor	46,663
29	Preston North End	A	3-1	Blanchflower Rowley Taylor	30,064
30	Tottenham Hotspur	H	2-0	Rowley Taylor	35,485

31	Burnley	A	0-2		29,576
32	Sunderland	A	2-0	Blanchflower Taylor	58,440
33	Wolverhampton Wanderers	H	1-0	Berry	38,939
34	Aston Villa	A	2-2	Taylor 2	26,023
35	Huddersfield Town	H	3-1	Blanchflower Rowley Viollet	40,181
36	Arsenal	A	1-3	Taylor	42,753
37	Cardiff City	H	2-3	Rowley Viollet	22,832
38	Blackpool	A	0-2		25,996
39	Charlton Athletic	H	2-0	Aston Viollet	31,876
40	Portsmouth	H	2-0	Blanchflower Viollet	29,663
41	Charlton Athletic	A	0-1		19,111
42	Sheffield United	A	3-1	Aston Blanchflower Viollet	29,189

• Final League Position: 4th in Division One

FA Cup

3	Burnley	A	3-5	Blanchflower Taylor Viollet	54,000

1954/55

	Opposition	H/A	Score	Scorers	Attn.
1	Portsmouth	H	1-3	Rowley	38,203
2	Sheffield Wednesday	A	4-2	Blanchflower 2 Viollet 2	38,118
3	Blackpool	A	4-2	Webster 2 Blanchflower Viollet	31,855
4	Sheffield Wednesday	H	2-0	Viollet 2	31,371
5	Charlton Athletic	H	3-1	Rowley 2 Taylor	38,105
6	Tottenham Hotspur	A	2-0	Berry Webster	35,162
7	Bolton Wanderers	A	1-1	Webster	44,661
8	Tottenham Hotspur	H	2-1	Rowley Viollet	29,212
9	Huddersfield Town	H	1-1	Viollet	45,648
10	Manchester City	A	2-3	Blanchflower Taylor	54,105
11	Wolverhampton Wanderers	A	2-4	Rowley Viollet	39,617
12	Cardiff City	H	5-2	Taylor 4 Viollet	39,378
13	Chelsea	A	6-5	Viollet 3 Taylor 2 Blanchflower	55,966
14	Newcastle United	H	2-2	Taylor Scoular og	29,217
15	Everton	A	2-4	Taylor Rowley	63,021
16	Preston North End	H	2-1	Viollet 2	30,063
17	Sheffield United	A	0-3		26,257
18	Arsenal	H	2-1	Blanchflower Taylor	33,373

19	West Bromwich Albion	A	0-2		33,931
20	Leicester City	H	3-1	Webster Rowley Viollet	19,369
21	Burnley	A	4-2	Webster 3 Viollet	24,977
22	Portsmouth	A	0-0		26,019
23	Aston Villa	H	0-1		49,136
24	Aston Villa	A	1-2	Taylor	48,718
25	Blackpool	H	4-1	Blanchflower 2 Edwards Viollet	51,918
26	Bolton Wanderers	H	1-1	Taylor	39,873
27	Huddersfield Town	A	3-1	Berry Edwards Pegg	31,408
28	Manchester City	H	0-5		47,914
29	Wolverhampton Wanderers	H	2-4	Edwards Taylor	15,679
30	Cardiff City	A	0-3		16,329
31	Burnley	H	1-0	Edwards	31,729
32	Everton	H	1-2	Scanlon	32,295
33	Preston North End	A	2-0	Byrne Scanlon	13,327
34	Sheffield United	H	5-0	Taylor 2 Berry Viollet Whelan	21,158
35	Sunderland	A	3-4	Edwards 2 Scanlon	43,882
36	Leicester City	A	0-1		34,362
37	Sunderland	H	2-2	Byrne Taylor	36,013
38	West Bromwich Albion	H	3-0	Taylor 2 Viollet	24,765
39	Newcastle United	A	0-2		35,540
40	Arsenal	A	3-2	Blanchflower 2 Goring og	42,754
41	Charlton Athletic	A	1-1	Viollet	13,149
42	Chelsea	H	2-1	Scanlon Taylor	34,933

• Final League Position: 5th in Division One

FA Cup

3	Reading	A	1-1	Webster	26,000
3R	Reading	H	4-1	Webster 2 Viollet Rowley	24,578
4	Manchester City	A	0-2		75,000

1955/56

	Opposition	H/A	Score	Scorers	Attn.
1	Birmingham City	A	2-2	Viollet 2	37,994
2	Tottenham Hotspur	H	2-2	Berry Webster	25,406
3	West Bromwich Albion	H	3-1	Lewis Scanlon Viollet	31,996
4	Tottenham Hotspur	A	2-1	Edwards 2	27,453

5	Manchester City	A	0-1		59,162
6	Everton	H	2-1	Blanchflower Edwards	27,843
7	Sheffield United	A	0-1		28,241
8	Everton	A	2-4	Blanchflower Webster	34,897
9	Preston North End	H	3-2	Pegg Taylor Viollet	33,078
10	Burnley	A	0-0		26,873
11	Luton Town	H	3-1	Taylor 2 Webster	34,409
12	Wolverhampton Wanderers	H	4-2	Taylor 2 Doherty Pegg	48,638
13	Aston Villa	A	4-4	Pegg 2 Blanchflower Webster	29,478
14	Huddersfield Town	H	3-0	Berry Pegg Taylor	34,150
15	Cardiff City	A	1-0	Taylor	27,795
16	Arsenal	H	1-1	Taylor	41,586
17	Bolton Wanderers	A	1-3	Taylor	38,109
18	Chelsea	H	3-0	Taylor 2 Byrne	22,192
19	Blackpool	A	0-0		26,240
20	Sunderland	H	2-1	Doherty Viollet	39,901
21	Portsmouth	A	2-3	Pegg Taylor	24,594
22	Birmingham City	H	2-1	Jones Viollet	27,704
23	West Bromwich Albion	A	4-1	Viollet 3 Taylor	25,168
24	Charlton Athletic	H	5-1	Viollet 2 Byrne Doherty Taylor	44,611
25	Charlton Athletic	A	0-3		42,040
26	Manchester City	H	2-1	Taylor Viollet	60,956
27	Sheffield United	H	3-1	Berry Pegg Taylor	30,162
28	Preston North End	A	1-3	Whelan	28,047
29	Burnley	H	2-0	Taylor Viollet	27,342
30	Luton Town	A	2-0	Viollet Whelan	16,354
31	Wolverhampton Wanderers	A	2-0	Taylor 2	40,014
32	Aston Villa	H	1-0	Whelan	36,277
33	Chelsea	A	4-2	Viollet 2 Pegg Taylor	32,050
34	Cardiff City	H	1-1	Byrne	44,693
35	Arsenal	A	1-1	Viollet	50,758
36	Bolton Wanderers	H	1-0	Taylor	46,114
37	Newcastle United	H	5-2	Viollet 2 Doherty Pegg Taylor	58,994
38	Huddersfield Town	A	2-0	Taylor 2	37,780
39	Newcastle United	A	0-0		37,395
40	Blackpool	H	2-1	Berry Taylor	62,277
41	Sunderland	A	2-2	McGuinness Whelan	19,865

| 42 | Portsmouth | H | 1-0 | Viollet | 38,417 |

● Final League Position: 1st in Division One

FA Cup

| 3 | Bristol Rovers | A | 0-4 | | 35,872 |

1956/57

	Opposition	H/A	Score	Scorers	Attn.
1	Birmingham City	H	2-2	Viollet 2	32,752
2	Preston North End	A	3-1	Taylor 2 Whelan	32,569
3	West Bromwich Albion	A	3-2	Taylor Viollet Whelan	26,387
4	Preston North End	H	3-2	Viollet 3	32,515
5	Portsmouth	H	3-0	Berry Pegg Viollet	40,369
6	Chelsea	A	2-1	Taylor Whelan	29,082
7	Newcastle United	A	1-1	Whelan	50,130
8	Sheffield Wednesday	H	4-1	Berry Taylor Viollet Whelan	48,078
9	Manchester City	H	2-0	Whelan Viollet	53,525
10	Arsenal	A	2-1	Berry Whelan	62,479
11	Charlton Athletic	H	4-2	Charlton 2 Berry Whelan	41,439
12	Sunderland	A	3-1	Whelan, Viollet og	49,487
13	Everton	H	2-5	Charlton Whelan	43,451
14	Blackpool	A	2-2	Taylor 2	32,632
15	Wolverhampton Wanderers	H	3-0	Pegg Taylor Whelan	59,835
16	Bolton Wanderers	A	0-2		39,922
17	Leeds United	H	3-2	Whelan 2 Charlton	51,131
18	Tottenham Hotspur	A	2-2	Berry Colman	57,724
19	Luton Town	H	3-1	Edwards Pegg Taylor	34,736
20	Aston Villa	A	3-1	Taylor 2 Viollet	42,530
21	Birmingham City	A	1-3	Whelan	36,146
22	Cardiff City	H	3-1	Taylor Whelan Viollet	28,607
23	Portsmouth	A	3-1	Edwards Pegg Viollet	32,147
24	Chelsea	H	3-0	Taylor 2 Whelan	42,116
25	Newcastle United	H	6-1	Pegg 2 Whelan 2 Viollet 2	44,911
26	Sheffield Wednesday	A	1-2	Taylor	51,068
27	Manchester City	A	4-2	Edwards Taylor Whelan Viollet	63,872
28	Arsenal	H	6-2	Berry 2 Whelan 2 Edwards Taylor	60,384

29	Charlton Athletic	A	5-1	Charlton 3 Taylor 2	16,308
30	Blackpool	H	0-2		42,602
31	Everton	A	2-1	Webster 2	34,029
32	Aston Villa	H	1-1	Charlton	55,484
33	Wolverhampton Wanderers	A	1-1	Charlton	53,228
34	Bolton Wanderers	H	0-2		60,862
35	Leeds United	A	2-1	Berry Charlton	47,216
36	Tottenham Hotspur	H	0-0		60,349
37	Luton Town	A	2-0	Taylor 2	21,227
38	Burnley	A	3-1	Whelan	341,321
39	Sunderland	H	4-0	Whelan 2 Edwards Taylor	58,725
40	Burnley	H	2-0	Dawson Webster	41,321
41	Cardiff City	A	3-2	Scanlon 2 Dawson	17,708
42	West Bromwich Albion	H	1-1	Dawson	20,357

● Final League Position: 1st in Division One

FA Cup

3	Hartlepool United	A	4-3	Whelan 2 Berry Taylor	17,264
4	Wrexham	A	5-0	Whelan 2 Taylor 2 Byrne	34,445
5	Everton	H	1-0	Edwards	61,803
6	Bournemouth	A	2-1	Berry 2	28,799
SF	Birmingham City*	N	2-0	Berry Charlton	65,107
F	Aston Villa**	N	1-2	Taylor	100,000

*Played at Hillsborough
** Played at Wembley

1957/58

	Opposition	H/A	Score	Scorers	Attn.
1	Leicester City	A	3-0	Whelan 3	40,214
2	Everton	H	3-0	T Taylor, Viollet og	59,103
3	Manchester City	H	4-1	Berry Edwards T Taylor Viollet	63.347
4	Everton	A	3-3	Berry Viollet Whelan	72,077
5	Leeds United	H	5-0	Berry 2 T Taylor 2 Viollet	50,842
6	Blackpool	A	4-1	Viollet 2 Whelan 2	34,181
7	Bolton Wanderers	A	0-4		48,003
8	Blackpool	H	1-2	Edwards	40,763
9	Arsenal	H	4-2	Whelan 2 Pegg T Taylor	47,142

10	Wolverhampton Wanderers	A	1-3	Doherty	48,825
11	Aston Villa	H	4-1	T Taylor 2 Pegg og	43,102
12	Nottingham Forest	A	2-1	Viollet Whelan	47,654
13	Portsmouth	H	0-3		38,253
14	West Bromwich Albion	A	3-4	T Taylor 2 Whelan	52,160
15	Burnley	H	1-0	T Taylor	49,449
16	Preston North End	A	1-1	Whelan	39,063
17	Sheffield Wednesday	H	2-1	Webster 2	40,366
18	Newcastle United	A	2-1	Edwards T Taylor	53,890
19	Tottenham Hotspur	H	3-4	Pegg 2 Whelan	43,077
20	Birmingham City	A	3-3	Viollet 2 T Taylor	35,791
21	Chelsea	H	0-1		36,853
22	Leicester City	H	4-0	Viollet 2 Charlton Scanlon	41,631
23	Luton Town	H	3-0	Charlton Edwards T Taylor	39,444
24	Luton Town	A	2-2	Scanlon T Taylor	26,458
25	Manchester City	A	2-2	Charlton Viollet	70,483
26	Leeds United	A	1-1	Viollet	39,401
27	Bolton Wanderers	H	7-2	Charlton 3 Viollet 2 Edwards Scanlon	41,141
28	Arsenal	A	5-4	T Taylor 2 Charlton Edwards Viollet	63,578
29	Nottingham Forest	H	1-1	Dawson	66,124
30	West Bromwich Albion	H	0-4		63,278
31	Burnley	A	0-3		37,247
32	Sheffield Wednesday	A	0-1		35,608
33	Aston Villa	A	2-3	Dawson Webster	16,631
34	Sunderland	H	2-2	Charlton Dawson	47,421
35	Preston North End	H	0-0		47,816
36	Sunderland	A	2-1	Webster 2	51,302
37	Tottenham Hotspur	A	0-1		59,836
38	Portsmouth	A	3-3	Dawson E Taylor Webster	39,975
39	Birmingham City	H	0-2		38,991
40	Wolverhampton Wanderers	H	0-4		33,267
41	Newcastle United	H	1-1	Dawson	28,393
42	Chelsea	A	1-2	E Taylor	45,011

• Final League Position: 9th in Division One

FA Cup

3	Workington	A	3-1	Viollet 3	21,000
4	Ipswich Town	H	2-0	Charlton 2	53,550
5	Sheffield Wednesday	H	3-0	Brennan 2 Dawson	59,848
6	West Bromwich Albion	A	2-2	E Taylor Dawson	58,250
6R	West Bromwich Albion	H	1-0	Webster	60,000
SF	Fulham*	N	2-2	Charlton 2	69,745
SF(R)	Fulham**	N	5-3	Dawson 3 Charlton Brennan	38,000
F	Bolton Wanderers***	N	0-2		100,000

*Played at Villa Park
**Played at Highbury
***Played at Wembley

1958/59

	Opposition	H/A	Score	Scorers	Attn.
1	Chelsea	H	5-2	Charlton 3 Dawson 2	52,382
2	Nottingham Forest	A	3-0	Charlton 2 Scanlon	44,971
3	Blackpool	A	1-2	Viollet	36,719
4	Nottingham Forest	H	1-1	Charlton	51,880
5	Blackburn Rovers	H	6-1	Charlton 2 Viollet 2 Scanlon Webster	65,187
6	West ham United	A	2-3	McGuinness Webster	35,672
7	Newcastle United	A	1-1	Charlton	60,670
8	West Ham United	H	4-1	Scanlon 3 Webster	53,276
9	Tottenham Hotspur	H	2-2	Webster 2	62,277
10	Manchester City	A	1-1	Charlton	62,912
11	Wolverhampton Wanderers	A	0-4		36,840
12	Preston North End	H	0-2		46,163
13	Arsenal	H	1-1	Viollet	56,148
14	Everton	A	2-3	Cope 2	64,079
15	West Bromwich Albion	H	1-2	Goodwin	51,721
16	Leeds United	A	2-1	Goodwin Scanlon	48,574
17	Burnley	H	1-3	Quixall	48,509
18	Bolton Wanderers	A	3-6	Dawson 2 Charlton	33,358
19	Luton Town	H	2-1	Charlton Viollet	42,428
20	Birmingham City	A	4-0	Charlton 2 Bradley Scanlon	28,658
21	Leicester City	H	4-1	Bradley Charlton Scanlon Viollet	38,482

22	Preston North End	A	4-3	Bradley Charlton Scanlon Viollet	26,290
23	Chelsea	A	3-2	Charlton Goodwin og	48,550
24	Aston Villa	H	2-1	Quixall Viollet	63,098
25	Aston Villa	A	2-0	Pearson Viollet	56,450
26	Blackpool	H	3-1	Charlton 2 Viollet	61,961
27	Newcastle United	H	4-4	Charlton Scanlon Quixall Viollet	49,008
28	Tottenham Hotspur	A	3-1	Charlton 2 Scanlon	48,401
29	Manchester City	H	4-1	Bradley 2 Goodwin Scanlon	59,846
30	Wolverhampton Wanderers	H	2-1	Charlton Viollet	62,794
31	Arsenal	A	2-3	Bradley Viollet	67,162
32	Blackburn Rovers	A	3-1	Bradley 2 Scanlon	40,401
33	Everton	H	2-1	Goodwin Scanlon	51,254
34	West Bromwich Albion	A	3-1	Bradley Scanlon Viollet	35,463
35	Leeds United	H	4-0	Viollet 3 Charlton	45,473
36	Portsmouth	H	6-1	Charlton 2 Viollet 2 Bradley og	52,004
37	Burnley	A	2-4	Goodwin Viollet	44,577
38	Portsmouth	A	3-1	Charlton 2 Bradley	29,359
39	Bolton Wanderers	H	3-0	Charlton Scanlon Viollet	61,528
40	Luton Town	A	0-0		27,025
41	Birmingham City	H	1-0	Quixall	43,006
42	Leicester City	A	1-2	Bradley	38,466

• Final League Position: 2nd in Division One

FA Cup

3	Norwich City	A	0-3		38,000

1959/60

	Opposition	H/A	Score	Scorers	Attn.
1	West Bromwich Albion	A	2-3	Viollet 2	40,076
2	Chelsea	H	0-1		57,674
3	Newcastle United	H	3-2	Viollet 2 Charlton	53,257
4	Chelsea	A	6-3	Bradley 2 Viollet 2 Charlton Quixall	66,579
5	Birmingham City	A	1-1	Quixall	38,220
6	Leeds United	H	6-0	Bradley 2 Charlton 2 Scanlon Viollet	48,407
7	Tottenham Hotspur	H	1-5	Viollet	55,402

8	Leeds United	A	2-2	Charlton og	34,048
9	Manchester City	A	0-3		58,300
10	Preston North End	A	0-4		35,016
11	Leicester City	H	4-1	Viollet 2 Charlton Quixall	41,637
12	Arsenal	H	4-2	Charlton Quixall Viollet og	51,626
13	Wolverhampton Wanderers	A	2-3	Viollet og	45,451
14	Sheffield Wednesday	H	3-1	Viollet 2 Bradley	39,259
15	Blackburn Rovers	A	1-1	Quixall	39,621
16	Fulham	H	3-3	Charlton Scanlon Viollet	44,063
17	Bolton Wanderers	A	1-1	Dawson	37,892
18	Luton Town	H	4-1	Viollet 2 Goodwin Quixall	40,572
19	Everton	A	1-2	Viollet	46,095
20	Blackpool	H	3-1	Viollet 2 Pearson	45,558
21	Nottingham Forest	A	5-1	Viollet 3 Dawson Scanlon	31,666
22	West Bromwich Albion	H	2-3	Dawson Quixall	33,677
23	Burnley	H	1-2	Quixall	62,376
24	Burnley	A	4-1	Scanlon 2 Viollet 2	47,253
25	Newcastle United	A	3-7	Quixall 2 Dawson	57,200
26	Birmingham City	H	2-1	Quixall Viollet	47,361
27	Tottenham Hotspur	A	1-2	Bradley	62,602
28	Manchester City	H	0-0		59,450
29	Preston North End	H	1-1	Viollet	44,014
30	Leicester City	A	1-3	Scanlon	33,191
31	Blackpool	A	6-0	Charlton 3 Viollet 2 Scanlon	23,996
32	Wolverhampton Wanderers	H	0-2		60,560
33	Nottingham Forest	H	3-1	Charlton 2 Dawson	35,269
34	Fulham	A	5-0	Viollet 2 Dawson Giles Pearson	38,250
35	Sheffield Wednesday	A	2-4	Charlton Viollet	26,821
36	Bolton Wanderers	H	2-0	Charlton 2	45,298
37	Luton Town	A	3-2	Dawson 2 Bradley	21,242
38	West Ham United	A	1-2	Dawson	34,969
39	Blackburn Rovers	H	1-0	Dawson	45,945
40	West Ham United	H	5-3	Charlton 2 Dawson 2 Quixall	34,676
41	Arsenal	A	2-5	Giles Pearson	41,057
42	Everton	H	5-0	Dawson 3 Bradley Quixall	43,823

• Final League Position: 7th in Division One

FA Cup

3	Derby County	A	4-2	Goodwin Charlton Scanlon og	33,297
4	Liverpool	A	3-1	Charlton 2 Bradley	56,736
5	Sheffield Wednesday	H	0-1		66,350

1960/61

	Opposition	H/A	Score	Scorers	Attn.
1	Blackburn Rovers	H	1-3	Charlton	47,778
2	Everton	A	0-4		51,602
3	Everton	H	4-0	Dawson 2 Charlton Nicholson	51,818
4	Tottenham Hotspur	A	1-4	Viollet	55,445
5	West Ham United	A	1-2	Quixall	30,506
6	Leicester City	H	1-1	Giles	35,493
7	West Ham United	H	6-1	Charlton 2 Viollet 2 Quixall Scanlon	33,695
8	Aston Villa	A	1-3	Viollet	43,593
9	Wolverhampton Wanderers	H	1-3	Charlton	44,458
10	Bolton Wanderers	A	1-1	Giles	39,197
11	Burnley	A	3-5	Viollet 3	32,011
12	Newcastle United	H	3-2	Dawson Setters Stiles	37,516
13	Nottingham Forest	H	2-1	Viollet 2	23,628
14	Arsenal	A	1-2	Quixall	45,715
15	Sheffield Wednesday	H	0-0		36,855
16	Birmingham City	A	1-3	Charlton	31,549
17	West Bromwich Albion	H	3-0	Dawson Quixall Viollet	32,756
18	Cardiff City	A	0-3		21,122
19	Preston North End	H	1-0	Dawson	24,904
20	Fulham	A	4-4	Quixall 2 Charlton Dawson	23,625
21	Blackburn Rovers	A	2-1	Pearson 2	17,285
22	Chelsea	A	2-1	Dawson Charlton	37,601
23	Chelsea	H	6-0	Dawson 3 Nicholson 2 Charlton	50,164
24	Manchester City	H	5-1	Dawson 3 Charlton 2	61,213
25	Tottenham Hotspur	H	2-0	Pearson Stiles	65,295
26	Leicester City	A	0-6		31,308
27	Aston Villa	H	1-1	Charlton	33,525
28	Wolverhampton Wanderers	A	1-2	Nicholson	38,526
29	Bolton Wanderers	H	3-1	Dawson 2 Quixall	37,558

30	Nottingham Forest	A	2-3	Charlton Quixall	26,850
31	Manchester City	A	3-1	Charlton Dawson Pearson	50,479
32	Newcastle United	A	1-1	Charlton	28,870
33	Arsenal	H	1-1	Moir	29,732
34	Sheffield Wednesday	A	1-5	Charlton	35,901
35	Blackpool	A	0-2		30,835
36	Fulham	H	3-1	Charlton Quixall Viollet	24,654
37	Blackpool	H	2-0	Nicholson og	39,169
38	West Bromwich Albion	A	1-1	Pearson	27,750
39	Burnley	H	6-0	Quixall 3 Viollet 3	25,019
40	Birmingham City	H	4-1	Pearson 2 Quixall Viollet	28,376
41	Preston North End	A	4-2	Charlton 2 Setters 2	21,252
42	Cardiff City	H	3-3	Charlton 2 Setters	30,320

• Final League Position: 7th in Division One

FA Cup

3	Middlesbrough	H	3-0	Dawson 2 Cantwell	49,184
4	Sheffield Wednesday	A	1-1	Cantwell	58,000
4R	Sheffield Wednesday	H	2-7	Dawson Pearson	65,243

League Cup

1	Exeter City	A	1-1	Dawson	14,494
1R	Exeter City	H	4-1	Quixall 2 (1 pen) Giles Pearson	15,662
2	Bradford City	A	1-2	Viollet	4,670

1961/62

	Opposition	H/A	Score	Scorers	Attn.
1	West Ham United	A	1-1	Stiles	32,628
2	Chelsea	H	3-2	Herd Pearson Viollet	45,847
3	Blackburn Rovers	H	6-1	Herd 2 Quixall 2 Charlton Setters	45,302
4	Chelsea	A	0-2		42,248
5	Blackpool	A	3-2	Viollet 2 Charlton	28,156
6	Tottenham Hotspur	H	1-0	Quixall	57,135
7	Cardiff City	A	2-1	Dawson Quixall	29,251
8	Aston Villa	A	1-1	Stiles	38,837
9	Manchester City	H	3-2	Stiles Viollet Ewing og	56,345

10	Wolverhampton Wanderers	H	0-2		39,457
11	West Bromwich Albion	A	1-1	Dawson	25,645
12	Birmingham City	H	0-2		30,674
13	Arsenal	A	1-5	Viollet	54,245
14	Bolton Wanderers	H	0-3		31,442
15	Sheffield Wednesday	A	1-3	Viollet	35,998
16	Leicester City	H	2-2	Giles Viollet	21,567
17	Ipswich Town	A	1-4	McMillan	25,755
18	Burnley	H	1-4	Herd	41,029
19	Everton	A	1-5	Herd	48,099
20	Fulham	H	3-0	Herd 2 Lawton	22,193
21	West Ham United	H	1-2	Herd	29,472
22	Nottingham Forest	H	6-3	Lawton 3 Brennan Charlton Herd	30,822
23	Blackpool	H	0-1		26,999
24	Aston Villa	H	2-0	Charlton Quixall	20,807
25	Tottenham Hotspur	A	2-2	Charlton Stiles	55,225
26	Cardiff City	H	3-0	Giles Lawton Stiles	29,200
27	Manchester City	A	2-0	Chisnall Herd	49,959
28	West Bromwich Albion	H	4-1	Charlton 2 Setters Quixall	32,456
29	Wolverhampton Wanderers	A	2-2	Herd Lawton	27,565
30	Birmingham City	A	1-1	Herd	25,817
31	Bolton Wanderers	A	0-1		34,366
32	Nottingham Forest	A	0-1		27,833
33	Sheffield Wednesday	H	1-1	Charlton	31,322
34	Leicester City	A	3-4	McMillan 2 Quixall	15,318
35	Ipswich Town	H	5-0	Quixall 3 Setters Stiles	24,976
36	Blackburn Rovers	A	0-3		14,623
37	Burnley	A	3-1	Brennan Cantwell Herd	36,240
38	Arsenal	H	2-3	Cantwell McMillan	24,258
39	Everton	H	1-1	Herd	31,926
40	Sheffield United	H	0-1		30,073
41	Sheffield United	A	3-2	McMillan 2 Stiles	25,324
42	Fulham	A	0-2		40,113

● Final League Position: 15th in Division One

FA Cup

3	Bolton Wanderers	H	2-1	Nicholson Herd	42,202

4	Arsenal	H	1-0	Setters	54,082
5	Sheffield Wednesday	H	0-0		59,533
5R	Sheffield Wednesday	A	2-0	Charlton Giles	62,969
6	Preston North End	A	0-0		37,521
6R	Preston North End	H	2-1	Herd Charlton	63,468
SF	Tottenham Hotspur	N*	1-3	Herd	65,000

*Played at Hillsborough, Sheffield

1962/63

	Opposition	H/A	Score	Scorers	Attn.
1	West Bromwich Albion	H	2-2	Herd Law	51,685
2	Everton	A	1-3	Moir	69,501
3	Arsenal	A	3-1	Herd 2 Chisnall	62,308
4	Everton	H	0-1		63,437
5	Birmingham City	H	2-0	Giles Herd	39,847
6	Bolton Wanderers	A	0-3		44,859
7	Leyton Orient	A	0-1		24,901
8	Bolton Wanderers	H	3-0	Herd 2 Cantwell	37,721
9	Manchester City	H	2-3	Law 2	49,193
10	Burnley	H	2-5	Law Stiles	45,954
11	Sheffield Wednesday	A	0-1		40,520
12	Blackpool	A	2-2	Herd 2	33,242
13	Blackburn Rovers	H	0-3		42,252
14	Tottenham Hotspur	A	2-6	Herd Quixall	51,314
15	West Ham United	H	3-1	Quixall 2 Law	29,204
16	Ipswich Town	A	5-3	Law 4 Herd	18,483
17	Liverpool	H	3-3	Giles Herd Quixall	43,810
18	Wolverhampton Wanderers	A	3-2	Law 2 Herd	27,305
19	Aston Villa	H	2-2	Quixall 2	36,852
20	Sheffield United	A	1-1	Charlton	25,173
21	Nottingham Forest	H	5-1	Herd 2 Charlton Giles Law	27,946
22	West Bromwich Albion	A	0-3		18,113
23	Fulham	A	1-0	Charlton	23,928
24	Blackpool	H	1-1	Herd	43,121
25	Blackburn Rovers	A	2-2	Charlton Law	27,924
26	Tottenham Hotspur	H	0-2		53,416
27	West Ham United	A	1-3	Herd	28,950

28	Ipswich Town	H	0-1		32,792
29	Fulham	H	0-2		28,124
30	Aston Villa	A	2-1	Charlton Stiles	26,867
31	Liverpool	A	0-1		51,529
32	Leicester City	H	2-2	Charlton Herd	50,005
33	Leicester City	A	3-4	Law 3	37,002
34	Sheffield United	H	1-1	Law	31,179
35	Wolverhampton Wanderers	H	2-1	Herd Law	36,147
36	Sheffield Wednesday	H	1-3	Setters	31,878
37	Burnley	A	1-0	Law	30,266
38	Arsenal	H	2-3	Law 2	35,999
39	Birmingham City	A	1-2	Law	21,814
40	Manchester City	A	1-1	Quixall	52,424
41	Leyton Orient	H	3-1	Charlton Law og	32,759
42	Nottingham Forest	A	2-3	Giles Herd	16,130

• Final League Position: 19th in Division One

FA Cup

3	Huddersfield Town	H	5-0	Law 3 Giles Quixall	47,703
4	Aston Villa	H	1-0	Quixall	52,265
5	Chelsea	H	2-1	Quixall Law	48,298
6	Coventry City	A	3-1	Charlton 2 Quixall	44,000
SF	Southampton	N*	1-0	Law	65,000
F	Leicester City	N**	3-1	Herd 2 Law	100,000

*Played at Villa Park, Birmingham
**Played at Wembley Stadium

1963/64

	Opposition	H/A	Score	Scorers	Attn.
1	Sheffield Wednesday	A	3-3	Charlton 2 Moir	
					32,177
2	Ipswich Town	H	2-0	Law 2	39,921
3	Everton	H	5-1	Chisnall 2 Law 2 Sadler	62,965
4	Ipswich Town	A	7-2	Law 3 Chisnall Moir Sadler Setters	28,113
5	Birmingham City	A	1-1	Chisnall	36,874
6	Blackpool	H	3-0	Charlton 2 Law	47,400

7	West Bromwich Albion	H	1-0	Sadler	50,453
8	Blackpool	A	0-1		29,806
9	Arsenal	A	1-2	Herd	56,776
10	Leicester City	H	3-1	Herd 2 Setters	41,374
11	Chelsea	A	1-1	Setters	45,351
12	Bolton Wanderers	A	1-0	Herd	35,872
13	Nottingham Forest	A	2-1	Chisnall Quixall	41,426
14	West Ham United	H	0-1		45,120
15	Blackburn Rovers	H	2-2	Quixall 2	41,169
16	Wolverhampton Wanderers	A	0-2		34,159
17	Tottenham Hotspur	H	4-1	Law 3 Herd	57,413
18	Aston Villa	A	0-4		36,276
19	Liverpool	H	0-1		54,654
20	Sheffield United	A	2-1	Law 2	30,615
21	Stoke City	H	5-2	Law 4 Herd	52,232
22	Sheffield Wednesday	H	3-1	Herd 3	35,139
23	Everton	A	0-4		48,027
24	Burnley	A	1-6	Herd	35,764
25	Burnley	H	5-1	Herd 2 Moore 2 Best	47,834
26	Birmingham City	H	1-2	Sadler	44,695
27	West Bromwich Albion	A	4-1	Law 2 Best Charlton	25,624
28	Arsenal	H	3-1	Herd Law Setters	48,340
29	Leicester City	A	2-3	Herd Law	35,538
30	Bolton Wanderers	H	5-0	Best 2 Herd 2 Charlton	33,926
31	Blackburn Rovers	A	3-1	Law 2 Chisnall	36,726
32	West Ham United	A	2-0	Herd Sadler	27,027
33	Tottenham Hotspur	A	3-2	Charlton Law Moore	56,392
34	Chelsea	H	1-1	Law	42,931
35	Fulham	A	2-2	Herd Law	41,769
36	Wolverhampton Wanderers	H	2-2	Charlton Herd	44,470
37	Fulham	H	3-0	Crerand Foulkes Herd	42,279
38	Liverpool	A	0-3		52,559
39	Aston Villa	H	1-0	Law	25,848
40	Sheffield United	H	2-1	Law Moir	27,587
41	Stoke City	A	1-3	Charlton	45,670
42	Nottingham Forest	H	3-1	Law 2 Moore	31,671

● Final League Position: 2nd in Division One

FA Cup

3	Southampton	A	3-2	Crerand Moore Herd	29,164
4	Bristol Rovers	H	4-1	Law 3 Herd	55,772
5	Barnsley	A	4-0	Law 2 Best Herd	38,076
6	Sunderland	H	3-3	Charlton Best Hurley og	63,700
6R	Sunderland	A	2-2 aet	Charlton Law	68,000
6RR	Sunderland	N*	5-1	Law 3 Chisnall Herd	54,952
SF	West Ham United	N**	1-3	Law	65,000

*Played at Leeds Road, Huddersfield
**Played at Hillsborough, Sheffield

1964/65

	Opposition	H/A	Score	Scorers	Attn.
1	West Bromwich Albion	H	2-2	Charlton Law	52,007
2	West Ham United	A	1-3	Law	37,070
3	Leicester City	A	2-2	Law Sadler	32,373
4	West Ham United	H	3-1	Best Connelly Law	45,123
5	Fulham	A	1-2	Connelly	36,291
6	Everton	A	3-3	Connelly Herd Law	63,024
7	Nottingham Forest	H	3-0	Herd 2 Connelly	45,012
8	Everton	H	2-1	Best Law	49,968
9	Stoke City	A	2-1	Connelly Herd	40,031
10	Tottenham Hotspur	H	4-1	Crerand 2 Law 2	53,058
11	Chelsea	A	2-0	Best Law	60,769
12	Burnley	A	0-0		30,761
13	Sunderland	H	1-0	Herd	48,577
14	Wolverhampton Wanderers	A	4-2	Law 2 Herd og	26,763
15	Aston Villa	H	7-0	Law 4 Herd 2 Connelly	35,807
16	Liverpool	A	2-0	Crerand Herd	52,402
17	Sheffield Wednesday	H	1-0	Herd	50,178
18	Blackpool	A	2-1	Connelly Herd	31,129
19	Blackburn Rovers	H	3-0	Best Connelly Herd	49,633
20	Arsenal	A	3-2	Law 2 Connelly	59,627
21	Leeds United	H	0-1		53,374
22	West Bromwich Albion	A	1-1	Law	28,126
23	Birmingham City	H	1-1	Charlton	25,721
24	Sheffield United	A	1-0	Best	37,295

25	Sheffield United	H	1-1	Herd	42,219
26	Nottingham Forest	A	2-2	Law 2	43,009
27	Stoke City	H	1-1	Law	50,392
28	Tottenham Hotspur	A	0-1		58,639
29	Burnley	H	3-2	Best Charlton Herd	38,865
30	Sunderland	A	0-1		51,336
31	Wolverhampton Wanderers	H	3-0	Charlton 2 Connelly	37,018
32	Chelsea	H	4-0	Herd 2 Best Law	56,261
33	Fulham	H	4-1	Connelly 2 Herd 2	45,402
34	Sheffield Wednesday	A	0-1		33,549
35	Blackpool	H	2-0	Law 2	42,318
36	Blackburn Rovers	A	5-0	Charlton 3 Connelly Herd	29,363
37	Leicester City	H	1-0	Herd	34,114
38	Leeds United	A	1-0	Connelly	52,368
39	Birmingham City	A	4-2	Best 2 Cantwell Charlton	28,907
40	Liverpool	H	3-0	Law 2 Connelly	55,772
41	Arsenal	H	3-1	Law 2 Best	51,625
42	Aston Villa	A	1-2	Charlton	36,081

• Final League Position: 1st in Division One

FA Cup

3	Chester	H	2-1	Kinsey Best	40,000
4	Stoke City	A	0-0		53,009
4R	Stoke City	H	1-0	Herd	50,814
5	Burnley	H	2-1	Crerand Law	54,000
6	Wolverhampton Wanderers	A	5-3	Law 2 Crerand Herd Best	53,581
SF	Leeds United	N*	0-0		65,000
SF(R)	Leeds United	N**	0-1		46,300

*Played at Hillsborough, Sheffield
**Played at the City Ground, Nottingham

1965/66

	Opposition	H/A	Score	Scorers	Attn.
1	Sheffield Wednesday	H	1-0	Herd	37,524
2	Nottingham Forest	A	2-4	Aston Best	33,744
3	Northampton Town	A	1-1	Connelly	21,140
4	Nottingham Forest	H	0-0		38,777

5	Stoke City	H	1-1	Herd	37,603
6	Newcastle United	A	2-1	Herd Law	57,380
7	Burnley	A	0-3		30,235
8	Newcastle United	H	1-1	Stiles	30,401
9	Chelsea	H	4-1	Law 3 Charlton	37,917
10	Arsenal	A	2-4	Aston Charlton	56,757
11	Liverpool	H	2-0	Best Law	58,161
12	Tottenham Hotspur	A	1-5	Charlton	58,051
13	Fulham	H	4-1	Herd 3 Charlton	32,716
14	Blackpool	A	2-1	Herd 2	4,703
15	Blackburn Rovers	H	2-2	Charlton Law	38,823
16	Leicester City	A	5-0	Herd 2 Best Charlton Connelly	34,551
17	Sheffield United	H	3-1	Best 2 Law	37,922
18	West Ham United	H	0-0		32,924
19	Sunderland	A	3-2	Best 2 Herd	37,417
20	Everton	H	3-0	Best Charlton Herd	32,624
21	Tottenham Hotspur	H	5-1	Law 2 Charlton Herd Beal og	39,270
22	West Bromwich Albion	H	1-1	Law	54,102
23	Liverpool	A	1-2	Law	53,790
24	Sunderland	H	1-1	Best	39,162
25	Leeds United	A	1-1	Herd	49,672
26	Fulham	A	1-0	Charlton	33,018
27	Sheffield Wednesday	A	0-0		39,281
28	Northampton Town	H	6-2	Charlton 3 Law 2 Connelly	34,986
29	Stoke City	A	2-2	Connelly Herd	36,667
30	Burnley	H	4-2	Herd 3 Charlton	49,982
31	Chelsea	A	0-2		60,269
32	Arsenal	H	2-1	Law Stiles	47,246
33	Aston Villa	A	1-1	Cantwell	28,211
34	Leicester City	H	1-2	Connelly	42,593
35	Sheffield United	A	1-3	Sadler	22,330
36	Everton	A	0-0		50,843
37	Blackpool	H	2-1	Charlton Law	26,953
38	West Ham United	A	2-3	Aston Cantwell	36,416
39	West Bromwich Albion	A	3-3	Aston A Dunne Herd	22,609
40	Blackburn Rovers	A	4-1	Herd 2 Charlton Sadler	14,513
41	Aston Villa	H	6-1	Herd 2 Sadler 2 Charlton Ryan	23,039

| 42 | Leeds United | H | 1-1 | Herd | 35,008 |

• Final League Position: 4th in Division One

FA Cup

3	Derby County	A	5-2	Best 2 Law 2 Herd	33,827
4	Rotherham United	H	0-0		54,263
4R	Rotherham United	A	1-0 aet	Connelly	23,500
5	Wolverhampton Wanderers	A	4-2	Law 2 Herd Best	53,500
6	Preston North End	A	1-1	Herd	37,876
6R	Preston North End	H	3-1	Law 2 Connelly	60,433
SF	Everton	N*	0-1		60,000

*Played at Burnden Park, Bolton

1966/67

	Opposition	H/A	Score	Scorers	Attn.
1	West Bromwich Albion	H	5-3	Law 2 Best Herd Stiles	41,343
2	Everton	A	2-1	Law 2	60,657
3	Leeds United	A	1-3	Best	45,092
4	Everton	H	3-0	Connelly Foulkes Law	61,114
5	Newcastle United	H	3-2	Connelly Herd Law	44,448
6	Stoke City	A	0-3		44,337
7	Tottenham Hotspur	A	1-2	Law	56,295
8	Manchester City	H	1-0	Law	62,085
9	Burnley	H	4-1	Crerand Herd Law Sadler	52,697
10	Nottingham Forest	A	1-4	Charlton	41,854
11	Blackpool	A	2-1	Law 2	33,555
12	Chelsea	H	1-1	Law	56,789
13	Arsenal	H	1-0	Sadler	45,387
14	Chelsea	A	3-1	Aston 2 Best	55,958
15	Sheffield Wednesday	H	2-0	Charlton Herd	46,942
16	Southampton	A	2-1	Charlton 2	29,458
17	Sunderland	H	5-0	Herd 4 Law	44,687
18	Leicester City	A	2-1	Best Law	39,014
19	Aston Villa	A	1-2	Herd	39,937
20	Liverpool	H	2-2	Best 2	61,768
21	West Bromwich Albion	A	4-3	Herd 3 Law	32,080
22	Sheffield United	A	1-2	Herd	42,752

23	Sheffield United	H	2-0	Crerand Herd	59,392
24	Leeds United	H	0-0		53,486
25	Tottenham Hotspur	H	1-0	Herd	57,366
26	Manchester City	A	1-1	Foulkes	62,983
27	Burnley	A	1-1	Sadler	40,165
28	Nottingham Forest	H	1-0	Law	62,727
29	Blackpool	H	4-0	Charlton 2 Law Hughes og	47,158
30	Arsenal	A	1-1	Aston	63,363
31	Newcastle United	A	0-0		37,430
32	Leicester City	H	5-2	Aston Charlton Herd Law Sadler	50,281
33	Liverpool	A	0-0		53,813
34	Fulham	A	2-2	Best Stiles	47,290
35	Fulham	H	2-1	Foulkes Stiles	51,673
36	West Ham United	H	3-0	Best Charlton Law	61,308
37	Sheffield Wednesday	A	2-2	Charlton 2	51,101
38	Southampton	H	3-0	Charlton Law Sadler	54,291
39	Sunderland	A	0-0		43,570
40	Aston Villa	H	3-1	Aston Best Law	55,782
41	West Ham United	A	6-1	Law 2 Best Charlton Crerand Foulkes	38,424
42	Stoke City	H	0-0		61,071

• Final League Position: 1st in Division One

FA Cup

3	Stoke City	H	2-0	Law Herd	63,500
4	Norwich City	H	1-2	Law	63,409

League Cup

2	Blackpool	A	1-5	Herd	15,570

1967/68

	Opposition	H/A	Score	Scorers	Attn.
1	Everton	A	1-3	Charlton	61,452
2	Leeds United	H	1-0	Charlton	53,016
3	Leicester City	H	1-1	Foulkes	51,256
4	West Ham United	A	3-1	Kidd Ryan Sadler	36,562
5	Sunderland	A	1-1	Kidd	51,527

6	Burnley	H	2-2	Burns Crerand	55,809
7	Sheffield Wednesday	A	1-1	Best	47,274
8	Tottenham Hotspur	H	3-1	Best2 Law	58,779
9	Manchester City	A	2-1	Charlton 2	62,942
10	Arsenal	H	1-0	Aston	60,197
11	Sheffield United	H	3-0	Aston Kidd Law	29,170
12	Coventry City	H	4-0	Aston 2 Best Charlton	54,253
13	Nottingham Forest	A	1-3	Best	49,946
14	Stoke City	H	1-0	Charlton	51,041
15	Leeds United	A	0-1		43,999
16	Liverpool	A	2-1	Best 2	54,515
17	Southampton	H	3-2	Aston Charlton Kidd	48,732
18	Chelsea	A	1-1	Kidd	54,712
19	West Bromwich Albion	H	2-1	Best 2	52,568
20	Newcastle United	A	2-2	Dunne Kidd	48,639
21	Everton	H	3-1	Aston Law Sadler	60,736
22	Leicester City	A	2-2	Charlton Law	40,104
23	Wolverhampton Wanderers	H	4-0	Best 2 Charlton Kidd	63,450
24	Wolverhampton Wanderers	A	3-2	Aston Charlton Kidd	53,940
25	West Ham United	H	3-1	Aston Best Charlton	54,498
26	Sheffield Wednesday	H	4-2	Best 2 Charlton Kidd	55,254
27	Tottenham Hotspur	A	2-1	Best Charlton	57,790
28	Burnley	A	1-2	Best	31,965
29	Arsenal	A	2-0	Best Storey og	46,417
30	Chelsea	H	1-3	Kidd	62,978
31	Coventry City	A	0-2		47,110
32	Nottingham Forest	H	3-0	Herd Brennan Burns	61,978
33	Manchester City	H	1-3	Best	63,004
34	Stoke City	A	4-2	Aston Best Gowling Ryan	30,141
35	Liverpool	H	1-2	Best	63,059
36	Fulham	A	4-0	Best 2 Kidd Law	40,152
37	Southampton	A	2-2	Best Charlton	30,079
38	Fulham	H	3-0	Aston Best Charlton	60,465
39	Sheffield United	H	1-0	Law	55,033
40	West Bromwich Albion	A	3-6	Kidd 2 Law	43,412
41	Newcastle United	H	6-0	Best 3 Kidd 2 Sadler	59,976
42	Sunderland	H	1-2	Best	62,963

● Final League Position: 2nd in Division One

FA Cup

| 3 | Tottenham Hotspur | H | 2-2 | Best Charlton | 63,500 |
| 3R | Tottenham Hotspur | A | 0-1 aet | | 57,200 |

1968/69

	Opposition	H/A	Score	Scorers	Attn.
1	Everton	H	2-1	Best Charlton	61,311
2	West Bromwich Albion	A	1-3	Charlton	38,299
3	Manchester City	A	0-0		63,052
4	Coventry City	H	1-0	Ryan	51,201
5	Chelsea	H	0-4		55,114
6	Tottenham Hotspur	H	3-1	Fitzpatrick 2 Beal og	62,649
7	Sheffield Wednesday	A	4-5	Law 2 Best Charlton	50,490
8	West Ham United	H	1-1	Law	63,274
9	Burnley	A	0-1		32,935
10	Newcastle United	H	3-1	Best 2 Law	47,262
11	Arsenal	H	0-0		61,843
12	Tottenham Hotspur	A	2-2	Crerand Law	56,205
13	Liverpool	A	0-2		53,392
14	Southampton	H	1-2	Best	46,526
15	Queen's ParkRangers	A	3-2	Best 2 Law	31,138
16	Leeds United	H	0-0		53,839
17	Sunderland	A	1-1	Hurley og	33,151
18	Ipswich Town	H	0-0		45,796
19	Stoke City	A	0-0		30,562
20	Wolverhampton Wanderers	H	2-0	Best Law	50,165
21	Leicester City	A	1-2	Law	36,303
22	Liverpool	H	1-0	Law	55,354
23	Southampton	A	0-2		26,194
24	Arsenal	A	0-3		62,300
25	Leeds United	A	1-2	Charlton	48,145
26	Sunderland	H	4-1	Law 3 Best	45,670
27	Ipswich Town	A	0-1		30,837
28	Wolverhampton Wanderers	A	2-2	Best Charlton	44,023
29	Manchester City	H	0-1		63,264

30	Everton	A	0-0		57,514
31	Chelsea	A	2-3	James Law	60,436
32	Queen's Park Rangers	H	8-1	Morgan 3 Best 2 Aston Kidd Stiles	36,638
33	Sheffield Wednesday	H	1-0	Best	45,527
34	Stoke City	H	1-1	Aston	39,931
35	West Ham United	A	0-0		41,546
36	Nottingham Forest	A	1-0	Best	41,892
37	West Bromwich Albion	H	2-1	Best 2	38,846
38	Nottingham Forest	H	3-1	Morgan 2 Best	51,952
39	Coventry City	A	1-2	Fitzpatrick	45,402
40	Newcastle United	A	0-2		46,379
41	Burnley	H	2-0	Best Waldron og	52,626
42	Leicester City	H	3-2	Best Law Morgan	45,860

● Final League Position: 11th in Division One

FA Cup

3	Exeter City	A	3-1	Fitzpatrick Kidd Newman og	18,500
4	Watford	H	1-1	Law	63,498
4R	Watford	A	2-0	Law 2	34,000
5	Birmingham City	A	2-2	Law Best	52,500
5R	Birmingham City	H	6-2	Law 3 Kidd Morgan Crerand	61,932
6	Everton	H	0-1		63,464

1969/70

	Opposition	H/A	Score	Scorers	Attn.
1	Crystal Palace	A	2-2	Charlton Morgan	48,610
2	Everton	H	0-2		57,752
3	Southampton	H	1-4	Morgan	46,328
4	Everton	A	0-3		53,185
5	Wolverhampton Wanderers	A	0-0		50,783
6	Newcastle United	H	0-0		52,774
7	Sunderland	H	3-1	Best Givens Kidd	50,570
8	Leeds United	A	2-2	Best 2	44,271
9	Liverpool	H	1-0	Morgan	56,509
10	Sheffield Wednesday	A	3-1	Best 2 Kidd	39,298
11	Arsenal	A	2-2	Best Sadler	59,498

12	West Ham United	H	5-2	Best 2 Burns Charlton Kidd	58,579
13	Derby County	A	0-2		40,724
14	Southampton	A	3-0	Best Burns Kidd	31,044
15	Ipswich Town	H	2-1	Best Kidd	52,281
16	Nottingham Forest	H	1-1	Best	53,702
17	West Bromwich Albion	A	1-2	Kidd	45,120
18	Stoke City	H	1-1	Charlton	53,406
19	Coventry City	A	2-1	Aston Law	43,446
20	Manchester City	A	0-4		63,013
21	Tottenham Hotspur	H	3-1	Charlton 2 Burns	50,003
22	Burnley	A	1-1	Best	23,770
23	Chelsea	H	0-2		49,344
24	Liverpool	A	4-1	Charlton Morgan Ure Yeats og	47,682
25	Wolverhampton Wanderers	H	0-0		50,806
26	Sunderland	A	1-1	Kidd	36,504
27	Arsenal	H	2-1	Morgan Sartori	41,055
28	West Ham United	A	0-0		41,643
29	Leeds United	H	2-2	Kidd Sadler	59,879
30	Derby County	H	1-0	Charlton	59,315
31	Ipswich Town	A	1-0	Kidd	29,755
32	Crystal Palace	H	1-1	Kidd	54,711
33	Stoke City	A	2-2	Morgan Sartori	38,917
34	Burnley	H	3-3	Best Crerand Law	38,377
35	Chelsea	A	1-2	Morgan	61,479
36	Manchester City	H	1-2	Kidd	59,777
37	Coventry City	H	1-1	Kidd	38,647
38	Nottingham Forest	A	2-1	Charlton Gowling	39,228
39	Newcastle United	A	1-5	Charlton	43,094
40	West Bromwich Albion	H	7-0	Charlton 2 Fitzpatrick 2 Gowling 2 Best	26,582
41	Tottenham Hotspur	A	1-2	Fitzpatrick	41,808
42	Sheffield Wednesday	H	2-2	Best Charlton	36,649

• Final League Position: 8th in Division One

FA Cup

| 3 | Ipswich Town | A | 1-0 | McNeil og | 29,552 |
| 4 | Manchester City | H | 3-0 | Kidd 2 Morgan | 63,417 |

5	Northampton Town	A	8-2	Best 6 Kidd 2	21,771
6	Middlesbrough	A	1-1	Sartori	40,000
6R	Middlesbrough	H	2-1	Charlton Morgan	63,418
SF	Leeds United	N*	0-0		55,000
SFR	Leeds United	N**	0-0		62,500
SF2R	Leeds United	N***	0-1		56,000
P-O	Watford	N****	2-0	Kidd 2	15,105

*Played at Hillsborough, Sheffield
**Played at Villa Park, Birmingham
***Played at Burnden Park, Bolton
**** Played at Highbury Stadium, London

League Cup

2	Middlesbrough	H	1-0	Sadler	38,939
3	Wrexham	H	2-0	Kidd Best	48,347
4	Burnley	A	0-0		27,959
4R	Burnley	H	1-0	Best	50,275
5	Derby County	A	0-0		38,895
5R	Derby County	H	1-0	Kidd	57,393
SF1	Manchester City	A	1-2	Charlton	55,799
SF2	Manchester City	H	2-2	Edwards Law	63,418

1970/71

	Opposition	H/A	Score	Scorers	Attn.
1	Leeds United	H	0-1		59,365
2	Chelsea	H	0-0		50,979
3	Arsenal	A	0-4		54,117
4	Burnley	A	2-0	Law 2	29,385
5	West Ham United	H	1-1	Fitzpatrick	50,643
6	Everton	H	2-0	Best Charlton	51,346
7	Liverpool	A	1-1	Kidd	52,542
8	Coventry City	H	2-0	Best Charlton	48,939
9	Ipswich Town	A	0-4		27,776
10	Blackpool	H	1-1	Best	46,647
11	Wolverhampton Wanderers	A	2-3	Gowling Kidd	38,629
12	Crystal Palace	H	0-1		42,979
13	Leeds United	A	2-2	Charlton Fitzpatrick	50,190

14	West Bromwich Albion	H	2-1	Kidd Law	43,278
15	Newcastle United	A	0-1		45,140
16	Stoke City	H	2-2	Law Sadler	47,451
17	Nottingham Forest	A	2-1	Gowling Sartori	36,364
18	Southampton	A	0-1		30,202
19	Huddersfield Town	H	1-1	Best	45,306
20	Tottenham Hotspur	A	2-2	Best Law	55,693
21	Manchester City	H	1-4	Kidd	52,636
22	Arsenal	H	1-3	Sartori	33,182
23	Derby County	A	4-4	Law 2 Best Kidd	34,068
24	Chelsea	A	2-1	Gowling Morgan	53,482
25	Burnley	H	1-1	Aston	40,135
26	Huddersfield Town	A	2-1	Aston Law	41,464
27	Tottenham Hotspur	H	2-1	Best Morgan	48,965
28	Southampton	H	5-1	Gowling 4 Morgan	36,060
29	Everton	A	0-1		52,544
30	Newcastle United	H	1-0	Kidd	41,902
31	West Bromwich Albion	A	3-4	Aston Best Kidd	41,112
32	Nottingham Forest	H	2-0	Best Law	40,473
33	Stoke City	A	2-1	Best 2	40,005
34	West Ham United	A	1-2	Best	38,507
35	Derby County	H	1-2	Law	45,691
36	Wolverhampton Wanderers	H	1-0	Gowling	41,886
37	Coventry City	A	1-2	Best	33,818
38	Crystal Palace	A	5-3	Law 3 Best 2	39,145
39	Liverpool	H	0-2		44,004
40	Ipswich Town	H	3-2	Charlton Best Kidd	33,566
41	Blackpool	A	1-1	Law	29,857
42	Manchester City	A	4-3	Best 2 Charlton Law	43,626

● Final League Position: 8th in Division One

FA Cup

| 3 | Middlesbrough | H | 0-0 | | 47,824 |
| 3R | Middlesbrough | A | 1-2 | Best | 41,000 |

League Cup

| 2 | Aldershot | A | 3-1 | Law Kidd Best | 18,509 |

3	Portsmouth	H	1-0	Charlton	32,068
4	Chelsea	H	2-1	Best Charlton	47,565
5	Crystal Palace	H	4-2	Kid 2 Charlton Fitzpatrick	48,961
SF1	Aston Villa	H	1-1	Kidd	48,889
SF2	Aston Villa	A	1-2	Kidd	58,667

1971/72

	Opposition	H/A	Score	Scorers	Attn.
1	Derby County	A	2-2	Gowling Law	35,886
2	Chelsea	A	3-2	Charlton Kidd Morgan	54,763
3	Arsenal	H	3-1	Charlton Gowling Kidd	27,649
4	West Bromwich Albion	H	3-1	Best 2 Gowling	23,146
5	Wolverhampton Wanderers	A	1-1	Best	46,471
6	Everton	A	0-1		52,151
7	Ipswich Town	H	1-0	Best	45,656
8	Crystal Palace	A	3-1	Law 2 Kidd	44,020
9	West Ham United	H	4-2	Best 3 Charlton	53,339
10	Liverpool	A	2-2	Charlton Law	55,634
11	Sheffield United	H	2-0	Best Gowling	51,735
12	Huddersfield Town	A	3-0	Best Charlton Law	33,458
13	Derby County	H	1-0	Best	53,247
14	Newcastle United	A	1-0	Best	52,411
15	Leeds United	H	0-1		53,960
16	Manchester City	A	3-3	Gowling Kidd McIlroy	63,326
17	Tottenham Hotspur	H	3-1	Law 2 McIlroy	54,058
18	Leicester City	H	3-2	Law 2 Kidd	48,757
19	Southampton	A	5-2	Best 3 Kidd McIlroy	30,323
20	Nottingham Forest	H	3-2	Kidd 2 Law	45,411
21	Stoke City	A	1-1	Law	33,857
22	Ipswich Town	A	0-0		29,229
23	Coventry City	H	2-2	James Law	52,117
24	West Ham United	A	0-3		41,892
25	Wolverhampton Wanderers	H	1-3	McIlroy	46,781
26	Chelsea	H	0-1		55,927
27	West Bromwich Albion	A	1-2	Kidd	47,012
28	Newcastle United	H	0-2		44,983
29	Leeds United	A	1-5	Burns	45,399

30	Tottenham Hotspur	A	0-2		54,814
31	Everton	H	0-0		38,415
32	Huddersfield Town	H	2-0	Best Storey-Moore	53,581
33	Crystal Palace	H	4-0	Charlton Gowling Law Storey-Moore	41,550
34	Coventry City	A	3-2	Best Charlton Storey-Moore	37,901
35	Liverpool	H	0-3		53,826
36	Sheffield United	A	1-1	Sadler	45,045
37	Leicester City	A	0-2		35,970
38	Manchester City	H	1-3	Buchan	56,362
39	Southampton	H	3-2	Best Kidd Storey-Moore	38,437
40	Nottingham Forest	A	0-0		35,063
41	Arsenal	A	0-3		49,125
42	Stoke City	H	3-0	Best Charlton Storey-Moore	34,959

• Final League Position: 8th in Division One

FA Cup

3	Southampton	A	1-1	Charlton	30,190
3R	Southampton	H	4-1 aet	Best 2 Sadler Aston	50,960
4	Preston North End	A	2-0	Gowling 2	27,025
5	Middlesbrough	H	0-0		53,850
5R	Middlesbrough	A	3-0	Morgan Charlton Best	39,683
6	Stoke City	H	1-1	Best	54,226
6R	Stoke City	A	1-2 aet	Best	49,192

League Cup

2	Ipswich Town	A	3-1	Best 2 Morgan	28,143
3	Burnley	H	1-1	Charlton	44,600
3R	Burnley	A	1-0	Charlton	27,511
4	Stoke City	H	1-1	Gowling	47,062
4R	Stoke City	A	0-0 aet		40,805
4RR	Stoke City	A	1-2	Best	42,249

1972/73

	Opposition	H/A	Score	Scorers	Attn.
1	Ipswich Town	H	1-2	Law	51,459
2	Liverpool	A	0-2		54,799

3	Everton	A	0-2		52,348
4	Leicester City	H	1-1	Best	40,067
5	Arsenal	H	0-0		48,108
6	Chelsea	H	0-0		44,482
7	West Ham United	A	2-2	Best Storey-Moore	31,939
8	Coventry City	H	0-1		37,073
9	Wolverhampton Wanderers	A	0-2		34,049
10	Derby County	H	3-0	Davies Morgan Storey-Moore	48,255
11	Sheffield United	A	0-1		37,347
12	West Bromwich Albion	A	2-2	Best Storey-Moore	39,209
13	Birmingham City	H	1-0	MacDougall	52,104
14	Newcastle United	A	1-2	Charlton	38,170
15	Tottenham Hotspur	H	1-4	Charlton	52,497
16	Leicester City	A	2-2	Best Davies	32,575
17	Liverpool	H	2-0	Davies MacDougall	53,944
18	Manchester City	A	0-3		52,050
19	Southampton	H	2-1	Davies MacDougall	36,073
20	Norwich City	A	2-0	MacDougall Storey-Moore	35,910
21	Stoke City	H	0-2		41,347
22	Crystal Palace	A	0-5		39,484
23	Leeds United	H	1-1	MacDougall	46,382
24	Derby County	A	1-3	Storey-Moore	35,098
25	Arsenal	A	1-3	Kidd	51,194
26	West Ham United	H	2-2	Charlton Macari	50,878
27	Everton	H	0-0		58,970
28	Coventry City	A	1-1	Holton	42,767
29	Wolverhampton Wanderers	H	2-1	Charlton 2	52,089
30	Ipswich Town	A	1-4	Macari	31,918
31	West Bromwich Albion	H	2-1	Kidd Macari	46,735
32	Birmingham City	A	1-3	Macari	51,278
33	Newcastle United	H	2-1	Holton Martin	48,426
34	Tottenham Hotspur	A	1-1	Graham	49,751
35	Southampton	A	2-0	Charlton Holton	23,161
36	Norwich City	H	1-0	Martin	48,593
37	Crystal Palace	H	2-0	Kidd Morgan	46,891
38	Stoke City	A	2-2	Macari Morgan	37,051
39	Leeds United	A	1-0	Anderson	45,450

40	Manchester City	H	0-0		61,676
41	Sheffield United	H	1-2	Kidd	57,280
42	Chelsea	A	0-1		44,184

• Final League Position: 18th in Division One

FA Cup

2	Wolverhampton Wanderers	A	0-1		40,005

League Cup

2	Oxford United	A	2-2	Charlton Law	16,560
2R	Oxford United	H	3-1	Best 2 Storey-Moore	21,486
3	Bristol Rovers	A	1-1	Morgan	33,957
3R	Bristol Rovers	H	1-2	McIlroy	29,349

1973/74

	Opposition	H/A	Score	Scorers	Attn.
1	Arsenal	A	0-3		51,501
2	Stoke City	H	1-0	James	43,614
3	Queen's Park Rangers	H	2-1	Holton McIlroy	44,156
4	Leicester City	A	0-1		29,152
5	Ipswich Town	A	1-2	Anderson	22,023
6	Leicester City	H	1-2	Stepney	40,793
7	West Ham United	H	3-1	Kidd 2 Storey-Moore	44,757
8	Leeds United	A	0-0		47,058
9	Liverpool	H	0-0		53,882
10	Wolverhampton Wanderers	A	1-2	McIlroy	32,962
11	Derby County	H	0-1		43,724
12	Birmingham City	H	1-0	Stepney	48,937
13	Burnley	A	0-0		31,976
14	Chelsea	H	2-2	Greenhoff Young	48,036
15	Tottenham Hotspur	A	1-2	Best	42,756
16	Newcastle United	A	2-3	Graham Macari	41,768
17	Norwich City	H	0-0		36,338
18	Southampton	H	0-0		31,648
19	Coventry City	H	2-3	Best Morgan	28,589
20	Liverpool	A	0-2		40,420
21	Sheffield United	H	1-2	Macari	38,653

22	Ipswich Town	H	2-0	Macari McIlroy	36,365
23	Queen's Park Rangers	A	0-3		32,339
24	West Ham United	A	1-2	McIlroy	34,147
25	Arsenal	H	1-1	James	38,589
26	Coventry City	A	0-1		25,313
27	Leeds United	H	0-2		60,025
28	Derby County	A	2-2	Greenhoff Houston	29,987
29	Wolverhampton Wanderers	H	0-0		39,260
30	Sheffield United	A	1-0	Macari	29,203
31	Manchester City	A	0-0		51,331
32	Birmingham City	A	0-1		37,768
33	Tottenham Hotspur	H	0-1		36,278
34	Chelsea	A	3-1	Daly McIlroy Morgan	29,602
35	Burnley	H	3-3	Forsyth Holton McIlroy	33,336
36	Norwich City	A	2-0	Greenhoff Macari	28,223
37	Newcastle United	H	1-0	McCalliog	44,751
38	Everton	H	3-0	McCalliog 2 Houston	48,424
39	Southampton	A	1-1	McCalliog	30,789
40	Everton	A	0-1		46,093
41	Manchester City	H	0-1		56,996
42	Stoke City	A	0-1		27,392

• Final League Position: 21st in Division One

FA Cup

| 3 | Plymouth Argyle | H | 1-0 | Macari | 31,810 |
| 4 | Ipswich town | H | 0-1 | | 37,177 |

League Cup

| 2 | Middlesbrough | H | 0-1 | | 23,906 |

1974/75

	Opposition	H/A	Score	Scorers	Attn.
1	Orient	A	2-0	Houston Morgan	17,772
2	Millwall	H	4-0	Daly 3 Pearson	44,756
3	Portsmouth	H	2-1	Daly McIlroy	42,547
4	Cardiff City	A	1-0	Daly	22,344
5	Nottingham Forest	H	2-2	Greenhoff McIlroy	40,671

6	West Bromwich Albion	A	1-1	Pearson	23,721
7	Millwall	A	1-0	Daly	16,988
8	Bristol Rovers	H	2-0	Greenhoff Prince og	42,948
9	Bolton Wanderers	H	3-0	Houston Macari McAllister og	47,084
10	Norwich City	A	0-2		24,586
11	Fulham	A	2-1	Pearson 2	26,513
12	Notts County	H	1-0	McIlroy	46,565
13	Portsmouth	A	0-0		25,608
14	Blackpool	A	3-0	Forsyth Macari McCalliog	25,370
15	Southampton	H	1-0	Pearson	48,724
16	Oxford United	H	4-0	Pearson 3 Macari	41,909
17	Bristol City	A	0-1		28,104
18	Aston Villa	H	2-1	Daly 2	55,615
19	Hull City	A	0-2		23,287
20	Sunderland	H	3-2	McIlroy Morgan Pearson	60,585
21	Sheffield Wednesday	A	4-4	Macari 2 Houston Pearson	35,230
22	Orient	H	0-0		41,200
23	York City	A	1-0	Pearson	15,567
24	West Bromwich Albion	H	2-1	Daly McIlroy	51,104
25	Oldham Athletic	A	0-1		26,384
26	Sheffield Wednesday	H	2-0	McCalliog 2	45,662
27	Sunderland	A	0-0		45,976
28	Bristol City	H	0-1		47,118
29	Oxford United	A	0-1		15,959
30	Hull City	H	2-0	Houston Pearson	44,712
31	Aston Villa	A	0-2		39,156
32	Cardiff City	H	4-0	Houston McIlroy Macari Pearson	43,601
33	Bolton Wanderers	A	1-0	Pearson	38,152
34	Norwich City	H	1-1	Pearson	56,202
35	Nottingham Forest	A	1-0	Daly	21,893
36	Bristol Rovers	A	1-1	Macari	19,337
37	York City	H	2-1	Macari Morgan	46,802
38	Oldham Athletic	H	3-2	Coppell Macari McIlroy	56,618
39	Southampton	A	1-0	Macari	21,866
40	Fulham	H	1-0	Daly	52,971
41	Notts County	A	2-2	Greenhoff Houston	17,320
42	Blackpool	H	4-0	Pearson 2 Greenhoff Macari	58,769

● Final League Position: 1st in Division Two

FA Cup

3	Walsall	H	0-0		43,353
3R	Walsall	A	2-3 aet	McIlroy Daly	18,105

League Cup

2	Charlton Athletic	H	5-1	Macari 2 Houston McIlroy Warman og	21,616
3	Manchester City	H	1-0	Daly	55,159
4	Burnley	H	3-2	Macari 2 Morgan	46,275
5	Middlesbrough	A	0-0		36,005
5R	Middlesbrough	H	3-0	McIlroy Pearson Macari	49,501
SF1	Norwich City	H	2-2	Macari 2	58,010
SF2	Norwich City	A	0-1		31,621

1975/76

	Opposition	H/A	Score	Scorers	Attn.
1	Wolverhampton Wanderers	A	2-0	Macari 2	32,348
2	Birmingham City	A	2-0	McIlroy 2	33,177
3	Sheffield United	H	5-1	Pearson 2 Daly McIlroy Badger og	55,949
4	Coventry City	H	1-1	Pearson	52,169
5	Stoke City	A	1-0	Dodd og	33,092
6	Tottenham Hotspur	H	3-2	Daly 2 Pratt og	51,641
7	Queen's Park Rangers	A	0-1		29,237
8	Ipswich Town	H	1-0	Houston	50,513
9	Derby County	A	1-2	Daly	33,187
10	Manchester City	A	2-2	Macari McCreery	46,931
11	Leicester City	H	0-0		47,878
12	Leeds United	A	2-1	McIlroy 2	40,264
13	Arsenal	H	3-1	Coppell 2 Pearson	53,885
14	West Ham United	A	1-2	Macari	38,528
15	Norwich City	H	1-0	Pearson	50,587
16	Liverpool	A	1-3	Coppell	49,136
17	Aston Villa	H	2-0	Coppell McIlroy	51,682
18	Arsenal	A	1-3	Pearson	40,102

19	Newcastle United	H	1-0	Daly	52,624
20	Middlesbrough	A	0-0		32,454
21	Sheffield United	A	4-1	Pearson 2 Hill Macari	31,741
22	Wolverhampton Wanderers	H	1-0	Hill	44,269
23	Everton	A	1-1	Macari	41,732
24	Burnley	H	2-1	Macari McIlroy	59,726
25	Queen's Park Rangers	H	2-1	Hill McIlroy	58,312
26	Tottenham Hotspur	A	1-1	Hill	49,189
27	Birmingham City	H	3-1	Forsyth Macari McIlroy	50,724
28	Coventry City	A	1-1	Macari	33,922
29	Liverpool	H	0-0		59,709
30	Aston Villa	A	1-2	Macari	50,094
31	Derby County	H	1-1	Pearson	59,632
32	West Ham United	H	4-0	Forsyth Macari McCreery Pearson	57,220
33	Leeds United	H	3-2	Daly Houston Pearson	59,429
34	Norwich City	A	1-1	Hill	27,787
35	Newcastle United	A	4-3	Pearson 2 Bird og Howard og	45,043
36	Middlesbrough	H	3-0	Daly Hill McCreery	58,527
37	Ipswich Town	A	0-3		34,886
38	Everton	H	2-1	McCreery Kenyon og	61,879
39	Burnley	A	1-0	Macari	27,418
40	Stoke City	H	0-1		53,879
41	Leicester City	A	1-2	Coyne	31,053
42	Manchester City	H	2-0	Hill McIlroy	59,517

• Final League Position: 3rd in Division One

FA Cup

3	Oxford United	H	2-1	Daly 2	41,082
4	Peterborough United	H	3-1	Forsyth McIlroy Hill	56,352
5	Leicester City	A	2-1	Daly Macari	34,000
6	Wolverhampton Wanderers	H	1-1	Daly	59,433
6R	Wolverhampton Wanderers	A	3-2 aet	B Greenhoff McIlroy Pearson	44,373
SF	Derby County	N*	2-0	Hill 2	55,000
F	Southampton	N**	0-1		100,000

* Played at Hillsborough, Sheffield

** Played at Wembley

League Cup

2	Brentford	H	2-1	McIlroy Macari	25,286
3	Aston Villa	A	2-1	Coppell Macari	41,447
4	Manchester City	A	0-4		50,182

1976/77

	Opposition	H/A	Score	Scorers	Attn.
1	Birmingham City	H	2-2	Coppell Pearson	58,898
2	Coventry City	A	2-0	Hill Macari	26,775
3	Derby County	A	0-0		30,054
4	Tottenham Hotspur	H	2-3	Coppell Pearson	60,723
5	Newcastle United	A	2-2	B Greenhoff Pearson	39,037
6	Middlesbrough	H	2-0	Pearson McAndrew og	56,712
7	Manchester City	A	3-1	Coppell Daly McCreery	48,861
8	Leeds United	A	2-0	Coppell Daly	44,512
9	West Bromwich Albion	A	0-4		36,615
10	Norwich City	H	2-2	Daly Hill	54,356
11	Ipswich Town	H	0-1		57,416
12	Aston Villa	A	2-3	Hill Pearson	44,789
13	Sunderland	H	3-3	B Greenhoff Hill Pearson	42,685
14	Leicester City	A	1-1	Daly	26,421
15	West Ham United	H	0-2		55,366
16	Arsenal	A	1-3	McIlroy	39,572
17	Everton	H	4-0	J Greenhoff Hill Macari Pearson	56,786
18	Aston Villa	H	2-0	Pearson 2	55,446
19	Ipswich Town	A	1-2	Pearson	30,105
20	Coventry City	H	2-0	Macari 2	46,567
21	Bristol City	H	2-1	B Greenhoff Pearson	43,051
22	Birmingham City	A	3-2	J Greenhoff Houston Pearson	35,316
23	Derby County	H	3-1	Houston Macari Powell og	54,044
24	Tottenham Hotspur	A	3-1	Hill Macari McIlroy	46,946
25	Liverpool	H	0-0		57,487
26	Newcastle United	H	3-1	J Greenhoff 3	51,828
27	Manchester City	H	3-1	Coppell Hill Pearson	58,595
28	Leeds United	H	1-0	Cherry og	60,612
29	West Bromwich Albion	H	2-2	Coppell Hill	51,053
30	Norwich City	A	1-2	Powell og	24,161

31	Everton	A	2-1	Hill 2	38,216
32	Stoke City	H	3-0	Houston Macari Pearson	53,102
33	Sunderland	A	1-2	Hill	38,785
34	Leicester City	H	1-1	J Greenhoff	49,161
35	Queen's Park Rangers	A	0-4		28,848
36	Middlesbrough	A	0-3		21,744
37	Queen's Park Rangers	H	1-0	Macari	50,788
38	Liverpool	A	0-1		53,046
39	Bristol City	A	1-1	J Greenhoff	28,864
40	Stoke City	A	3-3	Hill 2 McCreery	24,204
41	Arsenal	H	3-2	J Greenhoff Hill Macari	53,232
42	West Ham United	A	2-4	Hill Pearson	29,904

• Final League Position: 6th in Division One

FA Cup

3	Walsall	H	1-0	Hill	48,870
4	Queen's Park Rangers	H	1-0	Macari	57,422
5	Southampton	A	2-2	Macari Hill	29,137
5R	Southampton	H	2-1	J Greenhoff 2	58,103
6	Aston Villa	H	2-1	Houston Macari	57,089
SF	Leeds United	N*	2-1	Coppell J Greenhoff	55,000
F	Liverpool	N**	2-1	Pearson J Greenhoff	100,000

* Played at Hillsborough, Sheffield
** Played at Wembley

League Cup

2	Tranmere Rovers	H	5-0	Daly 2 Pearson Macari Hill	37,586
3	Sunderland	H	2-2	Pearson Clarke og	46,170
3R	Sunderland	A	2-2 aet	Daly B Greenhoff	46,170
3RR	Sunderland	H	1-0	B Greenhoff	47,689
4	Newcastle United	H	7-2	Hill 3 Nicholl Houston Coppell Pearson	52,002
5	Everton	H	0-3		57,738

1977/78

	Opposition	H/A	Score	Scorers	Attn.
1	Birmingham City	A	4-1	Macari 3 Hill	28,005

2	Coventry City	H	2-1	Hill McCreery	55,726
3	Ipswich Town	H	0-0		57,904
4	Derby County	A	1-0	Macari	21,279
5	Manchester City	A	1-3	Nicholl	50,856
6	Chelsea	H	0-1		54,951
7	Leeds United	A	1-1	Hill	33,517
8	Liverpool	H	2-0	Macari McIlroy	55,089
9	Middlesbrough	A	1-2	Coppell	27,526
10	Newcastle United	H	3-2	Coppell J Greenhoff Macari	39,144
11	West Bromwich Albion	A	0-4		53,055
12	Aston Villa	A	1-2	Nicholl	30,183
13	Arsenal	H	1-2	Hill	48,729
14	Nottingham Forest	A	1-2	Pearson	25,367
15	Norwich City	H	1-0	Pearson	48,729
16	Queen's Park Rangers	A	2-2	Hill 2	25,367
17	Wolverhampton Wanderers	H	3-1	J Greenhoff McIlroy Pearson	48,874
18	West Ham United	A	1-2	McGrath	20,242
19	Nottingham Forest	H	0-4		54,374
20	Everton	A	6-2	Macari 2 Coppell J Greenhoff Hill McIlroy	48,335
21	Leicester City	H	3-1	Coppell J Greenhoff Hill	57,396
22	Coventry City	A	0-3		24,706
23	Birmingham City	H	1-2	J Greenhoff	53,501
24	Ipswich Town	A	2-1	McIlroy Pearson	23,321
25	Derby County	H	4-0	Hill 2 Buchan Pearson	57,115
26	Bristol City	H	1-1	Hill	43,457
27	Chelsea	A	2-2	Hill McIlroy	32,849
28	Liverpool	A	1-3	McIlroy	49,094
29	Leeds United	H	0-1		49,101
30	Middlesbrough	H	0-0		46,332
31	Newcastle United	A	2-2	Hill Jordan	25,825
32	Manchester City	H	2-2	Hill 2	58,398
33	West Bromwich Albion	H	1-1	McQueen	46,329
34	Leicester City	A	3-2	J Greenhoff Hill Pearson	20,299
35	Everton	H	1-2	Hill	55,277
36	Aston Villa	H	1-1	McIlroy	41,625
37	Arsenal	A	1-3	Jordan	40,829

38	Queen's Park Rangers	H	3-1	Pearson 2 Grimes	42,677
39	Norwich City	A	3-1	Coppell Jordan McIlroy	19,778
40	West Ham United	H	3-0	Grimes McIlroy Pearson	54,089
41	Bristol City	A	1-0	Pearson	26,035
42	Wolverhampton Wanderers	A	1-2	B Greenhoff	24,774

● Final League Position: 10th in Division One

FA Cup

3	Carlisle United	A	1-1	Macari	
					21,710
3R	Carlisle United	H	4-2	Pearson 2 Macari 2	54,156
4	West Bromwich Albion	H	1-1	Coppell	57,056
4R	West Bromwich Albion	A	2-3 aet	Pearson Hill	37,086

League Cup

| 2 | Arsenal | A | 2-3 | McCreery Pearson | 36,171 |

1978/79

	Opposition	H/A	Score	Scorers	Attn.
1	Birmingham City	H	1-0	Jordan	56,139
2	Leeds United	A	3-2	Macari McIlroy McQueen	36,845
3	Ipswich Town	A	0-3		21,802
4	Everton	H	1-1	Buchan	53,982
5	Queen's Park Rangers	A	1-1	J Greenhoff	23,477
6	Nottingham Forest	H	1-1	J Greenhoff	53,039
7	Arsenal	A	1-1	Coppell	45,393
8	Manchester City	H	1-0	Jordan	55,301
9	Middlesbrough	H	3-2	Macari 2 Jordan	45,402
10	Aston Villa	A	2-2	Macari McIlroy	36,204
11	Bristol City	H	1-3	J Greenhoff	47,211
12	Wolverhampton Wanderers	A	4-2	J Greenhoff 2 B Greenhoff Jordan	23,141
13	Southampton	H	1-1	J Greenhoff	46,259
14	Birmingham City	A	1-5	Jordan	23,550
15	Ipswich Town	H	2-0	Coppell J Greenhoff	42,109
16	Everton	A	0-3		42,126
17	Chelsea	A	1-0	J Greenhoff	28,162

18	Derby County	A	3-1	Ritchie 2 J Greenhoff	23,180
19	Tottenham Hotspur	H	2-0	McIlroy Ritchie	52,026
20	Bolton Wanderers	A	0-3		32,390
21	Liverpool	H	0-3		54,910
22	West Bromwich Albion	H	3-5	B Greenhoff McIlroy McQueen	45,091
23	Arsenal	H	0-2		45,460
24	Manchester City	A	3-0	Coppell 2 Ritchie	46,151
25	Aston Villa	H	1-1	J Greenhoff	44,437
26	Queen's Park Rangers	H	2-0	Coppell J Greenhoff	36,085
27	Bristol City	A	2-1	McQueen Ritchie	24,583
28	Coventry City	A	3-4	Coppell 2 Mcilroy	25,382
29	Leeds United	H	4-1	Ritchie 3 Thomas	51,191
30	Middlesbrough	A	2-2	Coppell McQueen	20,138
31	Norwich City	A	2-2	Macari McQueen	19,382
32	Bolton Wanderers	H	1-2	Buchan	49,617
33	Liverpool	A	0-2		46,608
34	Coventry City	H	0-0		43,035
35	Nottingham Forest	A	1-1	Jordan	33,074
36	Tottenham Hotspur	H	1-1	McQueen	36,665
37	Norwich City	H	1-0	Macari	33,678
38	Derby County	H	0-0		42,546
39	Southampton	A	1-1	Ritchie	21,616
40	West Bromwich Albion	A	0-1		27,960
41	Wolverhampton Wanderers	H	3-2	Coppell 2 Ritchie	39,402
42	Chelsea	H	1-1	Coppell	38,109

● Final League Position: 9th in Division One

FA Cup

3	Chelsea	H	3-0	Coppell J Greenhoff Grimes	38,743
4	Fulham	A	1-1	J Greenhoff	25,229
4R	Fulham	H	1-0	J Greenhoff	41,200
5	Colchester United	A	1-0	J Greenhoff	13,717
6	Tottenham Hotspur	A	1-1	Thomas	51,800
6R	Tottenham Hotspur	H	2-0	McIlroy Jordan	55,584
SF	Liverpool	N*	2-2	Jordan B Greenhoff	52,524
SF(R)	Liverpool	N**	1-0	J Greenhoff	53,069
F	Arsenal	N***	2-3	McQueen McIlroy	100,000

* played at Maine Road, Manchester
** played at Goodison Park, Liverpool
*** played at Wembley

League Cup

2	Stockport County	A*	3-2	McIlroy J Greenhoff Jordan	41,761
3	Watford	H	1-2	Jordan	40,534

* played at Old Trafford, Manchester

1979/80

	Opposition	H/A	Score	Scorers	Attn.
1	Southampton	A	1-1	McQueen	21,768
2	West Bromwich Albion	H	2-0	Coppell McQueen	53,377
3	Arsenal	A	0-0		44,380
4	Middlesbrough	H	2-1	Macari 2	51,015
5	Aston Villa	A	3-0	Coppell Grimes Thomas	34,859
6	Derby County	H	1-0	Grimes	54,308
7	Wolverhampton Wanderers	A	1-3	Macari	35,503
8	Stoke City	H	4-0	McQueen 2 McIlroy Wilkins	52,596
9	Brighton & Hove Albion	H	2-0	Coppell Macari	52,641
10	West Bromwich Albion	A	0-2		27,713
11	Bristol City	A	1-1	Macari	28,305
12	Ipswich Town	H	1-0	Grimes	50,826
13	Everton	A	0-0		37,708
14	Southampton	H	1-0	Macari	50,215
15	Manchester City	A	0-2		50,067
16	Crystal Palace	H	1-1	Jordan	52,800
17	Norwich City	H	5-0	Jordan 2 Coppell Macari Moran	46,540
18	Tottenham Hotspur	A	2-1	Coppell Macari	51,389
19	Leeds United	H	1-1	Thomas	58,348
20	Coventry City	A	2-1	Macari McQueen	25,541
21	Nottingham Forest	H	3-0	Jordan 2 McQueen	54,607
22	Liverpool	A	0-2		51,073
23	Arsenal	H	3-0	Jordan McIlroy McQueen	54,295
24	Middlesbrough	A	1-1	Thomas	30,587
25	Derby County	A	3-1	McIlroy Thomas Powell og	27,783
26	Wolverhampton Wanderers	H	0-1		51,568

27	Stoke City	A	1-1	Coppell	28,389
28	Bristol City	H	4-0	Jordan 2 McIlroy Merrick og	43,329
29	Bolton Wanderers	H	2-0	Coppell McQueen	47,546
30	Ipswich Town	A	0-6		30,229
31	Everton	H	0-0		45,515
32	Brighton & Hove Albion	A	0-0		29,621
33	Manchester City	H	1-0	Thomas	56,387
34	Crystal Palace	A	2-0	Jordan Thomas	33,056
35	Nottingham Forest	A	0-2		31,417
36	Liverpool	H	2-1	J Greenhoff Thomas	57,342
37	Bolton Wanderers	A	3-1	Coppell McQueen Thomas	31,902
38	Tottenham Hotspur	H	4-1	Ritchie 3 Wilkins	53,151
39	Norwich City	A	2-0	Jordan 2	23,274
40	Aston Villa	H	2-1	Jordan 2	45,201
41	Coventry City	H	2-1	McIlroy 2	52,154
42	Leeds United	A	0-2		39,625

• Final League Position: 2nd in Division One

FA Cup

3	Tottenham Hotspur	A	1-1	McIlroy	45,207
3R	Tottenham Hotspur	H	0-1 aet		53,762

League Cup

2	Tottenham Hotspur	A	1-2	Thomas	29,163
	Tottenham Hotspur	H	3-1	Coppell Thomas Miler og	48,292
3	Norwich City	A	1-4	McIlroy	18,312

1980/81

	Opposition	H/A	Score	Scorers	Attn.
1	Middlesbrough	H	3-0	Grimes Macari Thomas	54,394
2	Wolverhampton Wanderers	A	0-1		31,955
3	Birmingham City	A	0-0		28,661
4	Sunderland	H	1-1	Jovanovic	51,498
5	Tottenham Hotspur	A	0-0		40,995
6	Leicester City	H	5-0	Jovanovic 2 Coppell Grimes Macari	43,229
7	Leeds United	A	0-0		32,539

8	Manchester City	H	2-2	Albiston Coppell	55,918
9	Nottingham Forest	A	2-1	Coppell Macari	29,801
10	Aston Villa	H	3-3	McIlroy 2 Coppell	38,831
11	Arsenal	H	0-0		49,036
12	Ipswich Town	A	1-1	McIlroy	28,572
13	Stoke City	A	2-1	Jordan Macari	24,534
14	Everton	H	2-0	Coppell Jordan	54,260
15	Crystal Palace	A	0-1		31,449
16	Coventry City	H	0-0		42,794
17	Wolverhampton Wanderers	H	0-0		37,959
18	Middlesbrough	A	1-1	Jordan	20,606
19	Brighton & Hove Albion	A	4-1	Jordan 2 Duxbury McIlroy	23,293
20	Southampton	H	1-1	Jordan	46,840
21	Norwich City	A	2-2	Coppell Bond og	18,780
22	Stoke City	H	2-2	Jordan Macari	39,568
23	Arsenal	A	1-2	Macari	33,730
24	Liverpool	H	0-0		57,049
25	West Bromwich Albion	A	1-3	Jovanovic	30,326
26	Brighton & Hove Albion	H	2-1	Macari McQueen	42,208
27	Sunderland	A	0-2		31,910
28	Birmingham City	H	2-0	Jordan Macari	39,081
29	Leicester City	A	0-1		26,085
30	Tottenham Hotspur	H	0-0		40,642
31	Manchester City	A	0-1		50,114
32	Leeds United	H	0-1		45,733
33	Southampton	A	0-1		22,698
34	Aston Villa	A	3-3	Jordan 2 McIlroy	42,182
35	Nottingham Forest	H	1-1	Burns og	38,205
36	Ipswich Town	H	2-1	Nicholl Thomas	46,685
37	Everton	A	1-0	Jordan	25,856
38	Crystal Palace	H	1-0	Duxbury	37,954
39	Coventry City	A	2-0	Jordan 2	20,201
40	Liverpool	A	1-0	McQueen	31,276
41	West Bromwich Albion	H	2-1	Jordan Macari	44,442
42	Norwich City	H	1-0	Jordan	40,165

• Final League Position: 8th in Division One

FA Cup

	Brighton & Hove Albion	H	2-2	Duxbury Thomas	42,199
3R	Brighton & Hove Albion	A	2-0	Nicholl Birtles	26,915
4	Nottingham Forest	A	0-1		34,110

League Cup

	Coventry City	H	0-1	31,656
2	Coventry City	A	0-1	18,946

1981-82

	Opposition	H/A	Score	Scorers	Attn.
1	Coventry City	A	1-2	Macari	19,329
2	Nottingham Forest	H	0-0		51,496
3	Ipswich Town	H	1-2	Stapleton	45,555
4	Aston Villa	A	1-1	Stapleton	37,661
5	Swansea City	H	1-0	Birtles	47,309
6	Middlesbrough	A	2-0	Birtles Stapleton	19,895
7	Arsenal	A	0-0		39,795
8	Leeds United	H	1-0	Stapleton	47,019
9	Wolverhampton Wanderers	H	5-0	McIlroy 3 Birtles Stapleton	46,837
10	Manchester City	A	0-0		52,037
11	Birmingham City	H	1-1	Coppell	48,800
12	Middlesbrough	H	1-0	Moses	38,342
13	Liverpool	A	2-1	Albiston Moran	41,438
14	Notts County	H	2-1	Birtles Moses	45,928
15	Sunderland	A	5-1	Stapleton 2 Birtles Moran Robson	27,070
16	Tottenham Hotspur	A	1-3	Birtles	35,534
17	Brighton & Hove Albion	H	2-0	Birtles Stapleton	41,911
18	Southampton	A	2-3	Robson Stapleton	24,404
19	Everton	H	1-1	Stapleton	40,451
20	Stoke City	A	3-0	Birtles Coppell Stapleton	19,793
21	West Ham United	H	1-0	Macari	41,291
22	Swansea City	A	0-2		24,115
23	Aston Villa	H	4-1	Moran 2 Coppell Robson	43,184
24	Wolverhampton Wanderers	A	1-0	Birtles	22,481
25	Arsenal	H	0-0		43,833

26	Manchester City	H	1-1	Moran	57,830
27	Birmingham City	A	1-0	Birtles	19,637
28	Coventry City	H	0-1		34,499
29	Notts County	A	3-1	Coppell 2 Stapleton	17,048
30	Sunderland	H	0-0		40,776
31	Leeds United	A	0-0		30,953
32	Liverpool	H	0-1		48,371
33	Everton	A	3-3	Coppell 2 Grimes	29,306
34	West Bromwich Albion	H	1-0	Moran	38,717
35	Tottenham Hotspur	H	2-0	Coppell McGarvey	50,724
36	Ipswich Town	A	1-2	Gidman	25,744
37	Brighton & Hove Albion	A	1-0	Wilkins	20,750
38	Southampton	H	1-0	McGarvey	40,038
39	Nottingham Forest	A	1-0	Stapleton	18,449
40	West Ham United	A	1-1	Moran	26,337
41	West Bromwich Albion	A	3-0	Birtles Coppell Robson	19,707
42	Stoke City	H	2-0	Robson Whiteside	43,072

• Final League Position: 3rd in Division One

FA Cup

3	Watford	A	0-1		26,104

League Cup

2	Tottenham Hotspur	A	0-1		39,333
	Tottenham Hotspur	H	0-1		55,890

1982/83

	Opposition	H/A	Score	Scorers	Attn.
1	Birmingham City	H	3-0	Coppell Moran Stapleton	48,673
2	Nottingham Forest	A	3-0	Robson Whiteside Wilkins	23,956
3	West Bromwich Albion	A	1-3	Robson	24,928
4	Everton	H	2-1	Robson Whiteside	43,186
5	Ipswich Town	H	3-1	Whiteside 2 Coppell	43,140
6	Southampton	A	1-0	Macari	21,700
7	Arsenal	H	0-0		43,198
8	Luton Town	A	1-1	Grimes	17,009
9	Stoke City	H	1-0	Robson	43,132

10	Liverpool	A	0-0		40,853
11	Manchester City	H	2-2	Stapleton 2	57,334
12	West Ham United	A	1-3	Moran	31,684
13	Brighton & Hove Albion	A	0-1		18,379
14	Tottenham Hotspur	H	1-0	Muhren	47,869
15	Aston Villa	A	1-2	Stapleton	35,487
16	Norwich City	H	3-0	Robson 2 Muhren	34,579
17	Watford	A	1-0	Whiteside	25,669
18	Notts County	H	4-0	Duxbury Robson Stapleton Whiteside	33,618
19	Swansea City	A	0-0		15,748
20	Sunderland	H	0-0		47,783
21	Coventry City	A	0-3		18,945
22	Aston Villa	H	3-1	Stapleton 2 Coppell	41,545
23	West Bromwich Albion	H	0-0		39,123
24	Birmingham City	A	2-1	Robson Whiteside	19,333
25	Nottingham Forest	H	2-0	Coppell Muhren	38,615
26	Ipswich Town	A	1-1	Stapleton	23,804
27	Liverpool	H	1-1	Muhren	57,397
28	Stoke City	A	0-1		21,266
29	Manchester City	A	2-1	Stapleton 2	45,400
30	Brighton & Hove Albion	H	1-1	Albiston	36,264
31	West Ham United	H	2-1	McGarvey Stapleton	30,227
32	Coventry City	H	3-0	Macari Stapleton Gillespie og	36,814
33	Sunderland	A	0-0		31,486
34	Southampton	H	1-1	Robson	37,120
35	Everton	A	0-2		21,715
36	Watford	H	2-0	Cunningham Grimes	43,048
37	Norwich City	A	1-1	Whiteside	22,233
38	Arsenal	A	0-3		23,602
39	Swansea City	H	2-1	Robson Stapleton	35,724
40	Luton Town	H	3-0	McGrath 2 Stapleton	34,213
41	Tottenham Hotspur	A	0-2		32,803
42	Notts County	A	2-3	McGrath Muhren	14,395

• Final League Position: 3rd in Division One

FA Cup

3	West Ham United	H	2-0	Stapleton Coppell	44,143
4	Luton Town	A	2-0	Moses Moran	20,516
5	Derby County	A	1-0	Whiteside	33,022
6	Everton	H	1-0	Stapleton	58,198
SF	Arsenal	N*	2-1	Robson Whiteside	46,535
F	Brighton & Hove Albion	N**	2-2	Stapleton Wilkins	100,000
FR	Brighton & Hove Albion	N**	4-0	Robson 2 Muhren Whiteside	92,000

*Played at Villa Park, Birmingham
**Played at Wembley

League Cup

2	Bournemouth	H	2-0	Redknapp og Stapleton	22,091
	Bournemouth	A	2-2	Muhren Coppell	13,226
3	Bradford City	A	0-0		15,568
3R	Bradford City	H	4-1	Moses Albiston Moran Coppell	24,507
4	Southampton	H	2-0	McQueen Whiteside	28,378
5	Nottingham Forest	H	4-0	McQueen 2 Coppell Robson	44,413
SF	Arsenal	A	4-2	Coppell 2 Whiteside Stapleton	43,136
	Arsenal	H	2-1	Coppell Moran	65,635
F	Liverpool	N*	1-2 aet	Whiteside	100,000

*Played at Wembley

1983/84

	Opposition	H/A	Score	Scorers	Attn.
1	Queen's Park Rangers	H	3-1	Muhren 2 Stapleton	48,742
2	Nottingham Forest	H	1-2	Moran	43,005
3	Stoke City	A	1-0	Muhren	23,704
4	Arsenal	A	3-2	Moran Robson Stapleton	42,703
5	Luton Town	H	2-0	Muhren Albiston	41,013
6	Southampton	A	0-3		20,674
7	Liverpool	H	1-0	Stapleton	56,121
8	Norwich City	A	3-3	Whiteside 2 Stapleton	19,290
9	West Bromwich Albion	H	3-0	Albiston Graham Whiteside	42,221
10	Sunderland	A	1-0	Wilkins	26,826
11	Wolverhampton Wanderers	H	3-0	Stapleton 2 Robson	41,880
12	Aston Villa	H	1-2	Robson	45,077

13	Leicester City	A	1-1	Robson	24,409
14	Watford	H	4-1	Stapleton 3 Robson	43,111
15	West Ham United	A	1-1	Wilkins	23,355
16	Everton	H	0-1		43,664
17	Ipswich Town	A	2-0	Crooks Graham	19,779
18	Tottenham Hotspur	H	4-2	Graham 2 Moran 2	33,616
19	Coventry City	A	1-1	Muhren	21,553
20	Notts County	H	3-3	Crooks McQueen Moran	41,544
21	Stoke City	H	1-0	Graham	40,164
22	Liverpool	A	1-1	Whiteside	44,622
23	Queen's Park Rangers	A	1-1	Robson	16,308
24	Southampton	H	3-2	Muhren Robson Stapleton	40,371
25	Norwich City	H	0-0		36,851
26	Birmingham City	A	2-2	Hogg Whiteside	19,957
27	Luton Town	A	5-0	Robson 2 Whiteside 2 Stapleton	11,265
28	Wolverhampton Wanderers	A	1-1	Whiteside	20,676
29	Sunderland	H	2-1	Moran 2	40,615
30	Aston Villa	A	3-0	Moses Robson Whiteside	32,874
31	Leicester City	H	2-0	Hughes Moses	39,473
32	Arsenal	H	4-0	Muhren 2 Robson Stapleton	48,942
33	West Bromwich Albion	A	0-2		28,104
34	Birmingham City	H	1-0	Robson	39,896
35	Notts County	A	0-1		13,911
36	Watford	A	0-0		20,764
37	Coventry City	H	4-	Hughes 2 McGrath Wilkins	38,524
38	West Ham United	H	0-0		44,124
39	Everton	A	1-1	Stapleton	28,802
40	Ipswich Town	H	1-2	Hughes	44,257
41	Tottenham Hotspur	A	1-1	Whiteside	39,790
42	Nottingham Forest	A	0-2		23,651

• Final League Position: 4th in Division One

FA Cup

| 3 | Bournemouth | A | 0-2 | | 14,782 |

League Cup

| 2 | Port Vale | A | 1-0 | Stapleton | 19,885 |

		H/A	Score	Scorers	Attn.
	Port Vale	H	2-0	Whiteside Wilkins	23,589
3	Colchester United	A	2-0	McQueen Moses	13,031
4	Oxford United	A	1-1	Hughes	13,739
4R	Oxford United	H	1-1 aet	Stapleton	27,459
4RR	Oxford United	A	1-2	Graham	13,912

1984/85

	Opposition	H/A	Score	Scorers	Attn.
1	Watford	H	1-1	Strachan	53,668
2	Southampton	A	0-0		22,183
3	Ipswich Town	A	1-1	Hughes	20,876
4	Chelsea	H	1-1	Olsen	48,398
5	Newcastle United	H	5-0	Strachan 2 Hughes Moses Olsen	54,915
6	Coventry City	A	3-0	Whiteside 2 Robson	18,312
7	Liverpool	H	1-1	Strachan	56,638
8	West Bromwich Albion	A	2-1	Robson Strachan	26,292
9	Aston Villa	A	0-3		37,131
10	West Ham United	H	5-1	Brazil Hughes McQueen Moses Strachan	47,559
11	Tottenham Hotspur	H	1-0	Hughes	54,516
12	Everton	A	0-5		40,742
13	Arsenal	H	4-2	Strachan 2 Hughes Robson	32,279
14	Leicester City	A	3-2	Brazil Hughes Strachan	23,840
15	Luton Town	H	2-0	Whiteside 2	41,630
16	Sunderland	A	2-3	Hughes Robson	25,405
17	Norwich City	H	2-0	Hughes Robson	36,635
18	Nottingham Forest	A	2-3	Strachan 2	25,902
19	Queen's Park Rangers	H	3-0	Brazil Duxbury Gidman	36,134
20	Ipswich Town	H	3-0	Gidman Robson Strachan	35,168
21	Stoke City	A	1-2	Stapleton	20,985
22	Chelsea	A	3-1	Hughes Moses Stapleton	42,197
23	Sheffield Wednesday	H	1-2	Hughes	47,625
24	Coventry City	H	0-1		35,992
25	West Bromwich Albion	H	2-0	Strachan 2	36,681
26	Newcastle United	A	1-1	Moran	32,555
27	Arsenal	A	1-0	Whiteside	48,612
28	Everton	H	1-1	Olsen	51,150

29	Tottenham Hotspur	A	2-1	Hughes Whiteside	42,908
30	West Ham United	A	2-2	Robson Stapleton	16,674
31	Aston Villa	H	4-0	Hughes 3 Whiteside	40,941
32	Liverpool	A	1-0	Stapleton	34,886
33	Leicester City	H	2-1	Robson Stapleton	35,590
34	Stoke City	H	5-0	Hughes 2 Olsen 2 Whiteside	42,940
35	Sheffield Wednesday	A	0-1		39,380
36	Luton Town	A	1-2	Whiteside	10,320
37	Southampton	H	0-0		31,291
38	Sunderland	H	2-2	Moran Robson	38,979
39	Norwich City	A	1-0	Moran	15,502
40	Nottingham Forest	H	2-0	Gidman Stapleton	41,775
41	Queen's Park Rangers	A	3-1	Brazil 2 Strachan	20,483
42	Watford	A	1-5	Moran	20,500

• Final League Position: 4th in Division One

FA Cup

3	Bournemouth	H	3-0	Strachan McQueen Stapleton	32,080
4	Coventry City	H	2-1	Hughes McGrath	38,039
5	Blackburn Rovers	A	2-0	Strachan McGrath	22,692
6	West Ham United	H	4-2	Whiteside 3 Hughes	46,769
SF	Liverpool	N*	2-2	Robson Stapleton	51,690
SF(R)	Liverpool	N**	2-1	Robson Hughes	45,775
F	Everton	N***	1-0	Whiteside	100,000

*Played at Goodison Park, Liverpool
**Played at Maine Road, Manchester
***Played at Wembley

League Cup

2	Burnley	H	4-0	Hughes 3 Robson	28,383
	Burnley	A	3-0	Brazil 2 Olsen	12,690
3	Everton	H	1-2	Brazil	50,918

1985/86

	Opposition	H/A	Score	Scorers	Attn.
1	Aston Villa	H	4-0	Hughes 2 Olsen Whiteside	49,743
2	Ipswich Town	A	1-0	Robson	18,777

3	Arsenal	A	2-1	Hughes McGrath	37,145
4	West Ham United	H	2-0	Hughes Strachan	50,773
5	Nottingham Forest	A	3-1	Barnes Hughes Stapleton	26,274
6	Newcastle United	H	3-0	Stapleton 2 Hughes	51,102
7	Oxford United	H	3-0	Barnes Robson Whiteside	51,820
8	Manchester City	A	3-0	Albiston Duxbury Robson	48,773
9	West Bromwich Albion	A	5-1	Brazil 2 Blackmore Stapleton Strachan	25,068
10	Southampton	H	1-0	Hughes	52,449
11	Luton Town	A	1-1	Hughes	17,454
12	Queen's Park Rangers	H	2-0	Hughes Olsen	48,845
13	Liverpool	H	1-1	McGrath	54,492
14	Chelsea	A	2-1	Hughes Olsen	42,485
15	Coventry City	H	2-0	Olsen 2	46,748
16	Sheffield Wednesday	A	0-1		48,105
17	Tottenham Hotspur	H	0-0		54,575
18	Leicester City	A	0-3		22,008
19	Watford	H	1-1	Brazil	42,181
20	Ipswich Town	H	1-0	Stapleton	37,981
21	Aston Villa	A	3-1	Blackmore Hughes Strachan	27,626
22	Arsenal	H	0-1		44,386
23	Everton	A	1-3	Stapleton	42,551
24	Birmingham City	H	1-0	C Gibson	43,095
25	Oxford United	A	3-1	C Gibson Hughes Whiteside	13,280
26	Nottingham Forest	H	2-3	Olsen 2	46,717
27	West Ham United	A	1-2	Robson	22,642
28	Liverpool	A	1-1	C Gibson	35,064
29	West Bromwich Albion	H	3-0	Olsen 3	45,193
30	Southampton	A	0-1		19,012
31	Queen's Park Rangers	A	0-1		23,407
32	Luton Town	H	2-0	Hughes McGrath	33,668
33	Manchester City	H	2-2	C Gibson Strachan	51,274
34	Birmingham City	A	1-1	Robson	22,551
35	Everton	H	0-0		51,189
36	Coventry City	A	3-1	C Gibson Robson Strachan	17,160
37	Chelsea	H	1-2	Olsen	45,355
38	Sheffield Wednesday	H	0-2		32,331

39	Newcastle United	A	4-2	Hughes 2 Robson Whiteside	31,840
40	Tottenham Hotspur	A	0-0		32,357
41	Leicester City	H	4-0	Blackmore Davenport Hughes Stapleton	38,840
42	Watford	A	1-1	Hughes	18,414

• Final League Position: 4th in Division One

FA Cup

3	Rochdale	H	2-0	Stapleton Hughes	40,223
4	Sunderland	A	0-0		35,284
4R	Sunderland	H	3-0	Olsen 2 Whiteside	43,402
5	West Ham United	A	1-1	Stapleton	26,441
5R	West Ham United	H	0-2		30,441

League Cup

2	Crystal Palace	A	1-0	Barnes	21,507
	Crystal Palace	H	1-0	Whiteside	26,118
3	West Ham United	H	1-0	Whiteside	32,056
4	Liverpool	A	1-2	McGrath	41,291

1986/87

	Opposition	H/A	Score	Scorers	Attn.
1	Arsenal	A	0-1		41,382
2	West Ham United	H	2-3	Stapleton Davenport	43,306
3	Charlton Athletic	H	0-1		37,544
4	Leicester City	A	1-1	Whiteside	16,785
5	Southampton	H	5-1	Stapleton 2 Olsen Davenport Whiteside	40,135
6	Watford	A	0-1		21,650
7	Everton	A	1-3	Robson	25,843
8	Chelsea	H	0-1		33,340
9	Nottingham Forest	A	1-1	Robson	34,828
10	Sheffield Wednesday	H	3-1	Davenport 2 Whiteside	45,890
11	Luton Town	H	1-0	Stapleton	39,927
12	Manchester City	A	1-1	Stapleton	32,440
13	Coventry City	H	1-1	Davenport	36,946
14	Oxford United	A	0-2		13,545

15	Norwich City	A	0-0		22,684
16	Queen's Park Rangers	H	1-0	Siveback	42,235
17	Wimbledon	A	0-1		12,112
18	Tottenham Hotspur	H	3-3	Davenport 2 Whiteside	35,957
19	Aston Villa	A	3-3	Davenport 2 Whiteside	29,205
20	Leicester City	H	2-0	C Gibson Stapleton	34,180
21	Liverpool	A	1-0	Whiteside	40,663
22	Norwich City	H	0-1		44,610
23	Newcastle United	H	4-1	Whiteside Stapleton Olsen P Jackson og	43,334
24	Southampton	A	1-1	Olsen	20,409
25	Arsenal	H	2-0	Strachan T Gibson	51,367
26	Charlton Athletic	A	0-0		15,482
27	Watford	H	3-1	McGrath Davenport Strachan	35,763
28	Chelsea	A	1-1	Davenport	26,516
29	Everton	H	0-0		47,421
30	Manchester City	H	2-0	Robson Reid og	48,619
31	Luton Town	A	1-2	Robson	12,509
32	Sheffield Wednesday	A	0-1		29,888
33	Nottingham Forest	H	2-0	McGrath Robson	39,182
34	Oxford United	H	3-2	Davenport 2 Robson	32,443
35	West Ham United	A	0-0		23,486
36	Newcastle United	A	1-2	Strachan	32,706
37	Liverpool	H	1-0	Davenport	54,103
38	Queen's Park Rangers	A	1-1	Strachan	17,414
39	Wimbledon	H	0-1		31,686
40	Tottenham Hotspur	A	0-4		36,692
41	Coventry City	A	1-1	Whiteside	23,407
42	Aston Villa	H	3-1	Blackmore Duxbury Robson	35,179

• Final League Position: 11th in Division One

FA Cup

3	Manchester City	H	1-0	Whiteside	54,294
4	Coventry City	H	0-1		49,082

League Cup

| 2 | Port Vale | H | 2-0 | Stapleton Whiteside | 18,906 |

	Port Vale	A	5-2	Moses 2 Stapleton Barnes Davenport	10,486
3	Southampton	H	0-0		23,639
3R	Southampton	A	1-4	Davenport	17,915

1987/88

	Opposition	H/A	Score	Scorers	Attn.
1	Southampton	A	2-2	Whiteside 2	21,214
2	Arsenal	H	0-0		42,890
3	Watford	H	2-0	McGrath McClair	38,582
4	Charlton Athletic	A	3-1	McClair Robson McGrath	14,046
5	Chelsea	H	3-1	McClair Strachan Whiteside	46,478
6	Coventry City	A	0-0		27,125
7	Newcastle United	H	2-2	Olsen McClair	45,137
8	Everton	A	1-2	Whiteside	38,439
9	Tottenham Hotspur	H	1-0	McClair	47,601
10	Luton Town	A	1-1	McClair	9,137
11	Sheffield Wednesday	A	4-2	McClair 2 Robson Blackmore	32,779
12	Norwich City	H	2-1	Davenport Robson	39,345
13	West Ham United	A	1-1	Gibson	19,863
14	Nottingham Forest	H	2-2	Robson Whiteside	44,669
15	Liverpool	H	1-1	Whiteside	47,106
16	Wimbledon	A	1-2	Blackmore	11,532
17	Queen's Park Rangers	A	2-0	Davenport Robson	20,632
18	Oxford United	H	3-1	Strachan 2 Olsen	34,709
19	Portsmouth	A	2-1	Robson McClair	22,207
20	Newcastle United	A	0-1		26,461
21	Everton	H	2-1	McClair 2	47,024
22	Charlton Athletic	H	0-0		37,257
23	Watford	A	1-0	McClair	18,038
24	Southampton	H	0-2		35,716
25	Arsenal	A	2-1	Strachan McClair	29,392
26	Coventry City	H	1-0	O'Brien	37,144
27	Derby County	A	2-1	Whiteside Strachan	20,016
28	Chelsea	A	2-1	Bruce O'Brien	25,014
29	Tottenham Hotspur	A	1-1	McClair	25,731
30	Norwich City	A	0-1		19,129

31	Sheffield Wednesday	H	4-1	McClair 2 Blackmore Davenport	33,318
32	Nottingham Forest	A	0-0		27,598
33	West Ham United	H	3-1	Strachan Anderson Robson	37,269
34	Derby County	H	4-1	McClair 3 Gibson	40,146
35	Liverpool	A	3-3	Robson 2 Strachan	43,497
36	Luton Town	H	3-0	McClair Robson Davenport	28,830
37	Queen's Park Rangers	H	2-1	Bruce Parker og	35,733
38	Oxford United	A	2-0	Anderson Strachan	8,966
39	Portsmouth	H	4-1	McClair 2 davenport Robson	35,105
40	Wimbledon	H	2-1	McClair 2	28,040

● Final League Position: 2nd in Division One

FA Cup

3	Ipswich Town	A	2-1	D'Avray og Anderson	23,012
4	Chelsea	H	2-0	Whiteside McClair	50,716
5	Arsenal	A	1-2	McClair	54,161

League Cup

2	Hull City	H	5-0	McGrath Davenport Whiteside Strachan McClair	25,041
	Hull City	A	1-0	McClair	13,586
3	Crystal Palace	H	2-1	McClair 2	27,283
4	Bury	A*	2-1	Whiteside McClair	33,519
5	Oxford United	A	0-2		12,658

*Played at Old Trafford

1988/89

	Opposition	H/A	Score	Scorers	Attn.
1	Queen's Park Rangers	H	0-0		46,377
2	Liverpool	A	0-1		42,026
3	Middlesbrough	H	1-0	Robson	40,422
4	Luton Town	A	2-0	Davenport Robson	11,010
5	West Ham United	H	2-0	Davenport Hughes	39,941
6	Tottenham Hotspur	A	2-2	Hughes McClair	29,318
7	Wimbledon	A	1-1	Hughes	12,143
8	Norwich City	H	1-2	Hughes	36,998
9	Everton	A	1-1	Hughes	27,005

10	Aston Villa	H	1-1	Bruce	44,804
11	Derby County	A	2-2	Hughes McClair	24,080
12	Southampton	H	2-2	Robson Hughes	37,277
13	Sheffield Wednesday	H	1-1	Hughes	30,867
14	Newcastle United	A	0-0		20,350
15	Charlton Athletic	H	3-0	Milne McClair Hughes	31,173
16	Coventry City	A	0-1		19,936
17	Arsenal	A	1-2	Hughes	37,422
18	Nottingham Forest	H	2-0	Milne Hughes	39,582
19	Liverpool	H	3-1	McClair Hughes Beardsmore	44,745
20	Middlesbrough	A	0-1		24,411
21	Millwall	H	3-0	Blackmore Gill Hughes	40,931
22	West Ham United	A	3-1	Strachan Martin McClair	29,822
23	Tottenham Hotspur	H	1-0	McClair	41,423
24	Sheffield Wednesday	A	2-0	McClair 2	34,820
25	Norwich City	A	1-2	McGrath	23,155
26	Aston Villa	A	0-0		28,332
27	Luton Town	H	2-0	Milne Blackmore	36,335
28	Nottingham Forest	A	0-2		30,092
29	Arsenal	H	1-1	Adams og	37,977
30	Millwall	A	0-0		17,523
31	Derby County	H	0-2		34,145
32	Charlton Athletic	A	0-1		12,055
33	Coventry City	H	0-1		29,799
34	Wimbledon	H	1-0	McClair	23,368
35	Southampton	A	1-2	Beardsmore	17,021
36	Queen's Park Rangers	A	2-3	Bruce Blackmore	10,017
37	Everton	H	1-2	Hughes	26,722
38	Newcastle United	H	2-0	McClair Robson	30,379

• Final League Position: 11th in Division One

FA Cup

3	Queen's Park Rangers	H	0-0		36,222
3R	Queen's Park Rangers	A	2-2 aet	Gill Graham	22,236
3RR	Queen's Park Rangers	H	3-0	McClair 2 (1 pen) Robson	46,257
4	Oxford United	H	4-0	Hughes Bruce Phillips og Robson	47,754
5	Bournemouth	A	1-1	Hughes	12,500

| 5R | Bournemouth | H | 1-0 | McClair | 52,422 |
| 6 | Nottingham Forest | H | 0-1 | | 55,052 |

League Cup

2	Rotherham United	A	1-0	Davenport	12,592
	Rotherham United	H	5-0	McClair 3 Robson Bruce	20,597
3	Wimbledon	A	1-2	Robson	10,864

1989/90

	Opposition	H/A	Score	Scorers	Attn.
1	Arsenal	H	4-1	Bruce Hughes Webb McClair	47,245
2	Crystal Palace	A	1-1	Robson	22,423
3	Derby County	A	0-2		22,175
4	Norwich City	H	0-2		39,610
5	Everton	A	2-3	McClair Beardsmore	37,916
6	Millwall	H	5-1	Hughes 3 Robson Sharpe	42,746
7	Manchester City	A	1-5	Hughes	43,246
8	Sheffield Wednesday	H	0-0		41,492
9	Coventry City	A	4-1	Hughes 2 Bruce Phelan	19,605
10	Southampton	H	2-1	McClair 2	37,122
11	Charlton Athletic	A	0-2		16,065
12	Nottingham Forest	H	1-0	Pallister	34,182
13	Luton Town	A	3-1	Wallace Blackmore Hughes	11,141
14	Chelsea	H	0-0		46,975
15	Arsenal	A	0-1		34,484
16	Crystal Palace	H	1-2	Beardsmore	33,514
17	Tottenham Hotspur	H	0-1		36,230
18	Liverpool	A	0-0		37,426
19	Aston Villa	A	0-3		41,247
20	Wimbledon	A	2-2	Hughes Robins	9,622
21	Queen's Park Rangers	H	0-0		34,824
22	Derby County	H	1-2	Pallister	38,985
23	Norwich City	A	0-2		17,370
24	Manchester City	H	1-1	Blackmore	40,274
25	Millwall	A	2-1	Wallace Hughes	15,491
26	Chelsea	A	0-1		29,979
27	Luton Town	H	4-1	McClair Hughes Wallace Robins	35,327

28	Everton	H	0-0		37,398
29	Liverpool	H	1-2	Whelan og	46,629
30	Sheffield Wednesday	A	0-1		33,260
31	Southampton	A	2-0	Gibson Robins	20,510
32	Coventry City	H	3-0	Hughes 2 Robins	39,172
33	Queen's Park Rangers	A	2-1	Robins Webb	18,997
34	Aston Villa	H	2-0	Robins 2	44,880
35	Tottenham Hotspur	A	1-2	Bruce	33,317
36	Wimbledon	H	0-0		29,281
37	Nottingham Forest	A	0-4		21,186
38	Charlton Athletic	H	1-0	Pallister	35,389

• Final League Position: 13th in Division one

FA Cup

3	Nottingham Forest	A	1-0	Robins	23,072
4	Hereford United	A	1-0	Blackmore	13,777
5	Newcastle United	A	3-2	Robins Wallace McClair	31,748
6	Sheffield United	A	1-0	McClair	34,344
SF	Oldham Athletic	N*	3-3	Robson Webb Wallace	44,026
SF(R)	Oldham Athletic	N*	2-1 aet	McClair Robins	35,005
F	Crystal Palace	N**	3-3 aet	Hughes 2 Robson	80,000
FR	Crystal Palace	N**	1-0	Martin	80,000

*Played at Maine Road, Manchester
**Played at Wembley

League Cup

2	Portsmouth	A	3-2	Ince 2 Wallace	18,072
	Portsmouth	H	0-0		26,698
3	Tottenham Hotspur	H	0-3		45,759

1990/91

	Opposition	H/A	Score	Scorers	Attn.
1	Coventry City	H	2-0	Bruce Webb	46,715
2	Leeds United	A	0-0		29,174
3	Sunderland	A	1-2	McClair	26,105
4	Luton Town	A	1-0	Robins	12,576
5	Queen's Park Rangers	H	3-1	Robins 2 McClair	43,427

6	Liverpool	A	0-4		35,726
7	Southampton	H	3-2	Blackmore Hughes McClair	41,288
8	Nottingham Forest	H	0-1		46,766
9	Arsenal	H	0-1		47,232
10	Manchester City	A	3-3	McClair 2 Hughes	36,427
11	Crystal Palace	H	2-0	Wallace Webb	45,724
12	Derby County	A	0-0		21,115
13	Sheffield United	H	2-0	Bruce Hughes	45,093
14	Chelsea	H	2-3	Hughes Wallace	37,836
15	Everton	A	1-0	Sharpe	32,400
16	Leeds United	H	1-1	Webb	40,927
17	Coventry City	A	2-2	Hughes Wallace	17,106
18	Wimbledon	A	3-1	Bruce 2 Hughes	9,644
19	Norwich City	H	3-0	McClair 2 Hughes	39,801
20	Aston Villa	H	1-1	Bruce	47,485
21	Tottenham Hotspur	A	2-1	Bruce McClair	29,399
22	Sunderland	H	3-0	Hughes 2 McClair	45,934
23	Queen's Park Rangers	A	1-1	Phelan	18,544
24	Liverpool	H	1-1	Bruce	43,690
25	Sheffield United	A	1-2	Blackmore	27,570
26	Everton	H	0-2		45,658
27	Chelsea	A	2-3	Hughes McClair	22,818
28	Southampton	A	1-1	Ince	15,701
29	Nottingham Forest	A	1-1	Blackmore	23,859
30	Luton Town	H	4-1	Bruce 2 McClair Robins	41,752
31	Norwich City	A	3-0	Bruce 2 Ince	18,282
32	Wimbledon	H	2-1	Bruce McClair	36,660
33	Aston Villa	A	1-1	Sharpe	33,307
34	Derby County	H	3-1	Blackmore McClair Robson	32,776
35	Manchester City	H	1-0	Giggs	45,286
36	Arsenal	A	1-3	Bruce	40,229
37	Crystal Palace	A	0-3		25,301
38	Tottenham Hotspur	H	1-1	Ince	46,791

• Final League Position: 6th in Division One

FA Cup

3	Queen's Park Rangers	H	2-1	Hughes McClair	35,065

| 4 | Bolton Wanderers | H | 1-0 | Hughes | 43,293 |
| 5 | Norwich City | A | 1-2 | McClair | 23,058 |

League Cup

2	Halifax Town	A	3-1	Blackmore McClair Webb	6,841
	Halifax Town	H	2-1	Anderson Bruce	22,295
3	Liverpool	H	3-1	Bruce Hughes Sharpe	42,033
4	Arsenal	A	6-2	Sharpe 3 Blackmore Hughes Wallace	40,844
5	Southampton	A	1-1	Hughes	21,011
5R	Southampton	H	3-2	Hughes 3	41,903
SF1	Leeds United	H	2-1	McClair Sharpe	34,050
SF2	Leeds United	A	1-0	Sharpe	32,104
F	Sheffield Wednesday	N*	0-1		77,612

*Played at Wembley

1991/92

	Opposition	H/A	Score	Scorers	Attn.
1	Notts County	H	2-0	Hughes Robson	46,278
2	Aston Villa	A	1-0	Bruce	39,995
3	Everton	A	0-0		36,085
4	Oldham Athletic	H	1-0	McClair	42,078
5	Leeds United	H	1-1	Robson	43,778
6	Wimbledon	A	2-1	Blackmore Pallister	13,824
7	Norwich City	H	3-0	Giggs Irwin McClair	44,946
8	Southampton	A	1-0	Hughes	19,264
9	Luton Town	H	5-0	McClair 2 Bruce Hughes Ince	46,491
10	Tottenham Hotspur	A	2-1	Hughes Robson	35,087
11	Liverpool	H	0-0		44,997
12	Arsenal	H	1-1	Bruce	46,594
13	Sheffield Wednesday	A	2-3	McClair 2	38,260
14	Sheffield United	H	2-0	Kanchelskis og	42,942
15	Manchester City	A	0-0		36,180
16	West Ham United	H	2-1	Giggs Robson	47,185
17	Crystal Palace	A	3-1	Kanchelskis McClair Webb	29,017
18	Coventry City	H	4-0	Bruce Hughes McClair Webb	42,549
19	Chelsea	A	3-1	Bruce Irwin McClair	23,120

20	Oldham Athletic	A	6-3	Irwin 2 McClair 2 Giggs Kanchelskis	18,947
21	Leeds United	A	1-1	Webb	32,638
22	Queen's Park Rangers	H	1-4	McClair	38,554
23	Everton	H	1-0	Kanchelskis	46,619
24	Notts County	A	1-1	Blackmore	21,055
25	Aston Villa	H	1-0	Hughes	45,022
26	Arsenal	A	1-1	McClair	41,703
27	Sheffield Wednesday	H	1-1	McClair	47,074
28	Crystal Palace	H	2-0	Hughes 2	46,347
29	Chelsea	H	1-1	Hughes	44,872
30	Coventry City	A	0-0		23,967
31	Sheffield United	A	2-1	Blackmore McClair	30,183
32	Nottingham Forest	A	0-1		28,062
33	Wimbledon	H	0-0		45,428
34	Queen's Park Rangers	A	0-0		22,603
35	Norwich City	A	3-1	Ince 2 McClair	17,489
36	Manchester City	H	1-1	Giggs	46,781
37	Southampton	H	1-0	Kanchelskis	43,972
38	Luton Town	A	1-1	Sharpe	13,410
39	Nottingham Forest	H	1-2	McClair	47,575
40	West Ham United	A	0-1		24,197
41	Liverpool	A	0-2		36,669
42	Tottenham Hotspur	H	3-1	Hughes 2 McClair	44,595

● Final League Position: 2nd in Division One

FA Cup

3	Leeds United	A	1-0	Hughes	31,819
4	Southampton	A	0-0		19,506
4R	Southampton	H	2-2*	Kanchelskis McClair	33,414

United lost 4-2 on penalties

League Cup

2	Cambridge United	H	3-0	Bruce Giggs McClair	30,934
	Cambridge United	A	1-1	McClair	9,248
3	Portsmouth	H	3-1	Robins 2 Robson	29,543
4	Oldham Athletic	H	2-0	Kanchelskis McClair	38,550

5	Leeds United	A	3-1	Blackmore Giggs Kanchelskis	28,886
SF1	Middlesbrough	A	0-0		25,572
SF2	Middlesbrough	H	2-1	Giggs Sharpe	45,875
F	Nottingham Forest	N*	1-0	McClair	76,810

*Played at Wembley

1992/93

	Opposition	H/A	Score	Scorers	Attn.
1	Sheffield United	A	1-2	Hughes	28,070
2	Everton	H	0-3		31,901
3	Ipswich Town	H	1-1	Irwin	31,704
4	Southampton	A	1-0	Dublin	15,623
5	Nottingham Forest	A	2-0	Giggs Hughes	19,694
6	Crystal Palace	H	1-0	Hughes	29,736
7	Leeds United	H	2-0	Bruce Kanchelskis	31,296
8	Everton	A	2-0	Bruce McClair	30,002
9	Tottenham Hotspur	A	1-1	Giggs	33,296
10	Queen's Park Rangers	H	0-0		33,287
11	Middlesbrough	A	1-1	Bruce	24,172
12	Liverpool	H	2-2	Hughes 2	33,243
13	Blackburn Rovers	A	0-0		20,305
14	Wimbledon	H	0-1		32,622
15	Aston Villa	A	0-1		39,063
16	Oldham Athletic	H	3-0	McClair 2 Hughes	33,497
17	Arsenal	A	1-0	Hughes	29,739
18	Manchester City	H	2-1	Hughes Ince	35,408
19	Norwich City	H	1-0	Hughes	34,500
20	Chelsea	A	1-1	Cantona	34,464
21	Sheffield Wednesday	A	3-3	McClair 2 Cantona	37,708
22	Coventry City	H	5-0	Cantona Giggs Hughes Irwin Sharpe	36,025
23	Tottenham Hotspur	H	4-1	Cantona Irwin McClair Parker	35,648
24	Queen's Park Rangers	A	3-1	Giggs Ince Kanchelskis	21,117
25	Nottingham Forest	H	2-0	Hughes Ince	36,085
26	Ipswich Town	A	1-2	McClair	22,068
27	Sheffield United	H	2-1	Cantona McClair	36,156
28	Leeds United	A	0-0		34,166

29	Southampton	H	2-1	Giggs 2	36,257
30	Middlesbrough	H	3-0	Cantona Giggs Irwin	36,251
31	Liverpool	A	2-1	Hughes McClair	44,374
32	Oldham Athletic	A	0-1		17,106
33	Aston Villa	H	1-1	Hughes	36,163
34	Manchester City	A	1-1	Cantona	37,136
35	Arsenal	H	0-0		37,301
36	Norwich City	A	3-1	Cantona Giggs Kanchelskis	20,582
37	Sheffield Wednesday	H	2-1	Bruce 2	40,102
38	Coventry City	A	1-0	Irwin	24,249
39	Chelsea	H	3-0	Cantona Hughes og	40,139
40	Crystal Palace	A	2-0	Hughes Ince	30,115
41	Blackburn Rovers	H	3-1	Giggs Ince Pallister	40,447
42	Wimbledon	A	2-1	Ince Robson	30,115

• Final League Position: 1st in the Premiership

FA Cup

3	Bury	H	2-0	Gillespie Phelan	30,668
4	Brighton & Hove Albion	H	1-0	Giggs	33,600
5	Sheffield United	A	1-2	Giggs	27,150

League Cup

6	Brighton & Hove Albion	A	1-1	Wallace	16,649
	Brighton & Hove Albion	H	1-0	Hughes	25,405
3	Aston Villa	A	0-1		35,964

1993/94

	Opposition	H/A	Score	Scorers	Attn.
1	Norwich City	A	2-0	Giggs Robson	19,705
2	Sheffield United	H	3-0	Keane 2 Hughes	41,949
3	Newcastle United	H	1-1	Giggs	41,829
4	Aston Villa	A	2-1	Sharpe 2	39,624
5	Southampton	A	3-1	Cantona Irwin Sharpe	16,189
6	West Ham United	H	3-0	Bruce Cantona Sharpe	44,613
7	Chelsea	A	0-1		37,064
8	Arsenal	H	1-0	Cantona	44,009

9	Swindon Town	H	4-2	Hughes 2 Cantona Kanchelskis	44,583
10	Sheffield Wednesday	A	3-2	Hughes 2 Giggs	34,548
11	Tottenham Hotspur	H	2-1	Keane Sharpe	44,655
12	Everton	A	1-0	Sharpe	35,430
13	Queen's Park Rangers	H	2-1	Cantona Hughes	44,663
14	Manchester City	A	3-2	Cantona 2 Keane	35,155
15	Wimbledon	H	3-1	Hughes Kanchelskis Pallister	44,748
16	Ipswich Town	H	0-0		43,300
17	Coventry City	A	1-0	Cantona	17,020
18	Norwich City	H	2-2	Giggs McClair	44,694
19	Sheffield United	A	3-0	Cantona Hughes Sharpe	26,746
20	Newcastle United	A	1-1	Ince	36,388
21	Aston Villa	H	3-1	Cantona 2 Ince	44,499
22	Blackburn Rovers	H	1-1	Ince	44,511
23	Oldham Athletic	A	5-2	Giggs 2 Bruce Cantona Kanchelskis	16,708
24	Leeds United	H	0-0		44,724
25	Liverpool	A	3-3	Bruce Giggs Irwin	42,795
26	Tottenham Hotspur	A	1-0	Hughes	31,343
27	Everton	H	1-0	Giggs	44,750
28	Queen's Park Rangers	A	3-2	Cantona Giggs Kanchelskis	21,267
29	West Ham United	A	2-2	Hughes Ince	28,832
30	Chelsea	H	0-1		44,745
31	Sheffield Wednesday	H	5-0	Cantona 2 Giggs Hughes Ince	43,669
32	Swindon Town	A	2-2	Ince Keane	18,102
33	Arsenal	A	2-2	Sharpe 2	36,203
34	Liverpool	H	1-0	Ince	44,751
35	Blackburn Rovers	A	0-2		20,886
36	Oldham Athletic	H	3-2	Dublin Giggs Ince	44,686
37	Wimbledon	A	0-1		28,553
38	Manchester City	H	2-0	Cantona 2	44,333
39	Leeds United	A	2-0	Giggs Kanchelskis	41,125
40	Ipswich Town	A	2-1	Cantona Giggs	22,559
41	Southampton	H	2-0	Hughes Kanchelskis	44,705
42	Coventry City	H	0-0		44,717

● Final League Position: 1st in the Premiership

FA Cup

3	Sheffield United	A	1-0	Hughes	22,109
4	Norwich City	A	2-0	Cantona Keane	21,060
5	Wimbledon	A	3-0	Cantona Ince Irwin	27,511
6	Charlton Athletic	H	3-1	Kanchelskis 2 Hughes	44,347
SF	Oldham Athletic	N*	1-1	Hughes	56,399
SF(R)	Oldham Athletic	N**	4-1	Giggs Irwin Kanchelskis Robson	32,311
F	Chelsea	N*	4-0	Cantona 2 Hughes McClair	79,364

*Played at Wembley
**Played at Maine Road, Manchester

League Cup

2	Stoke City	A	1-2	Dublin	23,327
	Stoke City	H	2-0	McClair Sharpe	41,387
3	Leicester City	H	5-1	Bruce 2 Hughes McClair Sharpe	41,344
4	Everton	A	2-0	Giggs Hughes	34,052
5	Portsmouth	H	2-2	Cantona Giggs	43,794
5R	Portsmouth	A	1-0	McClair	24,950
SF1	Sheffield Wednesday	H	1-0	Giggs	43,294
SF2	Sheffield Wednesday	A	4-1	Hughes 2 Kanchelskis McClair	34,878
F	Aston Villa	N*	1-3	Hughes	77,231

*Played at Wembley

1994/95

	Opposition	H/A	Score	Scorers	Attn.
1	Queen's Park Rangers	H	2-0	Hughes McClair	43,214
2	Nottingham Forest	A	1-1	Kanchelskis	22,072
3	Tottenham Hotspur	A	1-0	Bruce	24,502
4	Wimbledon	H	3-0	Cantona Giggs McClair	43,440
5	Leeds United	A	1-2	Cantona	39,396
6	Liverpool	H	2-0	Kanchelskis McClair	43,740
7	Ipswich Town	A	2-3	Cantona Scholes	22,559
8	Everton	H	2-0	Kanchelskis Sharpe	43,803
9	Sheffield Wednesday	A	0-1		33,441
10	West Ham United	H	1-0	Cantona	43,795
11	Blackburn Rovers	A	4-2	Kanchelskis 2 Cantona Hughes	30,260
12	Newcastle United	H	2-0	Gillespie Pallister	43,795
13	Aston Villa	A	2-1	Ince Kanchelskis	32,136

14	Manchester City	H	5-0	Kanchelskis 3 Cantona Hughes	43,738
15	Crystal Palace	H	3-0	Cantona Irwin Kanchelskis	43,788
16	Arsenal	A	0-0		38,301
17	Norwich City	H	1-0	Cantona	43,789
18	Queen's Park Rangers	A	3-2	Scholes 2 Keane	18,948
19	Nottingham Forest	H	1-2	Cantona	43,744
20	Chelsea	A	3-2	Cantona Hughes McClair	31,161
21	Leicester City	H	1-1	Kanchelskis	43,789
22	Southampton	A	2-2	Butt Pallister	15,204
23	Coventry City	H	2-0	Cantona Scholes	43,130
24	Newcastle United	A	1-1	Hughes	34,471
25	Blackburn Rovers	H	1-0	Cantona	43,742
26	Crystal Palace	A	1-1	May	18,224
27	Aston Villa	H	1-0	Cole	43,795
28	Manchester City	A	3-0	Cole Ince Kanchelskis	26,368
29	Norwich City	A	2-0	Ince Kanchelskis	21,824
30	Everton	A	0-1		40,011
31	Ipswich Town	H	9-0	Cole 5 Hughes 2 Ince Keane	43,804
32	Wimbledon	A	1-0	Bruce	18,224
33	Tottenham Hotspur	H	0-0		43,802
34	Liverpool	A	0-2		38,906
35	Arsenal	H	3-0	Hughes Kanchelskis Sharpe	43,623
36	Leeds United	H	0-0		43,712
37	Leicester City	A	4-0	Cole 2 Ince Sharpe	21,281
38	Chelsea	H	0-0		43,728
39	Coventry City	A	3-2	Cole 2 Scholes	21,885
40	Sheffield Wednesday	H	1-0	May	43,868
41	Southampton	H	2-1	Cole Irwin	43,479
42	West Ham United	A	1-1	McClair	24,783

● Final League Position: 2nd in the Premiership

FA Cup

3	Sheffield United	A	2-0	Cantona Hughes	22,322
4	Wrexham	H	5-2	Irwin 2 Giggs McClair og	43,222
5	Leeds United	H	3-1	Bruce Hughes McClair	42,744
6	Queen's Park Rangers	H	2-0	Irwin Sharpe	42,830
SF	Crystal Palace	N*	2-2	Irwin Pallister	38,256

SF(R)	Crystal Palace	N*	2-0	Bruce Pallister	17,987
F	Everton	N**	0-1		79,592

*Played at Villa Park, Birmingham
**Played at Wembley

League Cup

2	Port Vale	A	2-1	Scholes 2	18,605
	Port Vale	H	2-0	May McClair	31,615
3	Newcastle United	A	0-2		34,178

1995/96

	Opposition	H/A	Score	Scorers	Attn.
1	Aston Villa	A	1-3	Beckham	34,655
2	West Ham United	H	2-1	Keane Scholes	31,966
3	Wimbledon	H	3-1	Keane 2 Cole	32,226
4	Blackburn Rovers	A	2-1	Beckham Sharpe	29,643
5	Everton	A	3-2	Sharpe 2 Giggs	39,496
6	Bolton Wanderers	H	3-0	Scholes 2 Giggs	32,812
7	Sheffield Wednesday	A	0-0		34,101
8	Liverpool	H	2-2	Butt Cantona	34,934
9	Manchester City	H	1-0	Scholes	35,707
10	Chelsea	A	4-1	Scholes 2 Giggs McClair	31,019
11	Middlesbrough	H	2-0	Cole Pallister	36,580
12	Arsenal	A	0-1		38,317
13	Southampton	H	4-1	Giggs 2 Cole Scholes	39,301
14	Coventry City	A	4-0	McClair 2 Beckham Irwin	23,400
15	Nottingham Forest	A	1-1	Cantona	29,263
16	Chelsea	H	1-1	Beckham	42,019
17	Sheffield Wednesday	H	2-2	Cantona 2	41,849
18	Liverpool	A	0-2		40,546
19	Leeds United	A	1-3	Cole	39,801
20	Newcastle United	H	2-0	Cole Keane	42,024
21	Queen's Park Rangers	H	2-1	Cole Giggs	41,890
22	Tottenham Hotspur	A	1-4	Cole	32,852
23	Aston Villa	H	0-0		42,667
24	West Ham United	A	1-0	Cantona	24,197
25	Wimbledon	A	4-2	Cantona 2 Cole og	25,380

26	Blackburn Rovers	H	1-0	Sharpe	42,681
27	Everton	H	2-0	Giggs Keane	42,459
28	Bolton Wanderers	A	6-0	Scholes 2 Beckham Bruce Butt Cole	21,381
29	Newcastle United	A	1-0	Cantona	36,584
30	Queen's Park Rangers	A	1-1	Cantona	18,817
31	Arsenal	H	1-0	Cantona	50,028
32	Tottenham Hotspur	H	1-0	Cantona	50,157
33	Manchester City	A	3-2	Cantona Cole Giggs	29,668
34	Coventry City	H	1-0	Cantona	50,332
35	Southampton	A	1-3	Giggs	15,262
36	Leeds United	H	1-0	Keane	48,382
37	Nottingham Forest	H	5-0	Beckham 2 Cantona Giggs Scholes	53,926
38	Middlesbrough	A	3-0	Cole Giggs May	29,921

• Final League Position: 1st in the Premiership

FA Cup

3	Sunderland	H	2-2	Butt Cantona	41,563
3R	Sunderland	A	2-1	Cole Scholes	21,378
4	Reading	A	3-0	Cantona Giggs Parker	14,780
5	Manchester City	H	2-1	Cantona Sharpe	42,692
6	Southampton	H	2-0	Cantona Sharpe	45,446
SF	Chelsea	N*	2-1	Beckham Cole	38,421
F	Liverpool	N**	1-0	Cantona	79,007

*Played at Villa Park, Birmingham
**Played at Wembley

League Cup

2	York City	H	0-3		29,049
	York City	A	3-1	Scholes 2 Cooke	9,386

1996/97

	Opposition	H/A	Score	Scorers	Attn.
1	Wimbledon	A	3-0	Beckham Cantona Irwin	25,786
2	Everton	H	2-2	Cruyff og	54,943
3	Blackburn Rovers	H	2-2	Cruyff Solskjaer	54,178

4	Derby County	A	1-1	Beckham	18,026
5	Leeds United	A	4-0	Butt Cantona Poborsky og	39,694
6	Nottingham Forest	H	4-1	Cantona 2 Giggs Solskjaer	54,984
7	Aston Villa	A	0-0		39,339
8	Tottenham Hotspur	H	2-0	Solskjaer 2	54,943
9	Liverpool	H	1-0	Beckham	55,128
10	Newcastle United	A	0-5		35,579
11	Southampton	A	3-6	Beckham May Scholes	15,253
12	Chelsea	H	1-2	May	55,198
13	Arsenal	H	1-0	og	55,210
14	Middlesbrough	A	2-2	Keane May	30,063
15	Leicester City	H	3-1	Butt 2 Solskjaer	55,196
16	West Ham United	A	2-2	Beckham Solskjaer	25,045
17	Sheffield Wednesday	A	1-1	Scholes	37,671
18	Sunderland	H	5-0	Cantona 2 Solskjaer 2 Butt	55,081
19	Nottingham Forest	A	4-0	Beckham Butt Cole Solskjaer	29,032
20	Leeds United	H	1-0	Cantona	55,256
21	Aston Villa	H	0-0		55,133
22	Tottenham Hotspur	A	2-1	Beckham Solskjaer	33,026
23	Coventry City	A	2-0	Giggs Solskjaer	23,085
24	Wimbledon	H	2-1	Cole Giggs	55,314
25	Southampton	H	2-1	Cantona Pallister	55,269
26	Arsenal	A	2-1	Cole Solskjaer	38,172
27	Chelsea	A	1-1	Beckham	28,336
28	Coventry City	H	3-1	Poborsky 2ogs	55,230
29	Sunderland	A	1-2	og	22,225
30	Sheffield Wednesday	H	2-0	Cole Poborksy	55,267
31	Everton	A	2-0	Cantona Solskjaer	40,079
32	Derby County	H	2-3	Cantona Solskjaer	55,243
33	Blackburn Rovers	A	3-2	Cantona Cole Scholes	30,476
34	Liverpool	A	3-1	Pallister 2 Cole	40,892
35	Leicester City	A	2-2	Solskjaer 2	21,068
36	Middlesbrough	H	3-3	Keane G Neville Solskjaer	54,489
37	Newcastle United	H	0-0		55,236
38	West Ham United	H	2-0	Cruyff Solskjaer	55,249

● Final League Position: 1st in the Premiership

FA Cup

3	Tottenham Hotspur	H	2-0	Beckham Scholes	52,445
4	Wimbledon	H	1-1	Scholes	53,342
4R	Wimbledon	A	0-1		25,601

League Cup

3	Swindon Town	H	2-1	Poborsky Scholes	49,305
4	Leicester City	A	0-2		20,428

1997/98

	Opposition	H/A	Score	Scorers	Attn.
1	Tottenham Hotspur	A	2-0	Butt og	26,359
2	Southampton	H	1-0	Beckham	55,008
3	Leicester City	A	0-0		21,221
4	Everton	A	2-0	Beckham Sheringham	40,079
5	Coventry City	H	3-0	Cole Keane Poborsky	55,074
6	West Ham United	H	2-1	Keane Scholes	55,068
7	Bolton Wanderers	A	0-0		25,000
8	Chelsea	H	2-2	Scholes Solskjaer	55,163
9	Leeds United	A	0-1		39,952
10	Crystal Palace	H	2-0	Sheringham og	55,143
11	Derby County	A	2-2	Cole Sheringham	30,014
12	Barnsley	H	7-0	Cole 3 Giggs 2 Poborksy Scholes	55,142
13	Sheffield Wednesday	H	6-1	Sheringham 2 Solskjaer 2 Cole og	55,259
14	Arsenal	A	2-3	Sheringham 2	38,205
15	Wimbledon	A	5-2	Beckham 2 Butt Cole Scholes	26,309
16	Blackburn Rovers	H	4-0	Solskjaer 2 2 ogs	55,175
17	Liverpool	A	3-1	Cole 2 Beckham	41,027
18	Aston Villa	H	1-0	Giggs	55,151
19	Newcastle United	A	1-0	Cole	36,767
20	Everton	H	2-0	Berg Cole	55,167
21	Coventry City	A	2-3	Sheringham Solskjaer	23,054
22	Tottenham Hotspur	H	2-0	Giggs 2	55,281
23	Southampton	A	0-1		15,241
24	Leicester City	H	0-1		55,156
25	Bolton Wanderers	H	1-1	Cole	55,156

26	Aston Villa	A	2-0	Beckham Giggs	39,372
27	Derby County	H	2-0	Giggs Irwin	55,170
28	Chelsea	A	1-0	P Neville	35,411
29	Sheffield Wednesday	A	0-2		39,427
30	West Ham United	A	1-1	Scholes	25,892
31	Arsenal	H	0-1		55,174
32	Wimbledon	H	2-0	Johnsen Scholes	55,306
33	Blackburn Rovers	A	3-1	Beckham Cole Scholes	30,547
34	Liverpool	H	1-1	Johnsen	55,171
35	Newcastle United	H	1-1	Beckham	55,194
36	Crystal Palace	A	3-0	Butt Cole Scholes	26,180
37	Leeds United	H	3-0	Beckham Giggs Irwin	55,167
38	Barnsley	A	2-0	Cole Sheringham	18,694

• Final League Position: 2nd in the Premiership

FA Cup

3	Chelsea	A	5-3	Beckham 2 Cole 2 Sheringham	34,792
4	Walsall	H	5-1	Cole 2 Solskjaer 2 Johnsen	54,669
5	Barnsley	H	1-1	Sheringham	54,700
5R	Barnsley	A	2-3	Cole Sheringham	18,655

League Cup

3	Ipswich Town	A	0-2		22,173

1998/99

	Opposition	H/A	Score	Scorers	Attn.
1	Leicester City	H	2-2	Beckham Sheringham	55,052
2	West Ham United	A	0-0		26,039
3	Charlton Athletic	H	4-1	Solskjaer 2 Yorke 2	55,147
4	Coventry City	H	2-0	Johnsen Yorke	55,198
5	Arsenal	A	0-3		38,142
6	Liverpool	H	2-0	Irwin Scholes	55,181
7	Southampton	A	3-0	Cole Cruyff Yorke	15,251
8	Wimbledon	H	5-1	Cole 2 Beckham Giggs Yorke	55,265
9	Derby County	A	1-1	Cruyff	30,867
10	Everton	A	4-1	Blomqvist Cole Yorke og	40,079
11	Newcastle United	H	0-0		55,174

12	Blackburn Rovers	H	3-2	Scholes 2 Yorke	55,198
13	Sheffield Wednesday	A	1-3	Cole	39,475
14	Leeds United	H	3-2	Butt Keane Solskjaer	55,172
15	Aston Villa	A	1-1	Scholes	39,241
16	Tottenham Hotspur	A	2-2	Solskjaer 2	36,079
17	Chelsea	H	1-1	Cole	55,159
18	Middlesbrough	H	2-3	Butt Scholes	55,152
19	Nottingham Forest	H	3-0	Johnsen 2 Giggs	55,216
20	Chelsea	A	0-0		34,741
21	West Ham United	H	4-1	Cole 2 Solskjaer Yorke	55,180
22	Leicester City	A	6-2	Yorke 3 Cole 2 Stam	22,091
23	Charlton Athletic	A	1-0	Yorke	20,043
24	Derby County	H	1-0	Yorke	55,174
25	Nottingham Forest	A	8-1	Solskjaer 4 Cole 2 Yorke 2	30,025
26	Arsenal	H	1-1	Cole	55,171
27	Coventry City	A	1-0	Giggs	22,596
28	Southampton	H	2-1	Keane Yorke	55,316
29	Newcastle United	A	2-1	Cole 2	36,776
30	Everton	H	3-1	Beckham G Neville Solskjaer	55,182
31	Wimbledon	A	1-1	Beckham	26,121
32	Sheffield Wednesday	H	3-0	Scholes Sheringham Solskjaer	55,270
33	Leeds United	A	1-1	Cole	40,255
34	Aston Villa	H	2-1	Beckham og	55,189
35	Liverpool	A	2-2	Irwin Yorke	44,702
36	Middlesbrough	A	1-0	Yorke	34,665
37	Blackburn Rovers	A	0-0		30,436
38	Tottenham Hotspur	H	2-1	Beckham Cole	55,189

• Final League Position: 1st in the Premiership

FA Cup

3	Middlesbrough	H	3-1	Cole Irwin Giggs	52,232
4	Liverpool	H	2-1	Solskjaer Yorke	54,591
5	Fulham	H	1-0	Cole	54,798
6	Chelsea	H	0-0		54,587
6R	Chelsea	A	2-0	Yorke 2	33,075
SF	Arsenal	N*	0-0		39,217
SF(R)	Arsenal	N*	2-1	Beckham Giggs	30,223

| F | Newcastle United | N** | 2-0 | Scholes Sheringham | 79,101 |

*Played at Villa Park, Birmingham
**Played at Wembley

League Cup

3	Bury	H	2-0	Nevland Solskjaer	52,495
4	Nottingham Forest	H	2-1	Solskjaer 2	37,337
5	Tottenham Hotspur	A	1-3	Sheringham	35,702

1999/2000

	Opposition	H/A	Score	Scorers	Attn.
1	Everton	A	1-1	Yorke	39,141
2	Sheffield Wednesday	H	4-0	Cole Scholes Solskjaer Yorke	54,941
3	Leeds United	H	2-0	Yorke 2	55,187
4	Arsenal	A	2-1	Keane 2	38,147
5	Coventry City	A	2-1	Scholes Yorke	22,024
6	Newcastle United	H	5-1	Cole 4 Giggs	55,190
7	Liverpool	A	3-2	Cole 2ogs	44,929
8	Wimbledon	H	1-1	Cruyff	55,189
9	Southampton	H	3-3	Yorke 2 Sheringham	55,249
10	Chelsea	A	0-5		34,909
11	Watford	H	4-1	Cole 2 Irwin Yorke	55,188
12	Tottenham Hotspur	A	1-3	Giggs	36,072
13	Aston Villa	H	3-0	Cole Keane Scholes	55,211
14	Leicester City	H	2-0	Cole 2	55,191
15	Derby County	A	2-1	Butt Cole	33,370
16	Everton	H	5-1	Solskjaer 4 Irwin	55,193
17	West Ham United	A	4-2	Giggs 2 Yorke 2	26,037
18	Bradford City	H	4-0	Cole Fortune Keane Yorke	55,188
19	Sunderland	A	2-2	Butt Keane	42,026
20	Arsenal	H	1-1	Sheringham	58,293
21	Middlesbrough	H	1-0	Beckham	61,267
22	Sheffield Wednesday	A	1-0	Sheringham	39,640
23	Coventry City	H	3-2	Cole 2 Scholes	61,380
24	Newcastle United	A	0-3		36,470
25	Leeds United	A	1-0	Cole	40,160
26	Wimbledon	A	2-2	Cole Cruyff	26,129

27	Liverpool	H	1-1	Solskjaer	61,592
28	Derby County	H	3-1	Yorke 3	61,619
29	Leicester City	A	2-0	Beckham Yorke	22,170
30	Bradford City	A	4-0	Yorke 2 Beckham Scholes	18,276
31	West Ham United	H	7-1	Scholes 3 Beckham Cole Irwin Solskjaer	61,611
32	Middlesbrough	A	4-3	Cole Giggs Fortune Scholes	34,775
33	Sunderland	H	4-0	Solskjaer 2 Berg Butt	61,612
34	Southampton	A	3-1	Beckham Solskjaer og	15,245
35	Chelsea	H	3-2	Yorke 2 Solskjaer	61,593
36	Watford	A	3-2	Cruyff Giggs Yorke	20,250
37	Tottenham Hotspur	H	3-1	Beckham Sheringham Solskjaer	61,629
38	Aston Villa	A	1-0	Sheringham	

• Final League Position: 1st in the Premiership

FA Cup
Did not enter

League Cup

3	Aston Villa	A	0-3		33,815

2000/01

	Opposition	H/A	Score	Scorers	Attn.
1	Newcastle United	H	2-0	Cole Johnsen	67,477
2	Ipswich town	A	1-1	Beckham	22,007
3	West Ham United	A	2-2	Beckham Cole	25,998
4	Bradford City	H	6-0	Fortune 2 Sheringham 2 Beckham Cole	67,447
5	Sunderland	H	3-0	Scholes 2 Sheringham	67,503
6	Everton	A	3-1	Butt Giggs Solskjaer	38,541
7	Chelsea	H	3-3	Beckham Scholes Sheringham	67,568
8	Arsenal	A	0-1		38,146
9	Leicester City	A	3-0	Sheringham 2 Solskjaer	22,132
10	Leeds United	H	3-0	Beckham Yorke og	67,523
11	Southampton	H	5-0	Sheringham 3 Cole 2	67,581
12	Coventry City	A	2-1	Beckham Cole	21,079
13	Middlesbrough	H	2-1	Butt Sheringham	67,576

14	Manchester City	A	1-0	Beckham	34,429
15	Derby County	A	3-0	Butt Sheringham Yorke	32,190
16	Tottenham Hotspur	H	2-0	Scholes Solskjaer	67,583
17	Charlton Athletic	A	3-3	Giggs Keane Solskjaer	20,043
18	Liverpool	H	0-1		67,533
19	Ipswich Town	H	2-0	Solskjaer 2	67,597
20	Aston Villa	A	1-0	Solskjaer	40,889
21	Newcastle United	A	1-1	Beckham	52,134
22	West Ham United	H	3-1	Solskjaer Yorke og	67,603
23	Bradford City	A	3-0	Chadwick Giggs Sheringham	20,551
24	Aston Villa	H	2-0	G Neville Sheringham	67,533
25	Sunderland	A	1-0	Cole	48,260
26	Everton	H	1-0	og	67,528
27	Chelsea	A	1-1	Cole	34,690
28	Arsenal	H	6-1	Yorke 3 Keane Sheringham Solskjaer	67,535
29	Leeds United	A	1-1	Chadwick	40,055
30	Leicester City	H	2-0	Silvestre Yorke	67,516
31	Liverpool	A	0-2		44,806
32	Charlton Athletic	H	2-1	Cole Solskjaer	67,505
33	Coventry City	H	4-2	Yorke 2 Giggs Scholes	67,637
34	Manchester City	H	1-1	Sheringham	67,535
35	Middlesbrough	A	2-0	Beckham P Neville	34,417
36	Derby County	H	0-1		67,526
37	Southampton	A	1-2	Giggs	15,526
38	Tottenham Hotspur	A	1-3	Scholes	36,072

• Final League Position: 1st in the Premiership

FA Cup

3	Fulham	A	2-1	Sheringham Solskjaer	19,178
4	West Ham United	H	0-1		67,029

League Cup

3	Watford	A	3-0	Solskjaer 2 Yorke	18,871
4	Sunderland	A	1-2	Yorke	47,543

2001/02

	Opposition	H/A	Score	Scorers	Attn.
1	Fulham	H	3-2	van Nistelrooy 2 Beckham	67,534
2	Blackburn Rovers	A	2-2	Beckham Giggs	29,636
3	Aston Villa	A	1-1	og	42,632
4	Everton	H	4-1	Beckham Cole Fortune Veron	67,534
5	Newcastle United	A	3-4	Giggs van Nistelrooy Veron	52,056
6	Ipswich Town	H	4-0	Solskjaer 2 Cole Johnsen	67,551
7	Tottenham Hotspur	A	5-3	Beckham Blanc Cole Veron van Nistelrooy	36,038
8	Sunderland	A	3-1	Cole Giggs og	48,305
9	Bolton Wanderers	H	1-2	Veron	67,559
10	Leeds United	H	1-1	Solskjaer	67,555
11	Liverpool	A	1-3	Beckham	44,361
12	Leicester City	H	2-0	van Nistelrooy Yorke	67,651
13	Arsenal	A	1-3	Scholes	38,174
14	Chelsea	H	0-3		67,544
15	West Ham United	H	0-1		67,582
16	Derby County	H	5-0	Solskjaer 2 Keane Scholes van Nistelrooy	67,577
17	Middlesbrough	A	1-0	van Nistelrooy	34,358
18	Southampton	H	6-1	van Nistelrooy 3 Keane P Neville Solskjaer	67,638
19	Everton	A	2-0	Giggs van Nistelrooy	39,948
20	Fulham	A	3-2	Giggs 2 van Nistelrooy	21,159
21	Newcastle United	H	3-1	Scholes 2 van Nistelrooy	67,646
22	Southampton	A	3-1	Beckham Solskjaer van Nistelrooy	31,858
23	Blackburn Rovers	H	2-1	Keane van Nistelrooy	67,552
24	Liverpool	H	0-1		67,599
25	Bolton Wanderers	A	4-0	Solskjaer 3 van Nistelrooy	27,350
26	Sunderland	H	4-1	van Nistelrooy 2 Beckham P Neville	67,587
27	Charlton Athletic	A	2-0	Solskjaer 2	26,475
28	Aston Villa	H	1-0	van Nistelrooy	67,592
29	Derby County	A	2-2	Scholes Veron	33,041
30	Tottenham Hotspur	H	4-0	Beckham 2 van Nistelrooy 2	67,599

31	West Ham United	A	5-3	Beckham 2 Butt Scholes Solskjaer	35,281
32	Middlesbrough	H	0-1		67,683
33	Leeds United	A	4-3	Solskjaer 2 Giggs Scholes	40,058
34	Leicester City	A	1-0	Solskjaer	21,447
35	Chelsea	A	3-0	Scholes Solskjaer van Nistelrooy	41,725
36	Ipswich Town	A	1-0	van Nistelrooy	28,433
37	Arsenal	H	0-1		67,580
38	Charlton Athletic	H	0-0		67,571

• Final League Position: 3rd in the Premiership

FA Cup

| 3 | Aston Villa | A | 3-2 | van Nistelrooy 2 Solskjaer | 38,444 |
| 4 | Middlesbrough | A | 0-2 | | 17,624 |

League Cup

| 3 | Arsenal | A | 0-4 | | 30,693 |

2002/03

	Opposition	H/A	Score	Scorers	Attn.
1	West Bromwich Albion	H	1-0	Solskjaer	67,645
2	Chelsea	A	2-2	Beckham Giggs	41,841
3	Sunderland	A	1-1	Giggs	47,586
4	Middlesbrough	H	1-0	van Nistelrooy	67,464
5	Bolton Wanderers	H	0-1		67,623
6	Leeds United	A	0-1		39,622
7	Tottenham Hotspur	H	1-0	van Nistelrooy	67,611
8	Charlton Athletic	A	3-1	Giggs Scholes van Nistelrooy	26,630
9	Everton	H	3-0	Scholes 2 van Nistelrooy	67,629
10	Fulham	A	1-1	Solskjaer	18,103
11	Aston Villa	H	1-1	Forlan	67,619
12	Southampton	H	2-1	Forlan P Neville	67,691
13	Manchester City	A	1-3	Solskjaer	34,649
14	West Ham United	A	1-1	van Nistelrooy	35,049
15	Newcastle United	H	5-3	van Nistelrooy 3 Scholes Solskjaer	67,625
16	Liverpool	A	2-1	Forlan 2	44,250

17	Arsenal	H	2-0	Scholes Veron	67,650
18	West Ham United	H	3-0	Solskjaer Veron og	67,555
19	Blackburn Rovers	A	0-1		30,475
20	Middlesbrough	A	1-3	Giggs	34,673
21	Birmingham City	H	2-0	Beckham Forlan	67,640
22	Sunderland	H	2-1	Beckham Scholes	67,609
23	West Bromwich Albion	A	3-1	Scholes Solskjaer van Nistelrooy	27,129
24	Chelsea	H	2-1	Forlan Scholes	67,606
25	Southampton	A	2-0	Giggs van Nistelrooy	32,085
26	Birmingham City	A	1-0	van Nistelrooy	29,475
27	Manchester City	H	1-1	van Nistelrooy	67,646
28	Bolton Wanderers	A	1-1	Solskjaer	27,409
29	Leeds United	H	2-1	Silvestre og	67,135
30	Aston Villa	A	1-0	Beckham	42,602
31	Fulham	H	3-0	van Nistelrooy 3	67,706
32	Liverpool	H	4-0	van Nistelrooy 2 Giggs Solskjaer	67,639
33	Newcastle United	A	6-2	Scholes 3 Giggs Solskjaer van Nistelrooy	52,164
34	Arsenal	A	2-2	Giggs van Nistelrooy	38,164
35	Blackburn Rovers	H	3-1	Scholes 2 van Nistelrooy	67,626
36	Tottenham Hotspur	A	2-0	Scholes van Nistelrooy	36,073
37	Charlton Athletic	H	4-1	van Nistelrooy 3 Beckham	67,721
38	Everton	A	2-1	Beckham van Nistelrooy	40,168

• Final League Position: 1st in the Premiership

FA Cup

3	Portsmouth	H	4-1	van Nistelrooy 2 Beckham Scholes	67,222
4	West ham United	H	6-0	Giggs 2 van Nistelrooy 2 P Neville Solskjaer	67,181
5	Arsenal	H	0-2		67,209

League Cup

3	Leicester City	H	2-0	Beckham Richardson	47,848
4	Burnley	A	2-0	Forlan Solskjaer	22,034
5	Chelsea	H	1-0	Forlan	57,985
SF1	Blackburn Rovers	H	1-1	Scholes	62,740

SF2	Blackburn Rovers	A	3-1	Scholes 2 van Nistelrooy	29,048
F	Liverpool	N*	0-2		74,500

*Played at the Millennium Stadium, Cardiff

2003/04

	Opposition	H/A	Score	Scorers	Attn.
1	Bolton Wanderers	H	4-0	Giggs 2 Scholes van Nistelrooy	67,647
2	Newcastle United	A	2-1	Scholes van Nistelrooy	52,165
3	Wolverhampton Wanderers	H	1-0	O'Shea	67,648
4	Southampton	A	0-1		32,006
5	Charlton Athletic	A	2-0	van Nistelrooy 2	26,078
6	Arsenal	H	0-0		67,639
7	Leicester City	A	4-1	van Nistelrooy 3 Keane	32,044
8	Birmingham City	H	3-0	Giggs Scholes van Nistelrooy	67,633
9	Leeds United	A	1-0	Keane	40,153
10	Fulham	H	1-3	Forlan	67,727
11	Portsmouth	H	3-0	Forlan Keane Ronaldo	67,639
12	Liverpool	A	2-1	Giggs 2	44,159
13	Blackburn Rovers	H	2-1	Klberson van Nistelrooy	67,748
14	Chelsea	A	0-1		41,932
15	Aston Villa	H	4-0	Forlan 2 van Nistelrooy 2	67,621
16	Manchester City	H	3-1	Scholes 2 van Nistelrooy	67,643
17	Tottenham Hotspur	A	2-1	O'Shea van Nistelrooy	35,910
18	Everton	H	3-2	Bellion Butt Kleberson	67,642
19	Middlesbrough	A	1-0	Fortune	34,738
20	Bolton Wanderers	A	2-1	Scholes van Nistelrooy	27,668
21	Newcastle United	H	0-0		67,622
22	Wolverhampton Wanderers	A	0-1		29,396
23	Southampton	H	3-2	Saha Scholes van Nistelrooy	67,758
24	Everton	A	4-3	Saha 2 van Nistelrooy 2	40,190
25	Middlesbrough	H	2-3	Giggs van Nistelrooy	67,436
26	Leeds United	H	1-1	Scholes	67,744
27	Fulham	A	1-1	Saha	18,306
28	Manchester City	A	1-4	Scholes	47,284
29	Tottenham Hotspur	H	3-0	Bellion Giggs Ronaldo	67,644
30	Arsenal	A	1-1	Saha	38,184

31	Birmingham City	A	2-1	Ronaldo Saha	29,548
32	Leicester City	H	1-0	G Neville	67,749
33	Portsmouth	A	0-1		20,140
34	Charlton Athletic	H	2-0	G Neville Saha	67,477
35	Liverpool	H	0-1		67,647
36	Blackburn Rovers	A	0-1		29,616
37	Chelsea	H	1-1	van Nistelrooy	67,609
38	Aston Villa	A	2-0	Ronaldo van Nistelrooy	42,573

• Final League Position: 3rd in the Premiership

FA Cup

3	Aston Villa	A	2-1	Scholes 2	40,371
4	Northampton Town	A	3-0	Forlan Silvestre og	7,356
5	Manchester City	H	4-2	van Nistelrooy 2 Ronaldo Scholes	67,228
6	Fulham	H	2-1	van Nistelrooy 2	67,614
SF	Arsenal	N*	1-0	Scholes	39,939
F	Millwall	N**	3-0	van Nistelrooy 2 Ronaldo	71,350

*Played at Villa Park, Birmingham
**Played at the Millennium Stadium, Cardiff

League Cup

| 3 | Leeds United | A | 3-2 | Bellion Djemba-Djemba Forlan | 37,546 |
| 4 | West Bromwich Albion | A | 0-2 | | 25,282 |

2004/05

	Opposition	H/A	Score	Scorers	Attn.
1	Chelsea	A	0-1		41,813
2	Norwich City	H	2-1	Bellion Smith	67,812
3	Blackburn Rovers	A	1-1	Smith	26,155
4	Everton	H	0-0		67,803
5	Bolton Wanderers	A	2-2	Bellion Heinze	27,766
6	Liverpool	H	2-1	Silvestre 2	67,857
7	Tottenham Hotspur	A	1-0	van Nistelrooy	36,103
8	Middlesbrough	H	1-1	Smith	67,988
9	Birmingham City	A	0-0		29,221
10	Arsenal	H	2-0	Rooney van Nistelrooy	67,862
11	Portsmouth	A	0-2		20,190

12	Manchester City	H	0-0		67,863
13	Newcastle United	A	3-1	Rooney 2 van Nistelrooy	52,320
14	Charlton Athletic	H	2-0	Giggs Scholes	67,704
15	West Bromwich Albion	A	3-0	Scholes 2 van Nistelrooy	27,709
16	Southampton	H	3-0	Ronaldo Rooney Scholes	67,921
17	Fulham	A	1-1	Smith	21,940
18	Crystal Palace	H	5-2	Scholes 2 O'Shea Smith og	67,814
19	Bolton Wanderers	H	2-0	Giggs Scholes	67,867
20	Aston Villa	A	1-0	Giggs	42,593
21	Middlesbrough	A	2-0	Fletcher Giggs	34,199
22	Tottenham Hotspur	H	0-0		67,962
23	Liverpool	A	1-0	Rooney	44,183
24	Aston Villa	H	3-1	Ronaldo Saha Scholes	67,859
25	Arsenal	A	4-2	Ronaldo 2 O'Shea og	38,164
26	Birmingham City	H	2-0	Keane Rooney	67,838
27	Manchester City	A	2-0	Rooney og	47,111
28	Portsmouth	H	2-1	Rooney 2	67,989
29	Crystal Palace	A	0-0		26,201
30	Fulham	H	1-0	Ronaldo	67,959
31	Blackburn Rovers	H	0-0		67,939
32	Norwich City	A	0-2		25,522
33	Everton	A	0-1		37,160
34	Newcastle United	H	2-1	Brown Rooney	67,845
35	Charlton Athletic	A	4-0	Fletcher Scholes Smith Rooney	26,789
36	West Bromwich Albion	H	1-1	Giggs	67,827
37	Chelsea	H	1-3	van Nistelrooy	67,832
38	Southampton	A	2-1	Fletcher van Nistelrooy	32,066

• Final League Position: 3rd in the Premiership

FA Cup

3	Exeter City	H	0-0		67,551
3R	Exeter City	A	2-0	Ronaldo Rooney	9,033
4	Middlesbrough	H	3-0	Rooney 2 O'Shea	67,251
5	Everton	A	2-0	Fortune Ronaldo	38,664
6	Southampton	A	4-0	Scholes 2 Keane Ronaldo	30,971
SF	Newcastle United	N*	4-1	van Nistelrooy 2 Ronaldo Scholes	69,280
F	Arsenal	N*	0-0 aet		71,876

(United lost 4-5 on penalties)
*Played at the Millennium Stadium, Cardiff

League Cup

3	Crewe Alexandra	A	3-0	Miller Smith og	10,103
4	Crystal Palace	H	2-0	Richardson Saha	48,891
5	Arsenal	H	1-0	Bellion	67,103
SF1	Chelsea	A	0-0		41,492
SF2	Chelsea	H	1-2	Giggs	67,000

2005/06

	Opposition	H/A	Score	Scorers	Attn.
1	Everton	A	2-0	Rooney van Nistelrooy	38,610
2	Aston Villa	H	1-0	van Nistelrooy	67,934
3	Newcastle United	A	2-0	Rooney van Nistelrooy	52,327
4	Manchester City	H	1-1	van Nistelrooy	67,839
5	Liverpool	A	0-0		44,917
6	Blackburn Rovers	H	1-2	van Nistelrooy	67,765
7	Fulham	A	3-2	van Nistelrooy 2 Rooney	21,862
8	Sunderland	A	3-1	Rooney Rossi van Nistelrooy	39,085
9	Tottenham Hotspur	H	1-1	Silvestre	67,856
10	Middlesbrough	A	1-4	Ronaldo	30,579
11	Chelsea	H	1-0	Fletcher	67,864
12	Charlton Athletic	A	3-1	van Nistelrooy 2 Smith	26,730
13	West Ham United	A	2-1	O'Shea Rooney	34,755
14	Portsmouth	H	3-0	Rooney Scholes van Nistelrooy	67,684
15	Everton	H	1-1	Giggs	67,831
16	Wigan Athletic	H	4-0	Rooney 2 Ferdinand van Nistelrooy	67,793
17	Aston Villa	A	2-0	Rooney van Nistelrooy	37,128
18	West Bromwich Albion	H	3-0	Ferdinand Scholes van Nistelrooy	67,972
19	Birmingham City	A	2-2	Rooney van Nistelrooy	28,459
20	Bolton Wanderers	H	4-1	Ronaldo 2 Saha og	67,858
21	Arsenal	A	0-0		38,313
22	Manchester City	A	1-3	van Nistelrooy	47,192
23	Liverpool	H	1-0	Ferdinand	67,874
24	Blackburn Rovers	A	3-4	van Nistelrooy 2 Saha	25,484

25	Fulham	H	4-2	Ronaldo 2 Saha og	67,884
26	Portsmouth	A	3-1	Ronaldo 2 van Nistelrooy	20,206
27	Wigan Athletic	A	2-1	Ronaldo og	23,574
28	Newcastle United	H	2-0	Rooney 2	67,858
29	West Bromwich Albion	A	2-1	Saha 2	27,623
30	Birmingham City	H	3-0	Giggs 2 Rooney	69,070
31	West Ham United	H	1-0	van Nistelrooy	69,522
32	Bolton Wanderers	A	2-1	Saha van Nistelrooy	27,718
33	Arsenal	H	2-0	Park Rooney	70,908
34	Sunderland	H	0-0		72,519
35	Tottenham Hotspur	A	2-1	Rooney 2	36,141
36	Chelsea	A	0-3		42,219
37	Middlesbrough	H	0-0		69,531
38	Charlton Athletic	H	4-0	Richardson Ronaldo Saha og	73,006

• Final League Position: 2nd in the Premiership

FA Cup

3	Burton Albion	A	0-0		6,191
3R	Burton Albion	H	5-0	Rossi 2 Giggs Richardson Saha	53,564
3	Wolverhampton Wanderers	A	3-0	Richardson 2 Saha	28,333
5	Liverpool	A	0-1		44,039

League Cup

3	Barnet	H	4-1	Ebanks-Blake Miller Richardson Rossi	43,673
3	West Bromwich Albion	H	3-1	O'Shea Ronaldo Saha	48,924
5	Birmingham City	A	3-1	Saha 2 Park	20,454
SF1	Blackburn Rovers	A	1-1	Saha	24,348
SF2	Blackburn Rovers	H	2-1	Saha van Nistelrooy	61,636
F	Wigan Athletic	N*	4-0	Rooney 2 Ronaldo Saha	66,866

*Played at the Millennium Stadium, Cardiff

2006/07

	Opposition	H/A	Score	Scorers	Attn.
1	Fulham	H	5-1	Rooney 2 Ronaldo Saha og	75,115
2	Charlton Athletic	A	3-0	Fletcher Saha Solskjaer	25,422
3	Watford	A	2-1	Giggs Silvestre	19,453

4	Tottenham Hotspur	H	1-0	Giggs	75,453
5	Arsenal	H	0-1		75,595
6	Reading	A	1-1	Ronaldo	24,098
7	Newcastle United	H	2-0	Solskjaer 2	75,664
8	Wigan Athletic	A	3-1	Saha Solskjaer Vidic	20,631
9	Liverpool	H	2-0	Ferdinand Scholes	75,828
10	Bolton Wanderers	A	4-0	Rooney 3 Ronaldo	27,229
11	Portsmouth	H	3-0	Ronaldo Saha Vidic	76,004
12	Blackburn Rovers	A	1-0	Saha	26,162
13	Sheffield United	A	2-1	Rooney 2	32,584
14	Chelsea	H	1-1	Saha	75,948
15	Everton	H	3-0	Evra O'Shea Ronaldo	75,723
16	Middlesbrough	A	2-1	Fletcher Saha	31,238
17	Manchester City	H	3-1	Ronaldo Rooney Saha	75,858
18	West Ham United	A	0-1		34,966
19	Aston Villa	A	3-0	Ronaldo 2 Scholes	42,551
20	Wigan Athletic	H	3-1	Ronaldo 2 Solskjaer	76,018
21	Reading	H	3-2	Ronaldo 2 Solskjaer	75,910
22	Newcastle United	A	2-2	Scholes 2	52,302
23	Aston Villa	H	3-1	Carrick Park Ronaldo	76,073
24	Arsenal	A	1-2	Rooney	60,128
25	Watford	H	4-0	Larsson Ronaldo Rooney og	76,032
26	Tottenham Hotspur	A	4-0	Giggs Ronaldo Scholes Vidic	36,146
27	Charlton Athletic	H	2-0	Fletcher Park	75,883
28	Fulham	A	2-1	Giggs Ronaldo	24,549
29	Liverpool	A	1-0	O'Shea	44,403
30	Bolton Wanderers	H	4-1	Park 2 Rooney 2	76,058
31	Blackburn Rovers	H	4-1	Carrick Park Scholes Solskjaer	76,098
32	Portsmouth	A	1-2	O'Shea	20,223
33	Sheffield United	H	2-0	Carrick Rooney	75,540
34	Middlesbrough	H	1-1	Richardson	75,967
35	Everton	A	4-2	Eagles O'Shea Rooney og	39,682
36	Manchester City	A	1-0	Ronaldo	47,244
37	Chelsea	A	0-0		41,794
38	West Ham United	H	0-1		75,927

• Final League Position: 1st in the Premiership

FA Cup

3	Aston Villa	H	2-1	Larsson Solskjaer	74,924
4	Portsmouth	H	2-1	Rooney 2	71,137
5	Reading	H	1-1	Carrick	70,608
5R	Reading	A	3-2	Heinze Saha Solskjaer	23,821
6	Middlesbrough	A	2-2	Ronaldo Rooney	33,308
6R	Middlesbrough	H	1-0	Ronaldo	71,325
SF	Watford	N*	4-1	Rooney 2 Richardson Ronaldo	37,425
F	Chelsea	N**	0-1		89,826

*Played at Villa Park, Birmingham
**Played at Wembley

League Cup

3	Crewe Alexandra	A	2-1	Lee Solskjaer	10,046
4	Southend United	A	0-1		11,532

2007/08

	Opposition	H/A	Score	Scorers	Attn.
1	Reading	H	0-0		75,655
2	Portsmouth	A	1-1	Scholes	20,510
3	Manchester City	A	0-1		44,955
4	Tottenham Hotspur	H	1-0	Nani	75,696
5	Sunderland	H	1-0	Saha	75,648
6	Everton	A	1-0	Vidic	39,364
7	Chelsea	H	2-0	Tevez Saha (pen)	75,633
8	Birmingham City	A	1-0	Ronaldo	26,526
9	Wigan Athletic	H	4-0	Tevez Ronaldo 2 Rooney	75,300
10	Aston Villa	A	4-1	Rooney 2 Ferdinand Giggs	42,640
11	Middlesbrough	A	4-1	Nani Rooney Tevez 2	75,720
12	Arsenal	A	2-2	Gallas og Ronaldo	60,161
13	Blackburn Rovers	H	2-0	Ronaldo 2	75,710
14	Bolton Wanderers	A	0-1		25,028
15	Fulham	H	2-0	Ronaldo 2	75,055
16	Derby County	H	4-1	Giggs Tevez 2 Ronaldo	75,725
17	Liverpool	A	1-0	Tevez	44,459
18	Everton	H	2-1	Ronaldo 2 (1 pen)	75,749
19	Sunderland	A	4-0	Rooney Saha 2 (1 pen) Ronaldo	47,360

20	West Ham United	A	1-2	Ronaldo	34,966
21	Birmingham City	H	1-0	Tevez	75,459
22	Newcastle United	H	6-0	Ronaldo 3 Tevez 2 Ferdinand	75,965
23	Reading	A	2-0	Rooney Ronaldo	24,135
24	Portsmouth	H	2-0	Ronaldo 2	75,415
25	Tottenham Hotspur	A	1-1	Tevez	36,075
26	Manchester City	H	1-2	Carrick	75,970
27	Newcastle United	A	5-1	Rooney 2 Ronaldo 2 Saha	52,291
28	Fulham	A	3-0	Hargreaves Park Davies og	25,314
29	Derby County	A	1-0	Ronaldo	33,072
30	Bolton Wanderers	H	2-0	Ronaldo 2	75,476
31	Liverpool	H	3-0	Brown Ronaldo Nani	76,000
32	Aston Villa	H	4-0	Ronaldo Tevez Rooney 2	75,932
33	Middlesbrough	A	2-2	Ronaldo Rooney	33,952
34	Arsenal	H	2-1	Ronaldo (pen) Hargreaves	75,985
35	Blackburn Rovers	A	1-1	Tevez	30,316
36	Chelsea	A	1-2	Rooney	41,828
37	West Ham United	H	4-1	Ronaldo 2 Tevez Carrick	76,013
38	Wigan Athletic	A	2-0	Ronaldo (pen) Giggs	25,133

• Final League Position: 1st in the Premiership

FA Cup

3	Aston Villa	A	2-0	Ronaldo Rooney	33,630
4	Tottenham Hotspur	H	3-1	Tevez Ronaldo 2 (1 pen)	75,369
5	Arsenal	H	4-0	Rooney Fletcher 2 Nani	75,550
6	Portsmouth	H	0-1		75,463

League Cup

| 3 | Coventry City | H | 0-2 | | 74,055 |

2008/09

	Opposition	H/A	Score	Scorers	Attn.
1	Newcastle United	H	1-1	Fletcher	75,512
2	Portsmouth	A	1-0	Fletcher	20,540
3	Liverpool	A	1-2	Tevez	44,192
4	Chelsea	A	1-1	Park	41,760
5	Bolton Wanderers	H	2-0	Ronaldo (pen) Rooney	75,484

6	Blackburn Rovers	A	2-0	Brown Rooney	27,321
7	West Bromwich Albion	H	4-0	Berbatov Nani Ronaldo Rooney	75,451
8	Everton	A	1-1	Fletcher	36,069
9	West Ham United	H	2-0	Ronaldo 2	75,397
10	Hull City	H	4-3	Ronaldo 2 Carrick Vidic	75,398
11	Arsenal	A	1-2	Rafael	60,106
12	Stoke City	H	5-0	Ronaldo 2 Berbatov Carrick Welbeck	75,369
13	Aston Villa	A	0-0		42,585
14	Manchester City	A	1-0	Rooney	47,320
15	Sunderland	H	1-0	Vidic	75,400
16	Tottenham Hotspur	A	0-0		35,882
17	Stoke City	A	1-0	Tevez	27,500
18	Middlesbrough	H	1-0	Berbatov	75,294
19	Chelsea	H	3-0	Berbatov Rooney Vidic	75,455
20	Wigan Athletic	H	1-0	Rooney	73,917
21	Bolton Wanderers	A	1-0	Berbatov	26,021
22	West Bromwich Albion	A	5-0	Ronaldo 2 Berbatov Tevez Vidic	26,105
23	Everton	H	1-0	Ronaldo (pen)	75,399
24	West Ham United	A	1-0	Giggs	34,958
25	Fulham	H	3-0	Berbatov Rooney Scholes	75,437
26	Blackburn Rovers	H	2-1	Ronaldo Rooney	75,000
27	Newcastle United	A	2-1	Berbatov Rooney	51,636
28	Liverpool	H	1-4	Ronaldo (pen)	75,569
29	Fulham	A	0-2		25,652
30	Aston Villa	H	3-2	Ronaldo 2 Macheda	75,409
31	Sunderland	A	2-1	Macheda Scholes	45,408
32	Portsmouth	H	2-0	Carrick Rooney	74,895
33	Tottenham Hotspur	H	5-2	Ronaldo 2 (1 pen) Rooney 2 Berbatov	75,458
34	Middlesbrough	A	2-0	Giggs Park	33,767
35	Manchester City	H	2-0	Ronaldo Tevez	75,464
36	Wigan Athletic	A	2-1	Carrick Tevez	21,286
37	Arsenal	H	0-0		75,468
38	Hull City	A	1-0	Gibson	24,945

• Final League Position: 1st in the Premiership

FA Cup

3	Southampton	A	3-0	Gibson Nani Welbeck	31,901
4	Tottenham Hotspur	H	2-1	Berbatov Scholes	75,014
5	Derby County	A	4-1	Gibson Nani Ronaldo Welbeck	32,103
6	Fulham	A	4-0	Tevez 2 Park Rooney	24,662
SF	Everton	N*	0-0		88,141

(Manchester United lost 2-4 on penalties)
*Played at Wembley Stadium

League Cup

3	Middlesbrough	H	3-1	Giggs Nani Ronaldo	53,729
4	Queens Park Rangers	H	1-0	Tevez	62,539
5	Blackburn Rovers	H	5-3	Tevez 4 Nani	53,997
SF1	Derby County	A	0-1		30,194
SF2	Derby County	H	4-2	Nani O'Shea Ronaldo Tevez	73,374
F	Tottenham Hotspur	N*	0-0		88,217

(Manchester United won 4-1 on penalties)
*Played at Wembley Stadium

CHAPTER SEVEN

MANCHESTER UNITED IN EUROPE

1956/57 EUROPEAN CUP
Preliminary Round (1st Leg)
Sep 12 v RSC Anderlecht (away 2-0)
Scorers: Viollet, Taylor,
Wood Foulkes Byrne Colman Jones Blanchflower Berry Whelan Taylor Viollet Pegg

Preliminary Round (2nd Leg)
Sep 26 v RSC Anderlecht (home 10-0) (Aggregate 12-0)
Scorers: Viollet 4 Taylor 3 Whelan 2 Berry
Wood Foulkes Byrne Colman Jones Edwards Berry Whelan Taylor Viollet Pegg

Round 1 (1st Leg)
Oct 17 v Borussia Dortmund (home 3-2)* played at Maine Road
Scorers: Viollet 2 Pegg
Wood Foulkes Byrne Colman Jones Edwards Berry Whelan Taylor Viollet Pegg

Round 1 (2nd Leg)
Nov 21 v Borussia Dortmund (away 0-0) Aggregate 3-2
Wood Foulkes Byrne Colman Jones McGuinness Berry Whelan Taylor Edwards Pegg

Quarter Final (1st Leg)
Jan 16 v Athletico Bilbao (away 3-5)
Scorers: Taylor Viollet Whelan
Wood Foulkes Byrne Colman Jones Edwards Berry Whelan Taylor Viollet Pegg

Quarter Final (2nd Leg)
Feb 6 v Athletico Bilbao (home 3-0)* Aggregate 6-5 played at Maine Road
Scorers: Viollet Taylor Berry
Wood Foulkes Byrne Colman Jones Edwards Berry Whelan Taylor Viollet Pegg

Semi Final (1st leg)
Apr 11 v Real Madrid (away 1-3)
Scorers: Taylor
Wood Foulkes Byrne Colman Blanchflower Edwards Berry Whelan Taylor Viollet Pegg

Semi Final (2nd leg)
Apr 25 v Real Madrid (home 2-2) Aggregate 3-5
Scorers: Taylor Charlton
Wood Foulkes Byrne Colman Blanchflower Edwards Berry Whelan Taylor Charlton Pegg

1957/58 EUROPEAN CUP
Preliminary Round (1st leg)
Sep 25 v Shamrock Rovers (away 6-0)
Scorers: Taylor 2 Whelan 2 Pegg Berry
Wood Foulkes Byrne Goodwin Blanchflower Edwards Berry Whelan T Taylor Viollet Pegg

Preliminary Round (2nd Leg)
Oct 2 v Shamrock Rovers (home) 3-2 Aggregate 9-2
Scorers: Viollet 2 Pegg
Wood Foulkes Byrne Colman Blanchflower Edwards Berry Whelan T Taylor Webster Pegg

Round 1 (1st Leg)
Nov 20 v Dukla Prague (home 3-0)
Scorers: Webster Taylor Pegg
Wood Foulkes Byrne Colman Blanchflower Edwards Berry Whelan T Taylor Webster Pegg

Round 1 (2nd leg)
Dec 4 v Dukla Prague (away 0-1) Aggregate 3-1
Wood Foulkes Byrne Colman Jones Edwards Scanlon Whelan T Taylor Webster Pegg

Quarter Final (1st Leg)
Jan 14 v Red Star Belgrade (home 2-1)
Scorers: Colman Charlton
Gregg Foulkes Byrne Colman Jones Edwards Morgans Charlton T Taylor Viollet Scanlon

Quarter Final (2nd Leg)
Feb 5 v Red Star Belgrade (away 3-3) Aggregate 5-4
Scorers: Charlton 2 Viollet
Gregg Foulkes Byrne Colman Jones Edwards Morgans Charlton T Taylor Viollet Scanlon

Semi-Final (1st Leg)
May 8 v AC Milan (home 2-1)
Scorers: E Taylor (pen) Viollet
Gregg Foulkes Greaves Goodwin Cope Crowther Morgans E Taylor Webster Viollet Pearson

Semi-Final (2nd Leg)
May 14 v AC Milan (away 0-4) Aggregate 2-5
Gregg Foulkes Greaves Goodwin Cope Crowther Morgans E Taylor Webster Viollet Pearson

1963/64 EUROPEAN CUP-WINNERS' CUP
Round 1 (1st Leg)
Sep 25 v Willem II (away 1-1)
Scorers: Herd
Gregg A Dunne Cantwell Crerand Foulkes Setters Herd Chisnall Sadler Law Charlton

Round 1 (2nd Leg)
Oct 15 v Willem II (home 6-1) Aggregate 7-2
Scorers: Law 3 Charlton Chisnall Setters
Gregg A Dunne Cantwell Crerand Foulkes Setters Quixall Chisnall Herd Law Charlton

Round 2 (1st Leg)
Dec 3 v Tottenham Hotspur (away 0-2)
Gaskell A Dunne Cantwell Crerand Foulkes Setters Quixall Stiles Herd Law Charlton

Round 2 (2nd Leg)
Dec 10 v Tottenham Hotspur (home 4-1) Aggregate 4-3
Scorers: Charlton 2 Herd 2
Gaskell A Dunne Cantwell Crerand Foulkes Setters Quixall Chisnall Sadler Herd Charlton

Quarter Final (1st Leg)
Feb 26 v Sporting Club Lisbon (home 4-1)
Scorers: Law 3 Charlton
Gaskell Brennan A Dunne Crerand Foulkes Setters Herd Stiles Charlton Law Best

Quarter Final (2nd Leg)
Mar 18 v Sporting Club Lisbon (away 0-5) Aggregate 4-6
Gaskell Brennan A Dunne Crerand Foulkes Setters Herd Chisnall Charlton Law Best

1964/65 INTER CITIES FAIRS CUP
Round 1 (1st leg)
Sep 23 v Djurgardens IF (away 1-1)
Scorers: Herd
P Dunne Brennan A Dunne Crerand Foulkes Stiles Connelly Charlton Herd Setters Best

Round 1 (2nd Leg)
Oct 27 v Djurgardens IF (home 6-1) Aggregate 7-2
Scorers: Law 3 Charlton 2 Best
P Dunne Brennan A Dunne Crerand Foulkes Stiles Connelly Charlton Herd Law Best

Round 2 (1st Leg)
Nov 11 v Borussia Dortmund (away 6-1)
Scorers: Charlton 3 Herd Law Best
P Dunne Brennan A Dunne Crerand Foulkes Stiles Connelly Charlton Herd Law Best

Round 2 (2nd Leg)
Dec 2 v Borussia Dortmund (home 4-0) Aggregate 10-1
Scorers: Charlton 2 Connelly Law
P Dunne Brennan A Dunne Crerand Foulkes Stiles Connelly Charlton Herd Law Best

Round 3 (1st leg)
Jan 20 v Everton (home 1-1)
Scorers: Connelly
P Dunne Brennan A Dunne Crerand Foulkes Stiles Connelly Charlton Herd Law Best

Round 3 (2nd Leg)
Feb 9 v Everton (away 2-1) Aggregate 3-2
Scorers: Connelly Herd
P Dunne Brennan A Dunne Crerand Foulkes Stiles Connelly Charlton Herd Law Best

Quarter Final (1st leg)
May 12 v RC Strasbourg (away 5-0)
Scorers: Law 2 Connelly Charlton Herd
P Dunne Brennan A Dunne Crerand Foulkes Stiles Connelly Charlton Herd Law Best

Quarter Final (2nd Leg)
May 19 v RC Strasbourg (home 0-0) Aggregate 5-0
P Dunne Brennan A Dunne Crerand Foulkes Stiles Connelly Charlton Herd Law Best

Semi-Final (1st Leg)
May 31 v Ferencvaros (home 3-2)
Scorers: Herd 2 Law
P Dunne Brennan A Dunne Crerand Foulkes Stiles Connelly Charlton Herd Law Best

Semi-Final (2nd Leg)
Jun 6 v Ferencvaros (away 0-1) Aggregate 3-3
P Dunne Brennan A Dunne Crerand Foulkes Stiles Connelly Charlton Herd Law Best

Play-Off
Jun 16 v Ferencvaros (away 1-2)
Scorers: Connelly
P Dunne Brennan A Dunne Crerand Foulkes Stiles Connelly Charlton Herd Law Best

1965/66 EUROPEAN CUP
Preliminary Round (1st leg)
Sep 22 v HJH Helsinki (away 3-2)
Scorers: Connelly Herd Law
Gaskell Brennan A Dunne Fitzpatrick Foulkes Stiles Connelly Charlton Herd Law Aston

Preliminary Round (2nd Leg)
Oct 6 v HJH Helsinki (home 6-0) Aggregate 9-2
Scorers: Connelly 3 Best 2 Charlton
P Dunne Brennan A Dunne Crerand Foulkes Stiles Connelly Best Charlton Law Aston

Round 1 (1st Leg)
Nov 17 v ASK Vorwarts (away 2-0)
Scorers: Law Connelly
Gregg A Dunne Cantwell Crerand Foulkes Stiles Best Law Charlton Herd Connelly

Round 1 (2nd leg)
Dec 1 v ASK Vorwarts (home 3-1) Aggregate 5-1
Scorers: Herd 3
P Dunne A Dunne Cantwell Crerand Foulkes Stiles Best law Charlton Herd Connelly

Quarter Final (1st leg)
Feb 2 v Benfica (home 3-2)
Scorers: Herd Law Foulkes
Gregg A Dunne Cantwell Crerand Foulkes Stiles Best Law Charlton Herd Connelly

Quarter Final (2nd Leg)
Mar 9 v Benfica (away 5-1) Aggregate 8-3
Scorers: Best 2 Charlton Connelly Crerand
Gregg Brennan A Dunne Crerand Foulkes Stiles Best Law Charlton Herd Connelly

Semi-Final (1st Leg)
Apr 13 v FK Partizan Belgrade (away 0-2)
Gregg Brennan A Dunne Crerand Foulkes Stiles Best Law Charlton Herd Connelly

Semi-Final (2nd Leg)
Apr 20 v FK Partizan Belgrade (home 1-0) Aggregate 1-2
Scorers: Stiles
Gregg Brennan A Dunne Crerand Foulkes Stiles Anderson Law Charlton Herd Connelly

1967/68 EUROPEAN CUP
Round 1 (1st leg)
Sep 20 v Hibernians (Malta) (home 4-0)
Scorers: Sadler 2 Law 2
Stepney Dunne Burns Crerand Foulkes Stiles Best Sadler Charlton Law Kidd

Round 1 (2nd Leg)
Sep 27 v Hibernians (Malta) (away 0-0 Aggregate 4-0)
Stepney Dunne Burns Crerand Foulkes Stiles Best Sadler Charlton Law Kidd

Round 2 (1st leg)
Nov 15 v FK Sarajevo (away 0-0)
Stepney Dunne Burns Crerand Foulkes Sadler Fitzpatrick Kidd Charlton Best Aston

Round 2 (2nd Leg)
Nov 29 v FK Sarajevo (home 2-1) Aggregate 2-1
Scorers: Best Aston
Stepney Brennan Dunne Crerand Foulkes Sadler Burns Kidd Charlton Best Aston

Quarter Final (1st Leg)
Feb 28 v Gornik Zabzre (home 2-0)
Scorers: Kidd Florenski (og)
Stepney Dunne Burns Crerand Sadler Stiles Best Kidd Charlton Ryan Aston

Quarter Final (2nd Leg)
Mar 13 v Gornik Zabzre (away 0-1) Aggregate 2-1
Stepney Dunne Burns Crerand Sadler Stiles Fitzpatrick Charlton Herd Kidd Best

Semi-Final (1st Leg)
Apr 24 v Real Madrid (home 1-0)
Scorers: Best
Stepney Dunne Burns Crerand Sadler Stiles Best Kidd Charlton Law Aston

Semi-Final (2nd Leg)
May 15 v Real Madrid (away 3-3) Aggregate 4-3
Scorers: Foulkes Sadler Zocco (og)
Stepney Brennan Dunne Crerand Foulkes Stiles Best Kidd Charlton Sadler Aston

Final
May 29 v Benfica (at Wembley 4-1) aet
Scorers: Charlton 2 Best Kidd
Stepney Brennan Dunne Crerand Foulkes Stiles Best Kidd Charlton Sadler Aston

1968/69 EUROPEAN CUP
Round 1 (1st leg)
Sep 18 v Waterford (away 3-1)
Scorers: Law 3
Stepney (Rimmer) Dunne Burns Crerand Foulkes Stiles Best Law Charlton Sadler Kidd

Round 1 (2nd Leg)
Oct 2 v Waterford (home 7-1) Aggregate 10-2
Scorers: Law 4 Stiles Burns Charlton
Stepney Dunne Burns Crerand Foulkes Stiles Best Law Charlton Sadler Kidd

Round 2 (1st Leg)
Nov 13 v RSC Anderlecht (home 3-0)
Scorers: Law 2 Kidd
Stepney Brennan Dunne Crerand Sadler Stiles Ryan Kidd Charlton Law Sartori

Round 2 (2nd Leg)
Nov 27 v RSC Anderlecht (away 1-3) Aggregate 4-3
Scorers: Sartori
Stepney Kopel Dunne Crerand Foulkes Stiles Fitzpatrick Law Charlton Sadler Sartori

Quarter Final (1st leg)
Feb 26 v Rapid Vienna (home 3-0)
Scorers: Best 2 Morgan
Stepney Fitzpatrick Dunne Crerand James Stiles Morgan Kidd Charlton Law Best

Quarter Final (2nd Leg)
Mar 5 v Rapid Vienna (away 0-0) Aggregate 3-0
Stepney Fitzpatrick Dunne Crerand James Stiles Morgan Kidd Charlton Sadler Best

Semi-Final (1st Leg)
Apr 23 v AC Milan (away 0-2)
Rimmer Brennan Fitzpatrick Crerand Foulkes Stiles (Burns) Morgan Kidd Charlton Law Best

Semi-Final (2nd Leg)
May 15 v AC Milan (home 1-0) Aggregate 1-2

Scorers: Charlton
Rimmer Brennan Burns Crerand Foulkes Stiles Morgan Kidd Charlton Law Best

1976/77 UEFA CUP
Round 1 (1st leg)
Sep 15 v Ajax Amsterdam (away 0-1)
Stepney Nicholl Houston Daly (McCreery) B Greenhoff Buchan Coppell McIlroy
Pearson Macari Hill

Round 1 (2nd Leg)
Sep 29 v Ajax Amsterdam (home 2-0) Aggregate 2-1
Scorers: McIlroy Macari
Stepney Nicholl Houston Daly (Albiston) B Greenhoff Buchan Coppell McIlroy
McCreery Macari Hill (Paterson)

Round 2 (1st Leg)
Oct 20 v Juventus (home 1-0)
Scorers: Hill
Stepney Nicholl Albiston Daly (McCreery) B Greenhoff Houston Coppell
McIlroy Pearson Macari Hill

Round 2 (2nd Leg)
Nov 3 v Juventus (away 0-3) Aggregate 1-3
Stepney Nicholl Albiston Daly B Greenhoff Houston Coppell McIlroy (McCreery)
Pearson Macari (Paterson) Hill

1977/78 EUROPEAN CUP-WINNERS' CUP
Round 1 (1st Leg)
Sep 14 v AS Saint-Etienne (away 1-1)
Scorers: Hill
Stepney Nicholl Albiston McIlroy (Grimes) B Greenhoff (Houston) Buchan
McGrath McCreery Pearson Coppell Hill

Round 1 (2nd Leg)
Oct 5 v AS Saint-Etienne (home 2-0)* Aggregate 3-1
played at Home Park, Plymouth
Scorers: Coppell Pearson
Stepney Nicholl Albiston McIlroy B Greenhoff Buchan Coppell J Greenhoff
Pearson (McGrath) Macari Hill

Round 2 (1st Leg)
Oct 19 v FC Porto (away 0-4)
Stepney Nicholl Albiston McIlroy Houston (Forsyth) Buchan McGrath (Grimes)
McCreery Coppell Macari Hill

Round 2 (2nd Leg)
Nov 2 v FC Porto (home 5-2) Aggregate 5-6
Scorers: Coppell 2 Nicholl Murca 2 ogs
Stepney Nicholl Albiston McIlroy Houston Buchan McGrath Coppell Pearson McCreery Hill

1980/81 UEFA CUP
Round 1 (1st Leg)
Sep 17 v Widzew Lodz (home 1-1)
Scorers: McIlroy
Bailey Nicholl (Duxbury) Albiston McIlroy Jovanovic Buchan Grimes
J Greenhoff Coppell Macari Thomas

Round 1 (2nd Leg)
Oct 1 v Widzew Lodz (away 0-0) Aggregate 1-1 lost on away goals rule
Bailey Nicholl Albiston McIlroy Jovanovic Buchan (Moran) Grimes Coppell
Jordan Duxbury Thomas

1982/83 UEFA CUP
Round 1 (1st Leg)
Sep 15 v Valencia CF (home 0-0)
Bailey Duxbury Albiston Wilkins Buchan McQueen Robson Grimes
Stapleton Whiteside Coppell

Round 1 (2nd Leg)
Sep 29 v Valencia CF (away 1-2) Aggregate 1-2
Scorers: Robson
Bailey Duxbury Albiston Wilkins Moran Buchan (Macari) Robson Grimes
Stapleton Whiteside Moses (Coppell)

1983/84 EUROPEAN CUP-WINNERS' CUP
Round 1 (1st Leg)
Sep 14 v Dukla Prague (home 1-1)
Scorers: Wilkins
Bailey Duxbury Albiston Wilkins Moran McQueen Robson (Gidman)
Muhren (Moses) Stapleton Macari Gibson

Round 1 (2nd Leg)
Sep 27 v Dukla Prague (away 2-2) Aggregate 3-3 won on away goals rule
Scorers: Robson Stapleton
Bailey Duxbury Albiston Wilkins Moran McQueen Robson Muhren
Stapleton Whiteside Graham

Round 2 (1st Leg)
Oct 19 v Spartak Varna (away 2-1)
Scorers: Robson Graham
Bailey Duxbury Albiston Wilkins Moran McQueen Robson Muhren
Stapleton Whiteside Graham

Round 2 (2nd Leg)
Nov 2 v Spartak Varna (home 2-0) Aggregate 4-1
Scorers: Stapleton 2
Bailey Duxbury Albiston Moses Moran (Dempsey) McQueen Robson Macari
Stapleton Whiteside (Hughes) Graham

Round 3 (1st Leg)
Mar 7 v FC Barcelona (away 0-2)
Bailey Duxbury Albiston Wilkins Moran Hogg Robson Muhren Stapleton
Hughes (Graham) Moses

Round 3 (2nd Leg)
Mar 21 v FC Barcelona (home 3-0) Aggregate 3-2
Scorers: Robson 2 Stapleton
Bailey Duxbury Albiston Wilkins Moran Hogg Robson Muhren Stapleton
Whiteside (Hughes) Moses

Semi-Final (1st Leg)
Apr 11 v Juventus (home 1-1)
Scorers: Davies
Bailey Duxbury Albiston McGrath Moran Hogg Graham Moses
Stapleton Whiteside Gidman (Davies)

Semi-Final (2nd Leg)
Apr 25 v Juventus (away 1-2) Aggregate 2-3
Scorers: Whiteside
Bailey Duxbury Albiston Wilkins Moran Hogg McGrath Moses
Stapleton (Whiteside) Hughes Graham

1984/85 UEFA CUP
Round 1 (1st Leg)
Sep 19 v Raba Vasas ETO (home 3-0)
Scorers: Robson Muhren Hughes
Bailey Duxbury Albiston Moses Moran Hogg Robson Muhren
Hughes Whiteside Olsen

Round 1 (2nd Leg)
Oct 3 v Raba Vasas ETO (away 2-2) Aggregate 5-2
Scorers: Brazil Muhren
Bailey Duxbury Albiston Moses Moran Hogg Robson Strachan Hughes Brazil Olsen

Round 2 (1st Leg)
Oct 24 v PSV Eindhoven (away) 0-0
Bailey Gidman Albiston Moses Moran Hogg Robson Strachan Hughes Brazil Olsen

Round 2 (2nd Leg)
Nov 7 v PSV Eindhoven (home 1-0) aet Aggregate 1-0
Scorers: Strachan
Bailey Gidman Albiston Moses Moran (Garton) Hogg Robson Strachan
Hughes Stapleton (Whiteside) Olsen

Round 3 (1st Leg)
Nov 28 v Dundee United (home 2-2)
Scorers: Strachan Robson
Bailey Gidman Albiston Moses McQueen Duxbury Robson Strachan
Hughes Whiteside (Stapleton) Olsen

Round 3 (2nd Leg)
Dec 12 v Dundee United (away 3-2) Aggregate 5-4
Scorers: Hughes Muhren McGinnis og
Bailey Gidman Albiston Moses McQueen Duxbury Robson Strachan
Hughes Stapleton Muhren

Quarter Final (1st Leg)
Mar 6 v Videoton (home 1-0)
Scorers: Stapleton
Bailey Gidman Albiston Duxbury McGrath Hogg Strachan Whiteside
Hughes Stapleton Olsen

Quarter Final (2nd Leg)
Mar 20 v Videoton (away 0-1) aet lost 5-4 on penalties
Bailey Gidman Albiston Duxbury McGrath Hogg Robson (Olsen) Strachan
Hughes Stapleton Whiteside

1990/91 EUROPEAN CUP-WINNERS' CUP
Round 1 (1st leg)
Sep 19 v Pesci Munkas (home 2-0)
Scorers: Blackmore Webb
Sealey Irwin Blackmore Bruce Phelan Pallister Webb Ince (Sharpe)
McClair Robins (Hughes) Beardsmore

Round 1 (2nd Leg)
3 Oct v Pesci Munkas (away 1-0) Aggregate 3-0
Scorers: McClair
Sealey Anderson Donaghy Bruce Phelan Pallister Webb Blackmore
McClair Hughes Martin (Sharpe)

Round 2 (1st Leg)
23 Oct v Wrexham (home 3-0)
Scorers: Bruce Pallister McClair
Sealey Blackmore Martin Bruce Sharpe Pallister Webb Ince (Beardsmore)
McClair Hughes Wallace (Robins)

Round 2 (2nd Leg)
7 Dec v Wrexham (away 2-0) Aggregate 5-0
Scorers: Bruce Robins
Sealey Irwin Blackmore Bruce Phelan Pallister Webb Ince (Donaghy)
McClair (Martin) Robins Wallace

Round 3 (1st Leg)
6 Mar v Montpellier (home 1-1)
Scorers: McClair
Sealey Blackmore Martin (Wallace) Donaghy Phelan Pallister Robson
Ince McClair Hughes Sharpe

Round 3 (2nd Leg)
19 Mar v Montpellier (away 2-0) Aggregate 3-1
Scorers: Blackmore Bruce
Sealey Irwin Blackmore Bruce Phelan Pallister Robson Ince (Martin)
McClair Hughes Sharpe

Semi-Final (1st Leg)
10 Apr v Legia Warsaw (away 3-1)
Scorers: Bruce McClair Hughes
Sealey Irwin Blackmore Bruce Phelan (Donaghy) Pallister Webb Ince
McClair Hughes Sharpe

Semi-Final (2nd Leg)
24 Apr v Legia Warsaw (away 1-1) Aggregate 4-1
Scorers: Sharpe
Walsh Irwin Blackmore (Donaghy) Bruce Phelan Pallister Robson Webb
McClair Hughes Sharpe

Final
15 May v Barcelona at Rotterdam (2-1)
Scorers: Hughes 2
Sealey Irwin Blackmore Bruce Phelan Pallister Robson Ince McClair Hughes Sharpe

1991/92 EUROPEAN CUP-WINNERS' CUP
Round 1 (1st Leg)
18 Sep v Athinaikos (away 0-0)
Schmeichel Phelan Irwin Bruce Webb Pallister Robins Ince McClair
Hughes Beardsmore (Wallace)

Round 1 (2nd Leg)
2 Oct v Athinaikos (home 2-0) Aggregate 2-0
Scorers: McClair Hughes
Schmeichel Phelan Martin (Beardsmore) Bruce Kanchelskis Pallister
Robson Ince McClair Hughes Wallace (Robins)

Round 2 (1st Leg)
23 Oct v Athletico Madrid (away 0-3)
Schmeichel Parker Irwin Bruce Webb Pallister Robson Ince McClair (Martin)
Hughes Phelan (Beardsmore)

Round 2 (2nd Leg)
6 Nov v Athletico Madrid (home 1-1) Aggregate 1-4
Scorers: Hughes
Walsh Parker Blackmore Bruce Webb Phelan (Martin) Robson Robins (Pallister)
McClair Hughes Giggs

1992/93 UEFA CUP
Round 1 (1st Leg)
16 Sep v Torpedo Moscow (home 0-0)
Walsh Irwin Martin (G Neville) Bruce Blackmore Pallister Kanchelskis Webb
McClair Hughes Wallace

Round 1 (2nd Leg)
29 Sep v Torpedo Moscow (away 0-0) Aggregate 0-0 Lost on penalties
Schmeichel Irwin Phelan (Parker) Bruce Webb Pallister Wallace (Robson) Ince
McClair Hughes Giggs

1993/94 UEFA CHAMPIONS LEAGUE
Round 1 (1st Leg)
15 Sep v Honved (away 3-2)
Scorers: Keane 2 Cantona
Schmeichel Parker Irwin Bruce Sharpe Pallister Robson Ince Cantona
Keane Giggs (Phelan)

Round 1 (2nd Leg)
29 Sep v Honved (home 2-1) Aggregate 5-3
Scorers: Bruce 2
Schmeichel Parker Irwin (Martin) Bruce Sharpe Pallister Robson Ince (Phelan)
Cantona Hughes Giggs

Round 2 (1st Leg)
20 Oct v Galatasaray (home 3-3)
Scorers: Robson Cantona og
Schmeichel Martin Sharpe Bruce Keane Pallister Robson (Phelan) Ince
Cantona Hughes Giggs

Round 2 (2nd Leg)

3 Nov v Galatasaray (away 0-0) Aggregate 3-3 Lost on away goals rule
Schmeichel Parker Irwin Bruce Sharpe Phelan (G Neville) Robson Ince
Cantona Keane (Dublin) Giggs

1994/95 UEFA CHAMPIONS LEAGUE
Group A

14 Sep v IFK Gothenburg (home 4-2)
Scorers: Giggs 2 Kanchelskis Sharpe
Schmeichel May Irwin Bruce Sharpe Pallister Kanchelskis Ince Butt
Hughes Giggs

28 Sep v Galatasaray (away 0-0)
Schmeichel May Bruce Pallister Sharpe Kanchelskis Butt Keane Ince
Giggs (Parker) Hughes

19 Oct v Barcelona (home 2-2)
Scorers: Hughes Sharpe
Schmeichel May (Bruce) Irwin Parker Sharpe Pallister Kanchelskis Ince
Keane Hughes Butt (Scholes)

2 Nov v Barcelona (away 0-4)
Walsh Parker Irwin Bruce Kanchelskis Pallister Butt Ince Keane Hughes Giggs (Scholes)

23 Nov v IFK Gothenburg (away 1-3)
Scorers: Hughes
Walsh May (G Neville) Irwin Bruce Kanchelskis Pallister Cantona Ince
McClair Hughes Davies (Butt)

7 Dec v Galatasaray (home 4-0)
Scorers: Davies Beckham Keane Bulent og)
Walsh G Neville Irwin Bruce Keane Pallister Cantona Beckham McClair Butt Davies

1995/96 UEFA CUP
1st Round (1st Leg)
12 Sep v Rotor Volgograd (away 0-0)
Schmeichel G Neville Irwin Bruce Sharpe Pallister Beckham Butt
Keane (Davies) Scholes (Parker) Giggs

1st Round (2nd leg)
26 Sep v Rotor Volgograd (home 2-2) Aggregate 2-2 Lost on away goals rule
Scorers: Scholes Schmeichel
Schmeichel O'Kane (Scholes) Bruce Pallister G Neville Beckham (Cooke)
Keane Butt Sharpe Cole Giggs

1996/97 UEFA CHAMPIONS LEAGUE
Group C
11 Sep v Juventus (away 0-1)
Schmeichel G Neville Irwin Johnsen Poborsky (Solskjaer) Pallister
Cantona Butt Cruyff (Cole) Beckham Giggs (McClair)

25 Sep v Rapid Vienna (home 2-0)
Scorers: Solskjaer Beckham
Schmeichel G Neville Irwin Johnsen (May) Keane Pallister Cantona
Poborsky (Butt) Solskjaer (Cole) Beckham Giggs

16 Oct v Fenerbahce (away 2-0)
Scorers: Beckham Cantona
Schmeichel G Neville Irwin May Johnsen Pallister Cantona Butt
Solskjaer Beckham Cruyff (Poborsky)

30 Oct v Fenerbahce (home 0-1)
Schmeichel G Neville (P Neville) Irwin May Keane Johnsen Cantona
Butt Poborsky (Scholes) Beckham Cruyff (Solskjaer)

20 Nov v Juventus (home 0-1)
Schmeichel G Neville P Neville (McClair) May Keane Johnsen Cantona
Butt Solskjaer (Cruyff) Beckham Giggs

4 Dec v Rapid Vienna (away 2-0)
Scorers: Giggs Cantona
Schmeichel G Neville (Casper) Irwin May Keane (McClair) Pallister
Cantona Butt (Poborsky) Solskjaer Beckham Giggs

Quarter Final (1st Leg)
5 Mar v Porto (home 4-0)
Scorers: May Cantona Giggs Cole
Schmeichel G Neville Irwin May Johnsen Pallister Cantona Solskjaer Cole Beckham Giggs

Quarter Final (2nd Leg)
19 Mar v Porto (away 0-0) Aggregate 4-0
Schmeichel G Neville Irwin (P Neville) May Keane Pallister Cantona
Butt Solskjaer (Scholes) Beckham (Poborsky) Johnsen

Semi Final (1st Leg)
9 Apr v Borussia Dortmund (away 0-1)
Van der Gouw G Neville Irwin Johnsen Keane Pallister Cantona
Butt Solskjaer (Cole) Beckham Giggs (Scholes)

Semi Final (2nd Leg)
23 Apr v Borussia Dortmund (home 0-1) Aggregate 0-2
Schmeichel G Neville P Neville May (Scholes) Johnsen Pallister Cantona
Butt Cole Beckham Solskjaer (Giggs)

1997/98 UEFA CHAMPIONS LEAGUE
Group B
17 Sep v Kosice (away 3-0)
Scorers: Irwin Berg Cole
Schmeichel G Neville Irwin Berg Keane Pallister Beckham (McClair)
Butt Cole Scholes Poborsky

1 Oct v Juventus (home 3-2)
Scorers: Sheringham Scholes Giggs
Schmeichel G Neville Irwin Berg Johnsen Pallister Beckham
Butt (Scholes) Solskjaer (P Neville) Sheringham Giggs

22 Oct v Feyenoord (home 2-1)
Scorers: Scholes Irwin (pen)
Schmeichel Irwin P Neville G Neville Scholes Pallister Beckham
Butt Cole (Solskjaer) Sheringham Giggs

5 Nov v Feyenoord (away 3-1)
Scorers: Cole 3
Schmeichel G Neville Irwin (P Neville) Berg Scholes (Poborsky) Pallister
Beckham Butt Cole (Solskjaer) Sheringham Giggs

27 Nov Kosice (home 3-0)
Scorers: Cole Faktor og Sheringham
Schmeichel G Neville P Neville (Berg) Johnsen Scholes Pallister Beckham
Butt (Solskjaer) Cole Sheringham Giggs (Poborksy)

10 Dec v Juventus (away 0-1)
Schmeichel G Neville P Neville Berg Johnsen Pallister Beckham
Poborksy (McClair) Solskjaer (Cole) Sheringham Giggs

Quarter Finals (1st Leg)
4 Mar v Monaco (away 0-0)
Schmeichel G Neville Irwin (McClair) Berg P Neville Johnsen
Beckham Butt Cole Sheringham Scholes

Quarter Finals (2nd Leg)
18 Mar v Monaco (home 1-1)
Scorers: Solskjaer
Van der Gouw P Neville Irwin G Neville (Berg) Scholes (Clegg) Johnsen
Beckham Butt Cole Sheringham Solskjaer

1998/99 UEFA CHAMPIONS LEAGUE
Second Qualifying Round (1st Leg)
12 Aug v LKS Lodz (home 2-0)
Scorers: Giggs Cole
Schmeichel G Neville Irwin Johnsen Keane Stam Beckham Butt
Cole Scholes (Solskjaer) Giggs

Second Qualifying Round (2nd Leg)
26 Aug v LKS Lodz (away 0-0) Aggregate 2-0
Schmeichel Irwin P Neville Johnsen Keane Stam Beckham Butt Scholes
Sheringham Giggs (Solskjaer)

Group D
16 Sep v Barcelona (home 3-3)
Scorers: Giggs Scholes Beckham
Schmeichel G Neville Irwin (P Neville) Berg Keane Stam Beckham
Solskjaer (Butt) Yorke Scholes Giggs (Blomqvist)

30 Sep v Bayern Munich (away 2-2)
Scorers: Yorke Scholes
Schmeichel P Neville Irwin G Neville Keane Stam Beckham Scholes
Yorke Sheringham Blomqvist (Cruyff)

21 Oct v Brondby (away 6-2)
Scorers: Giggs 2 Cole Keane Yorke Solskjaer
Schmeichel Brown P Neville G Neville Keane Stam Scholes Blomqvist
Cole (Solskjaer) Yorke (Wilson) Giggs (Cruyff)

4 Nov v Brondby (home 5-0)
Scorers: Beckham Cole P Neville Yorke Scholes

Schmeichel P Neville (Brown) Irwin G Neville Keane Stam Beckham
Blomqvist (Cruyff) Cole (Solskjaer) Yorke Scholes

25 Nov v Barcelona (away 3-3)
Scorers: Yorke 2 Cole
Schmeichel Brown Irwin G Neville Keane Stam Beckham (Butt) Blomqvist
Cole Yorke Scholes

9 Dec v Bayern Munich (home 1-1)
Scorers: Keane
Schmeichel Brown Irwin (Johnsen) G Neville Keane Stam Beckham
Scholes Cole Yorke (Butt) Giggs

Quarter Finals (1st Leg)
3 Mar v Inter Milan (home 2-0)
Scorers: Yorke 2
Schmeichel G Neville Irwin Johnsen (Berg) Keane Stam Beckham
Scholes (Butt) Cole Yorke Giggs

Quarter Final (2nd Leg)
17 Mar v Inter Milan (away 1-1) Aggregate 3-1
Scorers: Scholes
Schmeichel G Neville Irwin Berg Johnsen (Scholes) Stam Beckham Keane
Cole Yorke Giggs (P Neville)

Semi Finals (1st leg)
7 Apr v Juventus (home 1-1)
Scorers: Giggs
Schmeichel G Neville Irwin Berg (Johnsen) Keane Stam Beckham
Scholes Cole Yorke (Sheringham) Giggs

Semi Finals (2nd Leg)
21 Apr v Juventus (away 3-2)
Scorers: Keane Yorke Cole
Schmeichel G Neville Irwin Johnsen Keane Stam Beckham Butt
Cole Yorke Blomqvist (Scholes)

Final
26 May v Bayern Munich at Barcelona (2-1)
Scorers: Sheringham Solskjaer
Schmeichel G Neville Irwin Johnsen Butt Stam Beckham
Blomqvist (Sheringham) Cole (Solskjaer) Yorke Giggs

1999/2000 UEFA CHAMPIONS LEAGUE
Group D
14 Sep v Croatia Zagreb (home 0-0)
Van der Gouw Clegg (Fortune) P Neville Berg Wilson (Sheringham) Stam
Beckham Scholes Cole Yorke Giggs

22 Sep v Sturm Graz (away 3-0)
Scorers: Keane Yorke Cole
Van der Gouw P Neville Irwin berg Keane (Wilson) Stam Beckham
Scholes Cole (Solskjaer) Yorke Cruyff (Sheringham)

29 Sep v Marseille (home 2-1)
Scorers: Cole Scholes
Van der Gouw Irwin P Neville Berg (Sheringham) Scholes Stam
Beckham Butt Cole (Clegg) Yorke Solskjaer (Fortune)

19 Oct v Marseille (away 0-1)
Bosnich P Neville Irwin Berg (Solskjaer) Keane Stam Beckham
Scholes Cole Yorke Giggs

27 Oct v Croatia Zagreb (away 2-1)
Scorers: Beckham Keane
Bosnich P Neville Irwin Berg Keane Stam Beckham Scholes (Greening)
Cole (Cruyff) Yorke (Solskjaer) Giggs

2 Nov v Sturm Graz (home 2-1)
Scorers: Solskjaer Keane
Bosnich G Neville Irwin (Higginbotham) Berg Keane May Greening (Cruyff)
Wilson (P Neville) Cole Solskjaer Giggs

SECOND STAGE
Group B
23 Nov v Fiorentina (away 0-2)
Bosnich G Neville Irwin Berg (P Neville) Keane Stam Beckham
Scholes Cole (Sheringham) Yorke (Solskjaer) Giggs

8 Dec v Valencia (home 3-0)
Scorers: Keane Solskjaer Scholes
Van der Gouw P Neville Irwin G Neville Keane Stam Beckham
Scholes (Butt) Cole (Yorke) Solskjaer Giggs

1 Mar v Bordeaux (home 2-0)
Scorers: Giggs Sheringham
Van der Gouw G Neville Irwin (Solskjaer) Silvestre Keane (Fortune) Stam
Beckham Butt Cole (P Neville) Sheringham Giggs (Solskjaer)

7 Mar v Bordeaux (away 2-1)
Scorers: Keane Solskjaer
Van der Gouw G Neville Irwin (Solskjaer) Silvestre Keane Stam
Beckham Butt Cole (Berg) Sheringham (Yorke) Giggs

15 Mar v Fiorentina (home 3-1)
Scorers: Cole Keane Yorke
Bosnich G Neville Irwin Berg Keane Stam Beckham Scholes Cole Yorke Giggs

21 Mar v Valencia (away 0-0)
Bosnich G Neville Irwin Berg Keane Stam Scholes Butt Solskjaer (Cruyff)
Sheringham Fortune

Quarter Finals (1st leg)
4 Apr v Real Madrid (away 0-0)
Bosnich G Neville Irwin (Silvestre) Berg Keane Stam Beckham
Scholes (Butt) Cole Yorke (Sheringham) Giggs

Quarter Finals (2nd Leg)
19 Apr v Real Madrid (home 2-3)
Scorers: Beckham Scholes (pen)
Van der Gouw G Neville Irwin (Silvestre) Berg (Sheringham) Keane Stam
Beckham Scholes Cole (Solskjaer) Yorke Giggs

2000/01 UEFA CHAMPIONS LEAGUE
Group G
13 Sep v Anderlecht (home 5-1)
Scorers: Cole 3 Irwin (pen) Sheringham
Barthez Irwin (P Neville) Silvestre Johnsen Keane G Neville Beckham
Scholes Cole (Yorke) Sheringham Giggs (Solskjaer)

19 Sep v Dynamo Kiev (away 0-0)
Van der Gouw Irwin Silvestre Johnsen Keane G Neville Beckham
Butt Cole (Solskjaer) Yorke (Sheringham) Giggs

26 Sep v PSV Eindhoven (away 1-3)
Scorers: Scholes (pen)
Van der Gouw P Neville Silvestre (Wallwork) Brown Keane G Neville
Greening (Giggs) Butt Solskjaer Yorke Scholes (Beckham)

18 Oct v PSV Eindhoven (home 3-1)
Scorers: Sheringham Scholes Yorke
Barthez Irwin (Brown) Silvestre Johnsen Keane G Neville
Beckham (Butt) Scholes Cole Sheringham (Yorke) Giggs

24 Oct v Anderlect (away 1-2)
Scorers: Irwin (pen)
Barthez Irwin (Solskjaer) Silvestre (Brown) G Neville Scholes Johnsen
Beckham Butt Cole Yorke Giggs

8 Nov v Dynamo Kiev (home 1-0)
Scorers: Sheringham
Barthez P Neville Irwin Brown Keane G Neville Beckham Butt Cole
Sheringham (Yorke) Giggs (Fortune (Silvestre)

SECOND STAGE
Group A
21 Nov v Panathinaikos (home 3-1)
Scorers: Sheringham Scholes 2
Barthez P Neville Silvestre Brown Keane G Neville Beckham Butt
Yorke Sheringham Scholes

6 Dec v Sturm Graz (away 2-0)
Scorers: Scholes Giggs
Barthez Irwin (P Neville) Silvestre Brown Keane G Neville Beckham
Butt (Giggs) Yorke (Solskjaer) Sheringham Scholes

14 Feb v Valencia (away 0-0)
Barthez G Neville Silvestre Brown Keane Stam Beckham (Butt)
Scholes Cole (Solskjaer) Sheringham Giggs

20 Feb v Valencia (home 1-1)
Scorers: Cole
Barthez G Neville Silvestre Brown Keane Stam Beckham Scholes
Cole Sheringham (Solskjaer) Giggs (Butt)

7 Mar v Panathinaikos (away 1-1)
Scorers: Scholes
Barthez G Neville Silvestre (Chadwick) Brown Keane Stam Beckham
P Neville (Sheringham) Cole (Solskjaer) Yorke Scholes

13 Mar v Sturm Graz (Home 3-0)
Scorers: Butt Sheringham Keane
Barthez Irwin Silvestre G Neville Keane Stam Chadwick Butt
Solskjaer Sheringham Scholes (Greening)

Quarter Final (1st Leg)
3 Apr v Bayern Munich (home 0-1)
Barthez G Neville Silvestre Brown Keane Stam Beckham (Yorke)
Scholes Cole Solskjaer Giggs

Quarter Final (2nd Leg)
18 Apr v Bayern Munich (away 1-2) Aggregate 1-3
Scorers: Giggs
Barthez G Neville Silvestre Brown (Chadwick) Keane Stam Scholes
Butt (Solskjaer) Cole Yorke (Sheringham) Giggs

2001/02 UEFA CHAMPIONS LEAGUE
Group G
18 Sep v Lille (home 1-0)
Scorers: Beckham
Barthez G Neville (Silvestre) Irwin Brown Keane Blanc Beckham Scholes
van Nistelrooy Veron Giggs (Solskjaer)

25 Sep v La Coruna (away 1-2)
Scorers: Scholes
Barthez G Neville Irwin Johnsen Keane Blanc Beckham (Cole) Scholes
van Nistelrooy (Solskjaer) Veron Giggs

10 Oct v Olympiakos (away 2-0)
Scorers: Beckham Cole
Barthez G Neville Irwin (Silvestre) Johnsen Keane Blanc Beckham Scholes
van Nistelrooy (Solskjaer) Veron (Cole) Giggs

17 Oct v La Coruna (home 2-3)
Scorers: Van Nistelrooy 2
Barthez G Neville Irwin (Solskjaer) Johnsen (Brown) Keane Blanc
Beckham Scholes (Cole) van Nistelrooy Veron Giggs

23 Oct v Olympiakos (home 3-0)
Scorers: Solskjaer Giggs Van Nistelrooy
Barthez G Neville Irwin Brown Butt (Solskjaer) Blanc Beckham
Scholes van Nistelrooy Veron Giggs

31 Oct v Lille (away 1-1)
Scorers: Solskjaer)
Carroll P Neville Irwin May (O'Shea) Butt Silvestre Beckham Scholes
Cole (Yorke) Solskjaer Fortune

SECOND STAGE
Group A
20 Nov v Bayern Munich (away 1-1)
Scorers: Van Nistelrooy
Barthez G Neville Irwin (Silvestre) Brown Keane Blanc Beckham Scholes
van Nistelrooy (Yorke) Veron Fortune

5 Dec v Boavista (home 3-0)
Scorers: Van Nistelrooy 2 Blanc
Barthez P Neville Silvestre G Neville (O'Shea) Keane Blanc Veron
Butt van Nistelrooy (Solskjaer) Yorke Scholes (Fortune)

20 Feb v Nantes (away 1-1)
Scorers: Van Nistelrooy (pen)
Barthez P Neville (Forlan) Silvestre G Neville Keane Blanc Beckham
Scholes van Nistelrooy Veron (Solskjaer) Giggs

26 Feb v Nantes (home 5-1)
Scorers: Beckham Solskjaer 2 Silvestre Van Nistelrooy (pen)
Barthez Irwin Silvestre G Neville Keane (Butt) Blanc (Johnsen)
Beckham Veron van Nistelrooy (Forlan) Solskjaer Giggs

13 Mar v Bayern Munich (home 0-0)
Barthez G Neville Silvestre Johnsen Keane Blanc Beckham Veron
van Nistelrooy Solskjaer (Forlan) Giggs

19 Mar v Boavista (away 3-0)
Scorers: Blanc Solskjaer Beckham (pen)
Barthez G Neville Silvestre Johnsen (P Neville) Scholes (Stewart)
Blanc (O'Shea) Beckham Butt Solskjaer Forlan Giggs

Quarter Final (1st Leg)
2 Apr v La Coruna (away 2-0)
Scorers: Beckham Van Nistelrooy
Barthez G Neville Silvestre Johnsen Keane (Fortune) Blanc Beckham (P Neville)
Butt can Nistelrooy (Solskjaer) Scholes Giggs

Quarter Final (2nd Leg)
10 Apr v La Coruna (home 3-2) Aggregate 5-2
Scorers: Solskjaer 2 Giggs
Barthez G Neville Silvestre Johnsen (Brown) Butt Blanc Beckham (Solskjaer)
Veron (P Neville) van Nistelrooy Fortune Giggs

Semi Final (1st Leg)
24 Apr v Leverkusen (home 2-2)
Scorers: Zivkovic og Van Nistelrooy (pen)
Barthez G Neville (P Neville) (Irwin) Silvestre Brown Scholes (Keane) Blanc
Veron Butt van Nistelrooy Solskjaer Giggs

Semi Final (2nd leg)
30 Apr v Leverkusen (away 1-1(Aggregate 3-3 Lost on away goals rule
Scorers: Keane
Barthez Brown (Forlan) Silvestre Johnsen (Irwin) Keane Blanc Veron
Butt (Solskjaer) van Nistelrooy Scholes Giggs

2002/03 UEFA CHAMPIONS LEAGUE
Group F
18 Sep v Maccabi Haifa (home 5-2)
Scorers: Giggs Solskjaer Veron Van Nistelrooy Forlan (pen)
Barthez (Ricardo) O'Shea Silvestre Ferdinand P Neville Blanc Beckham
Veron van Nistelrooy (Pugh) Solskjaer Giggs (Forlan)

24 Sep v Leverkusen (away 2-1)
Scorers: Van Nistelrooy 2
Barthez O'Shea (G Neville) Silvestre Ferdinand P Neville Blanc Beckham
Butt van Nistelrooy (Forlan) Veron (Solskjaer) Giggs

1 Oct v Olympiakos (home 4-0)
Scorers: Giggs 2 Veron Solskjaer
Barthez G Neville Silvestre Ferdinand Butt Blanc (O'Shea) Beckham Veron
Solskjaer Scholes (Forlan) Giggs (Fortune)

23 Oct v Olympiakos (away 3-2)
Scorers: Blanc Veron Scholes
Barthez G Neville Silvestre O'Shea P Neville Blanc Beckham (Chadwick)
Veron (Richardson) Forlan Scholes Giggs (Fortune)

29 Oct v Maccabi Haifa (away 0-3)
Ricardo G Neville Silvestre Ferdinand P Neville O'Shea Richardson (Nardiello)
Scholes Forlan (Timm) Solskjaer Fortune

13 Nov v Leverkusen (home 2-0)}
Scorers: Veron Van Nistelrooy
Ricardo O'Shea Silvestre Ferdinand Veron Blanc (G Neville) Beckham (Solskjaer)
Fortune van Nistelrooy Scholes Giggs (Chadwick)

SECOND STAGE
Group D
26 Nov v Basle (away 3-1)
Scorers: Van Nistelrooy 2 Solskjaer
Barthez P Neville Silvestre Brown Fortune O'Shea Solskjaer (Chadwick)
Veron (May) van Nistelrooy (Forlan) Scholes Giggs

11 Dec v La Coruna (home 2-0)
Scorers: Van Nistelrooy 2
Barthez G Neville O'Shea (Beckham) Brown P Neville (Forlan) Silvestre
Solskjaer Veron van Nistelrooy (Richardson) Scholes Giggs

19 Feb v Juventus (home 2-1)
Scorers: Brown Van Nistelrooy
Barthez G Neville Silvestre (O'Shea) Brown Keane Ferdinand Beckham Butt
van Nistelrooy Scholes (Solskjaer) Giggs (Forlan)

25 Feb v Juventus (away 3-0)
Scorers: Giggs 2 Van Nistelrooy
Barthez G Neville O'Shea (Pugh) P Neville Keane Ferdinand Beckham
Butt Solskjaer Forlan (Giggs) (van Nistelrooy) Veron

12 Mar v Basle (home 1-1)}
Scorers: G Neville
Carroll G Neville O'Shea Ferdinand P Neville Blanc (Scholes) Solskjaer
Butt Forlan Fletcher (Beckham) Richardson (Giggs)

18 Mar v La Coruna (away 0-2)
Ricardo Lynch Pugh Roche (Stewart) O'Shea Blanc Fletcher P Neville
Forlan (Webber) Giggs (Richardson) Butt

Quarter Final (1st Leg)
8 Apr v Real Madrid (away 1-3)
Scorers: Van Nistelrooy
Barthez G Neville (Solskjaer) Silvestre (O'Shea) Brown Keane Ferdinand
Beckham Butt van Nistelrooy Scholes Giggs

Quarter Final (2nd Leg)
23 Apr v Real Madrid (home 4-3) Aggregate 5-6
Scorers: Van Nistelrooy Helguera og Beckham 2
Barthez Brown O'Shea Ferdinand Keane (Fortune) Silvestre (P Neville)
Solskjaer Butt van Nistelrooy Veron (Beckham) Giggs

2003/04 UEFA CHAMPIONS LEAGUE
Group E
16 Sep v Panathinaikos (home 5-0)
Scorers: Silvestre Fortune Solskjaer Butt Djemba Djemba
Howard G Neville O'Shea (Fletcher) Ferdinand P Neville Silvestre Solskjaer (Bellion)
Butt (Djemba Djemba) van Nistelrooy Giggs Fortune

1 Oct v Stuttgart (away 1-2)
Scorers: Van Nistelrooy
Howard G Neville O'Shea (Fortune) Ferdinand (Forlan) Keane Silvestre Scholes
P Neville van Nistelrooy Giggs Ronaldo (Fletcher)

22 Oct v Rangers (away 1-0)
Scorers: P Neville
Howard G Neville O'Shea Ferdinand Keane Silvestre P Neville (Butt) Scholes
van Nistelrooy Giggs Fortune (Djemba Djemba)

4 Nov v Rangers (home 3-0)
Scorers: Forlan Van Nistelrooy 2
Howard G Neville Fortune Ferdinand Keane Silvestre Ronaldo P Neville
van Nistelrooy (Fletcher) Forlan (Bellion) Giggs (Kleberson)

26 Nov v Panathinaikos (away 1-0)
Scorers: Forlan
Howard O'Shea Fortune Ferdinand Butt Silvestre Ronaldo Fletcher (Bellion)
Forlan Kleberson Giggs

9 Dec v Stuttgart (home 2-0)
Scorers: Van Nistelrooy Giggs
Carroll G Neville O'Shea Ferdinand P Neville Silvestre Fletcher Scholes (Djemba Djemba)
van Nistelrooy (Forlan) Giggs (Bellion) Fortune

Knock-out round (1st Leg)
24 Feb v Porto (away 1-2)
Scorers: Fortune
Howard P Neville (O'Shea) Fortune G Neville Keane Brown Scholes
Butt van Nistelrooy Saha (Ronaldo) Giggs

Knock-out round (2nd Leg)
9 Mar v Porto (home 1-1) Aggregate 2-3
Scorers: Scholes
Howard P Neville O'Shea G Neville Butt Brown Djemba Djemba (Saha)
Fletcher (Ronaldo) (Solskjaer) van Nistelrooy Scholes Giggs

2004/05 UEFA CHAMPIONS LEAGUE
Third Qualifying Round (1st Leg)
11 Aug v Dinamo Bucharest (away 2-1)
Scorers: Giggs Alistar og
Howard G Neville Fortune Keane O'Shea Silvestre Fletcher (Miller)
Djemba Djemba Smith Scholes (Forlan) Giggs (P Neville)

Third Qualifying Round (2nd Leg)
25 Aug v Dinamo Bucharest (home 3-0) Aggregate 5-1
Scorers: Smith 2 Bellion
Howard G Neville (P Neville) Spector O'Shea Eagles Silvestre Fletcher
Djembe Djemba Smith (Bellion) Kleberson Ronaldo (Richardson)

Group D
15 Sep v Lyon (away 2-2)
Scorers: van Nistelrooy 2
Howard O'Shea (P Neville) Heinze Brown Keane Silvestre Ronaldo
Djemba-Djemba van Nistelrooy (Smith) Scholes Giggs

28 Sep v Fenerbahce (home 6-2)
Scorers: Giggs Rooney 3 van Nistelrooy Bellion
Carroll G Neville Heinze (P Neville) Ferdinand Kleberson Silvestre Bellion
Djemba-Djemba van Nistelrooy (Miller) Rooney Giggs (Fletcher)

19 Oct v Sparta Prague (away 0-0)
Carroll G Neville Heinze Brown O'Shea Silvestre Miller Scholes
van Nistelrooy Rooney (Saha) Giggs (Ronaldo)

3 Nov v Sparta Prague (home 4-1)
Scorers: Van Nistelrooy 4 (1 pen)
Carroll G Neville Heinze Ferdinand Keane Brown Ronaldo (Kleberson)
Miller van Nistelrooy Rooney Scholes (P Neville)

23 Nov v Lyon (home 2-1)
Scorers: G Neville Van Nistelrooy
Carroll G Neville (Brown) Heinze Ferdinand Keane (Fortune) Silvestre
Ronaldo Scholes van Nistelrooy (Fletcher) Rooney Smith

8 Dec v Fenerbahce (away 0-3)
Howard P Neville Fortune Brown (Pique) Miller (Eagles) O'Shea Fletcher
Djemba-Djemba Bellion Richardson (Spector) Ronaldo

Knock-out Round (1st Leg)
22 Feb v AC Milan (home 0-1)
Carroll G Neville (Silvestre) Heinze Ferdinand Keane Brown
Ronaldo (van Nistelrooy) Scholes Giggs Rooney Fortune (Saha)

Knock-out round (2nd Leg)
8 Mar v AC Milan (away 0-1) Aggregate 0-2
Howard Brown (Smith) Heinze Ferdinand Keane Silvestre Ronaldo
Scholes van Nistelrooy Rooney Giggs (Fortune)

2005/06 UEFA CHAMPIONS LEAGUE
Third Qualifying Round (1st Leg)
9 Aug v Debrecen (home 3-0)
Scorers: Rooney Van Nistelrooy Ronaldo
van der Sar G Neville O'Shea Keane (Park) Ferdinand Silvestre Fletcher
Scholes van Nistelrooy (Rossi) Rooney Ronaldo (Smith)

Third Qualifying Round (2nd Leg)
23 Aug v Debrecen (away 3-0) Aggregate 6-0
Scorers: Heinze 2 Richardson
van der Sar G Neville (Richardson) Heinze Brown Ferdinand Scholes (Bardsley)
Fletcher (Miller) van Nistelrooy Smith Giggs Ronaldo

Group D
14 Sep v Villareal (away 0-0)
van der Sar O'Shea Heinze (Richardson) Smith Ferdinand Silvestre Fletcher
Scholes van Nistelrooy (Park) Rooney Ronaldo (Giggs)

27 Sep v Benfica (home 2-1)
Scorers: Giggs Van Nistelrooy
van der Sar Bardsley Richardson Smith Ferdinand O'Shea Fletcher
Scholes van Nistelrooy Giggs Ronaldo

18 Oct v Lille (home 0-0)
van der Sar Bardsley O'Shea Smith Ferdinand Silvestre Fletcher Scholes
van Nistelrooy Giggs (Park) Ronaldo

2 Nov v Lille (away 0-1)
van der Sar O'Shea Silvestre Smith Ferdinand Brown Fletcher Richardson (Park)
van Nistelrooy Rooney Ronaldo (Rossi)

22 Nov v Villareal (home 0-0)
van der Sar Brown (G Neville) O'Shea Smith (Saha) Ferdinand Silvestre
Fletcher (Park) Scholes van Nistelrooy Rooney Ronaldo

7 Dec v Benfica (away 1-2)
Scorers: Scholes
van der Sar G Neville O'Shea (Richardson) Smith Ferdinand Silvestre
Ronaldo (Park) Scholes van Nistelrooy Rooney Giggs (Saha)

2006/07 UEFA CHAMPIONS LEAGUE
Group F
13 Sep v Celtic (home 3-2)
Scorers: Saha 2 (1 pen) Solskjaer
van der Sar G Neville Silvestre Carrick Ferdinand Brown Fletcher
Scholes (O'Shea) Saha Rooney (Richardson) Giggs (Solskjaer)

26 Sep v Benfica (away 1-0)
Scorers: Saha
van der Sar G Neville Heinze Carrick Ferdinand Vidic Ronaldo Scholes
Saha (Smith) Rooney (Fletcher) O'Shea

17 Oct v FC Copenhagen (home 3-0)
Scorers: Scholes O'Shea Richardson
van der Sar O'Shea Evra Carrick (Solskjaer) Brown Vidic Fletcher
Scholes (Richardson) Saha (Smith) Rooney Ronaldo

1 Nov v FC Copenhagen (away 0-1)
van der Sar Heinze (Evra) Silvestre O'Shea Brown Vidic (Ferdinand)
Ronaldo Carrick Solskjaer Rooney Fletcher (Scholes)

21 Nov v Celtic (away 0-1)
van der Sar G Neville Heinze (Evra) Carrick (O'Shea) Ferdinand Vidic
Ronaldo Scholes Saha Rooney Giggs

8 Dec v Benfica (home 3-1)
Scorers: Vidic Giggs Saha
van der Sar G Neville Evra (Heinze) Carrick Ferdinand Vidic
Ronaldo Scholes (Solskjaer) Saha Rooney Giggs (Fletcher)

Knockout Round (1st Leg)
20 Feb v Lille (away 1-0)
Scorers: Giggs
van der Sar G Neville Evra Carrick Ferdinand Vidic Ronaldo (Saha)
Scholes (O'Shea) Larsson Rooney Giggs

Knock-out Round (2nd Leg)
7 Mar v Lille (home 1-0) Aggregate 2-0
Scorers: Larsson
van der Sar G Neville Silvestre O'Shea Ferdinand Vidic Ronaldo (Richardson)
Carrick Larsson (Smith) Rooney (Park) Scholes)

Quarter Final (1st Leg)
4 Apr v AS Roma (away 1-2)
Scorers: Rooney
van der Sar Brown Heinze Carrick Ferdinand O'Shea Ronaldo
Scholes Solskjaer (Fletcher) Rooney Giggs (Saha)

Quarter Final (2nd Leg)
10 April v AS Roma (home 7-1) Aggregate 8-3
Scorers: Carrick 2 Smith Rooney Ronaldo 2 Eva
van der Sar Brown O'Shea (Evra) Carrick (Richardson) Ferdinand
Heinze Ronaldo Fletcher Smith Rooney Giggs (Solskjaer)

Semi Final (1st Leg)
24 Apr v AC Milan (home 3-2)
Scorers: Ronaldo Rooney 2)
van der Sar O'Shea Evra Carrick Heinze Brown Fletcher Scholes
Ronaldo Rooney Giggs

Semi-Final (2nd Leg)
2 May v AC Milan (away 0-3) Aggregate 3-5
van der Sar O'Shea (Saha) Heinze Carrick Brown Vidic Fletcher Scholes
Ronaldo Rooney Giggs

2007/08 UEFA CHAMPIONS LEAGUE
Group F
19 Sep v Sporting Lisbon (away 1-0)
Scorers: Ronaldo
van der Sar Brown Ferdinand Vidic Evra Ronaldo (Tevez) Carrick
Scholes Giggs (Anderson) Nani Rooney (Saha)

2 Oct v AS Roma (home 1-0)
Scorers: Rooney
Kuszczak O'Shea Ferdinand Vidic Evra Carrick Scholes Ronaldo
Nani (Giggs) Rooney (Anderson) Saha (Tevez)

23 Oct v Dynamo Kiev (away 4-2)
Scorers: Ferdinand Rooney Ronaldo 2
van der Sar (Kuszczak) Brown Ferdinand Vidic O'Shea Ronaldo
Anderson Fletcher Giggs (Simpson) Tevez (Nani) Rooney

7 Nov v Dynamo Kiev (home 4-0)
Scorers: Pique Tevez Rooney Ronaldo
van der Sar (Kuszczak) Simpson Pique (Evans) Vidic Evra Ronaldo
Carrick Fletcher Nani Rooney Tevez (Saha)

27 Nov v Sporting Lisbon (home 2-1)
Scorers: Tevez Ronaldo
Kuszczak O'Shea Ferdinand Vidic Evra Fletcher (Giggs) Carrick Anderson
Nani (Tevez) Ronaldo Saha (Hargreaves)

12 Dec v AS Roma (away 1-1)
Scorers: Pique
Kuszczak Simpson Pique Evans O'Shea (Brown) Eagles Fletcher
Carrick Nani Rooney (Dong) Saha

Knockout Round (1st Leg)
20 Feb v Olympique Lyonnais (away 1-1)
Scorers: Tevez
van der Sar Brown Ferdinand Vidic Evra Ronaldo Anderson
Hargreaves (Carrick) Scholes (Tevez) Giggs (Nani) Rooney

Knockout Round (2nd Leg)
4 Mar v Olympique Lyonnais (home 1-0)
Scorers: Ronaldo
van der Sar Brown Ferdinand Vidic Evra Ronaldo (Hargreaves)
Fletcher Carrick Anderson (Tevez) Nani Rooney

Quarter Final (1st Leg)
1 Apr v AS Roma (away 2-0)
Scorers: Ronaldo Rooney
van der Sar Brown Ferdinand Vidic (O'Shea) Evra Carrick Scholes
Anderson (Hargreaves) Ronaldo Park Rooney (Tevez)

Quarter Final (2nd Leg)
9 Apr v AS Roma (home 1-0)
Scorers: Tevez
van der Sar Brown Pique Ferdinand Silvestre Hargreaves Park
Carrick (O'Shea) Anderson (Neville) Giggs (Rooney) Tevez

Semi-Final (1st Leg)
23 Apr v Barcelona (away 0-0)
van der Sar Hargreaves Ferdinand Brown Evra Ronaldo Carrick
Scholes Park Rooney (Nani) Tevez (Giggs)

Semi-Final (2nd Leg)
29 Apr v Barcelona (home 1-0)
Scorers: Scholes
van der Sar Hargreaves Ferdinand Brown Evra (Silvestre) Ronaldo
Carrick Scholes (Fletcher) Park Nani (Giggs) Tevez

Final
21 May v Chelsea at Moscow (1-1 aet) Man Utd won 6-5 on penalties
Scorers: Ronaldo
van der Sar Brown (Anderson) Ferdinand Vidic Evra Hargreaves
Ronaldo Carrick Scholes (Giggs) Rooney (Nani) Tevez

2008/09 UEFA CHAMPIONS LEAGUE
Group E
17 Sep v Villareal (home 0-0)
van der Sar Neville Ferdinand Evans Evra Nani Fletcher Hargreaves (Anderson)
Park (Ronaldo) Rooney Tevez (Giggs)

30 Sep v Aalborg (away 3-0)
Scorers: Berbatov 2 Rooney
van der Sar Rafael (Brown) Ferdinand Vidic Evra Nani O'Shea
Scholes (Giggs) Ronaldo Berbatov Rooney (Tevez)

21 Oct v Glasgow Celtic (home 3-0)
Scorers: Berbatov 2 Rooney
van der Sar Neville (Brown) Evans Vidic O'Shea Ronaldo (Park) Fletcher
Anderson Nani Berbatov (Tevez) Rooney

5 Nov v Glasgow Celtic (away 1-1)
Scorer: Giggs
Foster Rafael (Evra) Ferdinand Vidic O'Shea Ronaldo Fletcher Carrick
Nani (Berbatov) Tevez (Rooney) Giggs

25 Nov v Villareal (away 0-0)
Kuszczak O'Shea Ferdinand Evans Evra Ronaldo Fletcher (Gibson)
Carrick (Tevez) Nani (Park) Anderson Rooney

10 Dec v Aalborg (home 2-2)
Scorers: Rooney Tevez
Kuszczak Neville (Rafael) Ferdinand Evans O'Shea Gibson (Scholes)
Anderson Giggs (Park) Nani Rooney Tevez

Knockout Round (1st Leg)
24 Feb v Inter Milan (away 0-0)
van der Sar O'Shea Ferdinand Evans Evra Fletcher Carrick Giggs
Park (Rooney) Berbatov Ronaldo

Knockout Round (2nd Leg)
11 Mar v Inter Milan (home 2-0)
Scorers: Ronaldo Vidic
van der Sar O'Shea Ferdinand Vidic Evra Ronaldo Carrick
Scholes (Anderson) Giggs Rooney (Park) Berbatov

Quarter Final (1st Leg)
7 Apr v Porto (home 2-2)
Scorers: Rooney Tevez
van der Sar O'Shea Vidic Evans (Neville) Evra Fletcher Carrick
Scholes (Tevez) Ronaldo Rooney Park (Giggs)

Quarter Final (2nd Leg)
15 Apr v Porto (away 1-0)
Scorer: Ronaldo
van der Sar O'Shea Ferdinand Vidic Evra Giggs Carrick Anderson (Scholes)
Rooney Berbatov (Nani) Ronaldo

Semi-Final (1st Leg)
29 Apr v Arsenal (home 1-0)
Scorer: O'Shea
van der Sar O'Shea Ferdinand (Evans) Vidic Evra Fletcher Carrick
Anderson (Giggs) Ronaldo Tevez (Berbatov) Rooney

Semi-Final (2nd Leg)
5 May v Arsenal (away 3-1)
van der Sar O'Shea Ferdinand Vidic Evra (Rafael) Fletcher Carrick
Anderson (Giggs) Park Ronaldo Rooney (Berbatov)

Final
27 May v Barcelona at Rome (0-2)
van der Sar O'Shea Ferdinand Vidic Evra Anderson (Tevez) Carrick
Giggs (Scholes) Park (Berbatov) Ronaldo Rooney

CHAPTER EIGHT

STATISTICS

FOOTBALL LEAGUE APPEARANCES

1	Bobby Charlton	604/2
2	Bill Foulkes	563/3
3	Ryan Giggs	484/79
4	Joe Spence	481
5	Alex Stepney	433
6	John Silcock	423
7	Paul Scholes	342/74
8	Tony Dunne	414
9	Jack Rowley	380
10	Gary Neville	362/18
11	Arthur Albiston	364/15
12	Martin Buchan	376
13	Denis Irwin	356/12
14	George Best	361
15	Brian McClair	296/59
16	Allenby Chilton	352
17	Mark Hughes	336/9
18	Bryan Robson	326/19
19	Sammy McIlroy	320/22
20	Lou Macari	311/18

FA CUP APPEARANCES

1	Bobby Charlton	78
2	Ryan Giggs	57/7
3	Bill Foulkes	61
4	Tony Dunne	54/1

5=	George Best	46
	Mark Hughes	45/1
	Roy Keane	44/2
	Denis Law	44/2
	Gary Neville	43/3
10	Brian McClair	39/6
11	Alex Stepney	44
12=	Pat Crerand	43
	Denis Irwin	42/1
14	Jack Rowley	42
15=	Steve Bruce	41
	Peter Schmeichel	41
	Paul Scholes	28/13
18	Martin Buchan	39
19=	Johnny Carey	38
	Gary Pallister	38
	Nobby Stiles	38
	Sammy McIlroy	35/3

LEAGUE CUP APPEARANCES

1	Bryan Robson	50/1
2	Brian McClair	44/1
3	Arthur Albiston	38/2
4	Mark Hughes	37/1
5	Gary Pallister	36
6	Alex Stepney	35
7=	Steve Bruce	32/2
	Mike Duxbury	34
	Ryan Giggs	28/6
10	Denis Irwin	28/3
11	Martin Buchan	30
12	Norman Whiteside	26/3
13=	Gary Bailey	28
	Sammy McIlroy	25/3
15=	Lou Macari	22/5
	Frank Stapleton	26/1
17=	George Best	25

	Clayton Blackmore	23/2
	Kevin Moran	24/1
	Willie Morgan	24/1
	John O'Shea	24/1

EUROPEAN APPEARANCES

1	Ryan Giggs	113/16
2	Paul Scholes	101/15
3	Gary Neville	103/8
4	David Beckham	79/4
5	Roy Keane	81/1
6	Ole Gunnar Solskjaer	36/45
7	Denis Irwin	73/2
8	Nicky Butt	58/13
9	Mikel Silvestre	61/8
10	John O'Shea	54/13
11	Phil Neville	43/22
12	Rio Ferdinand	60/1
13	Wes Brown	50/9
14	Cristiano Ronaldo	51/4
15	Bill Foulkes	52
16	Andrew Cole	43/7
17=	Ruud van Nistelrooy	45/2
	Wayne Rooney	44/3
19	Bobby Charlton	45
20	Darren Fletcher	34/9

OVERALL APPEARANCES

1	Ryan Giggs	697/109
2	Bobby Charlton	756/2
3	Bill Foulkes	685/3
4	Paul Scholes	497/108
5	Gary Neville	538/32
6	Alex Stepney	539
7	Tony Dunne	534/1
8	Denis Irwin	511/18
9	Joe Spence	510

10	Arthur Albiston	467/18
11	Roy Keane	458/22
12	Brian McClair	398/73
13	George Best	470
14	Mark Hughes	453/14
15	Bryan Robson	437/24
16	Martin Buchan	456
17	John Silcock	449
18	Gary Pallister	433/4
19	Jack Rowley	424
20	Sammy McIlroy	391/28

FOOTBALL LEAGUE GOALS

1	Bobby Charlton	199
2	Jack Rowley	182
3	Denis Law	171
4	Dennis Viollet	159
5	Joe Spence	158
6	George Best	137
7	Stan Pearson	127
8	Mark Hughes	120
9	David Herd	114
10	Tommy Taylor	112
11	Ryan Giggs	103
12	Paul Scholes	98
13	Ruud van Nistelrooy	95
14	Andrew Cole	93
15	Ole Gunnar Solskjaer	91
16=	Joe Cassidy	90
	Sandy Turnbull	90
18	George Wall	89
19	Brian McClair	88
20	Cristiano Ronaldo	84

FA CUP GOALS

1	Denis Law	34
2	Jack Rowley	26

3=	George Best	21
	Stan Pearson	21
5	Bobby Charlton	19
6	Mark Hughes	17
7	David Herd	15
8=	Brian McClair	14
	Ruud van Nistelrooy	14
10=	Cristiano Ronaldo	13
	Paul Scholes	13
12=	Charlie Mitten	11
	Wayne Rooney	11
14=	Eric Cantona	10
	Bob Donaldson	10
	Ryan Giggs	10
	Bryan Robson	10
	Joe Spence	10
	Sandy Turnbull	10
	Norman Whiteside	10

LEAGUE CUP GOALS

1	Brian McClair	19
2	Mark Hughes	16
3	Lou Macari	10
4=	George Best	9
	Steve Coppell	9
	Lee Sharpe	9
	Norman Whiteside	9
8=	Ryan Giggs	8
	Paul Scholes	8
10=	Bobby Charlton	7
	Brian Kidd	7
	Louis Saha	7
	Ole Gunnar Solskjaer	7
14=	Steve Bruce	6
	Sammy McIlroy	6
	Frank Stapleton	6
	Carlos Tevez	6

18=	Stuart Pearson	5
	Bryan Robson	5
20=	Gerry Daly	4
	Peter Davenport	4
	Gordon Hill	4
	Gordon McQueen	4
	Remi Moses	4
	Cristiano Ronaldo	4

EUROPEAN GOALS

1	Ruud van Nistelrooy	38
2	Denis Law	28
3	Ryan Giggs	26
4	Paul Scholes	23
5	Bobby Charlton	22
6	Ole Gunnar Solskjaer	20
7	Andrew Cole	19
8=	Cristiano Ronaldo	16
	Wayne Rooney	16
10	David Beckham	15
11=	David Herd	14
	Roy Keane	14
13	Dennis Viollet	13
14=	George Best	11
	John Connelly	11
	Tommy Taylor	11
	Dwight Yorke	11
18=	Mark Hughes	9
	Teddy Sheringham	9
20	Bryan Robson	8

OVERALL GOALS

1	Bobby Charlton	249
2	Denis Law	237
3	Jack Rowley	211
4=	George Best	179
	Dennis Viollet	179

6	Joe Spence	168
7	Mark Hughes	163
8	Ruud van Nistelrooy	150
9=	Ryan Giggs	148
	Stan Pearson	148
11	David Herd	145
12	Paul Scholes	142
13	Tommy Taylor	131
14	Brian McClair	127
15	Ole Gunnar Solskjaer	126
16	Andrew Cole	121
17	Cristiano Ronaldo	118
18	Sandy Turnbull	101
19=	Joe Cassidy	100
	George Wall	100